The Entrepreneur
and Small Business
Problem Solver

Other Books by William A. Cohen

THE EXECUTIVE'S GUIDE TO FINDING A SUPERIOR JOB (AMACON)
HIGH TECH MANAGEMENT (AMACON)
BUILDING A MAIL ORDER BUSINESS (John Wiley & Sons)
TOP EXECUTIVE PERFORMANCE (*with Nurit Cohen*) (John Wiley & Sons)
DIRECT RESPONSE MARKETING (John Wiley & Sons)
MAKING IT BIG AS A CONSULTANT (AMACON)
WINNING ON THE MARKETING FRONT (John Wiley & Sons)
DEVELOPING A WINNING MARKETING PLAN (John Wiley & Sons)
THE STUDENT'S GUIDE TO FINDING A SUPERIOR JOB (Avant Books)
THE PRACTICE OF MARKETING MANAGEMENT (Macmillan Publishing Co.)
THE ENTREPRENEUR AND SMALL BUSINESS FINANCIAL PROBLEM
  SOLVER (John Wiley & Sons)
THE ART OF THE LEADER (Prentice-Hall)

The Entrepreneur
and Small Business
Problem Solver
Second Edition

An Encyclopedic Reference and Guide

WILLIAM A. COHEN

JOHN WILEY & SONS

New York • Chichester • Brisbane • Toronto • Singapore

Library of Congress Cataloging in Publication Data:

Cohen, William A., 1937–
    The entrepreneur and small business problem solver / by William A.
Cohen.—2nd ed.
        p.   cm.
    Bibliography: p.
    ISBN 0-471-50123-9.—ISBN 0-471-50124-7 (pbk.)
        1. Small business—Handbooks, manuals, etc.   2. Entrepreneurship—
Handbooks, manuals, etc.   I. Title.
    HD62.7.C63   1989   89-32064
    658.022–dc 20   CIP

Printed in the United States of America

10 9 8 7 6 5 4 3 2 1

This book is dedicated to Barak and Nimrod,
who will take the entrepreneurial spirit
into whatever lifework they choose.

Acknowledgments

I wish to thank the U.S. Small Business Administration, the U.S. Department of Labor, the U.S. Copyright Office of the Library of Commerce, the U.S. Department of Commerce Patent and Trademark Office and many others, through whose courtesy many of the excellent checklists, bibliographies, sources, and other information published by the U.S. Government were obtained.

W. A. C.

Contents

Section I
Financial Problem Solving

1

The Legal Aspects of Going into Business

In this chapter, we will cover the essential legal aspects of going into business, including setting up the legal structure for your firm; obtaining business licenses and paying local taxes; dealing with the state board of equalization and resale permits; registering a fictitious name; setting up the books; and handling federal tax obligations and income taxes, Social Security taxes, excise taxes, unemployment taxes, state taxes, local taxes, and records for income tax reporting.

SELECTING THE LEGAL STRUCTURE FOR YOUR FIRM

There are several different legal structures for your firm from which you can choose. These are the sole proprietorship, the partnership, and the corporation. Each has its own particular advantages and disadvantages, depending on your situation. We'll look at each in turn.

THE SOLE PROPRIETORSHIP

The sole or single proprietorship is a business structure for a firm that is owned and operated by only one person. To establish a sole proprietorship, all you need to do is obtain whatever licenses are needed in your local area to begin operations. This means it is the easiest of the legal structures to set up, and it is also the most used form of small business legal structure.

Advantages of the Sole Proprietorship

Ease and speed of formation.   With the sole proprietorship, there are fewer formalities and legal restrictions. A sole proprietorship requires little or no government approval and you usually need to spend only a few minutes with your city or county clerk to obtain a relatively inexpensive business license.

Reduced expense.   The sole proprietorship is less expensive to set up than either a partnership or a corporation. This is because of the minimal license fees and legal help needed to set up this type of business organization.

Complete control.   Since in a sole proprietorship there are no partners or other owners to consult with, you have total control over the business, and

1

you can run it yourself as you see fit. You make all the decisions. There is no board of directors or any other boss except your customers to direct you, tell you what to do, supervise the decisions you make, or criticize your errors. As a result, you can quickly respond to business needs on a day-to-day basis. Win, lose, or draw, you are the whole show and what you say goes.

Sole recipient of profits. Since you are the sole proprietor, you are not required to share profits with anyone. The profits are all yours.

Relative freedom from government regulations and taxes. For taxes, the government treats you and your sole proprietorship as one. If you actually end up losing money over the first year, then having this form of legal structure is an advantage since you may deduct those losses on your tax return against any other income that you may have earned during the year. This can be especially valuable if you run your business part-time while at the same time you have cash flow from a position held within a larger company. Naturally, the same advantage continues if you must run in the red for several years. However, the 1987 tax rules state that you must make money in three out of five years. If not, the Internal Revenue Service (IRS) classifies what you are engaged in as a hobby and *not* a business. For a hobby, your tax deductible expenses are limited to the amount of income earned. Further, the expenses you report are reduced by 2% of your 1987 adjusted gross income.

Termination. Termination is also very easy with a sole proprietorship. You can liquidate your assets, pay your debts, turn out the light, and your entire operation is completely shut down. Or you can sell your business if you wish to do so with few restrictions. With a sole proprietorship, it is as easy to get out of business as it is to get into business.

Disadvantages of the Sole Proprietorship

Unlimited liability. One major disadvantage of the sole proprietorship is that you have unlimited personal liability in your business. This means that you are responsible for the full amount of business debts, which could exceed your total investment in the business. This liability extends to all your assets, such as home and car. If your business fails while owing money to various creditors, those monies that you still owe can be collected from your personal assets. Of course, you can lessen the risk of liability in the case of physical loss or personal injury by obtaining proper insurance coverage. This will be discussed in Chapter 3. Also, these liabilities may not be of substantial importance in your situation under certain conditions. If you borrow money for your business, the bank will usually require that you personally guarantee your loan. In this way, even if you are incorporated, you may become personally liable. For many types of businesses, the chance of your being sued because of a failure of your product is very slim. The manufacture and sale of greeting cards, personalized stationery, or costume jewelry are examples. Therefore, even though you are totally responsible, your risks may be minimal.

Total responsibility. Since in a sole proprietorship you are essentially a one-man band, you are limited to and by your own skills and capabilities. This means, for example, that you may not be able to take a long vacation or that your enterprise could be put in serious jeopardy, or even terminated, by a serious illness or something else that takes you away from your business for some extended period of time. The fact that only your skills and experiences are brought to the business means there are fewer resources available to your firm than to another firm in which more than one are contributing experiences and personal resources.

Difficulties with capital. Again, since you are but one individual, it may be more difficult to obtain capital for your business than it is for other types of legal business structures with more than one individual involved. Also, it is difficult to get financing, since you alone must make good a debt. As the investor sees it, if you have a partner, this doubles the chances of getting his or her money back. The bottom line is that the sole proprietorship is the most difficult business structure for which to obtain financing.

THE PARTNERSHIP

The partnership is also fairly easy to get into, although written articles of partnership are customarily executed with the help of an attorney. Many states have adopted a uniform partnership act that defines a partnership as an association of two or more persons to carry on as co-owners of a business for profit. The contract or articles developed for use in your partnership may be very simple or fairly complex. They typically cover the following aspects:

1. Absence and disability
2. Arbitration
3. Authority of individual partners in conduct of business
4. Character of partners including whether general or limited, active or silent
5. Contribution by partners both now and at a later period
6. Dissolution and winding up
7. Division of profits and losses
8. Draws and/or salaries
9. Duration of agreement
10. Employee management
11. Expenses and how to handle them
12. Name, purpose, and domicile of partnership
13. Performance by partners
14. Records and method of accounting
15. Release of debts
16. Required acts and prohibited acts
17. Rights of continuing partner
18. Sale of partnership interest
19. Separate debts
20. Settlement of disputes

Characteristics That Distinguish a Partnership from a Sole Proprietorship

Certain characteristics distinguish a partnership from a sole proprietorship and other business structures. These are as follows: (1) co-ownership of the assets,

(2) limited life of the partnership, (3) mutual agency, (4) share in management, (5) share in partnership profits, (6) unlimited liability of at least one partner.

Types of Partners

In a partnership there can be different types of partners which have different responsibilities to the business. An *active partner* is one who is active in the business. A *dormant partner* is inactive and not known or held out as a partner.

A *limited* or *special partner* is a partner who risks only his or her agreed investment in the business. A limited partner is usually not subject to the same extent as a general partner to the liabilities of the firm, nor does he or she participate in the management and control of the firm or in the conduct of the firm's business. The limited partner's obligations to the partnership are liable for partnership obligations only to the extent of the original partnership investment, a share of any recourse debt, and a possible obligation to make future investments. Of importance to the limited partner is that the Tax Reform Act of 1986 treats limited partnership interests as passive activities. Losses from passive activities are not deductible for alternative minimum tax purposes and are being phased out for regular tax purposes.

A *nominal partner* is not a partner in the sense of being a party to the partnership agreement. However, the nominal partner represents him- or herself as a partner or permits others to make representation by the use of his or her name. Therefore, under the law, a nominal partner is as liable as if he or she were a partner to another party who has acted on the reliance on the truth of true partnership. An *ostensible partner* is an individual who is active and is known as a partner. A *secret partner* is a partner who is active but is not known or presented to be a partner. A *silent partner* is inactive but may be known to be a partner. A *subpartner* is an individual who is not a member of the partnership but contracts with one of the partners and participates in the interest of the partner in the firm's business and profits.

Advantages of the Partnership

Additional capital to start your business.   Your partner or partners are themselves sources of additional capital.

Help in decision making.   Two heads are better than one, and so your partners provide additional resources and help in decision making and the work of the business.

Ease of formation.   The legal formalities and expenses are not great. Although they are greater than those of a sole proprietorship, they are less than those of the development and creation of a corporation. Like a proprietorship, a partnership is easy to set up. Usually, you obtain a business license from your county clerk or city clerk, and the cost for the license is the same as for the proprietorship license.

Relatively stable business life.   In a partnership situation, you have double the resources to apply in solving problems or in handling such mundane decisions as when to go on vacation. There is more stability built into a partnership structure than into that of a sole proprietorship.

Relative freedom from government control and special taxation.   As with the sole proprietorship, there is a minimum amount of paperwork associated with a partnership as opposed to a corporation. There is a form that you must fill out each year for the IRS known as Form 1065, U.S. Partnership Return of Income, but basically the monies you receive from the partnership are treated as ordinary income as are the monies you receive from a sole proprietorship. You can deduct losses in the partnership from other sources of income when you complete your income tax just as you can for a sole proprietorship.

Share in profits. All partners, to a greater or lesser degree, are motivated to apply their best abilities and put in the time by direct sharing of the profits from the business.

Flexibility. Like a sole proprietorship, a partnership is reasonably flexible in that it can respond rapidly to changing conditions of business. On the other hand, because more than one individual is involved, the decision-making process is less flexible than that of the sole proprietorship.

Disadvantages of the Partnership

All partners are bound by the actions of one partner. This is perhaps the major disadvantage of a partnership: you are liable for the actions and commitments of your partners. A single partner can expend the company's resources in a business commitment and all partners are liable to that commitment, whether they agree with it or do not agree.

Organizational problems. Organizational responsibilities must be clearly written into the articles of partnership or else you'll run into problems trying to figure out who's in charge of what and who has the final say on various business matters.

Unlimited liability of at least one partner. By law, at least one partner has unlimited liability, just as with a sole proprietorship. Other partners may have similar liabilities, depending upon what's written into the articles of partnership.

Relative difficulty in obtaining capital. For a partnership, you can obtain capital more easily than you can for a sole proprietorship. However, it is much more difficult to obtain capital for a partnership than it is for a corporation.

Disposing of partnership interests. Buying out one partner may be very difficult unless the terms have been stated in the written agreement contained in the articles that formed the partnership.

THE CORPORATION

Unlike the other business structures, the corporation is not a simple structure. Usually you must have the help of an attorney to incorporate, although there are several books that can enable you to set up your corporation by yourself. One book on this subject is *How to Form Your Own Corporation Without a Lawyer for Under $50*, by Ted Nicholas, published by the Enterprise Publishing Co., 1000 Oakfield Lane, Wilmington, Del. 19810. Since state laws differ regarding corporations, many books have been written by experts discussing how to incorporate in their various states. Frequently these books have tear-out forms for you to use. If you're interested, check a local bookstore and find out if such a book is available for your state.

Corporations that do business in more than one state must comply with the federal laws regarding interstate commerce and with the various state laws. These may vary considerably from state to state. In general, to form a corporation, subscriptions to capital stock must be taken and a tentative organization created. Then, approval must be obtained from the secretary of the state in which the corporation is to be formed. The approval is in the form of a charter for the corporation stating the powers and limitations of the particular enterprise.

Advantages of the Corporation

Limited liability.   Perhaps the major advantage that exists over the other two forms of business ownership and structure is limited personal liability. With a corporation, your liability is limited to the amount of your investment in the business. Accordingly, your creditors cannot take your personal holdings or assets should the corporation fail or be sued for more funds than are available in the corporation.

Ease in securing capital.   Various lenders, including banks, venture capitalists, and others, are generally much more willing to make loans to a corporation that has been operating successfully than to a sole proprietorship or a partnership. Also, capital may be obtained through issuance of various stocks and long-term bonds.

Increased resources available.   Since a corporation will generally include more than one individual in its organization, the corporation has the ability to make use of multiple skills and resources.

Corporate benefits.   As a corporation, you and other members in your business will be able to take advantage of fringe benefits such as pension plans, insurance, company cars, and so forth.

Permanence of existence.   A corporation has a life of its own and continues to exist and may do business even after the death or illness of the principal officer in the corporation.

Disadvantages of the Corporation

Paperwork.   There is a tremendous amount of paperwork associated with a corporation, for taxes and for other reasons. Getting this paperwork done takes time, effort, and money.

Government regulations.   Your activities in the corporation are limited by various laws of the government. In fact, of the three types of business structures, this is the one over which the government has the most control. You must make numerous reports to the federal, state, and local governments.

Inability to take losses as deductions.   As noted earlier, in both the partnership and the sole proprietorship, if you lose money in your business, these losses can be taken as deductions from other earned income at income tax time. However, this is not true with losses sustained by a corporation. Your corporation may lose money, but until such time as you sell your stock or the business fails, these losses cannot be taken against other earned income. (There is an exception to this in an S corporation which will be discussed later.)

Lessened control.   As pointed out earlier, corporations are very closely regulated by the state in which you are registered. This control can restrict your business activities. Furthermore, your corporation is required to have a board of directors and hold stockholders' meetings. Even though you can stack the board of directors in your favor so that you can still run the company, your control over your business and the decision-making process does suffer from this limitation.

Taxes.   Depending on your situation and the profits in your business, the fact that you are incorporated may be a disadvantage because of double taxation. Corporate profits are taxed once through the corporation itself as a taxable legal entity and a second time through your salary or when profits are distributed to you as a stockholder. You then pay tax on this as ordinary income. If profits are sufficiently high, this is of little consequence since you will be building your business and taking your money out later. However, if profits are not that high, you'll be losing money to Uncle Sam through taxation instead of saving it. Also, corporate tax rates are higher than individual tax rates. This began in 1988. A corporation pays taxes to a maximum of 34% unless it is in the 5% surtax range of $100,001 to $335,000, during which it pays 39% while it phases out its lower bracket. But for an individual, the maximum tax rate is only 28% unless he or she is in the 5% surcharge range, which for an individual begins at $71,900. The surcharges are levied to wipe out the benefits of the lower tax rates imposed at the lower levels of taxable income. Again, an S corporation can help.

A Guide to Decision Making

In summary, in considering which form of legal structure to adopt, you should weigh the following factors:

1. Cost
2. The value of partners in either a partnership or a corporation in both capital and personal resource contributions
3. Organizational flexibility
4. Stability of your business during illness or when you want to take time off
5. Risks associated with each type of organizational structure
6. The taxation situation
7. The influence of laws (federal, local, and state)
8. The importance of other factors that are peculiar to your business

HOW TO INCORPORATE A SMALL BUSINESS

In general, to incorporate a small business you should either see an attorney or refer to one of the books on self-incorporation discussed earlier. However, this section will provide you with an overall view of the process and what is required.

Generally, the first step in incorporating is preparation of a certificate of incorporation. Many states require that the certificate be prepared by three or more individuals who are legally qualified, but the current trend is to require only one incorporator.

Before a certificate of incorporation is filed, however, you must consider the location of the corporation since it has important bearing on taxation and other aspects of your business.

Most small and medium-size businesses obtain their charters from the state in which the greatest part of their business is conducted. However, sometimes there are advantages or benefits to be gained from incorporation in another state. To the state in which you are located, yours would be known as a "foreign corporation." Advantages may include lower state taxes, fewer restrictions on corporate powers and lines of businesses in which your company may engage, and lower capital requirements for incorporation. On the other hand, foreign incorporation may also have significant disadvantages. For example, under the laws in many states, you may be taxed twice, that is, by the state in which you incorporated and the state in which your business is located. Under the laws of some states, the property of a foreign corporation is subject to less favorable treatment than that of a corporation located in the state. Also, some states require a foreign corporation to obtain certification to do business in their state, and without this certification your corporation may be deprived of the right to sue in those states. Finally, there is no standard fee, and the fee for a corporation and the organizational tax charged for a corporation vary greatly from state to state.

Certificate of Incorporation

Many states have a standard certificate of incorporation form which you can use. You can obtain copies of this form from the designated state official who grants charters or, in some states, local stationery stores. Also, if you intend to incorporate by yourself and you obtain one of the books mentioned earlier, these forms will frequently be found as tear-outs. In most cases, the following information is required on these forms:

1. *Corporate name of the company.* The name chosen cannot be so similar to the name of any other corporation authorized to do business in the state as to lead to confusion. Also, the name that you choose may not be deceptive; it may not mislead the public. To save yourself much time, you can check out the availability of names through an official in your state whose job it is to handle such inquiries. You should do this prior to drawing up a certificate of incorporation. There are companies that will perform this service for you that you can locate either through the state offices or through the telephone book. In many states there are certain procedures that are used to reserve a name for your corporation. Again, the proper state official can supply you with this information.

2. *Purposes for which the corporation is formed.* Most states require very specific information in this section. You must state in precise language the purposes of your corporation. However, several states will allow you to use very broad language in stating the purpose of your corporation; the purpose can be written in such a way as to allow you to pursue virtually any lawful enterprise. There are advantages for stating the purpose of your corporation specifically and for stating it in general terms. The advantage in stating the purpose in general terms is that if the corporation decides to change its business, reincorporation will not be required. On the other hand, in dealing with financial institutions, a specific purpose will give a very

clear picture of what you are doing. Also, a specific purpose will prevent problems in qualifying your corporation to do business in other jurisdictions.

3. *Length of time for which the corporation is being formed.* Here you may indicate a certain number of years or you may indicate that the length of time is in perpetuity.

4. *Names and addresses of the incorporators.* This requirement is a simple one, although you should know that in some states one or even more of the incorporators are required to be residents of the state within which the corporation is being organized. You should check and find out what is required in the state in which you intend to incorporate.

5. *Location of the principal office of the corporation in the state of incorporation.* In those situations in which you decide to obtain your charter from another state, you will be required to have an office in that state. However, there is an alternative: you may have an agent in the state to act for you. The agent is required to represent your corporation, maintain a duplicate list of stockholders, and receive or reply to suits brought against the corporation in the state of incorporation.

6. *The maximum amount and type of capital stock that the corporation is authorizing for issue.* Under this paragraph, you indicate the capital structure of the corporation, including the number and the classification of shares and the rights, preferences, and limitations of each class of shares and stock.

7. *Capital required at time of incorporation.* Some states require that a specific percentage of the par value of the capital stock be paid in cash and placed in a bank to the corporation's credit before the certification of incorporation is submitted for approval.

8. *The names of the stockholders and the number of shares to which each stockholder subscribes.*

9. *The names and addresses of persons who will serve as directors until the first meeting of stockholders or until their successors are elected and qualify.* For purposes of expediting the filing of the articles, sometimes dummy incorporators are employed. These dummy incorporators are usually associated with a service company that performs this or with an attorney for the organizers. Typically they elect their successors and resign at the first meeting of the incorporators.

Assuming that the name of the proposed corporation is satisfactory, that the certificate contains the information required and is properly executed, and that there is nothing in the certificate or in the proposed activities of the corporation that violates any law of the state or public policy, the charter is issued. The next step is an officers' and stockholders' meeting.

Officers' and Stockholders' Meeting

The officers' and stockholders' meeting is necessary to complete the incorporation process. This very important meeting is usually conducted by an attorney or someone familiar with corporate organizational procedures. Three basic things are accomplished during this meeting. First, corporate bylaws are adopted. Second, a board of directors is elected. And third, the board of directors elects the officers who will actually run the corporation on a day-to-day basis. It is possible in a small corporation for members of the board of directors to be elected officers of the corporation.

Bylaws of the Corporation

The bylaws of the corporation repeat some of the items already covered in the certificate of incorporation, but they also cover additional points. These include the following: (1) location of the principal offices and other offices of the corporation; (2) the time, place, and required notice of annual and special meetings of stockholders, the quorum necessary at the meetings, and the voting privileges of the various stockholders; (3) the number of directors, their compensation, if any, their term of office, how to elect them, and the methods of creating and filling vacancies on the board of directors; (4) the time and place of regular and special directors' meetings, as well as notification and quorum requirements; (5) the process for selecting officers and their titles, duties, terms of office, and salaries; (6) the issuance and form of stock certificates, how to transfer them, and their control in the company books; (7) dividends, when they are declared, and by whom they may be declared; (8) the fiscal year of the corporation, the corporate seal, the authority to sign checks, and the preparation of an annual statement; (9) the procedure for amending the bylaws that have been established.

S CORPORATIONS

S corporations were created by Congress to give tax relief to small companies. Specifically, the purpose of the S corporation is to permit a small business corporation to have its income taxed to the shareholders as if the corporation were a partnership, if it so desires. The advantages of an S corporation are twofold: (1) It permits you to avoid the double tax feature of taxation of corporate income; (2) it permits you as a shareholder to have the benefit of offsetting business losses incurred by the corporation against your income. Thus, you have the advantage of the protection of incorporation as well as the tax advantage of a partnership.

You should be aware that it may or may not be to your advantage to have an S corporation if your corporation enjoys substantial profits under the new tax laws, since corporate tax rates are higher than personal tax rates. Therefore, even if you forecast profitability, it makes sense to take a closer look and to work closely with your accountant and tax attorney before passing up the S corporation.

In order to qualify as an S corporation, you must meet the following requirements: (1) you must have no more than 10 shareholders, all of whom are individuals or estates; (2) you must have no nonresident alien shareholders; (3) you must have only one class of outstanding stock; (4) all shareholders must consent to the election of an S corporation; and (5) a specified portion of the corporation's receipts must be derived from actual business activity rather than passive investments.

In an S corporation, no limit is placed on the size of the corporation's income and assets.

OBTAINING BUSINESS LICENSES

Local Licensing Requirements

For most small businesses, you will need only a local business license. This may mean either a municipal or county license or both. These are payable at your city or county hall. To get the license, you may be required to conform to certain zoning laws and to meet building codes and other regulations set by the local health, fire, or police department. Permits may be required by these agencies for activities that are considered hazardous to the community. If you are required to have special permits, you will be informed at the time of the purchase of your business license.

State Licensing Requirements

Some states require licensing for particular occupations, and licenses are granted according to standards of professionalism and ability. Usually the requirement for state licensing will be indicated at the time of your purchase of your local business license. However, for more specific information, check with your state's department of commerce.

Federal Licensing Requirements

The federal government regulates interstate commerce and also requires federal permits or licenses for any enterprise involving preparation of meat products for transportation or sale, operation of a common carrier, construction of a radio or TV station, production of drugs or biological products, operation of an investment advisory service, and certain other businesses. Again, you usually will be informed of the necessity of an additional license at the time of purchase of a local business license. However, to be certain, you can contact your local department of commerce, which is listed in the white pages of your telephone directory under "U.S. Government."

Dealing with the State Board of Equalization and Resale Permits

The state board of equalization is the government agency to which you pay state taxes which you collect if your state has a sales tax. Usually the same agency will enable you to secure a seller's permit which allows you to buy tangible personal property that you intend to resell without paying sales or use tax to your vendor. In order to do this, you must give your vendor a signed resale certificate showing your seller's permit number.

To obtain a seller's permit, contact the sales and use tax department of your state (address listed in Figure 1.1). If a fee is required for a seller's permit, the appropriate office listed will inform you. Sometimes this office requires some security from you for the payment of future tax, since this office is the one to which you pay sales tax if applicable. If so, the amount is determined at the time you make your application for the permit required. This security deposit protects the state, because if you fail to pay any sales tax due, the state can

ALABAMA
Department of Revenue
Sales and Use Taxes
Montgomery, Alabama 36130

ALASKA
Department of Revenue
Pouch S
Juneau, Alaska 99801

ARIZONA
Sales Tax Division
Phoenix, Arizona 85007

ARKANSAS
Sales and Use Tax Division
Department of Finance and
Administration
Little Rock, Arkansas 72201

CALIFORNIA
Department of Business Taxes
State Board of Equalization
P.O. Box 1799
Sacramento, California 95808

COLORADO
Department of Revenue
State Capitol Annex
Denver, Colorado 80203

CONNECTICUT
Sales, Use and Excise Tax Division
Hartford, Connecticut 06115

DELAWARE
State Division of Revenue
Wilmington, Delaware 19801

DISTRICT OF COLUMBIA
Department of Finance and Revenue
300 Indiana Avenue, N.W.
Washington, D.C. 20001

FLORIDA
Sales Tax Bureau
Department of Revenue
Tallahassee, Florida 32304

GEORGIA
Sales and Use Tax Unit
Department of Revenue
Atlanta, Georgia 30334

HAWAII
Department of Taxation
State Tax Office Building
425 Queen Street
Honolulu, Hawaii, 96813

IDAHO
Sales Tax Division
State Tax Commission
Boise, Idaho 83707

ILLINOIS
Department of Revenue
Springfield, Illinois 62706

INDIANA
Sales Tax Division
Department of Revenue
100 N. Senate Avenue
Indianapolis, Indiana 46204

IOWA
Division of Retail Sales and Use Tax
Department of Revenue
Lucas State Office Building
Des Moines, Iowa 50319

KANSAS
Sales and Compensating Tax Division
State Revenue Building
Department of Revenue
Topeka, Kansas 66612

KENTUCKY
Sales Tax Division
Department of Revenue
Frankfort, Kentucky 40601

LOUISIANA
Collector of Revenue
Baton Rouge, Louisiana 70821

MAINE
Sales Tax Division
Bureau of Taxation
Augusta, Maine 04330

MARYLAND
Retail Sales Tax Division
Treasury Department
301 W. Preston Street
Baltimore, Maryland 21201

MASSACHUSETTS
Sales and Use Taxes
Department of Corporations & Taxation
Boston, Massachusetts 02133

MICHIGAN
Sales and Use Taxes
Department of Treasury
Revenue Division
Treasury Building
Lansing, Michigan 48922

MINNESOTA
Sales and Use Tax Division
Department of Taxation
Centennial Office Building
St. Paul, Minnesota 55101

MISSISSIPPI
Sales and Use Tax Division
State Tax Commission
Jackson, Mississippi 39205

MISSOURI
Sales and Use Tax Bureau
P.O. Box 840
Jefferson City, Missouri 65102

Figure 1.1. Sales and use tax departments

NEBRASKA
   Sales and Use Tax Unit
   Department of Revenue
   Box 4818, State Capitol
   Lincoln, Nebraska 68509

NEVADA
   Nevada Tax Commission
   Carson City, Nevada 89701

NEW JERSEY
   Division of Taxation
   Department of the Treasury
   Trenton, New Jersey 08625

NEW MEXICO
   Revenue, Bureau of Revenue
   Santa Fe, New Mexico 87501

NEW YORK
   Sales Tax Bureau, State Tax Commission
   Department of Taxation and Finance
   Tax and Finance Building 9
   State Campus
   Albany, New York 12226

NORTH CAROLINA
   Sales and Use Tax Division
   Main Office—Revenue Building
   Raleigh, North Carolina 27611

NORTH DAKOTA
   Enforcement Director (Sales Tax)
   State Capitol Building
   Bismarck, North Dakota 58501

OHIO
   Sales and Excise Division
   Department of Taxation
   68 East Gay Street
   Columbus, Ohio 43151

OKLAHOMA
   Sales and Use Taxes
   Oklahoma Tax Commission
   2101 Lincoln Blvd.
   Oklahoma City, Oklahoma 73105

PENNSYLVANIA
   Bureau of Taxes for Education
   Department of Revenue
   Harrisburg, Pennsylvania 17128

RHODE ISLAND
   Department of Administration
   49 Westminster Street
   Providence, Rhode Island 02903

SOUTH CAROLINA
   Sales and Use Tax Division
   South Carolina Tax Commission
   Columbia, South Carolina 29201

SOUTH DAKOTA
   Sales and Use Tax Division
   Department of Revenue
   Pierre, South Dakota 57501

TENNESSEE
   Sales and Use Tax Division
   Department of Revenue
   War Memorial Building
   Nashville, Tennessee 37219

TEXAS
   Comptroller of Public Accounts
   Austin, Texas 78711

UTAH
   Auditing Division (Sales Tax)
   State Tax Commission
   201 State Office Building
   Salt Lake City, Utah 84114

VERMONT
   Department of Taxes
   State of Vermont
   P.O. Box 547
   Montpelier, Vermont 05602

VIRGINIA
   Sales and Use Tax Division
   Department of Taxation
   P.O. Box 6L
   Richmond, Virginia 23215

WASHINGTON
   Department of Revenue
   Olympia, Washington 98501

WEST VIRGINIA
   Sales and Use Taxes
   State Tax Department
   Charleston, West Virginia 25305

   Business and Occupation Tax
   State Tax Department
   Charleston, West Virginia 25305

WISCONSIN
   Income, Sales, and Excise Tax Division
   Department of Revenue
   P.O. Box 39
   Madison, Wisconsin 53702

WYOMING
   Sales and Use Tax Division
   State Tax Commission
   Cheyenne, Wyoming 82002

Figure 1.1. (Continued)

13

deduct the amount that you owe them from the security that you posted with them.

Clearly it is to your advantage not to leave a security deposit for your seller's permit at all. How much security is required, however, or whether any is required, depends on the information that you provide on the application form that they will give you to fill out. The security amount required may be less than $100. However, the requirement for security can vary in any state from no deposit at all to several thousand dollars. In some cases, where the security deposit required is very high, installment payment arrangements can be made. The minimum is generally required if you own your own home and have substantial equity in it, if the estimated monthly expenses of your business are low, if your estimated monthly sales are low, if you are presently employed and this is a part-time business, if you have no employees, and if you have only one place of business. According to your own situation, additional amounts may or may not be required.

FICTITIOUS NAME REGISTRATION

You may or may not need fictitious name registration. Whether or not you must file a fictitious business name statement and get the publicity as required in your state depends on the law in your area of operations. Usually you must file a fictitious name registration statement if the business name that you select is within the definition of the fictitious business name used in your geographic area. What this generally means is that you are using a name in doing business that is other than your own or those of partners whom you may be associated with, that the name varies from the corporate name, that it does not include the surnames of all owners, or that it implies the existence of additional owners.

Obtaining fictitious name registration is usually very easy, and the fact that you must register it should not be considered an impediment to selecting a name that people will notice and associate with your business. To find out the law in your state, consult your telephone book and contact the appropriate agency listed under city, county, or state government, and they will give you the information regarding the requirements in your area. Typically, there will be a small registration fee of $10 or so, and within a period of the registration you must publish notice of the fictitious trade name in a general circulation newspaper in the area where the business is located. This may cost you another $30. You then file an affidavit confirming such publication at the county clerk's office. In practice, this is a very easy matter. Frequently the form can be obtained at the office of the newspaper in which you intend to publicize your notice, and they will handle everything for you, including filing the affidavit after publication. The form is usually a simple one, and filling it out will take you less than five minutes. Some states will allow you to obtain more than one fictitious name on one form. For some types of businesses, such as certain types of consultancies or researchers, this is an advantage, since these firms may legally use any of the fictitious names that are listed on the form. Usually the fictitious name is good for about five years and then must be renewed. You are generally informed well ahead of expiration. If you use your own name as that of your business, fictitious name registration is not required, nor is it required if you use your corporate name in the business.

SETTING UP THE BOOKS

Good records in your business are necessary for several purposes, including taxes, measurement of management effectiveness and efficiency, uncovering employee theft, material waste, and obtaining loans.

Essential records should include the following: (1) a daily summary of cash receipts taken from sales receipts; (2) an expense ledger tallying both cash and checks disbursed for expenses such as rent, payroll, and accounts payable; (3) an inventory purchase journal showing shipments received, accounts payable, and cash available for future purchases; (4) an employee compensation record listing hours, pay, and withheld deductions for both part-time and full-time workers; (5) an accounts receivable record for credit sales. Forms suitable for these purposes are shown in Figures 1.2–1.6.

FEDERAL TAX OBLIGATIONS

There are four basic types of federal taxes. These are income taxes, Social Security taxes, excise taxes, and unemployment taxes. We will discuss each in detail.

Income Taxes

The amount of federal income taxes that you will owe depends on the earnings of your company, as well as the type of business or organizational structure you choose: sole proprietorship, partnership, or corporation. If you choose either the sole proprietorship or the partnership structure, your other income exemptions and nonbusiness deductions and credits will also be important factors. If you are a sole proprietor, your income tax is paid just as if you were working for someone else. The big difference is that your income is derived from the earnings of your business instead of from a salary or wage. You file the identical form that the individual taxpayer working for someone else files. The only difference here is that you file an additional form that in effect identifies items of expense and income from your business. That form is Schedule C of 1040, Profit or Loss from Business or Profession. If your business is a partnership, the partnership must file a return to reflect the income and expenses of the business, and you will report only your share of the profit on your return.

One important difference as an individual proprietor or a partner in a partnership is that you are required by law to pay federal income tax and self-employment tax as income is received. You do this by filing a Declaration of Estimated Tax (Form 1040ES) on or before April 15 of each year. This declaration is an estimate of the income and self-employment taxes you expect to owe based on expected income and exemptions. You then make payment on this estimate each quarter, on or by April 15, June 15, September 15, and January 15. At the time of each payment, adjustments to the estimates can be made. As the owner of a new business, you may be required to file a declaration on a date other than April 15 if your expected income or exemptions change during the year. One example of this might be if you stop working as an employee and your wages were subject to withholding. You would then be required to file a declaration as follows: If the change occurred after April 1 or before June 2, you must file by June 15. If the change occurred after June 1 and before

Day/Date

Item Sold or Service Performed	Amount	
Total amount received today		
Total amount received through yesterday		
Total amount received to date		

Figure 1.2. Form for daily summary of cash receipts

Date	To Whom Paid	Purpose	Check Number	Amount	
		Total expenditures			

Figure 1.3. Form for an expense ledger tallying both cash and checks disbursed

Expenditure Summary

Purpose	Total This Period		Total up to This Period		Total to Date	
Advertising						
Car and truck expense						
Commissions						
Contributions						
Delivery expense						
Dues and publications						
Employee benefit program						
Freight						
Insurance						
Interest						
Laundry and cleaning						
Legal and professional services						
Licenses						
Miscellaneous expense						
Office supplies						
Pension and profit sharing plan						
Postage						

Figure 1.3. (Continued)

Purpose	Total This Period		Total up to This Period		Total to Date	
Rent						
Repairs						
Selling expense						
Supplies						
Tax						
Telephone						
Traveling and entertainment						
Utilities						
Wages						
Totals						

Figure 1.3. (*Continued*)

Date	Inventory Ordered	Shipments Received/Date	Accounts Payable	Cash Available for Future Purchases
	Carried Forward			

Totals

Figure 1.4. Form for an inventory purchase journal

Name _____ Social Security No. _____

Date	Period Worked (hours, days, weeks, or months)	Wage Rate	Total Wages	Deductions					Net Paid
				Soc. Sec.	Fed. Inc. Tax	State Inc. Tax			

Totals

Figure 1.5. Form for an employee compensation record

Date	Customer/Client Name	Products/Services	Amount Owed	Payments Made/Date

Figure 1.6. Form for an accounts receivable record for credit sales

September 2, you must file by September 15. If the change occurred after September 1, then you must file by January 15 of the following year.

If you are incorporated, your estimated payments are made on April 15, June 15, September 15, and December 15.

If your business is a corporation not filing as an S corporation discussed previously, it pays taxes on its profits. Also, as an owner of the corporation, you pay an additional tax on the salary you receive or dividend that your corporation pays to you.

Income tax rates for a corporation are currently set as shown in Table 1.1.

The income tax return for a corporation is due on the 15th day of the third month following the end of each taxable year. The corporation may select as its taxable year a period that does not coincide with the calendar year.

Table 1.1   Corporate Tax Rates

Taxable Income	Tax Rate
$50,000 or less	15%
$50,001–$75,000	25
$75,001–$100,000	34
$100,001–$335,000	39[a]
Over $335,000	34

[a] The highest rate is 39% between income levels $100,001 and $335,000. This higher rate is used to phase out the benefits of the lower tax rates for income levels up to $75,000.

While income tax returns are typically filed annually, payment of the taxes is made on an "on-account" basis by most firms, quarterly. Every corporation whose estimated tax is expected to be $40 or more is required to make estimated tax payments.

It is extremely important that you have the necessary funds to pay your income taxes on time. To assist you in paying income taxes as well as other taxes, it is recommended that you use Figure 1.7, Worksheet for Meeting Tax Obligations, which was developed by the Small Business Administration.

Withholding Income Taxes

By law, you must withhold the federal income tax payments for your employees. These payments are passed on to the government periodically. This process begins when you hire a new employee. Your new employee must sign Form W-4, Employee's Withholding Allowance Certificate. On it, your employee lists the exemptions and additional withholding allowances that he or she claims. The completed Form W-4 certificate is your authority to withhold income tax in accordance with the withholding tables issued by the IRS. If an employee fails to furnish a certificate, you are required to withhold tax as if he were a single person with no withholding exemptions. Before December 1, you should ask your employees to file new exemption certificates for the following year if there has been a change in their exemption status since they last filed their certificates. At the end of the year, you are required to furnish each employee copies of Form W-2, Wage and Tax Statement, for him- or herself and each taxing jurisdiction, that is, the state and local government. The employee files a copy with his or her income tax return and keeps one. You, the employer, must also furnish a copy of Form W-2 to the IRS on or before February 28. For complete details of how to do this and the necessary forms, contact the local office of the IRS.

Withholding Social Security Taxes

In paying Social Security taxes, you also deduct the necessary tax that each employee owes. However, by law, you are required to match these deductions. If you are using Social Security for your own retirement, you must pay the tax

This worksheet is designed to help the owner-manager to manage his firm's tax obligations. You may want your accountant or bookkeeper to prepare the worksheet so you can use it as a reminder in preparing for and paying the various taxes.

Kind of Tax	Due Date	Amount Due	Pay to	Date for Writing The Check
Federal Taxes				
Employee income tax and Social Security tax				
Excise Tax				
Owner-manager's and/or corporation's income tax				
Unemployment tax				
State Taxes				
Unemployment taxes				
Income taxes				
Sales taxes				
Franchise tax				
Other				
Local Taxes				
Sales tax				
Real estate tax				
Personal property tax				
Licenses (retail, vending machine, etc.)				
Other				

Figure 1.7. Worksheet for meeting tax obligations

for yourself. If your type of business involves tips, an employee receiving cash tips of $20 or more in a month while working for you must report these tips to you for income tax and Social Security purposes. This must be accomplished on or before the 10th day of the following month. You then deduct the employee's Social Security income tax from wages due the employee. However, you are required to match only deductions you made on the employee's wages. You need not match the Social Security taxes you deduct on the employee's tips.

Remitting Federal Taxes

To remit federal taxes, you take two actions: (1) You report the income and Social Security taxes that you withheld from the employee's pay, and (2) you deposit the funds that you withheld.

To report withholding and Social Security remittances to the federal government, use Form 941. A return for each calendar quarter is due on the last day of the following month, that is, April 30, July 31, October 31, and January 31. In many cases, remittances of taxes are required before the due date of the return. These dates depend on your situation.

To make deposits, you complete Form 501, Federal Tax Deposits, Withheld Income and FICA Taxes. This form, with a check, is sent to the Federal Reserve Bank that serves your district or to a commercial bank that is authorized to accept tax deposits. Your local bank or a Federal Reserve Bank can give you the names of such commercial banks. In general, the smaller the amount of your tax liability, the less frequently you are required to make a deposit. The basic rules are as follows:

1.   If you have less than $200 liability per quarter, no deposit will be required. The total liability for the quarter will be remitted with the return on or before the last day of the month following the close of the quarter.

2.   If at the end of the first month in the quarter the cumulative liability is less than $200 but by the end of the second month it is $200 or more, the employer must deposit the cumulative amount by the 15th day of the third month in the quarter. The liability for the third month of the quarter may be remitted with the return that will be due on or before the last day of the month following the close of the quarter. If the cumulative liability does not reach $200 until the third month of the quarter, the total liability must be deposited by the last day of the month following the close of the quarter.

3.   For each of the first two calendar months in the quarter, if the cumulative liability for the quarter is $200 or more and less than $2,000, deposits will be required on or before the 15th day of the next month. For the last month in the quarter, employers will not have to deposit until the last day of the month following the close of the quarter.

4.   If on the 7th, 15th, 22nd, or last day of the month cumulative liability is $2,000 or more, a deposit will be required within the next three banking days.

Excise Taxes

Federal excise taxes are imposed on the sale or use of certain items or certain transactions and on certain occupations. Examples are occupational tax on retail dealers in beer, retail liquor dealers, and wholesale beer and liquor dealers. Diesel fuel and certain special motor fuels carry a retailer's excise tax. There are manufacturers' excise taxes on trucks and equipment and on petroleum products and firearms. If a business involves liquor, gambling, or firearms, it may be subject to an occupational excise tax. To determine whether or not you are subject to a federal excise tax, contact your local IRS office. Certain excise taxes are due without assessment or notice. With others, you must file a quarterly return on Form 720. When you owe more than $100 a month in excise taxes, you must make monthly deposits of that tax in a Federal Reserve Bank or other authorized depository. Semimonthly rather than monthly deposits of excise taxes are required if you are liable for more than $2,000 in excise taxes reportable on Form 720 for any month during the previous quarter.

Unemployment Taxes

If you paid wages of $1,500 or more in any calendar quarter or you had one or more employees on at least some portion of one day in each of 20 or more calendar weeks, either consecutive or nonconsecutive, your business is liable for federal unemployment taxes. If your liability from deposits of federal unemployment taxes exceeds $100 for any calendar quarter and preceding quarter, you must deposit the tax with an authorized commercial bank or a Federal Reserve Bank within one month following the close of the quarter. Each deposit must be accompanied by a preinscribed Federal Unemployment Tax Deposit Form, Form 508. A supply of these forms will be furnished to you automatically if you have applied for an employer identification number. But in any case, they must be obtained from the IRS where you file returns.

An annual return must be filed on Form 940 on or before January 31 following the close of the calendar year for which the tax is due. Any tax still due is payable with the return. You must file Form 940 on a calendar year basis even if you operate on a fiscal year basis. Form 940 may be filed on or before February 10 following the close of the year if all the required deposits are made on time, in full payment of the tax due, deposited on or before January 31. Usually the IRS will mail copies of Form 940 to you. However, if you fail to receive them, copies may be obtained from your local IRS office.

Obtaining an Employer's Identification Number

An employer's identification number is required on all employment tax returns to the federal government. You obtain this by filing a Form SS-4 with your regional Internal Revenue Service Center. Please note that this identification number is not the same as your Social Security number required on your individual income tax returns. At the time that you apply for an employer's identification number, you can request your business tax kit which is IRS 454. This tax kit has additional information on taxes pertinent to each particular business.

STATE TAXES

State taxes vary from state to state. However, the three major types are unemployment taxes, income taxes, and sales taxes. It is critical for you to know what your state taxes are and what your state requires you to pay as well as what it requires you to collect as an agent of the state. In some states, if you fail to remit withheld state taxes, you can be charged with embezzlement.

Every state has state unemployment taxes. The rules and requirements vary state by state; however, they usually are based on the taxable wage base of a quarter, and the rate of tax charged is determined by your unemployment experience coupled with the unemployment experience of your state.

State income taxes are imposed by many states. If your state does so, you are required to deduct this tax from your employees' wages just as you deduct the federal tax. Sometimes these taxes are assessed in a fashion similar to the assessment of the federal tax, and sometimes not. If the requirements differ, make sure that your records will allow you the necessary information for the state income taxes.

To meet the sales tax obligation, if your state has sales tax, you must act as if you were an agent. You collect the tax and pass it on to the appropriate state agency. This was discussed earlier in the section dealing with the state board of equalization and resale permits.

LOCAL TAXES

Counties, towns, and cities impose various kinds of taxes. These include real estate taxes, personal property taxes, taxes on groceries, receipts of businesses, and unincorporated business taxes. A business license is also a tax, although you may not have thought of it as such. Local taxes may actually include income tax for very large cities. To ensure that you are paying the proper taxes, check with your local tax authorities.

TAX CREDITS

Tax credits are credits against the income tax that you pay and, as such, they are not deductions but account for much more. The laws have changed considerably under the new tax rules. Most tax credits have been eliminated.

In general, the regular Investment Credit has been repealed for property placed in service after December 31, 1985. However, there are some limited exceptions having to do with transition property, amortizable forestation and reforestation expenses, and qualified progress expenditures. Transitional property is generally any property you placed in service after 1985 if on that date you had a binding written contract for its acquisition, construction, or reconstruction.

As this is being written, most of the old standby tax credits such as Business Energy Credit, Research Credit, Target Jobs Credit, and the like have been eliminated or extended at reduced rates. There are, however, a new low-income housing credit available for buildings placed in service after 1986 and a fuel tax credit for taxicabs. For the latest information on tax credits, call one of the toll-free numbers listed in Appendix VI or order the appropriate free government tax publication in this appendix. You can get any of the forms or publications by calling the IRS's special toll-free "Forms Only" telephone number: 1-800-424-3676.

OUTSIDE HELP

For help with the legal aspects of going into business, you may need an attorney and an accountant. Whenever there's a doubt about a legal question, an attorney's help should be sought. An accountant can help you determine what records to keep and advise on techniques so you don't pay unnecessary tax. Both accountants and lawyers can advise on changes in tax laws that may require adjustments in the kind of facts necessary for tax reporting. Although use of attorneys and accountants will cost additional money, they may save you much more than their fees, not only in the long run but also in the short run.

And, of course, don't forget the government itself by using the information contained in Appendix VI.

COMPUTER PROGRAMS

There are now a number of computer programs that can help a great deal in the preparation of your taxes. One that I've found very useful is TurboTax R published by ChipSoft, Inc., 5045 Shoreham Place, #100, San Diego, CA 92122. Among other things, the program contains a large library of IRS tax forms. This will permit you to print out the forms yourself without having to go to one of the IRS offices. Also, the forms are linked so that updating one form updates all.

ChipSoft also publishes a state tax supplement, so that once your federal forms are completed, interaction with their state program completes all of your state form requirements by punching a few buttons on your computer.

Items such as Estimated Tax Worksheets are automatically calculated, and various other options let you consider the consequences of various changes in your income tax planning for the coming year in just a few minutes.

If all of the above weren't enough, the program can be used to keep most of your business records for the coming year. This, of course, will significantly reduce your tax preparation time then. For more information about computer programs, see Chapter 8.

SOURCES OF ADDITIONAL INFORMATION

The Drafting of Corporate Charters and Bylaws, by Kurt Pantzer and Richard Deer, published by the Joint Committee on Continuing Legal Education of the American Law Institute and the American Bar Association, 4025 Chestnut Street, Philadelphia, PA 19104.

Tax and Business Organization of Small Business, by Jonathan Sobeloff, published by the Joint Committee on Continuing Legal Education of the American Law Institute and the American Bar Association, 4025 Chestnut Street, Philadelphia, PA 19104.

Tax Guide for Small Business, IRS Publication No. 334, published by the Superintendent of Documents, Washington, DC 20402.

Sources of Capital and How to Get a Loan

THE BEST SOURCE OF CAPITAL

The best source of capital for any new business is your own money. The reason it's best is that it's the easiest to make use of and, of course, it's also the quickest to get. In addition, you don't need to worry about paying the money back and you don't have to surrender equity in your business. You should recognize that many outside sources of capital will expect you to put up some of your own money before they will agree to invest. This gives these sources greater confidence that you will not easily give up when the going in your business gets rough, and also that you are as convinced that your idea will succeed as you appear to be.

OBTAINING MONEY FROM FRIENDS AND RELATIVES

Friends and relatives are also a good source of money. This is the second fastest, easiest, and cheapest source of cash that you need for your business, with fewer legal problems and with far less paperwork required. If you do raise money from friends and relatives, try not to surrender control of your business; that is, make this money a loan and do not give up stock in your business. If you do become partners with friends or relatives, you may find it difficult to keep them out of day-to-day operations and decision making. Unless they have know-how to contribute as well as money, there is no reason for their participation.

BORROWING FROM THE BANK

There are various types of bank loans, and the difficulty of getting them varies considerably. Basically, the bank is a very conservative lender that will insist on collateral and will want to be absolutely certain that it will get its money back from you. If you have money in a savings account, you can borrow against this money. The cost of such a loan is usually low, because the savings institution in which you have the money can use your savings as collateral until your loan is repaid. There is an advantage to this type of loan: the money you have in the savings account continues to draw interest while you have the loan, even while it is being held as collateral. Accordingly, if your money is normally earning 9½% interest and if the loan is costing you 15½%, the real cost of the loan is only 6% interest.

It might also be relatively easy for you to get a loan using your life insurance as collateral. This is possible if your life insurance policy has cash value. If so, you can generally obtain a loan up to 95% of the money that has been accumulated. With this type of life insurance loan, you don't actually have to repay the loan; you pay only the interest each year along with your premium. Of course, if you don't replace the money that you borrowed from your life insurance, that amount is deducted from the face value of the policy paid to any beneficiary.

Another type of bank loan that is relatively easy to get, if your credit is good, is a signature or personal loan for several thousand dollars. If you have dealt with the same bank for some time, sometimes you can get an even larger loan if the bank believes that you are a good risk. These types of loans are short term and usually must be paid off within from several months to several years. Depending on your negotiations with the bank, these loans may be paid off on an installment plan or in a lump sum at a specified time.

TYPES OF BANK LOANS

The *commercial loan* is a short-term loan from a bank that is usually paid off in a lump sum within a six-month period. Stocks and bonds, the cash value of life insurance, or a personal guarantee may be accepted as collateral for this type of loan. If the loan exceeds a certain amount, some banks will require that the borrower maintain a reserve of cash in a bank account. This reserve is known as a compensating balance. Its size will depend on a number of factors, but usually will not have to be more than 20% of the amount borrowed.

Accounts receivable financing is credit extended from the bank, unsecured, against money owed you by your customers. Usually the bank will advance you up to about 80% of the receivable value. You are required to sign the receivables over to the bank. When you receive payment, you send payments to the bank which credits this amount against your loan along with the interest agreed upon. Your customer is not involved in any way and pays you in the usual manner.

Inventory financing uses raw materials or finished goods in your inventory as collateral. You usually can get this type of loan only up to 50% of the value of the inventory.

Loans against real estate can usually be made for up to 75% of the property value and amortized over a fairly long period, in some cases up to 20 years. A bank will also provide residential mortgages and real estate refinancing.

If you intend to buy major equipment, banks will make *equipment loans* for up to about 80% of the equipment's value. The maximum length of this loan is usually five years or the maximum life of the equipment.

SMALL BUSINESS ADMINISTRATION LOANS

Small Business Administration (SBA) loans have been a good source of capital; however, they are far from automatic and, like any loan, they require a completed loan package developed by the entrepreneur or small businessperson. Completing the "Small Business Administration Business Plan and Qualifications Résumé"

(Appendix V) will help you with this. You should also allow yourself as long a lead time as you can from the time you apply for the loan. An SBA loan is not instantaneous.

By law, the SBA may not make a loan if you can obtain funds from a bank or other private source. Therefore, you must seek private financing before applying for an SBA loan. This means that you should apply to your bank or other lending institution for a loan, and if you live in a city with a population of more than 200,000, you are required to apply to two banks before applying for a direct SBA loan.

There are various types of SBA loans, and their structures change from time to time. Therefore, you should check with the local office of your SBA (see Appendix I) to get the latest information. However, there are basically two types of loans that you may qualify for: business loans and economic opportunity loans.

SBA business loans are for businesses, including farms, that are independently owned and operated and not dominant in their fields, that are unable to obtain private financing under reasonable terms, that are qualified as "small" under SBA size standards based on various factors. These factors are always under review. According to an SBA bulletin issued in July 1982:

> The Small Business Act of 1953 broadly defines a small business as independently owned and not dominant in its field. The act authorizes the administrator of the U.S. Small Business Administration (SBA) to establish more specific, industry-related criteria that can be used to identify the small business community in order to determine eligibility for SBA program benefits, procurement set-asides, regulatory exemptions, and other forms of federal assistance. The size standards developed through these criteria are of vital concern to every business that considers itself to be small.
>
> Existing size standards were developed through a consensus process with each industry. While these standards vary markedly between industries in order to reflect the specific characteristics of each industry, they lack an underlying comprehensive rationale or a cohesive logic. In some cases these standards reflect the special interests of procurement agencies, Congress, or the historical view of specific businesses.
>
> Currently, SBA utilizes a variety of measures for size determinations. The largest number of businesses in retail, service, wholesale, construction, and agriculture, for example, are measured by annual receipts criteria (averaged over 3 years). Manufacturing, research and development, and mining are measured by employee criteria. Criteria used to determine business size in other industries include such measures as the number of hospital beds and barrels of oil refined per day.
>
> In 1978, the SBA initiated a comprehensive study of its size standards, and as a result has announced that it intends to propose sweeping revisions. While these revisions are fundamentally a bureaucratic exercise, they are necessary in order to bring coherence to SBA's policies regarding loans, procurement assistance, and advocacy.
>
> On March 10, 1980, SBA issued its first advance notice of proposed size standard revisions. The SBA held ten regional hearings on the notice and received over 1,500 comments. Over 80 percent of these comments criticized the new measure. The Senate Select Committee on Small Business also held hearings on the notice on May 5, 1981, at which the public was once again invited to participate.
>
> On May 3, 1982, the SBA issued its second advance notice of proposed size standard revisions which reflected the comments received on the first proposal.

The May 3 notice uses one criteria for measuring business size—number of employees—but retains the annual receipts criteria for measuring business size in agriculture and construction. (Measuring employment in the agriculture industry presents problems of determining whether family members and relatives are considered employees. In construction the question is whether employees of subcontractors, which are used widely in this industry category, should be included in the employee count. Both problems were resolved by the annual receipts approach.)

The May 3 notice establishes a maximum employee limit above which a business is no longer considered by the SBA to be small. In the manufacturing industry, the proposed limit has been set at 500 employees. This is a significant reduction from the 2,500 employee ceiling proposed in the 1980 notice.

Upper limits were also imposed on the major industry categories in retail, wholesale, service, transportation, and finance. These ceilings, proposed in the May 1982 notice, range from 25 to 500 employees depending on the type of firm. (In the 1980 proposal, some ceilings were as low as 15 employees.)

This adjustment corrects one inequity noted by the Office of Advocacy regarding the first advance notice in 1980. For example, under that proposal, a large manufacturer with just under 2,500 employees would have been eligible for SBA assistance. At the same time, a retailer owning a hardware store with eight employees and a small grocery store with eight employees would have been classified as a large business, and no longer eligible for SBA assistance. The adjustment restores some equity among industry categories.

In addition, the May 3 notice clarifies SBA's intent to average full-time and part-time employees so that seasonal fluctuations in employment will not significantly affect a firm's size status. Those industries relying heavily on part-time employees were reviewed carefully, and standards were adjusted accordingly.

In the interest of administrative simplicity and uniformity, SBA has also proposed several procedural changes in its size standard regulations. These include:

Eliminating geographical differentials.

Basing all SBA size standard categories on the Office of Management and Budget's published Standard Industrial Classification codes, in lieu of written descriptions.

Eliminating broad-based non-manufacturing size standards and replacing them with industry-specific size standards.

Eliminating the special size standards for the surety bond guarantee program.

Increasing small business size standards by 25 percent for businesses located in labor surplus or redevelopment areas.

More recently, the SBA published the following criteria that define a small business:

Manufacturing. Maximum number of employees may range from 500 to 1,500 depending on the industry in which the applicant is engaged.

Wholesaling. Maximum number of employees not to exceed 500.

Services. Annual sales or receipts not exceeding $3.5 to $14.5 million, depending on the industry in which the applicant is primarily engaged.

Retailing. Annual sales or receipts not exceeding $3.5 to $13.5 million, depending on the industry.

Construction. General construction average annual receipts not exceeding $17 million for the three most recently completed fiscal years.

Special trade construction. Average annual receipts not exceeding $7 million for three most recently completed fiscal years, depending on the industry.

Agriculture. Annual receipts not exceeding $0.1 to $3.5 million.

Check with your SBA office for the official definition at the time of your loan application.

You can use the SBA business loan for conversion or expansion; purchase of equipment, facilities, machinery, supplies, materials; and working capital.

There are two basic types of SBA business loan. The first consists of loans made by private lenders, usually banks, and guaranteed by the SBA. By law, the SBA can guarantee a portion of a loan made by a bank or other private lender; however, the SBA's guaranty cannot exceed $500,000.

The second basic type of SBA business loan is made directly by the SBA. In general, these loans carry interest rates slightly lower than the going rate in private financial markets. They are available only to applicants unable to obtain either private financing or an SBA guaranteed or participation loan.

How much can you borrow? As indicated previously, the maximum for the SBA guarantee program is $500,000. But loans made directly by the SBA are much less: currently a maximum of $150,000. For regular business loans, the maximum maturity is 25 years. Working capital loans, however, are generally limited to 7 years. The SBA sets a maximum allowable interest rate that banks charge on guaranteed loans. There is a special type of loan known as an immediate participation loan in which the bank disburses part of the loan at current market interest rates and the balance comes directly from the SBA. Interest rates on the SBA's share of this loan and on direct loans are tied to the cost of money to the federal government and adjusted periodically. For another special loan known as a handicap assistance loan, the interest rate for the SBA's share is only 3%.

As collateral for an SBA loan, you may be required to put up a mortgage on land, buildings, and/or equipment, assignment of warehouse receipts for marketable merchandise, a mortgage on chattels or guarantees of personal endorsements, and, in some cases, assignment or current receivables.

Economic opportunity loans are similar to business loans except they are for low-income or disadvantaged persons who lack the opportunity to start or strengthen a small business and cannot obtain the necessary financing from other sources on reasonable terms. Usually these loans are limited to $100,000 to any one borrower. The money can be used for purposes similar to those stated for the business loan, and the interest rate is set by a statutory formula. Major differences here have to do with the maximum period of time for repayment of the loan. There is a maximum of 15 years, with a maximum of 10 years for a working capital loan. Also, the collateral that is required may be any worthwhile collateral that is available or will be acquired with the proceeds of the loan.

How to Apply for an SBA Loan

There are many companies around that will offer to carry out the entire SBA loan application procedure for you, for a fee. In most cases, you will be able to do the same job for yourself at a much lower cost. You should be aware that no preparer can guarantee that you will get your loan approved. Be wary of any company that even implies that your loan approval is assured if they prepare your loan package. The SBA recommends the following sequence to obtain one of their loans:

1. Prepare a current financial statement balance sheet listing all assets and all liabilities of your business.

2. Have a profit and loss statement for the preceding full year and for the current period to the date of the balance sheet.

3. Prepare a current personal financial statement of yourself as owner or each partner or stockholder owning 20% or more of the corporate stock in the business.

4. List collateral to be offered as security for the loan with your estimate of the present market value of each item.

5. State amount of loan requested and explain exact purposes for which it will be used.

6. Take this material with you and see your banker. Ask for a direct bank loan and, if refused, ask the bank to make the loan under the SBA's loan guarantee plan or to participate with the SBA in a loan. If the bank is interested in an SBA guarantee or participation loan, ask the banker to contact the SBA for discussion of your application. In most cases of guarantee or participation loans, the SBA will deal directly with the bank.

7. If a guarantee or participation loan is not available, write or visit the nearest SBA office and they will give you the additional information required.

For new businesses, follow these procedures:

1. Describe in detail the type of business to be established.

2. Describe experience and management capabilities.

3. Prepare an estimate of how much you or others have to invest in the business and how much you will need to borrow.

4. Prepare a current financial statement balance sheet listing all personal assets and all liabilities.

5. Prepare a current financial statement balance sheet listing all personal assets and all liabilities.

5. Prepare a detailed projection of earnings for the first year the business will operate.

6. List collateral to be offered as security for the loan, indicating your estimate of the present market value of each item.

7. Take this material and go see your banker. Ask for a direct bank loan and, if refused, ask the bank to make the loan under the SBA's loan guarantee plan or to participate with the SBA in a loan. If the bank is interested in the SBA guarantee or participation loan, ask the banker to contact the SBA for discussion of your application. In most cases of guarantee or participation loans, the SBA will deal directly with the bank.

8. If a guarantee or participation loan is not available, write or visit the nearest SBA office for additional information.

See Chapters 6 and 8 for information on preparation of financial statements.

OBTAINING MONEY FROM FACTORS

Obtaining money from factors involves the outright sale of your accounts receivable to another party. Essentially, you get paid cash on delivery of your product or service while your customers receive credit on terms that they require. This differs from accounts receivable financing in that factoring is not a loan. The factor actually purchases your accounts receivable for their full value, usually for up to 80% of their worth, at the time that you ship the goods. The remainder of their worth is given to you when your customers pay. The factor checks the credit of each of your customer's accounts and purchases these receivables from you without recourse, which means that the factor absorbs any bad debt losses. To compensate for these risks, factors typically charge a 1 to 2% fee for each invoice, plus interest, on the advance that they make to you. The total amount is usually greater than bank and commercial finance company rates for comparable loans. However, factors do not require as extensive a loan package as other lenders. Also, obtaining money from a factor can be fast, and sometimes once your credit references and other financial statements are supplied and the credit of the account has been confirmed, you can obtain money in as little as 24 hours.

FINANCE COMPANIES

Finance companies will assume a greater amount of risk in the loan than will banks. Whereas a bank may deny you the loan if you have a high degree of debt or may be running into financial difficulties, a commercial finance company makes loans on the strength of your collateral rather than your track record or potential. Commercial finance companies will make loans much as banks do to include equipment leasing and factoring. Naturally you will pay more money in interest for a commercial finance company loan than for a bank loan. Obtaining the loan usually requires several days up to a few weeks.

USING SUPPLIERS FOR A LOAN

Your suppliers are a frequently overlooked source of a loan. Suppliers may be those selling you stationery and printing supplies, or various components or materials that are used in something that you manufacture. In effect, a loan exists if your supplier will not require a payment until the delivery of supplies. In addition, sometimes suppliers will grant you 30, 60, or 90 days, or even more time to pay for whatever material you have purchased from them. Clearly, the effect is that of a loan, even though a loan as such has not been negotiated. Usually suppliers will give a discount for early payment of purchased supplies; typically, this discount is 2% for payment within 10 days. This 2% savings should be weighed against your need for funds in the business. You should never be afraid to ask for credit to enable you to pay later if you need this money for some important business purpose.

CREDIT CARD LOANS

Credit cards are another frequently overlooked source of "loans." Depending on the particular credit card and the amount of credit that you are permitted with that card, you may be able to get several thousand dollars, with which you can purchase supplies or materials for your business. This credit is easy to get and requires no special paperwork as long as you do not go above the amount that has been established for you with the particular credit card. Be careful of the interest rate on these, however; it can be extremely high, and you should weigh against the easy acquisition of this money the amount of interest charged.

EQUITY CAPITAL FINANCING

Equity capital financing is selling off a portion of your business to another investor who contributes capital and may or may not participate in the management of your business. Your business has no legal obligation for repayment of the amount invested or for payment of interest for the amount of the funds. The investor shares in the ownership of the business and is entitled to participate in any distribution of earnings through dividends in the case of corporations or any draw in the case of a partnership. How much the investor participates in the distribution of earnings depends on the number of shares that he or she holds; or in a partnership, the percentage of the business that the partnership owns. Since you do not have to pay a debt, equity financing may appear to be an easy way to obtain capital for your business. However, it has the following disadvantages:

1. The share in the success must be extended to other owners in your business.
2. You lose some control over your business. In some types of equity financing you will have to give up a majority control. You should most definitely consult your attorney before taking on any equity investors.

HOW TO VALUE EQUITY CAPITAL

A primary question once the decision has been made to use equity capital is how to value it. In a start-up situation, for example, it is fairly typical for the individual with the idea or product innovation to get 50% equity and the investors to get the other 50% equity. If the innovator also has capital to contribute, he is given the same proportion of equity for his additional capital as the investors are given for theirs. Although the 50-50 rule is fairly common, another way of doing this is to put some value on the contributions of the individual starting the company. For example, if a price tag can be put on patents that he or she is contributing, specific knowledge, and so forth, then this would help to place a value on the equity that is given to the investors in exchange for capital. Of course, all terms are negotiable and the valuation of the innovator's contributions versus capital contributions will vary from situation to situation.

VENTURE CAPITAL

Venture capital is generally used for relatively new businesses that are somewhat risky but that have both a successful track record and a clear potential for high growth and return on investment. Venture capital firms and individuals who venture their own capital are interested in many of the same factors that influence other lending organizations. That is, they want to know the results and ratios of past operations, how much money is wanted, what the money is wanted for, and financial projections. But venture capitalists will look much more closely at the features of the product or service being offered and the potential in the market than do many other lending organizations. As a result, venture capitalists very frequently have definite preferences for certain types of industries, certain types of products, and certain locations.

Before you even consider this source, you should know that venture capitalists are interested in being owners. That is, they will insist on an equity type of financing. Further, in most cases, venture capitalists will insist on owning more than 50% of the business. However, this may not be as critical a factor as it seems. Although in theory, the venture capitalist will control the company by owning a majority of the stock, these companies are normally not interested in running the business on a day-to-day basis, or in exerting their control so as to interfere in your business management.

Despite the fact that venture capitalists insist on equity financing and owning a controlling interest in the businesses they finance, they are usually in a buyers' market. Typically venture capital firms will receive hundreds, if not thousands, of proposals during the course of the year. They may reject 95%. It is important to remember, therefore, that in order to interest a venture capital firm in your business, you must do the selling. Understand that they are interested only in companies with some sort of track record and will invest only in firms that they believe can rapidly increase in sales and generate substantial profits with the money they provide. Typically, venture capital companies seek a return of three to five times their investment in only five to seven years. And, also typically, venture capital firms are interested in investment projects requiring an investment of from $250,000 up to about $2 million.

Selling the Venture Proposal

Inasmuch as 90% or more proposals to venture capital firms are rejected, you must do your homework and recognize what a venture capital firm is looking for when you prepare your venture proposal. This proposal should emphasize the market potential and competitive position of the company, along with its products, present and potential customers, suppliers, production costs, financial condition, and the character and competence of the management including experience and background.

The proposal should be upbeat without lying. Difficulties should be clearly indicated, but each problem stated should also include a solution. The proposal should be under 50 pages and should cover the following areas in detail: purposes and objectives of the project; the proposed financing, including the amount of money that you'll need, how the money will be used, and how you plan on structuring the financing; marketing, including the marketing segment that you are after, competitors that are in the market and how you will beat them, characteristics of the market, and costs of executing the marketing plan you are proposing. You should also have a history of your firm including the significant milestones since founding, prior financing, your success, company organization, financial relationships with banks and other lending institutions, and a detailed description of your product or service and the costs associated with it. As for financial statements, you should include balance sheets, income statements, and cash flows for the last three years, as well as projections for the next three years that include the effect with the proposed project for which financing is being obtained. You should also include an analysis of key factors that may affect the financial performance, as well as the result if the level of sales projected is not attained. You should have a complete list of shareholders in your company, the amounts invested to date, and the form of capitalization equity per debt. Biographical sketches or résumés containing the qualifications and experience of key owners and managers of the company should be included and should emphasize experience and accomplishments that have a bearing on the operation of your firm. You should include a list of your main suppliers and your main customers and problems that you anticipate or that are possible, as well as actions that you would take in the event that these problems become a reality. Finally, you should have a section detailing the advantages of your firm—its product, service, plans, personnel—and the project for which you need the money. Finally, you should emphasize why and how your unique advantages cannot fail but will surely result in success for this project.

For a list of venture capital companies, get a copy of *The Guide to Venture Capital Sources*, published by the Capital Publishing Corp., 10 South LaSalle Street, Chicago, IL 60603.

SMALL BUSINESS INVESTMENT COMPANIES AND MINORITY ENTERPRISE SMALL BUSINESS INVESTMENT COMPANIES

Small business investment companies, or SBICs, and minority enterprise small business investment companies, or MESBICs, are both regulated and sponsored by the SBA. In fact, the government puts up a great deal of the capital for these firms to invest in young companies. The major difference between the SBIC and the MESBIC is that the MESBIC must invest only in minority-owned and minority-managed firms. The rules and regulations are relaxed significantly for these firms and the money leveraging capabilities are increased significantly.

SBICs and MESBICs make both equity investments and long-term loans. These loans can be as large as their equity investments—30% of the MESBIC's private capitalization or 20% of the SBIC's private funds. Most of these loans are made for from 5 to 7 years, although they can go as high as 20 years, and they are generally made for business expansion purposes. Typical charges for SBIC and MESBIC loans are the going bank rate in your state, and both loans and equity investments from either SBICs or MESBICs will take from several weeks to several months.

You will find a list of SBICs in Appendix VII.

SMALL BUSINESS DEVELOPMENT COMPANIES

Small business development companies, or SBDCs, operate in the same fashion as SBICs except that they are capitalized entirely by private sources, including banks, large manufacturing firms, utility companies, transportation firms, and so forth. Like the SBICs and the MESBICs, they make loans on a long-term basis or purchase stock in the venture. Information on SBDCs can be obtained from your local chamber of commerce.

STATE BUSINESS AND INDUSTRIAL DEVELOPMENT CORPORATIONS

Many states have their own development corporations which are capitalized through funds from the state. These state business and industrial development corporations, or SBIDCs, make long-term loans rather than equity investments, specializing in from 5- to 20-year loans for the expansion of facilities and the purchase of equipment. SBIDC interests and priorities vary from state to state. Some are particularly interested in making high-risk loans for businesses that cannot otherwise obtain loans from banks. Others will only lend capital when the risk is minimal. To get more information on SBIDCs, check with your state business development office or chamber of commerce or the SBA office in your area.

LOCAL DEVELOPMENT COMPANIES

Local development companies (LDCs) are resident organized and capitalized. However, they solicit SBA and bank loans to buy or build facilities for local small businesses. Once they have identified small businesses in the local area that are in need, they are eligible for one SBA loan or guarantee up to $1 million annually, and unlimited bank loans for each small business they assist. Typically, an LDC supplies only 10% of a project's cost; the remainder must be obtained through combined SBA and bank loans or one SBA guarantee bank loan. Also, an LDC can finance all of a company's facilities, but it cannot supply working capital or fund the purchase of inventory supplies or freestanding fixtures and equipment.

High-risk ventures are good candidates for an LDC loan because the LDC and not the small business is the actual loan recipient. Some LDCs are nonprofit corporations and therefore will charge minimum interest on their 10% of the funds lent. Others that operate for a profit will charge rates that are comparable with those of banks.

In order to use and get an LDC loan, you must first be approved by the LDC using a standard loan package that is described at the end of the chapter. You are then evaluated by the SBA and then by the participating bank. Lead time for the LDC loan in its entirety is from two to four months.

To find out the LDCs in your area, consult Appendix I and contact the SBA field office in your area.

USE OF FINDERS IN LOCATING LOANS

Finders are individual financial consultants who are paid a percentage of the loan by you to locate a loan for you. These finders may be obtained by word of mouth from other entrepreneurs and small businesspeople or from your attorney, accountant, or banker. Sometimes finders can be found through advertisements in financial papers or the classified section of your local newspaper or the *Wall Street Journal*. Finders' fees vary greatly. They may be as low as 1% or as high as 15% or more. Therefore, if you use a finder, make certain that you ask for enough money in the loan to include the fee.

HOW TO DECIDE WHICH TYPE OF FUNDING TO USE

To determine which source of funding is best for you in your situation, you should consider the following factors primary. They are:

1. *Cost.* How much will each type of capital cost and how will each source affect the earnings of the present owners of the business?
2. *Risk.* How does each source of funding affect your business or expose it to risk?

3. *Flexibility.* What conditions imposed by each source of funding affect your flexibility either in seeking additional capital or in using the capital generated the way you wish and according to your best judgment?
4. *Control.* How is your present control of the business affected by the source of funding? Will loss of control prevent you from making operating and daily business decisions that you consider to be in your best interest?
5. *Availability.* Which sources are in fact available for you to use and which are not?

These five factors can be weighed according to your situation and all tradeoffs should be considered in order to arrive at the optimal method of funding for your particular situation.

PUBLIC STOCK OFFERINGS, MERGERS, AND CASHING IN

When your business is first organized, equity capital is usually secured from a combination of sources including your own personal savings and money from friends, relatives, and so forth. Then, as you grow, you will need additional capital through professional finders, venture capitalists, SBICs, and other sources. Finally, as very high levels of capital are needed, you will have basically two choices. One option is to merge with a larger company for an infusion of capital, and a second is to sell shares through public offering. The public offering seeks to attract a large number of investors to purchase stock. Both stock offerings and mergers provide a way in which you can cash in on your business. For example, a merger may entitle you to stock from the larger firm which can be held or turned into cash, plus a management position and salary if you desire to continue managing the enterprise that you started, or a fee over a period of years as a consultant or as part of an agreement not to compete with the firm with which you've merged. Selling capital stock of a corporation is closely regulated and can fail. It is done through your local investment banker when your enterprise is a corporation. And through the use of different types of stock, common versus preferred, you may retain your control over the corporation since while preferred stock has a priority of dividends it does not have a voting privilege as does common stock. Therefore, by retaining the majority of common stock in a corporation, you can retain control.

The banker prepares a detailed study of your projections and plans for your firm which he issues in the form of an offering. The investment banker's charges will depend on whether he guarantees sale of the full amount or whether the stock is sold on a "best efforts" basis. The first type of offering is usually reserved for large enterprises that have a considerable track record. The investment banker, for a fee, can also analyze your business plan and loan package and prepare an offering of your company's stock to its investment contacts. This private placement may be in the form of a stock equity or long-term debt, but it is not intended for public trading and therefore is not registered with the Securities and Exchange Commission (SEC).

THE LOAN PACKAGE

The loan package is extremely important for all types of loans. Figure 2.1 shows a loan package outline from the SBA itself. Figure 2.2 shows a loan package outline and example.

U.S. Small Business Administration

APPLICATION FOR BUSINESS LOAN

I. Applicant

30

Trade Name of Borrower		Street Address		
32		34		

City	County	State	Zip	Tel. No. (Inc. A/C)
36		37	39	

Employers ID Number	Date of Application	Date Application Received by SBA	Number of Employees (including subsidiaries and affiliates)
33		5	

Type of Business	Date Business Established	☐ Existing Business	At Time of Application _____
Bank of Business Account		☐ New Business ☐ Purchase Existing Business	If Loan is Approved _____

II. Management (Proprietor, partners, officers, directors and stockholders owning 20% or more of outstanding stock)

Name	Address	% Owned	Annual Comp.	*Military Service From	To	*Race	*Sex
			$				
			$				
			$				
			$				

*This data is collected for statistical purposes only. It has no bearing on the credit decision to approve or decline this application.

III. Use of Proceeds: (Enter Gross Dollar Amounts Rounded to Nearest Hundreds)	Loan Requested	SBA USE ONLY Approved	2 SBA Office Code	1 (1) SBA Loan Number
⑤ Land Acquisition	$			
⑥ New Plant or Building Construction				
⑦ Building Expansion or Repair				
⑧ Acquisition and/or Repair of Machinery and Equipment				
⑨ Inventory Purchase				
⑩ Working Capital (Including Accounts Payable)				
⑪ Acquisition of all or part of Existing Business				
⑫a Payoff SBA Loan				
⑫b Payoff Bank Loan (Non SBA Associated)				
⑫c Other Debt Payment (Non SBA Associated)				
⑬ All Other				
⑭ Total Loan Requested	$			
Term of Loan				

IV. Summary of Collateral:

If your collateral consists of (A) Land and Building, (D) Accounts Receivable and/or (E) Inventory, fill in the appropriate blanks. If you are pledging (B) Machinery and Equipment, (C) Furniture and Fixtures, and/or (F) Other, please provide an itemized list (labeled Exhibit A) that contains serial and identification numbers for all articles that had an original value greater than $500. Include a legal description of Real Estate offered as collateral.

	Present Market Value	Present Mortgage Balance	Cost Less Depreciation
A. Land and Building	$	$	$
B. Machinery & Equipment			
C. Furniture & Fixtures			
D. Accounts Receivable			
E. Inventory			
F. Other			
Total Collateral	$	$	$

V. Previous Government Financing: If you or any principals or affiliates have ever requested Government Financing (including SBA), complete the following:

Name of Agency	Amount	Date of Request	Approved or Declined	Balance	Status
	$			$	
	$			$	
	$			$	

③ Previous SBA Financing (Check One) ☐ (1) No ☐ (2) Repaid/Other ☐ (3) Present Borrower

④ Loan Number of 1st SBA Loan

VI. Indebtedness: Furnish the following information on all installment debts, contracts, notes, and mortgages payable. Indicate by an asterisk (*) items to be paid by loan proceeds and reason for paying same (present balance should agree with latest balance sheet submitted).

To Whom Payable	Original Amount	Original Date	Present Balance	Rate of Interest	Maturity Date	Monthly Payment	Security	Current or Delinquent
	$		$			$		
	$		$			$		
	$		$			$		
	$		$			$		

SBA Form 4 (9-81) REF SOP 50 10 1 PREVIOUS EDITIONS ARE OBSOLETE (OVER)

Figure 2.1. Loan package outline from the SBA.

All Exhibits must be signed and dated by person signing this form.

1. Submit SBA Form 912 (Personal History Statement) for each person e.g. owners, partners, directors, major stockholders, etc; the instructions are on SBA Form 912.

2. Furnish a signed current personal balance sheet (SBA Form 413 may be used for this purpose) for each stockholder (with 20% or greater ownership), partner, officer, and owner. Social Security number should be included on personal financial statement. Label this Exhibit B.

3. Include the statements listed below: 1, 2, 3 for the last three years; also 1, 2, 3, 4 dated within 90 days of filing the application; and statement 5, if applicable. This is Exhibit C (SBA has Management Aids that help in the preparation of financial statements.)

    1. Balance Sheet   2. Profit and Loss Statement
    3. Reconciliation of Net Worth
    4. Aging of Accounts Receivable and Payable
    5. Earnings projections for at least one year where financial statements for the last three years are unavailable or where requested by District Office.

       (If Profit and Loss Statement is not available, explain why and substitute Federal Income Tax Forms.)

4. Provide a brief history of your company and a paragraph describing the expected benefits it will receive from the loan. Label it Exhibit D.

5. Provide a brief description of the educational, technical and business background for all the people listed in Section II under Management. Please mark it Exhibit E.

6. Do you have any co-signers and/or guarantors for this loan? If so, please submit their names, addresses and personal balance sheet(s) as Exhibit F.

7. Are you buying machinery or equipment with your loan money? If so, you must include a list of the equipment and the cost. This is Exhibit G.

8. Have you or any officers of your company ever been involved in bankruptcy or insolvency proceedings? If so, please provide the details as Exhibit H. If none, check here ☐

9. Are you or your business involved in any pending lawsuits? If yes, provide the details as Exhibit I. If none, check here ☐

10. Do you or your spouse or any member of your household, or anyone who owns, manages, or directs your business or their spouses or members of their households work for the Small Business Administration, Small Business Advisory Council, SCORE or ACE, any Federal Agency, or the participating lender? If so, please provide the name and address of the person and the office where employed. Label this Exhibit J. If none, check here ☐

11. Does your business have any subsidiaries or affiliates? If yes, please provide their names and the relationship with your company along with a current balance sheet and operating statement for each. This should be Exhibit K.

12. Do you buy from, sell to, or use the services of any concern in which someone in your company has a significant financial interest? If yes, provide details on a separate sheet of paper labeled Exhibit L.

13. If your business is a franchise, include a copy of the franchise agreement and a copy of the FTC disclosure statement supplied to you by the Franchisor. Please include it as Exhibit M.

CONSTRUCTION LOANS ONLY

14. Include in a separate exhibit (Exhibit N) the estimated cost of the project and a statement of the source of any additional funds.

15. File all the necessary compliance documents (SBA Form Series 601). The loan officer will advise which forms are necessary.

16. Provide copies of preliminary construction plans and specifications. Include them as Exhibit O. Final plans will be required prior to disbursement.

DIRECT LOANS ONLY

17. Include two bank declination letters with your application. These letters should include the name and telephone number of the persons contacted at the banks, the amount and terms of the loan, the reason for decline and whether or not the bank will participate with SBA. In cities with 200,000 people or less, one letter will be sufficient.

AGREEMENTS AND CERTIFICATIONS

Agreement of Nonemployment of SBA Personnel: I/We agree that if SBA approves this loan application I/We will not, for at least two years, hire as an employee or consultant anyone that was employed by the SBA during the one year period prior to the disbursement of the loan.

Certification: I/We certify: (a) I/We have not paid anyone connected with the Federal Government for help in getting this loan. I/We also agree to report to the SBA Office of Security and Investigations, 1441 L Street N.W., Washington, D.C., 20416 any Federal Government employee who offers, in return for any type of compensation, to help get this loan approved.

(b) All information in this application and the Exhibits is true and complete to the best of my/our knowledge and is submitted to SBA so SBA can decide whether to grant a loan or participate with a lending institution in a loan to me/us. I/We agree to pay for or reimburse SBA for the cost of any surveys, title or mortgage examinations, appraisals etc., performed by non-SBA personnel provided I/We have given my/our consent.

(c) I/We give the assurance that we will comply with sections 112 and 113 of Title 13 of the Code of Federal Regulations. These Code sections prohibit discrimination on the grounds of race, color, sex, religion, marital status, handicap, age, or national origin by recipients of Federal financial assistance and require appropriate reports and access to books and records. These requirements are applicable to anyone who buys or takes control of the business. I/We realize that if I/We do not comply with these non-discrimination requirements SBA can call, terminate, or accelerate repayment of my/our loan. As consideration for any Management and Technical Assistance that may be provided, I/We waive all claims against SBA and its consultants.

I/We understand that I/We need not pay anybody to deal with SBA. I/We have read and understand Form 394 which explains SBA policy on representatives and their fees.

For Guaranty Loans please provide an original and one copy (Photocopy is Acceptable) of the Application Form, and all Exhibits to the participating lender. For Direct Loans submit one original copy of application and Exhibits to SBA.

It is against SBA regulations to charge the applicant a percentage of the loan proceeds as a fee for preparing this application.

If you make a statement that you know to be false or if you over value a security in order to help obtain a loan under the provisions of the Small Business Act, you can be fined up to $5,000 or be put in jail for up to two years, or both.

Signature of Preparer if Other Than Applicant

Print or Type Name of Preparer

Address of Preparer

If Applicant is a proprietor or general partner, sign below:

By:_____
                                       Date

If Applicant is a corporation, sign below:

Corporate Seal   Date

By:_____
             Signature of President

Attested by: _____
              Signature of Corporate Secretary

Figure 2.1. (Continued)

A SUGGESTED FORMAT FOR LOAN APPLICATIONS

Any presentation whose objective is to obtain a loan or investment capital should be prepared by the applicant so that any lender or investor has sufficient information from the presentation alone upon which to base a decision as to whether to make a loan or an investment. With this thought in mind, each of the following categories should be carefully considered for the presentation.

THE BUSINESS STRUCTURE

When was the business formed? Is it a sole proprietorship, partnership, or corporation. Who are the owners, and what percentage of the business does each own? Includes personal financial statement(s) of principal owners or partners. A statement as to the type of business the firm is engaged in or proposes. A condensed narrative of history of the firm's operation including copies of last three year-end financial statements of your business (balance sheets and operating statements) or for entire period of operation if less than three (3) years. Copy of most recent financial statement (not older than 90 days).

PERSONNEL

Brief resumes including the background of education and experience of the principals and key employees should be part of the presentation with special emphasis on their experience in the type of work in which the firm is to be engaged.

PHYSICAL FACILITIES

A statement of physical facilities available which should include the location, square footage, and the equipment. One list should show the facilities currently owned or available and the second list the facilities to be acquired. Each item on the list should be followed by the cost of that item.

SPECIAL ASSETS

This should contain a listing of patents, designs, copyrights, prosessing or manufacturing techniques with the estimated value of each.

PRODUCTS & SERVICES

A comprehensive statement of the products and/or services the firm will offer with special emphasis on any unique or advantageous features.

MARKETING INFORMATION

A statement of the total market potential within the area of the operation of the firm. Make a statement as to the present and anticipated competition with the relative advantages and disadvantages of the firm in meeting this competition. A statement to the expected amount of the total potential that the firm expects to obtain over a stated period of time. If possible include letters or other documents from prospective customers that indicated that they are willing to buy from your firm.

PLAN OF ACTION

A statement of the proposed actions for the coming year including expansion of facilities, hiring of personnel, advertising proposed, sales efforts proposed, production efforts proposed, and any direct action that the management plans to take.

USE OF LOAN FUNDS

How the funds applied for are to be used.

FORECASTS - BUDGETS

A projection by month for at least one year but not less than that period of time required to show a positive generation of cash (spendable money). This projection should include: sales, cost of sales, expenses, profits, income, disbursements, cash flow monthly and cash flow cumulative. In addition, if the firm will gross over $250,000 in sales during the next year a pro-forma balance sheet should be made as of the end of the first year forecast.

Figure 2.1. (Continued)

Form Approved
OMB No. 3245-0016

| 2 | SBA Office Code |

U.S. SMALL BUSINESS ADMINISTRATION
LENDER'S APPLICATION FOR GUARANTY
OR PARTICIPATION
(Numbers in circles or squares are SBA codes only)

SBA Loan Number
1
(1)

Name of Applicant:

| 30 | |

WE PROPOSE TO MAKE A (Check One)

	Lenders Share	SBA Share	Term of Loan	Monthly Payment
Guaranteed Loan	%	%	Years	$

	Lenders Share	SBA Share	Lenders Interest Rate	Payment Beginning
Immediate Participation Loan (Lender to make and service)	%	%	% Per Annum	_____ Months from Date of Note

Amount of Loan $

If Interest Rate is to be Variable

Base Rate: Spread:

Rate Adjustment
☐ Quarterly   ☐ Other (Specify)

Base Rate Source

TERMS AND CONDITIONS OF LENDER: *(Attach additional sheets if more space is needed.)*

I approve this application to SBA subject to the terms and conditions outlined above. Without the participation of SBA to the extent applied for we would not be willing to make this loan, and in our opinion the financial assistance applied for is not otherwise available on reasonable terms. I certify that none of the Lender's employees, officers, directors or substantial stockholders (more than 10%) have a financial interest in the applicant.

Signature: Title: Date:

Name of Lender	Telephone (Inc A/C)	Financial Institution I.D. Code
40		41

Street Address	City	State	Zip
42	43	44	45

FOR SBA USE ONLY

Loan Officers Recommendation

☐ Approve   ☐ Decline   State Reason(s)

Signature: Title: Date:
                                                                   3

Other Recommendation, if Required

☐ Approve   ☐ Decline   State Reason(s)

Signature: Title: Date:

THIS BLOCK TO BE COMPLETED BY SBA OFFICIAL TAKING FINAL ACTION

☐ Approve   ☐ Decline   State Reason(s)

Signature: Title: Date:

BUSINESS LOANS ONLY

4 Program Struct. Code	6 MTY (MOS)	9 SMR	46 No. of Employees	47 Franchise Code	48 New Bus 1-No 2-Yes	49 Women 1-No 2-Yes	50 Viet Vet. 1-No 2-Yes	51 Organ. Code 1-Indiv. 2-Part. 3-Corp.
10 City Code	11 State Code	12 Loan Type (1) Dir. (4) IPSBA (3) IPBK (7) Guar.	52 SIC Code	53 Location 1-Urban 2-Rural	54 EOL Family Income ($ Only) $	55 Poll. Code	56	
13 Sub Program Code	14 County Code	15						

SBA LOAN PAY OFFS: LIST ALL SBA LOANS BEING REFUNDED

			15a Loan Number	15b Loan Type	15c Loan Status	15d Amount
Loan Amount Approved	% Participation	Interest Rate	cc 11-20	cc 21 (1) Direct (2) Part. (3) Guar.	cc 22 (1) Curr. (4) C/D (2) P/D (5) Liq. (3) Del.	
16 SBA	19 %	21 %				$
17 Bank	20 %	22 %	cc 29-38	cc 39 (1) Direct (2) Part. (3) Guar.	cc 40 (1) Curr. (4) C/D (2) P/D (5) Liq. (3) Del.	$
18 Total			cc 11-20	cc 21 (1) Direct (2) Part. (3) Guar.	cc 22 (1) Curr. (4) C/D (2) P/D (5) Liq. (3) Del.	$

23 Minority Code	24 O/S SBA Loan 1-No 2-Yes	25 Const. Cont. Amt. $	IF MORE THAN 3 LOANS ARE PAID OFF ENTER TOTAL OF REMAINING LOANS	16 $
26 New Construction 1-No 2-Yes	27 Real Collateral 1-No 2-Yes	28	PRIOR SBA LOANS: LIST LOAN NUMBERS OF ALL PRIOR SBA LOANS TO BORROWER	
29	31 Soc. Sec. No.		17a cc 11-20 17b cc 21-30 17c cc 31-40	
33 Employer ID No.		35 Borrower Alpha Code		

SBA Form 4-I (9-81) REF SOP 50 10 1   PREVIOUS EDITIONS ARE OBSOLETE

Figure 2.1. (Continued)

INSTRUCTIONS: The information requested below must be supplied with the application package.

FINANCIAL SPREAD

BALANCE SHEET	As of	Fiscal Year Ends	AUDITED ☐	UNAUDITED ☐
		DEBIT	CREDIT	PRO FORMA
Assets				
Cash	$	$	$	$
Accounts Rec.				
Inventory				
Other				
Total Current Assets				
Fixed Assets				
Other Assets				
Total Assets	$	$	$	$
Liabilities & Net Worth				
Accounts Payable	$	$	$	$
Notes Payable				
Taxes				
Other				
SBA				
Total Current Liabilities	$	$	$	$
Notes Payable	$	$	$	$
SBA				
Other				
Total Liabilities	$	$	$	$
Net Worth	$	$	$	$
Total Liab. & Net Worth	$	$	$	$
Profit & Loss	YEAR	YEAR	YEAR	YEAR
Sales	$	$	$	$
Depreciation				
Income Taxes				
W/D Officer Comp.				
Net Profit After Tax/Deprec.	$	$	$	$

PRO FORMA SCHEDULE OF FIXED OBLIGATIONS

	YEAR 1	YEAR 2	YEAR 3	YEAR 4
	$	$	$	$

Lender should comment on the following (Continue on separate sheet if needed):

1. Balance sheet and ratio analysis - comment on trends, debt to worth and current ratio.
2. Lenders analysis of repayment ability.
3. Management skill of the applicant.
4. Collateral offered and lien position, and analysis of collateral adequacy.
5. Lenders credit experience with the applicant.
6. Schedule of insurance requirements, standby agreements and other requirements.

Lenders Analysis:

☆ U.S. Government Printing Office: 1981—352/853/5576

Figure 2.1. (Continued)

	Prior to Loan	1st Month	2nd Month	3rd Month	4th Month	5th Month	6th Month	7th Month	8th Month	9th Month	10th Month	11th Month	12th Month	Total for Year
1. Total Sales (Net)														
2. Cost of Sales **														
3. Gross Profit (line 1 minus line 2)														
4. Expenses (operating): *******														
5. Salaries (other than owner)														
6. Payroll Taxes														
7. Rent														
8. Utilities (incl. phone)														
9. Insurance														
10. Professional Services (i.e., acct.)														
11. Taxes & Licenses														
12. Advertising														
13. Supplies (for business)														
14. Office Supplies (forms, postage, etc.)														
15. Interest (on loans, contracts, etc.)														
16. Depreciation														
17. Travel (incl. operating costs of veh.)														
18. Entertainment														
19. Dues & Subscriptions														
20. Other														
21														
22. Total Expenses (add line 5 thru 21)														
23. Profit Before Taxes (line 3 minus 22)														
24. Income (cash received)														
25. Cash Sales														
26. Collection of Accounts Receivable														
27. Other														
28. Total Income (add lines 25, 26, & 27)														
29. Disbursements (cash paid out)														
30. Owner's Draw														
31. Loan Repayments (principal only)														
32. Cost of Sales (line 2)														
33. Total Expenses (minus line 16)														
34. Capital Expenditures (equip. bldgs, veh., leasehold impr.)														
35. Reserve for Taxes														
36. Other														
37. Total Disbursements (add line 30 thru 36)														
38. Cash Flow Monthly (line 28 minus 37)														
39. Cash Flow Cumulative (line 38 plus 39 of previous month).														

**Line—Cost of Sales: Retail—beginning inventory–purchase minus ending inventory
Manufacturing—cost of material, labor manufacturing

Figure 2.1. (Continued)

Statements Required by Laws and Executive Orders

Federal executive agencies, including the Small Business Administration are required to withhold or limit financial assistance, to impose special conditions on approved loans, to provide special notices to applicants or borrowers and to require special reports and data from borrowers in order to comply with legislation passed by the Congress and Executive Orders issued by the President and by the provisions of various inter-agency agreements. SBA has issued regulations and procedures that implemented these laws and executive orders and they are contained in Parts 112, 113 and 116, Title 13 Code of Federal Regulations Chapter 1, or SOP's.

This form contains a brief summary of the various laws and executive orders that affect SBA's business and disaster loan programs and gives applicants and borrowers the notices required by law or otherwise. The signatures required on the last page provide evidence that SBA has given the necessary notices, that the signatory understands that special information will be required in some cases and that he or she may be required to complete and submit reports to SBA.

Freedom of Information Act
(5 U.S.C. 552)

This law provides that, with some exceptions, SBA must supply information reflected in Agency files and records to a person requesting it. Information about approved loans that will be automatically released includes, among other things, statistics on our loan programs (individual borrowers are not identified in the statistics) and other information such as the names of the borrowers (and their officers, directors, stockholders or partners), the collateral pledged to secure the loan, the amount of the loan, its purpose in general terms and the maturity. Propriety data on a borrower would not routinely be made available to third parties. All requests undet this Act are to be addressed to the nearest SBA office and be identified as a Freedom of Information request.

Privacy Act
(5 U.S.C. 552a)

Disaster home loan files are covered by this legislation because they are normally maintained in the names of individuals. Business loan files are maintained by business name or in the name of individuals in their entrepreneurial capacity. Thus they are not files on individuals and, therefore, are not subject to this Act. Any person can request to see or get copies of any personal information that SBA has in the requestor's file. Requests for information about another party may be denied unless SBA has the written permission of the individual to release the information to the requestor or unless the information is subject to disclosure under the Freedom of Information Act. (The "Acknowledgement" section of this form contains the written permission of SBA to release information when a disaster victim requests assistance under the family and individual grant program.)

Under the provisions of the Privacy Act, loan applicants are not required to give their social security number. The Small Business Administration, however, uses the social security number to distinguish between people with a similar or the same name. Failure to provide this number may not affect any right, benefit or privilege to which an individual is entitled by law but having the number makes it easier for SBA to more accurately identify to whom adverse credit information applies and to keep accurate loan records.

Figure 2.1. (Continued)

NOTE: Any person concerned with the collection of information, its voluntariness, disclosure or routine use under the Privacy Act or requesting information under the Freedom of Information Act may contact the Director, Freedom of Information/Privacy Acts Division, Small Business Administration, 1441 L Street, N.W. Washington, D.C. 20416, for information about the Agency's procedures on these two subjects.

Right to Financial Privacy Act of 1978
(12 U.S.C. 3401)

This is notice to you, as required by the Right to Financial Privacy Act of 1978, of SBA's access rights to financial records held by financial institutions that are or have been doing business with you or your business, including any financial institution participating in a loan or loan guarantee. The law provides that SBA shall have a right of access to your financial records in connection with its consideration or administration of assistance to you in the form of a Government loan or loan guaranty agreement. SBA is required to provide a certificate of its compliance with the Act to a financial institution in connection with its first request for access to your financial records, after which no further certification is required for subsequent accesses. The law also provides that SBA's access rights continue for the term of any approved loan or loan guaranty agreement. No further notice to you of SBA's access rights is required during the term of any such agreement.

The law also authorizes SBA to transfer to another Government authority, any financial records included in an application for a loan, or concerning an approved loan or loan guarantee, as necessary to process, service or foreclose a loan or loan guarantee or to collect on a defaulted loan or loan guarantee. No other transfer of your financial records to another Government authority will be permitted by SBA except as required or permitted by law.

Flood Disaster Protection Act
(42 U.S.C. 4011)

Regulations issued by the Federal Insurance Administration (FIA) and by SBA implement this Act and its amendments. These regulations prohibit SBA from making certain loans in an FIA designated floodplain unless Federal flood insurance is purchased as a condition of the loan. Failure to maintain the required level of flood insurance makes the applicant ineligible for any future financial assistance from SBA under any program, including disaster assistance.

Executive Orders — Floodplain Management and Wetland Protection
(42 F.R. 26951 and 42 F.R. 2961)

The SBA discourages any settlement in or development of a floodplain or a wetland. This statement is to notify all SBA loan applicants that such actions are hazardous to both life and property and should be avoided. The additional cost of flood preventive construction must be considered in addition to the possible loss of all assets and investments in future floods.

Lead-Based Paint Poisoning Prevention Act
(42 U.S.C. 4821 et seq)

Borrowers using SBA funds for the construction or rehabilitation of a residential structure are prohibited from using lead-based paint (as defined in SBA regulations) on all interior surfaces, whether accessible or not, and exterior surfaces, such as stairs, decks, porches, railings, windows and doors, which are readily accessible to children under 7 years of age. A "residential structure" is any home, apartment, hotel, motel, orphanage, boarding school, dormitory, day care center, extended car facility, college or other school housing, hospital, group practice or community facility and all other residential or institutional structures where persons reside.

Figure 2.1. (Continued)

Equal Credit Opportunity Act
(15 U.S.C. 1691)

The Federal Equal Credit Opportunity Act prohibits creditors from discriminating against credit applicants on the basis of race, color, religion, national origin, sex, marital status, age (provided that the applicant has the capacity to enter into a binding contract); because all or part of the applicant's income derives from any public assistance program; or because the applicant has in good faith exercised any right under the Consumer Credit Protection Act. The Federal agency that administers compliance with this law concerning this creditor is the Federal Trade Commission, Equal Credit Opportunity, Room 500, 633 Indiana Avenue, N.W., Washington, D.C. 20580.

Civil Rights Legislation

All businesses receiving SBA financial assistance must agree not to discriminate in any business practice, including employment practices and services to the public, on the basis of categories cited in 13 C.F.R., Parts 112 and 113 of SBA Regulations. This includes making their goods and services available to handicapped clients or customers. All business borrowers will be required to display the "Equal Employment Opportunity Poster" prescribed by SBA.

Executive Order 11738 — Environmental Protection
(38 F.R. 25161)

The Executive Order charges SBA with administering its loan programs in a manner that will result in effective enforcement of the Clean Air Act, the Federal Water Pollution Act and other environmental protection legislation. SBA must, therefore, impose conditions on some loans. By acknowledging receipt of this form and presenting the application, the principals of all small businesses borrowing $100,000 or more in direct funds stipulate to the following:

1. That any facility used, or to be used, by the subject firm is not listed on the EPA list of Violating Facilities.

2. That subject firm will comply with all the requirements of Section 114 of the Clean Air Act and Section 308 of the Water act relating to inspection, monitoring, entry, reports and information, as well as all other requirements specified in Section 114 and Section 308 of the respective Acts, and all regulations and guidelines issued thereunder.

3. That subject firm will notify SBA of the receipt of any communication from the Director of the Environmental Protection Agency indicating that a facility utilized, or to be utilized, by subject firm is under consideration to be listed on EPA List of Violating Facilities.

Occupational Safety and Health Act
(15 U.S.C. 651 et seq)

This legislation authorizes the Occupational Safety and Health Administration in the Department of Labor to require businesses to modify facilities and procedures to protect employees or pay penalty fees. In some instances the business can be forced to cease operations or be prevented from starting operations in a new facility. Therefore, in some instances SBA may require additional information from an applicant to determine whether the business will be in compliance with OSHA regulations and allowed to operate its facility after the loan is approved and disbursed.

In all instances, signing this form as borrower is a certification that the OSHA requirements that apply to the borrower's business have been determined and the borrower is, to the best of its knowledge, in compliance.

Figure 2.1. (Continued)

Consumer Credit Protection Act

(15 U.S.C. 1601 et seq)

This legislation gives an applicant who is refused credit because of adverse information about the applicant's credit, reputation, character or mode of living an opportunity to refute or challenge the accuracy of such reports. Therefore, whenever SBA declines a loan in whole or in part because of adverse information in a credit report, the applicant will be given the name and address of the reporting agency so the applicant can seek to have that agency correct its report, if inaccurate. If SBA declines a loan in whole or in part because of adverse information received from a source other than a credit reporting agency, the applicant will be given information about the nature of the adverse information but not the source of the report.

Within 3 days after the consummation of the transaction, any recipient of an SBA loan which is secured in whole or in part by a lien on the recipient's residence or household contents may rescind such a loan in accordance with the "Regulation Z" of the Federal Reserve Board.

Applicant's Acknowledgement

My (our) signature(s) acknowledges receipt of this form, that I (we) have read it and that I (we) have a copy for my (our) files. My (our) signature(s) represents my (our) agreement to comply with the requirements the Small Business Administration makes in connection with the approval of my (our) loan request and to comply, whenever applicable, with the hazard insurance, lead based paint, civil rights or other limitations contained in this notice.

My (our) signature(s) also represents written permission, as required by the Privacy Act, for the SBA to release any information in my (our) disaster loan application to the Governor of my (our) State or the Governor's designated representative in conjunction with the State's processing of my (our) application for assistance under the Individual and Family Grant Program that is available in certain major disaster areas declared by the President.

Business Name
_____

_____ BY _____
Date   Name and Title

Proprietor, Partners, Principals and Guarantors

_____
Date   Signature
_____
Date   Signature
_____
Date   Signature
_____
Date   Signature

SBA Form 1261 (9-81) SOP 50-10-1

Figure 2.1. (Continued)

United States of America

SMALL BUSINESS ADMINISTRATION

STATEMENT OF PERSONAL HISTORY

Please Read Carefully - Print or Type

Each member of the small business concern requesting assistance or the development company must submit this form in TRIPLICATE for filing with the SBA application. This form must be filled out and submitted:

1. If a sole proprietorship, by the proprietor;
2. If a partnership, by each partner;
3. If a corporation or a development company, by each officer, director, and additionally, by each holder of 20% or more of the voting stock;
4. Any other person, including a hired manager, who has authority to speak for and commit the borrower in the management of the business.

Name and Address of Applicant (Firm Name)(Street, City, State and ZIP Code)

SBA District Office and City

Amount Applied for:

1. Personal Statement of: (State name in full, if no middle name, state (NMN), or if initial only, indicate initial). List all former names used, and dates each name was used. Use separate sheet if necessary.

First   Middle   Last

2. Date of Birth: (Month, day and year)

3. Place of Birth: (City & State or Foreign Country)

U.S. Citizen? ☐ yes   ☐ no

If no, give alien registration number:
#

4. Give the percentage of ownership or stock owned or to be owned in the small business concern or the Development Company.

Social Security No.

5. Present residence address

From   To   Address

City   State

Home Telephone No. (Include A/C)

Business Telephone No. (Include A/C)

Immediate past residence address

From   To   Address

BE SURE TO ANSWER THE NEXT 3 QUESTIONS CORRECTLY BECAUSE THEY ARE IMPORTANT.

THE FACT THAT YOU HAVE AN ARREST OR CONVICTION RECORD WILL NOT NECESSARILY DISQUALIFY YOU. BUT AN INCORRECT ANSWER WILL PROBABLY CAUSE YOUR APPLICATION TO BE TURNED DOWN.

6. Are you presently under indictment, on parole or probation?

☐ Yes   ☐ No   If yes, furnish details in a separate exhibit. List name(s) under which held, if applicable.

7. Have you ever been charged with or arrested for any criminal offense other than a minor motor vehicle violation?

☐ Yes   ☐ No   If yes, furnish details in a separate exhibit. List name(s) under which charged, if applicable.

8. Have you ever been convicted of any criminal offense other than a minor motor vehicle violation?

☐ Yes   ☐ No   If yes, furnish details in a separate exhibit. List name(s) under which convicted, if applicable.

9. Name and address of participating bank

The information on this form will be used in connection with an investigation of your character. Any information you wish to submit, that you feel will expedite this investigation should be set forth.

Whoever makes any statement knowing it to be false, for the purpose of obtaining for himself or for any applicant, any loan, or loan extension by renewal, deferment or otherwise, or for the purpose of obtaining, or influencing SBA toward, anything of value under the Small Business Act, as amended, shall be punished under Section 16(a) of that Act, by a fine of not more than $5000, or by imprisonment for not more than 2 years, or both.

Signature   Title   Date

It is against SBA's policy to provide assistance to persons not of good character and therefore consideration is given to the qualities and personality traits of a person, favorable and unfavorable, relating thereto, including behavior, integrity, candor and disposition toward criminal actions. It is also against SBA's policy to provide assistance not in the best interests of the United States, for example, if there is reason to believe that the effect of such assistance will be to encourage or support, directly or indirectly, activities inimical to the Security of the United States. Anyone concerned with the collection of this information, as to its voluntariness, disclosure or routine uses may contact the FOIA Office, 1441 "L" Street, N.W., and a copy of §9 "Agency Collection of Information" from SOP 4C 04 will be provided.

SBA FORM 912 (3-79) SOP 50 10 1 EDITION OF 5-78 WILL BE USED UNTIL STOCK IS EXHAUSTED

1. SBA FILE COPY

Figure 2.1.   (Continued)

Form Approved
OMB No. 100-R-0081

PERSONAL FINANCIAL STATEMENT

As of _____ , 19 ___.

Return to:

Small Business Administration

For SBA Use Only

SBA Loan No.

Complete this form if 1) a sole proprietorship by the proprietor; 2) a partnership by each partner; 3) a corporation by each officer and each stockholder with **20%** or more ownership; 4) any other person or entity providing a guaranty on the loan.

Name and Address, Including ZIP Code *(of person and spouse submitting Statement)*

This statement is submitted in connection with S.B.A. loan requested or granted to the individual or firm, whose name appears below:

Name and Address of Applicant or Borrower, Including ZIP Code

SOCIAL SECURITY NO. _____

Business *(of person submitting Statement)*

Please answer all questions using "No" or "None" where necessary

ASSETS		LIABILITIES	
Cash on Hand & In Banks . . . . $ _____		Accounts Payable . . . . $ _____	
Savings Account in Banks . . . . _____		Notes Payable to Banks . . . . _____	
U. S. Government Bonds . . . . _____		*(Describe below - Section 2)*	
Accounts & Notes Receivable . . . . _____		Notes Payable to Others . . . . _____	
Life Insurance-Cash Surrender Value Only . . _____		*(Describe below - Section 2)*	
Other Stocks and Bonds . . . . _____		Installment Account (Auto) . . . . _____	
(Describe - reverse side - Section 3)		Monthly Payments $ _____	
Real Estate . . . . _____		Installment Accounts (Other) . . . . _____	
(Describe - reverse side - Section 4)		Monthly Payments $ _____	
Automobile - Present Value . . . . _____		Loans on Life Insurance . . . . _____	
Other Personal Property . . . . _____		Mortgages on Real Estate . . . . _____	
(Describe - reverse side - Section 5)		*(Describe - reverse side - Section 4)*	
Other Assets . . . . _____		Unpaid Taxes . . . . _____	
(Describe - reverse side - Section 6)		*(Describe - reverse side - Section 7)*	
		Other Liabilities . . . . _____	
		(Describe - reverse side - Section 8)	
		Total Liabilities . . . . _____	
		Net Worth . . . . _____	
Total . . . . $ _____		Total . . . . $ _____	

Section I. Source of Income

(Describe below all items listed in this Section)

CONTINGENT LIABILITIES

Salary . . . . $ _____		As Endorser or Co-Maker . . . . $ _____	
Net Investment Income . . . . _____		Legal Claims and Judgments . . . . _____	
Real Estate Income . . . . _____		Provision for Federal Income Tax . . . . _____	
Other Income (Describe) * . . . . _____		Other Special Debt . . . . _____	

Description of items listed in Section I _____

_____

_____

_____

_____

_____

_____

* Not necessary to disclose alimony or child support payments in "Other Income" unless it is desired to have such payments counted toward total income.

Life Insurance Held *(Give face amount of policies - name of company and beneficiaries)* _____

_____

_____

_____

_____

_____

_____

_____

_____

SUPPLEMENTARY SCHEDULES

Section 2. Notes Payable to Banks and Others

Name and Address of Holder of Note	Amount of Loan		Terms of Repayments	Maturity of Loan	How Endorsed, Guaranteed, or Secured
	Original Bal.	Present Bal.			
	$	$	$		

Figure 2.1. (Continued)

Section 3. Other Stocks and Bonds: Give listed and unlisted Stocks and Bonds *(Use separate sheet if necessary)*

No. of Shares	Names of Securities	Cost	Market Value Statement Date Quotation	Amount

Section 4. Real Estate Owned. *(List each parcel separately. Use supplemental sheets if necessary. Each sheet must be identified as a supplement to this statement and signed).* *(Also advises whether property is covered by title insurance, abstract of title, or both).*

Title is in name of	Type of property
Address of property (City and State)	Original Cost to (me) (us) $ _____ Date Purchased _____ Present Market Value $ _____ Tax Assessment Value $ _____
Name and Address of Holder of Mortgage (City and State)	Date of Mortgage _____ Original Amount $ _____ Balance $ _____ Maturity _____ Terms of Payment _____

Status of Mortgage, i.e., current or delinquent. If delinquent describe delinquencies

Section 5. Other Personal Property. *(Describe and if any is mortgaged, state name and address of mortgage holder and amount of mortgage, terms of payment and if delinquent, describe delinquency.)*

Section 6. Other Assets. *(Describe)*

Section 7. Unpaid Taxes. *(Describe in detail, as to type, to whom payable, when due, amount, and what, if any, property a tax lien, if any, attaches)*

Section 8. Other Liabilities. *(Describe in detail)*

(I) or (We) certify the above and the statements contained in the schedules herein is a true and accurate statement of (my) or (our) financial condition as of the date stated herein. This statement is given for the purpose of: *(Check one of the following)*

☐ Inducing S.B.A. to grant a loan as requested in application, of the individual or firm whose name appears herein, in connection with which this statement is submitted.

☐ Furnishing a statement of (my) or (our) financial condition, pursuant to the terms of the guaranty executed by (me) or (us) at the time S.B.A. granted a loan to the individual or firm, whose name appears herein.

Signature	Signature	Date

Figure 2.1. (Continued)

Summary of Collateral

OFFERED BY APPLICANT AS SECURITY FOR LOAN AND SBA APPRAISER'S VALUATION REPORT

	EMPLOYER ID NO.
Name and Address of Applicant: (Include Zip Code) _____	
	SBA LOAN NO.

IMPORTANT INSTRUCTIONS FOR PREPARING THE LISTING OF
COLLATERAL OFFERED AS SECURITY FOR LOAN

Page 1. Summary Of Collateral Offered By Applicant As Security For The Loan: This is a summarization of the detailed listing on SBA Form 4, Schedule A. If collateral is to be acquired, with proceeds of loan describe the collateral in detail *on an attachment* to Schedule A with the notation "To be acquired".

Show exact cost. If assets were acquired from a predecessor company at a price other than cost less depreciation.

The figures to be entered in the net book value column must agree with the figures shown in the balance sheet, on page 2 of the application, except for the assets, if any, not being offered as collateral and non-business assets, if any, which are being offered to secure guarantees.

If a recent appraisal has been made of the collateral offered, it should be submitted with the application.

Any leases on land and buildings must be described, giving date and term of lease, rental, name and address of owner.

Page 2. Real Estate:

Item 1 - Land And Improvements: (a) legal description from deed on the land - location - city where deed is recorded. Book and page numbers of Official Records. Describe the land improvements such as paving, utilities, fence, etc. (b) cost of land when purchased.

Item 2 - Buildings: (a) general description, describe each building or structure on the land. Include size, type of construction, number of stories, date erected, use and condition. (b) amount of taxes and the assessed value from tax bills. (c) total amount of income received by owner from rental of the described property. (d) cost of building when purchased.

INADEQUATE OR POORLY PREPARED LOAN APPLICATION AND LISTING OF COLLATERAL ON PAGE 3 WILL CAUSE DELAY IN THE PROCESSING OF LOAN APPLICATIONS.

Page 3 - It is most **IMPORTANT** that applicants make an **ACTUAL PHYSICAL INVENTORY OF THE EQUIPMENT** being offered as collateral. **DO NOT TAKE FROM BOOK RECORDS.** Actually list each in accordance with the classification, e.g.: 1. Machinery and Equipment; 2. Automotive Equipment; 3. Office furniture and equipment; 4. Other—jigs, dies, fixtures, airplanes, etc.

Page 4 - Is a continuation of Equipment being offered.
Group items in accordance with the above classifications

Show: manufacturer or make, model and serial numbers, size, year, whether purchased new, used, or rebuilt.
BE SURE ITEMS LISTED CAN BE **READILY INSPECTED** BY SBA APPRAISERS.

SUMMARY			
Item	Cost	Net Book Value	Not to be used by applicant
1. Land and land improvements			
2. Buildings			
3. Machinery and Equipment			
4. Automotive Equipment			
5. Office furniture and equipment			
6. Other			
7. Total			
8. Real and chattel mortgages (Not to be paid from SBA loan req.) Attach details	X X X X		
9. Equity	X X X X		
10. To be acquired (Cost)		X X X X	
11. Total			

THE APPRAISER CERTIFIES that he has personally and thoroughly inspected the collateral as listed in this Report. Furthermore, as of _____ the market values shown in the above Summary are fair and reasonable as of that date. Additional comments are attached to this Report.

_____
SBA Appraiser's Signature   Date of Report

SBA Form 4 Schedule A (8-66) REF ND 510-1A previous editions of sheets 1, 2 and 3 are obsolete.

Figure 2.1. (Continued)

Real Estate

OFFERED BY APPLICANT AS SECURITY FOR LOAN AND SBA APPRAISER'S VALUATION REPORT

Name and Address of Applicant (include Zip Code) | Parcel number _____ | SBA LOAN No.

Title data: ☐ Title Insurance ☐ Abstract
☐ Other (indicate)

Address of Realty Offered _____

Realty in name of _____

Recorded Book_____ Page_____ County_____

1. Land and land improvements (Do not include buildings - see Sec. 2 below)

Cost_____   date acquired_____

Legal description (Attach if too long) *

* If available, attach plat survey.

2. Improvements   Cost (If separate from land) $_____

Building description: List each building separately with brief description and dimensions.

Income if Applicable.

Rent $_____ Month ☐ Annually ☐ Lease ☐ _____ Term.

| Assessed Value |
| Land _____ |
| Improvements _____ |
| Taxes _____ |

SBA Form 4 Schedule A (8-66) previous editions are obsolete

Figure 2.1. (Continued)

54

Personal Property (Chattels)

OFFERED BY APPLICANT AS SECURITY FOR LOAN AND SBA APPRAISER'S VALUATION REPORT

The following described chattels are located or headquartered at (include Zip Code) _____	EMPLOYER ID NO.
	SBA LOAN NO.
Above location is owned ( ) leased ( )	

It is most **IMPORTANT** that applicants make an **ACTUAL PHYSICAL INVENTORY OF THE EQUIPMENT** being offered as collateral. **DO NOT TAKE FROM BOOK RECORDS.** Actually list each item in accordance with the classification, e.g.:* 1. Machinery and Equipment 2. Automotive Equipment 3. Office furniture and equipment 4. Other - jigs, dies, fixtures, airplanes, etc.

Show: manufacturer or make, model and serial numbers, size, year, whether purchased new, used or rebuilt.

List chattels at different locations on separate sheets. * Description of _____	Model	Serial Number	New Used Rebuilt	NOT TO BE USED BY APPLICANT	
				Cond.	Market Value
Carry Totals of Each Classification to Page 1 (Summary) Lines 3, 4, 5, and 6.				Total	

INADEQUATE OR POORLY PREPARED LOAN APPLICATION AND LISTING OF COLLATERAL WILL CAUSE DELAY IN THE PROCESSING OF LOAN APPLICATIONS. BE SURE ALL ITEMS CAN BE READILY INSPECTED BY SBA APPRAISER.

I, _____ _____ ,
(Signature of owner, partner, or corporation officer)   (Title)

of the _____
(Name of Firm)

certify that the above machinery and equipment listing represents an *actual physical inventory* taken on (date) _____ .
Mark items (in column 2) with an asterisk if they are subject to conditional bills of sale or chattel mortgages the balance of which will not be paid off from an SBA loan. Carry total of such balances to line 8, page 1 (Summary).

SBA Form 4 Schedule A (8-66) previous editions are obsolete

Figure 2.1. (Continued)

Continuation of Personal Property (Chattels)
Description of_____

	Model	Serial Number	New Used Rebuilt	NOT TO BE USED BY APPLICANT	
				Cond.	Market Value
Carry Totals of Each Classification to Page 1 (Summary) Lines 3, 4, 5, and 6.				Total	

SBA Form 4 Schedule A (8-66) previous editions are obsolete

Figure 2.1. (Continued)

56

The Loan Package

The **outline of a complete loan package** below illustrates the type of detailed presentation sometimes required by lenders such as banks and the Small Business Administration. However, this degree of detail is often unnecessary for stable businesses already known to the lender. Many debt sources never require such complete documentation. Instead, they seek the particular information described in their respective sections of this report.

The **sample loan documentation** on the following pages demonstrates an acceptable rendition of **only the major parts** of a loan package. It does not represent the complete loan package outlined below, and it adheres to the business buyout format, rather than the forms for business start-up or expansion.

This particular example involves a hypothetical SBA-guaranteed bank loan.

SAMPLE LOAN PACKAGE OUTLINE

I. Summary

  A. Nature of business
  B. Amount and purpose of loan
  C. Repayment terms
  D. Equity share of borrower (equity/debt ratio after loan)
  E. Security or collateral (listed with market value estimates and quotes on cost of equipment to be purchased with the loan proceeds)

II. Personal information (on persons owning more than 20% of the business)

  A. Educational and work history
  B. Credit references
  C. Income tax statements (last three years)
  D. Financial statement (no older than 60 days)

III. Firm information (whichever is applicable below—A, B or C)

  A. New business
    1. Business plan (see outline of business plan sections page 9)
    2. Life and casualty insurance coverage
    3. Lease agreement

  B. Business acquisition (buyout)
    1. Information on acquisition
      a. Business history (include seller's name, reasons for sale)
      b. Current balance sheet (not over 60 days old)
      c. Current profit and loss statements (less than 60 days old)
      d. Business' federal income tax statements (past three to five years)
      e. Cash flow statements for last year
      f. Copy of sales agreement with breakdown of inventory, fixtures, equipment, licenses, goodwill and other costs
      g. Description and dates of permits already acquired
    2. Business plan
    3. Life and casualty insurance

  C. Existing business expansion
    1. Information on existing business
      a. Business history
      b. Current balance sheet (not more than 60 days old)
      c. Current profit and loss statements (not more than 60 days old)
      d. Cash flow statements for last year
      e. Federal income tax returns for past three to five years
      f. Lease agreement and permit data
    2. Business plan
    3. Life and casualty insurance

IV. Projections

  A. Profit and loss projection (monthly, for one year) and explanation of projections
  B. Cash flow projection (monthly, for one year) and explanation of projections
  C. Projected balance sheet (one year after loan) and explanation of projections

Figure 2.2. Loan package outline from *Financing Small Business.* (Reprinted with permission from Bank of America, NT & SA, "Financing Small Business," *Small Business Reporter,* Vol. 14, No. 10, Copyright 1980.)

1

SUMMARY OF LOAN APPLICATION

Applicant	Mr Sammy I Lee phone 555-3742
	3578 35th Avenue
	Oakland, California 94923
Eligibility	Applicant is of a socially and economically dis-
	advantaged group and qualifies for a loan under
	Small Business Administration requirements as to
	size and type of business
Amount Requested	$38,000
Term Requested	Five years, with no prepayment penalty
Interest Rate	Current small business rate
Security	Business assets
	Personal guarantee
	SBA's 90% guarantee
Debt/Equity Ratio— after loan	$38,000/$33,075
Purpose of Loan	Loan will enable applicant, Mr Sammy Lee, to pur-
	chase Good Times Liquor Store Sales price of
	$60,000 includes all furniture, fixtures and
	equipment, sign (in working condition), inven-
	tory, liquor license and goodwill (See Sales
	Agreement for other details) Cash payment re-
	quired is $60,000, no deposit has been paid to
	date

2

The table that follows shows how the purchase will be financed and the distribution of loan proceeds and equity

USE OF FUNDS	SOURCE OF FUNDS		
	Loan	Equity	Total
Purchase of Business			
Inventory	$28,000	$ 2,000	$30,000
Ice Machine		1,170	1,170
Wine Case		578	578
Deli Case		307	307
Appliances and Fixtures		374	374
Liquor License	10,000		10,000
Goodwill		17,571	17,571
Subtotal	$38,000	$22,000	$60,000
Other			
Station Wagon		$ 3,450	$ 3,450
Cash		7,625	7,625
Subtotal		$11,075	$11,075
TOTAL	$38,000	$33,075	$71,075

COLLATERAL AND CONDITIONS

The following are offered as collateral and conditions for the loan

1 Security interest under the uniform commercial code on all fixtures, equipment and inventory

2 Borrower will assign life insurance in the amount of the loan
   and keep it in force by punctual payments of required premiums

3 Second deed of trust on borrower's residence

4 Borrower will maintain hazard insurance in the amount and type
   required by lender with loss payable endorsement

5 Borrower will deliver to lender quarterly financial statements

6 All loan documents will be signed by spouse (mandatory for SBA
   loan only)

3

RESUME

Name	Sammy I Lee
Address	3578-35th Avenue
	Oakland, California 94923
Phone	555-3742
Personal	Born February 23, 1938
	Married
	Two children
Education	Oakland High School
	Oakland, California
	Merritt College
	Oakland, California
	A A degree in Accounting
	Hayward State College
	Hayward, California
	B A degree in Business Administration
Employment and Business Experience	Lee's Grocery Store (family store)
	325 9th Street
	Oakland, California
	Duties Served customers, checked
	groceries, made deliveries, stocked shelves
	1951 - 1959
	Standard Forms & Supplies
	1717 San Pablo Avenue
	Oakland, California
	Duties Managed office and kept books
	Supervised staff of three
	1959 - 1964

4

RESUME continued

Employment and Business Experience	Bay Area Auto Supply Co. Inc
	2905 Bayshore Avenue
	South San Francisco, California
	Duties Managed warehouse, filled
	orders, maintained inventory records
	1964 - 1970
	Sunshine Liquor Store
	7789 MacArthur Boulevard
	Oakland, California
	Duties Managed store
	1970 - 1972
	Happy Liquor Store
	1535 Scotch Street
	San Francisco, California
	Duties Managed store for brother
	1973 - present

PERSONAL CREDIT REFERENCES

Bank of America
Broadway-MacArthur Branch
Oakland, California

Savings Account   4578 - 02039
Checking Account   7641 - 02666

Golden East Savings and Loan
5546 Telegraph Avenue
Oakland, California

Auto Loan No 05532 - 14684
Home Loan No 308 - 055921

Figure 2.2. (Continued)

5

PERSONAL FINANCIAL STATEMENT

Assets

Cash on hand and in banks	$ 250
Savings account in banks	29.375
U S government bonds	12.000
Accounts and notes receivable	0
Life insurance cash value	0
Other stocks and bonds	540
Real estate	43.600
Automobile	3.450
Other personal property	0
Other assets	0
TOTAL ASSETS	$89.215

Liabilities

Accounts payable	$ 0
Notes payable to banks	0
Notes payable to others	0
Installment account (Auto)	0
Installment account (Other)	0
Loans on life insurance	0
Mortgages on real estate	28.473
Unpaid taxes	0
Other liabilities	0
TOTAL LIABILITIES	$28.473
NET WORTH	$60.742

6

BUSINESS PLAN

Name of Firm — Good Times Liquor Store

Owner-to-Be — Sammy I. Lee   Sole proprietor

Method of Acquisition — Buy-out

Type of Business — Retail liquor store with some grocery and delicatessen items

Hours of Operation — 9 a.m. to 10 p.m. Will be open seven days a week and on all holidays.

Location — 575 Bourbon Avenue San Francisco, California 94112

Above location is in an area suitable for retail trade, a very busy area with numerous other business establishments. Surrounded by home owners, is easily accessible by public transportation and personal conveyance.

Shopping area draws from a vicinity of approximately one square mile with a population of 47.347. (See attached data and map.)

Area includes such ethnic groups as Latinos, Filipinos, Blacks, Asians, Irish and Italians.

The above will be the target area for potential customers.

7

Potential of the Business — As of 1970, San Francisco had 196 liquor stores with yearly income of $53.709.000. (Of the 196 stores, 145 have employees on their payrolls. The yearly income of these 145 stores is $49.775.000. This brings the yearly average per store to $343.275.) With a population in San Francisco of 715.674 the yearly average spent by each person would be about $75. With a population in the sales area of 47.347 the potential income of the area would be $3.551.025. This appears to be an ample reservoir of customers to tap.

Source: 1970 census, population and housing. Prepared by San Francisco Department of City Planning, March, 1975. (See attached map.)

Competition — There is one other liquor store and one liquor/grocery store within a six-block radius.

History of Firm — Good Times Liquor Store is presently owned by Mrs. William Win who acquired sole proprietorship after the death of her husband about three years ago. The store has been in operation since 1935.

For the past three years the store has been run by Mr. Win's brother, brother-in-law and Mrs. Win.

Mrs. Win's physician has advised her to stop working so she has decided to sell the business. Her brother and brother-in-law are also nearing retirement and have no interest in running the business.

Sales Plan — Mr. Lee believes the store has declined in recent years due to lack of interest on the part of current owners. He feels that through new ownership the store could develop into a profitable business.

8

The store now closes at 8 p.m. Mr. Lee plans on extending the business hours from 9 a.m. to 10 p.m., an additional two hours per day. Also, he intends to be open seven days a week and on all holidays.

An innovation by Mr. Lee will be to sell cold sandwiches and magazines. The store has ample room for display of inventory and a back room for storage.

Mr. Lee will also utilize to better advantage the ice machine, wine case, delicatessen case and appliances and fixtures.

The atmosphere in the store could be made pleasant and comfortable with bright, new decoration.

Mr. Lee plans local advertising through the neighborhood newspaper, leafleting and door-to-door personal contact with his neighbors.

Managerial Capability — Mr. Lee has acquired the background to own and operate a liquor store through practical experience. He operated and managed his brother's liquor store on Scotch Street. Thus he is familiar with all aspects of the retail liquor business.

Personnel — The liquor store at present has three employees working as cashiers and clerks. Mr. Lee plans to use only one clerk. He and Mrs. Lee will work the other hours. This will be a savings of approximately $20.000 per year.

Prices and Margins — There are no problems of price cutting competition. Analysis of the historical data, however, shows that gross profit margins have fluctuated widely. Mr. Lee plans to bring this under control by keeping a close watch on inventory.

Figure 2.2. (Continued)

GOOD TIMES LIQUOR STORE
PREVIOUS YEAR AND PROJECTED PROFIT & LOSS STATEMENT

	1974 $	1974 %	1975 Oct	1975 Nov	1975 Dec	1976 Jan	Feb	Mar	Apr	May	June	July	Aug	Sept	Total	%
Gross Sales	203.491	100	15.000	15.500	15.500	16.000	16.500	16.500	17.000	17.500	17.500	18.000	18.500	19.000	202.500	100
Less Cost of Sales	171.812	84 4	11.250	11.625	11.625	12.000	12.375	12.375	12.750	13.125	13.125	13.500	13.875	14.250	151.875	75
Gross Profit	31.679	15 6	3.750	3.875	3.875	4.000	4.125	4.125	4.250	4.375	4.375	4.500	4.625	4.750	50.625	25
Controllable Expenses																
Salaries	27.184	13 3	600	600	600	600	600	600	600	600	600	600	600	600	7.200	3.6
Payroll Taxes	1.622	8	57	57	57	57	57	57	57	57	57	57	35	35	640	.3
Alarm Service	318	2	30	30	30	30	30	30	30	30	31	31	31	31	364	.2
Advertising	68	0	35	35	35	35	35	35	35	35	35	35	35	35	420	.2
Automobile	156	1	90	93	93	96	99	99	102	105	105	108	111	114	1.215	.6
Bad Debts	315	2	15	15	15	15	15	15	15	15	15	15	15	15	180	.1
Collection Fees	157	1	15	15	15	15	15	15	15	15	15	15	15	15	180	.1
Dues & Subscriptions	11	0	5	5	5	5	5	5	5	5	5	5	5	5	60	.0
Laundry & Linen	20	0	8	8	8	8	8	8	8	8	8	8	8	8	96	.0
Legal & Accounting	855	4	100	100	100	100	100	100	100	100	100	100	100	100	1.200	.6
Office Expense	134	1	10	10	10	10	10	10	10	10	10	10	10	10	120	.0
Professional Fees	96	0	8	8	8	8	8	8	8	8	8	8	8	8	96	.0
Maintenance & Repairs	662	3	50	50	50	50	50	50	50	50	50	50	50	50	600	.3
Store Supplies	262	1	25	25	25	25	25	25	25	25	25	25	25	25	300	.2
Telephone	456	2	46	46	46	46	46	46	46	46	46	46	46	46	552	.3
Utilities	1.336	7	90	90	90	90	90	90	90	90	90	90	90	90	1.080	.5
Miscellaneous	341	2	25	25	25	25	25	25	25	25	25	25	25	25	300	.2
Total Controllable Expenses	33.993	16 7	1.209	1.212	1.212	1.215	1.218	1.218	1.221	1.224	1.225	1.228	1.209	1.212	14.603	7.2
Fixed Expenses																
Depreciation	149	1	85	85	86	86	86	86	87	87	87	87	87	87	1.036	.5
Insurance	1.335	6	125	125	125	125	125	125	125	125	125	125	125	125	1.500	.7
Rent	2.400	1 2	300	300	300	300	300	300	300	300	300	300	300	300	3.600	1.8
Taxes & Licenses	1.744	9	150	150	150	150	150	150	150	150	150	150	150	150	1.800	.8
Interest on Loan			325	320	316	312	308	303	299	295	290	286	281	277	3.612	1.9
Total Fixed Expenses	5.428	2 8	985	980	977	973	969	964	961	957	952	948	943	939	11.548	5.7
TOTAL EXPENSES	39.421	19 5	2.194	2.192	2.189	2.188	2.187	2.182	2.182	2.181	2.177	2.176	2.152	2.151	26.151	12.9
Net Profit (Loss)	(7.742)	(3 1)	1.556	1.683	1.686	1.812	1.938	1.943	2.068	2.194	2.198	2.324	2.473	2.599	24.474	12.1

Figure 2.2. (Continued)

10

EXPLANATION OF PROJECTED PROFIT AND LOSS STATEMENT

Gross sales for each month and the year. Projections are based on analysis of previous monthly sales from sales tax returns. The business averaged $16,957 a month for 1974. Although sales for early 1975 (not shown) averaged just below $15,000, projections for the first year under new management show a return to 1974's level. This is attributed to staying open longer hours and more vigorous management.

Cost of sales. Projected at 75% of sales. This is based on data from the State Board of Equalization. Retail Sales Tax Division: The Robert Morris Associates Annual Statement Studies: Almanac of Business and Industrial Financial Ratios: Bank of America Small Business Reporter for Independent Liquor Stores: and contact with the industry.

Gross profit. This is the difference between sales and cost of sales.

Controllable expenses. Controlled expenses are itemized below.

Salaries. This will be reduced nearly $20,000 by eliminating two clerks. The owner and family will operate the necessary hours with one employee.

Payroll taxes. This includes employer's share of 5.85% on Social Security: 3.6% on up to $4,200 of unemployment tax.

Alarm service. For use of burglar alarm service.

Advertising. For advertising in local newspaper, printing flyers. For expense of station wagon to be used 75% of the time for deliveries, pickups, etc.

Bad debts. For direct write-offs of uncollectible accounts. Based on historical ex, erience of 0.1%.

Collection fees. Fees paid for collection of delinquent accounts. Based on historical experience of 0.1%.

Dues and subscriptions. For trade journals.

Laundry and linen. Smocks for clerks and restroom towels.

Legal and accounting services. For outside accountant and legal assistance. Based on historical costs plus added service.

Office expense. Includes stationery and miscellaneous office supplies like postage, etc.

Professional services. For outside technical advice and assistance. Based on historical experience.

Repairs and maintenance. Projected on historical experience of 0.3% of sales.

Stores supplies. For storeroom, cartons, etc.

Telephone. Projected on historical experience of 0.4% of sales.

Utilities. Electricity, gas, water, trash, etc. Projected on historical experience of 0.5% of sales.

Miscellaneous. For sundry items.

Total controllable expenses. Total of items from salaries through miscellaneous.

Fixed expenses. The detailed fixed expenses are itemized below.

Depreciation calculated by straight line depreciation method as follows:

Item	Cost	Life	Amount
Ice Machine	$1,170	10 yrs.	$ 117
Wine Case	578	5 yrs.	116
Delicates. Case	307	8 yrs.	38
Appliances & Fixtures	374	5 yrs.	75
1973 Chev. Sta.			
Wagon (personal)	4,600	5 yrs.	920 x 75% = 690
			$1,036

Insurance on inventory and building for fire and theft; also public liability, life insurance for loan and workers' compensation. Projected on historical experience of 0.7% of sales.

Rent. Based on new lease agreement at $300 per month.

Taxes and licenses. Property tax plus business license.

Interest on loan. Calculated on $38,000 loan requested, over five years at 10%.

Total fixed expenses. Sum of items from depreciation through interest on loan.

Total expenses. Sum of controllable expenses and fixed expenses.

Net profit or loss. Difference between gross profits and total expenses. Net earnings are expected to total over $24,000.

Figure 2.2. (Continued)

GOOD TIMES LIQUOR STORE

PROJECTED CASH FLOW

	1975 Oct.	Nov.	Dec.	Jan.	Feb.	March	April	May	1976 June	July	Aug.	Sept.	TOTAL
Cash on Hand and in Banks (before purchase of business)	29.625												29.625
Cash Sales	13.500	14.000	14.000	14.500	15.000	15.000	15.500	16.000	16.000	16.500	17.000	17.500	184.500
Sales Tax Collected	878	906	907	936	965	965	994	1.024	1.024	1.053	1.082	1.112	11.846
Payments on Accounts Rec.	0	1.500	1.500	1.500	1.500	1.500	1.500	1.500	1.500	1.500	1.500	1.500	16.500
Loan Injection	38.000												38.000
TOTAL Cash Available	82.003	16.406	16.407	16.936	17.465	17.475	17.994	18.524	18.524	19.053	19.582	20.112	280.471
Cash disbursement													
Owner's Draw	1.000	1.000	1.000	1.000	1.000	1.000	1.000	1.000	1.000	1.000	1.000	1.000	12.000
Payment on Inventory Purchases	0	11.250	11.625	11.625	12.000	12.375	12.375	12.750	13.125	13.125	13.500	13.875	137.625
Payroll & Withholding Taxes Payable (quarterly)	579			579			579			579			1.737
Sales Tax Payable	0	878	906	907	936	965	965	994	1.024	1.024	1.053	1.082	10.734
Purchase of Business	60.000												60.000
Total Operating Expenses Less: Payroll Taxes. Depreciation and Bad Debt Write-off	1.916	1.914	1.910	1.909	1.908	1.903	1.902	1.901	1.897	1.896	1.894	1.893	22.843
Loan Payment Principal	488	492	496	500	505	509	513	518	522	527	531	536	6.137
TOTAL Disbursements	63.404	15.534	15.937	16.520	16.349	16.752	17.334	17.163	17.568	18.151	17.978	18.386	251.076
Cash Flow Monthly	18.599	872	470	416	1.116	713	660	1.361	956	902	1.604	1.726	29.395
Cash Flow Cumulative	18.599	19.471	19.941	20.357	21.473	22.186	22.846	24.207	25.163	26.065	27.669	29.395	

Figure 2.2. (Continued)

11

EXPLANATION OF CASH FLOW PROJECTION

Cash on hand and in bank. From personal financial statement. $29,625.

Cash sales. Total sales less receivables due.

Sales tax collected. Estimated at 6.5% on 90% of cash sales.

Payments on A/R. Collections from accounts receivable of previous month. Mr. Lee's plan is to limit credit sales to no more than $1,500 a month.

Loan injection. This is the loan of $38,000 being requested.

Total cash available. The sum of items from cash on hand through loan injection.

Cash disbursements. detailed below.

Owner's draw of $1,000 per month is sufficient for owner to cover living expenses, income taxes and residential real estate loan payments. However, this could be adjusted depending on the business.

Cost of sales is taken from the projected profit and loss statement, the second line, allowing 30 days' credit from suppliers.

Payroll and withholding taxes payable projected on the basis of one employee. 11.7% Social Security, state and federal income taxes withheld: 3.6% on up to $4,200 for unemployment tax and disability tax withheld from employee.

Sales tax payable. Payments on sales tax collected for the previous month.

Purchase of business for $60,000. This is the use of the $38,000 loan that is being requested. Owner is providing $22,000 to complete the purchase from accessible cash.

Total operating expenses. Total expenses including loan interest payments.

Loan payment principal. Only the principal portion of the loan repayment is shown because the interest portion has already been included under fixed expenses. Payments are based on a five-year loan.

Total disbursements. The sum of items from owner's draw through loan payment principal.

Cash flow monthly. The difference between total cash available and total disbursements for each month represents a positive flow.

Cash flow cumulative. A $29,395 excess of current receipts over all current disbursements is expected for the 12-month period. This indicates a substantial cushion for repayment of the loan.

Figure 2.2. (Continued)

63

13

GOOD TIMES LIQUOR STORE

Projected Balance Sheet

Current Status (after purchase of business) vs. One Year Later

	I Oct. 1. 1975	II Oct. 1. 1976
ASSETS		
Current Assets		
Cash on Hand and in Bank	7,625	29,395
Accounts Receivable	0	1,500
Inventory	30,000	30,000
Total Current Assets	37,625	60,895
Fixed Assets		
1973 Vega Station Wagon	3,450	3,450
Ice Machine	1,170	1,170
Wine Case	578	578
Delicatessen Case	307	307
Appliances and Fixtures	374	374
Total	5,879	5,879
Less Allowance for Depreciation	0	(1,036)
Net Fixed Assets	5,879	4,843
Other Assets		
License (Market Value)	10,000	10,000
Goodwill	17,571	17,571
Total Other Assets	27,571	27,571
TOTAL ASSETS	71,075	93,309
LIABILITIES		
Current Liabilities		
Accounts Payable	0	14,250
Federal Income Tax Withheld	0	252
State Income Tax Withheld	0	33
Federal S.S. Tax Payable	0	210
State Disability Tax Payable	0	18
Sales Tax Payable	0	1,112
State Unemployment Tax Payable	0	22
Principal Payments Due, Long-Term Loan	6,137	6,794
Total Current Liabilities	6,137	22,691
Long-Term Loan	31,863	25,069
TOTAL LIABILITIES	38,000	47,760
NET WORTH	33,075	45,549
Total Liabilities Plus Net Worth	71,075	93,309

Figure 2.2. (Continued)

14

EXPLANATION OF PROJECTED BALANCE SHEET

ASSETS. Current, fixed and other.

Current assets. Detailed below.

Cash on hand and in bank. 1976 balance is taken from projected cash flow statement.

Accounts receivable. Determined by calculating charge sales ($18,000) and deducting receivables payments ($16,500).

Inventory. Projected on the basis that inventory would remain constant at $30,000.

Total current assets. Sum of 3 items above.

Fixed assets. Detailed below.

1973 Vega station wagon. Based on 75% of cost of $4,600, as it will be used on that percentage.

The values of the following fixed assets were taken from C-3 1974 income tax return (original cost).

Ice machine. $1,170

Wine case. $678

Delicatessen case. $307

Appliances and fixtures. $374

Total fixed assets. Sum of items from station wagon through appliances and fixtures.

Less allowance for depreciation. Amount taken from projected profit and loss statement.

Net fixed assets. Total fixed assets less allowance for depreciation.

Other assets. Detailed below.

License. Fair market value for license issued in 1935.

Goodwill. Amount of purchase price over assets acquired.

Total other assets. Sum of license and goodwill.

Total assets. Sum of current, fixed and other assets.

LIABILITIES. Current and long-term liabilities detailed below.

Current liabilities. Detailed below.

Accounts payable. Cost of sales less payments to suppliers.

Federal income tax withheld. From employee for the quarter—$252.

State income tax withheld. From employee for the quarter—$33.

Federal Social Security tax payable. 11.7% of wages for the quarter—$210.

State disability tax payable. Amount withheld from employee for the quarter—$18.

Sales tax payable. Sales tax collected for September.

State unemployment tax payable. 3.6% of balance of wages up to $4,200 (3.6% x $600), for July, 1976, only; August and September wages went beyond $4,200 maximum.

Principal payments due on long-term loan—amount payable within one year. Taken from cash flow projection then calculated for year beginning October 1, 1976.

Total current liabilities. Sum of items from accounts payable through long-term loan payments.

Long-term loan. Original $38,000 minus principal already paid as current liability.

Total liabilities. Sum of total current liabilities and balance on long-term loan.

Net worth. Total assets less total liabilities (owner's equity).

$33,075	October, 1975 Net Worth
+24,474	Projected net profit (bottom line, projected profit and
$57,549	loss statement)
-12,000	Owner's draw, cash flow statement
$45,549	October, 1976 Net Worth

Total Liabilities plus Net Worth should balance Total Assets.

Figure 2.2. *(Continued)*

SOURCES OF ADDITIONAL INFORMATION

Anatomy of a Merger, by Robert Q. Parsons and John Stanley Baumgartner, published by Prentice-Hall, Inc., Englewood Cliffs, NJ 07632.

Business Loans, 2nd edition, by Rich Stephan Hayes, published by CBI Publishing, Inc., 51 Sleeper Street, Boston, MA 02210.

Financing for Small and Medium-Sized Businesses, by Harry Gross, published by Prentice-Hall, Inc., Englewood Cliffs, NJ 07632.

Going Public, by Daniel S. Berman, published by Prentice-Hall, Inc., Englewood Cliffs, NJ 07632.

How to Borrow Your Way to a Great Fortune, by Tyler G. Hicks, published by Parker Publishing Co., West Nyack, NY 10994.

How to Finance a Growing Business, by Royce Diener, published by Frederick Fell Publishers, Inc., 386 Park Avenue, New York, NY 10016.

How to Negotiate a Business Loan, by Richard C. Below, published by Van Nostrand Reinhold Co., 135 Weston Street, New York, NY 10020.

Money Raising and Planning for the Small Business, by David L. Markstein, published by Henry Regnery Co., 114 West Illinois Street, Chicago, IL 60610.

Small Business Reporter, Vol. 13, No. 10, "Financing Small Business," published by the Bank of America, Department 3120, P.O. Box 37000, San Francisco, CA 94137.

Winning the Money Game, edited by Donald Dible, published by The Entrepreneur Press, Santa Clara, CA 95051.

3

Business Insurance

WHY BUSINESS INSURANCE IS NECESSARY

Business insurance is extremely important for your business because it provides a means of protection against many business risks. You pay a relatively small amount of money to insure your business against the loss of a far greater amount. It is not an understatement that the relatively small insurance fee that you pay may actually save your company from going under.

RISK MANAGEMENT

Use of insurance for a business is really a way of managing risk in your business. This means identifying and controlling the exposure of your business or your personal assets to loss or to injury. Proper risk management is done in a four-step process as follows:

1. Identify the risk to which your business will be subjected.
2. Evaluate the probability of the occurrence of each risk that you have identified, along with the cost to you should it occur and the cost of insurance coverage protecting you against this risk.
3. Decide the best way to allow for each risk: whether to accept all or part of it and whether to reduce the risk through insurance.
4. Control the risk by implementing what you have decided is the best method or combination of methods for each risk.

To identify each risk, you should think of everything that poses a threat to your business. This includes strikes by your employees; death or temporary ill health of key personnel; losses resulting from fire, earthquake, or some other natural calamity, through a product causing some injury and your being sued, and so forth. You should list every threat that you can think of.

Now you must decide whether each risk that you have listed describes an event that is likely or unlikely. Further, if the event is likely, what can it cost you or your firm? For example, if you are sued because of a defect in your product that causes injury, how much are you likely to be sued for? If you have a fire, what is the fire likely to destroy and what is the dollar value of what is destroyed? After doing this, then investigate the insurances involved and how much insurance would cost to protect your business in each case.

After finding the cost of insurance protection, you must decide the best way to handle each of the threats to your business. In other words, you make some decisions about each risk. In some cases you may be able to avoid the risk entirely by having someone else perform the task that leads to the risk. For example, you can avoid certain of the fire risks and risks of injury to your employees by subcontracting the manufacture of your product to someone else. Another alternative is spreading the risk. You can duplicate various valuable documents, keeping them in two different locations, so that if a fire destroys one set, the other set is still available. Some risks may be prevented. Safety equipment may prevent injury; sprinkler systems and fire alarms minimize the potential for loss from fire. Finally, you can transfer the risk. Transferring the risk is done through contracts entered into with insurance companies. The insurance companies assume the risk of losses due to fire and so forth in return for a payment of a fee. This fee is called a "premium." Finally, if the risk is slight, you may simply accept it as a cost of doing business.

After weighing all alternatives, you must take the action to implement the decision that you have made. In many cases some type of insurance will be the best course of action. Now the problem is to develop an overall insurance program to implement this decision.

DEVELOPING AN INSURANCE PROGRAM

Developing an insurance program requires three basic actions: (1) getting exact insurance costs; (2) developing an insurance plan for your business; and (3) getting professional advice. Let's look at each in turn.

Getting Exact Insurance Cost

In order to decide how to handle the risk, it is necessary to obtain a rough idea of insurance costs. However, before you actually purchase any insurance, you should investigate the methods by which you can reduce the cost of your coverage. These methods are listed below.

1. Use as high a deductible as you can afford.
2. Make certain there's no duplication in the various insurance policies that you have.
3. Buy your insurance in as large a unit as possible. Certain package policies are suitable for different types of small businesses.
4. Review your insurance program periodically to insure that your coverage is adequate and that your premiums are as low as possible, consistent with the protection that you seek.

Developing a Business Insurance Plan

As with other aspects of business, you must plan in order to manage your insurance program properly. In this way you will receive the necessary coverage at the lowest possible cost. Some general principles will help here. Think through what you want to accomplish with your insurance program, and write out clear statements of what you expect insurance to do for you and your firm. Try to select only one agent to handle your insurance. This fixes responsibility in one single individual or company. If you personally are not handling the insurance, make certain that whoever is handling it for your company understands the importance of his or her responsibility. Don't try to con your insurance agent. An insurance agent is like a doctor, attorney, or other professional. In order to give you maximum help, he or she should know everything possible about risks to your business and its exposure to loss. Be careful about under-insuring in areas that can cause major loss even if the probability of the loss's occurrence is small. Premiums vary depending upon probability. So if the probability of occurrence is small, the premium will probably be small as well. Keep accurate and complete records of your insurance policies as well as your premiums, losses, and loss recoveries. You can use this information as your business grows to make better decisions about insurance coverage in the future. Finally, make certain that your property is appraised periodically by independent appraisers. In this way you will know what your exposure to risk actually is.

Getting Professional Advice

Insurance, like any other aspect of your business, can be complex. You cannot expect to master it by yourself unless you have very limited coverages. Therefore, an agent who is professionally qualified, a broker, or some other consultant can be worth the fees that you pay for this service many times over—just as are fees you pay for the services of an attorney or an accountant or any other business professional.

THE THREE BASIC TYPES OF INSURANCE

There are three basic types of insurance. They are liability insurance, life and health insurance, and property insurance.

Liability Insurance

Any business is subject to laws governing negligence, and this includes negligence to customers, employees, or anyone else with whom you may happen to do business or with whom you have contact in the course of business, or who is on your property. If you are negligent, you fail to do something, and in the case of liability, negligence refers to failing to exercise a degree of care that may be expected or required under your particular situation or circumstances. An example might be failing to clear snow properly from the walkway in the entrance to your premises, or permitting a hazard to exist because of the man-ufacturing processes that you employ. You may be liable through negligence even if you have signs posted specifically warning of this hazard, or if you have cleaned the snow from the walkway to your own satisfaction. It may be that an accident occurs from carelessness on the part of the injured. It doesn't seem to make much difference. Many courts judge in favor of the plaintiff anyway; the business is assumed to be responsible for any accidents happening on the premises, even though the injured person's carelessness may contribute to the mishap.

But there are even more important kinds of liabilities to your business than accidents or mishaps that may occur on your premises. One example is product liability. You are liable for the effects of the product that you produce under almost every situation. Some years ago a firearm manufacturing company was successfully sued by someone who was injured by operating a firearm in a manner specifically noted in the manufacturer's manual provided with the gun as being extremely hazardous. There is also liability as a result of an automobile accident by one of your employees while on the job. The bottom line is that you may have to purchase separate liability protection against potential liabilities that are not included in a general comprehensive liability policy.

General Liability Coverages

In general, liability insurance policies cover the following types of losses:

1. Payments that are required due to bodily injury or damage to the property of others that you cause accidentally
2. Medical services necessary at the time of the accident
3. Costs of defending lawsuits that allege bodily injury or property damage including expenses in investigation and settlement
4. The cost of any court bonds or other judgments during appeal

There are various exclusions and limitations on most liability policies. Some policies may exclude obligations under workers' compensation laws since this is covered by special workers' compensation insurance, as we will discuss shortly. Also excluded may be damage to property of others that is in your care or control. This exclusion may usually be eliminated by payment of an extra premium. Finally, a major exclusion will include liability resulting from war, mishaps involving nuclear energy, blasting operations, and similar situations. Limits to liability may be on a per-person or on a per-accident basis. For example, automobile liability insurance may limit you to $100,000 per person injured or to a total of $400,000 in any one accident. This means that if two persons are injured in a single automobile accident for which you are covered by liability insurance and the judgments are $200,000 each, the policy will pay only $200,000 because of the limit of $100,000 per person. On the other hand, if four individuals were injured and the judgment is $100,000 each, the policy would cover the total amount. Other limitations may include a single limit applying to bodily injury and property damage, or in property liability insurance, or as a limitation on product liability that applies to a certain group or batch of bad products. You should be aware of all limitations before purchasing the insurance. Now let's look at several types of liability insurance.

Automobile Liability Insurance.   You will generally be required to maintain insurance on all automobiles or other vehicles that you operate as a part of your business. You should also know that you can be legally liable for accidents by vehicles owned by others, either employees, vendors, or even customers who are involved in these accidents while they are using their vehicles on behalf of your business.

Typical coverage for automobile liability insurance includes insurance for damages from collision, fire, theft, and other physical perils. Physical damage or perils can be subdivided into several types. These include collision damage, which can be insured separately from other types of losses. Collision insurance does not cover glass breakage and damage from falling objects, missiles, windstorms, hail, malicious mischief, and vandalism. With your automobile liability insurance you can insure all types of physical loss except collision by taking out a comprehensive policy. A comprehensive policy generally excludes only the following: losses from wear and tear; losses to tires unless owing to fire, malicious mischief, or vandalism arising from collision; loss from radioactive contamination; and loss from freezing or from mechanical or electrical breakdown. However, if any of these losses except for those covered by radioactive contamination result from theft, you are covered. The alternative to buying comprehensive insurance is to insure against each peril separately. You can probably imagine how complex this could become.

How much you have to pay for automobile insurance or physical damage insurance can vary widely depending on the vehicle, including its age, type, the territory including the location and distance traveled, and the age of the driver or drivers. Sometimes special physical damage rates can be obtained if you own more than one vehicle. These are called experience rates and give individual physical damage rates based upon experience over a period of several years. Other special physical damage rates can be obtained under safe driver plans or merit rates for which you as the individual owner may qualify. In these days of very high insurance rates, obtaining a policy that allows for a deductible amount will permit you to save a significant amount of money on your collision coverage. This means that you yourself assume the obligation for a certain amount of damage in the event of an accident. Let's say you agree to a $500 deductible coverage. If you suffer damage to $500, you receive no reimbursement from the insurance. You are assuming the risk to that amount. Above $500, the policy would cover your losses. Again, you must weigh your loss in the event of damage, the probability of occurrence, and other factors to develop a risk trade-off that will help you decide how much obligation you should assume in any given situation.

Product Liability Insurance. Product liability insurance is useful to you as a manufacturer or, in some cases, a retailer of products that may cause injury or damage to the user of the product. However, even though this is known as "product" liability insurance, services too can cause damage and may be subject to product liability laws. Today, judgments against physicians for incorrect or incompetent medical decisions are common. The insurance that physicians carry to protect them against judgments in such suits is a type of product liability insurance. In the same fashion, an automobile mechanic who does a repair job incorrectly could be liable for an injury caused due to the service performed. Product liability insurance can be very expensive depending on the likelihood of your product's causing injury or damage or even allowing it to happen if your product is protective in nature. However, the awards in the event of an injury or death caused by your product may be so high as to make such insurance imperative.

Workers' Compensation Insurance. Usually workers' compensation insurance is required by law. It protects the employer against liability in the event of an accident to the employee. By law, you are required to provide employees with a safe place to work, hire only competent employees so they will not endanger one another, provide safe tools to work with, and warn employees of any existing dangers that may exist or develop while they are doing their job for you. If you fail to take any of these actions, not only in your eyes but in the eyes of the court, you are liable for damage suits brought against you by your employees. The mere fact that you try to do these duties to the best of your ability is not sufficient, and under workers' compensation insurance an employee can collect payment for doctors' bills and medications, as well as hospital expenses and income payments for time lost beyond a specified minimum period. If injuries are received that result in permanent damage, the employee may collect a lump sum payment to compensate for that loss.

These workers' compensation awards are not automatic and are made on the basis of the hearing by a special examiner or board. At this board, you will have the right to be represented either directly or jointly with the insurance company. Awards made to the employee may be smaller in the case of carelessness by the employee or when the loss is the result of an injury caused by a fellow employee.

All-Inclusive Policies.   You may also purchase overall insurance that can cover exceptionally large liabilities above and beyond your basic coverage. Such a policy may cover a multimillion-dollar lawsuit for the loss of life in an accident on your premises. Fortunately these general coverages or umbrella policies are not as expensive as one might think because the insurance company which provides them need only fulfill the few claims that exceed the basic insurance coverage. The result is that for a relatively small cost these all-inclusive policies can protect you against extremely severe losses. As to whether you need such policies or not, it is important to read the fine print carefully and take the time to have the insurance agent explain to you exactly what you are covered for and exactly what you are not covered for under the basic insurance policies that you purchase.

Life and Health Insurance

Life and health insurance provides extra compensation to employees, owners, or the business itself for losses that are sustained as a result of illness or death. These are not required by law, but most businesses today do carry them for their employees—in addition to the basic workers' compensation insurance. You will probably have to carry such life and health insurance policies for your employees in order to be competitive with what is offered by other companies in your industry. Typical coverages for this type of policy include basic life insurance, basic health insurance, major medical insurance coverage, dental insurance, and even eyeglass insurance in some cases. Life insurance is used to provide financial protection to the employee's family in the event of the employee's death. Some group life insurance plans are tax deductible for you as the employer. Also, group coverage can frequently be obtained at lower rates even if your firm includes only one or two employees. Generally a life insurance policy is offered in conjunction with some form of basic health or major medical insurance.

Health and medical insurance may include basic hospitalization and medical plans, major medical plans, and disability plans. Basic hospitalization medical plans pay the cost of hospitalization, medical care, and medication during hospitalization, and they also pay for medical care outside of hospitals and diagnostic services such as blood tests, X rays, urinalyses, and so forth. These policies, in some cases, may be split between medical and surgical on one hand and hospitalization on the other. Usually basic medical insurance is less expensive in group plans, except in the case of small groups. If the group or firm has very few employees, it may be less expensive to cover them with individual policies. Again, here's a trade-off that you should calculate after speaking with your insurance agent.

Major medical or catastrophic plans are intended to meet the cost of catastrophic illnesses. They usually contain deductible clauses so that they apply only after the payments covered by basic medical and hospitalization plans. For the same reason that all-inclusive policies are not expensive, major medical plans are not expensive, even for small companies.

In some states, disability plans are required by the law. These plans pay the employees a proportion of their salary during temporary or extended absences due to illness or accidents that are work related.

It is possible to use life insurance annuities to provide pension benefits to your employees. These pension and retirement plans are frequently offered by many large and small companies, but they are complex and they can be very expensive. Therefore, you must be very careful about these plans to make sure that you will not have increasing premium payments and that your business has sufficient income to make pension payments over the long run. Pension plans are also subject to federal laws and IRS regulations. Therefore, they represent a major insurance decision for your firm, and you should be certain that the plan that you intend to adopt meets all federal requirements.

There is an alternative to pension retirement plans. The Individual Retirement Account (IRA) is available for employees, and you may qualify for the Keogh Plan as an owner. Because of tax deferments for various other reasons, these may be more advantageous to you than a very small pension plan. Check into these plans with your bank and insurance agent and again compute the trade-offs to yourself, your employees, and your firm.

Property Insurance

Property insurance protects against losses that may occur to your business property. This includes real property or buildings, personal property including machines, office supplies, and equipment, finished goods, and so forth. Property coverages that you may want to consider include the following:

1. Automobile damage collision insurance
2. Comprehensive property insurance
3. Crime insurance for theft, burglary, and/or robbery
4. Fire insurance
5. Flood insurance
6. Hail and windstorm insurance
7. Vandalism
8. Inland marine insurance

Automobile Damage Insurance.   Automobile damage insurance is usually included as part of the automobile liability insurance policy discussed earlier. Therefore, it is usually excluded from all-purpose property policies.

Comprehensive Property Insurance.   This is an all-risk policy that generally covers all perils except those that are specifically excluded and named in the policy. An all-risk policy has certain advantages:

1. You avoid gaps in your coverage since you know that you are covered for all perils not specifically excluded.

2. You are less likely to duplicate your coverage with additional policies than if you tried to get the same insurance by purchasing several different policies.

3. In general, it is easier to obtain settlement for lawsuits with an all-risk policy. This is because owning several policies that cover a single loss may lead to a conflict as to how much each policy is to contribute toward coverage of the loss.

4. The total premium on an all-risk policy is generally less than the same coverage obtained by several different policies.

The areas that all-risk policies do not usually cover include such items as accounting records, automobiles, cash, jewelry, machinery, manuscripts, and like items, which are protected by other types of policies.

Crime Insurance. Some types of crime insurance can be included in comprehensive all-risk policies. However, other types of crimes such as off-premise robberies, disappearance of money, employee theft, and embezzlement are not included. Typical types of crime insurance include burglary insurance covering your safes and inventory of merchandise; robbery insurance, which will protect you from loss of property, money, and securities by robbery either on or off the premises; comprehensive crime policies, which can cover other types of theft loss in addition to burglary and robbery, including destruction or disappearance of property; and storekeepers' burglary and robbery policies, which are designed specifically for small businesspersons and cover up to a certain amount of loss for each occurrence of certain types of crime such as inside robbery, outside robbery, stock burglary, kidnapping of the owner, and so forth.

Crime insurance rates are generally high. They do, of course, depend on many factors, including your type of business, the location, kinds of loss prevention measurements such as safes and burglar alarms, and various other factors.

Fidelity bonds are a type of insurance that protects you against a serious potential loss that is caused by a special kind of crime: dishonesty of your own employees. For example, an embezzler may steal small amounts from you over a number of years, but the grand total may be quite high. A fidelity bond can insure you against this type of theft. Furthermore, the act of requiring an employee to be bonded may itself discourage stealing. Also, the character investigation performed by the bonding company may disclose unfavorable facts about an employee, enabling you to take preventive measures before a theft can occur.

Fire Insurance. Fire insurance is standardized in the United States. A standard policy covers three basic perils: fire, lightning, and losses to goods temporarily removed from their premises because of the fire. For any additional perils you must pay extra. For example, a standard fire policy excludes theft and failure to protect the property after a fire. Also, a special policy that extends the standard fire policy is needed to cover loss by fire of accounts, bills, currency, deeds, evidence of debt, and securities.

Flood, Hail, Windstorm, and Vandalism. The perils of windstorm, hail, and vandalism are frequently covered under comprehensive all-risk property insurance policies discussed earlier. However, flood damage is not, and such a policy is usually purchased separately.

Inland Marine Insurance. The inland marine floater policy is designed for specialized types of retailers and wholesalers, including equipment dealers, furriers, jewelers, and launderers, that are not covered by general all-risk commercial property insurance because their property is highly susceptible to loss. The type of insurance available may be all risk or there may be specifically named peril contracts.

SPECIAL-PURPOSE INSURANCE COVERAGES

Various additional coverages can be obtained to protect you against the potential of large losses. These include the following:

1. Business interruption insurance
2. Credit insurance
3. Glass insurance
4. Key employee insurance
5. Power plant insurance
6. Profits and commission insurance
7. Rent insurance
8. Sprinkler leakage insurance
9. Surety bonds
10. Transportation insurance
11. FAIR plan program

Let's look at each of these in turn.

Business Interruption Insurance

Your business will lose money if you are shut down as a result of a major disaster including fire, earthquake, flood, or storm. Further, even after repairs have been made, you will have to continue paying expenses such as salaries of employees, taxes, and so forth, even though there may be little or no money coming in. Business interruption insurance can help you with this problem.

Credit Insurance

Credit insurance is of several types. Credit life insurance is generally used by retail firms that sell on credit. It insures that the outstanding debt of the customer will be paid off in the event of his or her death. Commercial credit insurance enables you to have an open account of credit that you can extend to buyers of merchandise for commercial purposes. Installment sales floaters protect you against loss that has a potential for occurring when a purchaser has not insured goods bought on credit. In other words, they assure you of payments for goods that you have already sold.

Glass Insurance

Glass insurance protects you against breakage of large and expensive plate glass windows, signs, and showcases.

Key Employee Insurance

Key employee insurance insures you against losses resulting from the death or total disability of a key employee in your firm, including owners and partners. Thus, if a good deal of business depends on a single individual in your firm, this potential loss can be insured.

Power Plant Insurance

Certain types of machinery that can explode are not covered under all-risk or comprehensive property insurance. Therefore, these require separate policies. This category includes power plants, boilers, and other like machinery or electrical equipment.

Profits and Commission Insurance

This type of insurance enables you to insure profits or commissions you would lose if some named peril destroyed the merchandise involved.

Rent Insurance

Rent insurance is insurance for rent on property that you lease. It will reimburse you if your tenant fails to pay.

Sprinkler Leakage Insurance

This insurance covers losses resulting from leakage from water sprinklers used in fire protection of your building.

Surety Bonds

Surety bonds enable you to compete on an equal basis with larger or better-known firms. Basically, surety bonds are a guarantee that you will carry out work according to contract. Typically, surety bonds are issued for persons or firms doing contract construction, for those connected with court actions, or for those seeking licenses or permits. The bond guarantees that you are honest and have the necessary ability and financial capacity to meet the obligations required. The surety bond will also back your credit and vouch for your ability to perform. As with a fidelity bond, the bonding firm will require extensive information about you. They also require you to put up collateral before the bond will be issued. In the event of loss, sureties have the right to collect from you any amount they are required to pay to the person or company protected. You can see how such bonds put you on an equal footing with much larger firms since your ability to perform is guaranteed even though you may not be known to the individual paying for the job.

Transportation Insurance

Transportation insurance covers you while transporting goods. Many businesspersons do not realize that common carriers are not always liable for losses to the goods that they may be carrying for you. For example, common carriers are not liable for loss from floods, storms, earthquakes, or other perils or acts of God which cannot reasonably be guarded against by the carrier. Therefore, transportation insurance is of some importance.

Two basic types of transportation insurance are *inland transit policy* and *blanket motor cargo policy*. Inland transit policy is most frequently used for land shipments. It covers those perils that are not the liability of the common carrier. The coverage includes collision, derailment, and acts of God. Pilferage is usually excluded, but theft of an entire shipping package or container can be covered. Typical exclusions for the inland transit policy are those arising from strike, riot, civil commotion, war, delay of shipment or loss of market, and leakage or breakage—unless caused by one of the perils insured against. Certain types of property are also excluded, including accounts, bills, deeds, evidences of debt, money, notes and securities, and exports after arrival at seaport. Certain coverages in these provisions can be negotiated. Rates for an inland transit policy vary widely. You can save insurance costs by using a released bill of lading which makes the common carrier liable for a relatively low dollar value of damage. This can result in a reduction in transit rates which is usually more than enough to pay for the inland policy insurance.

A blanket motor cargo policy is issued to truckers and to those who ship by truck. All states require truckers to have certain minimum coverages, including their legal liability for loss of a shipper's goods. Federal laws also require interstate truckers to carry certain coverages. As a shipper, you may wish to obtain your own coverage rather than rely solely on the truckers since these minimums may not offer you full protection. Also, even if the trucker carries more than the minimum required by law, you have no assurance that the policy cannot be voided by breach of warranty or exclusions of various types. Finally, of course, the trucker's policy will not cover acts of God. Therefore, blanket motor cargo policies can be obtained that cover fire, flood, collisions, explosions, and other perils. Typical exclusions for this type of policy are strikes, war, illegal trade, and civil commotion.

FAIR Plan Program

The FAIR (Fair Access to Insurance Requirements) plan is a riot insurance program established by the U.S. Housing and Urban Development Act of 1968. In states accepting the plan, the state, the insurance industry, and the federal government cooperate to make property insurance available in certain high-risk areas at moderate rates. If your business is in an area generally known to be subject to riots or serious vandalism, and you are unable to get adequate insurance in the normal manner or cannot get insurance without paying excessively high premiums, this plan may help you out. In fact, you may not be turned down because of being located in a riot-prone area subject to vandalism. It is therefore in your interest to find out whether your state has a FAIR plan and where to apply if this situation applies to you. To do so, contact your state insurance commissioner.

HOW TO BUY INSURANCE

Direct Writers and Agents

There are basically two different types of insurance sellers. These are the direct writer and the agent. The direct writer is a commissioned employee of the insurer. The business he or she writes belongs to the insurance company itself, which may turn it over to someone else who is also an employee of the firm. The agent is an independent businessperson who has negotiated with the insurer to represent him or her in a given territory. The agent is also compensated on a commissioned basis.

There are advantages in dealing with either the agent or the direct writer. An independent agent may represent many different insurers. Therefore, such an agent will be able to offer you a wide choice among a number of different coverages. Also, if this independent agent handles many different types of insurance, you need deal with only this one seller to obtain the same coverage that you would otherwise have to obtain from several different insurance sellers. Because the insurance agent may deal with a variety of different coverages, he or she may have greater knowledge of the overall field than a direct writer, who would be limited to the line of the employer insurance company. Finally, inasmuch as the business is all his or hers, the independent agent has a greater financial motivation to give you the best service possible.

Advantages in dealing with direct writers include lower costs, since the commission paid the direct writer by his or her own company is less than that paid the independent agent. Also, the direct writer becomes a specialist in whatever area or line of insurance he or she is handling. Thus, whereas the independent agent has general knowledge, the direct writer has in-depth, specialized knowledge in one area. This may be advantageous to you, depending on the type of insurance that you are interested in and your business situation.

How to Pick an Insurer

The decision to pick one insurer over another generally is based on four factors. These are cost, type of insurance offered, flexibility in coverage, and financial stability of the firm.

Cost. To evaluate the cost factor, set up a matrix as shown in Table 3.1. Using this matrix, you would select the insurer who offers the lower cost for the coverage and deductible that you decide on. Note that there may be more to it than just the lower premium to consider. Some insurers charge a lower initial premium. However, another insurer, which charges a higher premium, may pay a dividend to its policyholders. Therefore, to make an accurate comparison, you must compare not only the initial premium involved but also the probable size of dividend if one is being paid.

If the premium is extremely low, you should be particularly careful that this low premium is not made possible by extremely strict claim settlement policies,

Table 3.1 Decision Matrix for Insurance Based on Cost and Deductibles

Insurance Company	Coverage	Deductible Amounts			
		$ 500	$1000	$2000	
Insurance Company A	$80,000	$1400	$1200	$ 800	
	85,000	1460	1245	830	
	90,000	1520	1300	860	Required premiums less dividends
Insurance Company B	$80,000	$1525	$1300	$ 835	
	85,000	1580	1335	910	
	70,000	1670	1410	960	

the setting aside of inadequate loss reserves, or such low commissions to their agents that the agents will not be motivated to render quality service.

Type of Insurance Offered.   Some insurers may specialize in certain types of insurance, and even in insurance for a specific industry. If you choose an insurer offering this sort of specialization, you will obtain coverages that are specifically applicable to your business, and the cost of the coverages can be lower than that which other firms offer for a similar type of insurance.

Flexibility in Coverage.   Various insurers are able to tailor their policies specifically to the type of buyers that they envision. Also, some insurers will enable you to insert certain provisions that may affect the final premium you pay or other factors. In some cases and with some insurers, you may negotiate depending on your situation and an insurance rating calculated according to the likelihood of the occurrence of the event for which you are to be insured. All of these factors can affect both the exact type of insurance coverage that you receive and the cost of the premiums.

Financial Stability of the Firm.   In most cases, the agent representing the firm will be your normal source of information about it, and generally you will not be misled. In dealing with an agent with whom you have not dealt before, you must also recognize that the agent could have an ulterior motive for recommending one insurance company over another. For example, one insurance company may pay him or her more. In this and similar situations, it is important that you know that the insuring company recommended has financial stability. Be especially careful when a policy is issued that has a provision that allows policyholders to be assessed additional premiums if the resources of the insurer are insufficient to pay claims against it. You should check to see whether the proposed policy is assessable or not. In general, you should purchase assessable policies only when nonassessable policies are not available and never if the insurance firm is unstable financially. To check on the financial stability of an insurance firm other than through the agent, consult a publication known as *Best's Insurance Reports. Best's Insurance Reports* publishes ratings that describe firms' reliability in their dealings with policyholders, their size of net worth, and other important factors. Most ratings fall in the three highest classes, A+, A, and B+. If the company that you are investigating does not fall into one of these three classes, you should look at it much more closely.

How Much Deductible?

You can decide on how much deductible or which policy or coverage to purchase with the matrix method also. Let's consider the case of the deductibles in Table 3.1. Because of basic costs, we have already decided to do business with insurance company A, and now the question is how much deductible to take. First, we decide on how much insurance is adequate for our purposes. Let us assume that the answer is $80,000. Now we have three options: $500 deductible for a premium of $1,400, $1,000 deductible for a premium of $1,200, and $2,000 deductible for a premium of $800. Let us say that we calculate that on the average we will suffer a $500 loss every two years, a $1,000 loss once every four years, and a $2,000 loss once every six years. We can then make the following calculations. For the $500 deductible policy, we would pay six times

$1,400 or $8,400 for their premium plus three times $500 or $1,500 for the three losses during the six years, for a total of $9,900. If we chose $1,000 deductible, we would pay six times $1,200 or $7,200 for the premium and suffer an average of one and one-half losses during the six-year period. That is one and one-half times $1,000 or $1,500, for a total of $8,700. Or, considering our third option, $2,000 deductible, we would pay six times $800 or $4,800 for our premium and during the six-year period suffer one loss of $2,000, for a total of $6,800. Since $6,800 is lower than either $8,700 or $9,900, it would pay us to take the $2,000 deductible policy.

How to Save Money with Your Insurance

To save money in buying your insurance, you should do the following:

1. Get competitive bids on all of your policies, review them using the matrix system shown in Table 3.1, and compare the alternatives.
2. Don't rely totally on your agent. Review your alternatives to be sure that your agent has not neglected to suggest the best possible coverage for your situation.
3. Over a period of time, evaluate how your agent has performed in getting compensation for your losses.
4. Make certain that you evaluate the use of deductibles in your insurance program.
5. Check with your agent where you can reduce premiums through assuming certain obligations, for example, a sprinkler system, a burglar alarm system, and so forth.

SETTLING INSURANCE LOSSES

Notice of Loss

All insurance policies will require you to notify the insurer as soon as the loss occurs. Do not violate this rule; you may endanger your right of recovery. As soon as practicable after the loss occurs, make certain that the insurer is informed.

Proof of Loss

Insurers will require some proof of the loss that has occurred. Generally this will amount to some sort of documentation: accounting records, death certificate in the case of life insurance, a complete inventory of destroyed property in the case of fire insurance, and so forth. To do this, you should keep good records ahead of time and expect to have to prove the loss that occurred. However, do not delay the notice of loss in order to get the full proof. You will have a reasonable period in which to provide the proof required.

Paying for Losses

Your local agent is generally authorized to settle small claims. However, larger claims are usually handled by company representatives. The company representative's job is to evaluate the loss and arrive at the settlement that will compensate you in accordance with your policy.

Basic Insurer Options

Generally, the insurer has three options in order to fulfill the terms of the policy that you have taken. These include (1) paying a cash settlement for your loss, (2) repairing the property, or (3) replacing the property with goods of like kind and quality. A cash settlement is the most frequent means of settling the claim.

Arbitration

A careful reading of your policy will indicate arbitration procedures if you and your insurer do not agree on the amount to be paid in cases of loss. The general procedure is for each party to select an independent and competent appraiser as well as a disinterested party to act as judge. The appraiser assesses the loss separately and submits any differences between your value and the insurance company's to the judge or umpire. Usually no lawsuit can be initiated unless these arbitration procedures have been carried out first. Also, there is a limitation regarding the time when a lawsuit can occur. This information can be found in your insurance policy.

Potential Problems in Settlement

There are certain potential problems in settling your claim, and the time to consider them is when you purchase your insurance and not after the loss occurs. The main problems of this type are overlapping coverage, nonconcurrency, and spread-out coverage.

Overlapping Coverage. This means that two or more policies cover the same risk or property. Intentionally obtaining overlapping coverage is a mistake because it inflates your cost as well as hindering settlement when and if a loss occurs. What happens is this: If a loss occurs, each insurer may try to make its policy that which pays the excess over the other insurance policy. Thus, both end up denying the basic liability and resulting legal litigation may mean that you won't get a settlement for years. Be very careful about overlapping coverage. In some cases, it may be difficult if not impossible to avoid, but in every instance in which it can be avoided, do so.

Nonconcurrency. This refers to a discrepancy among different policies covering identical property. This occurs because of conflicting provisions of different policies or overlapping coverage. Again, a close reading of your policies before the loss occurs can help you avoid lots of difficulty later on.

Spread-Out Coverage. This refers to spreading out your insurance among several different agents. This increases the chances of overlapping coverage and nonconcurrency. It also means that no one agent is completely responsible for your entire insurance program. Spread-out coverage should be minimized or, if possible, eliminated. The only exception is the case where the advantages of using direct writers described earlier are so significant that they outweigh this major disadvantage.

COMMON INSURANCE TERMS

Beneficiary. A person who is designated to receive the face amount of the policy.

Cash value of policy. The amount of insurance a company will pay if the policy is canceled, generally in the case of life insurance.

Coverage. The type of loss for which a policy will pay you. For example, most liability policies will pay for the amount you become legally obligated to pay because of bodily injury or damage to property that you accidentally caused, and the expense of settling a liability suit.

Deductibles. Deductibles are a specified dollar amount and percentage of loss above which the insurance company will pay.

Face amount of policy. A life insurance term that refers to the amount paid by the insurance company in the event of the death of the insured.

Exclusions. The types of losses for which a policy will not pay.

Indemnity. A principle that permits you to collect only the actual amount of the loss and not an amount named in the policy as the policy limit. This concept prevents excessive insurance coverage.

Limitations. The maximum amount of payment that the policy will provide in the event of a loss.

Loan value of policy. This, again, has to do with life insurance and is the amount of insurance that the insurance company will loan if you wish to borrow against the cash value of the policy.

Paid-up policy. This is also a life insurance term. It is a policy in which no further premiums are required. It may also be a new policy for less than the face value of an older policy that is given to the insured in the event the insured desires to cancel the original policy and take a policy of less than the original face but pay no more premiums.

Premium. The amount paid to maintain the policy in force.

Subrogation. A principle under which the insured gives to the insurer the right of recovery against the liable third parties, to the extent that the insurer indemnifies the insured for loss.

INSURANCE CHECKLIST FOR SMALL BUSINESS

The following insurance checklist for small business was developed by Mark R. Greene, Distinguished Professor of Insurance at the University of Georgia.[1] This checklist will enable you to discover areas in which your insurance program can be improved, costs can be saved, and the effectiveness of your insurance can be increased. It will also serve as a guide on points to talk about with your insurance agent, broker, or other insurance counselor.

The points covered in the checklist are grouped under three general classes of insurance: (1) coverages that are essential for most businesses, (2) coverages that are desirable for many firms but not absolutely necessary, and (3) coverages for employee benefits. For each of the statements, put a check in the first answer column if you understand the statement and how it affects your insurance

[1] Mark R. Greene, *Insurance Checklist for Small Business*, Small Business Administration (1979).

program. Otherwise, check the second column. Then study your policies with these points in mind and discuss any questions you still have with your agent.

Essential Coverages

Four kinds of insurance are essential: fire insurance, liability insurance, automobile insurance, and workers' compensation insurance. In some areas and in some kinds of businesses, crime insurance, which is discussed under "Desirable Coverages," is also essential.

Fire Insurance

	No action needed	Look into this

1. You can add other perils—such as windstorm, hail, smoke, explosion, vandalism, and malicious mischief—to your basic fire insurance at a relatively small additional cost.

2. If you need comprehensive coverage, your best buy may be one of the all-risk contracts that offer the broadest available protection for the money.

3. The insurance company may indemnify you—that is, compensate you for your losses—in any one of several ways: (1) It may pay actual cash value of the property at the time of loss. (2) It may repair or replace the property with material of like kind and quality. (3) It may take *all* the property at the agreed or appraised value and reimburse you for your loss.

4. You can insure property you don't own. You must have an insurable interest—a financial interest—in the property *when a loss occurs* but not necessarily at the time the insurance contract is made. For instance, a repair shop or drycleaning plant may carry insurance on customers' property in the shop, or a person holding a mortgage on a building may insure the building although he doesn't own it.

5. When you sell property, you cannot assign the insurance policy along with the property unless you have permission from the insurance company.

6. Even if you have several policies on your property, you can still collect only the amount of your actual cash loss. All the insurers share the payment proportionately. Suppose, for example, that you are carrying two policies—one for $20,000 and one for $30,000—on a $40,000 building, and fire causes damage to the building amounting to $12,000. The $20,000 policy will pay $4,800; that is, $\frac{20,000}{50,000}$, or $\frac{2}{5}$, of $12,000. The $30,000 policy will pay $7,200; which is $\frac{30,000}{50,000}$, or $\frac{3}{5}$, of $12,000.

7. Special protection other than the standard fire policy is needed to cover the loss by fire of accounts, bills, currency, deeds, evidences of debt, and money and securities.

	No action needed	Look into this

8. If an insured building is vacant or unoccupied for more than 60 consecutive days, coverage is suspended unless you have a special endorsement to your policy canceling this provision.   ___   ___

9. If, either before or after a loss, you conceal or misrepresent to the insurer any material fact or circumstance concerning your insurance or the interest of the insured, the policy may be voided.   ___   ___

10. If you increase the hazard of fire, the insurance company may suspend your coverage even for losses not originating from the increased hazard. (An example of such a hazard might be renting part of your building to a drycleaning plant.)   ___   ___

11. After a loss, you must use all reasonable means to protect the property from further loss or run the risk of having your coverage canceled.   ___   ___

12. To recover your loss, you must furnish within 60 days (unless an extension is granted by the insurance company) a complete inventory of the damaged, destroyed, and undamaged property showing in detail quantities, costs, actual cash value, and amount of loss claimed.   ___   ___

13. If you and the insurer disagree on the amount of loss, the question may be resolved through special appraisal procedures provided for in the fire insurance policy.   ___   ___

14. You may cancel your policy without notice at any time and get part of the premium returned. The insurance company also may cancel at any time with a 5-day written notice to you.   ___   ___

15. By accepting a coinsurance clause in your policy, you get a substantial reduction in premiums. A coinsurance clause states that you must carry insurance equal to 80 or 90 percent of the value of the insured property. If you carry less than this, you cannot collect the full amount of your loss, even if the loss is small. What percent of your loss you can collect will depend on what percent of the full value of the property you have insured it for.   ___   ___

16. If your loss is caused by someone else's negligence, the insurer has the right to sue this negligent third party for the amount it has paid you under the policy. This is known as the insurer's right of subrogation. However, the insurer will usually waive this right upon request. For example, if you have leased your insured building to someone and have waived your right to recover from the tenant for any insured damages to your property, you should have your agent request the insurer to waive the subrogation clause in the fire policy on your leased building.   ___   ___

17. A building under construction can be insured for fire, lightning, extended coverage, vandalism, and malicious mischief.   ___   ___

	No action needed	Look into this

Liability Insurance

1. Legal liability limits of $1 million are no longer considered high or unreasonable even for a small business.

2. Most liability policies require you to notify the insurer immediately after an incident on your property that might cause a future claim. This holds true no matter how unimportant the incident may seem at the time it happens.

3. Most liability policies, in addition to *bodily* injuries, may now cover *personal* injuries (libel, slander, and so on) *if* these are specifically insured.

4. Under certain conditions, your business may be subject to damage claims even from trespassers.

5. You may be legally liable for damages even in cases where you used "reasonable care."

6. Even if the suit against you is false or fraudulent, the liability insurer pays court costs, legal fees, and interest on judgments *in addition to* the liability judgments themselves.

7. You can be liable for the acts of others under contracts you have signed with them. This liability is insurable.

8. In some cases you may be held liable for fire loss to property of others in your care. Yet, this property would normally not be covered by your fire or general liability insurance. This risk can be covered by fire legal liability insurance or through requesting subrogation waivers from insurers of owners of the property.

Automobile Insurance

1. When an employee or a subcontractor uses his own car on your behalf, you can be legally liable even if you don't own a car or truck yourself.

2. Five or more automobiles or motorcycles under one ownership and operated as a fleet for business purposes can generally be insured under a low-cost fleet policy against both material damage to your vehicle and liability to others for property damage or personal injury.

3. You can often get deductibles of almost any amount— say $250 or $500—and thereby reduce your premiums.

4. Automobile medical payments insurance pays for medical claims, including your own, arising from automobile accidents regardless of the question of negligence.

5. In most states, you must carry liability insurance or be prepared to provide other proof (surety bond) of financial responsibility when you are involved in an accident.

6. You can purchase uninsured motorist protection to cover your own bodily injury claims from someone who has no insurance.

	No action needed	Look into this

7. Personal property stored in an automobile and not attached to it (for example, merchandise being delivered) is not covered under an automobile policy. ___ ___

Workers' Compensation

1. Common law requires that an employer (1) provide his employees a safe place to work, (2) hire competent fellow employees, (3) provide safe tools, and (4) warn his employees of an existing danger. ___ ___

2. If an employer fails to provide the above, under both common law and workers' compensation laws he is liable for damage suits brought by an employee. ___ ___

3. State law determines the level or type of benefits payable under workers' compensation policies. ___ ___

4. Not all employees are covered by workers' compensation laws. The exceptions are determined by state law and therefore vary from state to state. ___ ___

5. In nearly all states, you are now legally *required* to cover your workers under workers' compensation. ___ ___

6. You can save money on workers' compensation insurance by seeing that your employees are properly classified. ___ ___

7. Rates for workers' compensation insurance vary from 0.1 percent of the payroll for "safe" occupations to about 25 percent or more of the payroll for very hazardous occupations. ___ ___

8. Most employers in most states can reduce their workers' compensation premium cost by reducing their accident rates below the average. They do this by using safety and loss-prevention measures. ___ ___

Desirable Coverages

Some types of insurance coverage, while not absolutely essential, will add greatly to the security of your business. These coverages include business interruption insurance, crime insurance, glass insurance, and rent insurance.

Business Interruption Insurance

1. You can purchase insurance to cover fixed expenses that would continue if a fire shut down your business—such as salaries to key employees, taxes, interest, depreciation, and utilities—as well as the profits you would lose. ___ ___

2. Under properly written contingent business interruption insurance, you can also collect if fire or other peril closes down the business of a supplier or customer and this interrupts your business. ___ ___

3. The business interruption policy provides payments for amounts you spend to hasten the reopening of your business after a fire or other insured peril. ___ ___

	No action needed	Look into this

4. You can get coverage for the extra expenses you suffer if an insured peril, while not actually closing your business down, seriously disrupts it.   —   —

5. When the policy is properly endorsed, you can get business interruption insurance to indemnify you if your operations are suspended because of failure or interruption of the supply of power, light, heat, gas, or water furnished by a public utility company.   —   —

Crime Insurance

1. Burglary insurance excludes such property as accounts, fur articles in a showcase window, and manuscripts.   —   —

2. Coverage is granted under burglary insurance only if there are visible marks of the burglar's forced entry.   —   —

3. Burglary insurance can be written to cover, in addition to money in a safe, inventoried merchandise and damage incurred in the course of a burglary.   —   —

4. Robbery insurance protects you from loss of property, money, and securities by force, trickery, or threat of violence on *or off* your premises.   —   —

5. A comprehensive crime policy written just for small businessmen is available. In addition to burglary and robbery, it covers other types of loss by theft, destruction, and disappearance of money and securities. It also covers thefts by your employees.   —   —

6. If you are in a high-risk area and cannot get insurance through normal channels without paying excessive rates, you may be able to get help through the federal crime insurance plan. Your agent or state insurance commissioner can tell you where to get information about these plans.   —   —

Glass Insurance

1. You can purchase a special glass insurance policy that covers all risk to plate-glass windows, glass signs, motion picture screens, glass brick, glass doors, showcases, countertops, and insulated glass panels.   —   —

2. The glass insurance policy covers not only the glass itself, but also its lettering and ornamentation, if these are specifically insured, and the costs of temporary plates or boarding up when necessary.   —   —

3. After the glass has been replaced, full coverage is continued without any additional premium for the period covered.   —   —

Rent Insurance

1. You can buy rent insurance that will pay your rent if the property you lease becomes unusable because of fire or other insured perils and your lease calls for continued payments in such a situation.   —   —

	No action needed	Look into this

2. If you own property and lease it to others, you can insure against loss if the lease is canceled because of fire and you have to rent the property again at a reduced rental. ___ ___

Employee Benefit Coverages

Insurance coverages that can be used to provide employee benefits include group life insurance, group health insurance, disability insurance, and retirement income. Key-man insurance protects the company against financial loss caused by the death of a valuable employee or partner.

Group Life Insurance

1. If you pay group insurance premiums and cover all employees up to $50,000, the cost to you is deductible for federal income tax purposes, and yet the value of the benefit is not taxable income to your employees. ___ ___

2. Most insurers will provide group coverages at low rates even if there are 10 or fewer employees in your group. ___ ___

3. If the employees pay part of the cost of the group insurance, state laws require that 75 percent of them must elect coverage for the plan to qualify as group insurance. ___ ___

4. Group plans permit an employee leaving the company to convert his group insurance coverage to a private plan, at the rate for his age, without a medical exam if he does so within 30 days after leaving his job. ___ ___

Group Health Insurance

1. Group health insurance costs much less and provides more generous benefits for the worker than individual contracts would. ___ ___

2. If you pay the entire cost, individual employees cannot be dropped from a group plan unless the entire group policy is canceled. ___ ___

3. Generous programs of employee benefits, such as group health insurance, tend to reduce labor turnover. ___ ___

Disability Insurance

1. Workers' compensation insurance pays an employee only for time lost because of work injuries and work-related sickness—not for time lost because of disabilities incurred off the job. But you can purchase, at a low premium, insurance to replace the lost income of workers who suffer short-term or long-term disability not related to their work. ___ ___

2. You can get coverage that provides employees with an income for life in case of permanent disability resulting from work-related sickness or accident. ___ ___

	No action needed	Look into this

Retirement Income

1. If you are self-employed, you can get an income tax deduction for funds used for retirement for you and your employees through plans of insurance or annuities approved for use under the Employees Retirement Income Security Act of 1974 (ERISA). ⸺ ⸺

2. Annuity contracts may provide for variable payments in the hope of giving the annuitants some protection against the effects of inflation. Whether fixed or variable, an annuity can provide retirement income that is guaranteed for life. ⸺ ⸺

Key-Man Insurance

1. One of the most serious setbacks that can come to a small company is the loss of a key man. But your key man can be insured with life insurance and disability insurance owned by and payable to your company. ⸺ ⸺

2. Proceeds of a key-man policy are not subject to income tax, but premiums are not a deductible business expense. ⸺ ⸺

3. The cash value of key-man insurance, which accumulates as an asset of the business, can be borrowed against and the interest and dividends are not subject to income tax as long as the policy remains in force. ⸺ ⸺

SOURCES OF ADDITIONAL INFORMATION

Business Insurance, 4th edition, by Edwin H. White and H. Chasman, published by Prentice-Hall, Inc., Englewood Cliffs, NJ 07632.

General Insurance, 9th edition, by John H. Magee, published by Richard D. Irwin, Inc., 1818 Ridge Road, Homewood, IL 60430.

General Insurance Guide, by B. G. Werbel, published by Werbel Publishing Co., 595 Old Willets Path, Smithtown, NY 11787.

Group Insurance Handbook, edited by Robert D. Eilers and Robert M. Crowe, published by Richard D. Irwin, 1818 Ridge Road, Homewood, IL 60430.

Insurance and Risk Management for Small Business, by Mark R. Greene, published by the Small Business Administration, Superintendent of Documents, Washington, DC 20402.

Life and Health Insurance Handbook, 3rd edition, edited by Davis W. Gregg and Vane B. Lucas, published by Richard D. Irwin, Inc., 1818 Ridge Road, Homewood, IL 60430.

Modern Life Insurance, 3rd edition, by Robert W. Osler, published by Macmillan Co., 866 Third Avenue, New York, NY 10022.

Risk and Insurance, 3rd edition, by Mark R. Greene, published by Southwestern Publishing Co., 5101 Madison Road, Cincinnati, OH 45227.

Risk Management and Insurance, 2nd edition, by C. Arthur Williams, Jr., and Richard M. Heins, published by McGraw-Hill Book Co., 1221 Avenue of the Americas, New York, NY 10020.

Risk Management: Concepts and Applications, by Robert I. Mehr and Bole A. Hedges, published by Richard D. Irwin, 1818 Ridge Road, Homewood, IL 60430.

4

Buying a Business

THE ADVANTAGES AND DISADVANTAGES OF BUYING A BUSINESS

Buying a business has both advantages and disadvantages when compared to starting your own business. Before deciding whether to buy a new business or to start one, it is important to consider all of the facts.

Advantages

1. Prior successful operation of a business increases your chances of success with the same business.
2. Prior successful operation at a specific location increases your chances of success at the same location.
3. If the business has been profitable or is headed toward profit, you will be profitable sooner than if you start up your own business.
4. The amount of planning that may be necessary for an ongoing business will probably be less than that for a new business.
5. You will already have established customers or clientele.
6. You will already have established suppliers.
7. You may already have inventory on hand and will not lose the time necessary for selecting, ordering, and waiting for the order to arrive before you can make your first sale.
8. Most necessary equipment is probably already on hand.
9. Most of the financing that will be necessary is for purchasing the business.
10. You may be able to buy the business at a bargain price.
11. You will acquire the benefit of the experience of the prior owner.
12. Much of the hard work of start-up is avoided, including finding the location, purchasing the equipment, and so forth.
13. If employees are on board, they are probably already experienced in the business.
14. You may be able to finance all or part of the purchase price through a note to the owner.
15. Existing records of the business may help you and guide you in running the business.
16. The business already has a track record for you to look at.

Disadvantages

1. You will inherit any bad will that exists because of the way the business has been managed.
2. The employees who are currently working for the company may not be the best or the best for you and the way you manage.
3. The image of the business is already established. This image will be difficult to change.
4. Precedents have already been set by the previous owners. They may be difficult to change.
5. Modernization may be needed.
6. The purchase price may create a burden on future cash flow and profitability.
7. It is possible that you can overpay due to misrepresentation or an inaccurate appraisal of what the business is worth.
8. The business location may be a drawback.
9. You may be liable for contracts entered into by the previous owners.

SOURCES OF OPPORTUNITIES TO PURCHASE A NEW BUSINESS

Before you can decide whether it is in your interest to buy a business or not, you have to look it over, and before you can do that, you must locate businesses for sale. Such businesses can be obtained from the following sources:

1. *Classified advertisements in newspapers.* The Sunday edition usually has a number of listings or try the *Wall Street Journal* under the classification "Business Opportunities."
2. *Classified or space advertisements in trade magazines.*
3. *Realtors.* You can find them in the yellow pages of the telephone directory.
4. *Business brokers.* They can also be found in the yellow pages of your telephone directory. (Note: When dealing with business brokers, check more than one. Some businesses may be handled on an exclusive basis and you will not be able to uncover all opportunities in your area by talking to one broker.)
5. *Chambers of commerce.* Some chambers of commerce maintain a buying and selling service for businesses in their area. Check with your local unit.
6. *Trade sources.* These include suppliers, distributors, manufacturers, trade associations, and so forth. Simply call up individuals who would be suppliers or distributors to the business that you would like to buy and ask if they know if the business is for sale.
7. *Professionals.* Check with attorneys, accountants, and bankers dealing with small business. They may know of a business of the type that you're interested in.
8. *Business owners.* Ask owners of the type of business in which you're interested. Small businesspeople are eager to help one another, sometimes even potential competitors, and they may know of a business that is for

sale. Also, there is always the outside chance that the very businessperson you are talking with wishes to sell his or her business. Anyway, it never hurts to ask.

HOW TO SIZE UP BUSINESS BUY OPPORTUNITIES

The Screening Evaluation

The first step in evaluating a business buy opportunity is a screening evaluation. During the screening evaluation, you want to learn some basic facts about the new business that is for sale. The basic purpose of the screening evaluation is to decide not whether you will purchase the business, but whether you will look at it further.

Initial contact with the owner of the business that you wish to purchase can usually be by telephone. On the telephone you can ask some basic facts about the business: its location, annual sales, and such information. Make certain that you take good notes during this conversation. If anything said by the owner obviously disqualifies the business, then you should drop the matter right then and there and not waste additional time. But if the phone conversation seems to indicate to you that it is worthwhile to investigate further, then you should take the second step, which is to make an appointment for an initial visit with the owner.

Again, you are still in the screening stage, and even on an initial visit the purpose is simply to know whether to proceed or to scratch this business off your list. During this visit you should look around, assess how the business looks, the clientele or customers who may come in, the attitude of the owner, and especially his or her capabilities and personal integrity. Ask the history of the business, how it was established, and other background information.

It is extremely important that you determine the real reason for selling. Almost invariably the owner will give you one of two reasons: ill health or impending retirement. This may be the truth, but it is imperative that you check it out. Too many times these reasons are given to cover up a poor investment. For example, sales could be declining. There could be a major change in the neighborhood that is causing business to be lost or to be less favorable than it once was. There could be new competition or new technology on the scene. Perhaps the products are obsolete or a key employee has been lost. The business could have problems with creditors. It is essential that you really dig to find out the true facts. Sometimes you may be able to solve the problem and thus turn the whole situation around to your advantage. You will have a real bargain if you pay very little for the business and turn it around rapidly. This is far from fantasy. In fact, some individuals actually make a business of buying unprofitable businesses and turning them around. However, in order to be able to do this, you must identify the precise problems that are causing the business to go wrong and, of course, you must be absolutely confident that you can correct them.

The In-Depth Analysis

If the business still interests you, your real work begins. Now you must analyze the business much more carefully. You must study local conditions yourself to see exactly what is happening. This includes asking other businesspeople in the area their opinion of the business and their opinion of the owner; talking to suppliers and hearing about their experiences in dealing with this owner and the business; talking to customers; speaking with trade associations and executives about the business; talking to key employees and, if you have the opportunity, talking to former employees. This is sometimes your most valuable source of information since former employees may be more ready to give you information than present employees are. You should also talk to the bank, call the Better Business Bureau to see whether customers have complained about the business, talk to executives at the chamber of commerce, and contact Dun & Bradstreet who, for a fee, can give you their own intelligence estimate of the business. A local office of Dun & Bradstreet can be found in the white pages. If you are living in a small town or area that doesn't have a local office, then call or write to: Dun & Bradstreet, 99 Church Street, New York, NY 10007.

Below we will discuss the aspects of the business you are considering buying that you will want to know *all* about before you decide.

Profits and Sales.   The main factor in analysis of profits and sales is not current or even past profits and sales, but what the future profit potential is. You can find out the owner's income from his or her business from federal or state income tax returns, records of bank deposits, and similar sources. You should also get actual figures on past profit sales, operating ratios, and other like information from the firm's books and auditor reports. You should go back at least five years, and the ratios obtained should be compared to industry ratios. It is advisable to have your accountant audit these business records for you.

If for any reason the seller cannot or will not supply records for your analysis, this should be a very clear warning signal to you that something is amiss.

Once these records have been obtained and audited, you should analyze for profitability with your improvements. But in doing this, don't dream. Be realistic. Your improvements can make a difference, but you won't be able to work miracles. You should also analyze expenses for the business and see whether they are in line for a business of this type. Once you have your figures and expenses straight, and your own plans for what you might do in order to increase profitability, you should project sales and profits forward for a period of one to two years. Then analyze these figures to see whether the investment that you must make will bring you a better return than would starting a similar business of your own from scratch.

When analyzing profits and sales, make good use of professional services including, as mentioned before, your accountant. But also bring in your lawyer, talk to your banker, and even consult your business insurance agent to make certain that the figures are factual and that your analyses are correct and realistic.

Inventory.   Look at the inventory and have an independent appraiser determine its value—examining the inventory for age, salability, quality, style, condition, and whether it is in line with the product line that you plan. These facts should determine the real value of the inventory to you. The questions you should ask yourself are: Can you sell this inventory? At what price? Do you have to clear out the inventory at a percentage of its supposed value at a loss to yourself? It's crucial to recognize exactly how much you will be able to receive for the inventory in dollars. You should also recognize that if the inventory is still being sold, this asset may not exist at the time you actually go to purchase. So, be sure that it does exist if you're going to pay for it.

Capital Equipment, Furniture, Fixtures, and the Building.   Again, the key is to find out the real market value of capital equipment. If it is old, must it be replaced? If it must be replaced, when must it be replaced? Is the equipment in good condition and modern? Can you actually make use of the equipment or will it just be sitting around taking up space? Will modifications to the equipment be needed? How much will they cost? It is important to inspect this equipment yourself and not just take the owner's word for or description of what you are getting.

Accounts Receivable.   You should check the accounts receivable closely. Look at how old each account is. The older the account is, the more difficult it will be to collect. Look for the credit standing of the accounts. Check the business to see how much is actually done on credit and what the credit collection rate is. If much business is done on credit with long payments, it will mean that you will have a shortage of working capital even if the accounts are eventually paid. Analyze the situation and think through the results if you employed a stricter credit policy. Would you lose some customers? What percentage of the customers and what percentage of sales could you be expected to lose?

Contracts.   Contracts, including leases on rented equipment or buildings, have value. Be sure to check the transferability of the contract to you as the buyer and, if the contract can be renewed, the terms of renewal. Check how long the lease is for. Talk to the landlord and ascertain his or her attitude toward the business and the current owner. Check all the terms and options of the contract and lease. If the location is important, this becomes even more vital.

Clientele.   What kinds of customers are you dealing with? Is it likely that these customers will stay with you once the business is transferred? Are key contracts transferable or will you lose them once you buy the business?

Customer Lists.   Customer lists can be extremely valuable and are most definitely so in any type of mail order business. In fact, in such a case, the customer list may constitute the major asset of the business. Make certain that you will own these lists yourself on purchase and that the seller will no longer have the right to use them. You should also obtain various specifics such as the size of the list, the number of first-time buyers by year, sales value of initial purchase, sales values of subsequent purchases as well as their frequency, attrition rate of the active list, and information on revenues from list rental.

Franchises.   Check the terms of the franchise. Note the exclusivity. Check also for the transferability of the franchise and note the original cost to the seller. All these are important factors in deciding the value of the franchise as an asset.

Good Will.   Good will has to do with the business's reputation, its established patronage, and its established image. Good will is worth something and should be considered an asset. But remember that an image cannot be readily changed no matter what it is, and that to be an asset "good will" must in fact be "good." Carefully evaluate this asset or lack of same based on your investigation with the Better Business Bureau, suppliers, customers, and so forth.

Key Personnel.   Personnel who know the business well can be extremely valuable to you if they intend to stay with the business. You should check to ascertain whether or not they do. You should also analyze the situation to find out what the effect will be if key personnel leave the business. Talk to the former owner and size him up as a businessperson. He may be the guiding light who alone is able to make the business profitable. Once he leaves, the business may collapse. Is he willing to consult for you for a period of time to ensure the business's continued success? Also, ask whether he is willing to sign a non-competing agreement so that he cannot compete in the same business against you once he has sold this business to you.

Proprietary Items.   These items include copyrights, trademarks, patents, secret processes, and even a business name. Again, you must look at the situation closely to decide the real value of these items. A mechanical patent, for example, is good for only 17 years. How long has the patent been in force? Also, patents vary greatly in value even once granted. They can be designed around. They can even be invalidated in the courts, in which case the patent may be absolutely worthless. Are such items essential to the business or not?

Suppliers.   Check business relations with suppliers. Make sure they will continue to supply you. You should also find out whether or not the business is committed to any supplier and how satisfactory each supplier has been in the past in supplying what was needed in a timely fashion.

Have your lawyer make sure that all assets claimed are written into and spelled out in the sale contract.

Liabilities.   Every aspect of the business thus discussed can be either positive or negative; it can be either an asset or a liability. But it is particularly important that you identify every liability. Look for unpaid bills, back taxes owed, pending lawsuits, and so forth. Again, you must get the help of professionals for your investigation, including a lawyer and an accountant. This costs money, but the money that you save may save the business or save your investment for the future. Every liability that you will assume in the business should be put in writing (this goes for assets, too!) and a statement in the sales contract should indicate that all claims against the business now shown are assumed by the seller of the business.

Competition.   It is extremely important to know what competition, both current and future, you may expect in this business. Again, you must do more than just talk to the current owner. Much can be revealed about competition by looking at sales trends over the past few years as well as talking to other businesses in your area or the trade association in which the business is a member.

The Market.   Is the market, including the community that is being served, growing or has the growth leveled off? Is the market actually on the decline? Watch for things like traffic routing, new shopping centers, or regulations that may affect your business. A highway, freeway, or expressway going through the area can totally change the market that was formerly served by businesses in the area. Also, look for changing neighborhoods. A neighborhood that is being renovated may have a positive effect on the business, but it may have a negative effect instead, so you must check this carefully.

Circumstances Unique to the Owner.   Sometimes a business is based on a particular owner, his or her family, the relations, religion, ethnic group, or membership in certain social or political organizations. These may be the reasons the business and sales are at a certain level. You, coming into this business and not being of the same ethnic group, religion, family, social group, or whatever, may lose a great portion of the former sales. This is not always the case, but again you should be aware of the possibility.

Manpower.   You should look not only at the key personnel discussed previously but also at workers employed in this business. Are qualified people employed and will they stay? Should they leave, are there sources of additional manpower available in the local area?

Waste.   Look for waste in the business. Sometimes this will help you purchase a real bargain. Is there unused machinery, for example? This is a waste. Are materials being wasted that could be resold or used in other manufacturing processes?

Location and Location History.   Never buy a business without investigating the location and the location history of the business. Some locations are poor for almost any business, and a history over a period of time, say 5 or 10 years, will reveal that one business after another has been in that location and then failed. If some businesses have failed and some have not, find which ones did and which did not. Knowing what types have been successful and what types have not can be extremely helpful as an indicator of your chances of success. Use the checklist contained in Figure 4.1 to help you.

City or Town
   1. Economic considerations
      Industry
         Farming
         Manufacturing
         Trading
      Trend
         Highly satisfactory
         Growing
         Stationary
         Declining
      Permanency
         Old and well established
         Old and reviving
         New and promising
         Recent and uncertain
      Diversification
         Many and varied industries
         Many of the same type
         Few but varied
         Dependent on one industry
      Stability
         Constant
         Satisfactory

         Average
         Subject to wide fluctuations
      Seasonality
         Little or no seasonal change
         Mild seasonal change
         Periodic—every few years
         Highly seasonal in nature
      Future
         Very promising
         Satisfactory
         Uncertain
         Poor outlook
   2. Population
      Income distribution
         Mostly wealthy
         Well distributed
         Mostly middle income
         Poor
      Trend
         Growing
         Large and stable
         Small and stable
         Declining
      Living status

Figure 4.1.   Location checklist. [From *Buying and Selling a Small Business*, by Verne A. Bunn, Small Business Administration (1969).]

Own homes
Pay substantial rent
Pay moderate rent
Pay low rent
3. Competition
　Number of competing stores
　　Few
　　Average
　　Many
　　Too many
　Type of management
　　Not progressive
　　Average
　　Above average
　　Alert and progressive
　Presence of chains
　　No chains
　　Few chains
　　Average number
　　Many well established
　Type of competing stores
　　Unattractive
　　Average
　　Old and well established
　　Are many people shopping outside
the community?
4. The town as a place to live
　Character of the city
　　Are homes neat and clean, or run
down and shabby?
　　Are lawns, parks, streets, and so on
neat, modern, and generally attractive?
　　Are adequate facilities available?
　　　Banking
　　　Transportation
　　　Professional services
　　　Utilities
　　　Schools
　　　Churches
　　　Amusement centers
　　　Medical and dental services
　　Is the climate satisfactory for the type
of business you are considering?
The Site
1. Competition
　Number of independent stores of the
same kind as yours
　　Same block
　　Same side of the street
　　Across the street
　Number of chain stores
　　In the same block
　　Same side of the street
　　Across the street

　　Kind of stores next door
　　Number of vacancies
　　　Same side of the street
　　　Across the street
　　　Next door
　Dollar sales of your nearest competitor
2. Traffic flow
　Sex of pedestrians
　Age of pedestrians
　Destination of pedestrians
　Number of passersby
　Automobile traffic flow
　Peak hours of traffic flow
3. Transportation
　Transfer points
　Highway
　Kind (bus, streetcar, auto, railroad)
4. Parking facilities
　Large and convenient
　Large enough but not convenient
　Convenient but too small
　Completely inadequate
5. Side of street
6. Plant
　Frontage and depth—in feet
　Shape of building
　Condition
　Heat—type, air conditioning
　Light
　Display space
　Front and back entrances
　Display windows
7. Corner location—if not, what is it?
8. Unfavorable characteristics
　Fire hazards
　Cemetery
　Hospital
　Industry
　Relief office
　Undertaker
　Vacant lot—without parking possibilities
　Garages
　Playground
　Smoke, dust, odors
　Poor sidewalks and pavement
　Unsightly neighborhood buildings
9. Professional men in block
　Medical doctors and dentists
　Lawyers
　Veterinarians
　Others
10. History of the site

Figure 4.1. (Continued)

Additional Projections.   After your initial projections of sales and profits, you should project expenses and capital requirements for the next year. Include seasonal demands and, most important, include the amount that you must take out of the business for your own living expenses. No business can be successful if the owner cannot make a reasonable living.

Special Requirements.   Check for licenses, permits, and other legal requirements for building, health, fire, and the like. This is especially important in some areas in which the local government will permit old businesses to operate under old laws, but upon sale they are considered new businesses and the new owners must abide by the new laws. Your attorney can help you out here.

Partnership Agreements.   Be especially careful of partnership agreements. Read Chapter 1 of this book over again since all of this information applies. Make sure that a new partnership agreement is signed that documents the obligations and liabilities of each partner, and know what you are getting into before you purchase the partnership.

Nature of the Business.   The type of business is most important and most certainly affects appraisal value. The business must be analyzed within the framework of the overall industry of which it is a part. Different aspects of a business are important in different industries: For a publication, circulation, prepaid subscriptions, and advertising are all important. In other industries, inventory turnover, size of a customer list, or the economic life of a client or customer may be critical.

History of the Business.   What has happened in the history of this firm? Has it defaulted on payments? Gone bankrupt? Been involved in legal problems? All may affect what the business may be worth to you.

Economic Outlook.   Economic conditions vary over time and geographic location. Regardless of a past history of successful operations, these conditions can seriously affect the future demand for a firm's products or services, its ability to borrow money or maintain its source of inventory or raw materials, and the like. They may increase the risks to you and should be analyzed and considered in your evaluation of the opportunity that purchase of the business represents.

HOW MUCH SHOULD YOU PAY?

In deciding how much to pay, of course, you must consider all the information that you have dug up about the business. Some businesses have special formulas for calculation of price that apply only to their industry. In order to discover these formulas for the business you are considering, check with business brokers. The IRS, which has issued guidelines for valuation, states that no one formula can be used as a rule of thumb for valuation. Here are some general ones that you should consider.

Asset Appraisal

Value the tangible assets with the help of an appraiser. Be careful here not to use replacement cost as a basis for determining value. Replacement cost is valid only in a very scarce supply situation. Only then would old assets have nearly the value of new assets. Usually the book value is used. This is the original cost less a reasonable depreciation amount. However, you should recognize that marginally useful equipment, equipment that is not useful at all, obsolete inventory, or other factors can further depreciate the book value of the asset. The value of intangible assets such as good will is negotiable. Usually in total they are priced at 10 to 20% of the value of the tangible assets, and almost always less than 50% of the tangible asset value. Don't forget to subtract liabilities in an asset appraisal method of determining price.

Future Earning Capitalization

Here, you estimate future profits over an agreed-upon period such as five years. Calculate a risk factor by comparison with the return for other known risks. Then divide the risk factor into the average yearly pretax profits. The result is the value of the business. For example, a bank may pay 10% interest. This represents a known return for a risk. If yearly pretax profits after deducting the owner's salary are $10,000, then you would divide $10,000 by 10%. This equals $100,000. If the business that you are considering purchasing is somewhat riskier, you may equate the risk factor with an investment having a return of 25%. In that case, you would divide $10,000 by 25% which would equal $40,000, which is considerably less.

Excess Earning Method

With the excess earning method, you would first value the tangible assets and then forecast annual profit. Next, you would estimate how many years it would take to establish a new and similar business and develop it to a similar level of profitability. Then you would determine a return on your investment. This return on investment can be either a return that you desire or a return that you can earn elsewhere. Now, multiply this return on investment by the value of the tangible assets. Add this to your salary. This gives you the total pretax profit that you expect. Subtract this sum from the annual profit forecast and multiply this times the number of years necessary to achieve similar profitability if you start a new business from scratch. This is the value of good will. Add this good will value to the tangible assets figure that you calculated in the beginning and this will result in the amount you should be willing to pay for the business. If subtraction from the annual profit forecast is a negative value, then you must subtract the good will figure from the tangible asset value that you've calculated. This means, of course, that the amount you should be willing to pay will be less than the tangible value of the assets that you calculated initially.

Let's look at an example. Assume that the value of tangible assets of the business is $100,000 and annual profit forecast is $50,000. To establish a similar business will take five years and you desire a return on your investment of 20%. Your annual salary is $38,000.

Step 1 $10,000 × 20% = $2,000
Step 2 $38,000
         + 2,000
         $40,000 total expected pretax profit
Step 3 $50,000 − $40,000 = $10,000
         $10,000 × 5 years = $50,000 value of good will

In other words, regardless of other formulas used, if the seller must sell now, what will sophisticated buyers bid for this business? Clearly you would not want to spend more than that value.

NEGOTIATION

Rule 1 of negotiation is to get a lawyer for closing this important contract. Your agreement in writing should cover the following points: (1) a complete description of what is being sold including the assets fully described; (2) the liabilities that you will assume including the statement that all liabilities not spelled out in the contract will be assumed by the seller; (3) a statement of how adjustments are to be handled at the time of closing, including inventory sold up to this point, payroll, and similar items; (4) the seller's warranties to protect the buyer against inaccurate or false information; (5) the exact date that the buyer will take possession of the business; (6) who will pay legal fees; (7) an agreement by the seller not to compete (for a fixed period of time and/or limited to certain geographical locations depending on the situation and the business); (8) the exact purchase price; (9) the method of payment; (10) the seller's obligation and assumption of risk prior to closing; and (11) the time, place, and procedure of closing.

Once agreement is reached with the seller, it is best to close as soon as possible. In this way, inventory will not be depleted as much and problems caused by transition will be minimized.

If at all possible, try to get a note from the seller. This means that rather than borrowing money from someone else, you borrow it from the seller. It may be possible to negotiate a lower rate of interest this way. Also, the more willing the seller is to take a note, the less risk to you, since his or her willingness indicates confidence that you will be successful in this business.

Be careful of "buy-back" contracts. These are contracts to buy back the business if the business is unsuccessful or doesn't reach a certain level of sales or profits. These contracts are not risk free and can be absolutely worthless if the seller is dishonest and leaves town.

INITIAL FINANCIAL ESTIMATES

To estimate the first year's income, you can use Figure 4.2. To estimate the first year's cash requirements and expenses, use Figure 4.3. These estimates will help you in your decision whether to buy or not, and will also tell you your financial requirements and assist in your planning.

CASH FLOW PROJECTIONS													
	Start-up or prior to loan	Month 1	Month 2	Month 3	Month 4	Month 5	Month 6	Month 7	Month 8	Month 9	Month 10	Month 11	Month 12	TOTAL
Cash (beginning of month) Cash on hand														
Cash in bank														
Cash in investments														
TOTAL CASH														
Income (during month) Cash sales														
Credit sales payments														
Investment income														
Loans														
Other cash income														
TOTAL INCOME														
TOTAL CASH AND INCOME														
Expenses (during month) Inventory or new material														
Wages (including owner's)														
Taxes														
Equipment expense														
Overhead														
Selling expense														
Transportation														
Loan repayment														
Other cash expenses														
TOTAL EXPENSES														
CASH FLOW EXCESS (end of month)														
CASH FLOW CUMULATIVE (monthly)														

Figure 4.2. Income statement

INCOME STATEMENT												
	Month 1	Month 2	Month 3	Month 4	Month 5	Month 6	Month 7	Month 8	Month 9	Month 10	Month 11	Month 12
Total net sales												
Cost of sales												
GROSS PROFIT												
Controllable Expenses Salaries												
Payroll taxes												
Security												
Advertising												
Automobile												
Dues and subscriptions												
Legal and accounting												
Office supplies												
Telephone												
Utilities												
Miscellaneous												
Total Controllable Expenses												
Fixed Expenses Depreciation												
Insurance												
Rent												
Taxes and licenses												
Loan Payments												
Total Fixed Expenses												
TOTAL EXPENSES												
NET PROFIT (LOSS) (before taxes)												

Figure 4.3. Cash flow projections

SOURCES OF ADDITIONAL INFORMATION

Buying and Selling a Small Business, by Verne A. Bunn, published by the Small Business Administration, U.S. Government Printing Office, Washington, DC 20402.

Guide to Buying or Selling a Business, by James M. Hanes, published by Prentice-Hall, Englewood Cliffs, NJ 07632.

How to Buy a Small Business, by Maxwell J. Mangold, published by Pilot Books, 347 Fifth Avenue, New York, NY 10016.

Tax Guide for Buying and Selling a Business, 2nd edition, by Stanley Hagendorf, published by Prentice-Hall, Englewood Cliffs, NJ 07632.

The Complete Guide to Buying and Selling a Business, by Arnold S. Goldstein, published by John Wiley & Sons, Inc., 605 Third Avenue, New York, NY 10158.

5

Leasing or Buying Equipment

LEASING, A VIABLE ALTERNATIVE TO PURCHASE

Leasing should always be considered as an alternative to purchase, if for no other reason than the fact that leasing does not require a large capital outlay. Because of this, more small businesses are leasing than ever before. Further, these small businesses are leasing all types of equipment, including motor vehicles, computers, furniture for the office, manufacturing machinery, testing equipment, and thousands of other items. But leasing is not always the answer, and in making a decision between leasing and buying equipment, you should understand the advantages and the disadvantages of leasing, and you should also make a thorough cash analysis. In this chapter, all aspects of the lease-or-buy question will be covered so that you may consider it from all angles and arrive at the correct decision for your situation. Bear in mind that the right choice can save you thousands and thousands of dollars.

LEASING TERMS AND WHAT THEY MEAN

Basically, a leasing is a long-term agreement to rent equipment, land, buildings, or any other assets. Although the terms *leasing* and *renting* are sometimes used interchangeably, there are differences between the two. *Rental* refers to short-term leasing, usually by the day, week, or month, and generally for a year or less. And leasing may offer lower payments to you due to associated tax benefits. Also, leasing permits 100% financing. This allows your company to conserve its capital for other purposes. The company that leases is known as a lessee. It makes periodic payments to the owner of this asset who is known as a lessor. Your payments cover the original cost of the equipment to the lessor and provide the lessor with a profit for this service. The period of the lease frequently approximates the depreciable life of the equipment that is leased.

TYPES OF LEASES

There are many different types of leases that you may encounter. Each possesses different advantages and disadvantages.

Conditional Sales Agreement

A conditional sales agreement can itself involve many different types of leases. With the basic type, the lessee is considered the owner, for tax purposes, from the very beginning of the lease. At the end of the conditional sale lease period, the terms of the contract are structured in such a fashion that the lessee's only practical option is to purchase the equipment at a predetermined price. This price is decided upon prior to initiating the lease through negotiations between the lessee and the lessor. It reflects both the residual value of the equipment and the size of the payments made by the lessee during the period of the lease. Some conditional sales agreement leases have "put and call" provisions in which the "put" is the minimum price that a lessee is obligated to pay for the leased equipment, and the "call" is a maximum price that the lessee may be obligated to pay for the equipment. The put and call provisions set limits for negotiation on the lessee's purchase price. The minimum price can protect the lessor if the equipment depreciates rapidly during the term of the lease. On the other hand, the maximum price protects the lessee from having to pay a purchase price much greater than the current fair market value of the equipment at the end of the lease.

Financial Lease

The financial lease is the most common. A financial lease is usually written for a term that does not exceed the economic life of the equipment. Typical provisions of the financial lease are (1) that periodic payments must be made by the lessee, (2) that ownership of the equipment will revert to the lessor at the end of the lease term, (3) that the lease is noncancelable and the lessee has a legal obligation to continue payments to the end of the term, and (4) that the lessee agrees to maintain the equipment.

Gross Lease

Under a gross lease, the lessor is responsible for expenses such as maintenance, taxes, and insurance.

Leverage Lease

Under a leverage lease, the lessor puts up part of the purchase price of the equipment, usually 20 to 40%, and borrows the rest from other lenders. The tax benefits of ownership go to the lessor, not to the investors. The leverage lease is a type of "true lease" that is discussed later. It is generally used for multimillion-dollar leases.

Net Lease

A net lease is the opposite of a gross lease. Under a net lease, the lessee is responsible for expenses such as those for maintenance, taxes, and insurance. The most common type of lease, the financial lease, is usually a net lease.

Nonpayout Lease

With the nonpayout lease, the lessor collects less than his equipment cost over the period of the lease. The nonpayout lease is not common, but it is sometimes used when asset durability is high and resale values are well established on the used equipment that is being leased. In the nonpayout lease, the lessor will take the equipment back and resell it or lease it again after the period of the lease.

Operating Lease

The operating or maintenance lease can usually be canceled under conditions spelled out in the lease contract. Maintenance of the asset is usually the responsibility of the lessor. Computer equipment is often leased using the operating or maintenance type of lease.

Payout Lease

The payout lease is the opposite of the nonpayout lease. Under the payout lease, the lessor does recover the original cost of the asset during the term of the lease.

Sale and Lease-Back Lease

The sale and lease-back lease is similar to the financial lease. With this type of lease, the owner of the equipment sells it to another party and simultaneously leases it back to use it for a specified term. This allows you to use the money normally tied up in an asset for other purposes. Buildings are typically leased with a sale and lease-back lease.

True Lease

A true lease is an agreement in which the leasing company owns the lease equipment at all times so that no equity is built up with the lease payments by the lessee. Therefore, if the lessee wants to buy the leased equipment at the end of the period of the lease, the purchase price is in addition to the scheduled payments.

Which Is Best?

To determine which type of lease is best for your situation, you should consider the following three questions for your business:

1. Does your business need the tax benefit of ownership to reduce current tax obligations? If so, then a conditional sales agreement may be the most cost-effective method of leasing.
2. Can the leasing company receive the tax benefits of ownership such as the investment tax credit, depreciation allowance, and interest deductions and in return reduce your lease payments?
3. What is the estimated residual value of the equipment at the end of the proposed lease term?

WHO LEASES?

The majority of leasing is done by commercial banks, insurance companies, and finance companies. In fact, many of these types of organizations have subsidiaries that are primarily concerned with equipment leasing, and can make lease arrangements for almost any equipment that you may need. The growth of the leasing industry into a billion-dollar business has also caused companies to be founded that specialize only in leasing. Some may do general leasing with any type of equipment, while others may specialize in certain types of equipment such as computers or farm machinery. Many such leasing companies offer their services through trade magazines and newspapers. They may also work closely with manufacturers and provide training and outside financing to enable leasing directly from the manufacturers' sales. This leads us to a third kind of lessor: the manufacturer. Many manufacturers offer a lease plan to their customers. Naturally such firms usually lease only the equipment that they themselves manufacture. Finally, while not lessors, there are lease brokers that act as intermediaries between lessors and lessees and lessors and financing sources. The broker determines the need of the prospective lessee and solicits bids from banks, leasing companies, and other financing sources. The broker's compensation usually comes from the organization furnishing the financing, although sometimes he or she may be paid as a consultant to the lessee.

THE ADVANTAGES AND DISADVANTAGES OF LEASING

As noted earlier, there are both advantages and disadvantages to leasing. Let's look at the advantages first:

1. *Use of an asset without a large initial cash outlay.*
2. *No down payment.* A loan may require 25% down where a lease is usually 100% financed, requiring no down payment whatsoever.
3. *No restrictions on a company's financial operations.* By comparison, a loan may restrict your operation by its terms.
4. *Payments spread over a longer period.* With a lease, payments may be spread over periods of several years, and therefore you have lower payments than loans permit.
5. *Protection against equipment obsolescence.* A lease will protect you against the risk of the equipment's becoming obsolete since the lessee can get rid of the equipment at the end of the term of the lease.
6. *Tax benefits.* There are tax benefits in leasing, among them deductibility of lease payments as operating expenses if the arrangement is a true lease. Also, all the investment tax credit is usually taken by the lessor, but it may help the lessee as well since the lessee may have reduced payments in return.
7. *Consulting advice from the leasing firm.* Because the lessor has considerable experience with the equipment that it leases, it can provide expert technical advice.
8. *Flexible payment schedules.* Payment schedules for leases can be constructed so that they coincide with cash flow earnings of the company or various seasonal activities, depending upon the situation.

9. *Restriction on claims in the event of bankruptcy.* While all entrepreneurs should think positively, it is a fact that in the event of bankruptcy, the claims of a lessor to your assets are much more restricted than those of general creditors.

Now, let's look at some of the disadvantages of leasing:

1. *Loss of certain tax benefits.* Tax benefits that go with the ownership of an asset will not be available to you as a lessee. However, this may be no disadvantage if you don't have enough tax or liability for such tax benefits of ownership to come into force.

2. *No economic value of an asset at end of lease term.* Since you do not own the asset as a lessee, in order to obtain the economic value of this asset at the end of the lease term you must purchase it. Frequently, the salvage value of a leased asset at the end of the lease term is much greater than you thought at the time of initiating the lease.

3. *Higher overall cost in purchase.* If you as lessee can currently use the tax benefits of ownership such as depreciation tax allowance, leasing may be more costly than purchase. It is for this reason that a thorough cash analysis must be performed and also that you be aware fully of the latest tax laws.

4. *Difficulty in lease termination.* In general, you cannot terminate a lease without a penalty, and most leases for capital equipment are noncancelable contracts. Therefore, if you were to complete an operation that used leased equipment, you would have to pay as much as if the equipment were used during the full term of the lease.

5. *Senior debt obligation.* Although in the event of bankruptcy claims of a lessor to the assets of a firm are more restricted than those of general creditors, a lease may be one of the first debts that can be claimed by a creditor.

ANALYSIS OF COST OF LEASE VERSUS PURCHASE

It is extremely important to analyze the cash flow over the period of time of a lease versus a purchase in order to have an accurate comparison in hard figures. This analysis compares the cost of the two alternatives by considering the timing of the payments, the tax benefits, the interest rate on the loan, the lease rate, and other financial factors. To perform this analysis, you must know certain basic facts or make certain assumptions. These include information about the equipment cost, the estimated economic life, the lease terms, and the tax. Now let's look at an example.

Equipment cost. $40,000.

Estimated economic life. 10 years.

Lease terms. Eight annual payments of $8,000. First payment is due on delivery. Lessee must maintain equipment.

Loan terms with purchase. Five years, 75% financing at 10% requiring five annual payments of $7,913.92. The first payment is due at the end of the first year.

Taxes. Lessee tax rate is 50%. Straight line depreciation is used.

Other facts. The equipment is needed for eight years. At the end of that period, if the decision has been made to purchase the equipment, it can be sold at a salvage value that is equal to the book value of the equipment (equipment cost less total depreciation). The average after-tax cost of capital to the lessee is 10%.

Before we begin the analysis, certain facts about this information should be noted. First, payments are usually made monthly. In this example, annual payments are used for simplification. However, exactly the same procedures would be used to analyze monthly payments.

Depreciation arises from recognition of the fact that, except for land, all capital assets have a finite life span after which they are worthless. When you do your taxes, depreciation expense is entered on your income statement, reducing reported profit. Thus, applying depreciation against profit represents a tax saving. Calculating depreciation of equipment involves estimating its life. Straight line depreciation means simply calculating the yearly depreciation by dividing the cost of the equipment by the number of years of its life. In this case, the equipment costs $4,000 per year. At the end of 10 years, the equipment would have a book value of zero. In theory, it would be worth nothing. In order to compare this lease with purchase, we must do our analysis over identical periods of time. Therefore, we will depreciate the equipment over a period of 8 years. At $4,000 per year, that's $4,000 times 8 years or $32,000. Book value, which is salvage value of the equipment at this time, would be equal to the cost of the equipment minus the depreciation, $40,000 minus $32,000 or $8,000.

The actual tax rate depends on taxable income. In this case, it is assumed that this works out to be 50%.

Factors such as maintenance costs need not be included in the analysis, since in the example the lessee would pay these costs if leasing or if purchasing. If, however, the lessor were responsible for maintenance, then this fact would be taken into account by showing estimated annual maintenance costs as a savings in the cash flow evaluation of lease cost.

The concept of cost of capital is important since it allows you to calculate the present value of future costs. It refers to the fact that there is a time value of money. This time value can be seen if you consider receiving $1,000 today or $1,500 five years from now. At first glance, you may prefer the $1,500. But then you would probably remember that you can get a rather high rate of interest by depositing the $1,000 in a bank today. In fact, after five years, at 15% interest, your $1,000 would be worth $2,011. To allow for the time value of money, we discount each year's cash flow to the present, using Table 5.1, Present Value of $1 Received at the End of n Number of Years.

Now, let's consider the cash flow evaluation of the loan. Note how the discount factors are extracted from Table 5.2 in column 9 and multiplied by the net cash flow in column 8 to result in the present value in column 10.

The appropriate interest rate or time value of money in this case is the after-tax cost of the loan. Since the loan cost is 10% and tax rate is 50%, 0.50 times 10% or 5% is the proper interest rate.

The cash flow evaluation of lease cost is shown in Table 5.3.

The final result of the analysis of leasing the equipment, $27,145.20, is the net present value of the costs of leasing. Now, if we compare this with the net present value of purchasing, we will know whether leasing or purchasing will

Table 5.1 Present Value of $1 at the End of *n* Number of Years

n/r	1%	2%	3%	4%	5%	6%	7%	8%	9%	10%	11%	12%	13%	14%	15%
1	.9901	.9804	.9709	.9615	.9524	.9434	.9346	.9259	.9174	.9091	.9009	.8929	.8850	.8772	.8696
2	.9803	.9612	.9426	.9246	.9070	.8900	.8734	.8573	.8417	.8264	.8116	.7972	.7831	.7695	.7561
3	.9706	.9423	.9151	.8890	.8638	.8396	.8163	.7938	.7722	.7513	.7312	.7118	.6931	.6750	.6575
4	.9610	.9238	.8885	.8548	.8227	.7921	.7629	.7350	.7084	.6830	.6587	.6355	.6133	.5921	.5718
5	.9515	.9057	.8626	.8219	.7835	.7473	.7130	.6806	.6499	.6209	.5935	.5674	.5428	.5194	.4972
6	.9420	.8880	.8375	.7903	.7462	.7050	.6663	.6302	.5963	.5645	.5346	.5066	.4803	.4556	.4323
7	.9327	.8706	.8131	.7599	.7107	.6651	.6227	.5835	.5470	.5132	.4817	.4523	.4251	.3996	.3759
8	.9235	.8535	.7894	.7307	.6768	.6274	.5820	.5403	.5019	.4665	.4339	.4039	.3762	.3506	.3269
9	.9143	.8368	.7664	.7026	.6446	.5919	.5439	.5002	.4604	.4241	.3909	.3606	.3329	.3075	.2843
10	.9053	.8203	.7441	.6756	.6139	.5584	.5083	.4632	.4224	.3855	.3522	.3220	.2946	.2697	.2472
11	.8963	.8043	.7224	.6496	.5847	.5268	.4751	.4289	.3875	.3505	.3173	.2875	.2607	.2366	.2149
12	.8874	.7885	.7014	.6246	.5568	.4970	.4440	.3971	.3555	.3186	.2858	.2567	.2307	.2076	.1869
13	.8787	.7730	.6810	.6006	.5303	.4688	.4150	.3677	.3262	.2897	.2575	.2292	.2042	.1821	.1625
14	.8700	.7579	.6611	.5775	.5051	.4423	.3878	.3405	.2992	.2633	.2320	.2046	.1807	.1597	.1413
15	.8613	.7430	.6419	.5553	.4810	.4173	.3624	.3152	.2745	.2394	.2090	.1827	.1599	.1401	.1229
16	.8528	.7284	.6232	.5339	.4581	.3936	.3387	.2919	.2519	.2176	.1883	.1631	.1415	.1229	.1069
17	.8444	.7142	.6050	.5134	.4363	.3714	.3166	.2703	.2311	.1978	.1696	.1456	.1252	.1078	.0929
18	.8360	.7002	.5874	.4936	.4155	.3503	.2959	.2502	.2120	.1799	.1528	.1300	.1108	.0946	.0808
19	.8277	.6864	.5703	.4746	.3957	.3305	.2765	.2317	.1945	.1635	.1377	.1161	.0981	.0829	.0703
20	.8195	.6730	.5537	.4564	.3769	.3118	.2584	.2145	.1784	.1486	.1240	.1037	.0868	.0728	.0611
21	.8114	.6598	.5375	.4388	.3589	.2942	.2415	.1987	.1637	.1351	.1117	.0926	.0768	.0638	.0531
22	.8034	.6468	.5219	.4220	.3418	.2775	.2257	.1839	.1502	.1228	.1007	.0826	.0680	.0560	.0462
23	.7954	.6342	.5067	.4057	.3256	.2618	.2109	.1703	.1378	.1117	.0907	.0738	.0601	.0491	.0402
24	.7876	.6217	.4919	.3901	.3101	.2470	.1971	.1577	.1264	.1015	.0817	.0659	.0532	.0431	.0349
25	.7798	.6095	.4776	.3751	.2953	.2330	.1842	.1460	.1160	.0923	.0736	.0588	.0471	.0378	.0304
26	.7720	.5976	.4637	.3607	.2812	.2198	.1722	.1352	.1064	.0839	.0663	.0525	.0417	.0331	.0264
27	.7644	.5859	.4502	.3468	.2678	.2074	.1609	.1252	.0976	.0763	.0597	.0469	.0369	.0291	.0230
28	.7568	.5744	.4371	.3335	.2551	.1956	.1504	.1159	.0895	.0693	.0538	.0419	.0326	.0255	.0200
29	.7493	.5631	.4243	.3207	.2429	.1846	.1406	.1073	.0822	.0630	.0485	.0374	.0289	.0224	.0174
30	.7419	.5521	.4120	.3083	.2314	.1741	.1314	.0994	.0754	.0573	.0437	.0334	.0256	.0196	.0151
35	.7059	.5000	.3554	.2534	.1813	.1301	.0937	.0676	.0490	.0356	.0259	.0189	.0139	.0102	.0075
40	.6717	.4529	.3066	.2083	.1420	.0972	.0668	.0460	.0318	.0221	.0154	.0107	.0075	.0053	.0037
45	.6391	.410	.2644	.1713	.1112	.0727	.0476	.0313	.0207	.0137	.0091	.0061	.0041	.0027	.0019
50	.6080	.3715	.2281	.1407	.0872	.0543	.0339	.0213	.0134	.0085	.0054	.0035	.0022	.0014	.0009

n/r	16%	18%	20%	22%	24%	26%	28%	30%	32%	34%	36%	38%	40%	45%	50%
1	.8621	.8475	.8333	.8197	.8065	.7937	.7813	.7692	.7576	.7463	.7353	.7246	.7143	.6897	.6667
2	.7432	.7182	.6944	.6719	.6504	.6299	.6104	.5917	.5739	.5569	.5407	.5251	.5102	.4756	.4444
3	.6407	.6086	.5787	.5507	.5245	.4999	.4768	.4552	.4348	.4155	.3975	.3805	.3644	.3280	.2963
4	.5523	.5158	.4823	.4514	.4230	.3968	.3725	.3501	.3294	.3102	.2923	.2757	.2603	.2262	.1975
5	.4761	.4371	.4019	.3700	.3411	.3149	.2910	.2693	.2495	.2315	.2149	.1998	.1859	.1560	.1317
6	.4104	.3704	.3349	.3033	.2751	.2499	.2274	.2072	.1890	.1727	.1580	.1448	.1328	.1076	.0878
7	.3538	.3139	.2791	.2486	.2218	.1983	.1776	.1594	.1432	.1289	.1162	.1049	.0949	.0742	.0585
8	.3050	.2660	.2326	.2038	.1789	.1574	.1388	.1226	.1085	.0962	.0854	.0760	.0678	.0512	.0390
9	.2630	.2255	.1938	.1670	.1443	.1249	.1084	.0943	.0822	.0718	.0628	.0551	.0484	.0353	.0260
10	.2267	.1911	.1615	.1369	.1164	.0992	.0847	.0725	.0623	.0536	.0462	.0399	.0346	.0243	.0173
11	.1954	.1619	.1346	.1122	.0938	.0787	.0662	.0558	.0472	.0400	.0340	.0289	.0247	.0168	.0116
12	.1685	.1372	.1122	.0920	.0757	.0625	.0517	.0429	.0357	.0298	.0250	.0210	.0176	.0116	.0077
13	.1452	.1163	.0935	.0754	.0610	.0496	.0404	.0330	.0271	.0223	.0184	.0152	.0126	.0080	.0051
14	.1252	.0985	.0779	.0618	.0492	.0393	.0316	.0253	.0205	.0166	.0135	.0110	.0090	.0055	.0034
15	.1079	.0835	.0649	.0507	.0397	.0312	.0247	.0195	.0155	.0124	.0099	.0080	.0064	.0038	.0023
16	.0930	.0708	.0541	.0415	.0320	.0248	.0193	.0150	.0118	.0093	.0073	.0058	.0046	.0026	.0015
17	.0802	.0600	.0451	.0340	.0258	.0197	.0150	.0116	.0089	.0069	.0054	.0042	.0033	.0018	.0010
18	.0691	.0508	.0376	.0279	.0208	.0156	.0118	.0089	.0068	.0052	.0039	.0030	.0023	.0012	.0007
19	.0596	.0431	.0313	.0229	.0168	.0124	.0092	.0068	.0051	.0038	.0029	.0022	.0017	.0009	.0005
20	.0514	.0365	.0261	.0187	.0135	.0098	.0072	.0053	.0039	.0029	.0021	.0016	.0012	.0006	.0003
21	.0443	.0309	.0217	.0154	.0109	.0078	.0056	.0040	.0029	.0021	.0016	.0012	.0009	.0004	.0002
22	.0382	.0262	.0181	.0126	.0088	.0062	.0044	.0031	.0022	.0016	.0012	.0008	.0006	.0003	.0001
23	.0329	.0222	.0151	.0103	.0071	.0049	.0034	.0024	.0017	.0012	.0008	.0006	.0004	.0002	.0001
24	.0284	.0188	.0126	.0085	.0057	.0039	.0027	.0018	.0013	.0009	.0006	.0004	.0003	.0001	.0001
25	.0245	.0160	.0105	.0069	.0046	.0031	.0021	.0014	.0010	.0007	.0005	.0003	.0002	.0001	.0000
26	.0211	.0135	.0087	.0057	.0037	.0025	.0016	.0011	.0007	.0005	.0003	.0002	.0002	.0001	
27	.0182	.0115	.0073	.0047	.0030	.0019	.0013	.0008	.0006	.0004	.0002	.0002	.0001	.0000	
28	.0157	.0097	.0061	.0038	.0024	.0015	.0010	.0006	.0004	.0003	.0002	.0001	.0001		
29	.0135	.0082	.0051	.0031	.0020	.0012	.0008	.0005	.0003	.0002	.0001	.0001	.0001		
30	.0116	.0070	.0042	.0026	.0016	.0010	.0006	.0004	.0002	.0002	.0001	.0001	.0000		
35	.0055	.0030	.0017	.0009	.0005	.0003	.0002	.0001	.0001	.0000	.0000	.0000			
40	.0026	.0013	.0007	.0004	.0002	.0001	.0001	.0000	.0000						
45	.0013	.0006	.0003	.0001	.0001	.0000	.0000								
50	.0006	.0003	.0001	.0000	.0000										

Table 5.2 Cash Flow Evaluation of Purchasing

(1) End of Year	(2) Payment	(3) Interest	(4) Principal Repayment (2) − (3)	(5) Outstanding Balance (5) − (4)	(6) Depreciation	(7) Tax Savings 50% × ((6) + (3))	(8) Net Cash Flow (2) − (7)	(9) Discount Factor from Table 5.1[a]	(10) Present Value (8) × (9)
0	$10,000.00			$30,000.00			$10,000.00	1.0000	$10,000.00
1	7,913.92	$3,000.00	$4,913.92	25,086.08	$4,000	3,500.00	4,413.92	0.9524	4,203.82
2	7,913.92	2,508.60	5,405.32	19,680.76	4,000	3,254.30	4,659.62	0.9070	4,226.28
3	7,913.92	1,968.07	5,945.85	13,734.91	4,000	2,984.03	4,929.89	0.8638	4,258.44
4	7,913.92	1,373.49	6,540.43	7,194.48	4,000	2,686.74	5,227.17	0.8227	4,300.97
5	7,913.92	719.44	7,194.48		4,000	2,359.72	5,554.20	0.7835	4,351.72
6					4,000	2,000.00	(2,000.00)	0.7462	(1,492.40)
7					4,000	2,000.00	(2,000.00)	0.7107	(1,421.40)
8	(8,000.00)[b]				4,000	2,000.00	(2,000.00)	0.6768	(1,353.60)
							(8,000.00)	0.4665	(3,732.00)
									$23,341.83

[a]Discount factor calculated at the average after tax cost of capital of 10%.

[b]Salvage value at the end of eight years.

Note: In the example, the interest portion of the loan payment is found by multiplying the loan interest rate of 10% by the outstanding loan balance for the previous period. Also, the outstanding balance is calculated by subtracting column 4 from column 5 of the preceding year. In the example, the net cost of leasing the equipment is $23,752.05 versus $23,341.83 if you buy the equipment by taking a loan. That's a net savings of $3,803.37 ($27,145.20 minus $23,341.83) if you purchase and take the loan. Clearly, doing this analysis will more than pay for itself.

112

Table 5.3 Cash Flow Evaluation of Lease Cost

(1) End of Year	(2) Lease Payment	(3) Tax Saving 50% × (2)	(4) Net Outlay (2) − (3)	(5) Discount Factor from Table 5.1	(6) Present Value (4) × (5)
0	$8,000	$4,000	$4,000	1.0000	$ 4,000.00
1	8,000	4,000	4,000	0.9524	3,809.60
2	8,000	4,000	4,000	0.9070	3,628.00
3	8,000	4,000	4,000	0.8638	3,455.20
4	8,000	4,000	4,000	0.8227	3,290.80
5	8,000	4,000	4,000	0.7835	3,134.00
6	8,000	4,000	4,000	0.7462	2,984.80
7	8,000	4,000	4,000	0.7107	2,842.80
8	—	—	—	—	—
					$27,145.20

cost more money. In this case, purchasing the equipment, including the loan, results in a present value of $23,341.83. Since this is less than $27,145.20, it would be less expensive to purchase. In fact, in this case, purchase represents a net savings of $3,803.37!

HOW TO CHOOSE A LEASING COMPANY

Leasing is a big business today. As pointed out earlier, the companies and firms, banks, and manufacturers that make up this industry comprise a very diverse group. There is a major trade organization called the American Association of Equipment Lessors, located at 5635 Douglas Avenue, Milwaukee, WI 53218. The association can provide you with membership rosters as well as information on leases and leasing trends. You can also look in your Yellow Pages for the various types of companies that lease, mentioned earlier. Because the industry is so competitive, you should definitely shop around. This means choosing several lessors that you may wish to deal with before making a decision to lease with one or another, or even before doing an analysis of a lease versus purchase. Look for two things:

1. The price or lease rate
2. The reputation of the lessor you may wish to deal with

The lease rate may vary greatly from company to company. Therefore, it is extremely important that you make this comparison with several potential lessors. Generally, the lease rate will depend on the following factors:

1. The period of the lease
2. The equipment that you wish to lease
3. The use of the equipment
4. The equipment's residual value
5. Evaluation of your credit as the lessee
6. Who uses the investment tax credit

Equally important are the reputation and reliability of the lessor. These may be checked in several ways: by talking to individuals who have leased similar equipment from the firm, by asking for references from the company in question, and by checking with the Better Business Bureau in your area to see if any complaints have been made against the company.

TERMS OF THE LEASE CONTRACT

Don't forget that a lease contract is a legal document that carries a long-term obligation. Therefore, it's crucial that you know exactly what the terms of this contract are and that they cover all the points that are important to you. Naturally, lease contracts will differ depending on the situation that is unique to your leasing arrangement. However, the major items that will be included in the contract are as follows:

1. The term of the lease (usually expressed as a period of months or years)
2. The rate (usually expressed in percentage of the total equipment cost paid on a monthly or quarterly basis)
3. The specific terms of the financial arrangement with the lessor
4. The disposition of the asset at the end of the term, as well as purchase options
5. The schedule of the value of the equipment for insurance and any special settlement terms in the event of damage or loss of the equipment
6. Who is responsible for maintenance and who is responsible for taxes
7. Who gets and is entitled to the investment tax credit
8. Substitution provisions if later designed equipment becomes available
9. Renewal options
10. Cancellation penalties
11. Any special terms and conditions (for example, a requirement that you keep the equipment in a certain location or other limitations pertaining to your use of the equipment leased)

HOW TO NEGOTIATE A LEASE

The general procedure in obtaining a lease is for the lessor to send a short, written proposal letter to the potential lessee after a verbal discussion. This proposed letter spells out the basic terms of the proposed lease. A sample proposal letter is shown in Figure 5.1. While negotiation really begins with the first verbal contact with the lessor, the receipt of a written document such as the proposal is a signal for more formal negotiations, and this document should be reviewed by both your attorney and your tax accountant to ensure that the proposed terms are in your best interest. Based on the negotiations and assuming that you receive credit approval, the lessor will next send you a formal commitment letter which includes the detailed terms and the conditions of the proposed lease. Such an example is shown in Figure 5.2. Again, you should have these terms thoroughly reviewed by your accountant and your attorney. Assuming the terms in the lease commitment received are acceptable to you,

June 25, 1990

ABC Manufacturing Company
1055 Buffalo Street
Los Angeles, CA 90009

Gentlemen:

Confirming the general terms of the leasing arrangement we discussed on June 18th, this letter contains a proposal covering the lease of a new plastic molding system with an approximate cost of $100,000. Please note that the figures are of rough order of magnitude only and should not be construed as a commitment on our part to lease for that amount.

	Option 1 (Lessor Retains Investment Tax Credit)	Option 2 (Lessee Receives Investment Tax Credit)	Option 3 (Conditional Sale)
Term:	3 years	3 years	3 years
Depreciation:	Retained	Retained	Lessee
Investment tax credit:	Retained	Lessee	Lessee
Monthly payment (per $1,000 of cost):	$33.33	$38.89	$40.27
Renewal option:	At fair market value	At fair market value	None
Purchase option:	At fair market value	At fair market value	6% of cost

All options provide for 100% financing. Lessee is responsible for providing acceptable insurance coverage and maintaining equipment.
As with all lease proposals, this proposal is subject to credit approval.
If I can answer any questions regarding this proposal, please do not hesitate to call.

Sincerely,
John J. Smith
President

Figure 5.1. Present Value of $1

July 5, 1990

Mr. James C. Fite
President
ZKC Enterprises
150 N. Duke Street
Los Angeles, CA 90009

Dear Mr. Fite:

In response to your invitation to submit a lease commitment on a Nutronic 521Z Computer, we are submitting this letter. On your request we agree to purchase for lease a Nutronic Model 521Z Computer if available as described below for amounts and terms as indicated.

1. Lessee: James C. Fite
   President
   ZKC Enterprises
   150 N. Duke Street
   Los Angeles, CA 90009

Figure 5.2. Formal commitment letter

2. Lessor: ABC Leasing Company
          1151 Pasadena Avenue
          Los Angeles, CA 90032

3. Lease: Nutronic Model 521Z Computer with standard equipment as furnished by the manufacturer. Cost not in excess of $150,000.

4. Term: Lease term shall commence on delivery date of the computer and shall continue for 48 months from the lease scheduling date.

5. Lease payments:
    a. Interim rent will begin to accrue on the date the funds for purchase are advanced by the lessor until execution of the lease schedule. Daily rate will be $0.25 per $1,000 of cost, payable monthly.
    b. Beginning January 1, 1991, periodic rents are to be annually in arrears at $310.60 per $1,000 of lessor's cost

6. Expiration of commitment: This commitment will expire unless it has been accepted on or before August 5, 1990.

7. Taxes and insurance: Lessee will pay all taxes except those which may be levied on the income of the lessor. Lessee will furnish physical damage and liability insurance in amounts acceptable to the lessor prior to the lessor's issuance of purchase orders.

8. Investment tax credit: Investment tax credit will be retained by lessor.

9. Renewal option: Lessee may renew lease at expiration of lease term for a period to be determined by agreement between both parties at the current lease term rental rate.

10. Purchase option: Lessee may purchase the equipment at the expiration of the lease term $30 per $1,000 of lessor's cost.

11. Security deposit: None required.

12. Warranties: None except furnished by manufacturer.

13. Delinquent charges: 12% per annum.

14. Guarantors: None required.

15. Commitment fee: None required.

If the above terms are acceptable, and you agree to accept this proposal, acceptance is indicated by signing below, completing the required insurance information, and returning the letter.

Sincerely,

John J. Smith
President

JAMES C. FITE   INSURANCE INFORMATION
This proposal is accepted on _____ day
of
_____ , 1990.   _____
                                                           agent

By: _____   _____
                                                          address
Title: _____

                                            _____
                                               telephone number
_____

Figure 5.2. *(Continued)*

116

you then sign this commitment. By your signature you accept the terms of the formal proposal contained in the commitment.

FINANCIAL TREATMENT OF LEASES

An important change has been made over the last several years regarding the financial and accounting treatment of leases. In previous years, financial leases were not included on the balance sheet. In fact, they were known as off-the-balance-sheet financing, even though they were listed in footnotes. However, not accounting for leases explicitly sometimes resulted in a failure to state operational assets and liabilities in a way that would convey a thorough understanding of the company's financial position. Accordingly, in 1977, the Financial Accounting Standards Board (FASB), which is the rule-making body for the accounting profession, changed its position and required that capital leases be recorded on the balance sheet directly and not as a footnote and listed as both an asset and as a liability. Therefore, leasing is far more likely to affect your credit rating now than before this change in accounting procedures.

WHEN SHOULD YOU REPLACE EQUIPMENT?

Closely linked with the decision whether to lease or to buy is the decision to replace or not to replace older equipment that you are currently using. This decision depends mainly on four major cost elements. These are:

1. Depreciation
2. Opportunity cost
3. Operating costs
4. Revenues

Let's look at each in turn.

Depreciation

As pointed out earlier, depreciation is the amount by which the asset decreases in value over the period of the life of the asset. The importance of depreciation as a cost element is the fact that you may deduct this depreciation from your tax. In a cost analysis it must be taken into consideration, as shown in the previous example comparing a lease and a purchase. Once the book value of the old equipment reaches zero, you no longer may depreciate the equipment; thus, newly purchased equipment may be depreciated and may have a significant effect on your cost analysis. In order to do this analysis, including depreciation on the new equipment, you must know the initial cost of the equipment, its estimated service life, and its expected salvage value at the end of that period. The difference between the initial cost and the expected salvage value at the end of the estimated service life represents the amount that the equipment will depreciate during this service life.

Opportunity Cost

As pointed out earlier in this book, there is a time value to money, because you have alternative uses to which this money can be put. If you own an asset, the fact of ownership has tied up some of your capital. If you had to borrow this capital, you have to pay for the use of this money. But the same is true even if you use your own money and do not borrow. In this case, the amount involved is not available for other investments that could bring you a return. Therefore, this opportunity cost is one of the costs of owning the equipment. You allow for cost of capital by using the discount factor in Table 5.1 as shown earlier in the comparison of the cash flow of leasing versus buying. The assumed percentage that you use for your opportunity cost depends on what return you would obtain with an alternate investment. For example, if such an investment would bring you a return of 20%, then 20% is the figure that you should use in your calculations.

Operating Costs

Operating costs may include expenditures for labor, materials, supervision, maintenance, and power to run the equipment. These costs may tend to be higher with old equipment over new, due either to wear and tear on the equipment as it is used or to the fact that new equipment is more sophisticated and therefore more efficient. Because of this, these costs must be considered in your analysis. Therefore, if you can save $5,000 in operating costs over your first year of use of a new piece of equipment replacing an old, this will most definitely affect your decision. There are two ways you can simplify your consideration of operating costs when doing your analysis. First, those costs that are the same for both the old and the new equipment can be ignored since they will cancel each other out in a comparison of the bottom line figure. Secondly, you can estimate only the differences between the operating costs of the old and those of the new equipment. In this way, your calculations for each type of equipment will be understated by the identical amount. Therefore, the difference between the total cost will remain the same and you will be able to make the comparison to recognize the more attractive economical alternative.

Revenues

Sometimes the revenues generated by the old equipment will be identical to those of the new equipment. If this is the case, then revenues may be ignored. However, in some cases, because of its improved capability, the new equipment can generate much greater revenues than the old. Let's say you calculate that new equipment output will result in an additional $5,000 from the sale of additional units manufactured for the same input over the old equipment. This $5,000 can be shown in your analysis in one of two ways: either the $5,000 is considered an additional cost that will be experienced when using the old equipment or you can use the $5,000 as a negative annual expense with the new equipment. Either one of these two methods will work to give you an accurate bottom line comparison. However, be sure not to use both methods in the same analysis. If you do, they will cancel each other out and you will not have an accurate comparison.

Now let's look at an example of the economic analysis of the equipment replacement decision. Table 5.4 shows the situation. Our current equipment has been fully depreciated so we have no depreciation. Also, the salvage value of our current equipment is zero. The new equipment that we wish to purchase

Table 5.4   Examples of an Economic Analysis of the Equipment Replacement Decision

	Current Equipment	New Equipment	
Cost to purchase	0	$50,000	−$50,000.00
Salvage value if sold	0	$5,000 after 10 years × 0.1615 (discount factor = from Table 5.1)	+ 807.50
Depreciation	0	$4,500/year (straight line method) × 50% × 4.1925 (discount factor from Table 5.5)	+ 9,433.12
Operating cost savings over old equipment	0	$7,000/year × 4.1925 (discount factor from Table 5.5)	+ 29,347.50
Additional revenues with new equipment	0	$1,000/year × 4.1925 (discount factor from Table 5.5)	+ 4,192.50
Tax rate = 50% Opportunity costs = 20%			
	0		−$ 6,219.38

will cost us $50,000, but it has a salvage value after 10 years of $5,000. Therefore, we can depreciate it over a 10-year period using the straight line method at $4,500 per year. There is also an operating cost savings over using the old equipment of $7,000 a year, and the new equipment will generate additional revenues without additional input of $1,000 per year. In this case, we will assume that our company is in the 50% tax rate bracket and that the opportunity costs are 20%, which means that we can earn 20% on our money if we invest it in something other than the purchase of new equipment. For this analysis we are going to use not only Table 5.1 but also Table 5.5. Look again at Table 5.4. The cost of purchase for the current equipment is zero. Salvage value, if sold, is zero. Depreciation is zero. The operating cost savings over old equipment is zero, and the additional revenues with new equipment are zero. Of course, there is no investment tax credit, so this is zero as well. With the new equipment, we have the following information: As indicated, the equipment costs $50,000. Since this is the net outlay, we will assign this a negative value. The salvage value we said was $5,000 after 10 years. We will use a discount factor that we obtained from Table 5.1 just as we did in the earlier example of the lease versus purchase analysis. At 20% interest, after 10 years, the factor comes out 0.1615. We multiply this times $5,000 to arrive at a positive $807.50. Depreciation is $4,500 a year. Since our tax rate is 50%, we multiply this times 50% to get $2,250, and multiply this in turn by a discount factor of 4.1925. This we take not from Table 5.1 but from Table 5.5, since this amount is not in one lump sum after the number of years but rather every year. This comes out to be $9,433.12. We said the operating cost, if we use the old equipment, was $7,000 per year. Again, this is a saving that occurs every single year, so we use Table 5.5 and the same identical factor of 4.1925. Multiply it again and you get a

Table 5.5 Present Value of $1 Received Annually

n/r	1%	2%	3%	4%	5%	6%	7%	8%	9%	10%	11%	12%	13%	14%	15%
1	.9901	.9804	.9709	.9615	.9524	.9434	.9346	.9259	.9174	.9091	.9009	.8929	.8850	.8772	.8696
2	1.9704	1.9416	1.9135	1.8861	1.8594	1.8334	1.8080	1.7833	1.7591	1.7355	1.7125	1.6901	1.6681	1.6467	1.6257
3	2.9410	2.8839	2.8286	2.7751	2.7232	2.6730	2.6243	2.5771	2.5313	2.4869	2.4437	2.4018	2.3612	2.3216	2.2832
4	3.9020	3.8077	3.7171	3.6299	3.5459	3.4651	3.3872	3.3121	3.2397	3.1699	3.1024	3.0373	2.9745	2.9137	2.8550
5	4.8534	4.7135	4.5797	4.4518	4.3295	4.2124	4.1002	3.9927	3.8897	3.7908	3.6959	3.6048	3.5172	3.4331	3.3522
6	5.7955	5.6014	5.4172	5.2421	5.0757	4.9173	4.7665	4.6229	4.4859	4.3553	4.2305	4.1114	3.9975	3.8887	3.7845
7	6.7282	6.4720	6.2303	6.0020	5.7864	5.5824	5.3893	5.2064	5.0330	4.8684	4.7122	4.5638	4.4226	4.2883	4.1604
8	7.6517	7.3255	7.0197	6.7327	6.4632	6.2098	5.9713	5.7466	5.5348	5.3349	5.1461	4.9676	4.7988	4.6389	4.4873
9	8.5660	8.1622	7.7861	7.4353	7.1078	6.8017	6.5152	6.2469	5.9952	5.7590	5.5370	5.3282	5.1317	4.9464	4.7716
10	9.4713	8.9826	8.5302	8.1109	7.7217	7.3601	7.0236	6.7101	6.4177	6.1446	5.8892	5.6502	5.4262	5.2161	5.0188
11	10.3676	9.7868	9.2526	8.7605	8.3064	7.8869	7.4987	7.1390	6.8051	6.4951	6.2065	5.9377	5.6869	5.4527	5.2337
12	11.2551	10.5753	9.9540	9.3851	8.8632	8.3838	7.9427	7.5361	7.1607	6.8137	6.4924	6.1944	5.9176	5.6603	5.4206
13	12.1337	11.3484	10.6350	9.9856	9.3936	8.8527	8.3577	7.9038	7.4869	7.1034	6.7499	6.4235	6.1218	5.8424	5.5831
14	13.0037	12.1062	11.2961	10.5631	9.8986	9.2950	8.7455	8.2442	7.7862	7.3667	6.9819	6.6282	6.3025	6.0021	5.7245
15	13.8650	12.8493	11.9379	11.1184	10.3797	9.7122	9.1079	8.5595	8.0607	7.6061	7.1909	6.8109	6.4624	6.1422	5.8474
16	14.7179	13.5777	12.5611	11.6523	10.8378	10.1059	9.4466	8.8514	8.3126	7.8237	7.3792	6.9740	6.6039	6.2651	5.9542
17	15.5622	14.2919	13.1661	12.1657	11.2741	10.4773	9.7632	9.1216	8.5436	8.0216	7.5488	7.1196	6.7291	6.3729	6.0472
18	16.3983	14.9920	13.7535	12.6593	11.6896	10.8276	10.0591	9.3719	8.7556	8.2014	7.7016	7.2497	6.8399	6.4674	6.1280
19	17.2260	15.6785	14.3238	13.1339	12.0853	11.1581	10.3356	9.6036	8.9501	8.3649	7.8393	7.3658	6.9380	6.5504	6.1982
20	18.0455	16.3514	14.8775	13.5903	12.4622	11.4699	10.5940	9.8181	9.1285	8.5136	7.9633	7.4694	7.0248	6.6231	6.2593
21	18.8570	17.0112	15.4150	14.0292	12.8211	11.7641	10.8355	10.0168	9.2922	8.6487	8.0751	7.5620	7.1015	6.6870	6.3125
22	19.6604	17.6580	15.9369	14.4511	13.1630	12.0416	11.0612	10.2007	9.4424	8.7715	8.1757	7.6446	7.1695	6.7429	6.3587
23	20.4558	18.2922	16.4436	14.8568	13.4886	12.3034	11.2722	10.3711	9.5802	8.8832	8.2664	7.7184	7.2297	6.7921	6.3988
24	21.2434	18.9139	16.9355	15.2470	13.7986	12.5504	11.4693	10.5288	9.7066	8.9847	8.3481	7.7843	7.2829	6.8351	6.4338
25	22.0232	19.5235	17.4131	15.6221	14.0939	12.7834	11.6536	10.6748	9.8226	9.0770	8.4217	7.8431	7.3300	6.8729	6.4641
26	22.7952	20.1210	17.8768	15.9828	14.3752	13.0032	11.8258	10.8100	9.9290	9.1609	8.4881	7.8957	7.3717	6.9061	6.4906
27	23.5596	20.7069	18.3270	16.3296	14.6430	13.2105	11.9867	10.9352	10.0266	9.2372	8.5478	7.9426	7.4086	6.9352	6.5135
28	24.3164	21.2813	18.7641	16.6631	14.8981	13.4062	12.1371	11.0511	10.1161	9.3066	8.6016	7.9844	7.4412	6.9607	6.5335
29	25.0658	21.8444	19.1884	16.9837	15.1411	13.5907	12.2777	11.1584	10.1983	9.3696	8.6501	8.0218	7.4701	6.9830	6.5509
30	25.8077	22.3965	19.6004	17.2920	15.3724	13.7648	12.4090	11.2578	10.2737	9.4269	8.6938	8.0552	7.4957	7.0027	6.5660
31	26.5423	22.9377	20.0004	17.5885	15.5928	13.9291	12.5318	11.3498	10.3428	9.4790	8.7331	8.0850	7.5183	7.0199	6.5791
32	27.2696	23.4683	20.3888	17.8735	15.8027	14.0840	12.6466	11.4350	10.4062	9.5264	8.7686	8.1116	7.5383	7.0350	6.5905
33	27.9897	23.9886	20.7658	18.1476	16.0025	14.2302	12.7538	11.5139	10.4644	9.5694	8.8005	8.1354	7.5560	7.0482	6.6005
34	28.7027	24.4986	21.1318	18.4112	16.1929	14.3681	12.8540	11.5869	10.5178	9.6086	8.8293	8.1566	7.5717	7.0599	6.6091
35	29.4086	24.9986	21.4872	18.6646	16.3742	14.4982	12.9477	11.6546	10.5668	9.6442	8.8552	8.1755	7.5856	7.0700	6.6166
40	32.8347	27.3555	23.1148	19.7928	17.1591	15.0463	13.3317	11.9246	10.7574	9.7791	8.9511	8.2438	7.6344	7.1050	6.6418
45	36.0945	29.4902	24.5187	20.7200	17.7741	15.4558	13.6055	12.1084	10.8812	9.8628	9.0079	8.2825	7.6609	7.1232	6.6543
50	39.1961	31.4236	25.7298	21.4822	18.2559	15.7619	13.8007	12.2335	10.9617	9.9148	9.0417	8.3045	7.6752	7.1327	6.6605

n/r	16%	18%	20%	22%	24%	25%	28%	30%	32%	34%	36%	38%	40%	45%	50%
1	.8621	.8475	.8333	.8197	.8065	.7937	.7813	.7692	.7576	.7463	.7353	.7246	.7143	.6897	.6667
2	1.6052	1.5656	1.5278	1.4915	1.4568	1.4235	1.3916	1.3609	1.3315	1.3032	1.2760	1.2497	1.2245	1.1653	1.1111
3	2.2459	2.1743	2.1065	2.0422	1.9813	1.9234	1.8684	1.8161	1.7663	1.7188	1.6735	1.6302	1.5889	1.4933	1.4074
4	2.7982	2.6901	2.5887	2.4936	2.4043	2.3202	2.2410	2.1662	2.0957	2.0290	1.9658	1.9060	1.8492	1.7195	1.6049
5	3.2743	3.1272	2.9906	2.8636	2.7454	2.6351	2.5320	2.4356	2.3452	2.2604	2.1807	2.1058	2.0352	1.8755	1.7366
6	3.6847	3.4976	3.3255	3.1669	3.0205	2.8850	2.7594	2.6427	2.5342	2.4331	2.3388	2.2506	2.1680	1.9831	1.8244
7	4.0386	3.8115	3.6046	3.4155	3.2423	3.0833	2.9370	2.8021	2.6775	2.5620	2.4550	2.3555	2.2628	2.0573	1.8829
8	4.3436	4.0776	3.8372	3.6193	3.4212	3.2407	3.0758	2.9247	2.7860	2.6582	2.5404	2.4315	2.3306	2.1085	1.9220
9	4.6065	4.3030	4.0310	3.7863	3.5655	3.3657	3.1842	3.0190	2.8681	2.7300	2.6033	2.4866	2.3790	2.1438	1.9480
10	4.8332	4.4941	4.1925	3.9232	3.6819	3.4648	3.2689	3.0915	2.9304	2.7836	2.6495	2.5265	2.4136	2.1681	1.9653
11	5.0286	4.6560	4.3271	4.0354	3.7757	3.5435	3.3351	3.1473	2.9776	2.8236	2.6834	2.5555	2.4383	2.1849	1.9769
12	5.1971	4.7932	4.4392	4.1274	3.8514	3.6059	3.3868	3.1903	3.0133	2.8534	2.7084	2.5764	2.4559	2.1965	1.9845
13	5.3423	4.9095	4.5327	4.2028	3.9124	3.6555	3.4272	3.2233	3.0404	2.8757	2.7268	2.5916	2.4685	2.2045	1.9897
14	5.4675	5.0081	4.6106	4.2646	3.9616	3.6949	3.4587	3.2487	3.0609	2.8923	2.7403	2.6026	2.4775	2.2100	1.9931
15	5.5755	5.0916	4.6755	4.3152	4.0013	3.7261	3.4834	3.2682	3.0764	2.9047	2.7502	2.6106	2.4839	2.2138	1.9954
16	5.6685	5.1624	4.7296	4.3567	4.0333	3.7509	3.5026	3.2832	3.0882	2.9140	2.7575	2.6164	2.4885	2.2164	1.9970
17	5.7487	5.2223	4.7746	4.3908	4.0591	3.7705	3.5177	3.2948	3.0971	2.9209	2.7629	2.6206	2.4918	2.2182	1.9980
18	5.8178	5.2732	4.8122	4.4187	4.0799	3.7861	3.5294	3.3037	3.1039	2.9260	2.7668	2.6236	2.4941	2.2195	1.9986
19	5.8775	5.3162	4.8435	4.4415	4.0967	3.7985	3.5386	3.3105	3.1090	2.9299	2.7697	2.6258	2.4958	2.2203	1.9991
20	5.9288	5.3527	4.8696	4.4603	4.1103	3.8083	3.5458	3.3158	3.1129	2.9327	2.7718	2.6274	2.4970	2.2209	1.9994
21	5.9731	5.3837	4.8913	4.4756	4.1212	3.8161	3.5514	3.3198	3.1158	2.9349	2.7734	2.6285	2.4979	2.2213	1.9996
22	6.0113	5.4099	4.9094	4.4882	4.1300	3.8223	3.5558	3.3230	3.1180	2.9365	2.7746	2.6294	2.4985	2.2216	1.9997
23	6.0442	5.4321	4.9245	4.4985	4.1371	3.8273	3.5592	3.3253	3.1197	2.9377	2.7754	2.6300	2.4989	2.2218	1.9998
24	6.0726	5.4509	4.9371	4.5070	4.1428	3.8312	3.5619	3.3272	3.1210	2.9386	2.7760	2.6304	2.4992	2.2219	1.9999
25	6.0971	5.4669	4.9476	4.5139	4.1474	3.8342	3.5640	3.3286	3.1220	2.9392	2.7765	2.6307	2.4994	2.2220	1.9999
26	6.1182	5.4804	4.9563	4.5196	4.1511	3.8367	3.5656	3.3297	3.1227	2.9397	2.7768	2.6310	2.4996	2.2221	1.9999
27	6.1364	5.4919	4.9636	4.5243	4.1542	3.8387	3.5669	3.3305	3.1233	2.9401	2.7771	2.6311	2.4997	2.2221	2.0000
28	6.1520	5.5016	4.9697	4.5281	4.1566	3.8402	3.5679	3.3312	3.1237	2.9404	2.7773	2.6313	2.4998	2.2222	2.0000
29	6.1656	5.5098	4.9747	4.5312	4.1585	3.8414	3.5687	3.3316	3.1240	2.9406	2.7774	2.6313	2.4999	2.2222	2.0000
30	6.1772	5.5168	4.9789	4.5338	4.1601	3.8424	3.5693	3.3321	3.1242	2.9407	2.7775	2.6314	2.4999	2.2222	2.0000
31	6.1872	5.5227	4.9824	4.5359	4.1614	3.8432	3.5697	3.3324	3.1244	2.9408	2.7776	2.6315	2.4999	2.2222	2.0000
32	6.1959	5.5277	4.9854	4.5376	4.1624	3.8438	3.5701	3.3326	3.1246	2.9409	2.7776	2.6315	2.4999	2.2222	2.0000
33	6.2034	5.5320	4.9878	4.5390	4.1632	3.8443	3.5704	3.3328	3.1247	2.9410	2.7777	2.6315	2.5000	2.2222	2.0000
34	6.2098	5.5356	4.9898	4.5402	4.1639	3.8447	3.5706	3.3329	3.1248	2.9410	2.7777	2.6315	2.5000	2.2222	2.0000
35	6.2153	5.5386	4.9915	4.5411	4.1644	3.8450	3.5708	3.3330	3.1248	2.9411	2.7777	2.6215	2.5000	2.2222	2.0000
40	6.2335	5.5482	4.9966	4.5439	4.1659	3.8458	3.5712	3.3332	3.1250	2.9412	2.7778	2.6316	2.5000	2.2222	2.0000
45	6.2421	5.5523	4.9986	4.5449	4.1664	3.8460	3.5714	3.3333	3.1250	2.9412	2.7778	2.6316	2.5000	2.2222	2.0000
50	6.2463	5.5541	4.9995	4.5452	4.1666	3.8461	3.5714	3.3333	3.1250	2.9412	2.7778	2.6316	2.5000	2.2222	2.0000

positive $29,347.50. We also said there were additional revenues generated with new equipment of $1,000 per year, and again, since this is a yearly amount, we will use the 4.1925 figure to arrive at $4,192.50. We sum all of these figures algebraically. That is, there is one outlay and one outlay only, and that is the negative $50,000 which we will pay for the purchase price. All the other figures are summed together to give us a negative $6,219.38, which is less than the zero cost of the current equipment. This tells us that purchase of this new equipment is not in our interest at the present time. If the sum of these figures were positive, this would tell us to purchase the new equipment.

What might cause the situation to change in the future? It might do so if the cost of purchase was reduced. If the operating savings or additional revenues went up, that might cause the situation to change. And of course, the same might happen if the opportunity cost percentage changed for some reason. If any one of these possibilities occurred, we should reevaluate and do a new analysis to see whether we should buy new equipment.

OTHER FACTORS TO CONSIDER IN THE REPLACEMENT DECISION

In addition to the straight economic analysis discussed above, other factors must be taken into consideration when you are deciding whether to replace current equipment or not. These include size of the investment required and whether you can manage it or not. You will note that in the above example it was assumed that cash was paid. Naturally, whether a loan would be required and what kind of loan could be obtained under what terms would also affect this decision. The safety and reliability of your current equipment must be considered. Equipment that is unsafe and that might cause injury to you or to your workers may be too much of a liability to continue with, even though a straight economic analysis might indicate that it is in your economic interest. In the same manner, reliability and downtime and how they might affect the flow of your goods and your customer's opinions of your company should also be considered. Interest and investment rates must always be considered, and so should what the trend is likely to be regarding such interest rates. Along the same lines, trends in development of equipment should be considered. It makes no sense to purchase a new piece of equipment if a similar amount of money will buy you much more in the not-too-distant future. Also, price and price trends should be considered. Additional features in the new equipment might also be weighed, even though there are no direct cost savings. Maybe the features just make it easier or more convenient to use. There is a value here to your business also, even though it may not be reasonable in economic terms.

SOURCES OF ADDITIONAL INFORMATION

Finance for the Nonfinancial Manager, by Herbert T. Spiro, published by John Wiley & Sons, Inc., 605 Third Avenue, New York, NY 10158.

Should You Lease or Buy Equipment? Management Aid 249, by Paul Lerman, available free from the Small Business Administration, P.O. Box 15434, Fort Worth, TX 76119.

The Equipment Replacement Decision, by Raymond R. Mayer, available free from the Small Business Administration, P.O. Box 15434, Fort Worth, TX 76119.

6

Financial Management

FINANCIAL MANAGEMENT—WHAT IT IS AND WHY IT IS IMPORTANT

Financial management includes a number of different functions:

1. Managing old and new assets so that every single asset contributes to the maximum extent possible toward the profitable operation of your business
2. Ensuring that the assets that you have are used in such a manner as to bring the maximum return possible on the money that you invest
3. Obtaining funds to finance additional assets
4. Evaluating the need for new assets
5. Repaying borrowed monies from profits that the same money has generated

These functions impact on your profitability and your survivability. For this reason, they are extremely important. One reason for owning and operating your own business is to make a good profit for yourself, and you will need good financial management to reach this goal.

Methods to help you with these functions are discussed throughout the book, not only in this chapter. However, in this chapter we will focus on items of particular concern for the small businessperson in handling financial management responsibilities. These include the definition and components of working capital, the tools of financial management necessary to accomplish any of the functions listed, analysis methods needed to find out whether or not you are performing adequately financially, and the break-even analysis which must be used for many of your business decisions prior to an investment. This chapter is one that you will refer to again and again, and using it in conjunction with other chapters such as that on record keeping will enable you to analyze what is going on in your business at all times. This will help you correct deficiencies and make your business increasingly more profitable.

WORKING CAPITAL

Small businesspersons are particularly concerned with the term *working capital*. It is the difference between your current assets and your current liabilities. It is the circulating lifeblood of your business. Research has shown that lack of control of this lifeblood is a primary cause of business failure in firms of all sizes. For this reason, you must understand the components of working capital. This understanding will allow you to be alert for change or the opportunity for change. A change in your business implies a change in the financial health of your company, either for better or for worse. Monitor these components to ensure that the end result in your company is for the better.

   1. *Cash and cash equivalents.*   Cash and cash equivalents comprise the most liquid form of current assets. This means it is the easiest to convert in form and to use. Cash equivalents are usually marketable securities or short-term certificates of deposit. You must maintain a well-planned cash budgeting system so that you will know whether the cash on hand in the form of cash and equivalents is adequate to meet current expenses as you must pay them—whether the timing relationship between cash inflow and outflow is favorable. Remember, it is fine that at the end of the year you would make a big profit, but if at any time during the year you have a sufficiently large negative cash flow, you could end up bankrupt. You should also know when peak cash needs may occur and the magnitude of borrowing that might be required to meet cash shortfalls. And, of course, your system should enable you to see when and how repayment will be accomplished.

   2. *Accounts receivable.*   As explained in an earlier chapter, in many cases your business will be required to extend credit to your customers or clients. However, this account must be closely watched, and you should note whether the amounts of accounts receivable are reasonable in relationship to your overall sales and the age of these accounts, and, of course, what action you can take to speed up collections and whether such accounts should be eliminated in the future. It may be of little help if sales are extremely high if most of your sales are in accounts receivable. Everyone may owe you money, but no one is paying!

   3. *Inventories.*   Frequently your inventory may make up better than 50% of your current assets. This is a significant amount and means that you must keep a close watch on this account. You should know whether the amount of inventory is reasonable in relation to sales and other operational characteristics of your business. A rapidity of turnover of inventory is important here and should be compared with that of other firms in your industry. Also, you should note whether any amount of inventory is invested in items that are not moving or are slow to move. On the other hand, are you losing sales due to an inadequate supply of inventory? Either situation implies action that you must take either to increase or to decrease your inventory.

   4. *Accounts payable and trade notes payable.*   One source of credit is trade credit. We talked about this earlier, and about how money you owe to suppliers actually is a form of loan. But unlimited amounts of credit would not be good for your business, even if you could obtain them. In this respect, you should note the amount of credit and how it compares with your purchases. What is your payment policy and how does it affect your credit rating? This could be extremely important to you in the future, even if it is not now. Also, note the possible advantages of discount, such as the "2% if paid within 10 days" discussed in an earlier chapter. Also of interest are the possible timing relationships between the payments on accounts payable and collections that you receive on accounts receivable.

   5. *Notes payable.*   Notes payable to banks or perhaps even to individual lenders or the former owner of your business are a major source of possible financing, and one that we discussed in Chapter 2. You must know whether the debt amount is reasonable in relationship to other types of financing such as equity financing of your firm. Also, you must know when various payments will fall due and whether funds are available to meet these payments on time.

6. *Accrued expenses and taxes payable.* Accrued expenses and taxes payable represent obligations of the firm as of the date that you prepare the balance sheet. These accrued expenses represent items such as salaries, interest payable, bank notes, insurance premiums payable, and so forth. Taxes payable are self-evident. But in both cases, it is extremely important that the magnitude, timing, and availability of funds be looked into very carefully. Taxes not paid on time, for example, can result in your firm's being closed down by the government until the taxes are paid.

To help you keep track of some of the items that are necessary in monitoring the elements of your working capital listed above, various ratio analyses have been developed and used over the years. These will be discussed shortly.

THE TOOLS OF FINANCIAL MANAGEMENT

Certain tools are available for you in accomplishing the functions needed in the financial management of your firm. These tools are as follows:

1. *Accounting records.* Accounting records are the basis of your financial management. At this point you may feel that keeping track of your business on a day-to-day basis and accounting for all transactions is too time consuming. Overall, you will save time and money doing this. Methods of keeping accurate and precise records are contained in Chapter 8.

2. *Financial records and reports.* These records and reports are also of great help in financial management. They include the balance sheet and the profit and loss statement as discussed in Chapter 8. These two financial statements are the basis for all financial analyses and are used by bankers and other investors in making loan evaluations and investment decisions. For this reason, you must understand these two documents and be able to explain each item that may appear in them. State and federal laws pertaining to taxation also require reports that can be put together only from the use of profit and loss and balance sheets. Finally, these two documents will be very helpful in accomplishing your financial analyses.

3. *Analysis techniques.* Techniques of analysis developed for financial management are the third set of tools that you will use in accomplishing this task. These tools include ratio analyses, return-on-investment guides, and break-even analysis. They will be discussed next.

RATIO ANALYSES

Ratio analyses are indicators that have been developed to help you to determine the state of health of various financial aspects of your business. They provide indications as to weaknesses and strengths in your financial operation as well as clues as to where and how to develop better financial performance. Such ratios also permit you to compare how you are doing with the performance of other similar businesses in your industry.

However, even with their importance and the considerable insight they provide, there are limitations to the use of ratio analyses. You must also consider the following limitations during your analysis:

1. The ratios are based on past performance. Therefore, you must balance their indications with what is happening now and what is likely to happen in your business in the future.
2. Ratios are frequently calculated for specific dates. If your business is seasonal, this factor must be considered.
3. Businesses are not perfectly comparable. Different items may be stated in different ways on financial statements. As a result, the financial ratios computed for your business may differ from those of the average in your industry for reasons other than performance.

Despite these limitations, financial ratios and ratio analyses may be of great help to you. Let's look at some of those available.

Measures of Liquidity

Liquidity is the ability to use the money available in your business. In general, the more liquid the better the state of financial health. However, this is a bit oversimplified as I will show you later. The ratios intended to measure liquidity in your business will tell you whether you have enough cash on hand plus assets that can be readily turned into cash to pay debts that may fall due during any given period. They will also tell you about how quickly they can be turned into cash.

The Current Ratio

The current ratio is possibly the best-known measure of financial health. It answers this question: Does your business have sufficient current assets to meet current debts with a margin of safety for possible losses due to uncollectible accounts receivable and other factors?

The current ratio is computed by using information on your balance sheet. You simply divide current assets by current liabilities. For example, if we consider the sample balance sheet in Figure 8.3, current assets are $155,000, and current liabilities are $90,000. Dividing $155,000 by $90,000 gives a current ratio of 1.7.

Now you may ask: Is this a good current ratio or is it not? You cannot determine this from the numerical value of 1.7 by itself, even though there is a popular rule of thumb that says that a current ratio of at least two to one is okay. The current ratio very much depends on your business and the specific characteristics of your current assets and liabilities. However, one major indication is a comparison with other companies in your industry. I'll give you sources for this information later in the chapter.

If after analysis and comparison you decide that your current ratio is too low, you may be able to raise it by the following actions:

1. Increase your current assets by new equity contributions.
2. Try converting noncurrent assets into current assets.
3. Pay some of your debts.

4. Increase your current assets from loans or other types of borrowing that have a maturity of at least a year in the future.

5. Put some of the profits back into the business.

The Acid Test or "Quick" Ratio

The "quick" ratio or acid test ratio is also an outstanding measure of liquidity. You calculate this ratio as follows: cash plus government securities plus receivables divided by current liabilities.

The company shown in Figure 8.3 has no government securities. Therefore, the numerator of this figure becomes $35,000 cash plus $55,000 in accounts receivable or $90,000. This is divided by current liabilities on the same balance sheet of $90,000 to result in an acid test ratio of 1.0.

The quick ratio concentrates on really liquid assets whose values are definite and well known. Therefore, the quick ratio will answer this question: If all your sales revenue disappears tomorrow, can you meet current obligations with your cash or quick funds on hand? Usually an acid test ratio of approximately 1.0 is considered satisfactory. However, you must also make this decision conditional on the following:

1. There should be nothing in the offing to slow up the collection of your accounts receivable.

2. The receipt of accounts receivable collections should not trail the due schedule for paying your current liabilities. In checking out this timing, you should consider payment of your creditors sufficiently early to take advantage of any discounts that are offered.

If these two conditions are not met, you will need an acid test ratio higher than 1.0. However, it is erroneous to believe that either the current or the acid test ratio should always be as high as possible. Only those from whom you have borrowed money would say this is so. Naturally, they are interested in the greatest possible safety of their loan. However, you do not want to have large sums of money lying idle and not earning you additional profits. If you do have idle cash balances and receivables and inventories that are out of proportion to your needs, you should reduce them. The key here is to be conservative enough to keep a safety pad and yet bold enough to take advantage of the fact that you have these resources which can be used to earn additional profits for you. Before you make this decision as to the right amount of liquidity, you should consider the two ratios discussed next, average collection period and inventory turnover.

Average Collection Period

The average collection period is the number of days that sales are tied up in accounts receivable. This number can be calculated by using your profit and loss statement or income statement as shown in Figure 8.4. First, take your net sales, which in Figure 8.4 are $1,035,000, and divide this figure by the days in your accounting period or 365. This equals $2,836, the average sales per day in the accounting period. Next take your accounts receivable, which you obtain from the balance sheet, Figure 8.3. Accounts receivable are $55,000. Divide $55,000 by the figure you just calculated ($2,836): $55,000 divided by $2,836 equals 19. This is the average number of days sales are tied up in receivables. It is also your average collection period.

This tells you how promptly your accounts are being collected considering whatever credit terms you are extending. It tells you two other things: (1) the quality of your accounts and notes receivable, that is, whether you are really getting paid rapidly or not, and (2) how good a job your credit department is doing in collecting these accounts.

Now the question is: Is the figure of 19 days good or not good? There is a rule of thumb that says the average collection period should not exceed one and one-third times the credit terms offered. Therefore, if your company offers 30 days to pay and the average collection period is only 19 days, you are doing very well. On the other hand, anything in excess of 40 days ($1\frac{1}{3} \times 30 = 40$) would show that you may have a problem.

Inventory Turnover

Inventory turnover will show you how rapidly your merchandise is moving. It will also show you how much capital you had tied up in inventory to support the level of your company's operations for the period that you are analyzing. To calculate inventory turnover, simply divide the cost of goods sold that you obtain from your income statement, Figure 8.4, by your average inventory. According to Figure 8.4, your income or profit and loss statement, the cost of goods sold equals $525,000. You cannot calculate your average inventory from Figure 8.3. You only know that for the period for which the inventory is stated, it equals $60,000. Let's assume that the previous balance sheet indicated that your inventory was $50,000. Then, the average inventory for the two periods would be $60,000 plus $50,000 divided by 2, or $55,000. Now, let's see what inventory turnover is: Cost of goods sold again was $525,000 divided by $55,000 equals 9.5.

This means that you turned your inventory 9.5 times during the year. Put another way, through your business operations you used up merchandise that totals 9.5 times the average inventory investment. Under most circumstances, the higher the turnover of inventory, the better, because it means that you are able to operate with a relatively small sum of money invested in this inventory. Another implication is that your inventory is the right inventory. That is, it is salable and has not been in stock too long. But, even here, you must consider that too high a figure may be a sign of a problem. Very high inventory may mean that you have inventory shortages, and inventory shortages soon lead to customer dissatisfaction and may mean a loss of customers to the competition in the long run.

Is 9.5 a satisfactory inventory turnover or not? Again, the desirable rate depends on your business, your industry, your method of valuing inventories, and numerous other factors that are unique to your situation. And, once again, it is helpful to study and compare your turnover rate with that of similar businesses of your size in your industry. Once you have been working and operating for some time, past experiences with inventory turnover will indicate what is good and what is not with less reliance on inventory comparisons.

Very frequently it is helpful to analyze not just your total inventory but specific inventory turnover for different products or even groups of products or product lines. This will show you which items are doing well and which are not. You may also prepare turnover analyses for much more frequent periods than a year. Even monthly or weekly periods may be necessary or required for perishable items or items that become obsolete very quickly. Thus, you will know to reorder those items that are truly "hot" items early and in plenty of time, and you will also know which items you should not order and which items you must order before their value goes down to a point where you can no longer sell them at all.

PROFITABILITY MEASURES

Measures of profitability are essential in your business if you are to know how much money you are making, whether you are making as much as you can, or whether you are making money at all. There are several different ratios that will assist you in determining this. These are the asset earning power, return on the owner's equity, net profit on sales, investment turnover, and finally, return on investment (ROI).

Asset Earning Power

Asset earning power is determined by the ratio of earnings before interest and taxes to total assets. From the income statement in Figure 8.4 we can see that total operating profit or income is $105,000. Total assets from the balance sheet, Figure 8.3, are $272,000. Therefore, $105,000 divided by $272,000 equals 0.39 or 39%.

Return on the Owner's Equity

Return on the owner's equity shows the return that you received in exchange for your investment in your business. To compute this ratio you will usually use the average equity for 12 months, if it is available, or, if not, the average of figures from two different balance sheets, your latest and the one preceding. Return on the owner's equity equals net profit divided by equity. Net profit from Figure 8.4 is $55,000. Equity from Figure 8.3 is $115,000. Assuming the equity from the period before is also $115,000, we will use this as an average. Therefore, return on the owner's equity equals $55,000 divided by $115,000, which equals 0.48 or 48%.

You can calculate a similar ratio by using tangible net worth in lieu of equity. Tangible net worth equals equity less any intangible assets such as patents and good will. If no intangible assets exist, then, of course, the two will be equal.

Net Profit on Sales

The net profit on sales ratio measures the difference between what you take in and what you spend in the process of doing business. Again, net profit was determined to be $55,000. Net sales from Figure 8.4 is $1,035,000. Therefore, net profit on sales equals 0.053 or 5.3%.

This means that for every dollar of sales the company has made a profit of 5.3¢.

The net profit on sales ratio depends mainly on these two factors: (1) operating costs and (2) pricing policies. Therefore, if this figure goes down, it could be because you have lowered prices or it could be because costs have been increasing at the same time that prices have remained stable.

Again, this ratio should be compared with figures from other similar businesses, and you should consider trends over a period of time. It is also useful to compare net profit on sales ratios for individual products to show which products or product lines should be given additional emphasis and which should be eliminated.

Investment Turnover

The investment turnover ratio is annual net sales to total assets. In this case, net sales of $1,035,000, divided by total assets of $272,000 from Figure 8.3, equals 3.8.

Again, investment turnover should be compared and watched for trends.

Return on Investment

There are several different ways of calculating return on investment. It is a very useful method of measuring profitability. One simple way is to take net profit and divide it by total assets. In this case, the net profit equals $55,000. Total assets are $272,000. Therefore, $55,000 divided by $272,000 equals 0.20 or 20%.

It is desirable here to have the highest net profit for the smallest amount of total assets invested. You can use this rate of return on investment for intercompany and interindustry comparisons, as well as pricing costs, inventory and investment decisions, and many other measurements of efficiency and profitability. However you use it, always be sure that you are consistent in making your comparisons; that is, be sure that you use the same definitions of net profit and assets invested.

Here are some additional measures of profitability using ROI:

1. *Rate of earnings on total capital employed equals net income plus interest and taxes divided by total liabilities and capital.* This ratio serves as an index of productivity of capital as well as a measure of earning power in operating efficiency.

2. *Rate of earnings on invested capital equals net income plus income taxes divided by proprietary equity and fixed liabilities.* This ratio is used as a measure of earning power of the borrowed invested capital.

3. *Rate of earnings on proprietary equity equals net income divided by total capital including surplus reserves.* This ratio is used as a measure of the yield on the owner's investment.

4. *Rate of earnings on stock equity equals net income divided by total capital including surplus reserves.* This ratio is used as a measure of the attractiveness of common stock as an investment.

5. *Rate of dividends on common stock equity equals common stock dividends divided by common stock equity.* This ratio is used to indicate the desirability of common stock as a source of income.

6. *Rate of dividends on common stock equity equals common stock dividend per share divided by market value per share of common stock.* The ratio is used as a measure of the current yield on investment in a particular stock.

SOURCES OF RATIO ANALYSES FROM ALL INDUSTRIES

In order to be able to compare your business with other businesses in your industry, it is necessary to obtain pertinent data on other businesses. Here are different sources for such information:

1. Dun & Bradstreet, Inc., Business Information Systems, 99 Church Street, New York, NY 10007. This firm publishes key business ratios in 125 lines annually. Legal copies can be obtained free on request.

2. Accounting Corporation of America, 1929 First Avenue, San Diego, CA 92101. This organization publishes *Parameter of Small Businesses* which classifies its operating ratios for various industry groups on the basis of gross volume.

3. National Cash Register Co., Marketing Services Department, Dayton, OH 45409. This firm publishes *Expenses in Retail Businesses* which examines the cost of operations in over 50 kinds of businesses obtained from primary sources, most of which are trade associations.

4. Robert Morris Associates, Philadelphia National Bank Building, Philadelphia, PA 19107. Robert Morris has developed and published ratio studies for over 225 lines of businesses.

5. The Small Business Administration. The SBA has a series of reports that provide expenses as a percentage of sales for many industries. While the reports do not provide strict ratio information, a comparison of percentage expenses will be very useful for your financial management.

6. Trade Asssociations. National associations which have published ratio studies in the past include the following:

American Association of Advertising Agencies, 666 Third Avenue, 13th Floor, New York, NY 10017

American Camping Association, 5000 State Road, 67N, Martinsville, IN 46151

American Financial Services Association, 1101 14th Street, NW, Washington, DC 20005

American Jewelry Marketing Association, 1900 Arch Street, Philadelphia, PA 19103

American Meat Institute, P.O. Box 3556, Washington, DC 20007

American Paper Institute, 260 Madison Avenue, New York, NY 10016

American Society of Association Executives, 1575 Eye Street, NW, Washington, DC 20005

American Supply Association, 20 North Wacker Drive, Suite 2260, Chicago, IL 60606

Bowling Proprietors Association of America, Box 5802, Arlington, TX 76011

Building Owners and Managers Association, International, 1250 Eye Street, NW, Suite 200, Washington, DC 20005

Door and Hardware Institute, 7711 Old Springhouse Road, McLean, VA 22102

Florists' Transworld Delivery Association/Interflora, 29200 Northwestern Highway, Southfield, MI 48037

Food Market Institute, Inc., 1750 K Street, NW, Suite 700, Washington, DC 20006

Foodservice Equipment Distributors Association, 332 South Michigan Avenue, Chicago, IL 60604

Independent Insurance Agents of America, 100 Church Street, 19th Floor, New York, NY 10007

Laundry and Cleaners Allied Trades Association, 543 Valley Road, Upper Montclair, NJ 07043

Material Handling Equipment Distributors Association, 201 Route 45, Vernon Hills, IL 60061

Mechanical Contractors Association of America, 5410 Grosvenor Lane, Suite 120, Bethesda, MD 20814

Menswear Retailers of America, 2011 Eye Street, NW, Washington, DC 20006

Motor and Equipment Manufacturers' Association, P.O. Box 1638, 300 Sylvan Avenue, Englewood Cliffs, NJ 07632

National American Wholesale Grocers' Association, 201 Park Washington Court, Falls Church, VA 22046

National Appliance and Radio—TV Dealers Association, 10 East 22nd Street, Lombard, IL 60148

National Art Materials Trade Association, 178 Lakeview Avenue, Clifton, NJ 07011

National Association of Accountants, P.O. Box 433, 10 Paragon Drive, Montvale, NJ 07645

National Association of Electrical Distributors, 28 Cross Street, Norwalk, CT 06851

National Association of Food Chains, 1750 K Street, Suite 700, Washington, DC 20006

National Association of Furniture Manufacturers, P.O. Box HP.7, High Point, NC 27261

National Association of Music Merchants, Inc., 5140 Avenida Encinas, Carlsbad, CA 92008

National Association of Plastics Distributors, 5001 College Boulevard, Suite 201, Leawood, KS 66211

National Association of Textile and Apparel Distributors, P.O. Box 1325, Melbourne, FL 32902

National Association of Tobacco Distributors, 1199 North Fairfax Street, Suite 701, Alexandria, VA 22314

National Automatic Merchandising Association, 20 North Wacker Drive, Chicago, IL 60606

National Beer Wholesalers Association, 5205 Leesburg Pike, Suite 505, Falls Church, VA 22041

National Confectioners Association of the United States, 645 North Michigan Avenue, Suite 1006, Chicago, IL 60611

National Decorating Products Association, 1050 North Linbergh Boulevard, St. Louis, MO 63132

National Electrical Contractors Association, Inc., 7315 Wisconsin Avenue, Bethesda, MD 20814

National Electrical Manufacturers Association, 2101 L Street, NW, Washington, DC 20037

National Farm and Power Equipment Dealers Association, 10877 Watson Road, P.O. Box 8517, St. Louis, MO 63826

National Grocers Association, 1825 Samuel Moore Drive, Reston, VA 22090

National Home Furnishings Association, 220 West Gerry Lane, Wood Dale, IL 60191

National Kitchen Cabinet Association, P.O. Box 6830, Falls Church, VA 22046

National Lumber and Building Material Dealers Association, 40 Ivy Street, SE, Washington, DC 20003

National Machine Tool Builders Association, 7901 Westpark Drive, McLean, VA 22102

National Office Products Association, 301 North Fairfax Street, Alexandria, VA 22314

National Paint and Coatings Association, 1500 Rhode Island Avenue, NW, Washington, DC 20005

National Paperbox and Packaging Association, 231 Kings Highway East, Haddonfield, NJ 08033

National Paper Trade Association, Inc., 111 Great Neck Road, Great Neck, NY 11021

National Parking Association, 1112 16th Street, NW, Suite 2000, Washington, DC 20036

National Restaurant Association, 311 First Street, NW, Washington, DC 20001

National Retail Hardware Association, 770 North High School Road, Indianapolis, IN 46214

National Retail Merchants Association, 100 West 31st Street, New York, NY 10001

National Shoe Retailers Association, 9861 Broken Land Parkway, Columbia, MD 21046

National Soft Drink Association, 1101 16th Street, NW, Washington, DC 20036

National Sporting Goods Association, Lake Center Plaza Building, 1699 Wall Street, Mount Prospect, IL 60056

National Tire Dealers and Retreaders Association, 1250 Eye Street, NW, Suite 400, Washington, DC 20005

National Wholesale Druggists' Association, 105 Oronoco Street, P.O. Box 238, Alexandria, VA 22313

National Wholesale Hardware Association, 1900 Arch Street, Philadelphia, PA 19103

North American Heating and Airconditioning Wholesalers Association, P.O. Box 16790, 1389 Dublin Road, Columbus, OH 43216

North American Wholesale Lumber Association, Inc., 2340 South Arlington Heights Road, Suite 680, Arlington Heights, IL 60005

Northeastern Retail Lumbermens Association, 339 East Avenue, Rochester, NY 14604

Optical Laboratories Association, P.O. Box 2000, Merrifield, VA 22116

Painting and Decorating Contractors of America, 7223 Lee Highway, Falls Church, VA 22046

Petroleum Equipment Institute, P.O. Box 2380, Tulsa, OK 74104

Petroleum Marketers Association, 1120 Vermont Avenue, Suite 1130, Washington, DC 20005

Printing Industries of America, Inc., 1730 North Lynn Street, Arlington, VA 22209

Scientific Apparatus Makers Association, 1101 16th Street, NW, Washington, DC 20036

Shoe Service Institute of America, 112 Calendar Court Mall, La Grange, IL 60525

Society of the Plastics Industry, Inc., The, 1275 K Street, NW, Suite 400, Washington, DC 20005

United Fresh Fruit and Vegetable Association, 727 North Washington Street, Alexandria, VA 22314

Urban Land Institute, 1090 Vermont Avenue, Washington, DC 20005

Wine and Spirit Wholesalers of America, Inc., 1023 15th Street, NW, Washington, DC 20005

BREAK-EVEN ANALYSIS

The break-even analysis is an excellent technique for determining the ultimate success of any project before you begin. The break-even analysis will tell you the following:

1. How many units you must sell in order to start making money
2. How much profit you will make at any given level of sales

3. How changing your price will affect profitability
4. How expense reductions of different types will affect profitability

To accomplish a break-even analysis, you must first separate the costs associated with your project into two types: fixed costs and variable costs.

Fixed costs are those expenses associated with the project that you would have to pay whether you sold one unit or 10,000 units or for that matter sold no units at all. For example, if you rented a garage to use in your business and the owner of the garage charged you $500 to rent the garage for the period of the project, then this would be a fixed cost for that period. You would have to pay the $500 whether or not you sold any products or many of your products. Research and development costs for a project or a product would also be considered a fixed cost, since this money would have to be paid whether or not you sold any of the product.

Variable costs vary directly with the number of units that you sell. If it costs you $1.80 to manufacture a unit, then that $1.80 is a variable cost. If postage for mailing your product to a customer is $1, then $1 is a variable cost. If you sell 10 units, then your postage cost will be 10 times $1 or $10. If you sell 100 units, your total variable cost for postage will be 100 times $1 or $100.

It is difficult to decide whether to consider some costs fixed or to consider them variable, and very frequently there is no single right answer. You must make this decision by yourself as the owner of the business. As a general guideline, if there is a direct relationship between cost and number of units sold, consider the cost variable. If you can find no relationship, then consider the cost fixed.

Total cost of your project will always equal total fixed costs plus total variable costs. Consider the following example for an item that you are going to sell.

Fixed costs:

Utility expense at $100 per month for 36 months	$3,600
Telephone at $200 per year for 3 years	600
Product development	1,000
Patenting expense	2,500
Total fixed costs	7,700

Variable costs:

Cost of product	$1 per unit
Cost of postage and packaging	50¢ per unit
Cost of advertising	$3 per unit
Total variable cost	$4.50 per unit

To calculate break-even, we start with profit. Profit is the number of units sold multiplied by the profit at which we are selling them less the number of units sold multiplied by the total variable cost minus the total fixed cost. Let's use an equation to make this a little easier to follow.

Let P equal profit, p equal price, U equal number of units sold, V equal variable cost, and F equal fixed cost. Then our equation becomes:

$$P = (U \times p) - (U \times V) - F$$

Or, we can simplify this to:

$$P = (U \times p - V) - F$$

Now, let's say we anticipate selling 1,000 units at $10 a unit. What would be the results? Substituting the values we have in our sample, we have:

$$P = (1{,}000 \times \$10 - \$4.50) - \$7{,}700 = \$5{,}500 - \$7{,}700 = -\$2{,}200$$

What is the significance of the minus number? This means that instead of making a profit, we have lost money, $2,200 to be exact. Now, we may want to know how many units we must sell in order to make money, or at what point we will stop losing money. This point at which we will either make money or lose money is called break-even. Beginning at this point, we will begin to show a profit. In order to calculate this, we use the break-even formula. In the break-even formula, using the same variables as above:

$$\text{Break-even} = F \div p - V$$

Since we know that F equals $7,700 and P equals $10 and V equals $4.50,

$$\text{Break-even} = \$7{,}700 \div \$610 - \$4.50 = 1{,}400 \text{ units}$$

This means if we don't change price or reduce expenses in any other way, we need to sell 1,400 units of this product before we start making any money.

However, there is an easier way to calculate this; we can use a break-even chart as shown in Figure 6.1. A break-even chart has a major advantage over the break-even and profit formulas. It shows us graphically the relationship of fixed and variable costs and total expenses to sales at all volumes of sales. This means that we can calculate profits at any level of sales right away.

To construct a break-even chart, follow these five steps:

Step 1: Get some graph paper and label the horizontal line on the bottom *Units sold*. Label the vertical line at the left of the graph *Dollars (sales and expenses)*. Divide each line into equal parts of dollars and units and label them appropriately.

Step 2: Analyze all of your costs for the project and decide whether each is fixed or variable. Decide on the period of sales for your project. Total your fixed variable costs.

Step 3. Draw a horizontal line to intersect the proper point on the vertical line to represent fixed costs, as at point A in Figure 6.1.

Step 4. Calculate the dollar value of sales for any unit number. For example, if you sell 2,000 units, how much is this in sales dollars? For the example, total sales volume would be 2,000 times $10 or $20,000. Plot this point at 2,000 units at $20,000 on the chart as point *a*. Put one end of a ruler at the zero point in the lower left corner of the chart and the other end at the point you have just plotted. This is total sales line B in Figure 6.1.

Step 5. Calculate the dollar value for variable costs for any unit number. For example, in this case variable cost is $4.50 per unit. At 2,000 units, total variable cost is 2,000 times $4.50 or $9,000. Add $9,000 to the fixed cost, in this case $7,700, to come up with $16,700. Plot this on the chart as *b* in Figure 6.1. Lay one end of the ruler at the point where the fixed cost line, A, intersects with

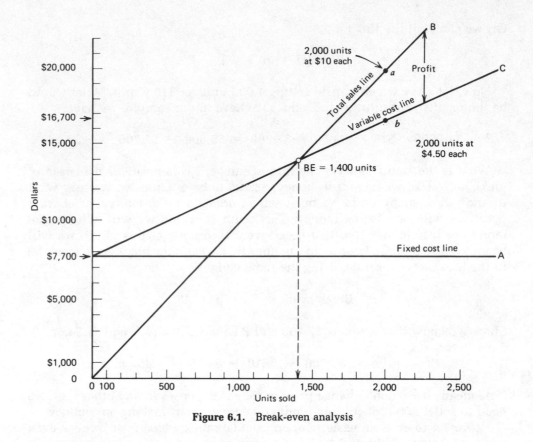

Figure 6.1. Break-even analysis

the vertical dollar scale, and the other at the point you just plotted. Draw a line to form the variable cost line, C, in Figure 6.1.

Now your break-even chart is complete. The point at which the total sales line or variable cost line intersects is a break-even point which you read on the horizontal unit scale at the bottom of the chart in Figure 6.1 as 1,400 units, just as we calculated before using the equation.

To calculate profit for any number of units you want, simply subtract the dollar value read opposite the profit point on the variable cost line, C, from the dollar value read opposite the profit point on the total sales line, B. For example, to calculate the profit if you sell 2,000 units, read right up from 2,000 units on the unit scale to point b on the variable cost line. Read straight across from point b to $16,700 on the vertical dollar scale. Now read straight out from 2,000 units on the unit scale to a point on the total sales line. Read straight across from point a to $20,000 on the vertical dollar scale. If you sell 2,000 units, $20,000 minus $16,700 equals $3,300. Do the same thing for any number of units to calculate profit.

Use break-even analysis any time you want to calculate the profit or how many units you must sell before you begin to make money.

There are some limitations to break-even analysis. These are as follows:

1. Break-even analysis shows profit at various levels of sales, but does not show profitability. Since there are always alternative uses for your firm's financial resources, it is impossible to compare products for profitability solely based

on break-even, whereas profitability should be one of the major points of consideration. For a profitability comparison, you must use one of the ratio analyses given to you earlier.

2. Break-even analysis does not allow you examination of cash flows, and it is generally accepted that the appropriate way to make investment or capital budgeting decisions is to consider the value of cash flows over a period of time and to discount this value using the cost of capital concept explained to you in Chapter 2. This cannot be done with break-even analysis, either.

CHECKLIST FOR PROFIT WATCHING

Financial management boils down to one major consideration: Are you making a profit or are you not? To assist you with this calculation, the SBA has published a checklist for profit watching, developed by Narendra C. Bhandari, associate professor of management, and Charles S. McCubbin, Jr., both of the University of Baltimore.[1] Use this checklist to be sure that you are doing everything possible to manage the financial resources of your firm effectively and efficiently.

Are You Making a Profit?

Analysis of Revenues and Expenses.   Since profit is revenues less expenses, to determine what your profit is you must first identify all revenues and expenses for the period under study.

	Yes	No

1. Have you chosen an appropriate period for profit determination?
For accounting purposes firms generally use a twelve-month period, such as January 1 to December 31 or July 1 to June 30. The accounting year you select doesn't have to be a calendar year (January to December); a seasonal business, for example, might close its year after the end of the season. The selection depends on the nature of your business, your personal preference, or possible tax considerations.

2. Have you determined your total revenues for the accounting period?
In order to answer this question, consider the following questions:
What is the amount of gross revenue from sales of your goods or service? **(Gross Sales)**
What is the amount of goods returned by your customers and credited? **(Returns and Rejects)**
What is the amount of discounts given to your customers and employees? **(Discounts)**
What is the amount of net sales from goods and services? **(Net Sales = Gross Sales − [Returns and Rejects + Discounts])**
What is the amount of income from other sources, such as interest on bank deposits, dividends from securities, rent on property leased to others? **(Nonoperating Income)**
What is the amount of total revenue? **(Total Revenue = Net Sales + Nonoperating Income)**

---

[1] Narendra C. Bhandari and Charles S. McCubbin, Jr., *Checklist to Profit Watching*, Small Business Administration (1980).

Yes   No
3. Do you know what your total expenses are?   —   —

Expenses are the cost of goods sold and services used in the process of selling goods or services. Some common expenses for all businesses are:

Cost of goods sold (Cost of Goods Sold = Beginning Inventory + Purchases − Ending Inventory)

Wages and salaries (don't forget to include your own—at the actual rate you'd have to pay someone else to do your job)

Rent

Utilities (electricity, gas, telephone, water, etc.)

Supplies (office, cleaning, and the like)

Delivery expenses

Insurance

Advertising and promotional costs

Maintenance and upkeep

Depreciation (here you need to make sure your depreciation policies are realistic and that all depreciable items are included)

Taxes and licenses

Interest

Bad debts

Professional assistance (accountant, attorney, etc.)

There are, of course, many other types of expenses, but the point is that *every* expense must be recorded and deducted from your revenues before you know what your profit is. Understanding your expenses is the first step toward controlling them and increasing your profit.

Financial Ratios

A **financial ratio** is an expression of the relationship between two items selected from the income statement or the balance sheet. Ratio analysis helps you to evaluate the weak and strong points in your financial and managerial performance.

4. Do you know your current ratio?   —   —

The **current ratio** (current assets divided by current debts) is a measure of the cash or near cash position (liquidity) of the firm. It tells you if you have enough cash to pay your firm's current creditors. The higher the ratio, the more liquid the firm's position is and, hence, the higher the credibility of the firm. Cash, receivables, marketable securities, and inventory are current assets. Naturally, you need to be realistic in valuing receivables and inventory for a true picture of your liquidity, since some debts may be uncollectible and some stock obsolete. Current liabilities are those which must be paid in one year.

5 Do you know your quick ratio?   —   —

Quick assets are current assets minus inventory. The **quick ratio** (or acid-test ratio) is found by dividing quick assets by current liabilities. The purpose, again, is to test the firm's ability to meet its current obligations. This test doesn't include inventory to make it a stiffer test of the company's liquidity. It tells you if the business could meet its current obligations with quickly convertible assets should sales revenues suddenly cease.

6. Do you know your total debt to net worth ratio?   —   —

This ratio (the result of total debt divided by net worth then multiplied by 100) is a measure of how the company can meet its total obligations from equity. The lower the ratio, the higher the proportion of equity relative to debt and the better the firm's credit rating will be.

Yes   No

7. Do you know your average collection period?

You find this ratio by dividing accounts receivable by daily credit sales. (Daily credit sales = annual credit sales divided by 360.) This ratio tells you the length of time it takes the firm to get its cash after making a sale on credit. The shorter this period the quicker the cash inflow is. A longer than normal period may mean overdue and uncollectible bills. If you extend credit for a specific period (say, 30 days), this ratio should be very close to the same number of days. If it's much longer than the established period, you may need to alter your credit policies. It's wise to develop an aging schedule to gauge the trend of collections and identify slow payers. Slow collections (without adequate financing charges) hurt your profit, since you could be doing something much more useful with your money, such as taking advantage of discounts on your own payables.

8. Do you know your ratio of net sales to total assets?

This ratio (net sales divided by total assets) measures the efficiency with which you are using your assets. A higher than normal ratio indicates that the firm is able to generate sales from its assets faster (and better) than the average concern.

9. Do you know your operating profit to net sales ratio?

This ratio (the result of dividing operating profit by net sales and multiplying by 100) is most often used to determine the profit position relative to sales. A higher than normal ratio indicates that your sales are good, that your expenses are low, or both. Interest income and interest expense should not be included in calculating this ratio.

10. Do you know your net profit to total assets ratio?

This ratio (found by multiplying by 100 the result of dividing net profit by total assets) is often called return on investment or ROI. It focuses on the profitability of the overall operation of the firm. Thus, it allows management to measure the effects of its policies on the firm's profitability. The ROI is the single most important measure of a firm's financial position. You might say it's the bottom line for the bottom line.

11. Do you know your net profit to net worth ratio?

This ratio is found by dividing net profit by net worth and multiplying the result by 100. It provides information on the productivity of the resources the owners have committed to the firm's operations.

All ratios measuring profitability can be computed either before or after taxes, depending on the purpose of the computations. Ratios have limitations. Since the information used to derive ratios is itself based on accounting rules and personal judgments, as well as facts, the ratios cannot be considered absolute indicators of a firm's financial position. Ratios are only one means of assessing the performance of the firm and must be considered in perspective with many other measures. They should be used as a point of departure for further analysis and not as an end in themselves.

Sufficiency of Profit

The following questions are designed to help you measure the adequacy of the profit your firm is making. Making a profit is only the first step; making enough profit to survive and *grow* is really what business is all about.

12. Have you compared your profit with your profit goals?

	Yes	No

13. Is it possible your goals are too high or too low? ___ ___

14. Have you compared your present profits (absolute and ratios) with the profits made in the last one to three years? ___ ___

15. Have you compared your profits (absolute and ratios) with profits made by similar firms in your line? ___ ___

A number of organizations publish financial ratios for various businesses, among them Dun & Bradstreet, Robert Morris Associates, the Accounting Corporation of America, NCR Corporation, and the Bank of America. Your own trade association may also publish such studies. Remember, these published ratios are only averages. You probably want to be better than average.

Trend of Profit

16. Have you analyzed the direction your profits have been taking? ___ ___

The preceding analyses, with all their merits, report on a firm only at a single time in the past. It is not possible to use these isolated moments to indicate the trend of your firm's performance. To do a trend analysis, performance indicators (absolute amounts or ratios) should be computed for several time periods (yearly for several years, for example) and the results laid out in columns side by side for easy comparison. You can then evaluate your performance, see the direction it's taking, and make initial forecasts of where it will go.

Mix of Profit

17. Does your firm sell more than one major product line or provide several distinct services? ___ ___

If it does, a separate profit and ratio analysis of each should be made:
To show the relative contribution by each product line or service;
To show the relative burden of expenses by each product or service;
To show which items are most profitable, which are less so, and which are losing money; and
To show which are slow- and fast-moving.

The profit and ratio analyses of each major item help you find out the strong and weak areas of your operations. They can help you to make profit-increasing decisions to drop a product line or service or to place particular emphasis behind one or another.

Records

Good records are essential. Without them a firm doesn't know where it's been, where it is, or where it's heading. Keeping records that are accurate, up-to-date, and easy to use is one of the most important functions of the owner-manager, his or her staff, and his or her outside counselors (lawyer, accountant, banker).

Basic Records

18. Do you have a general journal and/or special journals, such as one for cash receipts and disbursements? ___ ___

A general journal is the basic record of the firm. Every monetary event in the life of the firm is entered in the general journal or in one of the special journals.

Yes No

19. Do you prepare a sales report or analysis? — —
   (a) Do you have sales goals by product, department, and accounting
     period (month, quarter, year)? — —
   (b) Are your goals reasonable? — —
   (c) Are you meeting your goals? — —

If you aren't meeting your goals, try to list the likely reasons on a sheet of paper. Such a study might include areas such as general business climate, competition, pricing, advertising, sales promotion, credit policies, and the like. Once you've identified the apparent causes you can take steps to increase sales (and profits).

Buying and Inventory System

20. Do you have a buying and inventory system? — —
The buying and inventory systems are two critical areas of a firm's operation that can affect profitability.

21. Do you keep records on the quality, service, price, and promptness of delivery of your sources of supply? — —

22. Have you analyzed the advantages and disadvantages of:
   (a) Buying from suppliers? — —
   (b) Buying from a minimum number of suppliers? — —

23. Have you analyzed the advantages and disadvantages of buying through cooperatives or other such systems? — —

24. Do you know:
   (a) How long it usually takes to receive each order? — —
   (b) How much inventory cushion (usually called safety stock) to
   have so you can maintain normal sales while you wait for the order
   to arrive? — —

25. Have you ever suffered because you were out of stock? — —

26. Do you know the optimum order quantity for each item you need? — —

27. Do you (or can you) take advantage of quantity discounts for large size single purchases? — —

28. Do you know your costs of ordering inventory and carrying inventory? — —
The more frequently you buy (smaller quantities per order), the higher your average ordering costs (clerical costs, postage, telephone costs, etc.) will be, and the lower the average carrying costs (storage, loss through pilferage, obsolescence, etc.) will be. On the other hand, the larger the quantity per order, the lower the average ordering cost and the higher the carrying costs. A balance should be struck so that the minimum cost overall for ordering and carrying inventory can be achieved.

29. Do you keep records of inventory for each item? — —
These records should be kept current by making entries whenever items are added to or removed from inventory. Simple records on 3 × 5 or 5 × 7 cards can be used with each item being listed on a separate card. Proper records will show for each item: quantity in stock, quantity on order, date of order, slow- or fast-seller, and valuations (which are important for taxes and your own analyses).

Other Financial Records

30. Do you have an accounts payable ledger?   ___ ___

This ledger will show what, whom, and why you owe. Such records
should help you make your payments on schedule. Any expense not paid
on time could adversely affect your credit, but even more importantly such
records should help you take advantage of discounts which can help boost
your profits.

31. Do you have an accounts receivable ledger?   ___ ___

This ledger will show who owes money to your firm. It shows how much
is owed, how long it has been outstanding, and why the money is owed.
Overdue accounts could indicate that your credit granting policy needs to
be reviewed and that you may not be getting the cash into the firm quickly
enough to pay your own bills at the optimum time.

32. Do you have a cash receipts journal?   ___ ___

This journal records the cash received by source, day, and amount.

33. Do you have a cash payments journal?   ___ ___

This journal will be similar to the cash receipts journal but will show
cash paid out instead of cash received. The two cash journals can be combined,
if convenient.

34. Do you prepare an income (profit and loss or P & L) statement and
a balance sheet?   ___ ___

These are statements about the condition of your firm at a specific time
and show the income, expenses, assets, and liabilities of the firm. They are
absolutely essential.

35. Do you prepare a budget?   ___ ___

You could think of a budget as a "record in advance," projecting "future"
inflows and outflows for your business. A budget is usually prepared for a
single year, generally to correspond with the accounting year. It is then,
however, broken down into quarterly and monthly projections.

There are different kinds of budgets: cash, production, sales, etc. A cash
budget, for example, will show the estimate of sales and expenses for a
particular period of time. The cash budget forces the firm to think ahead
by estimating its income and expenses. Once reasonable projections are
made for every important product line or department, the owner-manager
has set targets for employees to meet for sales and expenses. You must plan
to ensure a profit. And you must prepare a budget to plan.

SOURCES OF ADDITIONAL INFORMATION

Accounting Handbook for Non-Accountants, by Clarence B. Nickerson, published by Cahners
Books International, Inc., 221 Columbus Avenue, Boston, MA 02116.

Finance for the Nonfinancial Manager, by Herbert T. Spiro, published by John Wiley & Sons, Inc.,
605 Third Avenue, New York, NY 10158.

Financial Handbook, edited by Jules I. Bogen, published by John Wiley & Sons, Inc., 605 Third
Avenue, New York, NY 10158.

Managerial Finance, 5th edition, by J. Fred Weston and Eugene F. Brigham, published by The
Dryden Press, Hinsdale, IL 60521.

Profit Strategies for Business, by Robert Rachlin, published by Marr Publications, P.O. Box 1421,
Radio City Station, New York, NY 10019.

7

Credit and Credit Collection

CREDIT IN TODAY'S ECONOMY

It is a fact of life in a modern economy that credit is necessary in most situations and for most businesses. This means that the basic problem is usually not whether or not to give credit, but how to manage the credit in such a fashion that the following objectives are achieved:

1. You have fewer dollars tied up in accounts receivable, allowing profitable application of these dollars in your business.
2. Your credit losses are minimized.
3. You have increased and maximized profits.
4. Your customers or clients will be encouraged to use your services or buy your goods.
5. Your company's investment in accounts receivable will be protected to the maximum extent possible.

CREDIT POLICY

To achieve the objectives outlined above, you must have a credit policy. This credit policy may be written down or not, but it must be communicated to your employees and your customers or clients. Cooke O'Neal, who is vice president of the National Association of Credit Management, notes the following factors that will influence your company's credit policy.

1. Nature and size of business
2. Overall business objectives
3. General policy of business
4. Product or service requirements
5. Channels of distribution
6. Classes of customers
7. Conditions of competition
8. Price of product or service
9. Expectations of customers

Your credit policy may be characterized by liberal extension of credit or strict extension of credit, liberal collection or strict collection, or your policy may fall somewhere between these two sets of extremes. You have to decide by weighing stimulation of sales on the one hand with failure to collect or exposure to a larger bad debt loss on the other. You must also consider the amounts in your accounts receivable and the working capital position of your business.

THE BASIC ELEMENTS OF YOUR CREDIT POLICY PROGRAM

The basic elements of your credit policy program are:

1. To whom credit will be extended
2. Credit terms
3. Problem detection
4. Collection procedures

To Whom Credit Will Be Extended

The extension of credit depends on several considerations, including personal judgment, investigation, credit applications, evaluation factors, the application evaluation, information verification, and applicant stability. Let's look at each in turn.

Personal Judgment.   Clearly, judgment plays an important part in determining whether you should grant credit or not, and many potential problems can be eliminated simply by exercising good judgment. For example, if an individual or a firm owes you a great deal of money and has been slow to pay in the past, or has not paid, it doesn't take any special insight to know that it is probably wise to refuse to give credit. If a firm or an individual appears low on cash, simply exercising good judgment may prevent a loss from bad debt. Remember that sales alone may not solve cash flow problems that you have in your business. In fact, building up sales but not collecting money may worsen your situation, since it drains time and resources that may profitably be used elsewhere. Therefore, when making a credit decision, consider your likelihood of getting paid. If the likelihood is small, don't grant credit.

Investigation.   Before making a decision on credit, you should get all of the facts. This means that for any sizable amount of credit you should do a thorough investigation. This will help protect you from an individual or a firm that really has no intention of paying at all, as well as those that are slow in paying. This may range from simply checking on a credit card number to be sure that the credit card has not been stolen and is still in force to a much more thorough probe involving the areas discussed in the following paragraphs.

Credit Applications.   Much information can be gained from a credit application, and for any sizable amount of credit an application such as those shown in Figures 7.1 and 7.2 should be required—and the information contained in it should be verified. In many cases, specific information may be required due to your situation, location, or industry. In that case the information shown in Figures 7.1 and 7.2 can be supplemented by the additional information needed.

DATE _____

NAME _____ AGE _____

ADDRESS _____ HOW LONG? _____

SINGLE _____

HOME PHONE _____ BUSINESS PHONE _____ MARRIED _____

DIVORCED _____

NUMBER OF DEPENDENTS _____

FORMER ADDRESS _____ HOW LONG? _____

EMPLOYER _____ PHONE NO. _____

ADDRESS _____ HOW LONG? _____

POSITION _____ MONTHLY INCOME _____ OTHER INCOME _____

PREVIOUS EMPLOYER _____ PHONE NO. _____

ADDRESS _____ HOW LONG? _____

BANK ACCOUNT (SAVINGS) _____ PHONE NO. _____

ADDRESS _____

BANK ACCOUNT (CHECKING) _____ PHONE NO. _____

ADDRESS _____

NAME OF SPOUSE _____ WHERE EMPLOYED? _____ MONTHLY INCOME _

DO YOU OWN AN AUTOMOBILE? ___ YEAR AND MODEL ___ WHEN PURCHASED

NEAREST RELATIVE WITH WHOM YOU ARE NOT LIVING _____

ADDRESS _____ RELATIONSHIP _____

REAL ESTATE OWNED (OTHER THAN HOME) _____

CREDIT REFERENCES

TYPE	REFERENCE	ADDRESS	MONTHLY PAYMENT	BALANCE OWED
HOME				
AUTOMOBILE				
CREDIT CARD				
CREDIT CARD				
OTHER				
OTHER				

IF GRANTED CREDIT, I AGREE TO PAY ALL BILLS IN ACCORDANCE WITH THE FOLLOWING TERMS:

_____

_____

SIGNED: _____

Figure 7.1. Personal credit application form

Evaluation Factors.   There are three basic factors to consider in evaluating a credit application. These are:

1. *The applicant's ability to pay.* This is based upon income and obligations.
2. *The applicant's willingness to pay.* This is determined from past credit history.
3. *The potential profitability of the account.* This is determined by your own analysis.

Remember that you will lose the cost of your product or the service if you do not collect on any account where credit is granted. When the cost is very high relative to the selling price, you must be particularly careful and assess such risk with great care.

COMPANY _____ PHONE NO. _____
ADDRESS _____
TYPES OF BUSINESS AND ORGANIZATION _____
_____
BANK _____ PHONE NO. _____
ADDRESS _____

TRADE REFERENCES

(Note: Do not use oil companies, credit cards, IBM, Xerox, or public utilities since these organizations will not confirm credit information.)

1. _____
_____

2. _____
_____

3. _____
_____

OWNERS AND/OR OFFICERS OF YOUR COMPANY

1. NAME _____ TITLE _____
2. NAME _____ TITLE _____
3. NAME _____ TITLE _____

PERSON TO BE CONTACTED WITH REGARD TO FINANCIAL COMMITMENTS

NAME _____ TITLE _____

It is understood that all purchases made during a given month are payable in thirty (30) days or no later than the end of the following month. Accounts not paid in accordance with these terms will be charged 13¾% monthly service charge equivalent to 20% annual interest.

DATE _____ AUTHORIZED SIGNATURE _____

AUTHORIZATION FOR BANK CREDIT INQUIRY

I hereby authorize _____ to disclose credit information to _____

for consideration of the establishment of trade credit.

NAME OF ACCOUNT _____ ACCOUNT NO. _____ AUTHORIZED SIGNATURE _
ESTIMATED MONTHLY CREDIT REQUIREMENTS _____
SALES TAX STATUS _____ TAXABLE _____ EXEMPT, RESALE PERMIT NO. _____
INDIVIDUALS IN YOUR COMPANY AUTHORIZED TO PLACE ORDERS

NAME _____ TITLE _____
NAME _____ TITLE _____
NAME _____ TITLE _____
NAME _____ TITLE _____
NAME _____ TITLE _____
NAME _____ TITLE _____

Figure 7.2. Business credit application form

Application Evaluation. In order to evaluate these factors, consider the following:

1. Amount of credit desired
2. The bank balances of the applicant
3. Current credit standing
4. Current income
5. Current position

6. Employment history
7. Job security
8. Other obligations, including loan payments, rent, and so forth
9. Personal assets
10. Time on the job

Applicant Stability. Whether you are dealing with an individual or a firm, the information contained on credit applications must be verified or it is worthless. You must be sure that it is current, that it is correct, and that it is complete and nothing has been left out. For individuals, places of employment, and other personal references regarding income, time on the job, and so forth can be verified fairly easily by a letter or telephone request. Bank references can be verified in the same manner, even though banks may be somewhat restrictive in the information they provide. However, they will usually confirm the existence of an account and give a broad, general range of the average balance. A bank may also indicate whether or not the account has been satisfactory. However, when checking out the facts concerning firms as opposed to individuals, other sources may be necessary. The following sources of credit information are useful for both firms and individuals depending upon the situation.

1. *Mercantile credit agencies.* These are agencies that are privately owned and operated. They collect, analyze, and evaluate credit information on business firms on a continuous basis. For a fee, they provide credit ratings based upon their observations. Perhaps the best known mercantile credit agency is Dun & Bradstreet. Dun & Bradstreet covers many fields and provides a reference book, credit reports, and other specific information to firms using its services. Information provided includes credit ratings, evaluation of financial strength, and other important credit information. Other mercantile agencies work in specialized areas; for example, the Lyon Furniture Mercantile Agency works the furniture industry, and the Jeweler's Board of Trade in that industry. In addition, the National Credit Office reports on several different trades including textiles, banking, metals, electronics, leather, furniture, paint, rubber, and chemicals.

2. *Credit bureaus.* Many credit bureaus are available for firms that need to check credit information on a frequent basis. Most local credit bureaus are affiliated with other national bureaus including the International Consumer Credit Association of the Associated Credit Bureaus of America. In this way, even if the individuals have moved into your area recently, frequently credit information is available on them. Credit bureaus will supply information including checks on newcomers in your area, written and telephone credit information on individuals, data on changes in customers' credit risk status, assistance in tracing customers who leave your area without providing forwarding information, and collection of poor risk accounts.

3. *Suppliers.* Suppliers in credit departments will frequently be willing to exchange information with you. This interchange can be extremely valuable to update your own records and warn you of situations where credit may negatively affect your business. You should also keep in touch with competitors and other firms that may be dealing with your customers. Frequently, an exchange of credit information can help out both sides, especially in a fluid situation where a customer's credit position may be changing rapidly.

4. *Department of Commerce.* The Department of Commerce will frequently provide assistance in checking out foreign firms that you may want to do business with. Check with the local office of the Department of Commerce which can be located under the heading "U.S. Government" in your telephone book.

CREDIT TERMS

The credit terms that you extend may have a significant effect on your sales as well as your profits. You should be familiar with the terms used in business sales contained in Figure 7.3. You should also consider the following points:

1. Insist on all or a portion of the money up front before you provide the goods or the services. In some industries this may not be possible. But you can always ask. If you have an extremely poor credit risk, it may be the only way to protect yourself from severe financial losses.

2. The use of credit cards is an excellent way to protect yourself, whether you are dealing with other firms or with individuals. Essentially, the credit card company, such as Visa or Master Card or others, grants the credit, and you get your money at once. The customer or client will have his credit needs met without your having to take any risk. Of course, you will pay a percentage of your sales for this service, and it is a factor you must consider. However, a lot of grief can be saved through the use of credit cards, and it is well worth taking the time to see if you can use them.

3. Remember that you are not obligated to grant credit. Therefore, never fool yourself into building up false sales when the chances of your getting paid are poor. If you're not going to get paid later on or if the time when you'll get paid is so far in the future that the sale is worthless to you, the only solution is to refuse credit.

4. Detecting problems must be an essential part of your credit and credit collection program. One way to do this is to calculate the average collection period. The average collection period is calculated by dividing your accounts receivable by the average daily credit sales. Let us say that your current outstanding accounts receivable are $10,000, and on the average your monthly credit sales are $3,000. First, you must calculate the average daily credit sales. This would be the monthly sales of $3,000 divided by 30 days or $100. Now, divide the accounts receivable of $10,000 by the average daily credit sales of $100. This equals the average collection period in days. In this example, we would have $10,000 divided by $100 equals 100 days. This means that on the average your customers are taking about 100 days to pay for their accounts. There is another way of calculating the average collection period using net credit sales which are determined by subtracting an estimated allowance for bad debts from your total annual sales.

Now that you have the average collection period for your accounts receivable, what do you do with it? You can make the following comparisons to determine whether or not a problem exists.

1. *Payment terms.* How does the average collection period compare with the terms of sale that you offer? If you reqeust payment within 100

Term	Explanation
3/10, 1/15, n/60	3 percent discount for first 10 days; 1 percent discount for 15 days; bill due net on 60th day.
M.O.M. (Middle of month)	Billing will be on the 15th of the month (middle of the month), including all purchases made since the middle of the previous month.
E.O.M. (End of month)	Bill at end of month, covering all credit purchases of that month.
C.W.O. or C.I.A. (Cash with order, or Cash in advance)	Orders received are not processed until advanced payment is received.
C.B.D. (Cash before delivery)	Merchandise may be prepared and packaged by the seller, but shipment is not made until payment is received.
C.O.D. (Cash on delivery)	Amount of bill will be collected upon delivery of goods.
S.D.—B.L. (Sight draft—Bill of lading)	A negotiable bill of lading, accompanied by the invoice and a sight draft drawn on the buyer, is forwarded by the seller to the customer's bank. The bill of lading is released by the bank to the customer only upon his honoring the draft.
2/10, n/30, *R.O.G. (Receipt of goods)	2 percent discount for 10 days; bill due net on 30th day—but both discount period and 30 days start from the date of receipt of the goods, not from the date of the sale.
2/10, n/30, M.O.M.	2 percent discount for 10 days; bill due net on 30th day—but both periods start from the 15th of the month following the sales date.
2/10, n/30, E.O.M.	2 percent discount for 10 days; bill due net on 30th day—but both periods start from the end of the month in which the sale was made.
8/10, E.O.M.	8 percent discount for 10 days; bill due net on 30th day—but both periods start from the end of the month following the sales date.

Sales date is the day that the shipment was made. It will generally be the same date shown on the invoice. In consumer credit, the sales date is the day the sale was made and may or may not coincide with the date of shipment.

* The owner–manager should keep in mind that 2/10, n/30 amounts to 36.5 percent in annual interest calculation:

$$\frac{2\%}{30 - 10} \times 365 = 36.5\%$$

Figure 7.3. Common business credit sales terms. [From Harvey C. Krentzman, *Managing for Profits*, Small Business Administration (1968).]

days and the average collection period is not greater than this, it indicates that your creditors are complying with your terms. If, on the other hand, the average collection period is greater than 100 days, they are not.

2. *Past history.* How does your current average collection period compare with that which you had in the past? Are things getting better or getting worse?

3. *Industry averages.* How does your average collection period compare with those of other companies in your industry? This will indicate whether your credit and collection policies are as effective as those of other companies and your competitors in your industry.

PROBLEM DETECTION

If the three preceding comparisons using your average collection period indicate that you do have a problem, your next step is to determine how *much* of a problem you have. This can be accomplished by comparing your actual receivables with a target level. Let us say that your terms of sale specify payment within 30 days, which compares with your industry average as well. This, then, would make a suitable target for your receivables. If your average daily credit sales are $100 as in the previous example, you could then calculate a target for your receivables by multiplying your average daily credit sales by the collection period of 30 days, in this case $100 times 30 days equals $3,000.

You would then compare this with your actual receivables. In the case above, actual receivables are $10,000. You then know that you have a problem that amounts to $10,000 minus $3,000 or $7,000.

The implication of problem detection is problem solving. That is, you take immediate action to reduce the collection period, the speed of conversion of your receivables to cash, to minimize the capital that you have tied up in accounts receivable and reduce the risk of uncollectible accounts.

COLLECTION PROCEDURES

The Fundamental Rule of Collection

The fundamental rule of collection is to minimize the time between the sale or performance of the service and the collection of the money. For example, Dr. Robert Kelley, a consultant and teacher, states in his book, *Consulting*, that a former graduate student of his conducted research having to do with the billing practices of professionals—doctors, dentists, and lawyers. This student found that professionals who request payment before the client leaves the office have 90 to 100% collection rates, and those who send monthly statements average 65% collection rates. Therefore, to increase your collection, minimize this time span.[1] Ask for the payment immediately after the services are performed or product sold.

Invoices

Invoice preparation is crucial to your collection procedures. Your invoices should be prepared promptly and accurately. Time is essential to eliminate one source of delay. Accuracy is necessary to eliminate another source: customer disputes with the information about which you have invoiced him or her. An invoice should clearly state the credit terms you have decided upon as described earlier.

[1] Robert E. Kelley, *Consulting*, Charles Scribner's Sons, New York (1981).

Statements

Statements keep customers advised of their account balances, and monthly statements should be submitted to all creditors with open accounts. The statement should summarize the amount owed previously as well as any additional activity in the account during the month. Figure 7.4 shows a properly prepared invoice, and Figure 7.5, a statement.

Delinquency Charges

In some types of businesses, delinquency charges are applied against late payments in order to discourage customers from allowing their accounts to become overdue. This normally involves a finance or service charge of between 1 and 1½% per month on all balances more than 30 days past due. However, in recent times of high inflation, many companies have raised these percentages.

Lateness Follow-Up

When your customers or clients do not pay, you should initiate a follow-up immediately. The longer an account becomes dated, the less the chance of a collection. Never be afraid to initiate these follow-up actions. Some people are

---

XYZ Manufacturing Company
1200 N. Applewood Drive, Fairview, CA 90076
Telephone: (805)789-6781

Terms: 2% discount for payment in 10 days. Total amount due in 30 days. There is a finance charge for amounts outstanding at 30 days or more of 1.5% per month (annual rate 18%).

Package No.	Quantity	Description	Unit Price	Total Price

Figure 7.4. Invoice.

XYZ Manufacturing Company
1200 N. Applewood Drive, Fairview, CA 90076
Telephone: (805)789-6781

Previous Charges and Credits

Balance from previous bill	$189.00	
Payments applied as of this date	100.00	
Balance	$ 89.00	$ 89.00

Current Charges and Credits

P.O. No. 1876 1000 envelopes	$ 55.00	
P.O. No. 1891 1000 business cards	15.00	
Current Charges	$ 70.00	$ 70.00
Total amount due		$159.00

TERMS: 2% discount for payment in 10 days. Total amount of current charges due in 30 days. There is a finance charge for amounts outstanding at 30 days or more of 1.5% per month (annual rate 18%).

Figure 7.5. Statement.

afraid to do so because they feel that a strict follow-up is a harassment of their customers and will hurt their business. Again, remember that you have no business without payment, and a good customer is not a good customer unless he or she actually pays for what was received. Some individuals are also afraid of pursuing a rigid collection policy for fear that this will hurt their reputation. It is highly unlikely that an individual who owes you money will want to advertise the fact that he hasn't been paying his bills.

A standard follow-up procedure for lateness in paying overdue or past-due accounts is generally a good idea. Such a policy makes it easier to implement the action required in an expeditious manner.

A typical follow-up procedure will be a telephone call, a letter or series of letters, or some combination of these two instruments, usually with the letters coming first.

Collection Letters

An initial collection letter should be used when the account becomes approximately 15 days past due. At this time, the account is not considered seriously delinquent; therefore the tone of the letter, while firm, should be moderate. If this letter is unsuccessful, a second letter should be sent approximately one month later. If this letter is unsuccessful as well, a third and stronger letter should be sent.

Figures 7.6–7.8 show an initial collection letter, a second collection letter, and a third collection letter. Note how the tone grows progressively stronger. The implication of action of a more serious nature is introduced as the letters progress. The exact wording that you use depends on the situation in which you find yourself, including your relationship with this particular customer, your industry, and so forth. But the basics are clear. Send the letters as indicated

---

Dear _____ :

We know that it is probably an oversight, but the amount of $400 owed us for consulting services performed for your company is overdue. Please send us your check immediately so we can update our records and mark you "paid in full . . . credit good."

Sincerely,

_____

Senior Partner

Figure 7.6. Initial collection letter.

Dear _____ :

Unfortunately, our Senior Partner, _____ , tells me that your account is in arrears in the amount of $400 for consulting services performed for your firm and also that a previous letter was sent to you pointing out this fact.

We would like to maintain you as a client and for you to maintain your good standing. However, your past-due bill must be paid immediately or further action will be taken in accordance with our policy.

Sincerely,

_____

President

Figure 7.7. Follow-up collection letter.

Dear _____ :

This is the final notice we intend to send you before initiating legal action. Your account is in arrears $400 for consulting services performed for your company. If this amount is not received within ten days to clear your account, we intend to initiate proceedings to recover this amount.

Sincerely,

_____

President

Figure 7.8. Second follow-up collection letter.

15 days after the account becomes due, and then at intervals of 30 days. A standard format can be adopted that will greatly reduce the time you spend doing this.

Use of the Telephone

The telephone can be used either with the letters or by itself. It can be even more persuasive since you will get immediate feedback and can respond directly to the information given by the individual. However, the basic methodology is the same, and if you make more than one call, each call should be firmer than the last. The disadvantages of a telephone call are that it consumes your time and that it is a direct confrontation and can sometimes be tricky.

If you use the telephone technique, you should again attempt to find out what the problem is. If the entire amount cannot be paid, find out how much can be paid over a reasonable period and how soon the initial payment of the amount can be expected.

Again, your telephone call should indicate to the creditor that you are aware that the payment has not been made, and that you do not intend that the creditor will get away with nonpayment.

External Collection Procedures

There are two external collection procedures that are available to you should the letter or telephone calls fail. These are collection agencies and courts of law.

Collection Agencies.   Collection agencies will collect past due accounts receivable for you. The advantages they offer are their experience, knowledge of persuasive collection techniques, and the additional emphasis that an outside agency gives to the collection procedure. While at first glance this may appear an easy way to take care of your problems, you should be aware of the fact that collection agencies usually will insist upon 25 to 50% of the amount that they succeed in collecting. Further, once you agree to work with a collection agency, you must make this percentage payment fee whether the debt is collected by you or through the agency.

Courts of Law.   A court of law is the final recourse for collection. If the amount is small enough, you may be able to go through a small claims court which, except for your time, will cost you nothing. However, for large amounts, you will have to sue for collection. This will take considerable money as well as time. Before making such a decision, you should consider both your chances of collection and the cost in time and money. Check with your attorney on this.

Credit Insurance

Credit insurance is available, but it is available only to manufacturers and wholesalers that sell to other business firms. This is because it is difficult to analyze the risk involved in selling to ultimate consumers, and because a retailer's need for credit insurance is not as great since the retailer's risk is spread among a greater number of customers. It is possible to insure some specific business accounts rather than getting general coverage. This is desirable since higher percentages of coinsurance are required for accounts that are considered to be high risk in order to discourage reckless credit by firms that are insured. Accounts are usually classified according to rating by Dun & Bradstreet or similar agencies, and the premiums will vary depending upon the account ratings assigned by these firms. For export accounts, credit insurance is available from the Foreign Credit Insurance Association. Check with your local Department of Commerce office.

Use of a Factor

If you are using the services of a factor, you can avoid maintaining credit and collection systems. This is because a factor establishes a working procedure for clearing credit for new customers and setting up credit limits for old customers, and for collecting accounts receivable; then the factor buys the accounts receivable outright from you. Naturally, this is going to cost you something, so once again, you must consider the costs as well as the benefits.

CREDIT AND COLLECTION POLICIES CHECKLIST[2]

The establishment of credit and collection policies which work well for your firm can be a major factor in your business's profitability and survivability. But, like any procedure, they must be reevaluated periodically in order to determine their effectiveness. To assist you in reviewing your current policies or in formulating new policies, the following credit and collection policies checklist is provided.

	Yes	No	Not Applicable
Credit Approval			
Is a written application required with every credit request?	—	—	—
Do you have a standard form for credit applications?	—	—	—
Is it completed personally by the applicant?	—	—	—
Is it reviewed for completeness?	—	—	—
Is all information verified for accuracy and timeliness?	—	—	—
Are applicants checked out with a credit bureau?	—	—	—
Does your evaluation consider income?	—	—	—
Does your evaluation consider fixed obligations?	—	—	—
Does your evaluation consider job stability?	—	—	—
Does your evaluation consider residential stability?	—	—	—
Does your evaluation consider credit history?	—	—	—
Does your evaluation consider bank balances?	—	—	—
Does your evaluation consider other assets?	—	—	—
Invoices			
Are invoices prepared promptly?	—	—	—
Is invoice preparation always accurate?	—	—	—
Are payment terms clearly stated?	—	—	—
Are customers' special instructions followed carefully?	—	—	—
Terms of Sale	—	—	—
Do you offer a cash discount?	—	—	—
Do you use a late payment penalty?	—	—	—
Is the time limit for payment clearly stated?	—	—	—
Statements	—	—	—
Are monthly statements submitted to all open accounts?	—	—	—
Are statements prompt and accurate?	—	—	—
Problems of Identification	—	—	—
Do you determine your average collection period on a regular basis?	—	—	—
Do you compare your collection period with industry averages?	—	—	—

[2] Developed by the U.S. Small Business Administration, author unknown.

	Yes	No	Not Applicable
Do you compare your current collection period with your previous experience?	—	—	—
Do you compare your collection period with your payment terms?	—	—	—
Do you have a monthly aging of all outstanding accounts?	—	—	—
When a problem is identified, is corrective action prompt and firm?	—	—	—

Follow-Up

	Yes	No	Not Applicable
Do you have a systematic procedure for follow-up on slow accounts?	—	—	—
Is there a standard sequence of follow-up letters?	—	—	—
Is the tone of these letters progressively stronger?	—	—	—
Do you use the telephone to contact delinquent accounts?	—	—	—
Is your telephone technique effective?	—	—	—
Do you offer special arrangements for collecting past-due accounts?	—	—	—
Do you have a late-payment penalty?	—	—	—
Do you put delinquent accounts on a C.O.D. basis?	—	—	—

External Resources

	Yes	No	Not Applicable
Do you have a working relationship with a collection agency?	—	—	—
Are accounts turned over automatically after a specific time period?	—	—	—
Do you refer the most serious delinquencies to an attorney?	—	—	—

SOURCES OF ADDITIONAL INFORMATION

Credit and Credit Collection for Small Business, by Donald R. Kitzing, published by AMACOM, a division of the American Management Association, 135 W. 50th Street, New York, NY 10020.

Credit Management Handbook, edited by William B. Abbott *et al.,* published by Credit Research Foundation, 3000 Marcus Avenue, Lake Success, NY 11040.

Credits and Collections: Management and Theory, 8th edition, by Theodore N. Beckman and Ronald S. Foster, published by McGraw-Hill Book Co., 1221 Avenue of the Americas, New York, NY 10020.

The Dun & Bradstreet Handbook of Credit and Collections, by Harold T. Redding and Guyon H. Knight III, published by Thomas Y. Crowell Co., 666 Fifth Avenue, New York, NY 10003.

Using Credit to Sell More, by Donald E. Miller, published by the National Association of Credit Management, 475 Park Avenue South, New York, NY 10016.

8

Record Keeping

WHY RECORDS ARE VITAL

Records are crucial to the success of your business. Even if you are successful initially, it is unlikely that you will be able to sustain this success without good records, since you will not know what is making your business successful. You need records to ensure that your business is profitable, and they should be kept from the very first day that you open your doors until such time as you sell your business to someone else or retire from it. Good records and record keeping are needed to make future plans for your company and to evolve strategies that will enable your business to grow rapidly and be successful in the future as well as to survive in the present. Without such records, your competition will eventually evolve strategies that you cannot counter since you will not know your position in the market or what is going wrong. Unfortunately, despite its importance, many small businesspeople use the shoebox approach to record keeping. That is, the only record of a sale or a purchase they make is a piece of paper tossed in a shoebox. At the end of the year, someone attempts to analyze the contents of the box. This isn't record keeping. It cannot enable a business to respond successfully to the day-to-day demands, problems, and opportunities that appear.

This chapter will help you avoid the shoebox approach and show you methods you can use not only to survive but also to make your business highly profitable. That these methods are made available to you does not mean that you shouldn't use the services of a good accountant. On the contrary, a good accountant can save you much additional money. A combination of using the methods described in this chapter and consulting an expert accountant will save you thousands and thousands of dollars throughout your business career, and may very well make the difference between mere survival and tremendous growth and success in your small business.

BASIC REQUIREMENTS

The basic requirements for your record-keeping system are four:

1. Your record system must be simple to use and to understand. If it's not simple to use, it will take much time and trouble to keep it updated, and if it is not easy to understand, you will waste time as will your accountant trying to figure it out. Since time is money, make sure your system is comprehensible.

2. Your record-keeping system should be accurate and relevant. "Accurate" means free of errors and conforming to whatever standards you have set for your record-keeping system. "Relevant" means pertinent to your business; be sure you are not wasting time recording information that you do not need.

3. Your record-keeping system should be consistent throughout. This means that whatever standard and structure you decide on should be adhered to throughout the system. This is not to say that if you find deficiencies in what you are doing you cannot change them. But it does mean that you should deviate from your standard methods only for good reasons and should maintain only one method of doing things.

4. Your system should ensure that records are kept in a timely fashion. This means that you must keep them current. If you do not, you will not be able to use this information effectively.

THE FOUR BASIC RECORDS REQUIRED

Just as there are four basic requirements, there are four basic records that are required for any good small business record-keeping system. These are:

1. Sales records
2. Cash receipts
3. Cash disbursements
4. Accounts receivable

Let's look at each in turn.

Sales Records

Sales records should be subdivided into convenient categories so that you can analyze them more easily later on. For example, you may subdivide your sales records into wholesale and retail sales, or you may subdivide them by geographic areas or by some other market segmentation.

Cash Receipts

Cash receipts represent cash actually received in the form of sales as well as collection of accounts receivable from monies formerly owed to you.

Cash Disbursements

Cash disbursements are monies paid out by you for your business. In general, you should pay by check except for small items which you can pay out of a petty cash fund. In keeping track of cash disbursements, always list the date, the check number, the amount, and the purpose for which the disbursement was made. Also, you may break the heading into different categories, such as office supplies, advertising, rent, utilities, and so forth.

The petty cash fund is set up simply by drawing a check for a certain amount, say, $50. The check is cashed and logged under the general heading of checks for the petty cash fund. The money is then placed in some convenient location so that you can use it easily as required. As payments are made for small items such as postage, bus fares, small amounts of supplies, and so forth, each item is listed on a special form that again lists the date of expenditure, the amount, and the purpose for which the money was spent. When the fund is nearly spent, the items are summarized and a check is drawn to cover the exact amount. In this way, when the new check is cashed, the fund is replenished. Doing this also means that at all times the cash that you have on hand in the petty cash fund, plus listed expenditures, will equal the amount of the fund.

Accounts Receivable

Accounts receivable are monies owed to you for services or goods supplied for which you have not yet been paid. To control the accounts receivable, be sure that all bills are sent when goods are shipped or services rendered and that they are mailed to correct addresses. Be especially careful of the larger accounts in your accounts receivable ledger. At the end of every month, you will age your accounts receivable. This means that you list accounts and enter amounts that are current, those unpaid for 30 days, and those unpaid for 60 days and longer. For those that are unpaid for 60 days or longer, you must find out exactly why these accounts are unpaid. In this way your system will help you in account control and collection. You should also pay attention to customer complaints about bills that you have sent. If you feel the complaint is justified, perhaps you should negotiate and propose a special adjustment or in some other way reach agreement with your customer. Do not delay in doing this. If the customer has not paid and is delinquent in his or her payment, then try to get a promise of payment on a specific date. If the payment is not received by that date, then you should again contact the customer and ask the customer to explain why, and obtain a new promise if necessary. If funds are still not forthcoming, many states have provisions for a small claims court for which a lawyer is not required and through which it is fairly easy to take a delinquent to task for nonpayment. You may try other means of intimidating the customer and getting him or her to pay, depending on the situation, the size of the account, future business anticipated with the same customer despite slowness in payment, whether you feel that you will ultimately be paid, and various other factors.

You should establish a definite figure below which you will not bother going after monies owed. Let us say you have decided that this figure is $10, and so you ask twice for the amount from the individual owing this to you and then you drop it. You do this because the trouble and time spent collecting are worth more than this amount. On the other hand, if letting one customer get away with nonpayment may lead others to expect they can do the same thing, then maybe even a small account will have to be gone after. Large accounts, of course, should be pursued vigorously to obtain payment.

Sometimes a new customer whom you do not know asks for credit. In this case, have your customer complete a simple form such as that shown in Figure 8.1, which lists the name, address, telephone number, place of employment, and bank and credit references of the individual who would like this credit. Make sure that the credit is warranted before you grant it, especially with larger amounts. Obviously, if the customer is an old customer of yours and has not paid his bill promptly, then you should think twice before granting credit or require a substantial amount up front.

Name			
Address		Years at this address _____	
Place of employment		Years at this employment _____	
Telephone			

	Name	Address	Telephone

Bank references

	Name	Address	Telephone

Credit references

Former employment

Figure 8.1. Sample credit form.

GENERAL RULES FOR KEEPING TRACK OF YOUR FINANCES AND YOUR BOOKKEEPING SYSTEM

Here are some general rules you should always follow no matter what system you adopt.

Always pay your business bills by check or through your petty cash fund. Never make disbursements out of your daily cash receipts.

Be certain that all incoming cash is recorded along with amounts, where the money came from, and the dates.

Never take money out of your daily cash receipts for your personal use, but instead, pay yourself a salary.

Use a business bank account for all your business funds and deposit all cash receipts in the account day by day as you receive them. Do not use your personal bank account for your business bank account, and keep your personal cash separate from cash generated from the business.

Periodically have your record-keeping system checked over by a certified public accountant (CPA).

SHOULD YOU USE CASH OR ACCRUAL BASIS FOR RECORDS?

Many small businesses will use a simple cash basis for bookkeeping. Which basis is used will depend on whether or not credit is granted to customers and the amount of inventory that is required. For example, if you are selling hamburgers, probably a credit system is not required, nor is inventory extensive. In this situation, you would probably use a cash basis for your records. On the other hand, with credit granted to customers and a more extensive inventory, the accrual basis would probably be better. With the accrual basis, each item is entered as earned or as the expense is incurred without regard to when the actual payments are made or received. This means that sales that are made on credit are written down at once in your books as sales and also in your accounts receivable records. At such time as the bills are actually collected, then your accounts receivable records are adjusted. Accruals are also made for expense items that are payable at times in the future. An example is yearly or periodic interest rates on loans. These accruals are made by entries explained later in this chapter.

WHICH METHOD OF DEPRECIATION SHOULD YOU ADOPT?

Depreciation is an expense of the business just as are rent, utilities, and salaries. Therefore, a charge to expenses should be made to cover depreciation of fixed assets other than land, which does not depreciate. Fixed assets may be defined as items that are normally in use for one year or longer. These may include buildings, equipment, tools, furniture, and other similar items. Most small businesses charge depreciation at the end of their fiscal year. However, if you have very substantial fixed assets such as a motel or hotel, you may want to calculate depreciation on a monthly basis. There are two basic methods of depreciation that you may use: (1) straight line depreciation and (2) the declining balance method of depreciation.

Straight Line Depreciation

Straight line depreciation is based on the expected life of the items for book purposes. Therefore, it is first necessary to estimate the total life of the item being depreciated. Let us say that you own a new building. A reasonable period of depreciation for a building is 20 years. This means that to depreciate the building 100%, you would depreciate it 5% a year. Other assets may have shorter periods of depreciation. Machinery may have an estimated life of 5 years. In this case, the item should be depreciated at 20% per year. An example of depreciations in a depreciation chart using the straight line method is shown in Figure 8.2.

Item	Date Purchased	Cost	Estimated Life	Yearly Depreciation	Accumulated Prior Depreciation	This Year's Depreciation	Total Accumulated Depreciation
Office	Jan. 1990	$100,000	20 years	5%	$25,000	$5,000	$30,000
Automobile	Jan. 1992	$10,000	5 years	20%	$6,000	$2,000	$8,000
Printing press	Mar. 1992	$5,000	10 years	10%	$1,416.67	$500	$1,916.67
Computer	July 1993	$2,000	4 years	25%	$750	$500	$1,250

Figure 8.2. Sample form for depreciation of assets using straight line method (year 1985). Note 1: To find yearly depreciation divide the estimated life into 1.0. Example: Estimated life = 20 years. 1.0/20 = 5%. Note 2: If purchase date is other than January, first year depreciation will be less than the full amount. Example: Purchase in March, 1982 (therefore, only 10 months depreciation in 1982). To adjust, if yearly depreciation is $500, then depreciation in 1982 would be 10/12 × $500 = $416.67

Declining Balance Method of Depreciation

The declining balance method of depreciation is used whenever quicker recovery of the investment is desirable. Using this method, your asset is depreciated by a certain percentage of the balance each year. However, if you use the declining balance method for tax-paying purposes, the IRS will not allow the rate of depreciation using the declining balance method to be greater than double the straight line rate of depreciation. This means that if yearly depreciation using the straight line method is computed at 5%, the asset would be depreciated at an annual rate of 10% using the declining balance method. If the yearly depreciation was 20%, then, using the declining balance method, 40% would be the figure. The difference in using the declining balance method is that the yearly depreciation is taken not of the total cost of the asset but rather of the remaining value.

A comparison of the two methods is shown in Table 8.1. Note that using the declining balance method, the remaining value approach never reaches zero. In the example, in both cases the asset cost $1,000 and the estimated year life is 5 years. This means that yearly depreciation using the straight line method is 20%, or, using the declining balance method, 40% of the remaining value of each year. The total depreciation after 5 years using the straight line method is $1,000, but since in the declining balance method it never will quite reach $1,000 and the remaining value will approach but will never equal zero, in this case it actually equals $922.24. In order to allow for this, the small businessperson should switch to the straight line depreciation method near the end of the asset's useful life. Therefore, in the example shown (the fourth and fifth year of life depreciating at $86.40 and $51.84, respectively), the $216 remaining value in the fourth year should be split up to $108 each, and therefore at the end of the period the depreciation would be $1,000 instead of the $922.24 shown.

The declining balance method permits the businessperson to take a heavy depreciation in the early years of the equipment's life. This is very desirable when the asset has a high rate of obsolescence and its market value accordingly decreases very rapidly.

Up to now, we've assumed the salvage of any equipment to be zero. However, this is usually not the case. That is, at the end of the depreciable period, the

Table 8.1 Depreciation: Declining Balance Method versus Straight Line Method

Asset cost = $1,000   Estimated life = 5 years
Yearly depreciation (straight line) = 1/5 = 20%
Yearly depreciation (declining balance) = 40% of remaining value each year

Year	Straight Line Depreciation	Declining Balance Remaining Value	Declining Balance Depreciation
1	(20% × $1,000) = $ 200	$1,000	(40% × $1,000) = $400
2	(20% × $1,000) = $ 200	$ 600	(40% × $ 600) = $240
3	(20% × $1,000) = $ 200	$ 360	(40% × $ 340) = $144
4	(20% × $1,000) = $ 200	$ 216	(40% × $ 216) = $ 86.40
5	(20% × $1,000) = $ 200	$ 129.60	(40% × $ 129.60) = $ 51.84
	$1,000		$922.24

equipment is probably worth something either for resale, trade-in, or scrap. This salvage value should be estimated at the time that the estimated life figure is established. This scrap or salvage value is then subtracted from the original cost of the equipment to give the amount to be depreciated over the estimated life. For example, if the automobile shown in Figure 8.2 had a salvage value of $5,000 after the 5-year period of estimated life, then only $5,000 should be depreciated rather than the $10,000 shown in the figure. If you fail to use a salvage value in your depreciation calculations, then this amount is recoverable by the IRS at such time as you do receive money for trade-in, scrap, or salvage.

WHICH BOOKKEEPING SYSTEM SHOULD YOU ADOPT?

Specialized bookkeeping systems are available for almost every business and industry. In order to see what is available in your area of interest, you should contact the trade organization that serves your business. You may also check with stationery and office supply stores. Usually either a general bookkeeping system or even one designed especially for your business will be available. The Small Business Administration has compiled a list of bookkeeping systems in two categories: systems designed for use in any retail or service establishment and systems designed for use in specific retail and service trades. This list will be found at the end of this chapter, along with a description of each system. You can also use the forms provided in Figures 1.2 to 1.6

THE NEED FOR GENERAL BOOKS AND JOURNALS

In addition to the basic records I've already discussed, you will need books for different journal entries. These are called general books. General entries of this type are used to record business transactions that do not involve cash. Examples would be accruals for depreciation and expenses that are due in the future.

Another book you should keep is called the general ledger. The general ledger is kept to record balances of assets, liabilities, and capital, and to accumulate sales and expense items. At the end of each fiscal year, your accounts are balanced and closed. Sales and expense account balances are transferred to the profit and loss account. The remaining asset, liability, and capital accounts provide the figures for the balance sheet. We will discuss this shortly. A typical classification of accounts for the general ledger follows:

1. Assets
2. Cash in banks
3. Petty cash fund
4. Accounts receivable
5. Materials and supplies
6. Prepaid expenses
7. Deposits
8. Land
9. Buildings
10. Tools and equipment
11. Automotive equipment

12. Furniture and fixtures
13. Reserve for depreciation (The reserve for depreciation is subtracted from the asset account. Technically this is known as a "credit" against the asset account.)
14. Liabilities
15. Accounts payable
16. Notes payable
17. Sales tax payable
18. FICA taxes payable
19. Federal withholding taxes
20. State withholding taxes
21. Unemployment taxes
22. Long-term debt and mortgages payable
23. Long-term debt SBA loan
24. Miscellaneous accruals
25. Capital accounts
26. Common capital stock
27. Preferred capital stock (for corporations only)
28. Proprietorship accounts (for a proprietorship)
29. Proprietorship withdrawals (for a proprietorship)
30. Retained earnings
31. Sales accounts
32. Retail sales
33. Wholesale sales
34. Sales services
35. Miscellaneous income
36. Expenses
37. Salaries and wages
38. Contract labor
39. Payroll taxes
40. Utilities
41. Telephone
42. Rent
43. Office supplies
44. Postage
45. Maintenance expense
46. Insurance
47. Interest
48. Depreciation
49. Travel expense
50. Entertainment
51. Advertising
52. Dues and contributions
53. Auto expense

54. Contributions
55. Electricity
56. Heat
57. Trade dues

Do not use too many different accounts. Tailor the accounts you use to your particular business. Sales should be broken down in a sufficient number of categories to provide a clear indication of your business. Different expense accounts should be used depending on the frequency of the individual expenses. Miscellaneous expenses are used for small unrelated expense items.

OTHER IMPORTANT RECORDS

Several other important records should be maintained by your business. These include an equipment list, insurance records, and payroll records.

Equipment List

An equipment list consists of all the permanent equipment used in the business. Don't bother keeping track of the small items, but do keep track of any item that is useful for a period of a year or longer and has some appreciable value to it. On your list you should show date purchased, the name of the supplier, description of the item, the number of the check with which the equipment was paid for, and the amount. This list is very useful for calculating depreciation as described earlier, as well as for reorder information, insurance preparation, and business functions.

Insurance Records

Insurance records are an absolute must. See Chapter 3 concerning business insurance for more details.

Payroll Records

Use Figure 1.5 to assist you in preparing payroll records. Yearly and quarterly reports of individual payroll payments must be made to state and federal governments. You must supply each individual employee a W-2 Form at the year's end showing total withholding payments made for the employee during that calendar year. A special employment card should be kept for each individual employee showing the individual's Social Security number, as well as name, address, telephone number, name of next of kin, and current address. Also on the form you should indicate whether the employee is married and the number of exemptions claimed. In this same file a W-4 Form should be on record which is completed earlier by the employee, as explained earlier in this book. A summary payroll should also be maintained showing the names, employee numbers, the rate of pay, hours worked, overtime hours if any, total pay, and the amount of deductions for FICA, withholding taxes, and deductions for insurance, pension, and/or savings plan. Use Figure 1.5 to maintain the records on individual employees, including rate of pay, Social Security number, and other information previously described. Enter the amounts for each pay period covering hours worked, gross pay, and the various deductions. At the end of each quarter, add up the amounts and the balance. These forms provide the needed information for quarterly and annual reports.

PREPARATION OF FINANCIAL STATEMENTS

There are two basic financial statements that you must either prepare yourself or have an accountant prepare. These statements are most important. One study showed that less than 7% of a group of failed businesses prepared these statements. These statements are (1) the balance sheet and (2) income statement. Both forms are prepared using the records that you've already accumulated.

The Balance Sheet

The balance sheet records the condition of your company at a single point in time. Therefore, the information contained on it is true on one specific date and on one specific date only. It is prepared usually at the close of the last day of the month and it answers the question: How does your company stand financially at this point in time? The balance sheet has two main sections. One section shows the assets, and the other shows the liabilities and owner's equity, which together represent claims against the assets. On the balance sheet, the total assets always equal the combined total of the liabilities and the owner's equity. It is from this fact that this particular financial statement gets its name.

A sample balance sheet is shown in Figure 8.3. Note that the assets are grouped into various subsections. These include current assets, long-term assets, fixed assets, and other assets. Current assets are cash and resources that can be converted into cash within 12 months of the date of the balance sheet. These include cash which is both money on hand and deposits in the bank, accounts receivable, inventory, temporary investments expected to be converted into cash within a year, and prepaid expenses. Long-term assets, which are also called long-term investments, are holdings that the business intends to keep for a year or longer, and typically yield interest for dividends including stocks, bonds, and savings accounts of a special type that are not to be touched for a term greater than a year. Fixed assets include the plant and equipment. These are the resources a business owns or acquires and uses in its operations, and are not intended for resale. Finally, we have other assets. These are resources that are not listed in any of the above categories. These include intangibles such as outdated equipment that is salable for scrap and trademarks or patents.

Now let's look at the liability section. Current liabilities are debts and obligations that are payable within 12 months. Typically they include accounts payable (amounts owed to suppliers for goods and services rendered in connection with business), notes payable (the balance of the principal due to pay off short-term debts for borrowed funds), interest payable, taxes payable, the current portion of long-term notes that are payable, and payroll (salaries and wages currently owed). Long-term liabilities are those notes for other liabilities due over a period exceeding 12 months. The amount listed is the outstanding balance less the current portion which is shown under current liabilities. Equity, which is also called net worth, is the claim of the owners on the assets of the business.

Income Statement		For the year ended December 31, 19 _____
Sales or revenue:		$1,040,000.00
Less returns and allowances		5,000.00
Net sales		$1,035,000.00
Cost of sales:		
Beginning inventory, Jan. 1, 19 __		250,000.00
Merchandise purchases	500,000.00	
Cost of goods available for sale		750,000.00
Less ending inventory, Dec. 31, 19 __		225,000.00
Total cost of goods sold		525,000.00
Gross profit		$ 510,000.00
Operating expenses:		
Selling and general and administrative		
Salaries and wages		180,000.00
Advertising		200,000.00
Rent		10,000.00
Utilities		5,000.00
Other expenses		10,000.00
Total operating expenses		405,000.00
Total operating income		$ 105,000.00
Other revenue and expenses		0
Pretax income:		$ 105,000.00
Taxes on income		50,000.00
Income after taxes but before extraordinary		
gain or loss		$ 55,000.00
Extraordinary gain or loss		0
Net income (or loss)		$ 55,000.00

Figure 8.3. Sample balance sheet for the XYZ Company

In a proprietorship or partnership, equity is each of the owners' original investment plus any earnings after withdrawal. Of course, in a corporation, the owners are the shareholders. The corporation's equity is the sum of the contributions plus earnings retained after paying dividends. The breakdown of equity includes capital stock, which is the total amount invested in the business in exchange for shares of stock, and retained earnings, which are the total accumulated net income less the total accumulated dividends declared since the corporation's founding. As noted earlier, the sum of the liabilities and equity must equal that of the assets. Note how this is true in Figure 8.3.

The Income Statement

The income statement, also known as the profit and loss statement, measures costs and expenses against sales revenues over a definite period of time, such as a month or a year, to show the net profit or loss of the business for the entire period covered by the statement. A sample income statement is shown in Figure 8.4. The first entry is sales or revenue. This is all the income coming into a business for services rendered or for goods sold. In addition to actual cash

Balance Sheet   December 31, 19 _____

Current assets:
  Cash $ 35,000.00
  Accounts receivable   55,000.00
  Inventory   60,000.00
  Temporary investments   3,000.00
  Prepaid expenses   2,000.00
    Total current assets $155,000.00
Long-term assets:
  Bonds $ 10,000.00
  Stocks   10,000.00
                                                                                                   $ 20,000.00
Fixed assets:
  Machinery and equipment $ 35,000.00
  Buildings   42,000.00
  Land   20,000.00
    Total fixed assets $ 97,000.00
Other assets:
  None   0
    Total other assets $272,000.00

Current liabilities:
  Accounts payable $ 36,000.00
  Notes payable   44,000.00
  Current portion of long-term notes   4,000.00
  Interest payable   1,000.00
  Taxes payable   3,000.00
  Accrued payroll   2,000.00
    Total current liabilities $ 90,000.00
Long-term liabilities:
  Notes payable $ 67,000.00
    Total long-term liabilities $ 67,000.00
Equity:
  Owner's equity $115,000.00
    Total equity $115,000.00
Total liabilities and equity $272,000.00

Figure 8.4.   Sample income statement for the XYZ Company

transactions, it reflects the amounts due from customers on accounts receivable, as well as equivalent cash values for merchandise or other tangible items if used as a payment. From this figure is subtracted the value of returned merchandise and allowances made for defective goods. The result is net sales. The next major column is cost of sales. Cost of sales equals the total amount of goods available less the inventory remaining at the end of the accounting period for which the income statement is constructed. Generally, service businesses such as a medical practice or a consultancy have no cost of sales. From the foregoing, the gross profit or gross margin is calculated. It is the difference between the cost of goods sold and the net sales. It is the business's profit before expenses and before taxes.

Operating expenses are the expenses of doing business. They generally fall into two major categories: (1) selling and (2) general and administrative expenses. Selling may include such things as salaries and wages, commissions, advertising, depreciation, and so forth. General and administrative expenses include salaries and wages of owners or senior managers, employee benefits, insurance, depreciation, and similar items.

The total operating expenses just calculated are now subtracted from the gross margin to show what the business earned before financial revenue and expenses, taxes, and extraordinary items.

Other revenue and expenses are income and expenses that are not generated by usual operations of the business. Typical items in this category are interest from investments and various financial expenses.

Total financial revenue less the expenses is now added to the total operating income. The result is pretax income. Taxes are then subtracted to develop income after taxes but before extraordinary items.

Extraordinary items are listed separately on the income statement. These are occurrences that are extremely unusual, cannot be foreseen, and are not generally expected to recur that generate either an income or a loss. Damage due to a storm or an earthquake, for example, might be considered an extraordinary loss. Adding in this final item results in the net income or net loss for the period of the income statement.

The balance sheet and the income statement are extremely important tools for you as a small businessperson. They are intended to represent a true and fair picture of the condition of your company for the period that they represent. However, because they are drawn up under conditions of uncertainty and some transactions are not complete at the time they are prepared, they should be used with caution and the judgment of both yourself and your accountant who may prepare them. You should bear this in mind when you use some of the financial tools presented in Chapter 6.

SMALL BUSINESS FINANCIAL STATUS CHECKLIST

The following is a checklist of what every owner/manager should know on a daily, weekly, and monthly basis. It was developed by John Cotton, a retired utility executive in Albuquerque, New Mexico.[1]

Daily

1. Cash on hand.
2. Bank balance (keep business and personal funds separate).
3. Daily summary of sales and cash receipts (see attached).
4. That all errors in recording collections on accounts are corrected.
5. That a record of all monies paid out, by cash or check, is maintained.

Weekly

1. Accounts receivable (take action on slow payers).
2. Accounts payable (take advantage of discounts).
3. Payroll (records should include name and address of employee, Social Security number, number of exemptions, date ending the pay period, hours worked, rate of pay, total wages, deductions, net pay, check number).

[1] John Cotton. *Keeping Records in Small Business.* The Small Business Administration (1976).

4. Taxes and reports to state and federal government (sales, withholding, Social Security, etc.).

Monthly

1. That all journal entries are classified according to like elements (these should be generally accepted and standardized for both income and expense) and posted to General Ledger.

2. That a profit and loss statement for the month is available within a reasonable time, usually 10 to 15 days following the close of the month. This shows the income of the business for the month, the expense incurred in obtaining the income, and the profit or loss resulting. From this, take action to eliminate loss (adjust mark-up? reduce overhead expense? pilferage? incorrect tax reporting? incorrect buying procedures? failure to take advantage of cash discounts?).

3. That a balance sheet accompanies the profit and loss statement. This shows assets (what the business has), liabilities (what the business owes), and the investment of the owner.

4. That the bank statement is reconciled. (That is, the owner's books are in agreement with the bank's record of the cash balance.)

5. That the petty cash account is in balance. (The actual cash in the petty cash box plus the total of the paid-out slips that have not been charged to expense total the amount set aside as petty cash.)

6. That all federal tax deposits, withheld income and FICA taxes (Form 501) and state taxes are made.

7. That accounts receivable are aged, i.e., 30, 60, 90 days, etc., past due. (Work all bad and slow accounts.)

8. That inventory control is worked to remove dead stock and order new stock. (What moves slowly? Reduce. What moves fast? Increase.)

SPECIALIZED RECORD-KEEPING SYSTEMS

Here is the list of specialized record-keeping systems compiled by staff members of the Office of Management Information and Training:

I. Systems Designed for Use in Any Retail or Service Establishment

Most of the record-keeping systems listed below are available from local stationery stores. If a particular system is not available from your local retail store, you may contact the publisher at the address given with each entry.

Blackbourn's General Business Bookkeeping System. Blackbourn Systems, Inc., 1821 University Ave., St. Paul, Minn. 55104. Provides for accounting inventory and personal records in quick, easy entries. Lists merchandise payments, record of sales and receipts on one side of the book, and operating expenses on the opposite page. Shows monthly record of sales; monthly balance sheets, showing cash on hand, amounts owed and due. Other sections include Accounts Payable, complete with discount columns: Inventory Sheets; Employee Social Security and Income Tax Records; Sales Record by Departments; Notes Receivable and Payable; Depreciation Schedule. Includes a list of suggested allowable tax deductions.

BINEX Automated Business Systems. 3102 "O" St., Sacramento, Calif. 95816. A complete computer-based report system able to provide an income statement, balance sheet, cash flow analysis, vendor analysis, and a variety of other information. BINEX also produces W-2 forms, provides the data for federal and state employment taxes, sales taxes, and provides a complete employee payroll history. Other systems include a customer follow-up for service station owners, a complete accounts receivable system, and address label system, and other analytic programs. Local BINEX users or franchises can assist with a complete business service. Because the family of computer programs is so complete and flexible, BINEX is able to provide to the small business owner the exact information desired at a price the business owner can afford.

Dome Simplified Monthly Bookkeeping Record, #612; Dome Simplified Weekly Bookkeeping Record #600. Dome Publishing Company, Dome Building, Providence, R.I. 02903. Available in stationery stores and chain stores. Contains the following forms sufficient for recording the results of one year's business: monthly record of income and expenses; annual summary sheet of income and expenditures; weekly payroll records covering 15 employees; individual employee compensation records. Also contains general instructions, specimen filled-in monthly record of income and expenses and list of 276 expenses which are "legal deductions" for federal income tax purposes. This record was designed by a CPA and fits every type and kind of business.

General Business System. General Business Services, Inc. 51 Monroe Street, Rockville, Md. 20850. Locally authorized business counselors provide complete, easy-to-maintain, preprinted manual, one-write or computerized record-keeping systems; custom designed for sole proprietors, partnerships, and corporations including a monthly profit and loss statement and proof of accuracy, meeting requirements of Internal Revenue Service. Service includes: review and analysis of particular record-keeping requirements; furnishing a complete set of records; personal instructions on use and maintenance of records; analysis of records and financial statements with guidance throughout the year; preparation of federal and state income tax returns, both business and personal, with guarantee of accuracy by professional staff at national office; tax advisory service by tax specialists for research and answers to income tax questions; monthly tax bulletin with money-saving ideas; and supplementary services by local business counselors as required. Also offers on an optional basis accounts receivable, computerized monthly billings, collection system for delinquent accounts, and tax preparation service for employed individuals.

Greenwood's Approved Business and Income Tax Record. The Greenwood Company, 712 South Federal St., Chicago, Ill. 60605. Contains the following forms: daily record of cash payments for month; monthly totals; yearly balance sheet; yearly profit and loss statements. Also includes filled-in specimen sheets. Individual and weekly payroll records are also available. Write for samples.

Ideal System: General Bookkeeping and Tax Record #3611. Dymo Visual Systems, Inc., P.O. Box 1568, Augusta, Ga. 30903. Designed for every type of business primarily offering a service (as opposed to merchandise). Examples would be acting, advertising, clubs, associations, and fraternal organizations.

Ideal System: Merchants Bookkeeping and Tax Record #3021. Dymo Visual Systems, Inc., P.O. Box 1568, Augusta, Ga. 30903. Designed for any retailer or wholesaler, for anyone buying at one price and reselling at another.

Ideal System: Weekly Bookkeeping and Tax Record #M-2025. Dymo Visual Systems, Inc., P.O. Box 1568, Augusta, Ga. 30903. For every business, profession, trade, farm, or ranch. Can be started any time. Pages for sample entries plus 52 sheets for weekly entries.

Ideal System: Payroll Record 1 to 25 Employees #M 1812; Payroll Record 1 to 50 Employees #M 2812. Dymo Visual Systems, Inc., P.O. Box 1568, Augusta, Ga. 30903. Both books provide one sheet for each employee. Column headings for both hourly-wage and salaried employees, all taxes and other withholdings.

Ideal System: Payroll Record #5812. Dymo Visual Systems, Inc., P.O. Box 1568, Augusta, Ga. 30903. For use with any bookkeeping system. Sheets for 50 employees. Can be expanded with additional sheets.

Ideal System: Double Entry Combined Journal #5831. Dymo Visual Systems, Inc., P.O. Box 1568, Augusta, Ga. 30903. This simplified journal ledger, used in conjunction with general ledger, provides for distribution of sales, cash, purchases, disbursements, and journal entries.

Ideal System: Double Entry General Ledger #5836. Dymo Visual Systems, Inc., P.O. Box 1568, Augusta, Ga. 30903. Used in conjunction with Combined Journal, provides all necessary records for any business, trade, profession, farm, or ranch.

Ideal System: Inventory Management System #5900. Dymo Visual Systems, Inc., P.O. Box 1568, Augusta, Ga. 30903. Shows at a glance your inventory position by item, what to order and when, its value, prime and alternate supplier.

Kolor-Key.   Moore Business Forms, Inc., P. O. Box 5252, Eastmont Station, Oakland, Calif. 94605. May be ordered through local Moore Business Forms representatives. System includes basic business forms (sales slip, invoice, statement, voucher check, purchase order, daily cash control, duplicate deposit slip); instructions for preparations and filing of forms; record-keeping aids. The system is adaptable to a wide range of businesses and can be easily modified as the business grows and forms need change.

Modern Merchant Simplified Bookkeeping.   The Johnson Systems, 828 North Broadway, Milwaukee, Wis. 53202. Contains the following forms sufficient for recording the results of two years' business: daily sales; expenses.

Practical Bookkeeping for the Small Business.   Henry Regnery Company, 180 North Michigan Ave., Chicago, Ill. Every aspect of business bookkeeping is presented and explained in detail: basic accounting reasoning and terms; the entire bookkeeping cycle, from the initial entry to closing the books; the correct uses of checking accounts and petty cash; making out payrolls, providing for deductions, and maintaining necessary payroll records; the IRS-approved cash-basis and accrual-basis bookkeeping methods; and how to figure state sales tax. Summary problems coordinate chapter information to facilitate complete understanding of this simple and accurate bookkeeping system.

Safeguard Business Systems, Inc.   Eric R. Haymen, General Market Mgr., 470 Maryland Drive, Fort Washington, Pa. 19034. Offers a number of one-write systems designed to save time and assist the small business owner with record-keeping activities. Systems are installed and serviced by local representatives. Also available are computerized financial reports through the business owner's accountant. All services and products are detailed in the "Business Systems Reference Manual," free on request.

Simplified Master System.   Simplified Business Services, Inc., 233 East Lancaster Avenue, Ardmore, Pa. 19003. Includes personalized business consultation services and preparation of federal and state income tax returns, also business advisory and tax questioning and answering service. Available through authorized local distributors or directly from the company. Monthly financial statements prepared and forwarded by mail for businesses wishing such services. Contains the following forms sufficient for record keeping: current business expenses; total employee weekly salaries; cash withdrawn for personal use by the owners or partners; daily cash receipts; summary of current business expenses; payments for notes, fixtures, and equipment; summary of monthly cash payments; payments for merchandise on everything bought to resell; summary of daily sales including charge sales; worksheets; income tax information sheet; balance sheet and statement of net worth on a comparative basis; monthly and accumulated profit and loss statements; stock and bond records; record of sales of business real estate or personal property; record of income from estates; record of real estate and property expenses and income; personal deduction records; real estate mortgage records; equipment and property inventory and depreciation records; inventory; notes payable; notes receivable; insurance records. Available in different editions for individuals, partnerships, and corporations. Includes (in addition to both forms and services) a business advisory service; business bulletins and instructions; business improvement ideas; management techniques and ideas and instructions on their use. See individual business listings on following pages for availability of special systems.

Marcoin—Busco Division—Business Management Services. MARCOIN, Inc., 1924 Cliff Valley Way, N.E., Atlanta, Ga. 30329, phone: 404-325-1200. MARCOIN "Daily Record System" with user's guide. One year supply of daily sheets with ring binders. National organization provides local and personal business counseling service. Trained counselors design and install a tailored record-keeping system to fit individual business needs. At owner's option, all federal, state and local taxes are prepared by competent MARCOIN representatives for the client. The basic management service includes a *monthly* departmentalized operating (profit) statement, financial statement and written analysis of each month's operation. In addition, MARCOIN'S Professional Counselor representatives each month discuss client's own business, review problems, and offer suggestions to improve operations, sales income, employee performance, and profits.

Whitehill Systems—Division of Small Business Advisors, Inc., 48 West 48th St., New York, N.Y. 10036, phone: 212-869-9642. A nationwide organization devoted to counseling small and medium size businesses with emphasis on record-keeping systems, computerized programs, and tax service. The programs include complete, easy to maintain, preprinted manual, one-write or computerized record-keeping system, custom designed to provide a monthly profit and loss statement and proof of accuracy, meeting requirements of the Internal Revenue Service. Locally authorized business counselors review and analyze record-keeping requirements; furnish a complete set of records; provide personal instructions on use and maintenance of records; analyze records and financial statements; provide guidance throughout the year. Federal and state income tax returns are prepared with a guarantee of accuracy by professional staff at the national office. Tax specialists in national office provide tax advisory service and answer income tax questions, publish a monthly tax bulletin including up-to-date tax information and money-saving ideas.

II. Systems Designed for Use in Specific Retail and Service Trades

Companies listed under this heading offer services for use in specific retail and service trades. Some of these systems are provided by trade associations. For example, see "Appliance Dealers." When an entry lacks a listing, such as General Business System, Safeguard Business Systems, Inc., and others, the listing can be found under Part I, Systems Designed for Use in Any Retail or Service Establishment.

Appliance Dealers

NARDA Simplified Bookkeeping System Instructions for Dealer Participants. National Appliance & Radio–TV Dealers Assn., 2 North Riverside Plaza, Chicago, Ill. 60606. To get started in the program, dealer must supply the beginning balances of each balance sheet account as of the date to begin the program. If dealer is starting up at any time other than the beginning of fiscal year, the beginning balances of all profit and loss statement accounts must be supplied. From then on, the dealer will record information in the four journals used as source documents for this program. These are: cash receipts journal, sales journal, purchase journal, and cash disbursements journal. Program also includes a manual containing step-by-step directions with illustrated entries. A revised fee for participating in the program is .002 of the dealer's monthly volume if a member of the association. Nonmembers are charged an additional 25 percent per month.

General Business System for Appliance Dealers.

Safeguard Business Systems, Inc. for Appliance Dealers.

Automobile Dealers

General Business System for Automobile Dealers.

Barber Shops

BINEX Automated Business Systems for Barber Shops.

Dome Simplified Weekly Bookkeeping Record #600; Dome Simplified Monthly Bookkeeping Record #612.

General Business System for Barber Shops.

Ideal System: Barber Shop Bookkeeping and Tax Record.

Modern Merchant Simplified Bookkeeping for Barber Shops.

Bars and Restaurants

Easy Bookkeeping Tax Systems: Bars and Restaurants.   Eric J. Engelhardt. Hampton Management Inc., P.O. Box 224, Greenville, N.Y. 11548. An elementary bookkeeping system which stresses daily and monthly analyses and business controls with the goal of increased profits through better business management. It is a do-it-yourself business kit, containing the following business forms and tax records: daily income and expenses; daily checks issued; summary of monthly income and expenses; the investment in fixtures, equipment, furniture; insurance, business and personal; ready-made financial reports, such as balance sheets and profit-and-loss statements; loan and note records; payroll book and record; personal tax deduction elementary tax guide, and ready-made envelopes to Internal Revenue Service; Social Security information; illustrated sample worksheets; monthly inventory controls; capital gains and investments; gross-profit chart; schedule of interest and dividend income; schedule of assets and depreciation records; personal instructions; preparation of federal and state tax returns with guarantee of accuracy—all of the above meeting the requirements of Internal Revenue Service.

Dome Simplified Weekly Bookkeeping Record #600; Simplified Monthly Bookkeeping Record #612.

General Business System for Bars and Restaurants.

Ideal Systems Tavern and Cafe Bookkeeping and Tax Record.

Modern Merchant Simplified Bookkeeping for Bars and Restaurants.

Safeguard Business Systems, Inc. for Bars and Restaurants.

Beauty Salons

Beautician Simplified Bookkeeping. The Johnson Systems, 828 North Broadway, Milwaukee, Wis. 53202. The Johnson Systems are simplified journals, designed especially for the small business owner. Easy to keep, the journal enables the business owner to prepare and to maintain accounting records, and prepare monthly balance sheet and profit and loss statements. It is also an approved U.S. federal and state income tax record and assists in the preparation of all quarterly and annual tax returns.

Dome Simplified Weekly Bookkeeping Record #600; Dome Simplified Monthly Bookkeeping Record #612.

Easy Bookkeeping Tax System for Beauty Salons. (See Bars and Restaurants.)

General Business System for Beauty Salons.

Ideal System: Beauty Shops.

Modern Merchant Simplified Bookkeeping for Beauty Salons.

NHCA Simplified Weekly Business Record. Dome Publishing Company, Inc., The Dome Bldg. Providence, R.I. 02903. Design for National Hairdressers and Cosmetologists Assoc., Inc., 3510 Olive St., St. Louis, MO 63103.

Safeguard Business Systems, Inc. for Beauty Salons.

Simplified Master System—Beauty Shop. Simplified Business Services, Inc.

Building Contractors

BINEX Automated Business Systems for Building Contractors. In addition to complete control of the financial statements listed in the general section, BINEX provides a report that allows a contractor to manage the sequence of expenses in a building project. Budgeted amounts can be compared with actual expenses as the project proceeds to help keep the costs under control. The job-cost program can be the difference between profit and loss on a project.

General Business System for Building Contractors.

Safeguard Business Systems, Inc. for Building Contractors.

Simplified Master System—Contractor. Simplified Business Services, Inc.

Practical Accounting and Cost Keeping for Contractors. Frank R. Walker Co., 5030 North Harlem Ave., Chicago, Ill. 60656. 7th ed. 1975. Includes estimating, job organization, time-keeping and cost-keeping methods, bookkeeping and accounting, Social Security records, etc.

Practical Bookkeeping Accounting Systems for Contractors. Frank R. Walker Co., 5030 North Harlem Ave., Chicago, Ill. 60656. Send for complete illustrated catalog with prices. A complete line of bookkeeping and accounting systems for contractors; also time sheets, payroll forms, estimate sheets, cost systems, etc.

Blackbourn Systems for Contractors' Job Analysis Pad No. 257; Job Cost Pad No. 155.

Credit Control and Billing System

American Billing Corp. National Headquarters, 4014 North 7th St., Phoenix, Az. 85014. A simple four-step third-party system for controlling accounts receivable, that is effective and easy to run. The ABC System is a time saver which increases cash flow, helps maintain business-like relations with credit clientele, increases efficiency in billing and credit operations, and is completely controlled by each user at point of use with no communications gaps or time delays. Low price of the system consistently produces a very low, cost/effective ratio, and it can be obtained in carbon sets for typing or in continuous format for computerized operations. The system is applicable wherever credit is extended, in both retail and wholesale establishments. It is being successfully used in animal hospitals, appliance stores, automobile dealers, auto parts dealers, camera stores, caterers, cleaners, clinics, clothing stores, contractors, dairies, dentists, doctors, employment agencies, floor covering stores, florists, fuel oil dealers, funeral homes, furniture stores, garages, glass shops, hardware stores, home improvement shops, hospitals, hotels, interior decorators, laundries, lawyers, lumber and building supply companies, newspapers, plumbers, printers, service stations, tool rental shops, TV sales and service, sporting goods shops, universities, upholsterers, veterinarians, and wholesalers.

Safeguard Business Systems, Inc. for Credit Control and Billing.

Credit Control and Receivable Billing System

American Accounting Credit Control Systems, Inc. (Western office) 1055 East Tropicana Ave., Las Vegas, Nev. 89109 (702) 736-6660. AACC is a completely self-contained credit control system which places direct control to the member. *A time saving method that* will apply overall efficiency to credit operation. The system recovers and increases cash flow while maintaining customer relations, using the *third-party intervention method* which gives the businessperson an effective system to properly extend credit, billing and follow-up procedure, generates prompt payment of accounts receivable. Includes a collection system proven throughout the collection industry without excessive commissions or charges. Letter forms are provided on an unlimited basis to members throughout the year. American Accounting guarantees the system. This fully tax deductible system is designed for every type of business in existence today. Among members are doctors, dentists, vets, chiropractors, plumbers, electricians, printers, drug stores, appliance stores, TV repair-sales, builder-contractors, hardware, florists, auto repair, service stations, carpet and drapery stores, photography studios, groceries, hotel-motels, and furniture stores. Mail inquiries for Eastern and Central time zones should go to P.O. Box 17149, Nashville, Tenn. All states in the Mountain and Pacific time zones should forward mail to P.O. Box 11311, Las Vegas, Nev. 89111.

Dairy Farm

General Business System for Dairy Farm.

Johnson Systems, The. 828 North Broadway, Milwaukee, Wis. All necessary records for two years' business.

Safeguard Business Systems, Inc. for Dairy Farm.

Simplified Master System for Dairy Farm. Simplified Business Services, Inc.

Drugstores

Easy Bookkeeping Tax System for Drug Stores. (See Bars and Restaurants.)

General Business System for Drug Stores.

Safeguard Business Systems, Inc. for Drug Stores.

Blackbourn Systems for Drug Stores (No. 170P).

Dry Cleaners, Tailors and Dyers

Easy Bookkeeping Tax System: Cleaners and Dyers. For general information see entry under Bars and Restaurants.

General Master Systems: Dry Cleaner or Tailor.

Simplified Master System for Dry Cleaner or Tailor. Simplified Business Services, Inc.

Farm and Ranch

Blackbourn Systems for Farmers and Ranchers (No. 715X).

Easy Bookkeeping Tax System: Farm and Ranch. For general information, see entry under Bars and Restaurants.

Johnson Systems for Farm and Ranch. See entry under Beauty Salons.

Safeguard Business Systems, Inc. for Farm and Ranch.

Florists

Guide to the FTDA Uniform Accounting System. Florists' Transworld Delivery Association, 29200 Northwestern Hwy., P.O. Box 2227, Southfield, Mich. 48037. A guide to simplified record keeping with sample forms. Available to members only.

Dome Simplified Weekly Bookkeeping Record #600; Dome Simplified Monthly Bookkeeping Record #612.

Easy Bookkeeping Tax System for Florists. See entry under Bars and Restaurants.

General Business System for Florists.

Safeguard Business Systems, Inc. for Florists.

Funeral Director

General Business System for Funeral Director.

Safeguard Business Systems, Inc. for Funeral Director.

Simplified Master Systems: Funeral Director. Simplified Business Services, Inc.

Furniture Stores

NRFA Uniform Accounting System. National Home Furnishings Association, 405 Merchandise Mart, Chicago, Ill. 60654. Contains the following forms sufficient for recording the results of one year's business: cash disbursements journal; cash receipts and sales journal; general journal; special analysis forms designed for specific secondary records. Also a "Guide to the System," containing step-by-step directions, with illustrated entries.

Safeguard Business Systems, Inc. for Furniture Stores.

Garage or Auto Repair

Dome Simplified Weekly Bookkeeping Record #600; Dome Simplified Monthly Bookkeeping Record #612.

General Business System for Garage or Auto Repair.

Safeguard Business Systems, Inc. for Garage or Auto Repair.

Simplified Master Systems: Garage or Auto Repair.   Simplified Business Services.

Gift Shops

General Business Systems for Gift Shops.

Safeguard Business Systems, Inc. for Gift Shops.

Grocery and Meat Stores

Blackbourn Systems for Grocery and Market Bookkeeping. No. 160X; No. 160P.

General Business Systems for Grocery and Meat Stores.

Modern Merchant Simplified Bookkeeping.   The Johnson Systems, 828 North Broadway, Milwaukee, Wis. 53202. Contains forms sufficient for recording results of two years' business.

Safeguard Business Systems, Inc. for Grocery and Meat Stores.

Hardware Stores

Blackbourn Systems for Hardlines Bookkeeping. No. 130P.

General Business System for Hardware Stores.

NRHA. Better Business Records.   National Retail Hardware Association, 964 North Pennsylvania St., Indianapolis, Ind. 46204. Price list available from Association; sale confined to members of state or national associations. Contains the following forms: daily record: expense distribution—cost of doing business; invoice and margin register, monthly and annual summary; profit-and-loss and financial statements; profit planning for business control forms. Also available: duplicate customers' ledger system and ledger sheets; sales books; envelopes; receipt books; order books; etc.; and *How to Keep Books without Being a Bookkeeper,* an instruction manual covering recommended accounting system for retail hardware stores.

NRHA Departmental Accounting System.   National Retail Hardware Association, 964 North Pennsylvania St., Indianapolis, Ind. 46204. Price list available from Association. Sale confined to members of state or national associations. Contains the following: system setup for eight departments: daily record; expense distribution; invoice and accounts payable record; monthly summary; monthly estimated profit and loss; year-end profit and loss and financial statements; profit planning and control sheets; instruction manual—*How to Keep Books Departmentally*—instruction manual on departmental system.

Safeguard Business Systems, Inc. for Hardware Stores.

Hotels

Blackbourn Systems for Hotel Guest Register, No. 703X. Hotel Guest Register No. 703P.

Simplified Master Systems for Hotels. Simplified Business Services, Inc.

Uniform System of Accounts for Hotels. Hotel Association of New York City, Inc., 141 West 51st St., New York, N.Y. 10019. 1977. A 128-page book containing the basic information required in establishing an accounting system in any hotel, large or small. The book contains a format for preparing a balance sheet and profit and loss statement and detailed explanations for recording financial transactions within the framework of these statements. Using the system will enable a hotel's operation to be compared with one of a similar size also using the system.

Jewelers and Watchmakers

General Business Systems for Jewelers and Watchmakers.

Safeguard Business Systems, Inc. for Jewelers and Watchmakers.

Modern Merchant Simplified Bookkeeping for Jewelers and Watchmakers.

Laundries

Easy Bookkeeping Tax System for Dry Cleaning and Coin-Op Laundries.

General Business System for Laundries.

Safeguard Business Systems, Inc. for Laundries.

Liquor Package Stores

Blackbourn Bookkeeping Systems for Liquor Store No. 91P.

General Business System for Liquor Package Stores.

Safeguard Business Systems, Inc. for Liquor Package Stores.

Simplified Master Systems. Simplified Business Services, Inc.

Men's Clothing and Furnishing

Inventory System: Store Supply Catalog pp. 72–107. National Clothier Corp., 1727 W. Devon, Chicago, Ill. 60660. 1977. Contains monitor stock status with systems designed for specific items; controls various departments with the aid of systems and publications covering different aspects of retail operations; financial and accounting procedures compiled by the financial and operations group of MRA and presented in manual form; operating experiences collected from nationwide sources and presented in annual business survey.

General Business System for Men's Clothing and Furnishing Stores.

Safeguard Business Systems, Inc. for Men's Clothing and Furnishing Stores.

Motels and Motor Hotels

An Account Book for Small Tourist and Resort Businesses. No. R-604. Robert W. McIntosh, 1953. 48 pp. Michigan State University, Tourist and Resort Service. A simplified account book for the use of motel operators. Instructions for use included. This book may be obtained from the Bulletin Office, P.O. Box 231, East Lansing, Mich. 48824.

Blackbourn Motel and Resort Bookkeeping No. 450P.

General Business Systems for Motels and Motor Hotels.

Safeguard Business Systems, Inc. for Motels and Motor Hotels.

Simplified Master Systems—Motels. Simplified Business Services, Inc.

Music Stores

NAMM Standard Accounting Manual for Music Stores. National Association of Music Merchants, Inc., 35 East Wacker Dr., Chicago, Ill. 60601. The aim of this manual is flexibility. The owner-manager may choose the accounts needed; use whichever forms desired; prepare reports and statements as often and as detailed as desired, and adopt segments of this system when convenient. Contains the following illustrations: general ledger; cash receipts journal; cash disbursements journal; accounts receivable ledger; accounts payable ledger; payroll journal; sales journal; purchase journal; property and equipment ledger; insurance register; general journal; and "railroaded" general ledger accounts.

General Business System for Music Stores.

Safeguard Business Systems, Inc. for Music Stores.

Nursing Homes

Blackbourn Nursing Homes and Hospitals. Book No. 270X.

Safeguard Business Systems, Inc. for Nursing Homes.

Simplified Master Systems—Nursing Homes. Simplified Business Services, Inc.

General Business System for Nursing Homes.

Office Supply and Stationery Stores

General Business System for Office Supply and Stationery Stores.

Safeguard Business Systems, Inc. for Office Supply and Stationery Stores.

Pest Control

Uniform Accounting Manual for Pest Control. National Pest Control Association. 8150 Leesburg Pike, Vienna, Va. 22180. 1965. 32 pp. Complete with chart of accounts, descriptions of the accounts by four size classifications.

Basic Bookkeeping System for Pest Control. National Pest Control Association, 8150 Leesburg Pike, Vienna, Va. 22180. 316 8½ × 11 preprinted looseleaf pages including income sheets, expense sheets, payroll records, general journal sheets, and profit and loss statements. Designed for the small firm (1–5 employees).

General Business System for Pest Control.

Safeguard Business Systems, Inc. for Pest Control.

Real Estate Business

BINEX Automated Business System. BINEX provides a report which can be used by a realtor to control rental properties which the realtor handles for others. This report tracks expenses, revenues, and computes the payment due the owner.

Blackbourn Real Estate Bookkeeping. No. 100X.

General Business System for Real Estate Business.

Ideal System: Real Estate Business Bookkeeping and Tax Record #3311. Dymo Visual Systems, Inc., P.O. Box 1568, Augusta, Ga. 30903. Designed for agents and brokers with special columns for sales, sales commission, rental commission, insurance commission, etc.

Income Property. The Johnson Systems, 828 North Broadway, Milwaukee, Wis. 53202. Contains the following forms sufficient for recording the results of two years' business: tenants' records; disbursements and expenses.

Safeguard Business Systems, Inc. for Real Estate Business.

Resorts and Tourist Business

Account Book for Small Tourist and Resort Business. See listing under Motels and Motor Hotels.

Blackbourn Motel and Resort Bookkeeping. No. 450P.

General Business System for Resorts and Tourist Business.

Safeguard Business Systems, Inc. for Resorts and Tourist Business.

Restaurants and Taverns (see also Bars and Restaurants)

Cafe and Restaurant Record. The Greenwood Company, 712 South Federal St., Chicago, Ill. 60605. Contains the following forms: daily purchase and expenses for months; record of daily sales; record of daily cash receipts; record of daily payments.

Restaurant Simplified Bookkeeping. The Johnson Systems, 828 North Broadway, Milwaukee, Wis. 53202. Contains the following forms sufficient for recording the results of two years' business: daily sales; daily food purchases; general overhead expense.

Simplified Master Systems—Restaurants. Simplified Business Services, Inc.

Tavern and Buffet Record. The Greenwood Company, 712 South Federal St., Chicago, Ill. 60605. Form 70A. Contains the following forms: daily purchases and expenses for month; record of daily sales; record of daily cash receipts; record of daily payments.

Uniform Systems of Accounts for Restaurants. National Restaurant Association. One IBM Plaza, Suite 2600, Chicago, Ill. 60611. A manual containing a system for all classifications of restaurants with detailed explanation of accounts and procedures.

Retail Stores and Service Firms

Easy Bookkeeping Tax System: General Retail and Service Firm. For general information, see entry under Bars and Restaurants.

General Business System for Retail Stores and Service Firms.

Safeguard Business System, Inc. for Retail Stores and Service Firms.

Service Stations and Garages

BINEX Automated Business Systems for Service Stations and Garages. A complete computer-prepared analysis of a service station is available from the local BINEX user or franchise. The report includes a monthly and year-to-date analysis of income and expenses, a complete statement of financial position, control of inventory, comparison with industry averages, complete payroll history including W-2 forms. All tax reports for federal and state employment taxes and state sales taxes can be prepared. In addition, the BINEX customer follow-up system mails postcards to customers thanking them for coming in to have their cars serviced or reminding them to do so. The combination of these two systems gives a service station owner the best information available to run his business.

Easy Bookkeeping Tax System: Service Stations. For general information, see entry under Bars and Restaurants.

Garage and Gas Station Record. The Greenwood Company, 210 South Federal St., Chicago, Ill. 60605. Form 50. Contains the following forms: daily purchases and expenses for month; record of daily sales; record of daily cash receipts; record of daily payments.

Safeguard Business Systems, Inc. for Service Stations and Garages.

Simplified Master Systems—Service Station. Simplified Business Services, Inc.

Service Station Simplified Bookkeeping. The Johnson Systems, 828 North Broadway, Milwaukee, Wis. 53202. Contains daily sales and expense forms sufficient for recording the results of two years' business.

Dome Simplified Monthly Bookkeeping Record, #612, and Dome Simplified Weekly Bookkeeping Record #600 for Service Stations and Garages.

Shoe Repair Shops

Shoe Service Shop Bookkeeping System. Shoe Service Institute of America, 222 West Adams St., Chicago, Ill. 60606. Contains the following forms sufficient for recording the results of one year's business: daily sales, purchases of materials and merchandise; operating expenses; monthly profit-and-loss statements; purchase of equipment and fixtures. Instructions included.

Safeguard Business Systems, Inc. for Shoe Repair Shops.

General Business System for Shoe Repair Shops.

Smaller Stores

Merchandise Control and Budgeting (M44566).   National Retail Merchants Association, 100 West 31st St., New York, N.Y. 10001. Explains the fundamentals of merchandise control planning and budgeting. Includes formulas to maintain proper ratios between stocks and customer demand. Illustrated with all necessary forms for maintaining profitable inventories and shows how to figure open-to-buy.

Retail Accounting Manual—Revised (C13276).   National Retail Merchants Association, 100 West 31st St., New York, N.Y. 10001. A publication with a chart of accounts flexible enough to accommodate the needs of multi-unit companies as well as individual single unit retail stores. In addition to serving the industry as a guide in the area of expense accounting and reporting, the revised manual places emphasis on merchandise accounting and management reporting. Separate chapters on the determination of gross margin, return on investment, and workroom accounting is covered in detail. A looseleaf reference book of 196 pages.

Retail Inventory Method Made Practical (C14370). National Retail Merchants Association, 100 West 31st St., New York, N.Y. 10001. 1971. Presents the fundamental operation involved in establishing and maintaining accurate inventories. Chapters clearly explain what the Retail Method of Inventory is and how it differs from the cost method, its advantages and disadvantages. Includes sample forms for recording merchandise transfers, sales, price changes, departmental merchandise statements, open-to-buy, and many more. Softcover, 70 pages.

Blackbourn Smaller Varied Business Bookkeeping No. 19X.

Safeguard Business Systems, Inc. for Smaller Stores.

General Business Systems for Smaller Stores.

Sporting Goods Dealers

NSGA Annual Cost of Doing Business Survey.   National Sporting Goods Association, 717 North Michigan Ave., Chicago, Ill. 60611. A 40-page compilation of sales, inventory, and operating ratios for a variety of sporting goods retailers, and institutional team distributors. Most data include average, median and hi-lo ratios, with separate compilations based on volume, size of outlets, regional locations, and makeup of retailers (pure retail or combination of retail-and-team). Selected composite balance sheet ratios are included.

General Business System for Sporting Goods Dealers.

Safeguard Business Systems, Inc. for Sporting Goods Dealers.

Television and Radio

General Business System for Television and Radio.

Safeguard Business System, Inc. for Television and Radio.

Television-Radio Sales and Service Record.   The Johnson Systems, 828 North Broadway, Milwaukee, Wis. 53202. Contains space and forms to record the following information sufficient to record two years' business: sales of new and used television and radio sets; daily charges of servicing and repairing of television and radio sets; merchandise purchases; repair parts; general overhead expenses.

Truckers and Motor Carriers

Blackbourn Truckers' Bookkeeping No. 350X.

General Business System for Truckers and Motor Carriers.

Safeguard Business Systems, Inc. for Truckers and Motor Carriers.

Simplified Master Systems—Trucking. Simplified Business Services, Inc.

COMPUTER PROGRAMS FOR FINANCIAL MANAGEMENT

There are many programs to assist you with record keeping for a small or expanding business. They range from the very simple, which cost only a few dollars to complicated spread sheets with powerful features costing hundreds of dollars. Programs to help you with all kinds of record keeping for a small business are constantly being developed, updated, and revised. And many are much easier to use than you might suspect. It's safe to say that if you have access to a computer, some program exists that suits your needs best and will most definitely increase your effectiveness and efficiency in the management of your enterprise.

My advice with most computer programs is to "try before buy." This means developing a relationship with your local software retailer. To give you some idea of what is available, here is a sampling of a few programs that can help you with small business record keeping.

ValueCalc is a simple and inexpensive program. With it, you can perform all types of numerical operations, including income statements, balance sheets, cost comparisons, and budgets. Three basic spreadsheets are furnished: an expense recorder, a gas mileage calculator, and a home budget. ValueCalc is published by Melody Hall Publishing Corp., Northbrook, IL 60065. MoneyCounts is another inexpensive record keeping system. Its capabilities include checking, credit card management, card management, budgeting, financial statements, graphics, financial data base, and a financial calculator. MoneyCounts is published by Parsons Technology, 6925 Surrey Drive NE, Cedar Rapids, IA 52402.

Quicken is a step up. It automates bill paying, organizes financial records, automatically categorizes expenses for business, taxes, or budgeting, reconciles bank statements, and will transfer your finances into Lotus 1-2-3, Symphony, or AppleWorks spreadsheets. It is also reputed to be 200% to 300% faster than less expensive financial software. Quicken is published by Intuit, 540 University Avenue, Palo Alto, CA 94301.

If you have needs for greater capabilities, ACCUPAC BPI Accounting is a full-function system with the capability of stepping up as your needs increase without changing systems. There are five separate modules: general accounting, accounts receivable, accounts payable, payroll, and inventory. In most cases you won't be interested in this package at start-up. There is, however, an ACCUPAC Easy which the manufacturer states is "simple, inexpensive accounting software designed for very small businesses that plan to grow." The less expensive version can be transferred to the more powerful version. ACCUPAC is published by Computer Associates, 1240 McKay Drive, San Jose, CA 95131.

Obviously this list is far from complete. There are literally hundreds of systems available. Since the pricing varies from less than $20 to more than

$1,000 for a complete system, you can see the reason for my earlier advice about trying what you are interested in before committing. A very powerful and sophisticated system can save you a lot of time and money if you really need it. If you don't, such a system will waste both. For many businesses the least expensive and simple system may be exactly what's wanted.

SOURCES OF ADDITIONAL INFORMATION

Financial Recordkeeping for Small Stores, Small Business Management Series No. 32, by Robert C. Ragan, published by the Small Business Administration, Washington, DC 20402.

Keeping Records in Small Business, Small Marketers Aids No. 155, by John Cotton, published by the Small Business Administration, Washington, DC 20402.

Record Keeping Systems Small Stores and Service Trade, Small Business Bibliography No. 15, by Nathan H. Olshan and Office of Management Information and Training staff, SBA, published by the Small Business Administration, Washington, DC 20402.

Section II
Marketing Problem Solving

9

Marketing Research

MARKETING RESEARCH—WHAT IT IS AND HOW IT CAN MAKE MONEY FOR YOU

Marketing research is the gathering, recording, and analyzing of information about problems relating to marketing. It will help you to identify who your market is as well as which methods will best satisfy the needs of your market. But it encompasses many other aspects of marketing, including new product introductions, pricing, advertising, consumer behavior, and so on. So important is marketing research that certain basic marketing strategies such as market segmentation, in which you identify a specific portion of the market and concentrate your resources on selling to that one segment, or product differentiation, in which you differentiate your product from that of a competitor in such a fashion as to best appeal to potential buyers, would be absolutely impossible without it.

Among the many things that marketing research will tell you are the following:

1. Who are your customers and who are your potential customers?
2. What kinds of people are your customers? (This includes demographic categories, such as age, income, and education, and psychographic categories such as interests and preferences.)
3. Where do your customers live?
4. Why do your customers buy?
5. Do they have the ability to pay?
6. Are you offering the kinds of goods and services that your customers want?
7. Are you offering your products or services at the best place, at the best time, and in the correct amounts?
8. Are your prices consistent with the value your customers place on the product or service that you are selling?
9. How are your promotional programs working?
10. What do your customers think of your business and its image?
11. How do your business and your business procedures compare with those of your competitors?[1]

---

[1] Adapted from J. Ford Laumer, Jr., James R. Harris, and Hugh J. Guffer, Jr., *Learning About Your Market*, Small Business Administration (1979).

Correct use of marketing research can mean amazing profits for your business and tremendous advantages over your competitors. A famous example of correct use of marketing research took place in the early 1960s. Ford, along with two other major American motor companies, had developed cars to compete with foreign cars such as the Volkswagen. Ford's entry had been the Falcon, introduced in 1959. As the years passed, the numbers of Ford Falcons that were sold began to decrease as a percentage of Ford's total sales. This was also true for the competing cars offered by the two other American companies. Ford might simply have concluded that American small cars were no longer wanted. Instead, Ford did marketing research to find out more about the falling off of Falcon sales. During this research, Ford discovered an interesting and important fact: while sales of the Falcon were declining, sales of sporty options such as bucket seats and a special interior were increasing. This was due primarily to the greater numbers of young adults who were purchasing the vehicle. Ford's careful study of the market research findings led the company to put out the Ford Mustang, introduced in 1965. This sporty vehicle demolished all previous records for sales and developed a new market after which competitors followed as best they could, some two to three years behind. The head of Ford's Mustang project was none other than a young engineer by the name of Lee Iacocca.

But successful use of marketing research is not limited to major companies such as Ford. Thousands of small firms and entrepreneurs have used marketing research successfully to carve out huge shares of their respective markets. An optical firm totally turned its company around and doubled sales within a year by identifying its customers. A mail order entrepreneur sold $10 million worth of a single product through marketing research techniques. A small computer firm successfully took on IBM for a segment of the total computer market and won through the correct application of marketing research.

In this chapter you will learn the same techniques used by these and other firms so successfully.

THREE IMPORTANT CATEGORIES OF MARKETING RESEARCH

Here are three categories of marketing research important to any small business: internal information, secondary research, and primary research. Let's look at each in turn.

Internal Information

Internal information is extremely useful because it is generally close at hand and costs you little or nothing to obtain. Therefore, before thinking about expensive field experiments or surveys, look at your own records and files. These include: sales records, receipts, complaints, all of the records noted in the record-keeping section of this book, and anything else which shows and tells about your customers and what they are interested in and what they buy. One source of information is your customers' addresses. This alone will tell a great deal about your customers, including where they live, their income, and their life styles. This information can be of great assistance to you in determining what your customers will be interested in buying. The most successful mail order firms make millions not by selling a single product once to a customer, but by selling numerous products to their customer list again and again.

Secondary Research

Secondary research concerns information already available outside your company. The key here is its availability. It has already been put together by someone else. This information may have been collected by other firms, by government agencies, and may be found in books, newspapers, and a host of other sources. But the important fact is that this information is already available. Someone else has done the work; that's why it's called "secondary" research. It costs you little or nothing to obtain. You don't have to design the survey method. You don't have to do the interviewing. And you don't have to spend time and resources collecting this information yourself. Where can you find this information? At the end of this chapter you will find over 100 sources of statistics, studies accomplished, and secondary research that you can analyze to obtain more facts regarding your customers. You can also purchase completed marketing research reports. Three firms that sell such reports are:

1. Cambridge Information Group
   Findex
   7200 Wisconsin Ave.
   Bethesda, Md. 20814
2. Mediamark Research, Inc.
   341 Madison Ave.
   New York, N.Y. 10017
3. Off-the-Shelf Publications, Inc.
   2171 Jericho Turnpike
   Commack, N.Y. 11725

Primary Research

Perhaps you have already looked at the cheaper and easier research methods—your internal records and secondary sources of information—and found that the specific information that you need simply isn't available. In this case, you must do the research yourself or hire someone else to do it for you. The means of getting this information, specifically tailored to your needs, is called primary research.

EXPLORATORY VERSUS SPECIFIC RESEARCH

There are two basic types of research that you should consider once the decision is made that primary research is necessary. One type is called *exploratory research* and the other is called *specific research*. Exploratory research is aimed at helping you to define the problem. It is typically done through in-depth interviews with a relatively small number of people. It tends to be open-ended. Questions are asked which invite detailed, lengthy answers from the respondents. These interviews tend to be nonstructured and freewheeling. One example of exploratory research was accomplished by a soup company sometime ago. A promotion for a new soup product had failed. The basic promotion had been a free pair of nylons if the customer would try the soup. The general question was: Why had the soup failed? In-depth interviews were conducted with a limited number of customers to discover the answer. From this limited research, the result was found that an image of "feet in soup" had resulted. This error in consumer behavior psychology had caused the promotion for the new product to fail.

Specific research is used when the basic problem has already been defined. It focuses on ways of solving the problem. Specific research typically uses much larger samples than exploratory research, and because of this it tends to be much more expensive. The interviews used with specific research are very structured, complete, and of formal design. Using the example of the soup, specific research would be conducted to find out what to do about the soup promotion, that is, what premium, if any, should be given to consumers for trying the new soup, and the respondent might be given a number of choices from which to select his or her preference.

THE MARKETING RESEARCH PROCESS

The marketing research process can be divided into certain steps. These steps are as follows:

1. Define the problem
2. Decide whether marketing research is needed
3. Identify objectives
4. State specific data to be obtained
5. Design the research instrument to be used
6. Decide on the sample
7. Collect the data
8. Tabulate and analyze
9. Draw conclusions and decide on courses of action

Define the Problem

You cannot proceed until you have a good definition of what your problem is, whether it be a new product introduction, identification of customers for a certain market, or whatever. This first step of the research process seems obvious and for this reason many people tend to overlook it. Yet, experts tell us that it is the most important step. When defining the problem, look beyond symptoms. Symptoms may be declining sales, declining profits, and so on. But you must ask yourself: Why are sales declining? Why are profits down? List every possible reason. Could your customers be changing? Is there new competition? List all possibilities, but focus on those that can be measured. These are the ones that you can do your marketing research on. Problems that cannot be measured are not candidates for marketing research.

Decide Whether Marketing Research Is Needed

As noted previously, if you cannot measure the influence on the problem, you cannot do marketing research. But even if measurement is possible, before you decide to invest your time and treasure in marketing research, you should consider several factors: (1) Is internal or secondary research available? (2) What in general will it cost in money, resources, and time to do the research?

If the research has already been done and is available free, it makes little sense to do it over. If the research can be obtained, but at too high a cost, higher than the increase in sales or profits that may result, the research is clearly not worthwhile. The same thing is true if it will take so long to get the information that you will not be able to use it. Therefore, always recognize that doing marketing research may not be the answer to the problem that you have defined. However, if thinking through the situation shows that you can accomplish research which will be of assistance in solving the problem, then proceed to the next step.

Identify Objectives

You should understand everything you can about the problem and the information you are seeking before proceeding. This will enable you to specify clearly the objective or objectives of the study that you are undertaking. You may have a single objective or you may have several. But, either way, you must state it or them in the clearest possible terms. For example: "The objective of this study is to determine who is buying memberships in health clubs within 10 miles of my location."

State Specific Data to Be Obtained

Now, you must decide on exactly what information you want to obtain. If you want to know who is purchasing memberships in health clubs in a 10-mile area, you may wish to know them by (1) income, (2) education, (3) age, (4) sex, (5) occupation, (6) employment, (7) precise geographical location, (8) what type of media they read, see, or listen to, and so forth. All of this information should be specified in this section.

Design the Research Instrument to Be Used

Now, you must decide how you will do the research. First, you must decide whether you wish to do exploratory or specific research. Then, you must decide where and how the information is to be obtained. Your questionnaire must motivate the respondents to supply the information you want, sometimes concealing the reasons for obtaining it so as not to introduce extraneous factors into the results. It can have several different forms: it may be a set of questions designed to be asked over the telephone or in a personal interview, or a survey going through the mail. Each form has advantages and disadvantages, and which one to use depends on your situation. For example, a mail survey must be as short as possible, or people won't respond. The same is true for the telephone interview. But a personal face-to-face interview can be as long as an hour or more. You must also consider the complexity of the questions you will ask. For most complex questions, a personal interview is necessary. If you are handling a touchy subject, the telephone interview may be extremely difficult because the respondent may hang up. Also, the personal interview may be risky because the individual making the interview may bias the reply. In a mail interview, since you are not there to obtain feedback, you must strongly motivate the individual to answer. A self-addressed, stamped envelope is almost a necessity, to enable the respondent to send the survey back to you easily. But you don't use a postage stamp. You would waste your money if the person did not answer. Instead, use a special reply permit indicia which you can obtain at your local post office. Even with this the respondents by mail will be far fewer than with other survey means. You must allow for this in the number of samples that you attempt to obtain. One survey that used all three methods had comparative responses as follows: mail, 15%; telephone survey, 70%; and personal interview, 80%. There are also tradeoffs regarding cost. Mail is probably the cheapest, followed by telephone. Personal interview is three times as costly as phone since an individual must go from place to place and must be compensated for his time. Use Figure 9.1 for a means of comparing the three methods in detail.

Once you've decided which type of questionnaire to construct, you must then begin to design it. usually the questionnaire should be divided into several sections. The first section contains the basic classification data, including the name of the respondent, the address, and so forth. Frequently this information can be filled in by the interviewer prior to the interview.

The introductory statement is usually the second section. It establishes rapport with the interviewee. Although it may be structured into the questionnaire section itself, if this is a personal or phone interview it should be put in the interviewer's own words so as not to sound stilted. Establishing this early rapport will make the difference between success or failure of the interview.

The next section may describe the product or service if the research has to do with your wares directly. Be careful of overselling the product here so as not to bias the results. The description should be complete and it should be factual. Generally, initial impression questions should appear first. They should be neither complicated nor personal. If the questionnaire is exploratory in nature, the questions should be open-ended without leading to any specific answers. If specific, the questions should give the respondent a choice of alternative answers. You may use attitude scales to determine the intensity of the respondents' feelings as in Figure 9.2.

It is important with products to determine buying intentions, because sometimes individuals will like a product but will not want to purchase it. If you can determine the reasons for this attitude, you may be able to make the changes necessary to make the product or service successful. Product appeals are necessary to determine how to promote the product effectively. This information will help you to determine what is important to emphasize and what is important to deemphasize. Pricing is also a very important aspect, and here you should attempt to determine a selective demand curve for your product or your service. That is, by asking your potential customers about the likelihood of their purchase of the product at different prices, you can later tabulate the results and know at which price the product is demanded more than at any other. It may be difficult to get exact answers for this question, but it will certainly help to give you a general idea of the price range. You should also determine distribution channels by asking the consumer where he or she would expect to find the product. Determine the advertising medium in which he or she would expect to see, hear, or read about the product or service advertised.

Certain information of a personal nature such as age, education, income, and the like should be left to the end of the questionnaire. You should be careful never to ask for a person's specific age or income or other information of this type, but rather indicate a range. Finally, at the end of the interview, deliver a friendly thank you. Your subjects are deserving of this.

Survey Aspect	Mail	Telephone	Personal Interview
Questionnaire			
Length of interview	The shorter the better	Short (15 minutes or less)	Longer (can be up to one hour or more; plus possible mail back). Usually maximum of 30 minutes.
Complexity of questions	May be moderately complex	Must be simple	Can be more complex; can use cards or props.
Flexibility	Poor (no feedback)	Fair	Excellent
Probing	Poor	Better	Best
Getting at reasons (determining "why")	Poor	Better	Best
Handling touchy subject	Relatively good	Risky: Respondent may hang up	Risky: Researcher or respondent may bias replies
Control of question order	Respondent may read ahead	Excellent	Excellent
Sample			
Sample bias	A real problem. Respondent usually higher in education and interest. Other biases uncertain.	Under-represents low income (no phone) and high income and others (not listed, especially in urban areas. But note random dialing)	Best. But occasionally a problem.
Sample of nonrespondents	Often necessary	Usually not necessary	Usually not necessary
List Availability	Must provide list of addresses.	Free, renewed annually	Area sampling a problem. Must get maps, population estimates by sub-areas.
Georgraphic clustering	Can be controlled by zip code	Sometimes (but usually not dangerous number of clusters)	Often if reasonably large.
Stratifying information	May have	Usually not available.	May have income, race, etc., by area (from Census, etc.).
Interviewing			
Response rate	Low: Can be as low as 15% or so for a single mailing to general public, higher for special groups, especially professionals, and for several mailings.	High: about 70%	High: about 80%
Interviewing bias and cheating by interviewer	None	Can occur. But supervisor can counteract to a considerable extent.	Can occur. Can telephone a sample of respondent's to check cheating.
Identity of Respondent	Not certain	Known	Known
Administration and Cost			
Cost	Low, especially if response rate is high and telephone sample of nonresidents not necessary.	Moderately expensive depending on area, and equipment used.	High: three or more times cost of mail or telephone.
Administrative load	Light	Heavier: must hire, train and supervise telephoners.	Heaviest: must hire train, supervise, check and pay at a distance.

Figure 9.1. Comparison of mail, telephone, and personal interview data collection. [Adapted from William A. Cohen and Marshall E. Reddick, *Successful Marketing for Small Business,* Figure 4.1, pgs. 50–51 (AMACOM: New York, 1981).

Nissan Attributes

1. Competitive purchase price	5. Serviceability
poor 1 2 3 4 5 6 7 8 9 excellent	poor 1 2 3 4 5 6 7 8 9 excellent
2. Fuel consumption	6. Distinctive modern styling and appearance
poor 1 2 3 4 5 6 7 8 9 excellent	poor 1 2 3 4 5 6 7 8 9 excellent
3. Durability	7. Riding comfort
poor 1 2 3 4 5 6 7 8 9 excellent	poor 1 2 3 4 5 6 7 8 9 excellent
4. Reliability	8. Handling characteristics
poor 1 2 3 4 5 6 7 8 9 excellent	poor 1 2 3 4 5 6 7 8 9 excellent

---

Figure 9.2. Example of measuring attitude intensity using scales.

Be certain that the information that you want is contained in your questionnaire. As mentioned previously, in some cases it may be necessary to conceal what you are actually after in order to obtain unbiased responses. For example, if you are trying to determine which one of a number of products is favored by the consumer and your product is one of these, it may be important to conceal the fact that you are representing one of the products indicated in the survey.

Always consider:

Whether your respondent has the information that you're asking.
Whether he or she has the necessary experience to provide you with an accurate answer.
Whether it is likely that he or she will remember in order to provide you with an accurate answer.
Whether he or she will have to work hard to get the information.
Whether he or she is likely to give you the information.
Whether he or she is likely to give you the true information.

There are many different types of questions that you may use in your questionnaire. Some which you may find useful are:

   1. *Open-ended.* This is where you ask the question and allow the respondent to talk at some length. The question is not structured and there is no one specific answer.
   2. *Multiple choice.* Here you give a number of different choices to your respondent. Each choice may be a different product or a different description of some information that you are trying to obtain. Or, in the case of demographics, it may simply be a different age group.
   3. *Forced choice.* Forced choice means that you give two choices, one or the other. Sometimes it is very difficult for a respondent to give a specific answer, but you may wish to have him or her choose one of two. An example is, "Do you primarily eat ice cream (1) at home, or (2) at an ice cream parlor?"
   4. *Semantic differential.* A semantic differential allows for an intensity of feelings about some statement. For example, if we are talking about ice

cream, you might ask a question such as this: "The XYZ brand of ice cream is . . . ?" You would then have an adjective scale ranging from "delicious" to "terrible." In between these two extreme points would be other adjectives such as "fair," and there would be different points on the scale such as in Figure 9.2

By analyzing a number of responses, you can come up with an average for each question.

Sequencing of your questions is extremely important. In general, your opening questions should motivate and not challenge your respondents psychologically. As pointed out earlier, identification items fit easily into this classification. Think of easing your respondent into the questionnaire.

Difficult questions should come in the body or at the end of the questionnaire. Why? First, your respondents are more at ease after they've answered some of the questions. Second, they are more accustomed to answering your questions and are less likely to hesitate in answering.

Another important point is that earlier questions will influence questions that follow. For example, the mention of a product in one question may influence the answer to a following question. Consider this question: "ABC Soap has recently changed its formulation to be even more cleansing. Have you used this new formulation?" Let's say your next question is: "What do you think of the new ABC Soap?" You can see how the first question will influence the next question.

A summary of these guides to questionnaire preparation is provided in Figure 9.3. Figure 12.1 in Chapter 12 is a consumer profile questionnaire which has a number of different questions which you may want to ask regarding demographics, psychographics, life style, social class, media use and interest, and other information. You can extract from this questionnaire when you design your own.

Decide on the Sample

Deciding on the sample means defining whom you will survey as well as how many people. Whom you survey will depend on your objectives and on the method of selection of your sample subjects. For example, you may use either random sampling or nonrandom sampling. If you use random sampling, every individual from the population surveyed has an equal chance at being selected. If you use nonrandom sampling, you may include groups containing certain specific individuals you wish to be sampled or surveyed, or you may simply obtain respondence by means of availability.

The sample size decision depends upon how much confidence you have or wish to have in your results. For 100% confidence you would need to sample everyone. But, of course, this isn't always possible or desirable. If you can't sample randomly or sample everyone, you may try systematic sampling. That means you sample every nth element in the total population. Let's say that you are sampling customers. Perhaps you talk to every 25th or every 50th customer. Another way of handling this problem is to subdivide the total universe of people that you want sampled into a few groups that are mutually exclusive. You would then randomly sample these smaller groups. Or, you could divide the total number of people into many groups and randomly choose some of the groups for sampling. Determining how many responses you need in order to reflect the nature of the total universe of individuals you are sampling depends upon the standard deviation or dispersion of the responses the consumer may

Very basic classification data can usually be filled in by the interviewer before the interview. Complicated or very personal classification data should go at the end of the questionnaire.

Name of respondent _____	Name of Interviewer _____
Address _____	Date _____
Phone _____	Time _____
Other (nonpersonal) relevant data _____	

The introductory statement establishes rapport with the interviewee. It should not be read, but rather put in the interviewer's own words. This introduction will make the difference between success and failure for the interview.

Good morning, my name is _____, and I am conducting a marketing study for a new product (service) called _____. The answers you give to the following questions will help determine whether or not to introduce this new product (service) idea, and what features to incorporate into the product. May I have a few minutes of your time?

Product descripton tells the interviewee about the product or service. It should be a complete description of the product. Do not try to eversell the product; that may bias the results.

The name of this product is _____. It is a _____, and its functions/purposes are _____.

The benefits of this product are _____.

Initial impression questions should appear first. They should be noncomplicated, nonpersonal, closed-end questions. Attitude scales are used to determine the intensity of the respondents' feelings.

1. What is your immediate reaction to this idea?

Positive	So-so	Negative
Great _____		
Like it very much _____		I do not particularly like it _____
Like it somewhat _____		I do not like it at all _____

Open-end questions are useful for determining why the person feels the way he or she does.

Why do you say that? Explain. _____

Buying intentions are important to determine. A person may like the idea, but not want to buy it. If one can determine why they would not, perhaps the product can be revised to meet more with their demands.

2. Which of the following best expresses your feeling about buying this product if it were available to you?

Positive	Negative
I'm absolutely sure I would buy it _____	I probably would not buy it _____
I'm almost sure I would buy it _____	I am almost sure I would not buy it _____
I probably would buy it _____	I am absolutely sure I would not buy it _____

Why do you say that? _____

3. Tell me, all things considered, what is there about this product idea that appeals to you most. What do you consider its most important advantages?

Appeal to Most	Advantages
1.	1.
2.	2.
3.	3.

Product appeals must be determine, so as to be able to effectively promote the product. Such information will indicate what to emphasize and what to de-emphasize.

4. How much do you think such a product would cost? _____

Pricing is an important aspect. Here one can determine a relative demand curve for the product. It is difficult for the consumer to answer this question precisely, but it should at least give the entrepreneur an idea of the price range.

5. Where would you expect to buy such a product? _____

The retail outlet, where the product would be most likely to be found, is important.

6. Where would you expect such a product to be advertised? _____

The advertising medium to use must also be determined. Sometimes consumers do not like a product for minor reasons, and when these reasons are eleviated, they will buy it. The more difficult, tiring questions should be placed at the end of the interview.

7. Are there any suggestions you would care to make that you think might improve this product? _____

Classification data of a personal nature should be asked at the end of the interview. Never ask for a person's specific age or income, because they will become suspicious of you and may become mad.

Classification data:
1. In what category does your age fall:
   below 15 _____
   16–21 _____
   22–29 _____
   30–49 _____
   50–60 _____
   over 60 _____

2. Please tell me where your total family income falls:
   below $5,000 _____
   $5,000–9,999 _____
   10,000–14,999 _____
   15,000–19,999 _____
   above 20,000 _____

3. Check one:
   Female; single _____ married _____
   Male; single _____ married _____

Thank you for your cooperation!

Always close with a friendly thank you. You may wish to interview them again.

Figure 9.3. Designing a questionnaire summary of rules.

give. If you are going to use a random sampling, one way of determining sample size is with the following method.

Let us say you have a new product on the market and have introduced it into your area in which there are 2,000 stores that are selling the product. The reports on the new product won't be in for a month, but you want to know how well this product is doing immediately in order to make investment and inventory decisions. One way, of course, is to survey all 2,000 stores. However, this would be needlessly expensive and time consuming. Another is to survey a certain number of stores at random. This would give us an answer which would be useful for decisions that we have to make.

The first step is to look at a few samples of the stores and calculate an average. Let us say we looked at five stores and they sold the following numbers of our new product: Store No. 1, 10 units; Store No, 2, 18 units; Store No. 3, 30 units; Store No. 4, 42 units; Store No. 5, 50 units. Added together, 150 units were sold, divided by 5 equals an average of 30 units.

The second step is to decide how much accuracy we want. Let's say the accuracy that we're happy with is plus or minus 10%. This is an arbitrary figure. We could have decided on plus or minus 15%.

The third step is to calculate an acceptable limit based on an accuracy that we calculated in the previous step. Plus or minus 10% times 30 units equals plus or minus 3 units. Therefore, acceptable units of accuracy in our case are plus or minus 3 units.

The fourth step is to estimate the standard deviation of our sample. Of any normal distribution, 68% of the units will fall within one standard deviation. We've looked at five stores. Therefore, 68% times 5 is 3.4. Since we can't use a partial store, we will say that 68% times 5 stores equals 3 stores. Now, let's look at Figure 9.4 with the stores noted on it. Figure 9.4 shows that on the left, Store No. 1 is 10 units. The next in the line is Store 2 with 18 units. Then comes Store No. 3 with 30, Store No. 4 with 42, and Store No. 5 with 50. The 3 units we're looking at would be stores in the center, Stores 2, 3, and 4; 18, 30, and 42 units, respectively. We can see that the difference between 18 and 30 is 12, and the difference between 30 and 42 is 12 as well. Therefore, the standard deviation would be 12.

For the fifth step, we calculate the required sample size using the following formula, which will provide the answer at a 95% confidence level:

$$n = \left(\frac{S}{I/1.96}\right)^2 + 1$$

where: n = sample size
S = standard deviation of sample
I = acceptable limits

In our example,

$$n = \left(\frac{12}{3/1.96}\right)^2 + 1 = 64 \text{ stores}$$

What will we do if we wished accuracy of 15% instead of 10%? In that case, the acceptable limits would be 15% times 30 equals plus or minus 4.5 instead of plus or minus 3.

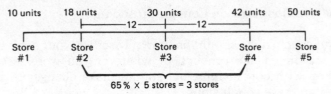

Figure 9.4. Calculating the standard deviation.

This approach is good only if our answer, 64 stores divided by the total number of stores, 2,000, is less than 5%. In our case, 64 divided by 2,000 equals 0.032, or 3.2%, which is less than 5%, so we're all right. But, let's say that instead of 2,000 stores, there were only 200 stores. What should we do then? In this case, we just adjust our answer. We do so using the following formula:

$$n^1 = \frac{n}{1 + \dfrac{n}{N}}$$

where n is our sample size, N is the total number of units surveyed, and n^1 is our adjusted sample size. In this case:

$$n^1 = \frac{n}{1 + \dfrac{n}{N}} = \frac{64}{1 + \dfrac{64}{200}} = 48.48 = \text{approx. } 48$$

If we had 200 stores selling the product instead of 2,000, we would sample 48 stores.

Collecting Data

Once the sample size has been decided upon, we can then begin to utilize the research tool that we have designed actually to collect data. Remember to be neat, courteous, and professional if you are doing this either in person or by telephone.

Tabulation and Analysis

In this step, the data that have been collected should be tabulated according to the specific questions that we have constructed to find information that we seek. This data can then be analyzed on a percentage basis to tell us the answers to our questions. For example, our demographic analysis may show us that the majority of our customers are ages 18 to 24, and that they are single. It may also show that most of our customers have graduated from high school and taken some college courses, and that they are mostly white-collar workers. This information can be extremely important. One local record shop had been carrying large stocks of classical records for years when most of its buyers were teenagers. A dress shop which was doing poorly was offering racks of expensive dresses which most of its customers could not afford.

Conclusions and Decisions on Courses of Action

At this point, conclusions should be drawn based on your analysis of the data as to your customers, the product, or whatever you were researching. You shouldn't stop with conclusions, but should make changes to increase your profits based on these conclusions.

Examples of Research You Can Do

The kind of marketing research you do is really limited only by your imagination. Some research can be done, even of the primary type, at very little cost except for your time. Here are some examples of simple research done by small businesses which greatly increased sales. These ideas were suggested by J. Ford Laumer, Jr., James R. Harris, and Hugh J. Guffey, Jr., all professors of marketing at Auburn University of Auburn, Alabama, in their booklet *Learning About Your Market*, published by the Small Business Administration.

    1. *License plate analysis.* In many states, license plates give you information about where car owners live. Therefore, simply by taking down the numbers of cars parked in your location and contacting the appropriate state agency, you can estimate the area from which you draw business. Knowing where your customers live can help you in your advertising or in targeting your approach to promotion. Through the same method you can find who your competitors' customers are.

    2. *Telephone number analysis.* Telephone numbers can also tell you the areas in which people live. You can obtain customers' telephone numbers from sales slips or credit card slips or checks. Again, knowing where they live will give you excellent information about their life styles.

    3. *Coded coupons.* The effectiveness of your advertising vehicle can easily be checked by coding coupons which can be used for discounts or inquiries about products. You can find out the areas that your customers come from, as well as which vehicle brought them your message.

    4. *People watching.* Simply looking at your customers can tell you a great deal abut them. How are they dressed? How old are they? Are they married or single? Do they have children or not? Many owners use this method intuitively to get a feel about their customers. However, a little sophistication with a tally sheet for a week can provide you much more accurate information simply, easily, and without cost. It may confirm what you've known all along, or it may change your picture of your typical customer completely.

CHECKLIST FOR APPRAISAL OF YOUR RESEARCH STUDY

Figure 9.5 is a complete checklist for appraisal of your research study. If you use it, your research should provide you with excellent results.

SOURCES OF SECONDARY RESEARCH

Following are more than 100 sources based on bibliographies but together by Lloyd M. DeBoer, Dean of the School of Business Administration at George

1. Review of research objectives
   a. In relation to the problem.
   b. In relation to previous research.
   c. In relation to developments subsequent to initiation of research.

2. Overall study design
   a. Are the hypotheses relevant? Consistent?
   b. Is the terminology relevant and unambiguous?
   c. Is the design a logical bridge from problem to solution?
   d. Are there any biases in the design that may have influenced the results?
   e. Was care taken to preserve anonymity, if needed?
   f. Were proper ethical considerations taken into account?
   g. Was the study well-administered?

3. Methods used
   a. Were the right sources used (populations sampled)?
   b. Do any of the data collection methods appear to be biased?
   c. What precautions were taken to avoid errors or mistakes in data collection?
   d. If sampling was used, how representative is the sample? With what margin of error?
   e. Were the data processed with due care? What precautions were taken to assure good coding?
   f. Are the categories used in tabulation meaningful?
   g. Were any pertinent tabulations or cross classifications overlooked? On the other hand, are the tabulations so detailed as to obscure some of the main points?
   h. Do the analytical (statistical) methods appear to be appropriate?
   i. Is the report well-executed in terms of organization, style, appearance, etc.?

4. Review of interpretations and recommendations
   a. Do they follow from the data? Are they well-supported?
   b. Are they comprehensive? Do they relate to the whole problem or only part of it?
   c. Are they consistent with the data? With existing information—other studies, executives' experiences, etc.?
   d. Were any relevant interpretations overlooked?

5. Responsibility for action and follow-up
   a. Will information receive due consideration from all those concerned?
   b. What are the implications of the results for action? Will all action possibilities be considered? (How do the results affect aspects of total operation outside the scope of the report?)
   c. Is an action program necessary? Will it be formulated?
   d. Is further information needed? If so, along what lines?
   e. Is responsibility for follow-up clearly assigned?
   f. Should a time be set for re-evaluation of the action program, e.g., to re-evaluate an innovation, or test a new package after introduction?

Figure 9.5.   Checklist for appraisal of your research study.

Mason University, Fairfax, Virginia, and the Office of Management and Training of the SBA and published by the Small Business Administration as a part of two booklets, *Marketing Research Procedure, SBB 9,* and *National Directories for Use in Marketing, SBB 13.*

Preliminary Sources

This section lists a wider range of reference sources to help locate pertinent materials for specific data. It is a good idea to consult one or more of them before investing substantial time or effort in any kind of market analysis.

Basic Library Reference Sources.   SBB-18. SBA Free. Contains a section on marketing information and guides to research.

Bureau of the Census Catalog. Bureau of the Census, U.S. Department of Commerce. Quarterly, cumulative to annual, with monthly supplements. GPO. Part I lists all publications issued by the Bureau of the Census. Part II lists available data files, special tabulations, and other unpublished materials. Both indexed.

Bureau of the Census Guide to Programs and Publications, Subjects and Areas. Bureau of the Census, Department of Commerce. GPO. Stock Number 0324-00196. On charts, describes the statistical information available in Census Bureau publications since 1968; defines geographic areas covered; outlines programs and activities. Indexed.

Note: Census data are issued initially in separate paperbound reports. Publication order forms are issued for reports as they become available and may be obtained from the Subscriber Service Section (Publications), Bureau of Census, Washington, D.C. 20233, or any U.S. Department of Commerce field office.

Directory of Federal Statistics for Local Areas: A Guide to Sources. Bureau of Census, U.S. Department of Commerce. GPO. Stock No. 003-024-01553-6. Gives detailed table-by-table descriptions of subjects for almost all types of areas smaller than States. Covers the whole range of local data—social, economic, technical—published by the U.S. Government. Bibliography with names and addresses of source agencies. Appendixes. Indexed.

Industrial Market Information Guide. Regular monthly column appearing in every issue. Crain Communications, Inc., 740 North Rush St., Chicago, Ill. 60611. Lists, in 32 market categories, over 600 items of market data annually. Most items available from business publications, Government agencies, and other publishers; some material for a limited period.

Measuring Markets: A Guide to the Use of Federal and State Statistical Data. Bureau of Domestic and International Business Administration, Department of Commerce. Revised periodically. GPO. Stock No. 003-025-00031. This is an excellent reference which not only describes Federal and State Government publications useful for measuring markets but also demonstrates the use of Federal statistics in market measurement.

Statistical Abstract of the United States. Bureau of Census, Department of Commerce. Annual. GPO. This is the most comprehensive and authoritative data book on the social, economic, and governmental characteristics of the United States. Special features include sections on recent national trends and an appendix on statistical methodology and reliability. Indexed. Appendix IV, *Guide to Sources of Statistics*, is arranged alphabetically by major subjects listing Government and private sources.

Statistics Sources: A Subject Guide to Data on Industrial, Business, Social, Educational, Financial, and Other Topics for the United States and Selected Foreign Countries. Gale Research Co., Book Tower, Detroit, Mich. 48226. Provides thousands of sources of statistics on about 12,000 subjects with 22,000 citations.

Consumer Market Information

This section lists references which provide information on products and services bought by individuals or households for home or personal use.

General Data

County and City Data Book.   Bureau of Census, Department of Commerce. GPO. A total of 195 statistical items tabulated for the U.S., its regions, and each county and State; 190 items for each city; and 161 items for 277 Standard Metropolitan Statistical Areas. Information is derived from latest available censuses of population, housing, governments, mineral industries, agriculture, manufactures, retail and wholesale trade, and selected services. Also includes data on health, vital statistics, public assistance programs, bank deposits, vote cast for President, and crime.

Statistics for States and Metropolitan Areas.   (A preprint from *County and City Data Book*). Bureau of Census, Department of Commerce. GPO. Presents data for 195 statistical items for the U.S, its regions, and each State, and 161 items for 277 Standard Metropolitan Statistical Areas.

Statistical Abstract of the United States.   Bureau of Census, Department of Commerce, GPO. Includes many consumer market statistics such as income, employment, communications, retail and wholesale trade and services, housing population characteristics by State and for large cities and standard metropolitan areas. More than 1,000 pages and hundreds of tables on such topics as gambling, daytime care for children, households with TV sets, Federal R&D obligations for energy development, franchised businesses, among others.

A Guide to Consumer Markets.   Annual. The Conference Board, Inc., Information Services, 845 Third Ave., New York, N.Y. 10022. Presents a detailed statistical profile of U.S. consumers and the consumer market. Contains data on population growth and mobility, employment, income, consumer spending patterns, production and sales, and prices.

E&P Market Guide.   Published annually in Fall. Editor & Publisher Company, 575 Lexington Ave., New York, N.Y. 10022. Tabulates current estimates of population, households, retail sales and for nine major sales classifications, income for States, counties, metropolitan areas, and 1,500 daily newspaper markets. Also lists specific information on major manufacturing, retailing, and business firms, transportation and utilities, local newspapers, climate, and employment, for newspaper markets. Includes State maps.

S&MM's Survey of Buying Power.   Revised annually in July. *Sales and Marketing Management*, 633 Third Ave., New York, N.Y. 10017. Information includes current estimates of population and households by income groups, total effective buying income, retail sales for major retail lines, and market quality indexes; given for all regions, States, counties, and metropolitan areas.

S&MM's Survey of Buying Power—Part II.   Revised annually in October. *Sales and Marketing Management*, 633 Third Ave., New York, N.Y. 10017. Gives population, income, retail sales, and buying income figures for television and newspaper markets in the United States and Canada. The data for television markets outlines the areas of dominant influence, while the newspaper markets information identifies both dominant and effective coverage areas.

Specific Data

Each of the reference sources listed above under *General Data* includes at least some *specific* market data. In addition, there are sources of data useful only for the appraisal and management of specific markets. Examples of some of these important market types are listed below.

Automotive Marketing Guide.   *Motor Age*, Chilton Way, Radnor, Pa. 19089. Number and relative importance (shown as percentage of U.S. total) of automotive wholesalers, franchised car dealers, repair shops, and service stations for counties, marketing areas, and States.

The New Yorker Guide to Selective Marketing.   Market Research Department, 25 West 43d St., New York, N.Y. 10036. Identifies and ranks markets for quality and premium-priced products and services available in the United States. Includes maps and statistics for 40 top-tier areas of best potential to sell premium-priced products. Gives statistics on high-income families, high-priced car registrations, expensive homes and various retail sales indices for top 40 and next 20 U.S. markets.

Survey of Industrial Purchasing Power.   Revised annually in April. *Sales and Marketing Management*, 633 Third Ave., New York, N.Y. 10017. A comprehensive look at the nation's key industrial markets. Included are a sales road map for the industrial marketer, an evaluation of the top 50 manufacturing counties, and statistics showing manufacturing activity by State, county, and 4-digit SIC code.

Sales and Marketing Management Survey of Selling Costs.   Revised annually in February. *Sales and Marketing Management*, 633 Third Ave., New York, N.Y. 10017. Contains data on costs of sales meetings and sales training, Metro sales costs for major U.S. markets, compensation, sales-support activities and transportation. There is also some cost information in the international area.

Business Market Information

This section lists references for all types of markets other than the consumer (individuals or household for personal use) markets. Some of the sources described in the *Consumer Market* sections of this *SBB* also provide data for *business* markets, such as commercial, farm, industrial, institutional, and Federal and State governments.

General Data

County Business Patterns.   Department of Commerce. Annual. GPO. Separate book for each State, District of Columbia, and a U.S. Summary. Reports provide figures on first quarter employment, first quarter payroll, annual payroll, number of establishments and number of establishments by employment size class for some 700 different U.S. business and industries by each county in the United States.

County and City Data Book.   Bureau of Census, Department of Commerce. GPO. Presents data on housing, population, income, local government financing, elections, agriculture, crime, etc., for States, cities, counties, and 277 Standard Metropolitan Statistical Areas.

Statistics for State and Metropolitan Areas.   (A preprint from *County and City Data Book*). Bureau of Census, Department of Commerce. GPO. Presents data for 195 statistical items for the U.S., its regions, and each State, and 161 items for 277 Standard Metropolitan Statistical Areas.

Statistical Abstract of the United States. Bureau of Census, Department of Commerce. Annual. GPO. Includes national and State data relating to business, industry, and institutional markets, as well as agriculture.

Specific Data

Automotive Marketing Guide. Motor Age, Chilton Way, Radnor, Pa. 19089. Number and relative importance (shown as a percentage of U.S. total) of automotive wholesalers, franchised car dealers, repair shops, and service stations for counties, marketing areas, and States.

Merchandising: Statistical Issue and Marketing Report. Annual. Billboard Publications, 1 Astor Plaza, New York, N.Y. 10036. Gives retail sales of major appliance types and number of appliance dealers by State and public utility service areas; also gives number of residential utility customers, and housing starts by State.

Maps

This section lists (1) maps that serve merely as a base for market analysis by providing geographic information, and (2) maps that themselves display marketing statistics. For ready reference, the maps are listed by publisher's name. Prices are shown when available.

American Map Company, Inc., 1926 Broadway, New York, N.Y. 10023. *Catalog of Cleartype and Colorprint Maps.* The catalog describes the types of maps (including plastic-surfaced maps for crayon presentations and maps on steel to accommodate magnetic markers). Company publishes U.S. base maps for depicting sales, markets, territories, distribution, statistics, and traffic data; detailed State, county, zip codes and township maps; and several types of atlases for use in analyzing national markets.

Rand McNally & Company, P.O. Box 7600, Chicago, Ill. 60680. Publishes a variety of maps and atlases. This publisher leases a *Commercial Atlas and Marketing Guide* which contains maps showing counties and cities, a road atlas, and statistical data on manufacturing, retail sales, and population. Standard metropolitan areas are shown. Includes a city index with information on transportation facilities, banks, and posted volume and an international section.

Sales Builders, 633 Third Ave., New York, N.Y. 10017. Publishes two sets of nine regional maps (11″ × 17″) which cover the 50 States and depict either retail sales or industrial sales information. Also publishes two 50-State Wall Maps (24½″ × 38″) which have county outlines and depict either the consumer or manufacturing data. For list of prices and order blank, write Sales Builders Division, *Sales and Marketing Management.*

U.S. Geological Survey, Department of the Interior, Washington, D.C. 20402. Publishes a variety of maps that show State and city areas. The following maps and a list (free) of other available maps may be ordered from the DISTRIBUTION SECTION, U.S. GEOLOGICAL SURVEY, 1200 South Eads St., Arlington, Va. 22202.

Map 2-A (54″ × 80″). Shows State and county boundaries and names. State capitals, and county seats in black, water features in blue.

Map 2-B (42″ × 65″). Same as above, without land tint background.

Map 3-A (42″ × 65″). Shows State boundaries and names. State capitals and principal cities in black, water features in blue.

Map 5-A (24½″ × 38″). Shows State and county boundaries and names, water features in black.

Map 7-A (20″ × 30″). Shows State boundaries and principal cities in black, water features in blue.

Map 11-A (13½″ × 20″). Shows State boundaries and principal cities in black, water features in blue.

Map 16-A (9½″ × 13″). Shows State boundaries and principal cities in black, water features in blue.

Contour Map—Map 7-B (20″ × 30″). State boundaries and principal cities in black, water features in blue, contours in brown.

Outline Map—Map 5-D (24½″ × 38″). State boundaries and names only.

Physical Divisions Map—Map 7-C (28″ × 32″). Physical divisions are outlined in red on the base map. Subdivisions and characteristics of each division are listed on the margin.

Locating Sources of National Lists

Other directories, new publications or revisions, may be located in one of the six following sources. Some of the selected directories, as well as the locating guides, are available for reference in public and university libraries.

1. *Mailing lists.* A major use of directories is in the compilation of mailing lists. Attention, therefore, is directed to another SBA Bibliography (SBB 29), "National Mailing-List Houses," which includes a selected compilation of both general line and limited line mailing-list houses that are national in scope. Also, consult Klein's *Directory of Mailing List Houses*—see listings under "Mailing-List Houses" for further description of these two publications.

2. *Trade associations and national organizations.* For those trades or industries where directories are not available, membership lists of trade associations, both national and local, are often useful. For names and addresses of trade associations, consult the following directory source—available at most business reference libraries: *Encyclopedia of Associations, Vol I., National Organizations of the United States,* Gale Research Co., Book Tower, Detroit. Mich. 48226. Published annually. Lists trade, business, professional, labor, scientific, educational, fraternal, and social organizations of the United States, includes historical data.

3. *Business periodicals.* Many business publications, particularly industrial magazines, develop comprehensive specialized directories of manufacturers in their respective fields. Names and addresses of business periodicals are listed (indexed by name of magazine and by business fields covered) in the *Business Publication Rates and Data* published monthly by Standard Rate and Data Service, 5201 Old Orchard Road, Skokie, Ill. 60077. Also, for listings of periodicals by subject index, consult the *Standard Periodical Directory* and for a listing by geographical areas, refer to *Ayer Directory of Publications.* Most libraries have one or more of these directories for reference.

4. *American directories.* Another source is *Guide to American Directories.* Published by B. Klein Publications, P.O. Box 8503, Coral Springs, Fla. 33065.

5. *F & S Index of Corporations and Industries.* It is available in most libraries. Indexes over 750 financial, trade, and business publications by corporate name and by SIC code. Published by Predicasts, Inc., 200 University Circle Research Center, 11001 Cedar Ave., Cleveland, Ohio 44106.

6. *The Public Affairs Information Service.* Available in many libraries, is published weekly, compiled five times a year and put into an annual edition. This is a selective subject list of the latest books, Government publications, reports, and periodical articles, relating to economic conditions, public conditions, public administration and international relations. Published by Public Affairs Information Service, Inc., 11 West 40th St., New York, N.Y. 10018.

Directories

The selected national directories are listed under categories of specific business or general marketing areas in an alphabetical subject index.

When the type of directory is not easily found under the alphabetical listing of a general marketing category, such as "jewelry," look for a specific type of industry or outlet, for example, "department stores."

Apparel

Fur Source Directory, Classified. Annually in June. Alphabetical directory of fur manufacturers in New York City area classified by type of fur; names, addresses, and telephone numbers for each. Also, lists pelt dealers, fur cleaners, fur designers, resident buyers and brokers and those engaged in fur repairing, processing, and remodeling. Fur Vogue Publishing Co., 127 West 30th St., New York, N.Y. 10001.

Hat Life Year Book (Men's). Annual. Includes classified list of manufacturers and wholesalers of men's headwear. Hat Life Year Book, 551 Summit Ave., Jersey City, N.J. 07306.

Knit Goods Trade, Davison's. Annual. Lists manufacturers of knitted products, manufacturers' agents, New York salesrooms, knit goods wholesalers, chain store organizations, department stores with names of buyers, discount chains, brokers and dealers, and rack jobbers. Davison Publishing Co., P.O. Drawer 477, Ridgewood, N.J. 07451.

Men's & Boys' Wear Buyers, Nation-Wide Directory of. (Exclusive of New York Metropolitan Area). Annually in November. More than 20,000 buyers and merchandise managers for 5,000 top department, family clothing and men's and boys' wear specialty stores. Telephone number, buying office, and postal zip code given for each firm. Also available in individual State editions. The Salesman's Guide, Inc., 1140 Broadway, New York, N.Y. 10001. Also publishes *Metropolitan New York Directory of Men's and Boys' Wear Buyers.* Semiannually in May and November. (Lists same information for the metropolitan New York area as the nationwide directory.)

Teens' & Boys' Outfitter Directory. Semiannually in April and October. (Pocket size.) List manufacturers of all types of apparel for boys and students by category, including their New York City addresses and phone numbers; also lists resident buying firms for out-of-town stores, and all trade associations related to boys' wear. The Boys' Outfitter Co., Inc., 71 West 35th St., New York, N.Y. 10001.

Women's & Children's Wear & Accessories Buyers, Nationwide Directory of (Exclusive of New York Metropolitan Area). Annually in February. Lists more than 25,000 buyers and divisional merchandise managers for about 5,000 leading department, family clothing and specialty stores. Telephone number and mail zip code given for each store. Also available in individual State editions. The Salesman's Guide, Inc., 1140 Broadway, New York, N.Y. 10001.

Appliances, Household

National Buyer's Guide. Annual. Lists manufacturers and distributors in home electronics, appliances, kitchens. Gives the products they handle, the territories they cover, and complete addresses for each distributor. Dealerscope, 115 Second Avenue Waltham, Mass. 02154.

Arts and Antiques

American Art and Antique Dealers, Mastai's Classified, Directory of. Lists 20,000 art museums, with names of directories and curators; art and antique dealers; art galleries; coin, armor, tapestry and china dealers in the United States and Canada. Mastai Publishing Co., 21 E 57th St., New York, N.Y. 10022.

Automatic Merchandising (Vending)

NAMA Directory of Members. Annually in July. Organized by State and by city, lists vending service companies who are NAMA members. Gives mailing address, telephone number, and products vended. Also includes machine manufacturers and suppliers. National Automatic Merchandising Association, 7 South Dearborn St., Chicago, Ill. 60603.

Automotive

Automotive Affiliated Representatives, Membership Roster. Annual. Alpha-geographical listing of about 400 member firms including name, address, telephone number, territories covered, and lines carried. Automotive Affiliated Representatives, 625 South Michigan Ave., Chicago, Ill. 60611.

Automotive Directory of Manufacturers and Their Sales Representatives, National. Annual. Alphabetical arrangement of manufacturers serving automotive replacement market. Where available, includes names and addresses of each manufacturers' representative showing territory covered. W. R. C. Smith Publishing Co., 1760 Peachtree Rd. N.W., Atlanta, Ga. 30357.

Automotive Warehouse Distributors Association Membership Directory. Annually. Includes listing of manufacturers, warehouse distributors, their products, pesonnel and territories. Automotive Warehouse Distributors Association, 1719 W. 91st Place, Kansas City, Mo. 64114.

Auto Trim Resource Directory. Nov. edition; annual issue of *Auto Trim News.* Alphabetical listing of name, address, and telephone number of auto trim resources and wholesalers who service auto trim shops. Has directory of product sources—listed by product supplied—with name and address of firm. Auto Trim News, 1623 Grand Ave., Baldwin, N.Y. 11510.

Credit and Sales Reference Directory. Three times annually. Available only to supplier-manufacturers on annual fee basis. Contains listings of 17,000 automotive distributors in the United States and Canada. Data include name and address of companies, and other pertinent information. Motor and Equipment Manufacturers Assn., MEMA Service Corp., 222 Cedar Lane, Teaneck, N.J. 07666.

Home Center, Hardware, Auto Supply Chains. Annually. Lists headquarter addresses, telephone numbers, number and types of stores and locations, annual sales volume, names of executives and buyers. Chain Store Guide Publications, 425 Park Ave., New York, N.Y. 10022.

Jobber Topics Automotive Aftermarket Directory. Annual. Lists 7,000 automotive warehouse distributors automotive rebuilders, manufacturers agents, automotive jobbers, associations, and manufacturers. The Irving-Cloud Publishing Co., 7300 N. Cicero Ave., Lincolnwood, Chicago, Ill. 60646.

Aviation

World Aviation Directory. Published twice a year. Spring and Fall. Gives administrative and operating personnel of airlines, aircraft, and engine manufacturers and component manufacturers and distributors, organizations, and schools. Indexed by companies activities, products, and individuals. Ziff-Davis Aviation Division, 1156 15th St., N.W.; Washington, D.C. 20005.

Bookstores

Book Trade Directory, American. Annual. Updated bimonthly. Lists retail and wholesale booksellers in the United States and Canada. Entries alphabetized by state (or province), and then by city and business mane. Each listing gives address, telephone numbers, key personnel, types of books sold, subject specialties carried, sidelines and services offered and general characteristics. For wholesale entries give types of accounts, import-export information and territory limitations. Edited by the Jacques Cattell Press. R. R. Bowker Company, 1180 Avenue of the Americas, New York, N.Y. 10036.

Multiple Book Store Owners, Directory of. Annually. Lists over 1,000 chains of book stores by state, city, and alphabetically by store within each city. Oldden Mercantile Corp., 560 Northern Blvd., Great Neck, N.Y. 11021.

Building Supplies

Building Supply News Buyers Guide. Annually. Classified directory of manufacturers of lumber, building materials, equipment, and supplies. Cahners Publishing Co., 5 S. Wabash Ave., Chicago, Ill. 60603.

Business Firms

Dun & Bradstreet Middle Market Directory. Annually in October. Lists about 31,000 businesses with net worth between $500,000 and $1,000,000. Arranged in three sections; alphabetically, geographically, and product classification. Gives business name, state of incorporation, address, telephone number, SIC numbers, function, sales volume, number of employees, and name of officers and directors. Marketing Services Division, Dun & Bradstreet, Inc., 99 Church St., New York, N.Y. 10007.

Dun & Bradstreet Million Dollar Directory. Annually in January. Lists about 46,000 businesses with a net worth of $1 million or more. Arranged in four sections; alphabetically, geographically, line of business, and officers and directors with the same information as detailed in the preceding entry. Marketing Services Division, Dun & Bradstreet, Inc., 99 Church St., New York, N.Y. 10007.

Buying Offices

Buying Offices and Accounts, Directory of. Annually in March. Approximately 230 New York, Chicago, Los Angeles, Dallas and Miami Resident Buying Offices, Corporate Offices and Merchandise Brokers together with 11,000 accounts listed under its own Buying Office complete with local address and alphabetically by address and buying office. The Salesman's Guide, Inc., 1140 Broadway, New York, N.Y. 10001.

China and Glassware

American Glass Review. Glass Factory Directory Issue. Annually. Issued as part of subscription (13th issue) to *American Glass Review*: Lists companies manufacturing flat glass, tableware glass and fiber glass, giving corporate and plant addresses, executives, type of equipment used. Ebel-Doctorow Publications, Inc., 1115 Clifton Ave., Clifton, N.J. 07013.

China Glass & Tableware Red Book Directory Issue. Annually. Issued as part of subscription (13th issue) to *China Glass & Tableware*. Lists about 1,000 manufacturers, importers, and national distributors of china, glass, and other table appointments, giving corporate addresses and executives. Ebel-Doctorow Publications, Inc., 1115 Clifton Ave., Clifton, N.J. 07013.

City Directories Catalog

Municipal Year Book. Annual. Contains a review of municipal events of the year, analyses of city operations, and a directory of city officials in all the States. International City Management Association, 1140 Connecticut Ave., N.W., Washington, D.C. 20036.

College Stores

College Stores, Directory of. Published every two years. Lists about 3,500 college stores, geographically with manager's name, kinds of goods sold, college name, number of students, whether men, women, or both, whether the store is college owned or privately owned. B. Klein Publications, P.O. Box 8503, Coral Springs, Fla. 33065.

Confectionery

Candy Buyers' Directory. Annually in January. Lists candy manufacturers; importers and United States representatives, and confectionery brokers. The Manufacturing Confectionery Publishing Co., 175 Rock Rd., Glen Rock, N.J. 07452.

Construction Equipment

Construction Equipment Buyer's Guide, AED Edition. Annual Summer. Lists U.S. and Canadian construction equipment distributors and manufacturers; includes company names, names of key personnel, addresses, telephone numbers, branch locations, and lines handled or type of equipment produced. Associated Equipment Distributors, 615 West 22d St., Oak Brook, Ill. 60521.

Conventions and Trade Shows

Directory of Conventions. Annually in January. Contains about 21,000 cross-indexed listings of annual events, gives dates, locations, names and addresses of executives in charge and type of group two years in advance. Successful Meetings Magazine, Directory Dept., 633 Third Ave., New York, N.Y. 10017.

Exhibits Schedule. Annually in January with supplement in July. Lists over 10,000 exhibits, trade shows, expositions, and fairs held throughout the world with dates given two years in advance. Listings run according to industrial classification covering all industries and professions; full information on dates, city, sponsoring organization, number of exhibits, attendance, gives title and address of executive in charge. Successful Meetings Magazine, Directory Dept., 633 Third Ave., New York, N.Y. 10017.

Dental Supply

Dental Supply Houses, Hayes Directory of. Annually in August. Lists wholesalers of dental supplies and equipment with addresses, telephone numbers, financial standing and credit rating. Edward N. Hayes, Publisher, 4229 Birch St., Newport Beach, Calif. 92660.

Department Stores

Department Stores. Annually. Lists headquarters address and branch locations, telephone numbers, number of stores, resident buying office, names of executives and buyers for independent and chain operators. Chain Store Guide Publications, 425 Park Ave., New York, N.Y. 10022.

Sheldon's Retail. Annual. Lists 1,700 large independent department stores, 446 large junior deartment store chains, 190 large independent and chain home-furnishing stores, 694 large independent women's specialty stores, and 270 large women's specialty store chains alphabetically by States and also major Canadian stores. Gives all department buyers with lines bought by each buyer, and addresses and telephone numbers of merchandise executives. Also gives all New York, Chicago, or Los Angeles buying offices, the number and locations of branch stores, and an index of all store/chain headquarters. Phelon, Sheldon & Marsar, Inc., 32 Union Sq., New York, N.Y. 10003.

Discount Stores

Discount Department Stores, Phelon's. Gives buying headquarters for about 2,000 discount stores, chains, drug chains, catalog showrooms, major jobbers and wholesalers; lines of merchandise bought, buyers' names, leased departments, addresses of leasees, executives, number of stores and price range.

Includes leased department operators with lines and buyers' names. Phelon, Sheldon & Marsar, Inc., 32 Union Sq., New York, N.Y. 10003.

Discount Department Stores.   Annually. Lists headquarters address, telephone number, location, square footage of each store, lines carried, leased operators, names of executives and buyers (includes Canada). Also special section on leased department operators. Chain Store Guide Publications, 425 Park Ave., New York, N.Y. 10022.

Drug Outlets—Retail and Wholesale

Drug Stores, Chain.   Annually. Lists headquarters address, telephone numbers, number and location of units, names of executives and buyers, wholesale drug distributors (includes Canada). Chain Store Guide Publications, 425 Park Ave., New York, N.Y. 10022.

Druggists—Wholesale.   Annually in March. Wholesale druggists in United States with full-line wholesalers specially indicated as taken from the *Hayes Druggist Directory.* Edward N. Hayes, Publisher, 4229 Birch St., Newport Beach, Calif. 92660.

Druggist Directory, Hayes.   Annually in March. Lists all the retail druggists in the United States, giving addresses, financial standing, and credit rating. Also publishes regional editions for one or more States. Computerized mailing labels available. Edward N. Hayes, Publisher, 4229 Birch St., Newport Beach, Calif. 92660.

Drug Topics Buyers' Guide.   Gives information on wholesale drug companies, chain drug stores headquarters, department stores maintaining toilet goods or drug departments, manufacturers' sales agents, and discount houses operating toilet goods, cosmetic, proprietary medicine or prescription departments. Drug Topics, Medical Economics Company, Oradell, N.J. 07649.

National Wholesale Druggists' Association Membership and Executive Directory.   Annually. Lists 800 American and foreign wholesalers and manufacturers of drugs and allied products. National Wholesale Druggists' Association, 670 White Plains Rd., Scarsdale, N.Y. 10583.

Electrical and Electronics

Electronic Industry Telephone Directory.   Annual. With order. Contains over 80,000 listings in White and Yellow Page sections. White pages: name, address, and telephone number of manufacturers, representatives, distributors, government agencies, contracting agencies, and others. Yellow Pages: alphabetic listings by 600 basic product headings and 3,000 sub-product headings. Harris Publishing Co., 2057-2 Aurora Rd., Twinsburg, Ohio 44087.

Electrical Wholesale Distributors, Directory of.   Detailed information on almost 5,000 listings, including name, address, telephone number, branch and affiliated houses, products handled, etc. Electrical Wholesaling, McGraw-Hill Publications Co., Dept. ECCC Services, 1221 Avenue of the Americas, New York, N.Y. 10020.

Who's Who in Electronics, including Electronic Representatives Directory.   Annual. Detailed information (name, address, telephone number, products handled, territories, etc.) on 7,500 electronic manufacturers, 500 suppliers, 3,500 independent sales representatives, and 2,500 industrial electronic distributors and branch outlets. Purchasing index with 1,600 product breakdowns for buyers and purchasing agents. Harris Publishing Co., 2057-2 Aurora Rd., Twinsburg, Ohio 44087.

Electrical Utilities

Electric Utilities, Electrical World Directory of. Annually in October. Complete listings of electric utilities (investor-owned, municipal, and government agencies in U.S. and Canada) giving their addresses and personnel, and selected data on operations. McGraw-Hill Publications Co., Inc., Directory of Electric Utilities, 1221 Avenue of the Americas, New York, N.Y. 10020.

Embroidery

Embroidery Directory. Annually in October-November. Alphabetical listing with addresses and telephone numbers of manufacturers, merchandisers, designers, cutters, bleacheries, yarn dealers, machine suppliers and other suppliers to the Schiffli lace and embroidery industry. Schiffli Lace and Embroidery Manufacturers Assn., Inc., 512 23d St., Union City, N.J. 07087.

Export and Import

American Register of Exporters and Importers. Annually. Includes over 30,000 importers and exporters and products handled. American Register of Exporters and Importers, Inc., 15 Park Row, New York, N.Y. 10038.

Canadian Trade Directory, Fraser's. June. Contains more than 12,000 product classifications with over 400,000 listings from 38,000 Canadian companies. Also lists over 10,000 foreign companies who have Canadian representatives. Fraser's Trade Directories, 481 University Ave., Toronto M5W 1A4, Ontario, Canada.

Flooring

Flooring Directory. Annually in November. Reference to sources of supply, giving their products and brand names, leading distributors, manufacturers' representatives, and associations. Flooring Directory, Harcourt Brace Jovanovich Publications, 1 East First St., Duluth, Minn. 55802.

Food Dealers—Retail and Wholesale

Co-ops, Voluntary Chains and Wholesale Grocers. Annually. Lists headquarters address, telephone number, number of accounts served, all branch operations, executives, buyers, annual sales volume (includes Canada and special "rack merchandiser" section). Chain Store Guide Publications, 425 Park Ave., New York, N.Y. 10022.

Food Brokers Association, National Directory of Members. Annually in July. Arranged by States and cities, lists member food brokers in the United States and Europe, giving names and addresses, products they handle, and services they perform. National Food Brokers Association, 1916 M St., N.W., Washington, D.C. 20036.

Food Service Distributors. Annually. Lists headquarters address, telephone number, number of accounts served, branch operations, executives and buyers for distributors serving the restaurant and institutional market. Chain Store Guide Publications, 425 Park Ave., New York, N.Y. 10022.

Fresh Fruit and Vegetable Dealers, The Blue Book of Credit Book and Marketing Guide.   Semiannually in April and October. (Kept up to date by Weekly Credit Sheets and Monthly Supplements.) Lists shippers, buyers, jobbers, brokers, wholesale and retail grocers, importers and exporters in the United States and Canada that handle fresh fruits and vegetables in carlot and trucklot quantities. Also lists truckers, truck brokers of exempt perishables with "customs and rules" covering both produce trading and truck transportation. Produce Reporter Co., 315 West Wesley St., Wheaton, Ill. 60187.

Frozen Food Fact Book and Directory.   Annual. Lists packers, distributors, suppliers, refrigerated warehouses, wholesalers, and brokers; includes names and addresses of each firm and their key officials. Contains statistical marketing data. National Frozen Food Association, Inc., P.O. Box 398, 1 Chocolate Ave., Hershey, Pa. 17033.

Grocery Register, Thomas'.   Annual. Volume 1: Lists supermarket chains, wholesalers, brokers, frozen food brokers, exporters, warehouses. Volume 2: Contains information on products and services; manufacturers, sources of supplies, importers. Volume 3: A-Z index of 56,000 companies. Also, a brand name/trademark index. Thomas Publishing Co., One Penn Plaza, New York, N.Y. 10001.

Quick Frozen Foods Directory of Wholesale Distributors.   Biennially. Lists distributors of frozen foods. Quick Frozen Foods, P.O. Box 6128, Duluth, Minn. 55806.

Supermarket, Grocery & Convenience Store Chains.   Annually. Lists headquarters address, telephone number, location and type of unit, annual sales volume, executives and buyers, cartographic display of 267 Standard Metropolitan Statistical Areas (includes Canada). Chain Store Guide Publications, 425 Park Ave., New York, N.Y. 10022.

Tea and Coffee Buyers' Guide, Ukers' International.   Biennial. Includes revised and updated lists of participants in the tea and coffee and allied trades. The Tea and Coffee Trade Journal, 18-15 Francis Lewis Blvd., Whitestone, N.Y. 11357.

Gas Companies

Gas Companies, Brown's Directory of International.   Annually in August. Includes information on every known gas utility company and holding company worldwide. Brown's Directory, Harcourt Brace Jovanovich Publications, 1 East First St., Duluth, Minn., 55802.

LP/Gas.   Annually in March. Lists suppliers, supplies, and distributors. Harcourt Brace Jovanovich Publications, 1 East First St., Duluth, Minn. 55802.

Gift and Art

Gift and Decorative Accessory Buyers Directory.   Annually in August. Included in subscription price of monthly magazine, *Gifts and Decorative Accessories.* Alphabetical listing of manufacturers, importers, jobbers, and representatives in the gift field. Listing of trade names, trademarks, brand names, and trade associations. Geyer-McAllister Publications, 51 Madison Ave., New York, N.Y. 10010.

Gift and Housewares Buyers, Nationwide Directory. Annually with semi-annual supplement. For 4,673 different types of retail firms lists store name, address, type of store, number of stores, names of president, merchandise managers, and buyers, etc., for giftwares and housewares. State editions also available. The Salesman's Guide, Inc., 1140 Broadway, New York, N.Y. 10001.

Gift & Tableware Reporter Directory Issue. Annual. Alphabetical listing by category of each (manufacturer, representative, importer, distributor, or jobber). Includes identification of trade names and trademarks, and statistics for imports, manufacturing, and retail sales. Gift & Tableware Reporter, 1 Astor Place, New York, N.Y. 10036.

Gift Shop Directory. Biennially. Lists 900 gift shops in the U.S. Resourceful Research, Box 642, F.D.R. Station, New York, N.Y. 10022.

Hardware

Hardware Wholesalers Guide, National. Annual. Alphabetical listing of manufacturers of hardware and building supplies. Where available, includes names and addresses of each manufacturer's representative showing territory covered. W.R.C. Smith Publishing Co., 1760 Peachtree Rd, N.W., Atlanta, Ga. 30357.

Hardware Wholesalers, Verified List of. Lists distributors (wholesale general hardware houses and hardware chain stores) serving the United States and Canada. Also lists manufacturers' agents handling hardware and allied lines. Chilton, Co., Chilton Way, Radnor, Pa. 19089.

Home Furnishings

The Antiques Dealer. Annual Directory Issue. Issued in September as part of subscription. Lists major wholesale sources by geographical section. Includes special listing for show managers, auctioneers, appraisers, reproductions, supplies and services. Ebel-Doctorow Publications, Inc., 115 Clifton Ave., Clifton, N.J. 07013.

Home Lighting & Accessories Suppliers. Directory issues. Semiannual. Issued in March and October as part of subscription. Lists names and addresses of suppliers to the lamp and lighting industry. Ebel-Doctorow Publications, Inc., 1115 Clifton Ave., Clifton, N.J. 07013.

Interior Decorator's Handbook. Semiannually. Published expressly for decorators and designers, interior decorating staff of department and furniture stores. Lists firms handling items used in interior decoration. Columbia Communications, Inc., 370 Lexington Ave., New York, N.Y. 10017.

Hospitals

American Hospital Association Guide to the Health Care Field. Annually in August. Lists registered hospitals, with selected data as well as listings of nursing homes, health related organizations, and professional schools. Includes international, national, regional, and state organizations and agencies. American Hospital Association, 840 North Lake Shore Dr., Chicago, Ill. 60611.

Hotels and Motels

Hotel-Motel Guide and Travel Atlas, Leahy's.   Annually. Lists more than 47,000 hotels and motels in the United States, Canada, and Mexico; includes room rates, number of rooms, and plan of operation. Also has extensive maps. American Hotel Register Co., 2775 Shermer Road, Northbrook, Ill. 60062.

Hotel Red Book.   Annually in May. Lists hotels in the United States, Canada, Caribbean, Mexico, Central and South America. Includes a section covering Europe, Asia, and Africa. Gives detailed information for each hotel. American Hotel Association Directory Corporation, 888 Seventh Ave., New York, N.Y. 10019.

Hotels Systems, Directory of.   Annually in July. Lists approximately 300 hotel systems in the Western Hemisphere. American Hotel Association Directory Corporation, 888 Seventh Ave., New York, N.Y. 10019.

Housewares

Housewares Reps Registry.   Annually in May. (Included with subscription to Housewares) Compilation of resources of the housewares trade, includes listing of their products, trade names, and a registry of manufacturers' representatives. Housewares Directory, Harcourt Brace Jovanovich Publications, 1 East First St., Duluth, Minn. 55802.

Jewelry

The Jewelers Board of Trade Confidential Reference Book.   Semiannually in March and September. Lists manufacturers, importers, distributors and retailers of jewelry; diamonds; precious, semiprecious, and imitation stones; watches; silverware; and kindred articles. Includes credit ratings. The Jewelers Board of Trade, 70 Catamore Blvd., East Providence, R.I. 02914.

Liquor

Wine and Spirits Wholesalers, Blue Book of.   Annually in December. Lists names of member companies; includes parent house and branches, addresses, and names of managers. Also, has register of suppliers, and gives State liquor control administrators, national associations, and trade press directory. Wine and Spirits Wholesalers of America, Inc., 2033 M St., N.W., Suite 400, Washington, D.C. 20036.

Mailing List Houses

Mailing List Houses, Directory of.   Lists more than 3,000 list firms, brokers, compilers, and firms offering their own lists for rent; includes the specialties of each firm. Arranged geographically. B. Klein Publications, P.O. Box 8503, Coral Springs, Fla. 33065.

National Mailing-List Houses.   (Small Business Bibliography 29). Lists selected national mailing list houses; includes both general line and limited line houses. Small Business Administration, P.O. Box 15434, Ft. Worth, Tex. 76119.

Mail Order Businesses

Mail Order Business Directory. Lists more than 6,300 names or mail order firms with buyers' names, and lines carried. Arranged geographically. B. Klein Publications, P.O. Box 8503, Coral Springs, Fla. 33065.

Manufacturers

MacRae's Blue Book. Annual. In five volumes: Volume 1—Corporate Index lists company names and addresses alphabetically, with 60,000 branch and/ or sales office telephone numbers. Volumes 2, 3, and 4—companies listed by 40,000 product classifications. Volume 5—company product catalogs. MacRae's Blue Book, 100 Shore Drive, Hinsdale, Ill. 60521.

Manufacturers, Thomas' Register of American. Annual. Volume 1–7— products and services; suppliers of each product category grouped by State and city. Vols. 9–14—manufacturers' catalogs. Thomas Publishing Co., One Penn Plaza, New York, N.Y. 10001.

Manufacturers' Sales Representatives

Manufacturers & Agents National Association Directory of Members. Annually in July. Contains individual listings of manufacturers' agents throughout the United States, Canada and several foreign countries. Listings cross-referenced by alphabetical, geographical and product classification. Manufacturers' Agents National Association, P.O. Box 16878. Irvine, Calif. 92713.

Mass Merchandisers

Major Mass Market Merchandisers, Nationwide Directory of. (Exclusive of New York, Metropolitan Area). Annually. Lists men's, women's, and children's wear buyers who buy for over 175,000 units—top discount, variety, super-market and drug chains; factory outlet stores; leased department operators. The Salesman's Guide, Inc., 1140 Broadway, New York, N.Y. 10001.

Mass Retailing Merchandiser Buyers Directory. Annually. Lists 7,000 man-ufacturers, mass retail chains, manufacturers' representatives, jobbers and wholesalers serving the mass retailing field. Merchandiser Publishing Co., Inc. 222 West Adams, Chicago, Ill. 60606.

Metalworking

Metalworking Directory, Dun & Bradstreet. Annually in May. Published in one national and five sectional editions. Lists about 44,000 metalworking and metal producing plants with 20 or more production employees. Arranged in four sections: geographically, line of business, alphabetically, and statistical courts summary. Marketing Services Division, Dun & Bradstreet, Inc., 99 Church St., New York, N.Y. 10007.

Military Market

Buyers' Guide. Annually. Listings grouped by systems served of suppliers names and addresses, military representatives and civilian brokerage firms that specialize in serving military stores are given. Military Market, 475 School St., S.W., Washington, D.C. 20024.

Nonfood Products

Non-Food Buyers, National Directory Of.   Annually. Alpha-geographical listing of 9,000 buyers of nonfood merchandise for over 336,000 outlets. United Publishing Co., 1372 Peachtree St., N.E., Atlanta, Ga. 30309.

Paper Products

Sources of Supply Buyers' Guide.   Lists mills and converters of paper, film, foil and allied products, and paper merchants in the United States alphabetically with addresses, principal personnel, and products manufactured. Also lists trade associations, brand names, and manufacturers' representatives. Advertisers and Publishers Service, Inc., P.O. Drawer 795, 300 N. Prospect Ave., Park Ridge, Ill. 60068.

Physicians and Medical Supply Houses

Medical Directory, American.   Volumes 1–4 gives complete information about all physicians in the United States and possessions—alphabetical and geographical listings. Volume 5—Directory of Women Physicians. American Medical Associations, 535 North Dearborn St., Chicago, Ill. 60610.

Physician and Hospital Supply Houses, Hayes' Directory of.   Annually in August. Listings of 1,850 U.S. wholesalers doing business in physician, hospital and surgical supplies and equipment; includes addresses, telephone numbers, financial standing, and credit ratings. Edward N. Hayes, Publisher, 4229 Birch St., Newport Beach, Calif. 92660.

Plumbing

Manufacturers' Representatives, Directory of.   Annually as a special section of the February issue of *The Wholesaler* magazine. Lists representatives of manufacturers selling plumbing, heating and cooling equipment, components, tools and related products, to this industry through wholesaler channels with detailed information on each. Scott Periodicals Corp., 135 Addison Ave., Elmhurst, Ill. 60126.

Premium Sources

Premium and Incentive Buyers, Directory of.   Annual in September. Lists over 16,000 executives for 12,000 firms with title, telephone number, address, and merchandise executive desires to buy in the premium, incentive and travel fields. The Salesman's Guide, 1140 Broadway, New York, N.Y. 10001.

Incentive Marketing/Incorporating Incentive Travel: Supply Sources Directory.   Annual in January. Contains classified directory of suppliers, and list of manufacturers' representatives serving the premium field. Also, lists associations and clubs, and trade shows. Incentive Marketing, 633 Third Ave., New York, N.Y. 10017.

Purchasing, Government

U.S. Government Purchasing and Sales Directory.   Booklet by Small Business Administration. Designed to help small business receive an equitable share of Government contracts. Lists types of purchases for both military and civilian needs, catalogs procurement offices by State. Lists SBA regional and branch offices. Order from Superintendent of Documents, U.S. Government Printing Office, Washington, D.C. 20402.

Refrigeration and Air Conditioning

Air Conditioning, Heating & Refrigeration News.   Dec. 31. Lists alphabetically and by products, the names of refrigeration, heating and air-conditioning manufacturers, trade names, wholesalers, and associations in the United States. Business News Publishing Co., P.O. Box 2600, Troy, Mich. 48084.

Air-Conditioning & Refrigeration Wholesalers Directory.   Annually. Lists alphabetically 950 member air-conditioning and refrigeration wholesalers with their addresses, telephone numbers, and official representatives by region, state, and city. Air-conditioning and Refrigeration Wholesalers, 22371 Newman Ave., Dearborn, Mich. 48124.

Restaurants

Restaurant Operators.   (Chain). Annually. Lists headquarters address, telephone number, number and location of units, trade names used, whether unit is company-operated or franchised, executives and buyers, annual sales volume for chains of restaurants, cafeterias, drive-ins, hotel and motel food operators, industrial caterers, etc. Chain Store Guide Publications, 425 Park Ave., New York, N.Y. 10022.

Roofing and Siding

RSI Trade Directory.   Annually in April. Has listing guide to products and equipment manufacturers, jobbers and distributors, and associations in the roofing, siding, and home improvement industries. RSI Directory, Harcourt Brace Jovanovich Publications, 1 East First St. Duluth, Minn. 55802.

Selling Direct

Direct Selling Companies, A Supplier's Guide to.   Information supplied by member companies of the Direct Selling Association includes names of contact persons, company product line, method of distribution, etc. Direct Selling Association, 1730 M Street, N.W., Washington, D.C. 20036.

Who's Who in Direct Selling.   Membership roster of the Direct Selling Association. Active members classified by type of product or service. Alphabetical listing gives name, address and telephone of firm, along with managing official. Direct Selling Association, 1730 M Street, N.W., Washington, D.C. 20036.

Shoes

Chain Shoe Stores Directory. Lists chain shoe stores at their headquarters including officers, buyers, lines carried, trading names of stores, number of operating units. The Rumpf Publishing Co., Div. of Nickerson & Collins Co., 1800 Oakton St., Des Plaines, Ill. 60018.

Shopping Centers

Shopping Centers in the United States and Canada, Directory of. Annual. Alphabetical listing of 16,000 American and Canadian shopping centers, location, owner/developer, manager, physical plant (number of stores, square feet), and leasing agent. National Research Bureau, Inc., 424 North Third St., Burlington, Iowa 52601.

Specialty Stores

Women's Specialty Stores, Phelon's. Lists over 18,000 women's apparel and accessory shops with store headquarters name and address, number of shops operated, New York City buying headquarters or representatives, lines of merchandise bought and sold, name of principal and buyers, store size, and price range. Phelon, Sheldon, & Marsar, Inc. 32 Union Sq., New York, N.Y. 10003.

Sporting Goods

Sporting Goods Buyers, Nationwide Directory of. Including semi-annual supplements. Lists over 4,500 top retail stores (23 different types) with names of buyers and executives, for all types of sporting goods, athletic apparel and athletic footwear, hunting and fishing, and outdoor equipment. The Salesman's Guide, Inc., 1140 Broadway, New York, N.Y. 10001.

The Sporting Goods Register. (Including jobbers, manufacturers' representatives and importers). Annual. Geographical listing of firms (name, address, buyers, types of goods sold, etc.) doing wholesale business in sporting goods merchandise and equipment. Similar data for Canadian firms. Alphabetical grouping of manufacturers' representatives and importers. The Sporting Goods Dealer, 1212 North Lindbergh Blvd., St. Louis, Mo. 63132.

The Sporting Goods Dealer's Directory. Annual. Lists about 5,000 manufacturers and suppliers. Also includes names of manufacturers agents, wholesalers and sporting goods associations and governing bodies of sports. The Sporting Goods Dealer, 1212 North Lindbergh Blvd., St. Louis, Mo. 63132.

Trailer Parks

Campground Directory, Woodall's North American Canadian Edition. Annually. Lists and star rates public and private campgrounds in North American continent alphabetically by town with location and description of facilities. Also lists more than 1,000 RV service locations. Regional editions available. Woodall Publishing Company, 500 Hyachinth Place, Highland Park, Ill. 60035.

Trucking

Trinc's Blue Book of the Trucking Industry and Trinc's Five Year Red Book. Retail price upon request. Together these two directories furnish comprehensive statistics on the trucking industry and individual truckers represented by about 3,500 Class I and Class II U.S. motor carriers of property. TRINC Transportation Consultants, P.O. Box 23091, Washington, D.C. 20024.

Variety Stores

General Merchandise, Variety and Junior Department Stores. Annually. Lists headquarters address, telephone number, number of units and locations, executives and buyers (includes Canada). Chain Store Guide Publications, 425 Park Ave., New York, N.Y. 10022.

Warehouses

Distribution Services, Guide to. Annually in July. Lists leading public warehouses in U.S. and Canada, as well as major truck lines, airlines, steamship lines, liquid and dry bulk terminals, material handling equipment suppliers, ports of the world and railroad piggyback services and routes. Distribution Magazine, Chilton Way, Radnor, Pa. 19089.

Public Refrigerated Warehouses, Directory of. Annually. Geographical listing of over 750 public refrigerated warehouse members. International Associations of Refrigerated Warehouses, 7315 Wisconsin Ave., N.W., Washington, D.C. 20014.

Stationers

Wholesale Stationers' Association Membership Roster. Annually. Alphabetical listing by company of over 300 wholesaler companies. Wholesale Stationers Assn., 3166 Des Plaines, Ill. 60018.

Textiles

Textile Blue Book, Davison's. Annual. Contains over 18,000 separate company listings (name, address, etc.) for U.S. and Canada. Firms included are cotton, wool, synthetic mills, knitting mills, cordage, twine, and duck manufacturers, dry goods commission merchants, converters, yarn dealers, cordage manufacturers' agents, wool dealers and merchants, cotton merchants, exporter, brokers, and others. Davison Publishing Co., P.O. Drawer 477, Ridgewood, N.J. 07451.

Toys and Novelties

Toys, Hobbies & Crafts Directory. Annually in June. Lists manufacturers, products, trade names, suppliers to manufacturers, supplier products, character licensors, manufacturers' representatives, toy trade associations, and trade show managements. Toys Directory, Harcourt Brace Jovanovich Publications, 1 East First St., Duluth, Minn. 55802.

Wholesalers and Manufacturers, Directory of. Contains information on wholesalers, manufacturers, manufacturers' representatives of toys, games, hobby, art, school, party, and office supply products. Toy Wholesalers' Association of America, 1514 Elmwood Ave., Evanston, Ill. 60201.

Other Important Directories

The following business directories are helpful to those persons doing marketing research. Most of these directories are available for reference at the larger libraries. For additional listings, consult the *Guide To American Directories* at local libraries.

AUBER Bibliography of Publications of University Bureaus of Business and Economic Research. Lists studies published by Bureaus of Business and Economic Research affiliated with American colleges and universities. Done for the Association for University Bureaus of Business and Economic Research. Issued annually. Previous volumes available, Bureau of Business Research, College of Business and Economics, West Virginia University, Morgantown, W.Va. 26506.

Bradford's Directory of Marketing Research Agencies and Management Consultants in the United States and the World. Give names and addresses of over 350 marketing research agencies in the United States, Canada, and abroad. Lists service offered by agency, along with other pertinent data, such as date established, names of principal officers, and size of staff. Bradford's Directory Of Marketing Research Agencies, P.O. Box 276, Department B-15, Fairfax, VA 22030.

Consultants and Consulting Organizations Directory. Contains 5,041 entries. Guides reader to right organization for a given consulting assignment. Entries include names, addresses, phone numbers, and data on services performed. Gale Research Company, Book Tower, Detroit, Mich. 48226.

Research Centers Directory. Palmer, Archie M., editor. Lists more than 5,500 nonprofit research organizations. Descriptive information provided for each center, including address, telephone number, name of director, data on staff, funds, publications, and a statement concerning its principal fields of research. Has special indexes. Gale Research Company, Book Tower, Detroit, Mich. 48226.

MacRae's Blue Book—Materials, Equipment, Supplies, Components. Annual. In five volumes: Vol. 1 is an index by corporations; Vols. 2–4 are a classification by products showing under each classification manufacturers of that item; Vol. 5 contains company catalogs. MacRae's Blue Book Company, 100 Shore Drive, Hinsdale, Ill. 60521.

Thomas' Grocery Register. Annual. Lists wholesale grocers; chain store organizations; voluntary buying groups; food brokers; exporters and importers of food products; frozen food brokers; distributors and related products distributed through grocery chains. Thomas Publishing Company, One Penn Plaza, New York, N.Y. 10001.

Thomas' Register of American Manufacturers. Annual. In 14 volumes: Vols. 1–7 contain manufacturers arranged geographically under each product, and capitalization or size rating for each manufacturer, Vol. 7 also lists brands names and their owners; Vol. 8 lists company addresses, phone numbers, and local offices; Vols. 9–14 contain company catalogs. Thomas Publishing Company, One Penn Plaza, New York, N.Y. 10001.

Other Sources

U.S. Small Business Administration, Washington, D.C. 20416. SBA issues a wide range of management and technical publications designed to help owner-managers and prospective owners of small business. (For general information about SBA, its policies and assistance programs, ask for *SBA—What It Is*, free on request to nearest SBA office.) Listings of currently available publications (free and for-sale) may be requested from SBA, P.O. Box 15434, Ft. Worth, Tex. 76119, or any of SBA's field offices. Ask for: SBA 115A—*Free Management Assistance Publications* and SBA 115B—*For-Sale booklets*. The lists are free and may be used for ordering the particular series listed, either the free series from SBA, or the for-sale series from the Superintendent of Documents (GPO).

Small Business Bibliography (8- to 12-page pamphlet). Each title in this series deals with a specific kind of business or business function, giving reference sources. It consists of an introduction that gives a description of the operation, listing of references applicable to the subject covered. Free.

  Statistics and Maps for National Market Analysis (SBB 12)
  National Directories for Use in Marketing (SBB 13)
  Basic Library Reference Sources (SBB 18)
  Advertising-Retail Store (SBB 20)

Management Aids for Small Manufacturers (4-8 page leaflet). Each title in this series discusses a specific management practice to help the owner-manager of small manufacturing firms with their management problems. Free.

  Using Census Data in Small Plant Marketing (MA 187)
  Locating or Relocating Your Business (MA 201)
  Finding a New Product for Your Company (MA 216)

Small Marketers Aids (4- to 8-page leaflet). Each title in this series gives guidance on a specific subject for owners of small retail, wholesale, and service business. Free.

  Measuring the Results of Advertising (SMA 121)
  Factors in Considering a Shopping Center Location (SMA 143)
  Using a Traffic Study to Select a Retail Site (SMA 152)
  Using Census Data to Select a Store Site (SMA 154)
  Advertising Guidelines for Small Retail Firms (SMA 160)

Small Business Management Series. Each booklet in this series discusses in depth the application of a specific management practice. The Series covers a wide range of small business subjects. Prices vary. GPO.

Office of Management and Budget, Executive Office Building, Washington, D.C. 20503.

Standard Industrial Classification Manual. GPO. Gives the definitions of the classifications of industrial establishments by the type of activity in which each is engaged and the resulting Industrial Classification Code. Very useful in classifying data collected from industrial firms so its classification is comparable to data reported by Government sources.

Bureau of the Census, Commerce Department, Suitland, Md 20233. Request list of publications from the Census Bureau. Publication order forms are issued for reports as they become available.

Census of Business: Retail-Area Statistics—U.S. Summary. GPO. Final figures from the Census of Retail Trade, includes statistical totals for each region, State, city and standard metropolitan area—tabulated by type of establishment.

County Business Patterns. GPO. A series of publications presenting first quarter employment and payroll statistics, by county and by industry. Separate reports issued for each of the 50 States, the District of Columbia, Puerto Rico, and outlying areas of the United States.

County and City Data Book. VTGB. GPO. Contains data for 50 States, 3141 counties or county equivalents, 243 SMSAs, 840 cities of 25,000 inhabitants or more, among others.

Directory of Federal Statistics for Local Areas, A Guide to Sources. GPO. Guide to local area socioeconomic data contained in 182 publications of 33 Federal agencies.

Directory of Federal Statistics of States, A Guide to Sources. GPO. Guide to State socio-economic data contained in more than 750 publications of Federal agencies.

Directory of Non-Federal Statistics for State and Local Areas. GPO. Guide to nonfederal sources of current statistics on social, political, and economic subjects for 50 States, the District of Columbia, Guam, Puerto Rico, and the Virgin Islands.

Standard Metropolitan Statistical Areas. GPO. Gives the criteria followed in establishing standard metropolitan statistical areas. Changes issued periodically as amendments.

Department of Commerce. Domestic and International Business Administration, Washington, D.C. 20230.

Measuring Markets: A Guide to the Use of Federal and State Statistical Data. GPO. Presents features and measurements of markets, types of useful data published by Federal and State Governments, case examples of market measurement by use of government data, and bibliographies.

SOURCES OF ADDITIONAL INFORMATION

Business Competition Intelligence, by William L. Sammon, Mark A. Kurland, and Robert Spitalnic, published by John Wiley & Sons, Inc., 605 Third Avenue, New York, NY 10158.

Business Research: Concept and Practice, by Robert G. Murdick, published by Richard D. Irwin, Inc., 1818 Ridge Road, Homewood, IL 60430.

Competition Intelligence, by Leonard M. Fuld, published by John Wiley & Sons, Inc., 605 Third Avenue, New York, NY 10158.

Do-It-Yourself Marketing Research, by George E. Breen, published by McGraw-Hill Book Co., 1221 Avenue of the Americas, New York, NY 10020.

Honomichl on Marketing Research, by Jack J. Honomichl, published by NTC Business Books, 4255 West Touhy Avenue, Lindenwood, IL 60646-1975.

A Manager's Guide to Marketing Research, by Paul E. Green and Donald E. Frank, published by John Wiley & Sons, Inc., 605 Third Avenue, New York, NY 10158.

Market and Sales Forecasting, by F. Keay, published by John Wiley & Sons, Inc., 605 Third Avenue, New York, NY 10158.

Marketing Research: A Management Overview, by Evelyn Konrad and Rod Erickson, published by AMACOM, a division of the American Management Association, 135 West 50th Street, New York, NY 10020.

Research for Marketing Decisions, by Paul E. Green and Donald S. Tull, published by Prentice-Hall, Inc., Englewood Cliffs, NJ 07632.

10

How to Find and Introduce a New Product

THE IMPORTANCE OF NEW PRODUCT INTRODUCTION

It is an unfortunate fact that eight out of ten new products fail in the marketplace. Yet, new product introduction is absolutely essential. Why is this so? Without new products your business cannot survive. You cannot continue to produce the old products that have made your company successful because of the product life cycle. The product life cycle shows that every product goes through the stages of introduction, growth, maturity, and decline. In this final phase, while sales may continue to be made, the product becomes more and more unprofitable. Now, naturally, life cycles are of different lengths for different products. Some life cycles are extremely long, such as those for the safety pin or the hairpin. Others, such as those for electronic calculators and electronic watches, are extremely short. However, no product or service can be offered in one form forever.

Of course, a company does not introduce a new product only because it is forced to do so. Below is a listing of some of the possible reasons for a company's decision to offer something new.

1. Your product has become noncompetitive because improvements in competitive products have rendered yours obsolete.
2. The use for which your product was created has either disappeared or has gone into decline.
3. Your product may be related to some phase of the national or local economy. This may be war or peace; it may be heavy industry, the military, energy, agriculture, or any other facet of economic life.
4. A new product may be desirable to take up excess plant capacity.
5. You may have surplus capital which you wish to utilize.
6. You may find the opportunity to utilize by-products and materials in the manufacture of other products.
7. You may want to make maximum use of your sales organization and have additional products which will allow you to amortize these overhead costs over a broader base.
8. You may be in a business that has cycles known as "peaks and valleys," either due to seasonal fluctuations or ordering phases. Sometimes these upswings and downturns can be leveled out by the use of new products which sell during the valleys.

9. You may wish to make use of marginal or partly used manpower or other facilities.

As noted earlier, the mortality of new product ideas is extremely high. Alan A. Smith, of the consulting firm of Arthur D. Little, Inc., of Cambridge, Massachusetts, researched the experience of 20 companies concerned with successful new product development. Here is the experience of these 20 companies.

There were 540 possibilities in the idea stage which were considered for research. 448 of these 540 were eliminated during initial screening of items which should be pursued. This left 92 which were selected for preliminary laboratory investigation. Only 8 of the 92 appeared sufficiently promising to warrant development, and 7 of the 8 were dropped as unsalable or unprofitable as determined during some process of development or introduction into the marketplace. Only 1 of these 7, or 1 out of the original 540 idea possibilities, was placed in regular production.

While many possibilities for new ideas and new products should be considered, you can see that 92 to 1 or even 8 to 1 is not a terrific success ratio, and much money was wasted finding the one product that was successful. In this chapter you will see how to increase your new products' success ratio dramatically.

THE ADVANTAGES OF NEW PRODUCT INTRODUCTION

Earlier we gave several reasons for introducing a new product. Here are some clear-cut advantages for new product development which should encourage you to look at new products and introduce them to the marketplace.

A new product may reduce your overhead by allowing you to amortize administrative sales, advertising and distribution costs over additional products.

Your new product may lead you into new markets which may be even greater than the current market which you are serving.

New products may add substantially to your profit as well as to the stability of your company.

New products may lead you into using distribution channels that will benefit your old product line and working together may synergistically help both.

Tax laws frequently encourage you and in effect share the cost of developing new products.

PRODUCT INTEREST CHECKLIST

I am going to give you a list of sources of new product ideas, but before you look these over, you should have a general idea of the type of product that you're looking for based on factors such as your company's strengths, market preference, the sales volume you desire, product status, the product configuration you may be interested in, and finance. This will give you a profile of product interest. The following checklist was developed by John B. Lang, technology utilization officer of the Small Business Administration in Los Angeles.[1] Use it to develop a profile of product interest.

[1] John B. Lang, *Finding a New Product for Your Company*, Small Business Administration (1980).

Your Company's Strengths

		Yes	No
1.	Is manufacturing your company's strength?		
2.	Do you prefer a highly automated production line?		
3.	Do you prefer a product with a high ratio of labor to production costs?		
4.	Are your production personnel highly skilled?		
5.	Are your industrial product designers exceptionally skilled?		
6.	Does your present equipment have a long usable life?		
7.	Is your present equipment largely underutilized?		
8.	Do you have a strong sales force?		
9.	Is your sales force hampered by too-narrow a product?		
10.	Do you have strong capability in a particular technology?		
11.	Does your company have cash or credit resources not used in your present operations?		
12.	Does your company have a reputation for high quality products?		
13.	Does your company have a reputation for low cost production?		

Market Preference

14.	Do you prefer a particular industry?		
15.	Do you prefer a product sold to retail consumers?		
16.	Do you prefer a product sold to industrial users?		
17.	Do you prefer a product sold to the government?		
18.	Do you prefer a product with long usage?		
19.	Will you accept a product that may be a fad item?		
20.	Do you prefer a consumable item?		
21.	Is there a distribution system (trade practice) you prefer?		
22.	Would you consider a product limited to a given locality? (Or a product in demand largely in overseas markets?)		
23.	Is a product that requires specialty selling desirable?		
24.	Is a product that needs mass merchandising suitable?		
25.	Do you intend overseas distribution?		
26.	Must your present sales department be able to sell a new product?		
27.	Are you willing to create a new or separate marketing department to sell a new product?		

Sales Volume Desired

28.	Have you determined the optimum annual volume from the product over the next 3 years?		

	Yes	No
29. Do you have any preference for a unit price range in a product?	_____	_____
30. Do you have 5 and 10 year volume objectives for a new product?	_____	_____
31. Will this product have to support its own sales organization?	_____	_____
32. Will the product support its own manufacturing equipment?	_____	_____
33. At what volume does a product exceed your company's capability?	_____	_____

Product Status

34. Will you accept an idea for a product?	_____	_____
35. Will you accept an unpatentable product?	_____	_____
36. Is a non-exclusive license of a patent acceptable?	_____	_____
37. Are you willing to develop an idea to a patentable stage?	_____	_____
38. Will you develop a patent without acceptable prototype?	_____	_____
39. Will you accept a product that has been on the market but is not yet profitable?	_____	_____
40. Will you license a patent?	_____	_____
41. Do you insist on owning the product's patent?	_____	_____
42. Will you enter a joint venture for a new product with another company?	_____	_____
43. Would you merge with or buy a company that has good products but needs your company's strengths in manufacturing, sales, finances, or management?	_____	_____

The Product Configuration

44. Are there any maximum size limitations to a product you can manufacture?	_____	_____
45. Would weight of a product be a factor?	_____	_____
46. Do warehousing facilities or yard space impose size limitation?	_____	_____
47. Does length of production time influence the desirability of a product?	_____	_____
48. Have you determined your equipment tolerance?	_____	_____
49. Do you have adequately trained personnel to do the job?	_____	_____
50. Would you prefer that a product be made of certain materials?	_____	_____
51. Are there manufacturing processes that should constitute the major portion of a new product?	_____	_____
52. Are there any manufacturing processes the product should not have?	_____	_____

		Yes	No
53.	Would a product requiring extensive quality control costs be desirable?	_____	_____

Finance

54.	Has an overall budget been established for a new product?	_____	_____
55.	Have separate budgets been established for finding, acquisition, development, market research, manufacturing, and marketing the new product?	_____	_____
56.	Has a time period been established by which a new product must become self-supporting, profitable, or capable of generating cash?	_____	_____
57.	Does the new product require a certain profit margin to be compatible with your financial resources or company objectives?	_____	_____
58.	Has external long-range financing been explored for your new product?	_____	_____
59.	Is the length of the sales cycle for the new product known?	_____	_____
60.	Do trade practices require you to furnish financial assistance, such as floor planning or dating plans, for distribution of your product?	_____	_____
61.	Have you determined average inventory to sales ratio for the new product?	_____	_____
62.	Have you determined average aging of accounts receivable for your new product?	_____	_____
63.	Does the product have seasonal aspects?	_____	_____

SCREENING QUESTIONS

Other questions you should ask yourself may be grouped by your company's operations, the potential market, concept marketability, and engineering production. These are shown in Figure 10.1[2] and are known as screening questions because they act as a screen to eliminate products that you shouldn't consider.

Profile of Product Interest

Your answers to the 63 questions can lead to a well thought-out guide as to the acceptability of any potential new product. A short condensed profile helps communicate your needs. Such a profile also indicates a high degree of professional management which sources of new products will welcome. For illustrative purposes a sample profile of the fictitious XYZ company follows.

[2] Adapted from Tom W. White, "Use Variety of Internal, External Sources to Gather and Screen New Product Ideas," *Marketing News*, September 10, 1983, p. 12.

Company Operations

- How compatible is the concept with the current product lines?
- Does it represent an environmental hazard or threat to our production facility and to the facilities of our neighbors?
- Would it unreasonably interrupt manufacturing, engineering or marketing activities?
- Could we meet the after-sale service requirements that would be demanded by customers?

Potential Market

- What is the size of the market?
- Where is the market located?
- What would be our potential market share?
- How diversified is the need for the product? Is it a one-industry or multi-industry product?
- How fast do we anticipate the market for the concept to grow?
- How stable would such a market be in a recession?

Concept Marketability

- Who would be our competitors?
- How good is their product?
- How well capitalized are potential competitors?
- How important is their product to the survival of their business?
- How is our product differentiated from the competition's? Will the differentiation provide a market advantage?
- Could we meet or beat the competition's price?
- Is the product normally sold through our current distribution channels or would we have to make special arrangements?
- Do we have qualified sales personnel?
- Do we have suitable means by which to promote the product?
- What would we anticipate to be the life expectancy of the product? Is it going to move through the various life cycle stages in six months, six years or sixty years?
- Will the product be offensive to the environment in which it will be used?

Engineering and Production

- What is the technical feasibility of the product?
- Do we have the technical capability to design it?
- Can it be manufactured at a marketable cost?

Figure 10.1. Screening questions. Adapted from Tom W. White, "Use Variety of Internal, External Sources to Gather and Screen New Product Ideas," *Marketing News* (September 16, 1983), p. 12.

- Will the necessary production materials be readily available?
- Do we have the production capabilities to build it?
- Do we have adequate storage facilities for the raw materials and completed product?
- Do we have adequate testing devices for proper quality control of the product?

Financial

- What is our required return on investment?
- What is our anticipated ROI for this product?
- Do we have the available capital?
- What would be the pay-back period?
- What is our break-even point?

Legal

- Is the product patentable?
- Can we meet legal restrictions regarding labeling, advertising, shipment, etc.?
- How significant are product warranty problems likely to be?
- Is the product vulnerable to existing or pending legislation?

Figure 10.1. *(Continued)*

The XYZ company, a defense-aerospace oriented precision metal stamping and machine shop, desires to acquire a product or product line to the following specifications:

Market—The product desired is one for use by industrial or commercial firms of a specific industry but not by the government or general public except incidentally.

Product—The product sought is one in which 60 percent of the total direct manufacturing cost consists of metal stamping and/or machining processes.

Price range—Open, but preferably the unit price to the user will be in the $100 to $400 range.

Volume—Open, but preferably a product which aggressively marketed will produce $500,000 in sales the first year with an annual potential sale of 3 to 5 million dollars.

Finance—Initial resources to $150,000 in addition to present plant capacity are available for manufacturing a new product.

Type of acquisition—Prefer royalties to a patent but will consider purchase of a patent, joint venture, merger, or purchase of a company outright.

EIGHTEEN SOURCES FOR NEW PRODUCTS

Any of these sources may give you a new product idea which will make you a fortune.

1. *Currently successful products.* Look at currently successful products, but be careful not to copy them. Copy only the concept. If you copy the idea exactly, you may be in violation of the law if the idea is covered by a patent, copyright, or other type of protection. But even if you don't copy an idea exactly, if your product is very much like another one, the individual who has introduced the product into the market has already captured a fair share, and you will be in the position of trying to take away that share.

2. *Inventor shows.* Many inventors are not good marketers. In fact, most inventions that are patented are never actually produced in quantity. At inventor shows you will have the opportunity to see hundreds of new products that the inventors would like to license for someone else to manufacture and sell for a royalty; perhaps they would like to sell the invention outright. You can find the inventor shows in your area by contacting your local chamber of commerce. Or, you can write to the Office of Inventions and Innovations, National Bureau of Standards, Washington, D.C. 20234, for a listing of the major inventor shows throughout the United States.

3. *Foreign products.* Foreign products are not always available in the United States, and frequently these products which are unfamiliar here may be outstanding and sell quite well. Also, every country would like to see the number of its exports increased. This points to one primary source of foreign products: the commercial attachés of foreign consulates and embassies. You can find the numbers of foreign consulates or embassies in your telephone book if you happen to live in or near a large city. If you do not live close enough to these offices to make calling feasible, get a copy of the *International Commerce Magazine Weekly*, published by the U.S. Department of Commerce. This magazine contains a license opportunity section in which many foreign-made products available for licensing in the United States are listed. To get a copy, contact the Department of Commerce's local field office which you will find in your telephone book. There are other books available that will help you if you are looking for products which you want to import. One is the *American Register of Exporters and Importers*, published by the American Register of Exporters and Importers Corp., 38 Park Row, New York, N.Y. 10038. Another is the *Directory of New York Importers*, published by Commerce Industry Association Institute, Inc., 65 Liberty St., New York, N.Y. 10005. Also, in your local library, you will find at least one directory of importers and exporters published annually for almost every country in the world. Check in the reference or business section of your library. There are also overseas trade publications which will help you. Some that are excellent sources of new product ideas are:

Hong Kong Enterprise, 3rd Floor, Connaught Center, Connaught Road Central, Hong Kong.

Made in Europe, P.O. Box 174027, D-6, Frankfurt am Main, West Germany.

Canada Commerce, Department of Industry, Trade and Commerce, Ottawa, Ontario, Canada K1A0H5.

Commerce in France at the Chamber, 21 Avenue George V, Paris 8E France.

Other foreign trade magazines can be found in your local library and will contain many additional products for you to manufacture or sell. Write to each and ask for a sample of the magazine.

4. *Newspapers.* Read the business opportunity section of your local paper as well as such publications as the *Wall Street Journal.* Very frequently individuals who have a product to sell will advertise. You can contact them to negotiate the best deal possible for a product that may be very successful. In addition, you may consider advertising in these publications yourself, or in trade magazines, stating that you are interested in acquiring certain types of new products.

5. *Local manufacturers.* Many manufacturers have created a product at one time or another that was no successful for his or her particular line of work or business, but which you may be able to make very successful. Simply call the president of each company and ask whether any old tooling exists for discontinued products from your line. Sometimes you can buy this tooling very cheaply, for perhaps only a couple hundred dollars, even though it may be worth $40,000 or more. This is one of Joe Cossman's secrets which helped to make him a multimillionaire. He frequently purchased old tooling from manufacturers, turned the product around, and made a fortune with it. Among the products acquired in this way were his famous Potato Spud Gun and Flippy the Frogman, both toy products which sold in the millions.

6. *NASA's Tech Briefs.* These bulletins are published periodically by the National Aviation and Space Administration. They describe new ideas, concepts, and patents for new products, all by-products of the space program. All of these are available for licensing from NASA. To get a copy of NASA's *Tech Briefs,* write to National Technical Information Service, U.S. Department of Commerce, Springfield, Va. 22151.

7. *Patent Abstracts Bibliography.* This semiannual publication lists NASA- and government-owned patents and applications for patents as a service to those seeking new licensable products for the commercial market. This may be ordered from the address above.

8. *New products from corporations.* You can write or contact major U.S. corporations. Most have research and development divisions which develop products the corporation has no interest in producing or selling. As a result, many have established special offices to market the licensing of their patents to individuals outside of their company. The titles of these individuals vary; however, you can usually get in touch with them by contacting any corporation which is large enough to have a research and development division and asking for the direct of patent licensing.

9. *Distress merchandise.* Every retailer has been in a situation where certain merchandise could not be sold. Under these circumstances, he cuts the price tremendously and then attempts to sell it at bargain rates. This material is called distress merchandise. When you see distress merchandise, if you think that you have a market for it, look at the product and see if there is a patent number on it. If there is, you can locate the inventor by purchasing a copy of the patent from the patent office. Or, if you live close to a depository for patents, you can look at the patent and find out the inventor's name and address at no cost at all. As I mentioned earlier, inventors are frequently poor marketers, and the fact that this is distress merchandise indicates that if the inventor still controls the patent, he or she may well be interested in licensing or outright sale. The address to write is U.S. Patent Office, Washington, D.C. 20231.

10. *The Official Gazette of the U.S. Patent Office.* This bulletin is published weekly and lists all the patents granted by the patent office. Annual subscriptions are available from the Superintendent of Documents, Government Printing Office, Washington, D.C. 20402. The gazette contains a section that lists one-time-only patents available for sale or licensing. Many libraries also subscribe to the *Official Gazette* of the U.S. Patent Office. Patent attorneys in your area also may know of new products recently patented and available for licensing.

11. *Expired patents.* In the United States, a patent is good for only 17 years. The only exception is an ornamental design patent which is good for 3½, 7, or 14 years. After that period, the patent is in the public domain and may be produced and sold by anyone. Also, you can look at the entire technology of any general product area by writing the patent office and asking for a list of all the patent numbers falling into a specified product area. The patent office will charge you for this service, but once you have the list of numbers you can go to a federal depository of patents which is usually located in a major library. All you need to do then is look up the patent number and you can get the full information. If the patent on the invention has expired, you are free to do with it as you want. If it has not expired, you may approach the inventor, getting his name and address from the patent, about licensing or purchasing the idea outright.

12. *Trade shows.* Like inventor shows, trade shows will have hundreds of products, some of which will be outstanding for your particular purposes. To find out about trade shows, get a copy of the *Directory of the United States Trade Shows, Expositions and Conventions.* Write to the United States Travel Service, U.S. Department of Commerce, Washington, D.C. 20230. Or, you may ask your local chamber of commerce about upcoming trade shows. Also, see Chapter 14.

13. *Old items from magazines.* If you look through an old Sears or Montgomery Ward catalog, you will notice how many of the products described therein are still of tremendous interest. You can also get good ideas from old magazines. Old mail order products are especially well suited for reissue. An afternoon spent in the library looking at old magazines may give you an idea which you may use as is or one to which you can give a new twist.

14. *Personalizing items.* People like to see items and like to buy items that have their names on them. This idea has been used again and again, every single day, to sell products of all sorts, from brass business card cases sold through the *Wall Street Journal* to briefcases, wallets, address labels, and paperweights. Do some research, because the field is far from exhausted. If you can find a product on which you can imprint someone's name, you probably have a winner.

15. *Commercial banks.* If you acquire all or part of another business, you may also acquire the products which that business controls. Many small companies will find outstanding products that may need the strength that your company can provide to become successful. This strength may have to do with personnel, facilities, equipment, know-how, marketing, or capital. Frequently, commercial banks will know of such a situation and can arrange the meeting between you and someone with a product that you might be interested in. The bank does this for no charge with the expectation of receiving banking business which might ensue from some sort of an arrangement.

16. *Small Business Investment Companies (SBICs) and investment bankers.* These companies are continually examining potential businesses, all of which have products of one sort or another. If you contact SBICs and investment bankers, they might well lead you to new products or an equity position in a business that has products which are desirable for your firm. You can obtain the latest list of SBICs from your local SBA office. A list of SBICs is also contained in the appendix of this book.

17. *Licensing brokers.* A licensing broker is a type of consultant having a wide range of contacts in the licensing field. They represent companies seeking licenses, that is, companies with products that they wish to license, as well as companies searching for products to license. They often have considerable experience in developing fair and reasonable licensing arrangements and can advise you or their client along these lines. You can locate licensing brokers through patent attorneys, in your local telephone book, and sometimes in your local newspapers under the Business Opportunities heading.

18. *The* Thomas Register of Manufacturers. This publication consists of several volumes listing manufacturers of all types of items in the United States. There are several such directories, and you can find them at your local library. You will find not only the names and addresses of the individuals running these companies, but also products that are available and the individuals to write about obtaining them. Every single page is a source of another potential product for your business.

HOW TO DECIDE WHICH NEW PRODUCT TO DEVELOP OR INTRODUCE

As you begin thinking about new product introduction and development, you will discover that there are many products among which to choose. Of course you can't develop them all; the problem then is deciding which products are best for your company. You may think that this will be fairly easy; you simply introduce those products that will bring you the most profit. However, the choice is *not* easy. You may have limited financial resources and a more profitable product will have to be passed over in favor of one that you can afford. Or, it may be important to you to recoup your investment rapidly. Then, too, you must consider the particular background and experience you have, either with the type of product or with marketplaces. Here are 10 different questions that you should ask yourself about each product you are considering.[3]

1. Is the product one which fits the company's needs, interests and abilities?
2. Is the chance of success good within the limits of reasonable time and expenditure?
3. Are the people connected with the project capable of carrying it to completion or can suitable people be hired?
4. Will a successfully completed project result in
   (a) New products?

---

[3] Alan A. Smith, *Technology and Your New Products*, Small Business Administration (1967), p. 11.

      (b) Improved products?
      (c) Reduced cost?

5. Is there a market for the new or improved product?
6. Is the market substantial and profitable?
7. Can the present marketing organization really sell the product?
8. Will the product expand the base of operations of the company?
9. Will the product fill a real need or will it be only a momentary fad?
10. Can the product be made with the present equipment? If not, can the estimated cost of tooling up be covered by increased sales?

These questions will help you screen out many products which will clearly be unsuited to your company or your particular situation.

Other factors which you must consider in comparing potential new products for development and for which you must obtain factual information or forecasts include the following:

Total profit
Profitability
The cost to develop
The market for the product
The life cycle, including estimated length
The cost of research and development
The plant overcapacity or undercapacity
The synergistic effect with other products in your product line
The cost of putting the product on the market
Technical know-how required
Labor skills required
Availability of raw materials
By-products that may be sold from the manufacture of this product
Good will
Marketing know-how available
Physical distribution facilities
Available distribution channels

You can see that deciding which product to introduce is no five-minute task, but the effort is worthwhile. You want the product you select to be a success.

Now, we are getting down to the serious assessment of the wisdom of spending money for one project over another. The end result is which potential products you will introduce and which you will not. First, list what factors you will use for comparison, those which you think are most important: high return on investment, a proprietary position, a large market share, low risk of failure in development, low risk of failure in marketing, huge demand, and so forth. Certain quantitative methods of comparison are also recommended. For example, you can calculate the total profit of a particular project if you can estimate its life cycle by using either the present value or internal rate of return methods shown you for comparison in the financial section of this book. You can compare the return for each investment, for each project, by dividing the projected return by the investment and choosing those projects which have the larger return.

If time to recoup your investment is important, compare using the pay-back formula, investment divided by the return per year. All of these various quantitative and nonquantitative comparisons are placed on a rating sheet as shown in Figure 10.2.

Now, you must determine factor weighting. You do this by taking your list of important factors and deciding which of these factors are more important than others. Let us say that you have four factors which you consider to be of equal importance. These four factors may be technical know-how, profitability, product synergism with other products in your product line, and marketing know-how. If these are your only factors and you consider them to be of equal importance, each would be assigned a weighting of 25%. The importance of the factors to you will be indicated by their percentages. Let's say that you consider profitability the main item, far and away the most important of the four factors. Perhaps you will assign it 50%. This then leaves 50% to be apportioned among the other three factors. You might assign 10% to technical knowhow, 20% to product synergism, and 20% to marketing know-how. In all cases, the total percentages assigned to all the different factors that you have listed should equal exactly 100%.

Now, look at each product you are considering and assign points to the project for each factor that you have listed. The points assigned are from 1 to 10. Those products that seem very good in relation to a particular factor receive 10 points. Those that are very poor receive only 1 point. For example, consider

RELEVANT FACTORS FOR SELECTING NEW PRODUCTS FOR INTRODUCTION

RELEVANT FACTOR	RELATIVE FACTOR WEIGHTING
DEMAND FOR PRODUCT	
1. Strength	3%
2. Period	3
3. Need	4
MARKET	
1. Size	6
2. Location	5
3. Competition	5
PRODUCT	
1. Compatibility with current line	1
2. Uniqueness of features	8
3. Price	4
4. Protection	3
COMPANY STRENGTHS	
1. Marketing	6
2. Location	2
3. Special facilities	4
4. Production	2
FINANCIAL CONSIDERATIONS	
1. Capital budgeting	8
2. ROI	8
3. Pay-back	8
4. Cash flow	8
PRODUCT DEVELOPMENT	
1. Technical risk	5
2. Producibility	4
3. Scheduling	3
TOTAL	100 %

Figure 10.2.   Relevant factors for selecting new products for introduction.

Factor	Relative Weight	Point Value	Final Value
Demand for product			
Strength	0.03	7	0.21
Period	0.03	3	0.09
Need	0.04	1	0.04
Market			
Size	0.06	4	0.24
Location	0.05	2	0.10
Competition	0.05	7	0.35
Product			
Compatibility with current line	0.01	6	0.06
Uniqueness of features	0.08	2	0.16
Price	0.04	1	0.04
Protection	0.03	1	0.03
Company Strengths			
Marketing	0.06	2	0.12
Location	0.02	8	0.16
Special facilities	0.04	1	0.04
Production	0.02	1	0.02
Financial Considerations			
Capital budgeting	0.08	5	0.40
ROI	0.08	4	0.32
Pay-back	0.08	3	0.24
Cash flow	0.08	2	0.16
Product Development			
Technical risk	0.05	1	0.05
Producibility	0.04	7	0.28
Scheduling	0.03	2	0.06
	1.00	Total point value for this product	3.17

Figure 10.3.   New product selection matrix (analysis for a simulated product).

technical know-how. If you have the technical know-how to develop a particular product easily, give it a 10-point rating. On the other hand, if you do not have the technical know-how to develop a certain product, you may give it a very low point score, perhaps only 1 or 2 points.

Now that you have completed the point assignments, you must multiply the weighting percentage by the points assigned. The result (shown in Figure 10.3) is a total point rating for this product. Now, you simply pick those products with the highest ratings. These are the ones you will introduce.

HOW TO BEAT YOUR COMPETITION IN NEW PRODUCT INTRODUCTION AND DEVELOPMENT

You may feel that because you are a small firm you have little or no chance to beat your larger competitors, especially in introducing a new product or a new service. This is wrong, and very frequently a small firm can win out over its competition. Here's how.

Ability to Make Decisions Fast

A small company, where one man or a few men make decisions, has an extremely big advantage in terms of time. Larger companies act slowly, because of a bureaucracy and many levels in the managerial chain of command, when making even simple decisions, while you can operate much more rapidly and efficiently. It is not unusual for a small firm to make a decision in one day that would take a large firm several months or even a year or more to make.

Lower Break-Even Point

Because a smaller firm carries a much lower overhead, the break-even point for your introduction of a new product or a new service will be much lower than that of a larger firm. Also, because as a smaller firm you can be more efficient, your break-even point can be lower than that of a larger competitor. As a result of this, many large firms cannot introduce certain new products or services unless the volume is sufficiently large. On the other hand, you are able to introduce products or services to service a smaller market. A volume that is tremendously profitable for you may be unprofitable for a larger company.

Regional Sales

For the same reason as above, many small firms can serve a specific region in their locality and provide much better customer service and a far more effective and efficient promotional effort than can their larger competitors. This is the reason that many local areas have their own brands of beer and other commodities. Further, in this local area, the small company frequently outsells the larger competitor many times over.

Custom-Made Quality Products

Large firms, because of their volume requirements, frequently cannot do custom work. And for the same reason, quality sometimes suffers. This leaves a nice niche for the smaller company that can do custom work with individuals or other companies that desire this type of product or service. Because of this, some small companies absolutely monopolize the custom-made quality markets in their industries. They charge high prices and make huge profit margins because they have developed this market, a market their bigger competitors cannot reach.

SOURCES OF HELP IN DEVELOPING AND INTRODUCING NEW PRODUCTS

Much of the work necessary in order to introduce a new product or service can be purchased by you, and other help can be obtained at no cost or very little cost. Here are some sources that will help you with your development and introduction of new products.

Management and Marketing Consultants

Management and marketing consultants exist which perform a wide range of services for you in the development and introduction of a new product. These services include evaluating potential sales, creating a marketing plan, setting up pricing, locating executives to run your programs, investigating material costs and sources, checking out competitive problems with which the new product will be faced, budgets, developing financial schedules, and other tasks.

Industrial Designers and Engineers

These individuals will help you to design the new product, help you make it more efficient, or allow you to produce it cheaper. They can improve the physical appearance of the product, making old products look new and visually appealing. They can redesign products, correct product defects, reduce noise vibration, reduce weight and bulk, eliminate hazards, reduce the number of parts, solve engineering problems, suggest new materials, and do many other similar types of work.

Patent Attorneys and Agents

Patent attorneys and agents can help you make patent searches and applications and help you with related patent, copyright, and trademark work.

Package Designers

Package designers will design the packaging of your product, including developing trademarks or logos, designing containers to hold the product, recommending sizes and shapes of packages, bottles, and enclosures, designing merchandise tags, advising on label requirements levied by city, state, or federal government, conducting drop tests for packaging, and so forth.

Advertising Agencies

Advertising agencies can handle your entire promotional effort, including writing copy, preparing graphics, suggesting other means of promotion, and suggesting which medium and vehicle to choose for your ad.

Marketing Research Firms

Marketing research firms can help you decide what new products to introduce. They offer preliminary consumer research, preliminary industrial research, exploratory research, and other means of determining whether it makes sense to introduce a new product at all.

All of the commercial firms above can be located either through the yellow pages under the appropriate headings or through engineering, marketing, or consultant trade associations. Before engaging any firm, it is wise to check their references; talk to at least three firms who have used their services. And you might also check with their trade association and with your local Better Business Bureau. Remember that this book shows you how to do many of these services yourself, if you desire, at a much reduced cost.

Noncommercial Sources

Some universities have centers funded by the National Science Foundation for helping inventors and innovators with their new product development and introduction into the marketplace. One of the better ones is the University of Oregon's Experimental Center for the Advancement of Invention and Innovation. Much of the information that the University of Oregon has is computerized. This allows the university to evaluate any new product idea on 33 different criteria and help you screen out bad ideas. Each submitted idea is evaluated against the following criteria: legality, safety, environmental impact, societal impact, potential market, product life cycle, usage for learning, product visibility, service, durability, new competition, functional feasibility, production feasibility, development status, investment cost, trend of demand, product line potential, need, promotion, appearance, price, protection, pay-back period, profitability, product interdependence, research and development, stability of demand, consumer, user compatibility, marketing research, distribution, perceived function, existing competition, and potential sales. The address is: Experimental Center for the Advancement of Invention and Innovation, College of Business Administration, 131 Gilbert Hall, University of Oregon, Eugene, OR 97403.

The Small Business Institute (SBI) is sponsored by the Small Business Administration and currently is located at 450 colleges and universities around the country. The help provided by the SBI is usually concerned with the business part of new product introduction, including marketing, finances, accounting, management problems, and so forth. Business students of the university supervised by professors provide this service to you free of charge. Contact your local Small Business Administration to learn more. The addresses of the SBA are listed in Appendix I.

The following two organizations may also be of assistance to you with your new product development and introduction problems: (1) the American Association of Small Research Companies, 8794 West Chester Pike, Upper Darby, PA 19082, and (2) the Association for the Advancement of Invention and Innovation, Suite 605, 1735 Jefferson Davis Highway, Arlington, VA 22202.

YOUR OWN PRODUCT SURVEY

You might also consider doing some simple marketing research to help yourself. Basically, you want to ask these questions:[4]

1. What do you think of the product concept?
2. Would you buy it?
3. How much do you think it should sell for?
4. How often would your purchase it?
5. Where would you expect to purchase it?
6. What additional features should the product have?
7. What features should be eliminated?
8. How would you expect to learn about the product's availability?
9. How large should the product be?
10. What color should the product be?
11. How would you use the product?
12. Are there benefits of this product over competing products or products that it might replace?
13. Would you buy this product to replace the current product you are using?

---

[4] William A. Cohen, *The Practice of Marketing Management* (Macmillan Publishing Co.: New York, 1988) p. 310.

TWENTY-ONE WARNING SIGNALS

Peter Hilton, founder of the New Product Institute and the president of Kastor, Hilton, Chesley, Clifford and Atherton, Inc., an advertising agency in New York, has documented 21 warning signals from the consumer, the trade, or company management that something is wrong with new product or new service introduction.[5] Action should be taken as soon as possible to correct the problem. If any of these occur as you begin new product introduction or development, stop, heed, and take the required action.

From the consumer:

1. The price is too high.
2. I don't know how to use it—I must be educated.
3. Certainly it's a better product, but it's not quite worth the extra money.

From the trade:

4. The product will have a low rate of turnover.
5. The product will disturb our business on established items, maybe destroy more business than it creates.
6. We are afraid of the servicing problems this new item may create.
7. The product is an unwanted addition to a field already crowded.
8. There is no retail shelf space or floor space available for this product.
9. The nature of the product is such that it must be sold in an odd size or shape ill suited to shipping or display facilities.
10. This product cannot be sold without individual demonstration.

From company management:

11. It is difficult to procure or procure consistently the right raw materials for this product.
12. It is difficult to project costs because the raw material market is subject to considerable price fluctuation.
13. Plant production would be seriously hampered if changes were made to handle the manufacture of this new product.
14. The product is good but impossible to package.
15. The patent situation is confused and we would be vulnerable.
16. The probably channel of distribution of this new product is not clearly defined.
17. To make salesmen's time available for this product would jeopardize our established line.
18. The new product does not hold promise of sufficient volume or frequency of purchase to maintain distribution.
19. The trademark situation is unsatisfactory.
20. Certain government regulations would make marketing of this product difficult.

[5] Peter Hilton, *New Product Introduction* (Small Business Administration: Washington, D.C., 1961).

21. With this product we would be competing in a field dominated by strong, aggressive companies with superior marketing resources.

SOURCES OF ADDITIONAL INFORMATION

Corporate Strategy and New Product Innovation, edited by Robert R. Rothberg, published by The Free Press, a division of Macmillan Publishing Co., Inc., 866 Third Avenue, New York, NY 10022.

Handbook of New Product Development, by Peter Hilton, published by Prentice-Hall, Inc., Englewood Cliffs, NJ 07632.

Innovation, by Richard Foster, published by Summit Books, a division of Simon & Schuster, Inc., 1230 Avenue of the Americas, New York, NY 10020.

Innovation, by Milton D. Rosenau, Jr., published by Lifetime Learning Publications, a division of Wadsworth, Inc., 10 Davis Drive, Belmont, CA 94002.

New Product Development Strategies, by Frederick D. Buggie, published by AMACOM, a division of the American Management Association, 135 West 50th Street, New York, NY 10020.

New Product Introduction for Small Business Owners, by Peter Hilton, published by the Small Business Administration, Washington, DC 20402.

New Products, New Profits, edited by Elibeth Marting, published by the American Management Association, 135 West 50th Street, New York, NY 10020.

Planning New Products, by Philip Marvin, published by the Penton Publishing Co., Cleveland, OH 44101.

Product Planning, edited by A. Edward Spitz, published by Auerbach Publishers, 121 North Broad Street, Philadelphia, PA 19107.

Technology and Your New Products, by Alan A. Smith, published by the Small Business Administration, Washington, DC 20402.

11

How to Price Your Products and Services

COST VERSUS PRICE

It is important to realize right from the start that it is the market, not your costs, that determines the price at which you can sell your product or service. Your costs only establish a floor below which you cannot sell your product or service and make any money. Therefore, in determining the price for your product or service, you should recognize that the relevant price is somewhere between the price floor that you established with your cost data and the price ceiling that is the maximum amount for which you could possibly sell your product or service.

THE IMPORTANCE OF THE PRICING DECISION

The decision on what price to ask for your product or service has a major influence in several important areas. These include the following:

1. *Profit.* The price you select determines how much profit you will make.

2. *Recouping your investment.* The price at which you decide to sell your product or service will determine how quickly you will be able to recover the investment you made in developing and marketing your product or service.

3. *Resources available for promotion.* Your price will help determine the amount of financial resources you have at any given time to compete in the marketplace.

4. *Ability to penetrate a new market.* *The price you select will determine whether or not you will be successful in getting into a new market.*

5. *Image.* The price you select creates an image of the product and of your business. A high price may imply status and quality. A low price may imply economy.

THE EMPHASIS ON NONPRICE COMPETITION

With the considerable importance of price in determining the success of your business, you would think that every single business owner and manager devotes a great deal of thought to pricing. However, this is not true. One reason is that, even in today's economy, many consumers have much larger disposable incomes than in the past. Therefore, price may be of less importance, depending upon what you are selling. Also, with the many sophisticated marketing techniques that are available today, many marketers feel that they don't need to use price as a means of attracting consumers. Some businesspeople give little thought to price because they are simply unaware of the sensitivity of demand in the marketplace to making changes in price, either upward or downward.

Perhaps those most aware are those dealing in direct response marketing. In this case, testing of all types, including the testing of different prices, is a must. Along these lines, I've had some experiences of my own. I once sold a four-volume set of booklets on how to become published as a writer for $19.95. During testing I reduced the price to $14.95, wondering whether the increased number of sales would make up for the loss in contribution of each individual set sold. Note that I assumed that sales would go up as price was reduced. The results were quite surprising. Not only did I lose money because of the $5 differential in price for each unit sold, but the total number of sales actually went down. When I increased the price to $19.95, sales went up to their former level.

Some businessmen avoid serious pricing decisions because they feel there are fewer worries if they maintain a single stable price. They don't have to change the prices of the items in their literature or catalog, they don't have to reevaluate inventories for accounting, they don't have to renegotiate contracts. To them, price just isn't worth the worry. I hope to convince you in this chapter that this is not a good way to handle pricing.

The fact that many business owners do not seriously price their products or services gives you an opportunity to make a great deal of money and win out over your competition by doing so.

WHEN SHOULD YOU CONSIDER PRICING OR REPRICING?

You should consider pricing or repricing what you are selling at any time, but especially in the following circumstances:

1. When you are introducing a new product or products
2. When there is an interrelated addition to your product line which may affect the pricing of older items already in the line
3. When you wish to penetrate a new market
4. When the competition has changed its price
5. During periods of inflation
6. During periods of depression
7. When you are about to change your strategy
8. When you are testing to find the "correct price"
9. When the product is in a different part of its life cycle

THE ECONOMIC THEORY OF PRICING

According to economic theory, price is determined according to the downward-sloping demand curve as shown in Figure 11.1. As prices increase, a smaller

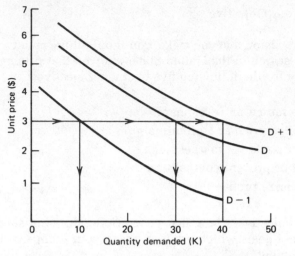

Figure 11.1. Downward-sloping demand curve.

quantity of the product or service is demanded by your customer. The implication of the downward slope of the demand curve is that it takes a lower price to sell more. However, note that according to a new demand curve, D+1, which is higher than the other demand curve, D, in Figure 11.1, for the same price you can sell more products. The implication of this higher demand curve is that in order to shift the demand from D to D+1 you must take additional action, such as increased advertising or a sweepstakes or some other form of promotion. However, at the same price you may also sell fewer products if the demand curve shifts to D−1 as shown in Figure 11.1. This can happen as technology causes obsolescence of your product. When the slide rule was first replaced by the hand-held calculator, the demand curve shifted downward, and eventually the slide rule could no longer be sold. This shift could also be caused by a product failure such as the crash of a certain model of aircraft. Now, at the same price, less of that model of aircraft will be sold.

Now, even though this is true, a firm can sometimes charge more and sell more product; this is what happened with the mail order product I mentioned earlier. This is true because of selective demand for a specific product and the way the product is perceived. Some factors here are distinctive features, perceived value, and status.

HOW TO PRICE A NEW PRODUCT

Let's look first at perhaps one of the most difficult pricing tasks that any manager of a small business or even a giant business faces: the pricing of a new product which is not yet in the market. To price a new product, there are three steps that you must take. These are as follows:

1. Determine your objective.
2. Find the demand versus the price.
3. Determine your basic pricing strategy.

Determining Your Objective

In any pricing decision that you make, you should think about what your overall objective is. Research in the United States showed that pricing decisions were made primarily for the following five business objectives:

1. To see a return on investment
2. To stabilize price and profit margin
3. To capture a target market share
4. To meet or prevent competition
5. To maximize profit

These pricing objectives show that your pricing decision should be based on a combination of goals which are internal to your company and the external market environment.

HOW TO ESTIMATE DEMAND VERSUS PRICE

Now that your basic objectives have been established, you must find some way to estimate the demand versus the price. The following methods have all been found effective in estimating this demand.

1. *Ask customers.* From asking a sufficient number of customers about various potential prices, you will get some idea of how much of your product can be sold at each price. You may also learn the percentages of your potential customers that will buy at each price. For example, a survey may show that 80% of your customers would buy the product if the price were $5, 20% if $7, and 10% if $10. This information will also give you some indication of the profits that you might expect. The drawback here is that people will now always respond truthfully. (See the Chapter 9 on marketing research for more details about this.)

2. *Comparison with close substitutes or a replacement item.* We may compare the item that we are going to introduce with similar items that are on the market today—what their prices are and how many are selling at those prices. If the product is totally new, then we may try to find a product which it is replacing. For example, if we are introducing a new type of electronic watch, we may derive some initial price demand curves from the old design.

3. *Cost savings.* Sometimes, especially with industrial products, a price can be calculated based on the cost savings possible with the adoption of a new product. If you are going to price in this fashion, it will be important for you to promote the cost savings to your prospective customers.

4. *Test marketing.* Test marketing of the product is an outstanding way to derive demand versus product price. All that is necessary is that the product be offered at various prices to the same market. Since this type of testing requires the customer actually to put money on the barrel head for the product, it is much more accurate than simply asking the potential customer whether he or she would or would not purchase.

Once quantitative figures can be established for demand at various prices that we may set, we will consider the various pricing strategies that may be adopted.

Pricing Strategies for a New Product

For a new product, there are three basic pricing strategies. These are:

1. A high price strategy known as skimming strategy
2. A low price strategy known as a penetration strategy
3. A meet-the-competition price strategy

Skimming Price Strategy. This strategy is used when the product is so new that basically there is no competition, or when you wish to give the product status through the price. You can skim the market using the high price, and later on, when competition enters the market, you can reduce the price to meet the competition. Such a strategy also enables you to have more resources available to meet the competition when that day comes.

Penetration Strategy. This strategy is used to get yourself into a new market by going in at a very low price. Some people will try your product simply because your price is significantly lower than the price that the competition is charging. Naturally, you must be very careful when using this strategy because of the implications regarding quality and the possibility of getting stuck with a low status image. Also, maintaining the low price with a lower contribution to profit margin means very, very high volume sales which cannot always be achieved. Many companies using this strategy do so only to get the product tried by prospective customers, and once it has been adopted by a sufficient number the price is raised and the strategy changed to a meet-the-competition price or an even higher price.

A Meet-the-Competition Strategy. According to this strategy, you are going to price your product or service at the same price as the competition's. If you are going to do this, you must have something else unique or people will not switch from the competition to your company unless they are thoroughly dissatisfied with the competition for some other reason. For example, perhaps you set the same price as your competition, but the quality of your product is much higher; or the reliability of your product is better; or your service is better and your employees more friendly. The point is that you must offer something different, something more than your competition, or people will have no reason to switch.

SECOND PHASE PRICING

After you have introduced a new product or service, you may or may not wish to maintain the same pricing that you used to introduce the product into the market. Perhaps you introduced a product that was totally new and for which you have no patent or other protection. After some time, the competition will enter the market with its new products which are similar to yours. Perhaps they will be using a penetration price, or some price which is lower than the one that you are offering. How do you react to this, a potential loss of your market? As mentioned earlier, perhaps your product has gone rapidly through the life cycle. Let us say you are selling an electronic calculator which technology has now rendered obsolete. In this case you may make the decision to do a remainder sale and sell everything out at a fraction of its initial high price, perhaps even at or below your cost. Whatever second phase strategy you will work out, you must begin to think ahead even as your introduce a new product.

Here is an excellent example of a second phase strategy. The individual who used it actually increased his price when the competition entered with a penetration price. During one summer season, marketing genius Joe Cossman introduced the now common sprinkler hose with hundreds of tiny holes placed in a flexible tubing to allow water to sprinkle the grass or flowers in any desired pattern. This unique plastic hose was easily duplicated and no patent protection was possible. Therefore, Cossman expected and had many competitors during the second summer season. However, Cossman's method of distribution was not to sell direct but instead to sell through grocery stores to which he gave an approximate 50% discount from retail price. Instead of reducing his price when the competition came in, Joe actually increased his retail price. He passed the increased profit margin on to his distributors, the grocery stores. This increased their profits, and at the same time the image of the Cossman sprinkler was that it was of higher quality than the products of the competition. Cossman's innovative price strategy extended his control of the market, and he made more profit the second year with competition than he did the first year without.

Always think through your situation regarding distribution and other important factors in developing an innovative pricing decision.

WHAT TO DO IF NO ONE BUYS

If the market will not take your product or your service at the price you have established, to cover your costs and to allow you to make a desired profit, you have five alternatives:

1. *Lower the price.* This means you are accepting less profit in the hope that more of your profit or service will be purchased.

2. *Increase the price.* This means that you are repositioning your product as compared with that of the competition so your product will be perceived by your potential customers as being of higher quality or better in some other fashion.

3. *Reduce your costs.* In this way you can maintain the price and still be profitable with the amount that you are selling.

4. *Drop the product completely.* This may sound drastic, but sometimes it is the wisest course.

5. *Differentiate your product from that of your competition.* This is the same sort of thing you must do if you establish a meet-the-competition price for a new product. That is, you emphasize quality, service, product performance, delivery time, financing arrangements, discounting, or some other aspect of importance to your customer.

PRICING POLICIES

There are three basic pricing policy categories. These are:

1. *Single price.* You have one price for all buyers regardless of timing, quantity purchase, and other factors

2. *Variable price.* Price is always open to negotiation

3. *Nonvariable price.* You offer the same price to all under similar conditions. Of course, under different conditions a different price is offered.

A single price has few advantages. The single price policy is used frequently in the consumer field or when selling to other small-purchase customers. The policy, of course, is easy to administer, and the emphasis then is always on nonprice appeals including all types of promotion such as face-to-face salesmen. Clearly, this policy will not be very attractive to individuals who buy in large quantity.

When selling to customers who make larger purchases, it is important to understand when it is best to have a nonvariable pricing policy or a variable pricing policy.

As noted earlier, a variable price can be negotiated. This has the following advantages. First, you can make adjustments to your price instantly during the process of negotiation. Secondly, you can be flexible in your dealings. Whatever the competition does can be countered immediately, and you can easily respond to other changes in the marketplace during the negotiation process. Finally, you can vary your appeal to be based on price or nonprice promotionals according to the situation.

However, a variable pricing policy also has many disadvantages. Since the resulting price charged will be different from one customer to another, the potential exists for bad feelings on the part of those customers who pay more for the same product or service. Also, for very large contracts, it will take time to negotiate. It is often said that time is money, and when your own time or the time of valuable people resources in your firm is spent, costs will not be insignificant. Sometimes having a variable price means that you will not be able to negotiate yourself, in which cases you must delegate the pricing decision to someone working for you. This means loss of your control over the pricing in your firm to a certain degree. The potential also exists for abuse in this delegation since some of your people may resort to what amounts to price cutting instead of actually "selling." Finally, there are some legal complications which may result, growing out of a law known as the Robinson-Patman Act. We will discuss the implications of this act for a variable pricing policy shortly.

A *nonvariable price* has advantages as well. Clearly, if simplifies the selling process since no one except you has any authority to vary the prices. There is an ease of administering such a policy, and it is clearly fair to all buyers. Naturally, you will avoid any legal complications of having a variable price, and you, of course, maintain control over the pricing decision.

DISCOUNT POLICIES

Discount policies can also affect sales in a very dramatic fashion. One entrepreneur, the inventor of a unique item used by pilots, lost thousands of dollars in potential orders from the government simply because he had no discount policy. Discount policy may be classified in the following ways:

1. *A promotional discount.*   This means special discounts to the consumer or perhaps within your distribution or organization to promote your product or your service.

2. *A trade discount.*   This is a discount on the basis of the position in the distribution channel, such as a discount offered to a retailer or a wholesaler if you are a manufacturer, or anyone between you and the ultimate consumer of your product or service.

3. *A quantity discount to encourage large orders.*   There are two types of quantity discounts. One is a noncumulative type which is based purely on the quantity ordered at a specific period of time. Another is the cumulative discount which is increased depending on quantities ordered by the same buyer over an indefinite period of time. Cumulative discounts tend to tie the buyer to the seller.

THE ROBINSON-PATMAN ACT OF 1936

The Robinson-Patman Act deals with price discrimination. Its intent is to regulate any tendency to injure competition. The implication is clear for any of your pricing policy decisions, and either the Federal Trade Commission or a private complainant can initiate action against you for your pricing policies if you sell at different prices to two or more competing customers engaged in interstate commerce and your acts have a tendency to injure competition. Now, there are certain defenses against these accusations. For example, it is not a violation of the act if you are selling at different prices because of cost differences, or if you have to lower the price to one customer to meet the competition, or if you have to lower the price because of changing market conditions. When in doubt, consult your attorney.

TWO CHECKLISTS FOR PRICING

The following checklists are provided to assist you in pricing. The first is a general pricing checklist for managers developed by Joseph D. O'Brien, associate professor of marketing at the College of Business Administration, Boston College, Boston, Massachusetts.[1] The second checklist is a special pricing checklist for small retailers developed by Bruce J. Walker, associate professor of marketing at Arizona State University, Tempe, Arizona.[2]

Checklist One: Examining Costs, Sales Volume, and Profits

The questions in this part should be helpful when you look at prices from the viewpoint of costs, sales volume, and profits.

---

[1] Joseph D. O'Brien, *A Pricing Checklist for Managers*, Small Business Administration (1972).
[2] Bruce J. Walker, *A Pricing Checklist for Small Retailers*, Small Business Administration (1979).

Costs and Prices

The small retailer who sets the price for an item by applying a standard markup may be overlooking certain cost factors which are connected with that item. The following questions are designed to help you gather information which should be helpful when you are determining prices on specific types of items.

		Yes	No
1.	Do you know which of your operating costs remain the same regardless of sales volume?	____	____
2.	Do you know which of your operating costs decrease percentage-wise as your sales volume increases?	____	____
3.	Have you ever figured out the breakeven point for your items selling at varying price levels?	____	____
4.	Do you look behind high gross margin percentages? (For example, a product with a high gross margin, may also be a slow turnover item with high handling costs. Thus is may be less profitable than lower margin items which turn over fast.)	____	____
5.	When you select items for price reductions, do you project the effects on profits? (For example, if a food marketer considers whether to run canned ham or rump steak on sale, an important cost factor is labor. Practically none is involved in featuring canned ham; however, a rump steak sale requires the skill of a meat-cutter and this labor cost might mean little or no profits.)	____	____

Pricing and Sales Volume

An effective pricing program should also consider sales volume. For example, high prices might limit your sales volume while low prices might result in a large, but unprofitable volume. The following questions should be helpful in determining what is right for your situation.

		Yes	No
6.	Have you considered setting a sales volume goal and then studying to see if your prices will help you reach it?	____	____
7.	Have you set a target of a certain number of new customers for next year? (If so, how can pricing help you to get them?)	____	____
8.	Should you limit the quantities of low-margin items which any one customer can buy when they are on sale? (If so, will you advertise this policy?)	____	____
9.	What is your policy when a sale item is sold out before the end of the advertised period? Do you allow disappointed customers to buy the item later at the sale price?	____	____

Yes   No

Pricing and Profits

Prices should help bring in sales which are profitable over the long pull. The following questions are designed to help you think about pricing policies and their effect on your annual profits.

10. Do you have all the facts on costs, sales, and competitive behavior?   _____   _____

11. Do you set prices with the hope of accomplishing definite objectives, such as a 1-percent profit increase over last year?   _____   _____

12. Have you set a given level of profits in dollars and in percent of sales?   _____   _____

13. Do you keep records which will give you the needed facts on profits, losses, and prices?   _____   _____

14. Do you review your pricing practices periodically to make sure that they are helping to achieve your profit goals?   _____   _____

Judging the Buyer, Timing, and Competitors

The questions in this part are designed to help you check your practices for judging the buyer (your customers), your timing, and your competitors.

The Buyer and Pricing Strategy

After you have your facts on costs, the next point must be the CUSTOMER—whether you are changing a price, putting in a new item, or checking out your present price practices. Knowledge of your customers helps you to determine how to vary prices in order to get the average gross margin you need for making a profit. (For example, to get an average gross margin of 35 percent, some retailers put a low markup—10 percent, for instance—on items which they promote as traffic builders and use high markup—sometimes as much as 60 percent—on slow-moving items.) The following questions should be helpful in checking your knowledge about your customers.

15. Do you know whether your customers shop around and for what items?   _____   _____

16. Do you know how your customers make their comparisons? By reading newspaper ads? Store shopping? Hearsay?   _____   _____

17. Are you trying to appeal to customers who buy on price alone? To those who buy on quality alone? To those who combine the two?   _____   _____

18. Do any of your customers tell you that your prices are in line with those of your competitors? Higher? Lower?   _____   _____

19. Do you know which item (or types of items) your customers call for even though you raise the price?   _____   _____

20. Do you know which items (or types of items) your customers leave on your shelves when you raise the price?   _____   _____

	Yes	No

21. Do certain items seem to appeal to customers more than others when you run weekend, clearance, or special-day sales?

22. Have you used your individual sales records to classify your present customers according to the volume of their purchases?

23. Will your customers buy more if you use multiple pricing? (For example, 3 for 39 cents for products with rapid turnover.)

24. Do your customers respond to odd prices more readily than even prices, for example, 99 cents rather than $1?

25. Have you decided on a pricing strategy to create a favorable price image with your customers? (For example, a retailer with 8,000 different items might decide to make a full margin on all medium or slow movers while featuring—at low price levels—the remaining fast movers.)

26. If you are trying to build a quality price image, do your individual customer records, such as charge account statements, show that you are selling a larger number of higher priced items than you were 12 months ago?

27. Do your records of individual customer accounts and your observations of customer behavior in the store show price as the important factor in their buying? Service? Assortments? Some other consideration?

Time and Pricing

Effective merchandising means that you have the right product, at the right place, at the right price, and at the *right time*. All are important, but timing is the critical element for the small retailer. The following questions should be helpful in determining what is the right time for you to adjust prices.

28. Are you a "leader" or a "follower" in announcing your price reductions? (The follower, even though he matches his competitors, creates a negative impression on his customers.)

29. Have you studied your competitors to see whether they follow any sort of pattern when making price changes? (For example, do some of them run clearance sales earlier than others?)

30. Is there a pattern to the kinds of items which competitors promote at lower prices at certain times of the month or year?

31. Have you decided whether it is better to take early markdowns on seasonal or style goods or to run a clearance sale at the end of the season?

32. Have you made regular annual sales, such as Anniversary Sales, Fall Clearance, or Holiday Cleanup, so popular

	Yes	No

that many customers wait for them rather than buying in season?

33. When you change a price, do you make sure that *all* customers know about it through price tags and so on?

34. Do you try to time price reductions so they can be promoted in your advertising?

Competition and Pricing

When you set prices, you have to consider how your competitors might react to your prices. The starting place is learning as much as you can about their price structures. The following questions are designed to help you check out this phase of pricing.

35. Do you use all the available channels of information to keep you up to date on your competitors' price policies? (Some useful sources of information are: things your customers tell you; the competitor's price list and catalogs, if he uses them; his advertising; reports from your suppliers; trade paper studies; and shoppers employed by you.)

36. Should your policy be to try always to sell above or below competition? Only to meet it?

37. Is there a pattern to the way your competitors respond to your price cuts?

39. Is the leader pricing of your competitors affecting your sales volume to such an extent that you must alter your pricing policy on individual items (or types of items) of merchandise?

40. Do you realize that no two competitors have identical cost curves? (This difference in costs means that certain price levels may be profitable for you but unprofitable for your competitor or vice versa.)

Practices Which Can Help Offset Price

Some small retailers take advantage of the fact that price is not always the determining factor in making a sale. They supply customer services and offer other inducements to offset the effect of competitors' lower prices. Delivery service is an example. Comfortable shopper's meeting place is another. The following questions are designed to help you take a look at some of these practices.

41. Do the items or services which you sell have advantages for which customers are willing to pay a little more?

42. From personal observation of customer behavior in your store can you tell about how much more customers will pay for such advantages?

	Yes	No

43. Should you change your services so as to create an advantage for which your customers will be willing to pay? _____ _____

44. Does your advertising emphasize customer benefits rather than price? _____ _____

45. Are you using the most common nonprice competitive tools? (For example, have you tried to alter your product or service to the existing market? Have you tried stamps, bonus purchase gifts, or other plans for building repeat business?) _____ _____

46. Should policies on returned goods be changed so as to impress your customers better? _____ _____

47. If you sell repair services, have you checked out your guarantee policy? _____ _____

48. Should you alter assortments of merchandise to increase sales? _____ _____

Checklist Two: Pricing Checklist for Small Retailers

1. Is the relative price of this item very important to your target customers? The importance of price depends on the specific product and on the specific individual. Some shoppers are very price-conscious, others want convenience and knowledgeable sales personnel. Because of these variations, you need to learn about your customers' desires in relation to different products. Having sales personnel seek feedback from shoppers is a good starting point. _____ _____

2. Are prices based on estimates of the number of units that consumers will demand at various price levels? Demand-oriented pricing such as this is superior to cost-oriented pricing. In the cost approach, a predetermined amount is added to the cost of the merchandise, whereas the demand approach considers what consumers are willing to pay. _____ _____

3. Have you established a price range for the product? The cost of merchandise will be at one end of the price range and the level above which consumers will *not* buy the product at the other end. _____ _____

4. Have you considered what price strategies would be compatible with your store's total retailing mix that includes merchandise, location, promotion, and services? _____ _____

5. Will trade-ins be accepted as part of the purchase price on items such as appliances and television sets? _____ _____

Supplier and Competitor Considerations

This set of questions looks outside your firm to two factors that you cannot directly control—suppliers and competitors.

Yes   No

6. Do you have final pricing authority? With the repeal of fair trade laws, "yes" answers will be more common than in previous years. Still, a supplier can control retail prices by refusing to deal with non-conforming stores (a tactic which may be illegal) or by selling to you on consignment. _____ _____

7. Do you know what direct competitors are doing price-wise? _____ _____

8. Do you regularly review competitors' ads to obtain information on their prices? _____ _____

9. Is your store large enough to employ either a full-time or part-time comparison shopper? These three questions emphasize the point that you must watch competitors' prices so that your prices will not be far out of line— too high or too low—without good reason. Of course, there may be a good reason for out-of-the-ordinary prices, such as seeking a special price image. _____ _____

A Price Level Strategy

Selecting a general level of prices in relation to competition is a key strategic decision, perhaps the most important.

10. Should your overall strategy be to sell at prevailing market price levels? The other alternatives are an above-the-market strategy or a below-the-market strategy. _____ _____

11. Should competitors' temporary price reductions ever be matched? _____ _____

12. Could private-brand merchandise be obtained in order to avoid direct price competition? _____ _____

Calculating Planned Initial Markup

In this section you will have to look *inside* your business, taking into account sales, expenses, and profits before setting prices. The point is that your initial markup must be large enough to cover anticipated expenses and reductions *and* still produce a satisfactory profit.

13. Have you estimated sales, operating expenses, and reductions for the next selling season? _____ _____

14. Have you established a profit objective for the next selling season? _____ _____

15. Given estimated sales, expenses, and reductions, have you planned initial markup? _____ _____
    This figure is calculated with the following formula:

$$\text{Initial markup \%} = \frac{\text{Operating expenses + reductions + profit}}{\text{Net sales + reductions}}$$

Yes   No

Reductions consist of markdowns, stock shortages, and employee and customer discounts. The following examples uses dollar amounts, but the estimates can also be percentages. If a retailer anticipates $94,000 in sales for a particular department, $34,000 in expenses, and $6,000 in reductions, and if the retailer desires a $4,000 profit, initial markup percentage can be calculated:

$$\text{Initial markup \%} = \frac{\$34,000 + \$6,000 + \$4,000}{\$94,000 + \$6,000} = 44\%$$

The resulting figure, 44 percent in this example, indicates what size initial markup is needed *on the average* in order to make the desired profits.

16. Would it be appropriate to have different initial markup figures for various lines of merchandise or services? You would seriously consider this when some lines have much different characteristics than others. For instance, a clothing retailer might logically have different initial markup figures for suits, shirts and pants, and accessories. (Various merchandise characteristics are covered in an upcoming section.) You may want those items with the highest turnover rates to carry the lowest initial markup.   _____   _____

Store Policies

Having calculated an initial markup figure, you could proceed to set prices on your merchandise. But an important decision such as this should not be rushed. Instead, you should consider additional factors which suggest what would be the best price.

17. Is your tentative price compatible with established store policies? *Policies* are written guidelines indicating appropriate methods or actions in different situations. If established with care, they can save you time in decision making and provide for consistent treatment of shoppers. Specific policy areas that you should consider are as follows: _____   _____

18. Will a one-price system, under which the same price is charged every purchaser of a particular item, be used on all items?   _____   _____

The alternative is to negotiate price with consumers.

19. Will odd-ending prices, such as $1.98 and $44.95, be more appealing to your customers than even-ending prices?   _____   _____

20. Will consumers buy more if multiple pricing, such as 2 for $8.50, is used?   _____   _____

	Yes	No

21. Should any leader offerings (selected products with quite low, less profitable prices) be used? _____ _____

22. Have the characteristics of an effective leader offering been considered? Ordinarily, a leader offering needs the following characteristics to accomplish its purpose of generating much shopper traffic: used by most people, bought frequently, very familiar regular price, and not a large expenditure for consumers.

23. Will price lining, the practice of setting up distinct price points (such as $5.00, $7.50, and $10.00) and then marking all related merchandise at these points, be used? _____ _____

24. Would price lining by means of zones (such as $5.00–$7.50 and $12.50–$15.00) be more appropriate than price points? _____ _____

25. Will cent-off coupons be used in newspaper ads or mailed to selected consumers on any occasion? _____ _____

26. Would periodic special sales, combining reduced prices and heavier advertising, be consistent with the store image you are seeking? _____ _____

27. Do certain items have greater appeal than others when they are part of a special sale? _____ _____

28. Has the impact of various sale items on profits been considered? Sale prices may mean little or no profit on these items. Still, the special sale may contribute to *total* profits by bringing in shoppers who may also buy some regular-price (and profitable) merchandise and by attracting new customers. Also, you should avoid featuring items that require a large amount of labor, which in turn would reduce or erase profits. For instance, according to this criterion, shirts would be a better special sale item than men's suits that often require free alterations. _____ _____

29. Will "rain checks" be issued to consumers who come in for special-sale merchandise that is temporarily out of stock? You should give particular attention to this decision since rain checks are required in some situations. Your lawyer or the regional Federal Trade Commission office should be consulted for specific advice regarding whether rain checks are needed in the special sales you plan. _____ _____

Nature of the Merchandise

In this section you will be considering how selected characteristics of particular merchandise affect a planned initial markup.

30. Did you get a "good deal" on the wholesale price of this merchandise? _____ _____

31. Is this item at the peak of its popularity? _____ _____

	Yes	No

32. Are handling and selling costs relatively great due to the product being bulky, having a low turnover rate, and/or requiring much personal selling, installation, or alterations? _____ _____

33. Are relatively large levels of reductions expected due to markdowns, spoilage, breakage, or theft? With respect to the preceding four questions, "Yes" answers suggest the possibility of or need for larger-than-normal initial markups. For example, very fashionable clothing often will carry a higher markup than basic clothing such as underwear because the particular fashion may suddenly lose its appeal to consumers. _____ _____

34. Will customer services such as delivery, alterations, gift wrapping, and installation be free of charge to customers? The alternative is to charge for some or all of these services. _____ _____

Environmental Considerations

The questions in this section focus your attention on three factors outside your business, namely economic conditions, laws, and consumerism.

35. If your state has an unfair sales practices act that requires minimum markups on certain merchandise, do your prices comply with this statute? _____ _____

36. Are economic conditions in your trading area abnormal? Consumers tend to be more price-conscious when the economy is depressed, suggesting that lower-than-normal markups may be needed to be competitive. On the other hand, shoppers are less price-conscious when the economy is booming, which would permit larger markups *on a selective basis.* _____ _____

37. Are the ways in which prices are displayed and promoted compatible with consumerism, one part of which has been a call for more straightforward price information? _____ _____

38. If yours is a grocery store, is it feasible to use unit pricing in which the item's cost per some standard measure is indicated? _____ _____

Having asked (and hopefully answered) more than three dozen questions, you are indeed ready to establish retail prices. When you have decided on an appropriate percentage markup, 35 percent on a garden hose for example, the next step is to determine what percentage of the still unknown retail price is represented by the cost figure. The basic markup formula is simply rearranged to do this:

Cost = Retail price − Markup
Cost = 100% − 35% = 65%

Yes   No

Then the dollar cost, say $3.25 for the garden hose, is plugged into the following formula to arrive at the retail price:

$$\text{Retail price} = \frac{\text{Dollar cost}}{\text{Percentage cost}} = \frac{\$3.25}{65\% \text{ (or .65)}} = \$5.00$$

One other consideration is necessary:

39. Is the retail price consistent with your planned initial markups? _____ _____

Adjustments

It would be ideal if all items sold at their original retail prices. But we know that things are not always ideal. Therefore, a section on price adjustments is necessary.

40. Are additional markups called for, because wholesale prices have increased or because an item's low price causes consumers to question its quality? _____ _____

41. Should employees be given purchase discounts? _____ _____

42. Should any groups of customers, such as students or senior citizens, be given purchase discounts? _____ _____

43. When markdowns appear necessary, have you first considered other alternatives such as retaining price but changing another element of the retailing mix or storing the merchandise until the next selling season? _____ _____

44. Has an attempt been made to identify causes of markdowns so that steps can be taken to minimize the number of avoidable buying, selling, and pricing errors that cause markdowns? _____ _____

45. Has the relationship between timing and size of markdowns been taken into account? In general, markdown taken *early* in the selling season or shortly after sales slow down can be smaller than *late* markdowns. Whether an early or late markdown would be more appropriate in a particular situation depends on several things: your assessment of how many consumers might still be interested in the product, the size of the initial markup, and the amount remaining in stock. _____ _____

46. Would a schedule of automatic markdowns after merchandise has been in stock for specified intervals be appropriate? _____ _____

47. Is the size of the markdown "just enough" to stimulate purchases? Of course, this question is difficult—perhaps impossible—to answer. Nevertheless, it stresses the point that you have to carefully observe the effects of different size markdowns so that you can eventually acquire some insights into what size markdowns are "just enough" for different kinds of merchandise.

	Yes	No

48. Has a procedure been worked out for markdowns on price-lined merchandise? _____ _____

49. Is the markdown price calculated from the off-retail percentage? This question gets you into the arithmetic of markdowns. Usually, you first tentatively decide on the percentage amount price must be marked down to excite consumers. For example, if you think a 25 percent markdown will be necessary to sell a lavender sofa, the dollar amount of the markdown is calculated as follows:

Dollar   Off-retail
markdown = percentage × Previous retail price

Dollar markdown = 25% (or .25) × $500. = $125.

Then the markdown is obtained by subtracting the dollar markdown from the previous retail price. Hence, the sofa would be $375.00 after taking the markdown.

50. Has cost of the merchandise been considered before setting the markdown price? This is not to say that a markdown price should never be lower than cost; on the contrary, a price that low may be your only hope of generating some revenue from the item. But cost should be considered to make sure that below-cost markdown prices are the *exception in your store rather than being so common that your total profits are really hurt.* _____ _____

51. Have procedures for recording the dollar amounts, percentages, and probable causes of markdowns been set up? _____ _____

Analyzing markdowns is very important since it can provide information that will assist in calculating planned initial markup, in decreasing errors that cause markdowns, and in evaluating suppliers.

You may be weary from thinking your way through the preceding sections, but don't overlook an important final question:

52. Have you marked the calendar for a periodic review of your pricing decisions? _____ _____

Rather than "laying an egg" due to careless pricing decisions, this checklist should help you lay a solid foundation of effective prices as you try to build retail profits.

SOURCES OF ADDITIONAL INFORMATION

Price and Price Policies, by Walton Hamilton, published by McGraw-Hill Book Co., 1221 Avenue of the Americas, New York, NY 10020.

Pricing Decisions in Small Business, by W. Warren Haynes, published by University of Kentucky Press, Lexington, KY 40506.

Pricing for Marketing Executives, by Alfred R. Oxenfeldt, published by Wadsworth Publishing Co., Inc., 10 Davis Drive, Belmont, CA 94002.

Pricing for Profit, by Curtis W. Symonds, published by AMACOM, a division of the American Management Association, 135 West 50th Street, New York, NY 10020.

Pricing for Profit and Growth, by Albert U. Bergfeld, James S. Earley, and William R. Knobloch, published by Prentice-Hall, Inc., Englewood Cliffs, NJ 07632.

Pricing Strategies, by Alfred R. Oxenfeldt, published by AMACOM, a division of the American Management Association, 135 West 50th Street, New York, NY 10020

A Robinson-Patman Primer, by Earl W. Kintner, published by Macmillan Publishing Co., 866 Third Avenue, New York, NY 10022.

12

Advertising and Publicity

THE IMPORTANCE OF ADVERTISING

Millions of dollars are spent on advertising every single year. In fact, you were exposed to about two million advertising messages from the time you were born until you reached the age of 21. To prove the strength of these messages, see if you can answer the questions. What is a Bulova? What is a Bic? What is Bayer? What is Rinso? What is Ivory? What is a Mustang? What is Prell? What is Lowenbrau? Unless you neither read, watch television, nor listen to the radio, you probably answered the majority of these questions without difficulty. Now, let's try one a little more difficult. What do the letters "LSMFT" stand for? Research has shown that a significant number of people can answer this question, even among those who are now in their early twenties. Yet, the advertising message which gave these letters has not been used for more than 30 years. "LSMFT" stands for "Lucky Strike Means Fine Tobacco," and the message hasn't been on the air since 1958!

Advertising is used for three basic purposes. These are:

1. To promote awareness of a business and its product or service
2. To stimulate sales directly
3. To establish a firm's image or modify a firm's image

YOU CAN COMPETE WITH THE BIG COMPANIES

Amazingly, even though some firms spend millions of dollars on their advertising every year, you can compete with them, and you can beat them if you get your money's worth for your advertising dollar. Why is this so? It is so because many firms, even large firms, do not advertise in a very efficient manner.

Let's look at some examples. For years, cigarette manufacturers fought to keep television advertising. When cigarettes were finally banned from advertising on television, tobacco companies predicted doom and stocks plunged. Yet, what happened to cigarette sales without television advertising? Sales went up? This showed that for more than 50 years, the million dollars that had been spent had largely been wasted through ineffective television advertising.

Some years ago a major company, Lestoil, developed a new spray cleaner. This new cleaner was a disinfectant that cleaned so well that household germs were killed instantly. In order to convey this message, this new product was advertised under the name "Clean and Kill." The result, however, was that the product was killed before the household germs. The advertising campaign was totally ineffective. Why? Possibly housewives, the buying agent for this product, thought that the product was some type of poison.

Just as there have been major disasters in advertising, there have been tremendously successful campaigns. Can you imagine a company bragging about not being first? Well, that's what Avis Rent-A-Car did some years ago. Their message was "We're No. 2," and therefore, "We try harder." This made it very difficult for Hertz. How could Hertz retaliate without appearing to be the villain? The campaign was tremendously effective, and Hertz lost much of the power that it should have had from being in first place.

Some years ago, Mercedes Benz produced its first diesel car of modern times. This was long before the time of the energy crunch. In fact, the diesel engine seemed to offer very few advantages since gasoline was relatively cheap. Even today, diesel fuel cannot be purchased everywhere, and then, some 25 years ago, diesel fuel was even more difficult to find. Also, diesel engines are very noisy compared with the standard gasoline engine. In despair, Mercedes Benz prepared to junk the production of the diesel engine car. But as a last resort, they turned the project over to a direct marketing expert by the name of Ed McLean. Ed McLean wrote a direct sales letter targeted to individuals who had the money and might be persuaded to buy a Mercedes Benz. This sales letter turned the supposed disadvantages of the diesel engine around and made them advantages. The fact that diesel fuel couldn't be found everywhere meant that the automobile was exclusive. The noise of the engine was promoted as positive evidence that the engine was running. This letter was sent out to consumers on well-chosen mailing lists. The campaign was so successful that Mercedes Benz actually had to reopen the production line and manufacture more diesel engine automobiles! This advertising success won Ed McLean the Golden Mailbox Award from the Direct Mail Marketing Association.

HOW TO DEVELOP AN ADVERTISING PROGRAM

Advertising will work as well as for a small firm as for a major multimillion-dollar corporation, if you use it correctly. To use advertising correctly, you must have an advertising program. To develop an advertising program, you must take the following steps:

1. Analyze the market.
2. Set concrete goals and objectives.
3. Set a budget.
4. Develop a creative strategy.
5. Choose your medium or media.
6. Evaluate the results.

Analyze the Market

To analyze the market, you've got to view your own product or service in terms of who can use it. That "who," whether it be male or female, child or senior citizen (or all of the above), is your target consumer (see Figure 12.1). Now, how are you going to reach him and/or her?

Along these lines, marketing and advertising experts have developed a very useful concept called *market segmentation*. If you use the market segmentation

CONSUMER PROFILE QUESTIONNAIRE

PERSONAL DEMOGRAPHIC INFORMATION

Mark the boxes that describe you.

1. Sex:
   - ☐ Male
   - ☐ Female

2. Age:
   - ☐ Under 6
   - ☐ 6 to 11
   - ☐ 12 to 17
   - ☐ 18 to 24
   - ☐ 25 to 34
   - ☐ 35 to 44
   - ☐ 45 to 54
   - ☐ 55 to 64
   - ☐ 65 & over

3. Martial Status:
   - ☐ Married
   - ☐ Single (never married)
   - ☐ Widowed
   - ☐ Divorced or separated

4. Education:
   - ☐ Grade school or less (grades 1–8)
   - ☐ Some high school
   - ☐ Graduated from high school (grades 9–12)
   - ☐ Some colleges
   - ☐ Graduated from college
   - ☐ Some postgraduate college work

5. Principal Language Spoken at Home:
   - ☐ English
   - ☐ Spanish
   - ☐ Other

6. Color:
   - ☐ White
   - ☐ Nonwhite

7. Employment:
   - ☐ Not employed outside the home
   - ☐ Employed outside the home
   - ☐ Employed full time (30 hours per week or more)
   - ☐ Employed part time (less than 30 hours per week)
   - ☐ Not employed—looking for work

8. Occupation:
   - ☐ Professional and technical
   - ☐ Managers, officials, and proprietors, except farm
   - ☐ Clerical
   - ☐ Sales
   - ☐ Craftsman
   - ☐ Foreman
   - ☐ Nonfarm laborers
   - ☐ Service workers
   - ☐ Private household workers
   - ☐ Farm managers
   - ☐ Farm laborers
   - ☐ Farm foreman
   - ☐ Armed services
   - ☐ Retired
   - ☐ Student
   - ☐ Other

9. Geographic Region:
   - ☐ Northeast
   - ☐ Metropolitan New York
   - ☐ Mid-Atlantic
   - ☐ East Central
   - ☐ Metropolitan Chicago
   - ☐ West Central
   - ☐ Southeast
   - ☐ Southwest
   - ☐ Metropolitan Los Angeles
   - ☐ Remaining Pacific

10. Geographic Area:
   - ☐ Central City
   - ☐ Urban Fringe (suburbs)
   - ☐ Town
   - ☐ Rural

Population of city or town:
   - ☐ 4 million or over
   - ☐ Between 4 and 1 million
   - ☐ Between 1 million and 500 thousand
   - ☐ Between 500 thousand and 250 thousand
   - ☐ Between 250 thousand and 50 thousand
   - ☐ Between 50 thousand and 35 thousand
   - ☐ Under 35 thousand

11. County Size:
   - ☐ A county—one of the largest markets
   - ☐ B county—not included in A but area over 150,000 population
   - ☐ C county—not included in A or B but area over 35,000
   - ☐ D county—all remaining counties under 35,000

HOUSEHOLD DEMOGRAPHIC INFORMATION

Answer these statements about your family:

12. Household Sizes:
   - ☐ 1 or 2 members
   - ☐ 2 or 3 members
   - ☐ 3 or 4 members
   - ☐ 5 or more members

13. Number of Children:
   - ☐ None
   - ☐ Two
   - ☐ Three or more

14. Ages of Youngest Child:
   - ☐ No child under 18
   - ☐ Youngest child 12 to 17
   - ☐ Youngest child 6 to 11
   - ☐ Youngest child 2 to 5
   - ☐ Youngest child under 2

15. Household income:
   - ☐ Under $5,000
   - ☐ $5,000 to $7,999
   - ☐ $8,000 to $9,999
   - ☐ $10,000 to $14,999
   - ☐ $15,000 to $24,999
   - ☐ $25,000 and over

16. Wage Earners in the Family:
   - ☐ Male head of household
   - ☐ Female head of household
   - ☐ Wife (non-head of household)
   - ☐ One child
   - ☐ Two children
   - ☐ Over three children

17. Home Ownership:
   - ☐ Own home
   - ☐ Rent home

Five years prior to survey date:
   - ☐ Lived in same home
   - ☐ Lived in different house
   - ☐ in same county
   - ☐ in different county

18. Dwelling Characteristics:
   - ☐ House (unattached)
   - ☐ Attached home
   - ☐ Apartment
   - ☐ Mobile home or trailer
   - ☐ Single family dwelling unit
   - ☐ Multiple family dwelling unit

SOCIAL CLASS INFORMATION

Mark the group your family belongs to.

19. ☐ The local elite with inherited wealth and family tradition.
20. ☐ Top executive or professional manager or owner.
21. ☐ Business, industrial, or professional manager or owner.
22. ☐ White-collar worker in industry or government and small business owner.
23. ☐ Semi-skilled worker in con-

Figure 12.1. Consumer profile questionnaire. (From *Advertising Today* by J. Douglas Johnson. Copyright © 1978 J. Douglas Johnson. Reprinted by permission of the publisher, Science Research Associates, Inc.)

struction or industry. Probably blue-collar union member.

24. ☐ Unskilled worker, perhaps unemployed.

PSYCHOGRAPHIC INFORMATION

Personality indicators

Mark the accurate statements about yourself.

It is my nature to:

25. ☐ Want to rival and surpass others.
26. ☐ Accept leadership and follow willingly.
27. ☐ Want things arranged, organized, secure, and predictable.
28. ☐ Want to be the center of attention.
29. ☐ Seek freedom, resist influence, and do things my own way.
30. ☐ Form friendships and participate in groups.
31. ☐ Want to understand others, examine their motives and my own.
32. ☐ Seek aid, help, and advice from others.
33. ☐ Want to control others and be the leader of groups.
34. ☐ Feel inferior, guilty, and accept blame easily.
35. ☐ Want to help others, be sympathetic and protective.
36. ☐ Look for new and different things to do.
37. ☐ Stick to a task and work hard to complete a job.
38. ☐ Am attracted by the opposite sex, go out and enjoy company.
39. ☐ Belittle, blame, attack, and want to punish people.
40. ☐ Have frequent daydreams and fantasies.
41. ☐ Experience times of tenseness, self-pity, and am restless or excitable.
42. ☐ Am self-confident in social, professional, and personal dealings.

LIFE-STYLE PREFERENCES AND ATTITUDES

Mark the answers that fit you best.

Leisure

43. ☐ Enjoy entertaining formally and going to movies, concerts, plays, dances, or dinner.
44. ☐ Habitually read newspapers, magazines, and books.
45. ☐ Spend a lot of time listening to music (not just as a background).
46. ☐ Think I have the right to do absolutely nothing some of the time.
47. ☐ Anxious to be busy, go out and see people, participate in sports and other activities.
48. ☐ Would rather study or work than "waste time" playing.

Cooking

49. ☐ Want to prepare good, healthy meals and think I am good at it.
50. ☐ Like convenience foods that are frozen, in cans, or packaged as mixes.
51. ☐ Judge my achievement on the basis of compliments I receive for enjoyable meals.
52. ☐ Try to stay out of the kitchen as much as possible and hate the drudgery of cooking.
53. ☐ Enjoy preparing fancy, exotic, or unusual dishes "from scratch" and serving them in an unusual way.

Family

54. ☐ Think the man should be the boss and run the family.
55. ☐ Think the woman should be the boss and run the family.
56. ☐ Believe marriage should be a partnership with no bosses.
57. ☐ Think children should be considered in most family decisions.
58. ☐ Believe parents should make an effort to teach children and spend time with them.

Dress

59. ☐ Like to wear casual, comfortable clothes.
60. ☐ Want to look fashionable and stylish.

Physical Condition

61. ☐ Am in very good health.
62. ☐ Have an overweight problem.
63. ☐ Always on some kind of a diet.
64. ☐ Watch the scale, eat intelligently, and exercise.
65. ☐ Feel sickly much of the time.
66. ☐ Use over-the-counter drugs for minor ailments.
67. ☐ Seldon take anything for a headache or an upset stomach.

Finances

68. ☐ Have money in the bank and feel secure.
69. ☐ Just about break even every month.
70. ☐ Am in debt but believe the bills can be paid.
71. ☐ Am not optimistic about the financial future.

Risk

72. ☐ Am conservative and do not take chances.
73. ☐ Will take a calculated risk.
74. ☐ Take chances just to see what will happen.

Buying Style

75. ☐ Pick the same brand of products habitually.
76. ☐ Think about the products I buy and select them because they satisfy.
77. ☐ Look for bargains, deals, premiums, and usually compare prices.
78. ☐ Want quality in a product and will pay extra to get it.
79. ☐ Choose advertised brands and do not take chances on unknown products or manufacturers.
80. ☐ Keep trying new products to see what they are like.
81. ☐ Buy what I need when I need it and when a store is handy.
82. ☐ Plan shopping carefully with a list of needs and make an excursion out of the trip.
83. ☐ Judge brands on the basis of ingredients, weight, and package size.
84. ☐ Never read the information on a package to find out what it contains.
85. ☐ Am attracted to a brand by its name, color of the package, and its design.
86. ☐ Usually buy what friends say is good.
87. ☐ Pay attention to advertisements and study them to make up my mind about what to buy.
88. ☐ Do not check into low-cost items much, but do shop intelligently and compare prices for high-priced products.
89. Respond to advertisements in:
    ☐ Newspaper
    ☐ Radio
    ☐ Magazine
    ☐ Television

Figure 12.1. (Continued)

MEDIA USE AND INTEREST

I use media at these times:	Newspaper		Magazines		Radio		Television	
	Day	Wkend	Day	Wkend	Day	Wkend	Day	Wkend
90. 6 A.M. to 10:00 A.M.	☐	☐	☐	☐	☐	☐	☐	☐
91. 10:00 A.M. to 3:00 P.M.	☐	☐	☐	☐	☐	☐	☐	☐
92. 3:00 P.M. to 7:00 P.M.	☐	☐	☐	☐	☐	☐	☐	☐
93. 7:00 P.M. to midnight	☐	☐	☐	☐	☐	☐	☐	☐
94. Midnight to 6:00 A.M.	☐	☐	☐	☐	☐	☐	☐	☐

I pay attention to these types of stories or programs:

	Newspaper	Magazine	Radio	Television
95. Local news	☐	☐	☐	☐
96. National news	☐	☐	☐	☐
97. Weather	☐	☐	☐	☐
98. Sports	☐	☐	☐	☐
99. Business and finance	☐	☐	☐	☐
100. Editorials and interviews	☐	☐	☐	☐
101. Classified	☐	☐	☐	☐
102. Daytime serials	☐	☐	☐	☐
103. Comics or comedy shows	☐	☐	☐	☐
104. Crime news or programs	☐	☐	☐	☐
105. Adventure	☐	☐	☐	☐
106. Quizzes or, game shows	☐	☐	☐	☐
107. Movies	☐	☐	☐	☐
108. Self-help stories	☐	☐	☐	☐
109. How-to-do-it	☐	☐	☐	☐
110. Theater arts, and entertainment	☐	☐	☐	☐
111. Editorials	☐	☐	☐	☐
112. Interviews	☐	☐	☐	☐
113. Travel	☐	☐	☐	☐
114. Police shows	☐	☐	☐	☐
115. Romantic programs	☐	☐	☐	☐
116. Sexy stories and pictures	☐	☐	☐	☐
117. Cooking programs and stories	☐	☐	☐	☐

USE OF A PARTICULAR PRODUCT OR SERVICE

(Statements must be adapted)

118. I am a
light _____
medium _____
heavy _____
or nonuser _____
119. I use your product/
service daily _____
once a week _____
once a month _____
once a year _____
120. I have used your product for a
short time _____
many years _____
121. I have tried similar products. The names are

_____

122. I use your product in combination with

_____
_____

123. I buy your product at a super-
market _____
drugstore _____
department store _____
discount store _____
hardware store _____
or other store _____
124. The quantity I buy at one time is
a single package _____
several packages _____
many packages _____

TRADE WITH A PARTICULAR STORE

125. I shop in your store
more than once a week _____
at least once a week _____
every two weeks _____
once a month _____
once a year _____
126. The distance from my home to your store is
less than five blocks _____
one mile away _____

two or three miles _____
five miles _____
over ten miles _____
127. I usually buy these types of products at your store:

_____
_____
_____
_____

128. The part of my shopping I do with your store is:
All _____
Most _____
129. My favorite stores that are similar to yours (and including it) are:
First choice _____
Second choice _____
Third choice _____
130. Each year I spend this amount in your store $_____

Figure 12.1. (Continued)

concept, instead of trying to sell to the entire market, you zero in on a specific segment of the population who are most interested and can best be served by buying your product or service. The segmentation concept makes sense. You cannot satisfy the entire market with one specific item, and further, you will always have limited resources with which to advertise and promote your products or services.

Advertisers use segmentation through their application of strategy: positioning strategy, media strategy, and creative strategy. *Positioning strategy* refers to how your product is positioned in comparison to the competition. For example, Colonel Sanders' Kentucky Fried Chicken was successful when aimed at buyers who are mainly housewives with a contemporary state of mind, busy, active, finding it hard to prepare meals for their family on a daily basis. Yet, at first, Kentucky Fried Chicken was a failure when positioned mainly as a countrified, folksy product.

Use of *media strategy* by advertising means selecting the appropriate medium or media to reach the segment that is most interested or would be most interested in buying your product. For example, why are beer, razors, and similar male-oriented products advertised on television during sporting events? Clearly because this is when and where the main user of these products is available as an audience for the advertising.

Creative strategy concerns the copy (writing) in the advertisement, the graphics, pictures, or photographs, and the ideas that combine these into an effective ad. For example, Mark O. Haroldsen wrote a book called *How to Wake Up the Financial Genius Within You.* His message for the opportunity-seeker's market in magazines such as *Salesman Opportunity, Spare Time Opportunities*, and the like, used the title of the book as the headline. Yet, in advertising in the *Wall Street Journal*, Haroldsen used an entirely different advertisement; the headline read: "How to Avoid Paying Taxes Legally." Why did he use this different creative strategy for the *Wall Street Journal*? In the first case he was appealing to individuals who wanted to grasp an opportunity to make money. In the *Wall Street Journal* he was appealing to professional managers and entrepreneurs who were already making money and were interested in reducing their considerable taxes.

Nowadays, advertisers segment the market in many ways. Here are just a few categories that you might consider for your product or service.

Age. Advertisers tend to spend the most money trying to gain the attention of individuals in the age group 18 to 34. Why do they do this? Because, statistically, this is the group that spends the most money on consumer products. However, this is certainly not true for all types of products or services. For example, record manufacturers go primarily to the age group 12 to 19, and those who sell luxury items appeal to the age group 34 to 49.

Sex. Here again you can see a segmentation. Mennen's Speed Stick underarm deodorant is sold to men. But women will buy an entirely different brand, although the chemical composition may be almost identical to that of Mennen's Speed Stick. Or, more obviously, men buy *Playboy*; women buy *Playgirl*.

Income, Education, and Occupation. Income, education, and occupation are frequently considered together because they are related. For instance, a medical doctor generally has a high income and a considerable education. However, this is not always true. Many blue-collar workers earn as much as or more than their white-collar counterparts. In fact, one of the problems that Robert Oppenheimer had when he headed the Manhatten Project, which developed the atom bomb, was that his electricians made as much as his scientists and engineers, and when his professionals discovered this they complained bitterly about this "inequity." Many tradesmen such as plumbers, certain mechanics, and others may make high salaries. And, of course, if you are self-employed you have the potential for making much more money than salaried professionals.

Geographic Location.   Here again, cold weather implies heavy clothing. Winter weather implies certain types of products just as sunny Miami or California implies other types of products. If you are selling disco clothes, your product would direct you to the location of your potential sales.

Marital Status and Family Size.   Here again, certain types of products and services will segment according to these factors. Video dating services, travel and tour services, singles bars, nightclubs, will all segment the market in advertising depending on marital status. Certain types of products are segmented by family size when a giant economy size is offered.

Ethnic Group.   Segmentation is accomplished by ethnic group because some groups prefer certain types of products over others. Soybean products, for example, such as tofu or soybean milk, are sold mainly to Asian communities. Certain types of delicatessen products are sold mainly to Jewish, Italian, or German communities. Other types of foods, cosmetic products, or luxury items must also be segmented by ethnic group.

Subculture.   Subcultures such as "disco youth" or "over 65" can also be effectively segmented from the mass market and therefore advertised to. For example, for the over-65 group, market research has shown a greater tendency to do comparison shopping, to buy mainly nationally known name brands, and to shy away from shops that are felt to cater exclusively to older customers. In fact, some years ago, a nationally known baby food company lost millions of dollars in sales because it introduced a special line of senior foods which was ignored by its intended market.

Social Class.   Different social classes tend to prefer and read different types of publications. For example, *Reader's Digest* and *Ladies' Home Journal* are in one class; *Time* and *Sports Illustrated* in another; *New Yorker* and Vogue magazine in yet another.

Of the categories previously discussed, age, sex, marital status, family size, income, education, and occupation, and geographical location are all known as *demographic* factors. Subculture, ethnic group, and social class are known as social culture factors. There is also more and more segmentation done for advertising in psychographics and life style categories. These include activities, interests, and opinions, product usage, new product adoption behavior, and family decision making. To accomplish segmentation by psychographics or life style factors, special research is done which measures aspects of human behavior including what products or services are consumed, the activities, interests, and opinions of respondents, special value systems, personality traits and conception of self, and attitudes toward various product classes.

Recently, additional special groups have been identified as being especially good targets for segmentation. Some of these new groups are as follows.

College Students. There are more than 11 million college students. Individuals selling to this market have made million of dollars, going back to computer dating which itself originated with a college student in 1966. This student became a millionaire prior to graduation through market segmentation.

The Latino Market. This is a viable market which has become so strong that special courses in marketing to this segment have been offered at some of the nation's largest universities. It includes more than 15 million people.

Divorces. While divorce may not be desirable in any society, it is a fact in ours. The average marriage today lasts only six years. As a result, divorcees today are one-half of the single population.

Individuals Living Together. Today, individuals who are living together constitute a segment in themselves. Their number approaches two million.

The Working Woman. Today, two-thirds of women are working, and more than 50% of mothers are working; this is a truly gigantic segment.

Health. There's a tremendous interest in health in the United States. Vitamin sales have doubled in 10 years. The readership of magazines pertaining to health, such as *Prevention*, is steadily growing, with new magazines and newsletters appearing every day. There are 60 million individuals in the United States who are overweight, and two-thirds of these individuals are women. As a result, diet books and other products and services are of continual interest to this segment. There is almost always at least one diet book on *The New York Times* Best Seller List.

Children with Money. Today, children ages 6 through 11 receive allowances the average of which approaches more than $100 a year. The result is $2.5 billion dollars in spendable income, making this segment a tremendous buying force.

Sports Enthusiasts. Jogging, tennis, bicycling, swimming, and even the martial arts are nosing out more traditional sports such as football and basketball in popularity. There is a tremendous interest in all sports and a tremendous market segment to be served.

Spiritual and Mind Power. Recent popular interest in such subjects as yoga, mysticism, Transcendental Meditation, Scientology, and Silva Mind Control has made this a leading and increasingly large segment of the population. Further, this group constitutes a segment which is completely separate from religion in the traditional sense.

In order to learn how best to reach your customer, some sort of market research will be necessary. One way of doing this is with your own survey of your customers or potential customers. A form for you to use is shown in Figure 12.1, a consumer profile questionnaire.

A book which will help you is *Do It Yourself Marketing Research*, by George Edward Breen, published by McGraw-Hill Book Co., 1221 Avenue of the Americas, New York, N.Y. 10020.

Set Concrete Goals and Objectives

Once your analysis is completed, your job is to establish the goals and objectives of your advertising program. What do you want to happen? You should answer the question in precise, concrete terms so that you can measure your results at a later time. And by when do you want it to happen? Give a specific time frame. For example, a suitable advertising objective might be to increase the number of males ages 15 to 25 who walk into your retail establishment and make a purchase by 20% over the next three months. That says precisely who, what, and when.

The Advertising Budget

Once goals and objectives have been established, you must look to your advertising budget. In some cases your budget will be established before goals and objectives due to your limited resources. It will be a given, and you may have to modify your goals and objectives. If money is available, you can work the other way around and see how much money it will take to reach the goals and objectives you have established.

The professionals use different methods of establishing an advertising budget. These are as follows:

Percentage of anticipated or past year's sales

The arbitrary approach

Quantitative models

Objective and task approach

Affordable approach

Competitive approach

Of these methods, a recent survey shows that the most popular method used today is that of *percentage of anticipated sales*. This means that you must forecast your sales for the future period and then allocate a fixed percentage. This fixed percentage is usually found by comparing other firms advertising in your industry that are of your size and have a similar product. Obviously, this method has an advantage over taking a fixed percentage of a past year's sales since you are looking to the future. On the other hand, it says little about the advertising program and has nothing to do with the objectives and goals that you have established.

The *arbitrary approach* means simply that you pull a figure out of the air and decide that this is how much money will be devoted to advertising. This method has little to recommend it.

Quantitative models can be extremely sophisticated. However, their complexity and the fact that so many factors must be considered mean that it is little used and probably not desirable or even workable for a small firm. As a matter of fact, even by major firms the quantitative model method is little used.

With the *objective and task* approach, you relate your budget to the goals and objectives you have established. While the percentage of sales or profits or percentage of any approach first determines how much you'll spend without much consideration of what you want to accomplish, this method establishes what you must do in order to meet your objectives—only then do you calculate its cost. For a small firm, it must frequently be used with the affordable approach since in some cases, and as mentioned previously, you may set objectives which can only be reached at a much higher budget than you can afford. In this case, you must scale down your objectives.

In order to use the objective and task method, you break down the cost of your budget by calendar periods, by media, and perhaps by sales areas. Breakdown by calendar periods means that you divide the advertising plan on a monthly or weekly basis. Media breakdown denotes how much money you will place in each advertising medium, such as television, radio, newspaper, direct mail, and so forth. Sales areas are the areas in which you will spend your advertising budget. That is, if you are going after different market segments simultaneously under one advertising program, you have to decide how much money each market segment will get. Use the form in Figure 12.2 to assist you in preparing your advertising budget.

With the *affordable approach*, you don't go for the optimal, but only what your firm can afford.

Finally, we have the *competitive approach*. With this approach, you analyze how much the competitor is spending and spend more, the same, or less depending upon your objectives.

Cahners Publishing Company publishes a booklet *Work Book for Estimating Your Advertising Budget*. The guidelines in the work book are based on ten decision rules which define conditions requiring higher advertising expenditures. The research which resulted in these decision rules was conducted for Cahners by the Strategic Planning Institute of Cambridge, Massachusetts. These 10 decision rules as to when higher expenditure is required are:

1. When you seek to maintain or increase market share
2. When you seek higher new product activity

Account	Month		Year to Date	
	Budget	Actual	Budget	Actual

Media
  Newspapers
  Radio
  TV
  Literature
  Direct Mail
  Other
Promotions
  Exhibits
  Displays
  Contests
  Sweepstakes
Advertising Expense
  Salaries
  Supplies
  Stationery
  Travel
  Postage
  Subscriptions
  Entertainment
  Dues				

Totals				

Figure 12.2. Advertising budget. [Adapted from *Advertising Guidelines for Small Retail Firms*, by Ovid Riso, SMA 160, Small Business Administration (1980)].

3. When you seek faster growing markets
4. When you seek lower plant capacity
5. When you seek lower unit price
6. For products that do not represent a major purchase for your customers in terms of total dollars
7. If your products are either high (or premium) priced or low (or discount) priced
8. If your products are of higher quality
9. If you have broad product lines
10. If your products are standard as opposed to made-to-order

If you would like a free copy of this workbook, you can get a copy from Cahners Publishing, 221 Columbus Avenue, Boston, MA 02116.

Creative Strategy

Creative strategy involves what you will say in your advertising message, how you will say it, and any artwork that is included. Unless you are a professional in this area, or your ad is very simple, it is better to get expert, professional help in preparing creative work. You can find these professionals fairly easily in your phone book. For artwork, look under Artists—Commercial or Advertising Artists. Do the same for photography and for copywriters.

If you intend to write your own copy, I would recommend the book *How to Write a Good Advertisement*, by Victor O. Schwab. This is published by the Wilshire Book Co., 12015 Sherman Rd., North Hollywood, CA 91605.

If you are going to write your own copy, follow the following guidelines.

First, make the headline appeal to self-interest, offer exciting news, or rouse interest in your consumer. The headline should be positive, not negative. The headline should suggest that the reader can obtain something easily and quickly. Make the headline stress the most important benefit of your product or your service, and write it so that it grabs the reader's attention and causes him or her to read further. Also, be sure that the headline is believable and, of course, when you begin to write the body of the copy, make sure that the headline does in fact tie in with what you write later.

In the copy content itself, you should try to gain interest immediately. If you have enough room in your copy, use a story or a startling or unusual statement or quote; use news if you don't have enough room. Show the benefits and advantages that appeal to emotional needs to such an extent that you offer and what you say are made irresistible. If you can, add credibility to your copy through the use of testimonials. These are statements made by other people who have used your product or service and are happy with it.

Always remember when you are writing copy that you are writing to communicate, and therefore write it in a conversational tone and keep your copy moving right along. Use short words, short sentences, and short paragraphs, and lots of subheadings throughout. If you want your copy to be read, make it interesting and make it easy to read. I have found that Rudolf Flesch's book, *The Art of Readable Writing*, published by Harper and Row Publishers, Inc., to be of considerable help here.

These principles in copywriting should apply whether your advertisement is to appear in print or on radio or television. Only minor modifications should be necessary depending on limitations of these different media.

Medium and Vehicle Selection

Each of the different advertising *media* categories (print, television, radio, etc.) has several vehicles: magazine or newspaper, and which type; what sort of radio television show, and so on. There are four major considerations when you make your selection of medium (assuming you're using just one) and vehicle. These are as follows:

1. *Budget match.* Which medium and vehicle you use must be consistent with the money that you have available for use in your budget.

2. *Medium and vehicle and target consumer match.* The medium and vehicle that you select must be seen, heard, or read by your target consumer market.

3. *Medium and vehicle market mix relationship.* Which medium and vehicle you select also must be reflected in the emphasis that you give to the marketing mix. The marketing mix is made up of various inputs of product, price, the distribution method that you use, and promotional factors. What is the relationship between medium and vehicle and market mix? Let's take a new product. With a new product you may choose to use TV as your medium because with TV you can reach the most people in the shortest amount of time. Also, the product must fit the medium or vehicle. Some years ago, entrepreneur Joe Cossman sold over one million plastic shrunken heads. Obviously *Vogue* magazine was never considered a vehicle for this particular product. In the same way, high price denotes a certain medium and vehicle, as does low price. Similar matching must be followed with distribution and promotional factors.

4. *Creative medium and vehicle marriage.* Certain appeals are best for certain media and vehicles, as mentioned previously using the example of Mark O. Haroldsen's book, *How to Wake Up the Financial Genius Within You.* To reach those interested in getting rich quick, the vehicle selected was *Specialty Salesmen* and similar magazines. To reach those interested in tax shelters, the vehicle selected was the *Wall Street Journal*.

The Categories of Media. The categories of media should all be considered as you plan for your advertising campaign. These include:

1. Print (newspapers, magazines)
2. Broadcasts (radio, TV)
3. Direct mail (letters addressed directly to lists of potential buyers in your target consumer market group)
4. Specialty items (pens, pencils, or other gadgets with the name of your firm embossed on them)
5. Directories (yellow pages advertisements, advertisements in association membership directories, and so forth)
6. Outdoor (billboards, transit posters)
7. Movie theater advertisement
8. Various others, such as matchbook covers

Audience. One publication that will greatly assist you in planning your campaign is the *Standard Rate and Data Service* or SRDS. The SRDS publishes a set of periodically updated volumes including :

1. Consumer magazines
2. Farm publications
3. Business publications
4. Newspapers
5. Weekly newspapers
6. Network radio and TV
7. Spot radio and TV
8. Transit
9. Mailing lists

While major advertisers and advertising agencies are the usual subscribers to SRDS, many libraries carry these volumes. You will find them extremely useful in matching your target audience and selecting the media and vehicles that you can use.

Making Intermediate Comparisons.   Each medium has its advantages and its disadvantages for your particular situation. For example, television, which has a broad reach and offers opportunities for a dynamic demonstration, is expensive and does not allow for demographic selectivity to any great extent. Newspapers may be relatively cheap; however, they offer little secondary readership, limited color facilities, and little demographic selectivity possibilities. To assist you in making intermedia comparisons, consider Figure 12.3, the advertising media comparison chart developed by the Bank of America.

Advertising Planning Concepts.   Some of the concepts that you should consider in your planning, in addition to cost, are reach versus frequency; continuity; target market, marketing and advertising objectives; the marketing mix of product, price, promotion and distribution, and promotional variables; competitive advertising activity; the size of your budget; and your creative strategy.

All of these have been discussed previously except for reach versus frequency and continuity.

Reach versus Frequency.   Reach is the total number of households that will be exposed to an advertising message in a particular vehicle or medium over a certain period of time. It is expressed as a percentage of the total universe of households. Frequency is the number of exposures to the same message each household receives. Therefore, average frequency would equal the total exposures for all households sampled, divided by the reach. Even at tremendous expense, you cannot reach 100% of your target market. Therefore, the key is trying to estimate the point at which additional dollars should go into frequency after the optimal reach has been achieved. Some pointers that will assist you in making this decision are as follows:

Go for greater reach

1. . . . when you're introducing a new product to a mass market and want as many people as possible to know about it.
2. . . . when your advertising message is so compelling that most people will react to the initial exposure.
3. . . . when your product or service message is in itself newsworthy and will itself demand attention.

ADVERTISING MEDIA

Medium	Market Coverage	Type of Audience	Sample Time/Space Costs
Daily Newspaper	Single community or entire metro area; zoned editions sometimes available.	General; tends more toward men, older age group, slightly higher income and education.	Per agate line, weekday; open rate: Circ: 8,700: $ .20 19,600: $ .35 46,200: $ .60 203,800: $ 1.60
Weekly Newspaper	Single community usually; sometimes a metro area.	General; usually residents of a smaller community.	Per agate line; open rate: Circ: 3,000: $ .35 8,900: $ .50 17,100: $ .75
Shopper	Most households in a single community; chain shoppers can cover a metro area.	Consumer households.	Per agate line; open rate: Circ: 10,000: $ .20 147,000: $ 2.00 300,000: $ 3.20
Telephone Directories	Geographic area or occupational field served by the directory.	Active shoppers for goods or services.	Yellow Pages, per half column; per month: Pop: 14-18,000: $ 15.00 110-135,000: $ 35.00 700-950,000: $ 100.00
Direct Mail	Controlled by the advertiser.	Controlled by the advertiser through use of demographic lists.	Production and mailing cost of an 8½" × 11" 2-color brochure; 4-page, 2-color letter; order card and reply envelope; label addressed; third class mail: $.33 each in quantities of 50,000.
Radio	Definable market area surrounding the station's location.	Selected audiences provided by stations with distinct programming formats.	Per 60-second morning drive-time spot; one time: Pop: 400,000: $ 35.00 1,100,000: $ 90.00 3,500,000: $ 150.00 13,000,000: $ 300.00
Television	Definable market area surrounding the station's location.	Varies with the time of day; tends toward younger age group, less print-oriented.	Per 30-second daytime spot; one time; nonpreemptible status: Pop: 400,000: $100.00 1,100,000: $300.00 3,500,000: $500.00 13,000,000: $600.00
Transit	Urban or metro community served by transit system; may be limited to a few transit routes.	Transit riders, especially wage earners and shoppers; pedestrians.	Inside 11" × 28" cards; per month: 50 buses: $ 125.00 400 buses: $1,000.00 Outside 21" × 88" posters; per month: 25 buses: $1,850.00 100 buses: $7,400.00
Outdoor	Entire metro area or single neighborhood.	General; especially auto drivers.	Per 12' × 25' poster; 100 GRP* per month: Pop: 21,800: $ 125.00 386,000: $ 135.00 628,900: $ 150.00
Local Magazine	Entire metro area or region; zoned editions sometimes available.	General; tends toward better educated, more affluent.	Per one-sixth page, black and white; open rate: Circ: 25,000: $ 310.00 80,000: $ 520.00

*Several boards must be purchased for these GRPs.

Figure 12.3. Advertising media comparison chart. (Reprinted with permission from Bank of America, NT & SA, "Advertising Small Business," *Small Business Reporter*, Vol. 15, No. 2, Copyright © 1976, 1978, 1981.)

Go for higher frequency

1. ... when your competitor is going for high frequency against the same segment as you.

2. ... when you are seeking direct response; that is, when you want individuals to order the product or respond to the service directly from the ad.

COMPARISON CHART

Particular Suitability	Major Advantage	Major Disadvantage
All general retailers.	Wide circulation.	Nonselective audience.
Retailers who service a strictly local market.	Local identification.	Limited readership.
Neighborhood retailers and service businesses.	Consumer orientation.	A giveaway and not always read.
Services, retailers of brand-name items, highly specialized retailers.	Users are in the market for goods or services.	Limited to active shoppers.
New and expanding businesses; those using coupon returns or catalogs.	Personalized approach to an audience of good prospects.	High CPM.
Businesses catering to identifiable groups; teens, commuters, housewives.	Market selectivity, wide market coverage.	Must be bought consistently to be of value.
Sellers of products or services with wide appeal.	Dramatic impact, wide market coverage.	High cost of time and production.
Businesses along transit routes, especially those appealing to wage earners.	Repetition and length of exposure.	Limited audience.
Amusements, tourist businesses, brand-name retailers.	Dominant size, frequency of exposure.	Clutter of many signs reduces effectiveness of each one.
Restaurants, entertainments, specialty shops, mail-order businesses.	Delivery of a loyal, special-interest audience.	Limited audience.

Figure 12.3. (Continued)

3. . . . when you want your target consumer to act within a certain limited time period.

4. . . . when there isn't too much to differentiate what you are offering from what your competition is selling.

Continuity. Continuity has to do with the length of time that your medium schedule should run. Obviously, you can run a medium schedule continuously or periodically; once a day, once a week, or even more infrequently. Here again, you should consider the various factors that may influence success as a tradeoff against cost and limited resources. For funding optimal frequency, experts have developed something called the "three-hit theory." The basis of the theory is that there is an optimal range after which you are wasting money. This range, according to the theory, is three receipts of your message or "hits." Three hits will insure that the customer learns of your product or service through your advertising message. To get the three hits, you need 11 to 12 potential advertising exposures. Therefore, the average potential frequency should be 11 to 12 times.

Once you have decided upon the medium (or media), you must then decide upon the vehicle(s). To do this, you use demographics, that is, the demographic research that you have done against that supplied by the vehicle in question. And in this regard, you should know that every magazine or television or radio show can offer a current demographic profile of its readership or listenership. It is therefore a question of matching up their information with your research of your target customer.

Negotiating and Special Discounts.   Many small business advertisers don't realize that they could advertise for much less than they are doing now if they knew about the special negotiating possibilities and discounts which are offered. These include the following:

1. Mail order discounts
2. PI (per inquiry) deals
3. Frequency discounts
4. Stand-by rates
5. Help if necessary
6. Remnants and regional editions
7. Barter
8. Bulk buyers
9. Seasonal discounts
10. Spread discounts
11. An in-house agency
12. Cost discounts

If you are a mail order advertiser, many magazines realize that you must make money directly from your ad or you cannot stay in business and will not advertise again. In addition to this, with this type of advertising, it is easy to know immediately whether you are doing well and whether it made money for you. Accordingly, many magazines will give special *mail order discounts*, sometimes up to 40%, to mail order advertisers. Therefore, if the advertisement normally costs you $200, you need only pay $120. This is a big discount and certainly nothing to pass by. Even for many national mail order advertisers, it may spell the difference between a profitable ad and failure.

A *PI deal* is one in which you agree to pay the publication only for those inquiries or sales that the ad itself brings in. This may be on the radio, television, or in a magazine. As a result, in return for this agreement, the magazine will run your advertisement with no money from you up front. Certainly this is a major advantage for a small businessperson. Usually the mail is sent to the vehicle which will sort it and keep the records for you. At other times the ad is keyed and the mail sent directly to you. You must turn a percentage of each order over to the vehicle at fixed periods that you agree upon. If the orders go to the vehicle, they will send you the names of those who order so that you can respond and send the product to the customer. They will also send that amount owed you for each product. A typical PI deal will usually cost something like 50% of the selling price to the publication vehicle.

Frequently it is difficult to locate PI deals, and you need to talk to the salesperson representing the vehicle. Few magazines, radio stations, or television stations like their regular advertisers to know that they accept PI deals, so don't expect them to be advertised as such. They are not easy to find, but they are worth the trouble of looking for them.

Most media will offer *frequency discounts*. Therefore, if you advertise more than once or more than what is standard, you can expect a lower cost than what you might otherwise achieve. Be careful, however, in committing yourself to long-range advertising programs until you know whether or not the campaign is going to work.

Most vehicles are committed to publication or broadcast on a regular basis. At certain times, all advertising may not be sold outright up to the last minute. The vehicle therefore has a choice: it can either sell this advertising at a greatly reduced amount—*stand-by rate*—or put in some sort of editorial content which does not generate additional profits. To get the stand-by rate, you must first let the different vehicles know that you are interested in this type of a deal, and they must be able to get hold of you quickly by telephone. Sometimes a stand-by rate is available only after you advertise with this publication or station for some time. Then, the people know you and trust you. This is important since the deal is closed verbally—no money from you in advance. The advantage of the stand-by rate is well worth it. Again, you may pay as little as 40 to 50% of the normal cost of advertising.

Help if necessary, is applicable usually to mail order advertisers and again, is in recognition of the fact that the mail order advertiser must make money from the ad in order to stay in business. What it means is that if the ad is not profitable, the publication may agree to run the ad and repeat it if necessary until you at least break even. Help may not assist you in making additional money, but it sure can prevent you from losing a lot of money. Therefore, you should always check into the possibility of help-if-necessary deals if you are a mail order advertiser.

Many national magazines today will allow advertisers to buy space only in certain regional editions rather than in every edition which appears nationally. This situation works to your advantage in reduced advertising costs, and sometimes the regional editions will not be sold out in advertising and space may go begging. You can get *remnants in regional editions* at a discount of as much as 50%. To locate remnant advertising possibilities, talk to salespeople representing the advertising vehicle.

Sometimes a publication or station may be willing to *barter*, that is, to take products or services in exchange for advertising. This occurs where the vehicle has an interest other than publishing or broadcasting. Barter is a great way to go since it allows you to increase sales without using up capital resources.

Bulk Buyers are purchasers of huge amounts of advertising from advertising media. Because of the quantity in which it is bought, they pay much less. The bulk buyer then resells the advertising space. The price you pay to a bulk buyer will vary greatly and it will be negotiable. Toward the end of the advertising period, if this space isn't sold, you may be able to get discounts as large as 50% of what you would normally pay.

Certain media do not do well during certain seasons of the year. As a result, during these periods they offer substantial *seasonal discounts* over their normal rate. If your product or service sells well during that season, you should seriously consider seasonal discounts in your advertising. On the same principle, your product may cost a great deal to sell during prime time on television or radio. However, there may be no need to sell during prime time. In fact, your product may sell better in other than prime time. Therefore, you should consider nonprime time discounts much in the line of seasonal discounts.

If you are a big advertiser and advertise on two or three pages or more of a particular issue of a magazine, you may be able to get a special *spread discount*. This may or may not be on the vehicle's rate card which describes its advertising costs, so you must ask about it. Again, discounts can run as high as 50% of the normal cost.

Advertising agencies get an automatic 15% discount from any vehicle in which they place your ad. This is one way they have of making their money. As a result, many small businesspeople form their own *in-house agency* to take advantage of the 15% discount for themselves. Most vehicles say they will not deal with inhouse agencies and will not accept advertising from them at the 15% discount. However, what they are really saying is that they will do this as long as you're not obvious about the fact that you are an in-house agency. Therefore, for the cost of registration of a name other than that of your regular company, and some specially printed stationery with this name, you can get a 15% discount every single time you advertise. To recapitulate:

1. Select a name for your in-hour advertising agency which is different from the name of your regular firm.
2. Have special stationery printed up with the in-house agency's name.
3. Do not volunteer the fact that you are an in-house agency. Merely indicate that you're placing the ad for the company indicated and give other instructions in accordance with the rate card or the *Standard Rate and Data Service* publication.

Many advertisers overlook the fact that most vehicles will give a 2% *cash discount* for payment of cash within the first ten days. However, if you do not take this discount, very few vehicles will automatically return your money. So, look for this information in materials supplied in the information on the rate card which you request from the vehicle. If you can get a 2% discount, you can save a lot of money. Even small firms are saving as much as $50,000 a year this way, once they become large advertisers.

Evaluation of Results

Unless you know how well your advertising is doing, much or all of your money could be totally wasted. Therefore, it is important to establish some measurements of the effectiveness of your advertising. There are several methods of doing this. They are:

1. Direct response
2. Involuntary methods

3. Recognition and awareness tests
4. Recall tests
5. Focus group tests

Direct Response. This is probably the best means of measuring the effectiveness of your advertising, because you measure actual responses to your ad. In order to do this, all you need do is code the advertisement so that you'll know which response is from which advertisement. A typical code uses "Suite," "Room," "Drawer," or sometimes even different initials before the name of the company, or different initials after the box number. For example, a letter can stand for the vehicle in which the advertisement appears, and a digit following the letter can denote the month. Let us say that you advertised in *Outdoor Life* magazine in January. "A" could stand for *Outdoor Life*, and the digit "1" could stand for advertisement in January. The simple addition to your address of "Suite A-1" or "Room A-1" would tell you immediately the vehicle and the exact advertisement.

Involuntary Methods. These methods of measuring advertisement effectiveness are usually pretesting methods. They record involuntary responses over which neither the subject nor the researcher has control. They are objective, but they are also expensive. They are also done in an unnatural setting. One device, called a pupilometer, measures the dilation of the pupil while the individual is observing advertising. The device is unwieldy and uncomfortable, and it certainly isn't the way that the reader usually sees advertising. One very simple involuntary method is called the "down the chute" test. It consists of having someone read advertising copy while you watch his eyes. If there are no problems with comprehension or readability, it is presumed that the individual's eyes will keep moving from left to right, left to right, as he goes line by line down the page. But if the pupils stop moving, there could be a problem, and at this point you should ask the reader what he is reading. You note the problem and then continue the procedure.

Recognition and Awareness Tests. In recognition and awareness tests, consumers who have read or seen an advertisement are asked whether they remember the ad. One limitation is the possibility of confusion of your ad with similar ads, and the sample size used is usually small compared to the total number of readers.

The oldest type of recognition test is a readership test called the "Starch." In the Starch system, the interviewer shows the magazine to the subject, and if the subject says he or she has read it, the interviewer goes through the magazine ad by ad with the subject indicating whether he or she has "noted the ad," which means has seen it; "associated it," which means he or she remembers the brand name; or "read most," which means that he or she has read at least half of the copy. The Starch system reports the percentage of ads "noted," "associated," and "read most" for each subject.

Awareness tests measure the cumulative effect of advertising. Test subjects are consumers in the target consumer group for the ad. First, demographic information is gathered to determine if they are likely customers. Then, they are asked the question: "Have you seen the ads lately for (name of product)? The problem with this type of test is that there are too many variables which can affect the response.

Recall Tests.   In a typical recall test, the prospects are first screened and asked questions about their attitude. They are then asked to watch a program, while those in a control group are asked similar questions but do not watch. The effectiveness of recall is determined later when brand awareness is measured in both groups and the results are compared.

Focus Group Tests.   The focus group has grown as a method of pretesting in recent years. It is relatively low budget in that 8 to 10 representative consumers are invited in. It is therefore not a quantitative measure but rather a qualitative measure of reactions to help you decide whether to run one ad or another.

The small businessperson can adopt many of these methods to help in determining the effectiveness of advertising. The key is to keep your methods simple, hold down costs, and be careful about drawing inferences if you use a very small sample size.

SHOULD YOU EMPLOY AN ADVERTISING AGENCY?

Whether or not to employ an advertising agency depends a great deal on how large a company you have and what an advertising agency can do for you. Many of the things that an advertising agency can do, such as media selection, copywriting, supplying artwork, and so forth, you may do for yourself, in which case it may be better to establish your own in-house agency as described earlier and save 15%. On the other hand, all these activities take up your resources, and an agency can tie everything together and can probably do a more professional job for you. The problem here is that many of the best agencies will only work for your firm when you become a major advertiser. If you are big enough, the services provided by an agency may cost you nothing since the agency receives 15% commission from the medium or media used. If you are not a major advertiser, the agency will bill you for services rendered on an hourly, daily, or project basis.

If you do decide to employ an advertising firm, do not engage the first one that you contact. First, talk to the principals of the agency and get some definite information about them. This should include: the size of the agency, that is, last year's billing, how long the principals have been with the agency, their general philosophy of positioning, whether they deal mainly with industrial accounts or with consumer accounts, and what some of their accounts are. You should also query them to find out in which areas of your business they would like to become involved. Some agencies will handle everything for you. Others will develop and place your ads, and that's it. Ask who at the agency would be working directly on your account and his or her title, and who would be responsible for supervision on a day-to-day basis. You should also ask for representative accounts, accounts similar to yours with which the advertising agency has experience so that you may contact those firms. Naturally, you should ask about compensation arrangements. If you are going to be doing a considerable amount of advertising, it is perfectly legitimate to ask for a speculative presentation by the agency. In fact, you should ask for a proposal from several different agencies. During these speculative presentations, you can get a feel for what the agency can do and whether you like or do not like the people and services you will be paying for. There are, however, certain disadvantages to asking several agencies for proposals. They will have competitive information on your firm, and some agencies will see this as exploitive inasmuch as they obviously must pay for this proposal whether or not they get your business. In general, it is better not to ask for a speculative proposal unless the agency is a serious candidate.

Consider the following factors in making your decision to "hire" an agency:

1. Is the agency size consistent with your needs and growth plans?
2. Is the agency's philosophy of positioning compatible with your own?
3. Is the agency's management strength compatible with your firm?
4. Is the agency's ability to offer overall marketing counsel good?
5. Is there a similarity among the agency's other accounts and your firm?
6. Do you have a good opinion of the account team assigned from the agency to be responsible for working with you and doing your advertising?
7. Does the agency have a good research capability?
8. Does the agency have a good creative capability?
9. Does the agency have a good media planning capability?
10. Is the agency in good financial shape?
11. How did the references check out?

Of course, as mentioned earlier, one of the problems that you will have as a small firm is interesting an agency in working with you. One way to do this is to stress your tremendous growth potential. If you don't have much cash, try barter. That is, trade your product or services for their services. Finally, you could offer stock in your company in exchange for their services.

HOW TO GET FREE ADVERTISING THROUGH A PUBLICITY RELEASE

Every magazine is constantly looking for new ideas, new news, and new information to tell its readers. So, whenever you have a new product or service or something different happens with regard to your current product or service that might be of interest to a magazine's readers, many magazines will be happy to publicize it for you and will charge you nothing. This has an additional advantage. Editorial coverage of your product or service is usually more effective than your own advertising. You should understand that magazines will not run every single idea or product publicity release which you submit. In order to reach those that will, you must run a direct mail campaign. Your campaign package should consist of three basic elements:

1. A sales letter to the editor
2. Suggested editorial material about your new product or service (called the "release")
3. Either the product itself or a 4-by-5-inch glossy photograph of the product (Generally a photograph is just as good, unless your product is a book or a booklet.)

Figure 12.4 is a letter to the editor for free advertising for a body armor product I sold several years ago. Follow this general format when asking for free advertising in a letter. Do not mention that you may become a paid advertiser later. If you are sending money to the magazine for a paid advertisement, do not send it with a letter to the editor requesting free editorial mention. Do not mention whether you're currently an advertiser in the magazine.

```
Mr. A. B. Jones
Editor
World Military Gazette
101 New State Drive
New York NY 10065

Dear Mr. Jones:

I am writing to you because my company, Global Associates, has just
developed a new product which will have a tremendous effect on cas-
ualty reduction in military operations. This new product is a per-
sonal protective body armor which is half the weight of current mod-
els but gives slightly more than double the level of protection.

This amazing armor is called "KPC Composite," and it is soft and flex-
ible although it has five times the tensile strength of steel. A
special patented carrier has been developed for the KPC Composite
material. The whole unit is called "The Commando MK III Armor
Jacket."

I know that your readers will be interested in knowing not only of
the existence of this life-saving garment, but also that indi-
vidual soldiers can order their own Commando MK III Armor Jackets
directly from Global Associates at $300 per unit, insurance and
postage costs included. I have enclosed a publicity release along
with a photograph for your use if desired.

                                                  Sincerely,



                                                  President
                                                  GLOBAL ASSOCIATES
```

Figure 12.4.   Letter to the editor for a publicity release.

Figure 12.5 shows a typical publicity release that might accompany a letter such as the one shown in Figure 12.4. Note that the publicity release is typed and need not be printed. Figure 12.6 shows a photograph of the product. Photographs can be reproduced in quantity rather cheaply, although usually not by a standard commercial photographer. For example, a 4-by-5-inch glossy in quantities of 100 can be obtained for as little as 30¢ a copy by a duplicate photograph service which you can find in your yellow pages. One that I have used and recommend is Duplicate Photo Laboratories, Inc., P.O. Box 2670, 1522 North Highland Ave., Hollywood, CA 90028.

HOW TO GET NEWSPAPERS ALL OVER THE COUNTRY TO GIVE YOU FREE PUBLICITY

Another type of promotion you can do is one that I did for my book *Building a Mail Order Business* (John Wiley & Sons, 1982, 1985). I wrote to editors of the family or general interest sections of newspapers all over the country. I offered each exclusive use in their geographic area of a short article I had written called "Can Anyone Make a Million Dollars in Mail Order?" Naturally I mentioned my book. You can see my letter in Figure 12.7 and a sample of the results in Figure 12.8. Note that the editor changed the title in this instance. This got me

New Body Armor Announced

Global Associates, a body armor company, announced the development of a new personal protective body armor today. The new armor, known as KPC Composite, is half the weight of current body armor, but offers twice the level of protection. The armor also has the unusual properties of being soft and flexible although it displays five times the tensile strength of steel. The armor has defeated projectiles travelling as fast as 2000 feet per second. It has also been tested against and has stopped various small-arm ammunition, including .38 caliber, .45 caliber, .22 magnum, 9mm, .41 magnum, and .44 magnum. A special patented carrier has been designed for the armor and designated the Commando MK III Armor Jacket. This garment itself has many unusual features. It is worn like a jacket, with a closure in the front. This permits increased ventilation during use and allows the armor to be donned or doffed without removing the helmet or other headgear. In addition, a special lockstrap suspension system has been developed. Although the straps cannot be pulled apart, under emergency conditions the armor can be completely jettisoned in less than three seconds. For normal armor closure, a protected slide fastener is provided. The entire ensemble comes in three sizes—small, medium, and large. It weighs just 4½ pounds. Interested buyers can purchase the Commando MK III Armor Jacket by sending $300 to Global Associates, 56 N. Sierra St., Pasadena, California 91109

Figure 12.5. Publicity release.

Figure 12.6. The Body Armor Product.

WILEY SERIES ON BUSINESS STRATEGY
JOHN WILEY & SONS, INC., 605 THIRD AVENUE,
NEW YORK, N.Y. 10158

Series Editor:

DR. WILLIAM A. COHEN

Recent research that I completed has uncovered a business that can be run out of the home on a part time basis, yet which can and has produced a number of millionaires. In fact, its current sales volume exceeds $100 billion every year, and it is so lucrative that more than half of the "Fortune 500" companies are engaged in it.

The business that I am referring to is the mail order business . . . and readership demand for information about the subject is so great that many major book publishers including McGraw-Hill, Prentice-Hall and Harper and Row have published a book on the subject. Several of these publishers have more than one book in print. Interestingly, almost every book stays in print over the years and continues to sell. For example, one of Prentice-Hall's books on mail order is in its 24th printing. John Wiley has just published my book entitled BUILDING A MAIL ORDER BUSINESS: A COMPLETE MANUAL FOR SUCCESS.

The reason that I am writing to you is that I have just completed a short article which explores the question, "Can Anyone Make a Million Dollars in the Mail Order Business?" I know that the answer, which is based on the research that I did for my book, will surprise you. It certainly surprised me . . . and I know that it will surprise and interest your readers as well.

I am enclosing this article for your review. I can offer it to you on an exclusive basis to your newspaper in your city. However, like many hot items which may be due in part to present economic conditions, the demand for this information is time sensitive. Therefore, I can only reserve my offer to you for 30 days. Please let me hear from you as soon as possible.

Sincerely,

William A. Cohen, PhD
Professor of Marketing

Figure 12.7. Letter to newspaper editors.

living

Imagination is the key to making a million

By DR. WILLIAM A. COHEN

More than eighty years ago, Richard Sears and Julius Rosenwald got together to build Sears, Roebuck & Co. into what would eventually become a $10 billion corporation. In the process, these two entrepreneurs built themselves into the world's first mail order millionaires.

Since the time of Sears' beginning, countless part time and full time entrepreneurs have been attracted by the apparent ease with which inexperienced business people could enter this profession of selling products through the mail and emerge with a fortune. What is surprising is not that many have failed. Many have. But the unexpected fact is that in both good times and bad, many have succeeded.

Just before the depression of 1929, a young man by the name of Robert Collier wrote a book in less than two months called, "The Secret of the Ages." In the first six months after writing the book, Collier made more than a million dollars selling the book solely through the mail. He went right on selling the book through the 1929 depression. In fact, although the book has never appeared on any best seller list, it wouldn't surprise me if "The Secret of the Ages," was one of the biggest sellers of all time since it has never been withdrawn and is still being sold through the mail today.

Now it could be that Collier's achievement was a fluke . . . if so many others hadn't done the same thing with similar products.

Brainerd Mellinger, famous for his self-published course on import-export, built a huge multi-million dollar business around his product. Joe Karbo wrote his book. "The Lazy Man's Way to Riches" in 1973. Before he died in 1980, he sold more than a million copies at ten dollars each. His family continues to sell the book today.

Melvin Powers, a famous mail order publisher in North Hollywood, started with a single small book on hypnotism. Today he has more than 400 books in print and has sold millions of books in the interim.

Of course, there are a great many products besides books which are sold through the mail. In a recent year, more than $2.7 billion in general merchandise including home furnishings, housewares and gifts were sold as well as another billion dollars each in ready to wear clothing and collectibles. This is the stamping ground of mail order wizards like Joe Sugarman in Chicago who built a $50 million a year business selling electronic products in only seven years right out of his garage.

Sixty-nine year old A. J. Masuen of LeMars, Iowa, went from door-to-door salesman to more than $1 million a year selling first aid kits and supplies through a mail order catalog. Two high school boys, Len and Rick Hornick started their multi-million dollar mail order business selling hand-carved wooden ducks to hunters and collectors. Today they employ more than 100 expert craftsmen to make their ducks, and they mail out a 32-page catalog to almost a million customers four times a year.

What qualities does the would-be mail order entrepreneur need? Three qualities are ab-

solutely essential: imagination, persistence, and a high degree of honesty. Imagination is needed in order to be able to visualize the special appeal which will compel a potential customer to buy your product. If you have imagination, you can sell almost anything by mail.

Mail order pro Ed McLean proved this by selling thousands of an unpopular model of a Mercedes-Benz automobile which conventional automobile dealers hadn't been able to sell. Mail order experts Hank Burnett, Christopher Stagg, and Dick Benson proved it by selling sixty airplane tickets at $10,000 each for an around-the-world flight. But perhaps the king is Joe Cossman. With no more business experience than being an ex-serviceman. Cossman sold 2,118,000 ant farms, 1,583,000 potato spud guns, 1,600,000 imitation shrunken heads, and 1,508,000 home garden sprinklers and many other products . . . all by mail.

Persistence is required because success is rarely instantaneous and there are always obstacles and set-backs. Cossman spent over a year working on his kitchen table encountering false leads, problems, and failures at the same time holding down a full time job during normal working hours before he finally hit his first success. And even that first successful project required hard work and numerous obstacles that had to be overcome. Less persistent entrepreneurs would have quit long before.

Absolute honesty is required because a successful mail order business is built on trust, repeat sales, and satisfied customers.

After all, you are asking your customers to send money, sometimes a great deal of money, to someone he does not know and cannot see. Cheat your customer even a little, and you've lost that customer forever. Without repeat customers, you might just as well invest your time and energy in a dried up oil well. The potential for a successful enterprise might have existed once, but now its gone for good.

The basic principles which you must understand to be successful in mail order have to do with product selection, structuring your offer, testing, where and when to advertise, and what to put into your advertisements. It takes a book to do justice to all of these subjects in detail, so we'll look only at the rudiments.

While it is true that a mail order expert can sell just about anything through the mail, some products just naturally make better mail order products than others. To increase your chances of picking a winner, look for a product that is light weight, nearly unbreakable, has a broad appeal to a large segment of the population, and has a large margin for profit. This last requirement means you have to be able to buy low, and sell high. Believe me, you are going to need this high profit margin in order to pay for your advertising costs, and at first to pay for your mistakes during the learning process.

You should try to get a product which allows you to sell it at three or four times the cost of the product to you. Now clearly you can't do this with a high priced product. But for most

products under $25 this should be your goal.

This brings us to the important subject of testing. Successful mail order dealers test almost everything. They test which offer is best. They test different types of appeals. The test different prices. And they test different media in which to advertise. Testing is mail order's secret weapon. It is also the secret which allows a mail order operator to fail with four products out of five and still walk away with a million dollars or more.

How is it done? You spend a little money for a test. A complete failure tells you to drop the whole project. A marginal failure or a marginal success says to experiment and rework some aspect of the project. A major success gives you the green light for a larger investment. In this way you can afford to lose a little money on several dismal failures. But when your testing indicates a clear success, you can move immediately to capitalize on what you know to be a winner. The idea is not to risk a lot of money until you are certain of success.

While there are no guarantees, the potential does exist for just about anyone to make a million dollars or more in this business if they have imagination, persistence, and honesty and if they follow the basic principles that have proven to be successful.

(Dr. Cohen is professor of marketing at California State University, Los Angeles. He has just published a book entitled, "Building A Mail Order Business: A Complete Manual For Success," which is in its second printing.)

Figure 12.8. Resulting newspaper notice.

countrywide newspaper coverage and eventually led to numerous appearances on radio and TV. The result was that we sold thousands of books that we would not otherwise have sold.

SOURCES OF ADDITIONAL INFORMATION

How to Advertise—A Handbook for Small Business, by Sandra Linville Dean, published by Enterprise Publishing, Inc., 725 Market Street, Wilmington, DE 19801.

How to Advertise and Promote Your Business, by Connie McClung Siegel, published by John Wiley & Sons, Inc., 605 Third Avenue, New York, NY 10058.

How to Be Your Own Advertising Agency, by Herbert J. Holtje, published by AMACOM, a division of the American Management Association, 135 West 50th Street, New York, NY 10020.

How to Get Big Results from a Small Advertising Budget, by Cynthia S. Smith, published by Hawthorne Books, Inc., 260 Madison Avenue, New York, NY 10016.

How to Write a Good Advertisement, by Victor O. Schwab, published by Wilshire Book Co., 12015 Sherman Road, North Hollywood, CA 91605.

Risk Free Advertising, by Victor Wademan, published by John Wiley & Sons, Inc., 605 Third Avenue, New York, NY 10158.

Tested Advertising Methods, by John Caples, published by Reward Books, Englewood Cliffs, NJ 07632.

The Successful Promoter, by Ted Schwarz, published by Contemporary Books, Inc., 180 North Michigan, Chicago, IL 60601.

13

Personal Selling

THE IMPORTANCE OF PERSONAL SELLING

As a method of promotion, personal selling of your product should have major consideration. Unlike other methods of promotion, including advertising, publicity releases, contests, and sweepstakes, personal selling involves face-to-face communication and feedback. That gives it a tremendous edge.

THE ADVANTAGES OF PERSONAL SELLING

There are six advantages that personal selling has over other promotional methods. These are as follows:

1. *More flexibility.*   Your salespeople can vary and tailor the sales presentations they make depending upon the customers' needs, behavior, motives, and special situations.
2. *Immediate feedback.*   Salespeople can vary their presentation and approach depending upon the reaction as they proceed.
3. *Market pinpointing.*   Much advertising is wasted because you pay for sending your message to individuals who may be readers or viewers of a vehicle but are not real prospects for your goods or service. With face-to-face, personal selling, greater pinpointing of the target consumer is possible than with any other means of promotion.
4. *On-the-spot sales.*   Personal selling is the only method of promotion with which you can sell the product and receive money immediately.
5. *Not just sales.*   Your salespeople can perform other necessary services while making sales calls. For instance, they can do customer research, relay customer complaints, develop credit information, and verify the reality of customer prospects.
6. *No time limit.*   An advertisement gets read. It either does its work or is disregarded. But until they get thrown out, your salespeople can keep trying to make the sale.

THE BIG DISADVANTAGE OF PERSONAL SELLING

Face-to-face selling has one single disadvantage, and it is a big one. That is: its high cost. The cost of recruiting, motivating, training, and operating a sales force is not low. Finding the caliber of people necessary to do the job may be extremely expensive. As energy costs have skyrocketed, so has the cost of each individual sales call. In many parts of the country today, a single sales call costs $150 or even more.

Because of this major limitation, sales forces and face-to-face selling must be used wisely and efficiently. This chapter will show you how to accomplish this.

WHAT DIFFERENT SALES JOBS DO SALESPEOPLE DO?

Salespeople do a variety of different types of sales jobs. Some sales jobs simply require order taking rather than actually persuading an individual to buy something. Others require the sale of complicated, sophisticated, and expensive machinery. The different sales jobs are sometimes placed into seven groups.

Group 1: Product delivery persons. With this type of sales position, selling is actually secondary to delivering the product, be it milk, fuel oil, soft drinks, or whatever. This type of salespeople rarely originates sales. Therefore, a persuasive personality is not required, although an individual who performs good service and is reasonably pleasant may ultimately increase sales over a period of time.

Group 2: Inside order-takers. Inside order-takers are salespeople who generally work inside, behind retail counters. In this case, and in the majority of situations, the customer has already entered the store in order to buy. These salespeople primarily service the customer. Sales can be increased by the order-taker's helpful attitude, but usually not significantly so.

Group 3: Outside order-takers. Outside order-takers are salespeople who work in the field outside of the store. Their job generally involves calling on retail food establishments. They do little or no selling, but, like the salespeople in the first group, are primarily delivery people.

Group 4: Missionary salespeople. The primary job of missionary salespeople is to build good will while performing promotional activities or providing other services to a customer. Examples of these types of salespeople are those detail men and women who service physicians and the pharmaceutical industry. They may or may not be expected or even permitted to solicit orders.

Group 5: Technical salespeople. Technical salespeople such as sales engineers don't need persuasive powers so much as they need technical, in-depth knowledge of the product or service which they can display when dealing with the customer. No matter how persuasive, a technical salesperson cannot be successful without this technical background. Therefore, technical knowledge is the foremost trait required for salespeople in this group.

Group 6: Creative sellers of tangibles. These are salespeople that must sell tangible products through creative selling. That is, they must actually persuade people to purchase. Now, we are getting into a more difficult sales job since the customer may not be aware of a need for the product or how the product can satisfy his or her needs better than other products or services he or she is currently using. The creative seller may sell a product which is also technical; however, in this case persuasiveness and other sales traits are as important as or more important than the technical knowledge. Sellers of tangible products sell everything from encyclopedias to airplanes.

Group 7: Creative sellers of intangibles. This is probably the most difficult of sales positions. Not only must the salesperson be persuasive and be able to sell, but he or she must sell a product which is not easily demonstrated and cannot be shown to or touched by the customer. Products that fall into the intangibles category include such items as insurance, consulting services, and advertising.

Knowing what kind of salesperson you want is very important. If you get the wrong type for your sales job, you will either fail to get sales or waste money on qualifications you do not need.

THREE KEYS TO IMPROVING SALES BY DEVELOPING A SUPERIOR SALES FORCE

Your sales force can do a poor, mediocre, or terrific job in selling for you. It all depends on you and your ability to develop your sales force. Here are three keys to success:

1. *Selection.* You've got to find the best salespeople. It is a challenging problem, but if you succeed, it will make a major contribution to the overall sales ability of your organization.

2. *Training.* Once you have superior people, your superior people must be given the correct training to enable them to maximize their sales ability.

3. *Compensation.* Compensation plans depend on many factors. They are critical in sales because compensation is what motivates your salespeople and makes them perform. Performance cannot be measured simply in terms of sales volume. While the importance of sales volume cannot be overemphasized, other factors may be very important to your organization. These factors may include service, providing information to customers and creating good will.

Selecting Salespeople

To begin the selection process, you must identify what type of salesperson you need. Next, you must establish a job description and specification. Armed with a job description and specification, you can search for sources of available salespeople and finally implement your selection system.

Sources of Salespeople. While you can use sources described earlier in your recruiting and selection of a sales force, salespeople fall into a special category. For example, a research study in the insurance industry revealed that there were four primary sources for prospective insurance salespeople:

1. Salespeople personally known by the hiring sales manager
2. Individuals with influence
3. Individuals selected from the present sales force and given new geographical territories or sent to new locations
4. Salespeople recruited through direct mail advertising

Which of these groups do you think did best? Those recruited from the present sales force did five times as much business the first month as those recruited cold through direct mail advertising. Also of interest is the fact that it took six times as long to complete negotiations and start the new sales recruits doing business from groups 3 and 4 as it did to start those from groups 1 and 2.

Other sources of salespeople which you should consider in your sales force recruiting are as follows:

1. *Those working for you who are not currently in sales.* Be alert for the bright, persuasive individual with a "sales-type personality" who is interested in selling. Such an individual may be moved from another position in your company to become very effective for you in a sales position.

2. *Word of mouth from present customers.* Your current customers may assist you by recommending effective salespeople.

3. *Local schools and universities.* New graduates are always looking for opportunities, and sales is a great way to start. If you have such an opportunity, schools and colleges will assist you in finding candidates from among their students.

4. *Recommendations from your present sales force.* Your present sales force frequently comes in contact with other salespeople from other companies and in other industries. They may have some excellent recommendations for new recruits.

The Six Elements of a Sales Force Selection System. The six elements of your selection system are as follows:

1. Application forms
2. References
3. The interview
4. Intelligence and aptitude tests
5. Physical examination
6. Field observations of candidates

While application forms, references, and interviewing have all been discussed in an earlier chapter, it is important to realize that here the most important qualities in a candidate are his or her readiness and ability to sell. Therefore, you should not hesitate to emphasize this aspect, especially in checking on references and in the personal, face-to-face interview.

In fact, in order to make the personal interview more objective, some interviewers of potential salespeople use a form having a semantic differential intensity scale to note differences. In this manner, various attributes can be more or less objectively rated immediately through judgment. A typical judgment chart is shown in Figure 13.1.

As recommended in an earlier chapter, the prospective candidate should be interviewed by more than one individual in your firm so that opinions can be compared. This is especially true when seeking salespeople who must have considerable persuasive abilities, who must actually inform and persuade people regarding their needs and wants and the ability of the product or the service to fulfill them. First, you want some objective opinion about this ability. But second, if the candidate has it, you don't want to miss some key point because of his or her ability to persuade you.

1. General appearance										6. Imagination									
poor	1	2	3	4	5	6	7	8	9	excellent	poor	1	2	3	4	5	6	7	8	9	excellent

2. Dress										7. Attitude toward work									
poor	1	2	3	4	5	6	7	8	9	excellent	poor	1	2	3	4	5	6	7	8	9	excellent

3. Verbal communication										8. Intelligence									
poor	1	2	3	4	5	6	7	8	9	excellent	poor	1	2	3	4	5	6	7	8	9	excellent

4. Manners										9. Ability to sell himself or herself									
poor	1	2	3	4	5	6	7	8	9	excellent	poor	1	2	3	4	5	6	7	8	9	excellent

5. Persuasiveness										10. Overall handling of interview									
poor	1	2	3	4	5	6	7	8	9	excellent	poor	1	2	3	4	5	6	7	8	9	excellent

Figure 13.1.   A semantic differential intensity scale for use in interviewing potential sales personnel.

Tests, physical examinations, and field observations have not been discussed previously for other types of jobs. They are particularly important, however, for sales positions. Because the sales job itself may require considerable field work, good health and personal appearance may have a direct bearing on success or failure. Therefore, if the job is at all demanding physically, a physical examination should be required prior to hiring. There are types of intelligence and aptitude tests for selling that were extremely popular in the late 1950s and early 1960s. They are currently controversial since they are far from perfect and many eliminate a few excellent candidates while allowing some poor candidates to get through. However, psychological testing will eliminate candidates who are totally unsuited for selling. Administering these tests has one additional advantage. It will impress the potential employee of the importance that you place on the sales position. This can have a motivational effect on the candidates you hire.

Remember, be very careful with psychological testing. Have a professional evaluate the results. You can find such psychological testers listed in your yellow pages of the telephone book under Aptitude and Employment Testing. Do not attempt to purchase the test and evaluate the results on your own. One firm that did this eventually discovered that candidates it hired who got top scores on a test were much poorer performers than those who scored less well.

For some very important positions, on-the-job observation may be necessary to determine whether the salesperson is suitable or not. This can be done through a conditional hire. An acceptable performance under personal observation is made one of the criteria for permanent hire.

Do's and Don't's of Salespeople Selection

Kenneth Grubb, president of Kenneth Grubb Associates of Princeton, New Jersey, developed the following list of do's and don't's for selection of salespeople.[1]

In thinking about tips on selecting salesmen, look first at the "Do's."

[1] Kenneth Grubb, *Tips on Selecting Salesman MA No. 196*, Small Business Administration (1976).

Do—Write a Job Description

The starting point in selecting salespeople is a job description. You should, if you haven't already done so, spell out the duties and responsibilities required for your selling job.

This description should define the type of selling that the job requires. Do you sell a product, a service, or a combination of the two? Selling a service, or a product and its related service, often requires your salesman to have a technical background or an aptitude for absorbing technical information.

As a counterpart to the job description, main specifications should also be prepared. Spell out in as much detail as you can the abilities and qualities which an applicant needs to be successful in selling your product or service. There is no substitute for knowing what you are looking for.

Do—Select for Initiative and Perseverance

Initiative and perseverance are vital to successful selling. Salespeople have to be self-starters because they are among the least supervisable of employees whether "on the road" or on the sales floor.

They either make themselves work, or they don't. At best, evaluation and incentive plans are a poor substitute for spontaneous self-drive, and self-policing. You or your sales manager, if you have one, cannot generate initiative in a dead battery.

How much of a self-starter you need depends on the job to be done. If your salespeople check into the office each morning, for example, they can be reminded, if necessary, to call on particular accounts. But if they are on the road all week, they have to remind themselves.

Do—Look for Reliability

An applicant salesman must be reliable because you will have to trust him to do his job. He also will have to gain the confidence of customers. The test of his reliability is their reactions to him. It boils down to his being a "straight shooter."

"Straight shooting" starts at home. In encouraging salesmen to do the right thing, three rules of thumb may be useful. First, the owner-manager should not fool himself about what his policies are. For example, if he has to withhold certain information for competitive reasons from his salesmen, he should not kid himself or them by pretending that they have all the information.

Second, the owner-manager should keep in mind that any failures in ethics which a salesman possesses will usually be turned first against his employer. If a company condones shady practices when they favor the company, the salesman is likely to use this attitude as license to put his own interests above those of the company.

Third, to many customers and to the public, almost the only "picture" they get of a company is the salesman whom they see. Moreover, they often see through a salesman more quickly than either the salesman or his company may believe. If he is not reliable, customers may realize it before the owner-manager does.

Do—Seek Mental Ability

The amount of brainpower which a salesman needs depends on the selling job. Some jobs require only enough mentality to memorize sales talks and put one foot in the door. Other jobs require a high degree of imagination, intelligence, and sometimes technical education.

In many small companies, the difference between a large and a small sales volume lies in the salesman's ability to understand quickly the key points in a customer's problem and to come up with an imaginative solution. Other small companies build a big sales volume on the salesman's ability to see new ways to redesign particular products. Such ingenuity enables the owner-manager to get a jump on his competitors. In selecting a salesman, make sure his mental ability matches the requirements of selling your product.

Do—Look for Willingness to Travel

If extensive travel is part of your selling job, make sure that the applicant is willing to travel. If he doesn't know it already, make him aware that the comforts and pleasures of normal home and social life are often impossible in a travelling job.

Your objective is to forestall trouble. If the wife wants her husband at home, or he wants to be with his family, all sorts of problems ensue.

On the other hand, some men like travel. They don't like the routine of calling on the same customers over short periods. They like to be away because it's so nice to come back. They like the attention they get from their families when they return from their trips.

When this is the case, you're lucky. This type of "travel-happy" salesman docsn't need the "diversions of the road" which can tarnish a company's reputation.

Do—Look for Willingness to Take Punishment

Many salesmen are paid to take punishment from which other employees would shrink. They receive rough and even rude treatment from the hard-to-see prospect, not to mention his secretary and other office help with instructions to keep salesmen away from his door.

Sometimes a salesmanager hands out, in a different way, as much punishment as the salesman receives from customers. At best, the push for large quotas turns into a battle of wits between the salesman and his boss.

In some companies, the punishment includes the risk of alcoholism. The owner-manager feels—not always correctly—that his salesmen must drink freely with all customers. When, and if, this is part of the selling job, applicants should be told.

Do—Select Emotionally Balanced People

Selling is often a sort of schizophrenic job. The demands and pressures split some men in two.

Most salesmen have to appear cheerful and unworried during frequent discouragements. For example, they have to be polite to a rude prospect when they prefer not to be.

Even with the most pleasant customers, the salesman often has to repress his desires in their favor. He may have to lean over backwards to satisfy some customers. Often he has to listen when he prefers to talk. A liking for people helps to cushion the pressures. When a salesman likes people, it is easier for him to put his preferences in the background when he needs to.

The pressures on salesmen are bad enough when times are good. They can become terrific when there is a temporary drought in sales. The boss may blame him and push for sales—sometimes where none are to be had. To add insult to injury, sometimes the factory may let him down on delivery dates he has promised customers. In addition, some customers—often big volume accounts—may jump on the bandwagon. They seem to sense that the salesman is "down" and try to browbeat him.

Under such topsy-turvy pressures, only an emotionally balanced person can survive. If a salesman is inclined to upset easily, he may start acting less than rationally. Or he may quit his job, and you lose your investment in him.

Whether the pressures are heavy or light, the effective salesman has to surmount them. Preoccupation with his own problems make him insensitive to the unspoken shifts in attitudes and interests of his customers. Also he needs to be emotionally mature to handle success—to resist the temptation to coast during good times.

In selecting salesmen, the "don't's" are as important as the "do's." A few of the negative aspects follows. They may remind you of others that are peculiar to your situation.

Don't—Pick Only for Selling Skills

Contrary to folklore, skills and experience in selling may be the last thing to look for in selecting a salesman. If you already have a successful sales organization, your best bet is probably to select people who can be trained in your methods. When the candidate's other qualifications (for example, he knows your industry and the needs of customers) are sound, he can usually be taught the necessary selling techniques fairly quickly.

On the other hand, when you hire an "experienced" salesman, you may be buying trouble. He may have to unlearn old ways before learning new ones. "Experience" includes bad practices, tricks, habits, and abuses which may handicap him in learning your ways of selling. For example, he may be in the habit of overstocking customers.

In a fairly new company, the owner-manager may have to hire experienced salesmen because no one in his company really knows how to sell. If such is your case, make sure that you select salesmen whose skills and experience are sound for your type of selling job.

Don't—Pick for Control of Accounts

Some owner-mangers are tempted to hire men from competitors on the theory that such salesmen bring business with them. If you are thinking in that direction, keep in mind that there is a strong tendency to exaggerate the extent to which salesmen can "take customers with them" and hold such business.

Don't—Pick for Trade Secrets

Some companies hire a competitor's salesman for the information they hope to gain rather than for the selling the man can do.

The owner-manager who hires with the expectation of gaining trade secrets or accounts should keep one fact in mind. That fact is: Benedict Arnolds are always available to the highest bidder. Money draws them from one company to another.

Don't—Pick Only for Wide Acquaintance

The owner-manager who hires a salesman because he is widely known among potential customers may be kidding himself. He may be the kind of salesman from whom customers run if they see him coming. His faults may outweigh the advantages of knowing the prospects you are trying to reach. Worthwhile prospects are ready to listen to salesmen who show promise of helping them to have fewer headaches and make more money.

Don't—Expect the Impossible

Some owner-managers expect their salesmen to do the impossible. They do little planning and preparation and expect the salesman to "steam roll" his way to a large sales volume. Even the best salesman is handicapped when the home office makes faulty marketing plans, such as insufficient advertising or a tight billing policy.

Often, when an owner-manager expects to get by with little or no planning, he picks men who have strong compulsions to get ahead fast. "We pay a high commission," he says, "and expect top results." The salesman drives himself, often sacrificing his personal life, to make such big money. Some individuals crack under such pressure. Addicted to big money, others change jobs for greener pastures.

In this same vein, an owner-manager should not expect his salesmen to do what he wouldn't do himself. For example, he would not himself be a doormat for customers to wipe their feet on. Nor would be deliberately lie to customers.

It is important also to caution your men about leading customers to expect the impossible. For example, a salesman should not sell more than you can ship. Nor should he "oversell" a customer on the benefits of your products.

Finally, in not expecting the impossible, if you hire a relative as a salesman, do it with your eyes open. It is one thing if he has proved his ability by selling for another company. It is another thing if his most prominent talent is kinship with you.

Intentionally Suggestive

These do's and don't's are suggestive. You may think of others that are pertinent to your situation.

Keep in mind the importance of doing your own thinking about the kind of salesmen you need. They develop procedures that will help in selecting individuals who meet the requirements of your situation.

In selecting salesmen, there is always the question: How do you tell whether the candidate is qualified? How does the owner-manager determine whether the candidate has: initiative, reliability, mental ability, and other requirements for the job?

You have to make a judgment based on what you can learn about the candidate. His application blank gives you some information. You get additional facts and impressions about his past performance by talking at length with him. Sometimes you may test him by asking critical questions about your industry and its customers. Or you might use tests which are prepared by firms that specialize in their preparation.

Above all, it is important to check his references before making a decision. Use the telephone or a face-to-face contact because a former employer may be too busy, or reluctant, to express himself freely in writing.

Training Salespeople

There are four main areas in which training will contribute to success of your sales force regardless of the type of selling in which they are engaged. These four main areas are as follows:

1. Knowledge
2. Work habits
3. Selling skills
4. Attitude

Knowledge. A salesperson must have knowledge of the product, knowledge of the company, knowledge of the sales environment, and knowledge of the entire environmental situation in which he or she is operating. Only with knowledge can the sales individual best explain the product or the service to the customer.

Work Habits. The salesperson's work habits are responsible for great success stories as well as great failures. An individual's work habits can also spell the difference between sales success and failure in your company. With sales calls as expensive as they are, a salesperson who makes few calls a day can ruin you in short order. Making calls is a matter of mental attitude and selling work habits.

Selling Skills. There are so-called "natural salespeople." But, while some individuals may be naturally better suited for selling than others, sales skills can be learned and mastered by many people. These skills include establishing rapport and empathy, making effective presentations, handling objections, closing, and so forth.

Attitude. A critical factor in performance in selling is attitude. In fact, it is so important that many books by successful salespersons emphasize this one factor. Elmer G. Leterman, who sold over $300 million worth of life insurance policies more than 30 years ago, said in his book, *The New Art of Selling*,[2] that the first law of creative success is to quit looking outside ourselves for solutions to our problems. In other words, it is the salesperson's attitude that spells success or failure.

Methods of Training Salespeople. There are several methods which you can use to train your salespeople to become sales "superstars."

[2] Elmer G. Leterman, *The New Art of Selling*, Harper and Brothers, New York (1957).

1. *Indoctrination training.* With indoctrination training, you give your salespeople basic orientation on the sales job and how it is done. In many cases, your sales manager will accompany the new salesperson to help him learn the job through observation. As the salesperson gets more and more experience, he or she takes over more and more of the job, and finally the manager backs off entirely and the salesperson is on his or her own.

2. *Job rotation training.* Job rotation training is generally for larger companies. A salesperson spends a certain amount of time in a variety of jobs which may include positions in the factory, in production, in research and development, in the office, and in a sales branch. This way he or she gets a better idea of how the salesperson's job fits into other company operations.

3. *In-class training.* When field experience cannot be easily given, or sometimes even if it is, classes can be conducted to train salespeople how to do their job. This training is particularly effective for providing new information on products, the company, the market, and so forth. The classroom can also be used for motivation. Also, selling skills can be taught and experienced through various types of role-playing. However, in-class training is time consuming. In a very small company, extensive classroom training may take too many of your resources. Even so, one multimillion-dollar executive recruiting operation started with a solid week of training for everyone hired and maintains this policy to this day.

4. *Sales meetings.* Sales meetings act as a training ground for new employees who are salespeople as well as older ones. In sales meetings, they can trade experiences and build friendly competition. You can also give additional or new training to help salespeople increase their job effectiveness.

5. *Seminars.* Many training companies around the country have training programs especially designed to train new salespeople. There are many training organizations, both national and local, which can provide training needs for your salespeople. These companies can be located in your telephone book in the yellow pages under Training—Sales or Sales Training headings. An investment of this type can pay off tremendously in the effectiveness of your new sales employees.

Compensating the Salesperson

The compensation plan for salespeople is particularly important, and is has definite aims. These aims include encouraging the highest volume of sales for your most profitable items while at the same time providing motivation and incentive for your salespeople to work harder. Specifically, your compensation plan must have objectives both for your company and for your salespeople.

Objectives for your salespeople:

1. To receive compensation in direct proportion to sales accomplishments
2. To be compensated for time spent with the customer which does not directly result in sales, such as "missionary" work and service to the customer.
3. To have provisions for security, retirement, and possible seasonal or other slumps in selling
4. To receive compensation on a par with what could be earned selling for other companies or for other lines of products or services

5. To have a sense of *esprit de corps*, not only in the sales force but with other employees.

Objectives for your company:

1. To motivate and inspire your salespeople to increase sales
2. To encourage your salespeople to sell high-profit items
3. To enable your firm to maintain the maximum of profit consistent with other factors including compensation for your salespeople which meet all criteria listed as objectives
4. To maintain the maximum control possible over your sales force and your salespeople's activities
5. To encourage cooperation among your salespeople and with other functional areas and people in your company
6. To encourage company *esprit de corps*

The Three Basic Means of Compensating a Sales Force.   There are three basic means of compensating a sales force. These are: (1) salary, (2) commission, and (3) combination plans. Each has its advantages and its disadvantages.

With a *salary* plan, you have an arrangement whereby you pay a defined amount of money, weekly, monthly, or annually, in return for whatever work is required by the sales force. It has the following advantages:

1. It is easy for the company to budget and administer.
2. Since the compensation is guaranteed so long as the salesperson works for you, it allows for the greatest amount of control over your sales force.
3. It is generally easier to recruit salespeople for this type of compensation plan.
4. Since compensation is guaranteed, extravagant promises or overselling by your salespeople will be discouraged.
5. It is easier to arrange for your salespeople to accomplish nonselling activities since their "time is not money."
6. The system encourages the maximum cooperation among salespeople and other members of your company.
7. It is easier to transfer salespeople to other territories using this plan.

However, this compensation plan also has disadvantages:

1. There is a lack of incentive for high sales.
2. Salary is a fixed cost unrelated to sales revenue.
3. So-called "super" salespeople are rarely attracted by a straight salary since they can make much more money on a commission system.
4. If business activity is declining, it is very difficult to adjust salaries. You generally are forced to discharge some of your salespeople. This means morale problems and additional costs for training and hiring when business conditions improve.
5. Salaries must be paid whether or not there are sales.

Straight salary plans are usually most useful under any of four conditions:

1. For compensating new salespeople who are not yet ready to assume their full responsibilities
2. For compensating missionary salespeople whose duties are not to make an immediate sale, but whose work eventually leads to sales over a period of months or even years
3. For opening new territories in which you have not formerly been selling
4. For sales of sophisticated or technical products requiring lengthy negotiations

A compensation plan using sales *commissions* is simply an agreement on your part to pay the salesperson a percentage of each dollar of a product or service sold. In such a plan, the salesperson is usually entirely on his or her own. A successful salesperson can make a lot of money. An unsuccessful salesperson makes nothing. In some states the straight commission plan has been modified since minimum wages must be paid. However, the basic principle is the same. The amount earned is directly related to sales made.

Advantages of the commission plan are as follows:

1. A company with limited capital can fully staff its sales force without high overhead commitments.
2. This method provides direct incentive for high sales.
3. A commission plan attracts more aggressive and persuasive salespeople since these are the only ones that can make it work successfully.
4. The costs of sales are automatically reduced if and when sales decline.

Naturally, the commission plan has its disadvantages, although at first it may appear that the system is absolutely ideal for any company. The disadvantages of the commission system of compensation are as follows:

1. There is a great deal of difficulty getting salespeople to devote time to sales tasks which may be important to your company but for which no commission is paid.
2. There is great danger in overselling the customer and possibly incurring customer ill will.
3. There is a great deal of bookkeeping involved.
4. There is potentially greater difficulty in recruiting.
5. There is less cooperation within the company among salespeople and among other functional areas.

Because of the potential difficulties with straight commission plans, modifications have been made. Here are the primary changes that have been introduced.

With the *commission against draw* modification of the straight commission, a salesperson is allowed to draw a certain amount of money ahead of his or her sales against commissions that will be earned later. This sales advance or draw allows the salesperson to have living expenses even during a slump. As soon as the first commissions are earned, they are used to pay the draw that the salesperson has already been advanced.

With the *modified commission scale*, a commission rate is established by a series of steps. It is frequently used with the draw in order to help the salesperson pay off the money advanced as rapidly as possible. In order to do this, a higher commission may be paid on the first sales until the money advanced is covered; then the commission rate may drop to lower levels or steps depending upon the scale that is constructed. Of course, this is also advantageous to the company if sales are greater than anticipated since the commission will be less on the higher amount of sales. The approach, however, does have a disadvantage; some companies take the opposite tactic and increase commission percentage for higher amounts of sales. In some cases this increase is effected through a bonus plan, a bonus being paid for effort resulting in increased sales or sales above a certain set goal or quota. Let us say that you are paying 10% commission and have established the quota for salespeople of $20,000 in sales per month. The bonus would come into play if this $20,000 per month were exceeded. Perhaps you would offer an additional 5% bonus for sales exceeding the quota. Thus, if a salesperson only met this quota, he or she would receive $20,000 times 10% or $2,000 commission. But for sales of $30,000 a month, your salesperson would receive $30,000 times 10% or $3,000, plus an additional 5% of the $10,000 difference between $20,000 and $30,000, or an additional $500. Therefore, the total amount of compensation would be $3,000 plus $500 or $3,500.

Commission plans work well under the following circumstances:

1. Where considerable incentive and motivation are needed to get high sales
2. Where very little missionary work or other sales assistance that does not have to do with closing out a sale is required
3. Where the company is not so strong financially that is can afford large amounts of overhead to compensate salespeople whether or not sales are made
4. Where salespeople can operate independently

Combination plans offer a fixed compensation element plus a variable element made up of a commission on sales or a bonus based on volume. In combination plans, the fixed portion is a salary. The variable portion is used to motivate sales and to achieve many of the benefits of the commission type of compensation plan. The variable element of the combination plan may include payments on sales volume, payments on a performance evaluation, a combination of volume and a performance evaluation, or some type of bonus.

The advantages of combination plans are:

1. Flexibility in dealing with the overall job of selling the company's product or service
2. Flexibility in making changes in territory assignment or assignment of customers
3. Choice among the various factors that will motivate the salespeople to work independently to achieve high sales
4. Ability to group salespeople for team selling situations of major products while applying direct incentive as well as salary compensation to motivate this performance

The disadvantages of combination plans are:

1. Complexity in construction of the plan
2. Amount of time required for administration and bookkeeping
3. Difficulty of explaining the plan to salespeople
4. The need for constant review to be sure that the factors that are being used as part of the overall compensation are doing what they are supposed to be doing

The combination plan can work well for many companies, but in order to use it you must balance the best features of the salary plan and the commission plan while at the same time trying to eliminate their disadvantages. This isn't always easy and requires considerable thinking and planning ahead of time. It should be used when (1) a complex selling task is to be rewarded, and (2) factors other than volume are considered important and yet an incentive element is definitely required.

HOW TO MEASURE THE PERFORMANCE OF YOUR SALES PERSONNEL

Until you know how your sales force is performing, you have no way of making meaningful changes which will improve performance. Therefore, it is necessary to develop means of evaluation. In general, this is done through two means: judging quantitative factors and judging qualitative factors. Quantitative factors generally are easier since they are specific and objective. Sales volume either goes up or it does not. You see the results in black and white. Qualitative factors must rely much on subjective judgment. However, in many types of sales operations, qualitative factors must be considered because of the importance of their influence on company objectives.

Quantitative Factors

The following are factors in sales that are useful in comparing quantitative performance:

1. Sales volume segmented as to areas, products, customer groups, and so forth
2. Sales volume as a percentage of a predetermined quota or calculated territorial potential
3. Gross profit
4. Sales that may be segmented by number of orders, average size, or similar factors
5. Closing ratio (a ratio of the number of sales closes divided by the number of calls made)
6. Percentage of new accounts sold
7. Number of new accounts sold
8. Number of new accounts sold divided by number of new accounts called on

Qualitative Factors

The following are factors which should be considered in evaluating your sales force on a qualitative basis:

1. Analytical ability
2. Company knowledge
3. Competition knowledge
4. Customer relations
5. Decision-making ability
6. General attitude
7. General knowledge of sales environment, the customer, legal aspects, and the product
8. Health
9. Organization and management of time
10. Personal appearance
11. Personality
12. Preparation for presentations and sales calls
13. Product knowledge

HOW TO IMPROVE YOUR SALESPERSON'S PERFORMANCE

Raymond O. Loen of R. O. Loen Company, Management Consultants of Lake Oswego, Oregon, developed the following guide to bringing about improvements in sales performance in three steps.[3] These three steps are planning, measuring, and correcting. Use this to help you improve your salesperson's performance.

Planning

Get the sales representative's agreement about goals to attain or exceed for the next year:

1. Total profit contribution in dollars
2. Profit contribution in dollars for:
   Each major profit line
   Each major market (by industry or geographical area)
   Each of 10–20 target accounts (for significant new and additional business)

Get the sales representative's agreement about expenses to stay within for the next year:

1. Total sales expense budget in dollars
2. Budget in dollars for: travel, customer entertainment, telephone, and other expenses

[3] Raymond O. Loen, *Measuring Sales Performance MA 190*, Small Business Administration (1978).

Measuring

Review at least monthly the sales representative's record for:

1. Year-to-date progress toward 12-month profit contribution goals
2. Year-to-date budget compliance

Correcting

Meet with sales representatives if his or her record is 10 percent or more off target. Review the number of calls made on each significant account plus what he or she feels are his or her problems and accomplishments. In addition, you may need to do some of the following to help improve performance:

—Give more day-to-day help and direction.
—Accompany on calls to provide coaching.
—Conduct regular meetings on subjects which representatives want covered.
—Increase sales promotion activities.
—Transfer accounts to other sales representatives if there is insufficient effort or progress.
—Establish tighter control over price variances allowed.
—Increase or reduce selling prices.
—Add new products or services.
—Increase financial incentives.
—Transfer, replace, or discharge.

WHETHER TO USE SALES TERRITORIES

A sales territory is a geographical area in which a salesperson does his or her business. His or her activities may be limited in certain areas or may not be. Further, he or she may or may not have an exclusive over a certain area. Establishing sales territories has the following advantages:

1. It fixes precise performance responsibilities.
2. It helps a salesperson to organize his time.
3. It helps maximize customer service.
4. It cuts down on overlapping of sales efforts.
5. It fosters competition and comparison among salespeople in different territories.
6. It helps equalize opportunities in various territories among different salespeople.
7. It makes for adaptation of certain background personality factors and desires of salespeople to their customers.
8. It helps control the overall sales operation.
9. It ensures that all of your salespeople have ample opportunities to sell.
10. It helps maintain total and efficient coverage of your entire market.

However, in certain circumstances, it is better not to limit your salespeople to distinct territories. This may be true if you don't have sufficient salespeople to cover all the territories that might be available, or if certain of your salespeople seem to operate better when they are freewheeling, and maybe you can get best results out of all of them if you do not establish territorial rights. Sometimes you will not be able to establish territory divisions fairly. In this case it is better not to establish them at all. And in some industries, such as executive recruiting, for example, it may make sense not to establish territories in a geographical sense but rather to group your salespeople depending upon the functions of the various individuals whom they are trying to recruit. Finally, if you are introducing a new product and you want to saturate the market as quickly as possible, the restrictions of sales territories may slow some of your people down.

HOW TO ESTABLISH SALES TERRITORIES

1. If you're going to establish sales territories, it is important first to establish them in a fair fashion. Therefore, there must be some basis of comparison. Usually, a market index or indices relating to the product or the service that you are selling are selected. These indices are usually based on one or more demographic factors, such as income, which would represent buying power or segments of the population which would be interested in the product or the service. For example, if you were selling a high-priced automobile, how many families in the area or the potential area which would constitute a geographical territory could afford such a car? Or, if you had a product that went in the home, how many homes are in the territory which uses such a product? Sometimes a combination of different factors is used with a weighting system applied depending upon the relative importance of the factor. In this fashion, territories are divided with indices resulting in approximately the same sales potential.

2. The next problem is to determine how wide an area a salesperson can handle. Factors such as distance, call frequency, as well as numbers that a salesperson can process must all be considered. This will impact on the size of the different territories that are divided, and will also let you know how many salespeople you will need to cover a particular area.

3. At this point you may begin allotting the various territories based on market potential to salesmen. Various adjustments may be necessary depending upon local conditions, demand, competition, transportation factors, the product, and other of the strategic and environmental variables that we will discuss in Chapter 15. For example, if a newer product is being sold, the territory may be expanded to give the salesperson having to sell this new product greater opportunity to sell a profitable volume. Each factor for adjustment should be considered on an individual basis so that the net result is territories which have essentially identical market potential and number of accounts that can be serviced by the salesperson. Territory allotment should be done so that the servicing of the territories will be profitable to you and profitable to the individual doing the selling.

WHETHER TO USE A SALES REPRESENTATIVE

A sales representative is a special type of sales agent who is independent and sells for a number of different companies for the commission that he or she is paid. Selling using a sales representative has some particular advantages for a small firm with a limited product line. First, you don't have to pay money up front to hire salespeople to sell your product. You pay only the commission after the product is sold. Second, you do not have to recruit except to locate the sales representative. And third, with a limited product line and your own salespeople, you must amortize the cost of selling over a limited line of products. Each call is therefore that much more costly and less profitable. There are other advantages to using a sales representative. These include:

1. Immediate entry into a specific territory or a more general market
2. Regular calls on your customers and prospects
3. Quality salesmanship with no need for you to train
4. The fact that cost is a predetermined selling expense, a percentage of sales as their commissions

However, there are also advantages that you must consider if you are going to use a sales representative:

1. You have limited control over a sales agent as opposed to a salesperson, who is your own employee, who reports to you, whom you train, and who is dependent directly upon you for compensation.
2. On very large volumes of sales, the selling expense will be large, much larger than it would be with your own employees.
3. An independent agent's allegiance to your products and your company is not total since he or she also serves other clients who are selling similar (but noncompeting) products or services. Therefore, such individuals must have special incentives to push your products over others.
4. If and when you terminate a contract with a sales representative, the sales representative may take your customer with him or her to a new client who is a competitor.

HOW TO SELECT A SALES REPRESENTATIVE

If you do decide that a sales representative is worthwhile employing for your business, you must get someone who is right for you, right for your company, and will build profits. Therefore, selecting a sales representative should not be done hastily. Edwin E. Bobrow, of Bobrow-Lewell Associates, Inc. of New York, recommends that you ask yourself the following questions in matching an agent to your company's character and image.[4]

What sort of selling skills are necessary for selling my products? Does the agent need technical knowledge and experience in addition to personal selling ability?
What marketing functions, if any, do I need in addition to selling?
Must the agent service my product as well as sell it?
Do I need a one-man or one-woman agency or an organization? If the latter, how large an organization?

[4] Edwin E. Bobrow, *Is the Independent Sales Agent for You? MA 200*, Small Business Administration (1978).

What is the agent's record of success in products and territories similar to mine?

How long has the agent been in business? What is the agent's reputation? How well can I trade on it?

Are the other lines carried by the agent compatible with mine? Will the agent's contract for his or her existing lines help gain entry for my line?

Is the trade the agent specializes in the one I want to reach?

Does the agent cover the geographic area I need covered and in what depth?

Do the character, personality, values, and integrity of our two organizations correspond?

Can the "reps" who are the employees of the sales agent sales manage their own territories or will they need management and guidance from the agent? Or from me?

Is the agent the type who merely follows instructions or does the agent have a reputation for offering constructive suggestions? Which type do I need?

Is the chemistry right? Will we enjoy working together?

In my own businesses I have employed a special form that all potential manufacturers' representatives or sales representatives are required to complete. This is shown in Figure 13.2. You may incorporate it or design a similar one for your own firm.

SOURCES FOR FINDING SALES REPRESENTATIVES

The following are sources of sales representatives for your company:

1. The Manufacturers and Agents National Association (P.O. Box 16878, Irvine, CA 92713) publishes a directory which may be available in your public library. It is called *The Manufacturers and Agents National Association Directory of Members.*
2. *The Directory of Manufacturers Agents* is published by McGraw-Hill Book Co., 1221 Avenue of the Americas, New York, NY 10020.
3. Recommendations from customers, sales managers of noncompeting companies, as well as editors, salesmen, and trade magazines can all be useful.
4. If you are exporting, contact the Department of Commerce. They may be able to find a manufacturers' representative for you abroad through their computerized system.
5. You can place classified ads in trade magazines whose readership includes the type of manufacturers' representatives that you are seeking.

IMPORTANT ADVICE ABOUT WORKING WITH A SALES REPRESENTATIVE

It's better to have a written contract with an agent so that both sides know exactly what they are going to do. Typically, this contract should spell out that either side may terminate the relationship with the other given 30 days' notice.

GLOBAL ASSOCIATES
Protective Armor Systems
56 N. SIERRA ST.
PASADENA, CALIFORNIA 91109
U. S. A.

Representative's Application Form

This application is for sales representatives of Global Associates' armor product lines on a commission basis for the territory indicated.

Name of firm _____

Address _____

_____

_____

Year established _____ Number of salespeople _____ Annual sales _____

Managers' or partners' names _____

_____

Territory covered _____

Territory desired _____

References _____

_____

_____

Firms now represented/products

_____

_____

_____

_____

Figure 13.2. Form for evaluating potential sales reprentative.

When dealing with a new sales representative, you should also be very choosy about granting wide territories. Unfortunately, a few sales representatives will take many more territories than they actually can service well, and some that they do not work in at all. But remember that under the terms of the contract, any sales made in any of those territories, whether directly or indirectly by the sales representative, will ensure him or her of a commission. Therefore, until you understand the situation fully, it is better to limist sales to those territories in which the sales representative has accomplished sales in the past, so that you can be reasonably sure he or she will be able to do so for you in the future.

Even after you have begun a relationship with a sales representative, look for ways to maximize the relationship. Seek ways that you can promote your products or your service with the agent. Remember that you are dealing with a human being, and it is not simply a matter of dropping the whole thing in the agent's lap and letting him or her run. You must give encouragement and reason to excel. You must motivate this individual who is selling for you. Never forget that his or her prime incentive is to build his or her own company. Your sales representative cannot afford to push your products or your services if they are unprofitable. Therefore, you must do what you can to insure that these products or services are profitable. Get feedback regarding customer relations and what features are liked and what features are not, and how your products and services can be improved.

Always involve the sales representative in all phases of your marketing. Invite him or her back for meetings either annually or semiannually at your company. Take his or her suggestions regarding packaging, promotion, and marketing. Make your manufacturer's representative or sales agent a part of your team.

However, with all of this information, do not burden your sales agent with confusing details. He or she must go out and make the sale. So, make your instructions and your aids clear-cut in order to make it easier for your representative to achieve this goal.

SOURCES OF ADDITIONAL INFORMATION

How I Raised Myself from Failure to Success in Selling, by Frank Bettger, published by Prentice-Hall, Englewood Cliffs, NJ 07632.

How to Develop Successful Salesmen, by Kenneth B. Haas, published by McGraw-Hill Book Co., 1221 Avenue of the Americas, New York, NY 10020.

How to Sell Well, by James F. Bender, published by McGraw-Hill Book Co., 1221 Avenue of the Americas, New York, NY 10020.

The Lacy Techniques of Salesmanship, by Paul J. Micali, published by Hawthorne Books, Inc., 260 Madison Avenue, New York, NY 10016.

Management of the Sales Force, by William J. Stanton and Richard H. Buskirk, published by Richard D. Irwin, Inc., 1818 Ridge Road, Homewood, IL 60430.

The New Art of Selling, by Elmer G. Leterman, published by Bantam Books, Inc., 666 Fifth Avenue, New York, NY 10019.

The Sales Managers Handbook, 13th edition, edited by John C. Aspley, published by The Dartnell Corp., 4660 Ravenswood Avenue, Chicago, IL 60640.

Sales Planning and Control, by Richard D. Crisp, published by McGraw-Hill Book Co., 1221 Avenue of the Americas, New York, NY 10020.

14

How to Make Money with Trade Shows

WHAT IS A TRADE SHOW?

Trade shows have been held since medieval times, providing sellers with an opportunity to get together to display their products. It has been estimated that there are over 35,000 trade events in the United States alone every year, and more than 7,800 trade shows. Taking proper advantage of the unique potential offered by a trade show can make a great deal of extra money for you by boosting your sales. On the other hand, incorrect use of this promotional opportunity will waste your money, time, and resources.

ADVANTAGES OF TRADE SHOWS

Trade shows offer unique advantages over other means of promotion. Here are a few:

1. You can meet with many of your customers and potential customers at one time. You can demonstrate your products and give your customers an opportunity to see and handle them.
2. You can meet with your sales representatives and bring them up to date on your latest products, techniques, and plans, and you can also locate new sales representatives.
3. You can promote your company image in a certain business or industry.
4. Because the trade show itself will be promoted to interest a certain target group of potential customers, you will be furnished with a pre-selected audience having interests matched with your products or services.
5. You can rapidly test new products to see whether there is interest from customers and sales representatives.
6. You can distribute additional information regarding your products or services to qualified buyers, potential buyers, sales representatives, and other interested people.
7. You will be able to reach some people who ordinarily are not accessible.
8. Other companies in your industry, both competitors and suppliers, will often be demonstrating their products at the same trade show. This gives you a look at your competition as well as the opportunity to talk to the top people in firms important to your business.

9. You will be able to develop inquiries and leads for expanding your mailing list into new markets which you haven't yet entered.
10. You will be able to make large numbers of potential contacts in a relatively short interval of time.
11. You will complement your other promotional activities through your trade show participation.

SETTING OBJECTIVES

In order to maximize the benefits that you will receive, it is necessary that you set definite objectives prior to your participation. That is, you should sit down and work out exactly what you wish to accomplish by your participation in the trade show. Study the list below and consider which objectives are applicable in your case.

1. To test market a new product
2. To recruit new sales personnel or new sales representatives or dealers
3. To develop new sales territories or new distribution channels
4. To encourage your customers to bring their technical problems to you for solutions
5. To introduce new products or new services or policies
6. To make sales
7. To demonstrate equipment which could not otherwise be shown easily to a customer
8. To bring together your representatives, internal sales and marketing people, and other key executives for conferences during the trade show
9. To expand your list of potential customers
10. To check on your competition and what they are offering
11. To increase the morale of your sales personnel and representatives and encourage them to work together
12. To build your company's image in the industry
13. To demonstrate your interest in and support of the sponsoring association

Please note that this list of objectives is not all-inclusive. There may be other goals or objectives which are unique to your situation, and which you should identify prior to trade show participation.

HOW TO DECIDE WHICH TRADE SHOWS TO ATTEND

With the large number of trade shows being held worldwide every year, it is clear that you cannot attend them all. It is therefore extremely important that those that you do attend are the most beneficial in boosting your sales and accomplishing others of the objectives that you establish. In order to make your plans, you must first know what shows are going to be held. The following are sources of information:

1. *Successful Meetings Magazine*, 1422 Chestnut St., Philadelphia, PA 19102, publishes an annual exhibit schedule.

2. *A Trade Show Convention Guide* is available from Budd Publications, Box 7, New York, NY 10004.
3. *World Meetings, United States and Canada*, and *World Meetings Outside the United States and Canada* are directories available from the Macmillan Publishing Co., 866 Third Ave., New York, NY 10022.
4. *Exhibits Schedule* is published by Bill Communications, Inc., 633 Third Ave., New York, NY 10017.
5. Check your trade or industry magazine. Frequently a calendar of upcoming trade shows and conventions is furnished.

From any of these sources, make a list of shows that interest you and seem to be for your business. Then, write the management of each show and ask for the literature that it has prepared. Specifically, you are interested in obtaining answers to the following questions:

1. Who has attended in the past and who are the people that these shows attract
2. How many attend
3. The geographical areas from which the attendees come
4. The industries and markets the attendees represent
5. The job titles and responsibilities held by the attendees
6. The topics of seminars, workshops, and events that may be offered at the show
7. The physical location of various exhibit booths available and the location relative to other events going on, entrances, exits, and so forth
8. Other services provided by the show sponsors

You should keep in mind that the information provided to you is a sales document and will therefore present everything in the best possible light. Therefore, one additional source of information obtained from this document which you can and must put to use is the list of prior exhibitors. If you contact these individuals, you can ask directly whether they were able to reach their objectives and whether they think your needs will be met by the trade show in question. Ask a lot of questions. The more you can learn about the show, the more information you have to make your decision.

Harvard professor Thomas V. Bonoma recommends making trade show spending decisions according to a nine-cell matrix as shown in Figure 14.1. Note that the idea is to look at your communication strength versus the strengths of the trade show in three areas: getting customers, keeping customers, and other objectives. This tells you whether you should make a high, low, or maintenance investment in the show.

HOW TO CALCULATE THE SPACE YOU WILL NEED FOR YOUR EXHIBIT

In order to calculate how much space you will need, you must consider your objectives and what will go into your exhibit. Every display, exhibit, or piece of furniture will require a certain amount of square footage. In addition, you will probably have salespeople on duty in the booth, and they too will require space. Therefore, you must decide how many salespeople you should have and how much footage you should allow for this.

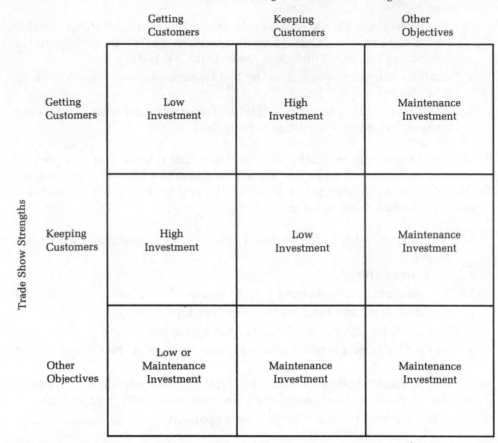

Figure 14.1. Making Trade Show Spending Decisions. Source: Adapted from Thomas V. Bonoma, "Get More Out Of Your Trade Shows," *Harvard Business Review*, Vol. 61 (January-February, 1983), p. 82, Exhibit II.

Robert B. Konikow, public relations counsel for the Trade Show Bureau in New York City, recommends finding out first how many of the people visiting the trade show are likely prospects. You do this using the prospects that you received in the mail from the trade show. Try to ascertain the number of visitors with meaningful titles or groups that you would be interested in talking with. Clearly, you won't be able to get all of these people to your booth, but you should be able to fit at least half of them. Take the total number of prospects of the type you are seeking and divide by two. Divide this number by the total number of hours the show will be open. From this calculation you can obtain the average number of visitors per hour.

A salesperson can typically handle approximately 15 prospects per hour. This is a good figure to use for your next calculation unless your own experience has shown that your salespeople handle more or less. Take the hourly visitor rate you have calculated previously and divide it by 15. From this you will get the average number of salespeople you should have on duty in your booth to handle the number of visitors you expect.

For each sales representative you have on duty, you must allow approximately 50 square feet of space. With less than 50 feet of space, the visitor will have a feeling of being crowded. But with more space, the visitor gets a feeling of loneliness and is unwilling to intrude on your salespeople! So, multiply the number of salespeople that you have calculated by 50 and you will get the amount of clear space that you will need. Add this to the space that you've calculated previously for your demonstration equipment and furniture and you will come up with how large a booth you are likely to need in square feet.

Let's look at an example of this. Let's assume that your furniture and equipment which you are going to display occupy 5 square feet of space. Let us say that you have decided from the prospectus that 1,200 prospects are likely to attend the show. Dividing this figure by 2 gives you 600, the number likely to visit your booth. Further, the show will be open a total of 20 hours. Dividing 600 by 20 gives you 30 visitors per hour. Dividing the 30 visitors per hour by the 15 prospects that a salesperson can see per hour on the average gives us 2 salespeople who should be on duty. Multiply 50 by 2 to get 100 square feet of space necessary for your salespeople. 100 plus 5 for the furniture and equipment you're going to display equals a total of 105 square feet necessary. Now, as it happens, most standard booths are 10 by 10, or 100 square feet. The extra 5 square feet can be easily absorbed and a standard booth will fill your bill. On the other hand, if the amount of space you need is much larger then the standard size, perhaps you should consider either two standard booths or an irregularly sized booth, if available.

HOW TO DESIGN YOUR DISPLAY

You must design your display to meet your own requirements as well as to conform to the requirements of the trade show. You should also consider the following factors:

1. You cannot show more than your budget will allow.
2. You want to attract only good prospects who will meet the objectives you have established.
3. You want to demonstrate the uniqueness of whatever it is that you are selling.

You must consider your booth just as you would an advertisement. That is, it must first attract attention, then gain interest, then create a desire to step in, and finally encourage action by your prospects, whether he or she is a potential customer, potential sales representative or whatever.

Remember that just as the headline in a good display or space advertisement attracts a reader to a specific ad, your trade show booth should, through its appearance, attract the people you want to see to your booth. It is best to use live demonstrations and other displays that are different from those of your competition and demonstrate benefits to your customers or to the prospects you are trying to attract. Participation demonstrations will gain added interest and are much better than static exhibits or presentations which prospects merely watch.

Demonstrations can be very simple and yet still carry the message across to the audience you wish to reach. A manufacturer of a new safety lens, much more protective than the ordinary safety lens, developed a simple but highly effective demonstration. He arranged a table like a small shooting gallery with a pellet gun mounted in a transparent, protective case. The handle and trigger of the gun were exposed so that it could be fired. A regular safety lens and this manufacturer's lens could be shot by interested prospects. The regular safety lens shattered easily. This manufacturer's new safety lens did not. This was the hit of this particular trade show and resulted in numerous sales. Go to other trade shows in your area even if you are not exhibiting and check out the exhibits which are attracting large numbers of prospects. This will give you many good ideas when you design your own exhibit.

THINGS TO DO BEFORE THE SHOW

After you have selected your trade show or (shows), designed your exhibit, and made other arrangements, you can greatly increase your ability to capitalize on a trade show's advantages if you venture into some of the following preshow activities:

1. Feature a unique item. Focus the activities around this unique item, brought in especially for the show. Naturally, the unique item should support the objectives that you have established previously.

2. Contact local media for publicity. Write letters to newspapers, radio and television stations, and other media in the city where the trade event will be held. With the letter, send a publicity release as described in Chapter 12. Feature the unique item you have developed for the show and ask to have your publicity release printed. Make yourself available for personal interviews.

3. Publicize to your industry. Send the publicity release that you have developed on your unique item for the show to all trade magazines in your field. Again, promote this unique product or service to the maximum extent possible and ask to have your publicity release printed.

4. Mail special letters with publicity release to your customers, sales representatives, and others who may be interested. Give them a special invitation to see you at your booth and see your new item or the item you are promoting. Be sure that you indicate the exact location of your booth.

5. Send letters with the publicity release and with your invitation to other interested parties who might not normally attend a trade show for your particular industry or association. For example, if you were a small book publisher and exhibiting a special health food diet cookbook at a certain exhibit, you might also do a mailing to all the health food stores in the city in which the show is being held. These individuals might not normally attend a book or publisher's trade show, but a special invitation promoting an item they are interested in might get them there and to your booth.

6. Obtain and prepare additional promotional material, such as posters in your show windows or stickers to affix to your normal correspondence, which announce the fact that you will be in a certain trade show. This will have the additional advantage of promoting your image to your customers and suppliers even if they do not go to the show.

7. Prepare brochures or other information about your products or services to distribute to prospects at the show. Make sure this information is to the point, directly relates to what you are selling, and, of course, is interesting. However, unless your product is highly technical and is an expensively priced item, do not go overboard on this. Remember that there are many show attendees who do nothing more than collect brochures and throw them away later.

You should also be concerned with the following tasks, many of the details of which were probably covered in the prospectus sent to you by the trade organization. They are important, so don't neglect them.

1. Be sure that you have insurance covering your trade show activities.
2. Prepare and prefabricate as much of your booth as possible prior to shipping. Labor costs at shows for doing this are expensive.
3. Be sure you've timed your packing and shipping so everything arrives well ahead of time.
4. Select your booth location. The better locations sometimes cost more money. However, many experts say that the location of the booth is a major factor in trade show success.
5. Be sure that you have your hotel reservations and also a rental car reserved if you will need it.
6. Have an emergency plan concocted in case your booth is lost or delayed in shipment. You might be able to fall back on displays put up through your local representatives or other equipment that you might carry with you. Always remember, "Expect the best but be prepared for the worst."
7. Have certain items duplicated and carry them with you in case they are lost or damaged in shipment, and have a tool kit for emergency repairs.

THINGS TO DO DURING THE SHOW

In order to maximize the benefits of a trade show, you should not simply go and have a good time. You should make a list of specific things which you intend to do and then do them. Your list may include the following:

1. Contact the local media if they haven't already contacted you after a mailing. Try to get additional exposure through interviews, appearing on television and radio talk shows, and so forth.

2. Contact local customers, suppliers, and other interested prospects. If you cannot do this face to face, use your telephone. Personal contact while you are in town will be of considerable assistance to your business.

3. Meet and talk with other exhibitors. Sell to them, if possible. Think creatively about ways in which other exhibitors may help you in your business. One exhibitor made thousands of dollars in sales simply by noting that his product fit naturally as a lead-in item to a higher-priced item sold by another exhibitor. His proposal was to give this other exhibitor exclusive sales rights in his industry, which was totally different from the industry for which the product was usually sold. Be alert to opportunities at exhibits.

4. Use your local sales representatives to the maximum extent possible. They will be able to profit heavily from the fact that you are exhibiting in their city. They can help you prepare your booth and be your local contact point.

During the exhibit, you will meet many people and will obtain sales cards from many. It is a sad fact that when you talk to many people, one after the other, you will not remember later what these business cards are for. One way of dealing with this problem is to write what the individual wants on the back of the business card as soon as you receive it. An even better way is to use a pocket tape recorder and record this information.

The Trade Show Business at P.O. Box 797, East Orleans, MA 02643, publishes a number of research reports on trade shows which you can obtain by writing them or calling (617) 240-0177. All except those with an "RS" designation are free for a self-addressed stamped envelope. Those designated "RS" are $50 a copy.

Audience Characteristics

The Effect of Economic Recessions on Trade Shows (RR #1050). This study was undertaken to determine what effect business recessions have on the quality and quantity of attendees at trade shows. The report provides an insight into the changes which have taken place in the industry, using 1968 as the base year.

An Audience Conversion Study The World of Concrete (RR #1040). A before and after analysis of one of the nation's major industrial expositions—evaluating attendees' plans to purchase versus actual purchases.

Corporate Executives' Perceptions of Trade Expositions—Factors Which Influence Attendance Decisions (RR #1030, October, 1986). An analysis of new studies by B. R. Blackmarr & Associates, management consultants, which sought out the attitudes of and comments from decision makers who do not regularly attend trade shows. These studies, which identify decision makers' rationales for non-attendance, contain significant information for show management and exhibitors—all of whom are seeking to attract corporate management executives, those individuals who are perceived to control key purchase decisions.

Attendee Purchase Behavior at a Retail Trade Show—Who Are the Buyers? (RR #1020). This study, undertaken for the Bureau by Georgia State University, looks at the attendees at a major retail buying show. It provides an audience overview of who attends, what they purchase, how they arrive at their buying decisions and how much they spend.

An Audience Survey of the 1985 National Plastics Exposition (RR 1010/April 1986). A dramatic analysis of the Society of the Plastics Industry's Chicago Exposition providing data on buying plans on product category, and projecting total sales generated by this major industry event.

Dispelling the Myths of Participating in Overseas Expositions (May 1986). A concise booklet listing the seven myths which tend to restrain exhibitors from taking advantage of the selling opportunities in overseas trade fairs. $1.00

Trade Shows in Black and White (April 1986). A 24 page booklet on trade show marketing. This thoughtful analysis was prepared as a reference for college faculty and students on trade shows. In addition to providing background and case history data on this marketing medium it defines the way in which it performs as a marketing alternative for improving an organization's competitive position. $8.50 + $1.50 Shipping and Handling.

Coping With Trade Show Overloads: Strategies For Participants by Audry J. Mahler and Ann Duke (March 1986). Trade shows invite participants to investigate current industry trends, products, and projections. This article presents a model for setting goals, planning a strategy, implementing the plan and measuring the results. Follow Mahler & Duke's model and you will "win the jackpot" at the next trade show you attend.

Do You Know How Much You Can Accomplish by Attending a Trade Show (January 1986). A concise guide to assist show visitors in getting the maximum return from show attendence.

Trade Show Selections Criteria (RR23/RS23/October 1984). An analysis of the most important factors in exhibitors' selection of which trade shows they select for participation.

Trade Show Marketing—Adjusting to the Needs of a Changing Market Place by Lewis P. Johnson (October 1984). As trade shows gain recognition as a marketing medium, exhibitors as well as other members of the exhibit community, must revise their thinking to capture the maximum return on their exhibit investment. This report defines the industry changes and the new opportunities these changes provide.

Characteristics at Regional and National Trade Shows (RR21/RS21/May 1984). Questionnaires returned by 18,341 visitors at 30 regional and 31 national trade shows are studied to determine audience quality, job function, distance traveled to reach show, other shows attended, time spent in exhibits, etc..

The Source for Unknown Prospects (RR22/RS22/May 1984). A study of visitors to 13 regional and 15 national shows indicates that the vast majority of them had not been called on by salespeople from companies whose exhibits they had visited. The study also compares traffic density and the performance of booth personnel at regional and national trade shows.

The Bottom Line (1983). A twelve minute film presentation demonstrates why the trade show, properly positioned in the exhibitor's marketing plan, provides a cost effective means of securing sales objectives. For purchase: ¾" or ½" VHS/ $50 16mm Print/$150

The Exhibition Validation Council—An Efficient Marketing Tool (January 1982). A descriptive brochure explains the functioning of the Exhibition Validation Council and the EVC Marketing Report Form. This program, designed to simplify the reporting of trade show audience data for exhibitors, was developed by the Trade Show Bureau to fill exhibitors' growing need for audience validation data.

Exhibitor Profiles

Characteristics of Specific Shows Each of the following studies examines the audience at a single show, looking at its buying influences, show experience, time spent on floor, etc.

Radiological Society of North America (RR16/RS16/July 1982)

New York Gift Show (RR15/RS15/July 1982)

Office Automation Conference (RR10/RS10/July 1981)

New York National Boat Show (RR9/RS9/July 1981)

AWS Welding Show (RR8/RS8/April 1981)

National Computer Conference (RR6/RS6/August 1980)

The Trade Show Audience (RR3). What is the make-up of the people who attend trade shows? Here is an analysis of visitors to 22 shows.

Reaching the Unknown Prospect (RR2). An analysis of the trade show audience's buying influence level—identifying the percentage of buyers not normally reached by the sales personnel.

Why Some Exhibits Pay Off, by Arthur L. Friedman. Success through trade show participation is no accident. This report, adapted from a presentation at "Meeting World," utilizes a series of case histories to help exhibitors maximize their return on show investment.

Trade Show Audio-Visuals: How Slides, Films, Sound and Video Can Add Impact to an Exhibit, by Don S. Vaughn. This analysis, reprinted from an article prepared for *Marketing Communications,* reviews the importance of audio-visuals in trade show marketing—providing detailed "how to" information to insure the maximum return on the show investment.

The Exhibit Management Function—Perceptions of Exhibit Management and Marketing Executives (RR #2040, November, 1986). An authoritative report by the Center for Marketing Management Studies, Southern Methodist University, on the exhibit management function—focusing on the ways exhibit management perceive the function and comparing it with the perceptions of their marketing management.

How is the Exhibit Dollar Spent (RR #2030, November, 1986). This cost analysis defines the ways in which exhibitors allocate their expenditures for the various elements making up the exhibit budget. In addition, it provides the current cost information on the various type of exhibits utilized.

Trade Shows Continue to Reach Prospects Less Expensively Than Personal Sales Calls (RR #2020 Cost Analysis, July 1986). The Trade Show Bureau's fifth cost analysis—comparing McGraw Hill's "Cost of an Industrial Sales Call" with "The Average Exhibit Cost Per Visitor Reached."

Exhibit Management Practices—Setting Objectives and the Evaluation of Results (RR #2010, July 1986). An extensive analysis by the Department of Marketing, University of Massachusetts at Boston, of exhibit management practices, with particular emphasis on the setting of objectives and the evaluation of show results.

You've Got an Uncle in the Overseas Trade Show Business (March, 1986). Traditionally wary of Government programs, U.S. companies, especially small-to-medium-sized firms, often overlook the assistance available to make their presence in an overseas trade show a success. Government services can make the experience a productive one.

An Analysis of Foreign Attendees and U.S. Exhibitors at American Trade Shows (RS26-$10/May 1985). An overview of foreign attendees perceptions of U.S. trade shows and their exhibitors.

Advertising Agency Involvement in Trade Shows (RR25/RS25/October 1984). An analysis of how advertising agencies perceive trade shows, how they are, or plan to be, involved with this marketing medium.

Sources of Information About Trade Shows and Expositions (M98F/May 1984). A list of associations, books, periodicals, and audio-visuals concerned with the trade show.

The Exhibitor/Their Trade Show Practices (RR19/RS19/June 1983). A study of the organizations and practices of companies that participate in trade shows, with 1982 compared to 1978.

Trade Show Industry Growth 1972–1981; Projected Growth 1981–1991 (RR17/ January 1983). An examination of ten year's activity, and a projection, based on responses from show managers, on what lies ahead.

Speakers Directory (M93/November, 1981). A geographical list of men and women who can speak with authority on various aspects of the industry.

How Should Exhibitors React to a Recession (RR5/RS5/April, 1980). An appraisal of exhibitor practices prior to and immediately following a recession.

What Makes a Trade Show? (M92). The script of a speech written by Hub Erickson, this gives a look at the forces that must be harnessed to produce a successful trade show.

Show Categories

Trade Shows: Opportunities to Sell, by Jenny Tesar (April, 1987). A case study of the Sporting Equipment Super Show. The emphasis at trade expositions is on sales results, and nowhere is this more evident than in modern major retail shows. Here cost effectiveness is the focus for attendees and exhibitors alike: an opportunity to capitalize on the efficiencies offered at a dominant industry gathering.

Market Research—Vital Ingredient for a Successful Trade Exposition (RR #3010, April, 1987). This report shows how the Institute of Food Technologies utilizes innovative market research to increase the value of their trade exposition to exhibitors and attendees alike.

The Trade Show Marketplace—New Growth, New Dimensions, by Robert Black, Founding Publisher, Tradeshow Week (December 1986). In a presentation developed for the Exposition Service Contractors Association, one of the industry's foremost authorities and statesmen, provides an incisive overview of the trade show industry.

Trade Show Space Usage—Convention Center Space Capacity, by Robert Black, Founding Publisher, Tradeshow Week (November, 1986). What are the facts on trade show growth? And can these growth trends be relied on to project convention center requirements for the future? This report provides answers to these questions.

The Trade Show Industry—Management and Marketing Career Opportunities, by Robert Black, Founding Publisher of Tradeshow Week. A reprint of a lecture presented on November 19, 1986, at Cornell University under the auspices of the Cornell University Department of Communications. This presentation reports on the growth and dynamism of the trade show industry and the career opportunities it provides.

A Formula for Determining Exhibit Staff and Space Needs, by Jenny Tesar. In an article for Successful Meetings, Jenny Tesar reviews the tested formula developed by Exhibit Surveys, Inc. of Middletown, New Jersey, to determine trade show staffing and space requirements.

Exposition Hall Industry—The 1986 Annual Report—Laventhol & Horwath. A detailed analysis of operating performance of all convention facilities with over 100,000 square feet of exhibit space.

Can Your Property Attract Trade Shows? A reprint of an August 1986 article from "Hotel and Resort Industry" that lists the ways experienced hotel operators capture this meaningful business.

The Effect of Booth Location on Exhibit Performance and Impact (RR20/RS20/ October 1983). According to this study, the location of the exhibit within the hall is neither a positive nor a negative factor.

How to Boost Your Exhibit's Propect Appeal (RR13/RS13/July 1982). A study by Robert T. Wheeler, Jr. examines what exhibitors can do before and during a show to get more qualified visitors to their space.

20 Ways to Turn a So-So Show Into a Bonanza (M105/1981). Robert Letwin, in *Successful Meetings,* lists essential steps you should take to get a good return on your investment in a trade show exhibit.

On Being an Exhibitionist! (M103/March 1981). This reprint from *Medical Conference Planner,* by Jan M. Spieczny, claims that a blend of showmanship, sellmanship and salesmanship is essential to get the most out of your exhibit dollar.

What Makes Visitors Remember Your Trade Show Exhibit (RR11/RS11/December 1980). This study looks at the effect of a number of characteristics on the proportion of visitors who remember a booth, including booth personnel, company awareness, industry leadership, and exhibit approach.

The Why and the How of Trade Show Exhibiting (S901). The qualities of the trade show visitor that make him a good prospect, and how to reach him economically and effectively, are outlined in this article by Don Vaughn, from *Sales & Marketing Management.*

Exhibiting at Trade Shows (M245). Originally published by the Small Business Administration, this brochure by Robert B. Konikow is designed for the small company which is considering trade show participation for the first time.

Sales Topics

1986 Radiological Society of North America—Exhibit Personnel Behavioral Study and Traffic Floor Analysis (RR #4000). Attendees' evaluation of booth personnel performance at the world's largest health care conference.

Does Your Staff Practice "Booth-personship?" (June 1986). Reprint from *Business Marketing* of an article by Bob Dallmeyer on the importance of understanding the uniqueness of trade show selling.

You Make the Difference—A Guide to Getting Sales Results Through Trade Shows (June, 1986). The second edition of the Bureau's most popular publication. Tips on how to maximize sales at trade shows. Thirteen page booklet. $1.00 per copy.

How Trade Shows Continue to Influence Sales (RR28/RS28/January 1986). U.S. Trade Shows are moving closer to their European counterparts as important sales vehicles. This conversion study of the 1984 National Computer Conference compares the dynamic sales results of the 1984 show with that held in 1978–79.

An Invitation to Join The Bureau. A listing of the Bureau's objectives and services, along with a Sustaining Member Application Blank.

How Much Must You Spend to Reach a Prospect? A graphic comparison of the cost of an industrial sales call ($229.70) with the cost of an exhibit to reach a prospect.

How Much Will it Cost to Book An Order? An evaluation of McGraw-Hills number of sales calls to book an order (5.5 sales calls, $1,263) with the cost to close a trade show lead (0.8 sales calls, $290).

What is the Cost to Book an Order From A New Customer? The most difficult and costly presentation is the one made to a new customer. This brief analysis compares the cost of securing an order based on a trade show lead ($290) against the efforts of sales personnel ($1,490).

Measuring Trade Show Results (January 1984). A member of one of the nation's foremost exhibit research firms, Jonathan M. Cox, in this reprint from *Successful Meetings*, focuses on the most important element in any marketing activity— evaluation results.

What a Lead Conversion Program Should Do For You (January 1984). In this penetrating analysis from *The Exhibitor*, Charyn Ofstie details how knowledgeable exhibitors can cover the costs of a lead-tracking program with the conversion of one qualified lead.

Number of Calls to Close a Trade Show Lead (RR18/RS18/April 1983). The report provides, for the first time, data on the number of follow-up calls—only 0.8, on the average!—required to close a trade show lead.

How to Improve Sales Success at Trade Shows (M102/1981). Reprint from *Meetings & Conventions* of an article by Michael J. Hatch on techniques to improve the effectiveness of trade show participation.

Spotlight Your New Product Via Tradeshows (M104). An article by Robert B. Konikow, reprinted from *Marketing Times*, outlines the special requirements of new product introduction at a trade show.

Marketing/Communications

Trade Show Lead Systems—A Faster Track to Sales, by Charyn Ofstie (RR #5000). Lead generation is one of the most important trade show benefits. Following through on those leads is particularly critical—and often over-looked. This report provides a precise and defined method to insure the full return on the show investment.

Success in Trade Show Exhibiting—It's Dependent On An Application of Marketing Skills—Skillfully Applied, by Gerald Sanderson. Successful participation in a major trade exposition requires the dedicated application of a variety of marketing skills. Failure to do the "necessary homework" can result in frustration and failure—evidenced by some exhibitors in the high technology field. Gerald Sanderson provides an insight into the elements which do guarantee success and provides the reasons why these elements must be addressed.

The NCC, A Grand Daddy Trade Show, AT&T—A Case Study, by Edward A. Chapman, Jr. Changing markets and buyer needs, along with exhibitor belt tightening, are having a great impact on our largest exhibit showcases, including the venerable National Computer Conference. This is the story of how a group of exhibit managers in one industry have gathered together to try and help both themselves and their show managers meet the challenge. Volatility is creating a new kind of partnership, where their show managers work more closely together to produce the results they want; where exhibitors work harder than ever to create their own marketing communications events tied in with the shows. This is the story of one company and its approach to a single show.

Pre-Show Promotion: Its Role in New Product Introduction (March 1986). Pre-show promotion is an essential ingredient in introducing new products. Mark Noble, in a case history, explains how through effective brand marketing, product positioning, and a dynamic pre-show promotion campaign, a company can introduce a new product line in a very mature and competitive market. He chronicles his company's success in bringing 94 out of 100 key prospects to their trade show booth. Over half of these accounts now carry their product.

The Effect of Advertising on Booth Traffic (RR27/RS27/October 1985). An analysis of the relationship between advertising consistency and booth traffic / a study of exhibitors at the Food Exposition of the Institute of Food Technologists— comparing booth traffic of those exhibitors who advertised in the Institute's "Food Technology," with those exhibitors who did not advertise.

Changes in the Trade Show Industry, by Don S. Vaughn (October 1985). An industry overview prepared for the 57th Summer Meeting of the National Association of Exposition Managers. This penetrating analysis reviews where the industry has been, where it is going, and some trends and areas of concern for the future.

Awaken the Sleeping Giant by Unleashing the Power of Trade Shows, by Robert Firks. This thoughtful analysis, adapted from a presentation prepared for the Association of Railroad Advertising Managers, defines the marketing elements which must be applied to insure the most profitable trade show participation.

The Role of an Advertising Agency in the Clients' Trade Show Programs
A Case Study—Anderson & Lambke. Hans Ullmark, Executive Vice President of Anderson & Lembke, an international network of business-to-business agencies, describes how Anderson & Lembke took an unconventional route to introduce a new product for a client into a closed market. Through an aggressive preshow promotion program, they achieved 100% turnout of their prospects at a key trade show.

A Case Study—The Barth Group. Katrine Barth, President of the Barth Group, an advertising and public relations firm, details the ways in which the agency participates in its clients' trade show programs. In addition to the Barth Group's work in advertising and promotion, it creates marketing strategies and special events for the nation's major trade show producers.

A Case Study—Cummings Advertising, Inc. This report is based on an interview with Quentin Barclay, President of Cummings Advertising, Inc. Cummings, located in Rockford, Illinois, is a medium-sized agency which is deeply involved in the trade show activity of its clients. While its clients are in many industrial fields, the greatest concentration is in food processing.

A Case Study—Forum Communications. Steve Swandbeck, President of Forum Communications, Inc., an advertising and public relations firm specializing in international trade, provides an insight into a unique aspect of trade show marketing. Forum is involved in marketing Hanover Fairs, the West German trade show organization, to the U.S. marketplace, as well as using their American expertise to help other European clients exhibit successfully in the United States.

A Case Study—O'Neal & Prelle. William O'Neal, President of O'Neal & Prelle, an advertising agency based in Hartford, Connecticut, describes his company's involvement in the trade show programs of its clients—making the trade show part of a firm's overall marketing and communications program. He demonstrates that trade show programs deserve the creative input that an advertising agency can provide.

A Case Study—Simms & McIvor. Simms & McIvor, an advertising agency in Bound Brook, New Jersey, is closely involved in its clients' trade show programs. With many of its clients in the pharmaceutical and health care field, McIvor reveals some valuable insights about preshow and show promotion for health care shows. He shows how an advertising agency can make the trade show program a dynamic and vital part of its clients' entire marketing plan.

THINGS TO DO AFTER THE SHOW

The trade show itself will generate many potential sources of business for you. But you must follow up immediately in order that all this potential business does not grow cold. Consider the following suggestions:

1. Write up another publicity release and mail it to all prospects that you met during the show. If the show provides a registration list of the names of companies and other persons attending the show, use this and add it to your mailing list.

2. Mail a publicity release to all your sales representatives throughout the country and promote your participation at the show to them. If you got good results during the trade show, let your sales representatives know about it. It will stimulate them to do more and better work for you.

3. Go over the business cards that you obtained and make certain that each one is individually handled and that what the prospect wanted is furnished.

4. Go over the objectives you established for the trade show and ask yourself whether these objectives were met. This will provide you with important information as to whether the trade show was worthwhile and whether you should attend next year. If you decide that this trade show was worthwhile, start planning immediately. Make reservations right away.

SOURCES OF ADDITIONAL INFORMATION

Creative Selling Through Trade Shows, by Al Hanlon, published by Hawthorne Books, Inc., 260 Madison Avenue, New York, NY 10016.

The Exhibit Medium, by David Maxwell, published by *Successful Meetings Magazine*, 1422 Chestnut Street, Philadelphia, PA 19102.

How to Get Big Results from a Small Advertising Budget, by Cynthia S. Smith, published by Hawthorne Books, Inc., 260 Madison Avenue, New York, NY 10016.

How to Participate Profitably in Trade Shows, by Robert B. Konikow, published by Dartnell Corp., 4660 Ravenswood Avenue, Chicago, IL 60640.

Trade Show Exhibit Planning Guide, published by Guideline Publishing Co., 5 Holmes Road, Lexington, MA 02173.

15

How to Develop a Marketing or Business Plan

A MARKETING PLAN CAN MAKE YOU RICH

For a small business, the marketing plan and the business plan are identical.*
Both must have hard financial information. This plan is essential for efficient
and effective marketing of any product or service, and every entrepreneur or
small business marketer should be able to develop a marketing plan that will
ultimately lead to success. Seeking a project success without a marketing plan
is much like trying to navigate a ship through rather perilous waters with the
competition shooting at you and with neither a map nor a clear idea of your
destination. Therefore, the time it takes to develop a marketing plan is well
worthwhile and will allow you to visualize clearly both where you want your
business to go and what you want it to accomplish. At the same time, a marketing
plan maps out the important steps necessary to get from where you are now
to where you want to be at the conclusion of the planning period. Further, you
will have thought through how long it will take to get where you want to go
and what resources in money and personnel will be needed and must be allocated
from within your company. In fact, to obtain this allocation of resources, a
competent and thoroughly thought-out plan is essential. Without a marketing
plan, you will not even know whether you have reached your objectives or
not!

WHAT A MARKETING PLAN WILL DO FOR YOU

A marketing plan accomplishes the following:

1. Acts as a road map
2. Assists you with management control
3. Helps you in briefing new employees and other personnel recently assigned
   to the project
4. Helps you in your briefings to higher management and in obtaining
   allocations of resources
5. Enables you to see problems and opportunities that may lie along the
   pathway to project success

* Note: An alternative approach for developing a marketing plan can be found in the appendix.

330

A Marketing Plan as a Road Map

If you were traveling from point A to point B and you had never been to point B before, you would almost certainly consult a road map if you had any distance at all to travel. If you didn't use a map, you could drive around in circles for hours trying to locate point B, and if you couldn't ask anyone for directions, you probably would not get there. Unfortunately, some marketers attempt to do the same thing in the marketplace. The usual result is failure. However, with a marketing plan used as a road map, everything is made much simpler. You can follow a precise route from where you are presently to where you want to go. Of course, sometimes something occurs during the travel which is not foreseen on the map—perhaps the road is closed or blocked, requiring the driver to take a detour. Even when this happens, the map assists the driver by helping him or her choose the best alternative route to the destination. The marketing plan, or the marketing road map, works in the same way. A marketing plan, which documents and shows exactly how to reach carefully defined business goals, serves the same function as a road map for the driver of a car and will enable you to reach corporate goals much quicker and with much less effort and more efficient utilization of resources than would otherwise be possible.

Management Control

Previously I indicated that even the driver of a motor vehicle with a road map may find it necessary to take a detour because of unplanned circumstances. This may be because the road is being repaired or because the weather makes the most direct route to the destination impassable. In the same way, as you are in the process of starting up and implementing the project, you will encounter various problems that cannot be foreseen. In fact, it is almost certain that nothing will go exactly as planned. However, in thinking through your project and laying out a full and complete plan, you will be able to spot many potential problems ahead of time. Furthermore, inasmuch as you have a documented plan leading directly to the goals you have established, you will be able to see clearly the difference between what is happening during implementation and what you had planned to happen. This gives you control of the situation and lets you see more clearly the corrective action necessary to keep your project on the proper course to achieve the goals you have set.

A good analogy here is an aircraft flight. For almost every aircraft flight the pilot is required to file a flight plan that he or she has developed. This flight plan specifies all information, including course headings, distances, air and ground speed, fuel, time enroute, emergency airfields, and other factors, for the specific destination the pilot has decided on. Using the flight plan, the pilot can compare actual course and progress in the air with the course and progress planned before the flight. The pilot can analyze this information rapidly to make the best decisions in minimum time. So important is this aspect of management control in flight planning that for some military flights an air crew spends as much time planning the flight on the ground as it spends flying in the air.

The necessity for both a flight plan and a marketing plan can be illustrated by Clausewitz, the great German strategic thinker. According to Clausewitz, although detailed planning must always be done, plans never go exactly as foreseen after they were developed. The difference, according to Clausewitz, is called "battle friction." Battle friction is encountered by the pilot in the air and the driver on the ground in going from point A to point B. But the important point that Clausewitz makes and the reason that the flight planner, the driver, and the corporate strategist must develop good plans is that once the battle, the flight, or the trip or journey has started, little time may be available for decision making. A decision under high-density traffic in the air may sometimes need to be made within minutes or even seconds to avoid a catastrophe. In the same way, once you have developed the plan and its execution begins, the pressures on the firing line of the marketing battlefield deriving from competition and other environmental variables make it crucial for you to come up with good decisions fairly rapidly. A marketing plan lets you think through most potential problem situations ahead of time, so that competent decisions can be made quickly when the plan is implemented under the pressures of the time and the competitive environment.

The marketing plan will give you management control over the particular project in your business just as a flight plan gives the pilot management control over the airplane and flight.

Briefing New Employees and Other Personnel

Many times you will wish to inform other people regarding the project, its progress toward its goals and objectives, and the way you intend on reaching them. Such individuals may be new employees who you have recently hired for the project. Having a ready reference does more than simply allow for easy briefing. It enables you to document and show the objectives that you have set and how and when the plan envisions reaching them. It will show them where they fit into the "big picture" and not only will assist in motivating them but also will help them to do a better job for you and for implementation of the plan. In addition, once you organize and document the material in a marketing plan, you have it for all time. You will not need to run around to assemble the information every time you wish to discuss it or tell someone new about it.

Obtaining Money

No organization has unlimited resources. Therefore, projects must be allocated resources according to the overall benefit to the organization. When you develop a marketing plan, you will be able to demonstrate exactly how the money and resources will be used to reach the goals and objectives established. The marketing plan in itself is documented proof that every aspect of the situation has been thought through.

For this reason, many businesspersons prepare a business or marketing plan to help them obtain investment capital for their business. Sources of this capital frequently say that, without question, the success in obtaining capital is primarily due to the quality of the business plan prepared. Business plans and marketing plans are really identical if the business concerns a single project, product line, or group of products considered at the same time. Success in obtaining money and the green light to go ahead with the plan are frequently primarily dependent on the marketing plan prepared. Sources of capital are approached by hundreds of entrepreneurs who seek capital every month. The only differentiating factors are the entrepreneurs themselves and what they want to do with the money. This is expressed in the marketing plan.

Seeing Problems and Opportunities

The requirement to sit down and think through a marketing plan will help you see all the problems and opportunities in any business situation. Thus it is not so important that a business situation has problems. This is always true. More important is the fact that these problems can be anticipated, and solutions worked out ahead of time. In this way you can develop your plans to take advantage of the opportunities, to solve the problems that arise, and to avoid potential threats or obstacles to achieving your objectives.

THE STRUCTURE OF THE BUSINESS/MARKETING PLAN

A good marketing plan will contain a number of different sections. Marketing plans are situational, and additional sections can be added to those listed below or can be included as appendixes. But almost all marketing plans contain the following:

1. Executive summary
2. Table of contents
3. Background and description of the business
4. Organization of company or project
5. Situation analysis
6. Problems and opportunities
7. Objectives
8. Marketing strategy
9. Marketing tactics
10. Budget
11. Financial plans
12. Strategy implementation time schedule

Let's look at each in turn.

Executive Summary

The executive summary is an overall view of your project and its potential, including what you want to do, how much money is needed for the project, how much money the project will make, and such financial measurements as return on investment. The executive summary is extremely important and should not be overlooked. As implied by its title, it is an overview or abstract of the entire plan. The target audience is the top-management executive such as the individual making the decision as to whether to loan you money or not. As this individual goes through your marketing plan, he or she will frequently skip over parts of the plan which are not of interest. Only certain sections will be read; most will only be scanned. However, the executive summary will always be read. Therefore, it is important that you present the essence of your plan as clearly and succinctly as possible. Using a few short paragraphs or a maximum of two or three pages, describe the thrust of what the plan purports to do, the objectives and goals to be achieved, and the overall strategy so that any reader can instantly understand what you are trying to do and how you propose to do it.

Table of Contents

You may wonder about the inclusion of the discussion of something as mundane as a table of contents under a subject as important as a marketing plan. However, you will find that the table of contents is extremely important. As indicated previously, most executives at the top levels of management will not read the entire plan in detail but, rather, will read only the executive summary and areas that are of particular interest to them. For example, a finance executive will surely read the finance section, while she or he may well skip over sections pertaining to product development, sales, or marketing. However, an executive oriented toward marketing will certainly take particular note of what you have to say in these sections. It is not enough to ensure that every subject area pertaining to the project is covered in your plan. You have to make it as easy as possible for the executive who is looking for his or her topics of interest to find them quickly. If you do this through a table of contents, many executives will make a cursory attempt to locate the information they want. If they cannot do so, they will assume it is not there. This results in a negative impact on these executives from what might otherwise be a brilliant marketing plan. Therefore, do not neglect to include a thorough table of contents as part of your plan.

Background and Description of Project

In this paragraph you give the details of your project, including what it is, how it is going to be run, and, most importantly, why it will be successful. What differential advantage does it have over other similar projects either in your own company or the companies of your competition? This differential advantage is crucial. Without it there is no reason to invest in this project, since without a competitive advantage over your competition, you cannot win. Unless the project has advantages over other projects, they should be funded, and not yours. The differential advantage should be clearly spelled out, be it a unique product, lower cost, better service, closer location to markets, unique expertise, and so forth.

Project Organization

In this section you should detail exactly how the project will be organized, including who will report to whom in collateral organizations if its a large project. Include a résumé of the principal project leaders in an appendix. These should zero in on experience, education, or background that specifically supports assigned positions in your plan.

Situation Analysis

The situation analysis has several subsections, all of which are important and should be included and discussed as a part of your marketing plan. These should include demand for your product or service, target market, competition, unique advantages, legal restrictions if any, and any and all other situational variables that you feel are important to successful completion of the project.

Demand includes both the need for your project or service and the extent of this need. This need may be very basic if your product is a food staple. On the other hand, products or services may satisfy psychological needs that are not necessarily obvious. A brass case for business cards has been on the market for several years and is sometimes advertised in the *Wall Street Journal*. The brass case has sold for as much as $20 or more, although in recent years the price has been reduced as it has gone through its product life cycle. The initials of the purchaser are frequently engraved free of charge. Now the question is, Is a brass case for business cards purchased primarily to protect business cards or to promote the status of the owner? Inasmuch as inexpensive plastic cases to protect business cards are frequently used as sales promotion giveaways and card cases are also frequently supplied free with the cards, chances are this product is purchased primarily to satisfy status needs. Whatever the needs satisfied by your product or service, they should be carefully considered and documented under this section. Indicate whether the product is a repeat product which will be purchased again and again by your customers, such as typewriter ribbon, or whether the product or service is a one-time need which is unlikely to be repeated, such as the purchase of a home. Also note whether the product or service is likely to continue to be sold over a long period of time or whether it is more likely to be a short-lived fad. Finally, what are the trends here? Is the demand for the product growing, leveling off, or declining?

The target market is the market that you intend to seek for your product or your service. Naturally, the larger the potential market, the better. But there are several different strategies you may follow. It might be advantageous to offer your product only to a certain segment of the total potential market. This is called a "strategy of market segmentation," and it offers a major advantage in certain situations, for you can concentrate all your resources on satisfying the specific needs of a certain segment of the market and can gear your promotional campaign to this segment. You will be stronger against this market segment than your competition will be if it spreads itself, its resources, and its promotional campaign across the total potential mass market. Because of this strategy and other possible strategies, you should note very carefully the market segments that make up the target market you intend to pursue, including the size of each market segment.

The importance of competition should never be underestimated. It is the only noncontrollable variable in your situation that will competitively react to your activities. Regardless of what product or service you offer, you will always have competition, even if the competition does not offer the exact same product or service. For example, home swimming pools may be indirect competition for health studios; however, they must be considered competition because the product or service fulfills the same need in your potential customers that your product or service fulfills. Perhaps you sell burglar alarms. Is your competition only other other firms selling burglar alarms? The answer is no. Other firms which fulfill the need for security must be considered competition. Such firms may offer iron bars to be installed over the windows, security guards, or watchdogs. All are indirect competition. Therefore, when you begin to analyze the competition for your product or service, be sure that you include all potential competitors, not just the direct competition of firms producing the identical product or service.

When you analyze your competition, you should also consider the fact that your competition will never remain static and will react to your marketing strategy if it proves effective. If you introduce a new product into the marketplace that competes with some other firm already there, you can be assured that if your product is successful, you will not be ignored. Your competition will then initiate an action in response in order to try to overcome your success. You might expect your competition to do something with the price of the product, to change the product, or to change its advertising. Therefore, you must, when you analyze your competition, think ahead as to what actions your competition might take, just as you would if you were in a chess game—only more thoroughly; not only because the stakes are higher but also because you will usually have more than one business opponent.

Your firm is not the same as any other firm. It is unique. So is your project. As pointed out earlier, you must sell this differential, or competitive, advantage. If you have no differential advantage, there is no reason to buy from you and you cannot win. In this section, emphasize the differential advantage from the point of view of your potential buyer. Some of these advantages have already been discussed, including specialized knowledge, lower prices, a totally unique product, additional services, and so forth. It is important to think through and write down these advantages in your marketing plan, so you will be certain not to overlook any and so you can exploit them to the maximum extent with the strategies you decide on. Remember, also, that although every single organization for any product or service has its advantages over competitors, if they are not identified in the marketing plan, they will probably not be exploited. And if they are not exploited, it is as if they did not exist.

Legal restrictions should always be noted in your marketing plan if they are applicable. They don't always exist, but if they do, you must consider them and note them down, not only so that they will not be overlooked but also so that others will know what they are and what their impact will be on other projects within the company. Every applicable restriction should be noted carefully, along with licenses and other legal obligations necessary for you to do business. You should do the research necessary to be absolutely certain that you meet your legal obligations. There is an additional advantage in documenting everything here: Sometimes someone going over your marketing plan will note something that you have forgotten and that in itself can save you a great deal of time, money, and allocation of important company resources, as well as your reputation as a corporate strategist.

Some years ago an entrepreneur invested thousands of dollars in marketing to mix wine and fruit juice to produce a canned drink, not realizing that government tax made the cost of such a drink prohibitive unless the company itself manufactured the wine. The entrepreneur who eventually made this product an incredible success researched and documented this crucial legal restriction and developed a strategy that allowed for the restriction.

Other important situation variables should also be noted. These may be anything that you consider important to your business situation and to the success of your marketing plan. Let us say your product is seasonal and sold only in the summer or during Christmas holidays or during the football season. In such a case, there are special problems, including expensive overhead during the off-season, peak periods of sale, and so forth. Thus seasonality, in this case, would be an important situational variable.

Problems and Opportunities

Problems and opportunities are really different sides of the same coin. Many people make millions of dollars because when they note a problem, they also note within this problem a unique opportunity for success. Listerine is a mouthwash having a rather harsh taste. In the words of the advertisement of the competition, it tastes "mediciny." However, Listerine managed to make this problem an opportunity. The company realized that many consumers feel that if a mouthwash has a harsh taste, it must be harsher on germs, whereas if a mouthwash taste sweet or, in the words of a Listerine ad, tastes like "soda pop," it may not be killing germs nearly as well. Look for the opportunity in every problem that you find. And in this section specify both problems you have found and their solutions and any opportunities inherent in them that your company can take advantage of.

Objectives

Objectives should be stated explicitly. They may be defined by stating the volume to be sold in dollars or units, and they may also include financial measurements, such as return on investment or some other profitability measure. If more than one objective is stated, be certain that the objectives do not conflict. For example, sometimes if a market share is specified as your objective, this can be reached only through a negative impact on short-term profitability. So if you specify more than one objective, check to be sure that one objective can be achieved only at the expense of another.

Marketing Strategy

Strategy for marketing your product should be stated as developed in previous chapters. What exactly are you going to do to reach your objectives?

Marketing Tactics

Marketing tactics refer to how you will carry out the strategy, that is, the different tasks involved, including who will do them, what they will cost, and when they will be done. Marketing tactics can be described in the budget and the financial plans, as well as in the next section, Strategy Implementation Time Schedule.

Budget. As indicated previously, every single strategy costs resources. It is very important to indicate exactly what these resources are in hard dollar amounts. For this reason, it is essential to establish a budget for your total marketing plan for the project, including exactly how much each single task will cost and when these funds will be required. The "Strategy Implementation Time Schedule" section shows one way of describing the budget.

Financial plans. The financial-plan section should include not only the budget for the strategies and tactics required but also the projected income statement, as shown in Figure 15.1; a cash-flow projection as shown in Figure 15.2; and a balance sheet, as shown in Figure 15.3. Use of these forms is mandatory for most marketing plans. Financial plans give the entire financial picture for your project and will assist you not only with management control but also in allowing individuals who decide on the allocation of resources to your project or to other projects to have the complete financial picture.

Using a Break-Even Analysis

Sometimes it is also useful to put a break-even analysis in this section. A "break-even analysis" is a method for evaluating relationships between sales revenues,

MONTHS AFTER START-UP

	Month 1	Month 2	Month 3	Month 4	Month 5	Month 6	Month 7	Month 8	Month 9	Month 10	Month 11	Month 12
Total net sales												
Cost of sales												
Gross Profit												
Controllable expenses												
Salaries												
Payroll taxes												
Security												
Advertising												
Automobile												
Dues and subscriptions												
Legal and accounting												
Office supplies												
Telephone												
Utilities												
Miscellaneous												
Total controllable expenses												
Fixed expenses												
Depreciation												
Insurance												
Rent												
Taxes and licenses												
Loan Payments												
Total fixed expenses												
Total Expenses												
Net Profit (Loss) (before taxes)												

Figure 15.1. Income statement for marketing plan.

MONTHS AFTER START-UP

	Month 1	Month 2	Month 3	Month 4	Month 5	Month 6	Month 7	Month 8	Month 9	Month 10	Month 11	Month 12	Total
Cash (beginning of month)													
Cash on hand													
Cash in bank													
Cash in investments													
Total cash													
Income (during month)													
Cash sales													
Credit sales payments													
Investment income													
Loans													
Other cash income													
Total income													
Total Cash and Income													
Expenses (during month)													
Inventory or new material													
Wages													
Taxes													
Equipment expense													
Overhead													
Selling expense													
Transportation													
Loan repayment													
Other cash expenses													
Total Expenses													
Cash-Flow Excess (end of month)													
Cash-Flow Cumulative (monthly)													

Figure 15.2. Cash-flow projection for marketing plan.

———— — , 19 ——

	Year I	Year II
Current Assets		
Cash	$ ————	$ ————
Accounts receivable	————	————
Inventory	————	————
Fixed Assets		
Real estate	————	————
Fixtures and equipment	————	————
Vehicles	————	————
Other Assets		
License	————	————
Goodwill	————	————
Total Assets	$ ————	$ ————
Current Liabilities		
Notes payable (due within 1 year)	$ ————	$ ————
Accounts payable	————	————
Accrued expenses	————	————
Taxes owed	————	————
Long-Term Liabilities		
Notes payable (due after 1 year)	————	————
Other	————	————
Total Liabilities	$ ————	$ ————
Net Worth (Assets *minus* Liabilities)	$ ————	$ ————

Total Liabilities *plus* Net Worth should *equal* Assets

Figure 15.3. Balance sheet for marketing plan.

fixed costs, and variable costs. The break-even point is the point at which the number of units sold covers all costs of developing, producing, and selling the product. Above this point you will make money, and below it you will lose money. It is one excellent measurement for determining the ultimate success of the project before you begin. In sum, the break-even analysis will tell you the following:

1. How many units you must sell in order to start making money
2. How much profit you will make at any given level of sales
3. How changing your price will affect profitability
4. How expense reductions at different levels of sales will affect profitability

To accomplish a break-even analysis, you must first separate the costs associated with your project into two categories: fixed costs and variable costs.

"Fixed costs" are those expenses associated with the project that you would have to pay whether you sold 1 unit or 10,000 units or, for that matter whether you sold any units at all. For example, if you rented a building for use in your project and the owner of the building charged you a thousand dollars to rent the building for the period of the project, then this would be a fixed cost for that period. You would have to pay the thousand dollars whether or not you sold any products or many products. Research and development costs for a project or a product would also be considered a fixed cost, and this money would have to be paid whether or not you sold any product.

"Variable costs" vary directly with the number of units that you sell. If it costs you $1.80 to manufacture a unit, then that $1.80 is considered a variable cost. If postage for mailing your product to a customer is $1, then 1 is a variable cost. If you sell 10 units, then your postage cost is 10 times $1, or $10. If you sell 100 units, your total variable cost for postage would be 100 times $1, or $100.

It is difficult to decide whether to consider some costs fixed or to consider them variable, and very frequently there is no single right answer. You must make this decision either by yourself or with the help of corporate financial experts. As a general guide, if there is a direct relationship between cost and number of units sold, consider the cost variable. If you cannot find such a relationship, consider the cost fixed.

The total cost of your project will always equal the sum of the fixed costs plus the variable costs. Consider the following example for an item which you are going to sell for $10. How much profit would you make if you sold 1000 units?

Fixed Costs

Utility expense at $300 per month for 12 months	=	$3600
Telephone at $50 per month for 1 year	=	600
Product development cost	=	1000
Rental expense	=	2500
Total fixed costs	=	$7700

Variable Costs

Cost of product	=	$1.00/unit
Cost of postage and packaging	=	0.50/unit
Cost of advertising	=	3.00/unit
Total variable costs	=	$4.50/unit

To calculate break even, we start with an equation for profit. Total profit *equals* the number of units sold *multiplied* by the price at which we are selling them *less* the number of units sold *multiplied* by the total variable cost and that answer *minus* the total fixed cost. If P equals profit, p equals price, U equals the number of units sold, V equals variable costs, and F equals fixed costs, then our equation becomes:

$$P = (U \times p) - (U \times V) - F$$

Or we can simplify this to:

$$P = U(p - V) - F$$

Substituting the values given in our example, we have:

$$P = 1000(\$10.00 - \$4.50) - \$7700 = \$5500 - \$7700 = -\$2200$$

What is the significance of a minus number? This means that instead of making a profit, we have lost money—$2200 to be exact. Now we may want to know how many units we must sell in order to make money, or at what point we will stop losing money. This point at which we will either make money or lose money is called "break even." Beginning at this point we will show a profit. In order to calculate this, we use the break-even equation. And the break-even equation, using the same variables from above, is $P = U(p - V) - F$. At break even, profit by definition $= 0$. Thus, if we transpose terms and let $P = 0$, break even $=$

$$\frac{F}{p - V}$$

Since we know that F equals $7700, p equals $10, and V equals $4.50, break even equals:

$$\frac{\$7700}{\$10 - \$4.50} = 1400 \text{ units}$$

This means if we don't change price or reduce expenses in any way, we need to sell 1400 units of this product before we can start making any money. However there is an easier way to calculate this. We can use the break-even chart shown in Figure 15.4. A break-even chart is a major advantage over the break-even and profit equation. It shows us graphically the relationship between profits and sales volume.

There are some limitations to break-even analysis:

1. Break-even analysis shows profit at various levels of sales but does not show profitability. Since there are always alternative uses for your firm's financial resources, it is impossible to compare products for profitability solely on the basis of break even, yet profitability should be one of the major points of consideration. For a profitability comparison, you must use one of the financial ratio analyses.

2. Break-even analyses do not allow you to examine cash flow. It is generally accepted that one appropriate way to compare investment or capital budgeting alternatives is to consider the value of cash flows over a period of time and to discount the cost of capital by an appropriate percentage. This cannot be done with break-even analyses either.

The Strategy Implementation Time Schedule

The final section in your marketing plan should be a time schedule showing an overview of your strategy implementation and the time when each task will be completed. This is shown in Figure 15.5. The strategy implementation time schedule is extremely important, letting you know when you are supposed to do what, and it will greatly assist you in management control, as well as showing any reader of your marketing plan that you really know what you are doing.

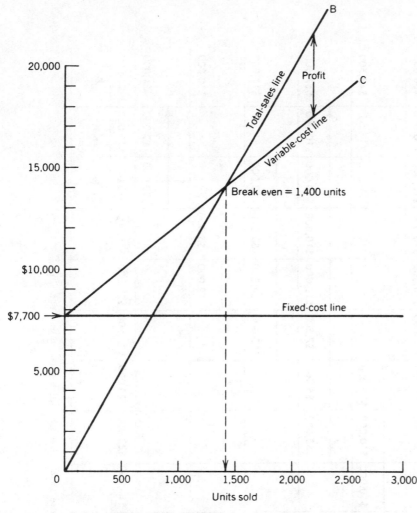

Figure 15.4. Break-even analysis chart.

Hints for Writing Your Marketing Plan

Some general comments about writing a marketing plan follow:

   1. *Establish your credibility.*   Remember that your firm and this project have unique advantages; if not, you should not proceed with the project. State these advantages clearly.

   2. *Document supporting facts about new concepts or ideas.*   Remember that not everyone reading your marketing plan has your knowledge or experience. Therefore, new concepts or ideas should be carefully documented and described from established sources.

   3. *Be optimistic, but be truthful.*   There are always disadvantages or problems, but if you can anticipate them and indicate how you will overcome them, it will not only help in implementing the marketing plan at the appropriate time but will assist in convincing readers that your marketing plan can be implemented.

Weeks after Project Initiation

Task	1	2	3	4	5	6	7	8	9	10	11	Total
Development and placement ads	$5,000	$5,000	$5,000	$5,000	$5,000	$5,000	$10,000	$10,000	$10,000	$10,000	$10,000	$80,000
Product manufacture, model I		$5,000	$7,500	$10,000	$10,000	$10,000						$42,500
Product manufacture, model II					$5,000	$5,000	$7,500	$10,000	$10,000	$10,000	$10,000	$57,500
Schedule promotional model II							$3,000	$3,000	$3,000	$3,000		$12,000
Running new contribution channel								$5,000	$5,000			$10,000
Phase-out promotion model I										$2,000	$2,000	$4,000
Monthly totals	$5,000	$10,000	$12,500	$15,000	$20,000	$20,000	$20,500	$28,000	$28,000	$25,000	$22,000	$206,000

Total for project strategy

Figure 15.5. Strategy implementation time schedule.

4. *Emphasize your uniqueness.* You have something that is different in some way than what everyone else has. Play up this difference.

5. *Make sure your marketing plan is workable.* It is essential to have a marketing plan, but it is useless if it is not workable. After you've gone through and completed the plan, be sure that the plan fits together and that each part is reasonable and can work. Be especially critical of the cash-flow and financial aspects, as well as the anticipated sales. One of the biggest problems of marketing plans is sales realism; that is, the strategist sometimes anticipates much higher sales than can realistically be expected. Analyze your plan by asking yourself what would happen if sales were 20, 30, 40, or even 50% less than you have forecast. Analyze your costs to make sure they are also realistic. Just as sales are frequently inflated during marketing planning, costs are sometimes deflated.

6. *Update your plan.* No marketing plan is "good forever." Further, the planning is never perfect, as you cannot foresee all circumstances that you will encounter at the start. Therefore, as the plan is implemented, it will have to be revised to be kept up to date. This is not to say that your plan has to be changed daily; however, you should be on top of conditions that are changing, and the plan should be adjusted accordingly as appropriate. To do this, you should first be alert to the changes that come about in your industry, market, customers, competition, technology, and so forth. Second, check your plan against these changes to make sure that the plan is still workable and to determine what revisions are necessary in your plan.

MARKETING PLAN DEVELOPMENT FORM

To assist you in developing your marketing plan, a special marketing plan development form has been put developed and is shown in Figure 15.6. It begins by listing required information for your plan, including characteristics of customer identification; location; segments of market; growth trends; consumer attitudes and buying habits; size of market in dollars and numbers; needs of market; industry pricing; technological trends; threats and opportunities; distribution factors and structure; key success factors; identification of competing companies; size, trend, and share of market of each competitor; customers' perception of competition; comparison of competitive features; pricing in features; comparison of promotional distribution of competitor products; competitor strengths and weaknesses; competitor strategies; processes and materials; business and economic conditions; social factors; political factors; government factors; legal constraints; and internal resources for marketing, engineering, and financial resources. The form also has additional spaces for other information required to put your marketing plan together. Spaces are also allowed for listing how and where information is to be obtained and the name of an individual responsible for obtaining this information.

To assist you in strategy development, the strategy development form using the functional approach (Figure 15.7) includes price promotion and distribution promotion aspects and asks you to write a description of the strategy and then to indicate an overall cost allocation for implementing it.

The marketing plan is one of the most powerful tools of the corporate strategist for planning. Literally billions of dollars have been made or lost through its use, misuse, or nonuse. Correctly put together, the marketing plan will guide

Product _____

Required Information for Plan	How/Where Information to Be Obtained	Individual Responsible
Market Characteristics		
Customer identification and location		
Segments of market		
Growth trends		
Consumer attitudes and buying habits		
Size of market in dollars and numbers		
Needs of market		
Industry pricing		
Technological trends, threats, and opportunities		

Distribution factors and structure

Key success factors

Competition
Identification of competing companies

Size, trend, and share of market of each competitor

Customers' perception of competition

Comparison of competitive products, pricing, and features

Figure 15.6. Marketing plan development form. (Copyright © 1983 by William A. Cohen.)

347

Product _____

Required Information for Plan	How/Where Information to Be Obtained	Individual Responsible
Comparison of competitive products, promotion and distribution		
Competitor strengths and weaknesses		
Competitors' strategies		
Manufacturing and Engineering Factors Processes and materials		
Environmental Climate Business, economic conditions		
Social factors		
Political factors		

Governmental factors

Legal constraints

Internal Resources
Marketing

Engineering

Financial resources

Figure 15.6. (Continued)

	Description of Strategy	Cost ($)
Product		
Price		
Distribution		
Promotion		

Figure 15.7. Strategy development form (functional approach). (Copyright © 1983 by William A. Cohen.)

your project from start-up to successful realization of your goals and objectives. It is totally worthy of your best efforts in putting it together.

SOURCES OF ADDITIONAL INFORMATION

Basics of Successful Business Planning, by William R. Osgood, published by the American Management Association, 135 West 50th Street, New York, NY 10020.

Building Your Business Plan, by Harold J. McLaughlin, published by John Wiley & Sons, Inc., 605 Third Avenue, New York, NY 10158.

Developing a Winning Marketing Plan, by William A. Cohen, published by John Wiley & Sons, Inc., 605 Third Avenue, New York, NY 10158.

The Executive Guide to Operational Planning, by George L. Morrisey, Patrick J. Below, and Betty L. Acomb, published by Jossey-Bass Publishers, 433 California Street, San Francisco, CA 94104.

How to Prepare and Present a Business Plan, by Joseph R. Mancuso, published by Prentice-Hall, Inc., Englewood Cliffs, NJ 07632.

The Marketing Plan, by William M. Luther, published by AMACOM, a division of the American Management Association, 135 West 50th Street, New York, NY 10020.

Planning for Nonplanners, by Darryl J. Ellis and Peter P. Pekar, Jr., published by AMACOM, a division of the American Management Association, 135 West 50th Street, New York, NY 10020.

The Practice of Marketing Management, by William A. Cohen, published by Macmillan Publishing Co., 866 Third Avenue, New York, NY, 10020.

Winning on the Marketing Front, by William A. Cohen, published by John Wiley & Sons, Inc., 605 Third Avenue, New York, NY 10058.

Section III
Management Problem Solving

16

Recruiting Employees

Since recruiting can have a major impact on the future, effectiveness and efficiency of your firm, this activity is among the most important to which you can devote yourself as the head of your own company. This process can be divided into four basic steps:

1. Establishing personnel requirements
2. Establishing job specifications
3. Recruiting
4. Hiring

ESTABLISHING PERSONNEL REQUIREMENTS

The first step in the improvement process is to plan ahead for your company's needs. To do this, it is best to set a time period of from several months to a year and decide what your organization's objectives will be during this period and what the attainment of these objectives will involve. For example, if you are expanding, will you require more salespeople over the coming months or years? More production people? Are you going to develop a new product and will you need more technical people? Whatever future activities you plan, you must insure that you have the necessary personnel on board. Now is the time to start laying out your future personnel requirements.

The way to establish these personnel requirements is first to establish what your company is going to do and then to break down the overall objective into smaller steps or tasks. You then describe the kind of individual you will need to perform the task and estimate how many labor-hours will be needed from that person for each month over the period that you have selected. For additional details on how to accomplish this, see Chapter 18. If you already have individuals in your company who can do the job, you merely indicate this. But if you do have needs in the personnel area, the method shown in the chart in Figure 16.1 will enable you to lay them out clearly so that you will know exactly when you need new employees and the particular skills that they will need to have.

In some cases your need will be unforeseen, because of a termination, someone leaving, or unexpected new business. When this happens, you must readjust your forecasts, or in the case of new business, complete a new chart to help you determine the personnel requirements of the job. With the forecast chart, you will always know your requirements in detail.

Project/Task	Type of Individual Required	Hours of Work Estimated by Month											
		Jan.	Feb.	Mar.	Apr.	May	June	July	Aug.	Sep.	Oct.	Nov.	Dec.
Monthly Labor Requirements by Title (1)													
Current Labor Resources on Hand (2)													
Additional Labor Required (1) — (2)													

Figure 16.1. Chart for forecasting labor requirements.

ESTABLISHING JOB SPECIFICATIONS

At this point, you should have a list of individuals you need for the coming year as well as the month that they should be hired.

Your task now is to write a detailed description of the job you want these individuals to perform along with other factors that you consider important. For this purpose, you can use Figure 16.2, the job specification form, which details the job title, to whom the individual will report, the background on why you need the individual, the tasks that the individual will perform, desired prior experience, desired education, special problems, factors that would definitely exclude a candidate from consideration regardless of other qualifications or accomplishments, travel requirements, salary range, other compensation, and some ideas about why someone should take the job.

Figure 16.3 shows a completed job specification form. Note that even in the form the requirements are not cast in iron. You may change the job title at any time, and tasks can be added or reduced in number or in scope. Prior experience and education also should be flexible since it is what you want the individual to do and not what he or she has done already that is important. Past experience and education are important only as indicators of potential to perform work. For this reason, requirements such as a certain number of years of experience should always be flexible. The salary that you intend to pay should be noted as a range rather than as a specific value, but even the range should be considered only as a guideline, and as you interview and talk to various candidates,

1. **Job title:** _____   2. **Required by:** _____

3. **Reporting to:** _____

4. **Background:** _____

_____

_____

_____

5. **Required Tasks:** _____

_____

_____

_____

_____

6. **Desired prior experience:** _____

_____

_____

_____

7. **Desired education:** _____

_____

_____

8. **Special problems:** _____

_____

Figure 16.2. Job specification form.

_____

_____

9. **Factors that would definitely exclude a candidate from consideration:** _____

_____

_____

10. **Travel requirements:** _____

11. **Salary range:** _____

12. **Other compensation:** _____

_____

_____

13. **Why should someone take this job?** _____

_____

_____

_____

_____

Figure 16.1. (*Continued*)

you can begin to narrow the salary range that you consider appropriate. Information about the advantages of taking the job is also very important, because it allows you to put yourself in the candidate's shoes and see things from his or her perspective. Why would the type of individual that you have specified here want to go to work for you? If there are few perceived advantages, you are not going to get the kind of individual you want. If you want good people, then there should be sufficient reasons motivating them to work for your company rather than going somewhere else or staying at their present place of employment. This section will be very useful for you in your recruiting, whether you do it yourself or go through someone else, such as a personnel agency, counselor, or headhunter.

1. **Job title:** Copywriter   2. **Required by:** Jan 1st, 1987

3. **Reporting to:** Creative Director

4. **Background:** The amount of copywriting required for ads for our client has

increased to such a degree that our one copyrwiter can no longer handle it

by himself. As a result, we are suffering delays up to 30 days causing

considerable dissatisfaction with our service. Therefore our need is urgent.

5. **Required tasks:** The individual will be responsible for all copywriting

having to do with industrial sales. This includes space advertising, direct

mail, telephone, and television.

6. **Desired prior experience:** This individual must have prior experience

with copywriting for industrial products and services. Two to five years would

probably be ideal, but if the individual is really talented, we could take

someone with only one year's experience.

7. **Desired education:** College graduate. Journalism,

english, marketing, communications, advertising,

business, or psychology. However, the field isn't important.

Figure 16.3. Completed job specification form.

8. **Special problems:** The creative director is sometimes hard to get along with.

We don't want any temperamental genius.

9. **Factors that would definitely exclude a candidate from consideration:**

No college degree. Less than one year's experience as a copywriter. Too sensitive

or temperamental.

10. **Travel requirements:** Maximum 5% of time.

11. **Salary range:** $25,000–30,000 per year.

12. **Other compensation:** Health and life insurance. Retirement plan.

21 days' paid vacation per year.

13. **Why should someone take this job?** As proved by this hire, we are a growing

company. Therefore there is an opportunity for growth into management. We are

giving more days of paid vacation than anyone else in the industry (standard

is 14 days). This will be our expert for industrial copywriting. The creative

director is a graphic designer, and the other copywriter will deal only with

consumer products.

Figure 16.3. *(Continued)*

RECRUITING

Sources of Personnel

The following are all sources of personnel which you should consider:

1. Personnel currently in your own company
2. Personnel in other companies
3. Newly graduated individuals or students about to graduate from colleges or universities

4. Currently unemployed individuals
5. Job shop companies

Personnel Currently in Your Own Company.   Staffing from within your own company is a good idea in many instances, and certainly when personnel for tasks required are currently available. This not only saves you money in recruiting but can also motivate all of your employees if the new job is a promotion and the individual within your company can handle the job. There are additional advantages. An individual recruited internally is already familiar with the practices, procedures, personnel, policy, special characteristics, and other employees of your company. Therefore, in general, there will be less time required to bring the individual up to speed for the job that you want him to perform. However, when recruiting from your own company, you must be concerned with who will take over the job that the individual was doing. You must also be sure that the change of job will create no problems. Does the individual really want the job? Do not automatically assume this to be the case, even if it means a promotion. Will other employees present problems that this individual must deal with in his or her new role? This is something else you must consider.

Personnel from Other Companies.   In many instances, the necessary personnel do not exist within your own company and you must go outside the organization to recruit them. Going outside the organization has advantages. If you have sufficient time, you can hire an individual who has been successful in an identical or similar job with another company. This can increase his chances of success in the job that you have planned. In addition, bringing new people into your company will also bring in new ideas that they have picked up from other companies. Of course, there are disadvantages to recruiting outside of your company. These include the additional expense, the fact that the new personnel are unfamiliar with your company's way of operating, and possibly dissatisfaction on the part of current employees.

In our society, it is generally accepted that an individual can move from one company to another if the new company can offer a better job opportunity, and that any individual is free to go from one company to another for personal betterment. However, in considering individuals from other companies, you should attempt to ascertain his or her current state of mind, because it will affect the candidate's readiness to come to your company and it will also influence how you handle the employment interview. Remember, just because an executive recruiter is successful in going into a firm and pulling out an individual for a specific job, this does not mean that the individual was unhappy in his or her job. Quite the opposite may have been true. The individual may have been perfectly happy in his or her old job, and executive recruiters often argue that these individuals make the best new employees; if they were happy in their former employment they should be happy in your employ as well. With a job candidate who is currently happily employed, you need to present the job situation in its best light. This is where your reasons why someone should take this job are very important.

Newly Graduated Individuals or Students About to Graduate from Colleges or Universities.   Most individuals newly graduated from institutions of higher learning go to larger companies, since larger companies offer training programs which initiate them into the industry and functional area they have chosen and can usually offer higher salaries. Also, because large companies send recruiters out all over the country in search of newly graduated talent, it is difficult for you as a small company to compete for this source of candidates. However, you can offer certain advantages to a college graduate that a larger company cannot offer. These include the possibility of rapid advancement, better visibility to top management, and more responsibility earlier. In fact, many individuals from college consider small companies more fun to work in and even seek them out. Further, if there are colleges or universities close by, you will not even have to bear a heavy travel expense to do this type of recruiting. All you need to do is to call the placement offices of colleges and universities in your geographical area. By emphasizing what you have to offer, you can successfully (and inexpensively) compete with larger companies for many top quality college graduates.

Currently Unemployed Individuals.   A potential employee for your company may be currently unemployed because he or she was fired, quit, or was laid off from a previous job. None of these reasons need reflect unfavorably on your candidate. However, it should be routine to find out as much as you can about the former employment and why the individual left the former job. Many companies do not like to hire unemployed individuals, preferring individuals who are currently holding a job. However, this is a prejudice which has no validity. Many unemployed individuals are outstanding candidates, even for high-level jobs in your company.

Job Shop Companies.   Job shop companies are known by various names, some less than flattering, but they are a source of skilled temporary help, even though in many large companies job shop individuals are used for periods as long as a year or more. What the job shop offers you is an individual who is rented out to you on an as-needed basis. The job shop company hires the individual and pays all fringe benefits concerned as well as salary. The advantage to the individual is that he or she is paid at a slightly higher rate than if he or she were working for one company and is guaranteed continued employment with less chance of a layoff from work than might otherwise be the case. To you, the advantage is that you will have personnel for short-term projects but you will not need to retain them when there is no more work for them. Of course, there is a disadvantage as well, and that is that it is difficult to make a "job shopper" an integral part of your company. He or she is unlikely to be as committed to your goals as your permanent employees since the term of employment is most definitely limited. Also, it is more difficult to control proprietary information with your company when you're using job shoppers. For more details on this, see Chapter 18.

Selection of the Right Recruiting Method

The recruiting methods that you should use will depend on many factors including your company, industry, the type of employee you seek, the job market at the time that you're doing your recruiting, and how long you are willing to look.

The methods discussed in the following paragraphs each have their own advantages and disadvantages. Some methods are very time consuming: advertising in certain magazines read by individuals owning the specialty for which you're looking, for example. The lead time for the ad to appear may be several months. Other methods may be very expensive: executive recruiting firms, for instance. You may be expected to pay as much as 30% of the annual compensation of the candidate in return for the firm's finding you a suitable candidate. Even employment agencies will require a fee of from 10 to 15% of annual compensation for their services. Some methods such as word of mouth which costs nothing are fine if you are not in a hurry, but may not be desirable at all if you need someone at once.

Word-of-Mouth Recruiting

Word of mouth is perhaps the easiest and the least expensive recruitment method. You or someone in your employ simply calls around to likely sources such as friends and professional associates and asks them if they would be interested in the position that you have, or if they know someone else who would be who meets the qualifications that you seek. This method has several advantages. As indicated before, it doesn't cost anything. It is also easy. There is no special procedure involved; anyone can do it. And either you know the individual yourself or your friends or associates know the individual. However, there are also disadvantages with this type of recruiting campaign. First, you will not reach as many potential candidates as you might otherwise. Also, if you are receiving recommendations from people who are friends of the candidate, the qualifications of the candidate may be somewhat colored by this relationship. If for one reason or another you want your hiring to be done without the knowledge of others, potential competitors or potential customers, you will not be able to use word of mouth. Finally, this process may not work very quickly.

Advertising for Candidates

Advertising for new candidates is expensive, but if your advertisement is reasonably well put together it will bring in applicants to fill the position for which you are advertising. If you are in a hurry, then you will probably run display or classified advertisements in the business section of your local paper or the *Wall Street Journal*. On the other hand, if you have time, then it may be wise to consider advertising in professional magazines that are read by individuals in the desired field. Such magazines may require a month to six weeks or more of lead time before the advertisement appears.

It is possible when you advertise to keep secret the fact that you are searching for new employees to fill certain designated positions. You can run a "blind ad" which gives a box number instead of the name of your company. The box number is provided by the newspaper or magazine that you have chosen. For a slight additional fee, they will collect all the responses to your ad and forward them to you. When considering a blind advertisement versus an open advertisement, however, you must also recognize that a blind advertisement will pull fewer responses than an open advertisement, since some potential candidates will be concerned about the identity of the advertiser. Needless to say, they have no desire for their present company to know that they have responded as a potential candidate for a new job.

If you are going to advertise, you should know what the competition is for the employees you seek to hire. This competition can be readily assessed by viewing the help wanted section of the Sunday edition of your local newspaper. Check the classified ads under the appropriate job description and also the display ads in the business section. By studying competitive ads you will get a general idea of what jobs are being offered in your geographical area. It is important once again for you to ask yourself the question: "Why should someone respond to my ad and go to work for me?" Use the information that you've put together in your job specification form to construct an ad that's interesting and well written, one that will attract many qualified candidates for the job that you are seeking to fill. Use the AIDA formula. AIDA stands for attention, interest, desire, and action. You write your ad with a headline to attract attention. Elaborate on the headline with job benefits to arouse interest and then state more benefits and the qualifications you are seeking. Finally, invite the prospective job candidate to act by asking for his or her résumé and salary history.

One major advantage of advertising is that you will be able to locate candidates fairly rapidly for the position. Also, the method is reasonably certain. Unless the competition is overwhelming, your ad is really poorly constructed and written, or the terms that you advertise are just not competitive, you are going to get enough responses to enable you to fill the position.

The biggest disadvantage of advertising as a method of securing candidates is the cost. Even a single display ad can run a thousand dollars or more. Another disadvantage is the fact that you will only reach candidates who are seeking a position. This would appear to be an advantage—isn't that what you want, after all, individuals who are looking for work? However, for some positions, you may want to recruit individuals who are perfectly happy and content and performing well for other companies. This may be especially true for high-level jobs. You will not reach such individuals through advertising since they will not be looking in the employment section of newspapers. Also, even if by chance such an individual reads your ad, rarely will the information be sufficient an enticement to encourage this candidate to make up a résumé to send to you. Finally, if you are seeking a job specialty which is in great demand at the time of your search, you may not be able to find sufficient potential candidates or qualified candidates through advertising.

Government Employment Agencies

Government employment agencies, local and state, may be of assistance in finding suitable employees for your company. The quality of candidates that they provide varies widely from place to place and time to time. Candidates from government employment agencies generally appear to be somewhat less well qualified for professional positions than candidates from other sources. The reason for this is that many professionals do not register with government employment agencies except as a last resort. However, it is always worthwhile checking with government employment agencies. It costs you nothing and you may find just the right candidate.

Employment Agencies and Executive Recruiters

Although employment agencies and executive recruiters are collectively known as headhunters and in both cases you pay money for their services, the two differ in a number of ways.

Executive recruiters or executive search firms in general go after higher level candidates than do employment agencies. In theory, executive recruiters or search firms will actually go into other companies by telephone and find and recruit exactly the right candidate for you. For these services, you may pay 30% of the annual compensation or more. Many times these firms will operate only on retainer, and you must pay them a basic fee whether or not a candidate is sent to you that you ultimately hire. For this reason, this type of recruiter should be reserved for very top candidates and used only at a time when you can afford this special service.

Employment agencies may recruit from other companies as well, but they tend to rely primarily on applicants who register with them, and while some may require a retainer in the same way as search firms, most operate on contingency only. This means that you only pay the employment agency if you hire a candidate that the employment agency sends to you for an interview. Obviously this has major advantages for the small firm which cannot afford to finance a search which may not be successful. Each individual agency has its own fee schedule; they generally start at a low 10% and may go as high as 30%.

The difference today between an executive search firm and an agency is in some cases very blurred. Many executive search firms work on contingency as well as on retainer. Many employment agencies will recruit for very top level positions that pay $100,000 a year or more, even though the average employee that they place makes much less. However, many states require that any organization that recruits candidates compensated below a certain amount must obtain a state agency license, while above that amount an agency license is unnecessary.

There are also agencies around that collect fees from the individual job applicant. You must be much more careful with the candidates that you interview coming from this source because the agency is far more likely to try to sell you a candidate than to send you the best person available for the job.

If you are dealing with a professional recruiter, whether he is in a search firm or an agency, this source of candidates can offer a number of advantages to you. For one thing, you can be very precise in the requirements that you set for potential candidates. This can save you a great deal of time screening numerous résumés and interviewing applicants who are not qualified for the job. Also, if you yourself recruit from a competing firm, you can run into legal difficulties. However, if a search firm or employment agency does this for you, you are probably off the hook legally. Finally, there is usually some type of guarantee if you hire the candidate and he or she quits work after a short period of time, or for some reason proves to be unsatisfactory. This is something you most definitely should investigate prior to giving the okay to any type of headhunter. Guarantees may run up to as long as a year, with the firm required to return your money or to recruit a new candidate for you.

One final word of caution on using a headhunter or search firm. Get some idea before you pay a retainer as to how fast the recruiter is going to work and when you can expect to interview the first candidate.

You should expect any personnel agency, employment agency, or search firm that you deal with to screen the candidates for you. How much screening you get really depends upon the agency involved. On the low end, if you are paying something like 10%, probably all you're going to get is basic screening of résumés. On the high end, with an executive search firm on a retainer, you can expect many candidates to be approached, some candidates to be screened face to face, references to be checked, and three to five candidates, all of whom meet your qualifications, to be submitted to you for your consideration. Other firms' services will fall somewhere in the middle. Perhaps references will be checked, candidates will be talked to and screened, but the screening will not be done in as thorough a manner as would be the case if you were paying on a retainer basis.

Another organization that you should consider contacting is a national organization known as "Forty Plus." This is a self-help agency composed of individuals who have reached the age of 40 or older and who are currently unemployed. These individuals pay a small fee and may donate their time to helping out the organization. The result is that you will see qualified candidates, and even if you hire them, you pay nothing.

If you're going to use a headhunter, it is well to talk to other small business-people who have also used headhunters since the quality varies so much.

Recruiting through the Schools

School recruiting is an excellent way for a small businessperson to acquire outstanding candidates for professional positions. For one thing, such candidates are frequently well trained, having received their bachelor's degree or an advanced degree, and eager to start work. They can be easily motivated to do a good job for you and yet their salaries are much lower than you would have to pay for a more experienced but perhaps less well qualified employee.

As pointed out earlier, you do not need to run around the country recruiting as does a major company. In fact, you need not do any face-to-face recruiting at all. If you are fortunate enough to live near a large city where there are many colleges and universities, place a telephone call to the career development office or to the department that teaches a subject likely to produce candidates for the job that you have open. This can produce very good results. Over the phone, you should indicate that you have a position open, what the qualifications are, some advantages for coming to work for you, and where you can be reached in order to set up an interview.

Depending upon how lucrative the position is and the job market in your area for these new graduates, you may or may not get a number of candidates for your job. However, this is a very easy way to recruit, and a very inexpensive one. You should not overlook it when seeking potential employees.

Professional Associations

Many professional associations will allow you to place recruiting advertisements in their newsletters or will act as a clearinghouse for job openings as a service to the members of the association. In many cases, this will cost you nothing—a major advantage for using this method. The disadvantage, as with many other low-cost methods, is that there are no assurances that you will get large numbers of candidates. In fact, you may not receive any applicants at all for the job. But you should consider professional associations as a supplemental source of job candidates.

Some Additional Recruiting Tips

1. Make sure you know exactly what you are looking for and the skills required, and develop a complete job specification as on the form shown everytime it's necessary for you to do recruiting.

2. Make certain that whoever answers the phone at your company has full information about the position so that he or she can answer inquiries about it if you are unavailable.

3. If your recruiting is going to bring in large numbers of résumés of candidates, then set minimum standards for these candidates and establish a list of these minimum standards so that someone else can screen these inquiries for you.

4. Let your other employees know about the position and give them a brief description from your job specification so that they can do free recruiting for you.

5. Select your recruiting methods based on your particular situation, but be certain to use all appropriate means of bringing in job candidates, especially those that are free.

6. If an advertisement under one heading fails to bring in an adequate number of qualified candidates, then try a different job heading or a slightly different job title.

7. If you decide to use a recruiter or an employment agency, visit the firm so that you can know better the headhunter who will be working for you. Also, ask if they can supply you with three names of clients not in your business who have been happy with their operation whom you may contact.

8. If you do a great deal of hiring, conduct an audit from time to time to see what your hiring costs are and which recruiting methods work best.

9. When you receive job applicants from organizations or associations which do not get paid, be certain to thank them for their time and effort in referring candidates or applicants to you.

HIRING

The hiring process consists of three steps: screening, interviewing, and making the offer. Let's look at each in turn.

Applicant Screening

If you used an employment agency or a search firm, the applicants have already been screened prior to the interview. In this case, you will be presented with a number of candidates and the amount of work that you will have to do along these lines is greatly reduced. On the other hand, if you've used any of the other methods, then you will have received résumés—sometimes quite a few. For example, a really good job at the professional level may bring in 500 to 800 résumés if you are located in a large urban area. Going through this number of résumés is a time-consuming and exacting task. However, if you establish basic requirements and communicate them to someone else, it may be easier and less expensive for a secretary or some other employee of yours to go through these résumés for you and reduce them to a reasonable amount. If the initial screening fails to weed out very many, then you can tighten up on the requirements and continue screening until you have a workable number. Remember that interviewing a candidate for a job also takes time. Therefore, the initial screening should pare the number of candidates down so that you see no more than 6 to 10. Some companies have the personnel manager do the initial screening, selecting 10 candidates from the résumés, and then the personnel manager sees these 10 himself or herself, and selects five candidates who will be interviewed by the executive doing the hiring. Use your own judgment in this, but don't spend all of your time interviewing, especially if it is not for a top-level job.

Opinions differ as to whether you should talk to references of the applicants prior to the interview. My feeling is not to do so until mutual interest has been established. Even if you only call three references for each candidate, when you are considering five candidates, that's 15 different telephone calls. Also, many candidates or applicants will not give you references until mutual interest is established as a result of the interview. The reason for this is that they do not want their references bothered by every single company with whom they interview. However, regardless of when you do a reference check, make certain that it is done prior to hiring. In fact, if you delay the reference check until after the offer, the offer should be contingent upon favorable references. Perhaps the best method is to interview the candidates and get permission to check references of one or two candidates you are seriously interested in. Assuming the references check out, you can extend the offer. Regardless of when the reference check is made, the following items should be checked:

1. How long the reference has known the candidate
2. Under what circumstances he or she has known the candidate
3. The candidate's personal qualities—honesty, reliability, dependability, and so forth
4. The candidate's general background
5. Specific items that you feel are relevant to this particular position, including years on the job, managerial experience if applicable, and what exactly the individual accomplished while working on the job

Don't be surprised if occasionally a reference does not check out, even though the candidate appears outstanding for the job. Sometimes a reference that the candidate feels will be a good one turns out to be a negative one because of jealousy or some other reason. When that happens, look at the overall situation. If two out of three references are positive and only one is bad, you might want to get back and ask for additional references. On the other hand, if the general pattern of references is bad, you may wish to drop the candidate.

Another thing you must not overlook when checking references is questioning individuals who have supervised the candidate in the past. A candidate would have to be very foolish to give you the name of someone he knows will not give a good reference. However, he or she doesn't always have the same control when dealing with former employers.

Interviewing the Candidate

To get the maximum out of the interview, you must prepare for and plan the interview ahead of time.

One of the most important steps and one that is frequently overlooked is to be sure that you will not be continually interrupted during the interview. If you are, your train of thought will be broken, and the candidate will be impressed with your lack of consideration for him or her. It may cause the candidate to turn down the offer even though he or she is ideal for the job.

If you have time prior to the interview, mail out a job applicant's form about a week before the interview and ask the candidate to complete the form and return it to you. The job applicant's form is more valuable than a résumé in that it forces the candidate to list more complete information in some sort of chronological order. A clever applicant for a job can structure his or her résumé around your requirements and keep information that may negatively affect his or her chances at the job out of your reach. But it is to your advantage to get all the information that you can. A suitable form is shown in Figure 16.4.

Before the actual interview, you should review this application form and the résumé and other information you have about the candidate. Write down information that you feel is missing that you want to get from the candidate. Also, review the candidate's background against your job specification form very carefully and develop a list of questions you want to ask. Write down a syllabus for the candidate's interview. Also, put down things that you wish to take place. Doing this planning ahead of time will make the interview most fruitful for you and for the candidate. It will show your interest in seeing that he or she will be happy in the position, and he or she will learn something about the company and have an easier time making his or her decision to come to work for you.

If possible, arrange for the candidate to be interviewed by at least two other individuals in your company beside yourself. Select these individuals carefully—individuals who have a good understanding of what the job will require and what the company is looking for. Such multiple interviewing has many advantages. For one thing, it brings in someone else's opinion. Also, sometimes other interviewers will pick up things that you did not. Finally, it allows the candidate to meet other members of your company and gives the candidate a better idea of what your company is like and what's going to be required of him or her as a part of the job.

You want the candidate to relax as much as possible. Do not put the candidate under pressure unless being under pressure is part of the job. Here is the general procedure to follow. First, ask very general and open questions to get the candidate to talk. Also, note those aspects of the candidate that you would like to know more about and write these down. Then, ask the more specific and detailed questions you wrote down during your planning. Get the candidate to do most of the talking. At some point you should try to find out what you can about the candidate's current or former compensation and what salary figure he or she has in mind for the position. Finally, even if you do not have a company tour, let the candidate know that you are interested by telling him or her more about the job and its importance to the company, fringe benefits, and so forth. Promise that you will get back to the candidate as soon as a decision is made, but do not make an offer at this time, no matter how good the candidate seems. Always wait to think it over and if possible to compare notes with other interviewers.

If the candidate is a skilled interviewee, he or she will have done considerable homework and learned everything possible about your company and the job. The interviewee may even have made up a list of questions to ask you. The purpose of these questions is to exhibit his or her alertness and interest. The candidate may also wish to learn exactly what you want so that he or she can best answer your questions when you ask them. Do not allow yourself to be drawn into answering questions in detail until you have your own questions answered.

PROFESSIONAL EMPLOYMENT APPLICATION 1-93122 R7

PERSONAL RECORD

LAST NAME | FIRST NAME | MIDDLE OR MAIDEN NAME | SOCIAL SECURITY NUMBER | DATE

PRESENT ADDRESS: STREET NO. | STREET | APT.# | CITY | STATE | ZIP | AREA CODE | PHONE | DATE OF BIRTH MO DAY YEAR

PERMANENT ADDRESS: STREET NO. | STREET | APT.# | CITY | STATE | ZIP | AREA CODE | PHONE | MARITAL STATUS S M W D SEP

TYPE OF WORK DESIRED | DATE AVAIL. FOR EMPL. | NO. DEPENDENTS

SECURITY CLEARANCE ☐ YES ☐ NO IF YES, SHOW: | LEVEL | ISSUING AUTHORITY | DATE | U.S. CITIZEN | BIRTH CERTIF. AVAILABLE? | WOULD YOU OBJECT TO A PHYS. EXAM. BY OUR DR.?

NAME ANY PHYSICAL DISABILITIES | HEIGHT | WEIGHT | TIME LOST FROM WORK DURING LAST TWELVE MONTHS DUE TO ILLNESS | PRESENT DRAFT CLASSIFICATION | RESERVE STATUS ☐ ACTIVE ☐ INACTIVE ☐ READY ☐ STANDBY

MILITARY SERVICE BRANCH | PRINCIPAL MILITARY EXPERIENCE | MILITARY RANK | MILITARY SERVICE DATES FROM TO | TYPE OF DISCHARGE

MILITARY SERVICE BRANCH | PRINCIPAL MILITARY EXPERIENCE | MILITARY RANK | MILITARY SERVICE DATES FROM TO | TYPE OF DISCHARGE

MILITARY SERVICE BRANCH | PRINCIPAL MILITARY EXPERIENCE | MILITARY RANK | MILITARY SERVICE DATES FROM TO | TYPE OF DISCHARGE

HAVE YOU EVER WORKED FOR ANY LTV COMPANY? ☐ YES ☐ NO | FROM | TO | WHAT DIVISION? | TYPE OF WORK

EDUCATION —

HIGH SCHOOL NAME | HIGH SCHOOL CITY | HIGH SCHOOL STATE | HIGH SCHOOL GRADUATION DAY MONTH YEAR | YEARS OF H.S. COMPLETED

COLLEGE/UNIVERSITY		YEARS ATTENDED	MAJOR FIELD OF EDUCATION	HOURS FOR DEGREE		OVERALL CUM GRD POINT (A-4.0)	YEAR GRADU-ATED	DEGREE
NAME	CITY AND STATE	FROM MO/YR TO MO/YR		COMP.	REQ'D			

DID YOU GRADUATE FROM COLLEGE? ☐ YES ☐ NO | AVERAGE NUMBER HOURS WORKED DURING SCHOOLING _____ PER WEEK | PERCENTILE CLASS STANDING: UPPER ☐ 10% ☐ 25% ☐ 50% ☐ 75% | PERCENT COLLEGE EXPENSES EARNED

LIST ANY OTHER INFORMATION SUCH AS PUBLICATIONS, INVENTIONS, SCIENTIFIC AWARDS, FRATERNITIES, HONORARIES, ETC.
LIST ANY SPECIAL COURSES IN MATH OR SCIENCE WHICH YOU HAVE TAKEN THAT MAY OR MAY NOT BE RELATED TO YOUR BACKGROUND.

PROFESSIONAL ORGANIZATIONS					LICENSE/PROF. CERT.		
NAME		FROM	TO	OFFICES HELD	NUMBER	STATE	FIELD CODE

EMERGENCY NOTIFICATION NAME | STREET ADDRESS | CITY | STATE ZIP | A C PHONE | RELATION

DO NOT WRITE BELOW THIS SPACE. SKIP TO REVERSE SIDE

HIRE TYPE CODE | MONTHS OF EXPER. | STARTED WORK | OCCUPATION GROUP AND DASH NUMBER | VETERAN CODE | NHR CODE | INTERVIEWER'S CODE | H/S CODE

SHIFT CODE | UNIT | JOB CODE | GRADE | LOC. CODE | RATE | EMPLOYEE NUMBER

THE AGE DISCRIMINATION ACT OF 1967 PROHIBITS DISCRIMINATION ON THE BASIS OF AGE WITH RESPECT TO INDIVIDUALS WHO ARE AT LEAST 40 BUT LESS THAN 65 YEARS OF AGE.

Figure 16.4. Job applicant's form.

EMPLOYMENT RECORD
1-93122 R7 (BP)

THIS MUST BE COMPLETED EVEN IF A RESUME IS ATTACHED. START WITH YOUR MOST RECENT EMPLOYMENT AND LIST ALL JOBS YOU HAVE HELD, INCLUDING MILITARY SERVICE. COVER ALL YOUR TIME SINCE LEAVING SCHOOL, WHETHER EMPLOYED OR NOT. BE SURE TO GIVE CORRECT ADDRESSES OF PREVIOUS EMPLOYERS. ADDITIONAL INFORMATION MAY BE PLACED ON A SEPARATE SHEET AND ATTACHED.

MAY WE CONTACT YOUR PRESENT EMPLOYER? [ ] YES [ ] NO

EMPLOYER _____ PHONE NO. _____

ADDRESS _____

NAME AND TITLE OF SUPERVISOR _____

YOUR POSITION AND DUTIES _____

RATE OF PAY MONTHLY		EMPLOYED		TOTAL MONTHS
STARTING	ENDING	FROM MO YR	TO MO YR	

REASON FOR LEAVING _____

NO. HRS/WK WORKED

EMPLOYER _____ PHONE NO. _____

ADDRESS _____

NAME AND TITLE OF SUPERVISOR _____

YOUR POSITION AND DUTIES _____

RATE OF PAY MONTHLY		EMPLOYED		TOTAL MONTHS
STARTING	ENDING	FROM MO YR	TO MO YR	

REASON FOR LEAVING _____

NO. HRS/WK WORKED

EMPLOYER _____ PHONE NO. _____

ADDRESS _____

NAME AND TITLE OF SUPERVISOR _____

YOUR POSITION AND DUTIES _____

RATE OF PAY MONTHLY		EMPLOYED		TOTAL MONTHS
STARTING	ENDING	FROM MO YR	TO MO YR	

REASON FOR LEAVING _____

NO. HRS/WK WORKED

EMPLOYER _____ PHONE NO. _____

ADDRESS _____

NAME AND TITLE OF SUPERVISOR _____

YOUR POSITION AND DUTIES _____

RATE OF PAY MONTHLY		EMPLOYED		TOTAL MONTHS
STARTING	ENDING	FROM MO YR	TO MO YR	

REASON FOR LEAVING _____

NO. HRS/WK WORKED

RELATIVES EMPLOYED BY LTV AEROSPACE CORPORATION

NAME	RELATIONSHIP	WHERE EMPLOYED

LIST FOUR REFERENCES OTHER THAN RELATIVES AND FORMER EMPLOYERS WHO HAVE KNOWN YOU FOR AT LEAST FIVE YEARS

NAME	ADDRESS (STREET, CITY, STATE, ZIP)	OCCUPATION	A/C	PHONE

CAN YOU TAKE SHORTHAND? _____ TYPE? _____ READ AIRCRAFT BLUEPRINTS? _____ LIST OFFICE AND FACTORY MACHINES YOU

WPM _____ WPM _____ READ SCHEMATICS? _____ CAN OPERATE _____

SCORE _____ SCORE _____

FOREIGN LANGUAGE ABILITY

LANGUAGE	SPEAK	UNDER-STAND	READ	WRITE
	[ ]	[ ]	[ ]	[ ]
	[ ]	[ ]	[ ]	[ ]
	[ ]	[ ]	[ ]	[ ]

STARTING SALARY EXPECTED

I CERTIFY THAT, TO THE BEST OF MY KNOWLEDGE AND BELIEF, THE ANSWERS AND STATEMENTS ON THIS FORM ARE CORRECT WITHOUT OMISSIONS OF ANY KIND. I UNDERSTAND THAT ANY FALSE INFORMATION CONTAINED IN THE APPLICATION IS CAUSE FOR DISCHARGE AT ANY TIME.

_____
APPLICANT'S SIGNATURE

Figure 16.4. (Continued)

Here are some tips you should consider in any interview that you conduct to recruit new employees for your company.

1. Make the applicant feel comfortable and attempt to establish a friendly, personal relationship.

2. Make certain that you ask the questions that you have listed prior to the interview before the applicant asks questions of you.

3. Make certain the applicant has the necessary qualifications for the job.

4. Determine whether the applicant has the personal characteristics required for the job.

5. Try to discover what the applicant's attitude toward the position in your company is. Remember, you are looking for someone for a long-term relationship and do not want the person you hire to quit after a few weeks or a few months.

6. Always let the applicant do more talking than you do. In fact, a good way to start is to ask the candidate to tell you something about him- or herself.

7. Take notes on any information that you think is important or that you may wish to talk or ask about later.

8. Make sure you probe to get some idea of what the applicant is seeking in the way of compensation. This may affect your own tactics when making the offer later on.

9. Make sure any questions you ask conform with equal employment opportunity practices.

10. You should know and be able to explain everything about the job, including the basic duties, the salary range, the fringe benefits, any overtime hours expected, possibility of travel, and so forth.

Equal Employment Opportunity Laws

Equal employment opportunity laws state that you may not discriminate against an applicant on the basis of the applicant's race, religion, sex, national origin, or age. Some of the laws in the purview of equal opportunity employment are discussed below.

Equal Pay Act of 1963. This act prohibits employers from paying lower wages to an employee involved in producing, buying, or selling goods because of the sex of the employee. The act makes it illegal for employers to discriminate against employees on the basis of sex by paying lower wages to employees of one sex who within the same establishment perform equal work on a job requiring equal skill, effort, and responsibility, and who are performing under similar working conditions except where payment is based on:

1. The seniority system
2. A merit system
3. A system which measures earnings by quantity or quality of production
4. A differential based on any factor other than sex

Title VII, Civil Rights Act of 1964. This act is intended to eliminate any form of discrimination in employment based upon an individual's race, color, religion, sex, or national origin. Specifically, Title VII states that it shall be unlawful employment practice for an employer to:

1. Fail or refuse to hire or to discharge any individual or otherwise discriminate against any individual with respect to compensation, terms, conditions or privileges of employment because of such individual's race, color, religion, sex or national origin, or 2. Limit, segregate or classify employees (or applicants for employment) in any way which would deprive or tend to deprive any individual of employment opportunities or otherwise adversely affect his or her status as an employee because of such individual's race, color, religion, sex or national origin.

The Age Discrimination and Employment Act of 1967.   This act prohibits discrimination on the basis of age against individuals who are between the ages of 40 and 64, inclusive, with the exception of cases in which age is a bona fide occupational qualification. For example, certain federal statutory and regulatory requirements impose compulsory age limitations on a few occupations for the safety of the public. Positions such as those requiring actors for youthful or elderly roles or persons who will advertise or promote products aimed toward youthful or elderly clientele often cannot be filled by individuals other than those in the appropriate age range.

The Equal Employment Opportunity Act of 1972.   This act gives the Equal Employment Opportunity Commission the authority to file suits in federal courts against violators of the Civil Rights Act. The 1972 amendment also extends the coverage of the Title VII act to employment relationships in most government agencies, and states that employers who follow federally approved affirmative action plans for 12 months cannot be denied or suspended from a government contract without a special hearing.

How to Be an Equal Opportunity Employer.   According to the Small Business Administration, to employ fairly you do not have to remember a lot of regulations. There's only one basic rule that you must keep in mind. The questions you ask, verbally or in writing on an employment form or in any other fashion, and any other test you administer must be relevant to the work for which the applicant is applying. Also, you must recognize that even if you do not intend to discriminate, if you ask the wrong questions you may cause an applicant to believe that you are prejudiced and the applicant may file a complaint against you. If you are found guilty of discrimination, even though you are a small business, size is no defense. You may be sued. Therefore, be very careful. To ask for the following information is considered discriminatory unless for some reason the information being gathered for employment is job related and essential for occupational qualification, or necessary for national or state security. Note that some of these questions may have been asked in the past, and you may consider them very innocent. Remember, they may be considered discriminatory.

1. Marital status
2. Birthplace
3. Age
4. Religion
5. How or when citizenship was attained

6. Extracurricular and nonprofessional affiliations or memberships in organizations

7. Wife's maiden name

8. Applicant's maiden name

9. Relatives [Note: After employment, you may request names of persons (do not specify relatives) who should be notified in case of an accident or emergency.]

10. How skill in foreign language was acquired

11. Arrests for crime (It is illegal to discharge or refuse to hire an employee who answers arrest record questions falsely. You may, however, ask questions regarding whether or not a person was ever *convicted* of a crime.)

12. Children

13. Physical size and weight

14. Garnishments of wages or salaries

15. Bond refusals

16. Possessions (whether applicant owns a home, car, etc.)

17. Spouse's job or father's/mother's job

18. Requesting a photograph of the applicant

Making the Offer

Once you have settled on a single candidate to make the offer to, state your offer either by telephone or in person. Generally, assuming the amount is fair, you should open at from 10 to 15% lower than what you think the person will accept. Some candidates will state a minimum figure which is really the maximum amount they feel they can get, and they may be perfectly willing to accept 10 to 15% less if this is a fair amount and not lower than the approximate going rate for the work. If the person is inflexible regarding the amount that he or she wants and you really wish to hire the candidate, then you can always allow yourself to be negotiated up to a higher figure in your predetermined range.

If the candidate asks for an unreasonably high figure which is well out of your range, you can explain to the candidate that while you want to hire him or her, the salary is too high and is not reasonable considering the going rate. Offer what you think the job is worth and emphasize other positive aspects of the job such as promotion opportunities, fringe benefits, and so forth.

Always keep in mind that your objective during negotiations is not to hire at the lowest figure possible, as even if you succeed in doing this it will probably make for an unhappy employee, and that you definitely don't want. Rather, your objective is to hire at the lowest fair price.

What to Do with Candidates You Do Not Hire

You should always endeavor to let unsuccessful candidates or applicants down gently. After all, they've gone to considerable trouble for you, submitting résumés, being interviewed, and allowing their references to be checked. Every candidate who has seen you in a face-to-face interview should be contacted after you have made your decision. You should explain to each that while he or she was an outstanding finalist for the job, you have made the decision to hire someone else. Thank him or her for coming for the interview. If the statement is true, tell the unsuccessful candidate that you would like to consider him or her for future positions with the company. In this way, you keep on good terms with everyone that you contact and can even use some of the unsuccessful candidates as potential candidates for future jobs. This could be extremely important if something went wrong with the deal you've already struck. If for any reason the candidate you hire cancels out prior to beginning work, you don't want to start from the beginning all over again.

SOURCES OF ADDITIONAL INFORMATION

Finding and Hiring the Right Employee, Small Marketers Aids No. 106, by Rudolph Raphelson, published by the Small Business Administration, Washington, DC 20402.

Hiring the Right Man, Small Marketers Aids No. 106 (no author listed), published by the Small Business Administration, Washington, DC 20402.

Improving Personnel Selection Through New Approaches to Classification, published by the U.S. Office of Personnel Management, Washington, DC 20044.

Management's Talent Search, by Paul W. Maloney, published by the American Management Association, 135 West 50th Street, New York, NY 10020.

Recruiting and Selecting Employees, A Self-Instruction Booklet (no author listed), published by the Small Business Administration, Washington, DC 20402.

The Selection Process, by M. M. Mandell, published by the American Management Association, 135 West 50th Street, New York, NY 10020.

17

Protecting Your Idea

This chapter discusses ways in which the small businessperson can protect him or herself from competitors and potential competitors. In some cases he or she may be able to get the exclusive right to some invention, product, service, or name which can be applied to his or her business and no other. Clearly this is of no small value for the small businessperson, and this chapter is one of the most important.

WHAT IS A PATENT?

A patent for an invention is a grant by the government to an inventor which permits him or her certain rights. In the United States, a patent is granted by the government acting through the Patent and Trademark Office. The patent is good for 17 years from the date on which it was issued, except for patents on ornamental designs which are granted for terms of 14 years. The term may be extended by a special act of Congress, but this occurs extremely rarely. Once the patent expires, the inventor has no control over his invention, and anyone has the free right to use it. You should also understand that the right inferred by the government to the patent grant extends only throughout the United States and its territories and possessions. That is, a U.S. patent does not give you protection in foreign countries. For such protection, you must obtain a separate patent in each country for which protection is desired. What you gain with a patent is the right to exclude others from making, using, or selling your invention.

WHAT CAN BE PATENTED?

According to the patent law, which was first enacted in the United States in 1790, any person who "invents or discovers any new and usable process, machine, manufacture or composition of matter, or any new and useful improvements therefore, may obtain a patent."

Note that the statute refers to "composition of matter." This relates to chemical compositions and may include mixtures of ingredients as well as new chemical compounds. However, the Atomic Energy Act of 1954 excludes the patenting of inventions solely for the utilization of special nuclear material or atomic energy for atomic weapons.

The statute also specifies that the subject matter must be "useful." This means that whatever it is that you have invented must have a useful purpose and that it must be able to perform its intended purpose.

The courts have made various interpretations of this statute, and through these interpretations they have defined the limits of the subject matter which can be patented. The courts have ruled that methods of doing business, such as management by objectives, cannot be patented. Similarly, printed matter cannot be patented. Also, with regard to mixtures of ingredients, a patent cannot be granted unless there is more to the mixture than the effect of the individual components. Therefore, the combination of two or more components or ingredients in a single concoction cannot be patented unless the synergistic effect of the ingredients or components causes some greater or other benefit.

The statute says also that the invention must be new to be patentable. The invention cannot be patented if "(a) the invention was known or used by others in this country or patented or described in a printed publication in this or a foreign country before the invention thereof by the applicant for a patent, or (b) the invention was patented or described in a printed publication in this or a foreign country or in public use or sale in this country more than one year prior to the application for a patent in the United States." This means that if the invention for which you seek a patent has been described in a printed publication anywhere in the world or if it has been in public use or on sale in this country before the date that the applicant made his invention, a patent cannot be issued. If the invention has been described in a printed publication anywhere or has been in public use or on sale in this country more than one year before the date on which an application for a patent is filed in this country, a valid patent cannot be obtained.

It is important to note here that it's immaterial when the invention was made or whether the printed publication or public use was by the inventor himself or by someone else. Therefore if you, the inventor, describe the invention in a printed publication such as a magazine, use the invention publicly, or place the invention on sale, you must apply for a patent before a year has gone by or your right to a patent will be lost.

Your invention must also be sufficiently different from a similar invention that has gone before. Even if what you seek to patent involves a few differences over a similar invention, a patent may be refused if the differences are "obvious." According to the Patent and Trademark Office, the subject matter which you seek to patent must be sufficiently different from what was described before or used before so that it may be said to amount to invention over the prior art, and small advances that would be obvious to a person having ordinary skill in the art are not considered inventions capable of being patented by this interpretation. For example, simply substituting one material for another material would not enable you to patent an idea as an invention.

WHO CAN APPLY FOR A PATENT?

According to the law, only the inventor may apply for a patent on an object, with certain exceptions. If the inventor is dead, the application may be made by those who are legally authorized to represent him. If the inventor is insane or is otherwise under legal guardianship, his guardian may represent him. If an inventor is missing or refuses to apply for a patent, a joint inventor or a person having a proprietary interest in the invention may apply on behalf of the missing inventor. If a person who is not the inventor applies for a patent and is granted one, this patent would be void. Also, if an individual states that he is the inventor of an item and in fact he is not, he is subject to legal prosecution. If two or more persons make an invention jointly then they can apply as joint inventors.

Even through it is possible for an inventor to prepare the application for his own patent, this is not recommended. The procedures are very complex, and even if a patent is granted, it is unlikely that an untrained individual will secure all the rights he could to protect his invention through the patent. If you do decide to patent your invention by yourself, I would recommend reading one of the books available on this subject. One such is *Patent It Yourself!*, by David Pressman, published by Nolo Press, 950 Parker St., Berkeley, CA 94710.

Most inventors employ the services of persons known as patent attorneys or patent agents. Only certain patent attorneys and patent agents are authorized to practice before the Patent and Trademark Office, and this office maintains a register of these attorneys and agents. Those listed meet certain qualifications and demonstrate them by passing an examination. The difference between patent attorneys and patent agents is that patent attorneys are also attorneys at law. Patent agents are not. Both are fully qualified for preparing an application for a patent and conducting the prosecution in the Patent and Trademark Office. However, patent agents cannot conduct patent litigation in the courts or perform various other services which the local jurisdiction considers to be practicing law. You can get a complete list of those attorneys and agents registered to practice before the U.S. Patent and Trademark Office by from the Superintendent of Documents, Washington, D.C. 20402, or through any district office of the U.S. Department of Commerce. You can also find a patent attorney through the yellow pages of your local phone book. Once you employ a patent attorney or an agent, you execute a power of attorney or authorization of agent. This must be filed in the Patent and Trademark Office, and is usually part of the application papers. Once an attorney has been appointed, the Patent and Trademark Office won't communicate with you directly, but will conduct all correspondence with your attorney, although, of course, you are free to contact the office concerning the status of your application. You can remove the attorney or agent from your patent case by revoking the power of attorney.

PROTECTING YOUR IDEA PRIOR TO PATENTING

How do you protect your idea prior to its patenting? One recommended method of protecting your invention is to get a close friend or someone who understands your invention to sign his or her name on a dated diagram or written description of the invention. In fact, you can do this during the process of your inventing. Every couple of days, as your work progresses, you can have someone sign as a witness to your notes. This will provide evidence of the time you came up with your idea or invention in case of a dispute with others as to who developed the invention first. Another way of protecting your invention prior to patenting is through a program established by the U.S. Patent and Trademark Office. This is known as the Disclosure Document Program. You file a disclosure document with the patent office which remains on file. This protects you for a two-year period. The current fee for this service is only $6.00. If you are interested in this program, you can get a copy of the pamphlet called *The U.S. Patent Office's Disclosure Document Program* by writing to the U.S. Department of Commerce, Patent and Trademark Office, Washington, D.C. 20231.

PATENT PROCEDURES

One of the first steps in patenting, before you begin to prepare the application, is to insure that you have established "novelty." According to the patent office, this is one of the most crucial and difficult determinations to make, and it involves two things. First, you must analyze your device according to standards specified by the patent office, and second, you must see whether or not anyone else has patented the device first. The only sure way of accomplishing the second requirement is to make a search of the patent office files.

Analyzing Your Device

You should analyze your device according to the standards of what is patentable. As pointed out earlier, for a device to be patentable, it must be (1) a new, useful, and unobvious process, machine, manufacture, or composition of matter, or a new, useful, and unobvious improvement thereof; (2) a new and unobvious original and ornamental design for an article manufacturer such as a new airplane design (3) a distinct and new variety of plant, not propagated as tubes, which are asexually reproduced.

The following are not patentable: (1) an idea by itself; (2) a method of doing business; (3) printed matter; (4) an inoperable device; (5) an improvement in a device which is obvious or the result of mere mechanical skill.

Here are four government tests for novelty: (1) whether or not the device is known or used by others in this country before the invention of the applicant; (2) whether or not it was patented or described in a printed publication in this or a foreign country before the invention by the applicant; (3) whether or not it was described in a printed publication more than one year prior to the date of application for patent in the United States; (4) whether or not it was in public use or on sale in this country more than one year prior to the date of application for a patent in the United States.

Searching Existing Patents and Technical Literature

A search room is provided at the Scientific Library of the Patent and Trademark Office (the address is Crystal Plaza, 2021 Jefferson Davis Highway, Arlington, VA) where you may search and examine U.S. patents granted since 1836. In the search room, patents are arranged according to the Patent and Trademark Office classification system which includes over 300 subject classes and 64,000 subclasses. The search room also contains a set of U.S. patents arranged in numerical order and a complete set of the *Official Gazette*, the official journal relating to patents and trademarks which has been published weekly since January 1872. By searching in these classified patents, it is possible to determine whether an invention for the same or a similar device has already been granted before you actually file a patent application. It is also possible to obtain the information contained in patents relating to any field of endeavor that you desire.

However, it is not necessary for you or your attorney to travel personally to Virginia to make a search of Patent and Trademark Office files. Arrangements can be made with someone else in Arlington to do this for you. You may also order from the Patent and Trademark Office copies of lists of original patents or of cross-reference patents contained in the subclasses comprising the field of search, and inspect the printed copies of the patents in a library which has a numerically arranged set of patents. These libraries, designated as Patent Depository Libraries, receive current issues of U.S. patents and maintain collections of earlier patents. In some cases they go all the way back to 1790! These libraries are:

State	Name of Library	Telephone Contact
Alabama	Auburn University Libraries	(205) 826-4500 Ext. 21
	Birmingham Public Library	(205) 226-3680
Alaska	Anchorage Municipal Libraries	(907) 264-4481
Arizona	Tempe: Noble Library, Arizona State University	(602) 965-7609
	Little Rock: Arkansas State Library	(501) 371-2090
California	Irvine: University of California, Irvine Library	(714) 856-7234
	Los Angeles Public Library	(213) 612-3273
	Sacramento: California State Library	(916) 322-4572
	San Diego Public Library	(619) 236-5813
	Sunnyvale: Patent Information Clearinghouse*	(408) 730-7290
Colorado	Denver Public Library	(303) 571-2122
Connecticut	New Haven: Science Park Library	(203) 786-5000
Delaware	Newark: University of Delaware Library	(302) 451-2965
Florida	Fort Lauderdale: Broward County Main Library	(305) 357-7444
	Miami-Dade Public Library	(305) 375-2665
Georgia	Atlanta: Price Gilbert Memorial Library, Georgia Institute of Technology	(404) 894-4508
Idaho	Moscow: University of Idaho Library	(208) 885-6235
Illinois	Chicago Public Library	(312) 269-2865
	Springfield: Illinois State Library	(217) 782-5430
Indiana	Indianapolis-Marion County Public Library	(317) 269-1741
Louisiana	Baton Rouge: Troy H. Middleton Library, Louisiana State University	(504) 388-2570
Maryland	College Park: Engineering and Physical Sciences Library, University of Maryland	(301) 454-3037
Massachusetts	Amherst: Physical Sciences Library, University of Massachusetts	(413) 545-1370
	Boston Public Library	(617) 536-5400 Ext. 265
Michigan	Ann Arbor: Engineering Transportation Library, University of Michigan	(313) 764-7494
	Detroit Public Library	(313) 833-1450
Minnesota	Minneapolis Public Library & Information Center	(612) 372-6570

State	Name of Library	Telephone Contact
Missouri	Kansas City: Linda Hall Library	(816) 363-4600
	St. Louis Public Library	(314) 241-2288 Ext. 390
Montana	Butte: Montana College of Mineral Science and Technology Library	(406) 496-4284
Nebraska	Lincoln: University of Nebraska-Lincoln, Engineering Library	(402) 472-3411
Nevada	Reno: University of Nevada Library	(702) 784-6579
New Hampshire	Durham: University of New Hampshire Library	(603) 862-1777
New Jersey	Newark Public Library	(201) 733-7815
New Mexico	Albuquerque: University of New Mexico Library	(505) 277-5441
New York	Albany: New York State Library	(518) 474-7040
	Buffalo and Erie County Public Library	(716) 856-7525 Ext. 267
	New York Public Library (The Research Libraries)	(212) 714-8529
North Carolina	Raleigh: D. H. Hill Library, N.C. State University	(919) 737-3280
Ohio	Cincinnati & Hamilton County, Public Library of	(513) 369-6936
	Cleveland Public Library	(216) 623-2870
	Columbus: Ohio State University Libraries	(614) 422-6286
	Toledo/Lucas County Public Library	(419) 255-7055 Ext. 212
Oklahoma	Stillwater: Oklahoma State University Library	(405) 624-6546
Oregon	Salem: Oregon State Library	(503) 378-4239
Pennsylvania	Philadelphia: The Free Library	(215) 686-5330
	Pittsburgh: Carnegie Library of Pittsburgh	(412) 622-3138
	University Park: Pattee Library, Pennsylvania State University	(814) 865-4861
Rhode Island	Providence Public Library	(401) 521-8726
South Carolina	Charleston: Medical University of South Carolina Library	(803) 792-2371
Tennessee	Memphis & Shelby County Public Library and Information Center	(901) 725-8876
	Nashville: Vanderbilt University Library	(615) 322-2775
Texas	Austin: McKinney Engineering Library, University of Texas	(512) 471-1610
	College Station: Sterling C. Evans Library, Texas A & M University	(409) 845-2551
	Dallas Public Library	(214) 749-4176
	Houston: The Fondren Library, Rice University	(713) 527-8101 Ext. 2587
Utah	Salt Lake City: Marriott Library, University of Utah	(801) 581-8394
Virginia	Richmond: Virginia Commonwealth University Library	(804) 257-1104
Washington	Seattle: Engineering Library, University of Washington	(206) 543-0740

State	Name of Library	Telephone Contact
Wisconsin	Madison: Kurt F. Wendt Engineering Library, University of Wisconsin	(608) 262-6845
	Milwaukee Public Library	(414) 278-3247

All of the above-listed libraries offer CASSIS (Classification And Search Support Information System), which provides direct, on-line access to Patent and Trademark Office data.
* Collection organized by subject matter.

The Patent and Trademark Office has also prepared a microfilm list of the numbers of the patents issued in each of the subclasses, and many libraries have purchased copies of these lists. If your library has these lists and a copy of the Manual of Classification, and also a set of patent copies or the *Official Gazette*, you can begin your search without communicating with the Patent and Trademark Office at all.

A patent search can save you a lot of time and trouble by letting you know beforehand whether or not your device is patentable. It will also indicate to you whether superior devices have been patented which may already be in production, or similar technologies which may be profitable to you or your company.

THE APPLICATION FOR A PATENT

The application for a patent is made to the commissioner of patents and trademarks. It includes the following: (1) a written document which comprises a specification of description and claims and an oath or declaration; (2) a drawing in those cases in which a drawing is possible; and (3) the filing fee.

There are some general requirements with regard to the form in which the application is submitted. The specification and oath of declaration must be in the English language and must be legibly written or printed in permanent ink on one side of the paper. The patent office prefers a typewritten application on legal-size paper, 8 to 8½ by 10½ to 13 inches, a line and a half or double spaced, with margins of one inch on the left-hand side and at the top. Various forms for patent applications are shown in Figures 17.1 through 17.11.

All applications are numbered in regular order and the applicant is informed of the serial number and filing date of the complete application by filing receipt. The filing date of the application is the date on which a complete and acceptable application is received at the Patent and Trademark Office, or the day on which the part completing such application is received if you have previously sent in an incomplete or a defective application.

The Specification

The specification must include a written description of the invention and of the manner and process of making and using it, and is required to be in such full, clear, concise, and exact terms as to enable any persons skilled in the art to which the invention pertains or with which it is most nearly connected to make and use the same invention. The specification must describe the precise invention for which a patent is being solicited, and it should be done in such a manner as to distinguish it from other inventions and from prior inventions. You must also describe the best method that you can think of for carrying out your invention. In the case of improvements, the specifications must particularly point out the part or parts of the process or device or whatever to which your improvement relates, and the description should be in such a form that the reader will have a complete understanding of it. The title of the invention should be as short and specific as possible, and it should appear as a heading

To the Commissioner of Patents and Trademarks:

Your petitioner, ..., a citizen of the United States and a resident of ...., State of ...., whose post-office address is ...., prays that letters patent may be granted to him for the improvement in ...., set forth in the following specification; and he hereby appoints ...., of ...., (Registration No. ....), his attorney (or agent) to prosecute this application and to transact all business in the Patent and Trademark Office connected therewith. (If no power of attorney is to be included in the application, omit the appointment of the attorney.)

[The specification, which includes the description of the invention and the claims, is written here.]

........................., the above-named petitioner, being sworn (or affirmed), deposes and says that he is a citizen of the United States and resident of ...., State of ...., that he verily believes himself to be the original, first and sole inventor of the improvement in .... described and claimed in the foregoing specification; that he does not know and does not believe that the same was ever known or used before his invention thereof, or patented or described in any printed publication in any country before his invention thereof, or more than one year prior to this application, or in public use or on sale in the United States more than one year prior to this application; that said invention has not been patented or made the subject of an inventor's certificate in any country foreign to the United States on an application filed by him or his legal representatives or assigns more than twelve months prior to this application; that he acknowledges his duty to disclose information of which he is aware which is material to the examination of this application; and that no application for patent or inventor's certificate on said invention has been filed by him or his representatives or assigns in any country foreign to the United States, except as follows: ....

....
(Inventor's full signature)

State of........................
County of .... } ss:

Sworn to and subscribed before me this .... day of ...., 19.....

....
(Signature of notary or officer)

[SEAL]

....
(Official character)

Figure 17.1. Patent application, sole inventor; power of attorney, oath.

on the first page of the specification, if it does not appear otherwise at the beginning of the application. Immediately following the claims, in a separate paragraph, it is necessary to write a brief abstract of the technical disclosure in the specification under the heading. Abstract of the Disclosure. Before the detailed description, you write a brief summary of the invention indicating its nature and substance which may include a statement of the object of the invention. When there are drawings, each drawing should have a brief description of the several views, and your detailed description of your invention should refer to the different views by specifying numbers of the figures. You should conclude with one or more claims in which you point out very clearly the subject matter which you regard as your invention. These claims are the operative part of the patent. Both novelty and patentability are judged by the claims, and when a patent is granted, questions of infringement are judged by the courts on the basis of the claims.

In summary, here is the order of arrangement for your specification: (1) title of invention (you may incorporate in this part the name, citizenship, and residence of the applicant and the title of the invention in one grouping); (2) cross-reference to related applications, if any; (3) a brief summary of the invention; (4) a brief description of the several views of the drawings, if you have included

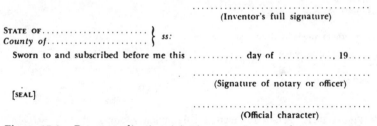

To the Commissioner of Patents and Trademarks:

Your petitioners, ... and .... , citizens of the United States and residents, respectively, of .... , State of .... , and of .... , State of .... whose post-office addresses are, respectively, ... and .... pray that letters patent may be granted to them, as joint inventors, for the improvements in .... set forth in the following specifications; and they hereby appoint .... , of .... (Registration No. ....), their attorney (or agent), to prosecute this application and to transact all business in the Patent and Trademark Office connected therewith. (If no power of attorney is to be included in the application, omit the appointment of the attorney.)

[The specification, which includes the description of the invention and the claims, is written here.]

.... and .... , the above-named petitioners, being sworn (or affirmed), depose and say that they are citizens of the United States and residents of .... , State of .... that they verily believe themselves to be the original, first and joint inventors of the improvement in .... described and claimed in the foregoing specification; that they do not know and do not believe that the same was ever known or used before their invention thereof, or patented or described in any printed publication in any country before their invention thereof, or more than one year prior to this application, or in public use or on sale in the United States for more than one year prior to this application; that said invention has not been patented or made the subject of an inventor's certificate in any country foreign to the United States on an application filed by them or their legal representatives or assigns more than 12 months prior to this application; that they acknowledge their duty to disclose information of which they are aware which is material to the examination of this application, and that no application for patent or inventor's certificate on said invention has been filed by them or their representatives or assigns in any country foreign to the United States, except as follows: ....

....
(Inventor's full signature)

STATE OF...................... ⎫
                             ⎬ ss:
County of..................... ⎭

Sworn to and subscribed before me this .... day of .... , 19.....

....
(Signature of notary or officer)

[SEAL]

....
(Official character)

Figure 17.2. Patent application, joint inventors; power of attorney, oath.

drawings as part of your invention; (5) a detailed description; (6) claim or claims; and (7) abstract of the disclosure.

Oath or Declaration and Signature

The oath or declaration from you as the applicant and inventor is required by statute. You must make an oath or declaration that you believe yourself to be the original and first inventor of the subject matter of the application, and must make various other allegations required by statute and various allegations required by the Patent and Trademark Office rules. Forms of oaths are shown in Figure 17.1, through 17.6 and in Figure 17.11. This oath will be sworn to by the inventor before a notary public or other officer authorized to administer oaths. A declaration may be used in lieu of an oath, as part of the original application for a patent involving designs, plants, and other patentable inventions. This application must be signed by you as the inventor in person or by a person entitled by law to make application on your behalf. A full first or middle name of each inventor without abbreviation, and a middle or first initial, if any, are required. Your mailing address is also required. Blank forms of applications are not supplied by the Patent and Trademark Office, but you can use those shown in the figures.

Drawings

In most cases you will have to furnish a drawing with your application. The drawing must show every feature of the invention specified in your claims, and is also required by the patent office to conform to a particular form. The patent office specifies the size of the sheet on which the drawing is made, the type of paper, the margins, and other details relating to the making of the drawing. They do this because the drawings are printed and published in a uniform, standard style which the patent office issues, and also because the

TO THE COMMISSIONER OF PATENTS AND TRADEMARKS:

    Your petitioner, A .... B ...., a citizen of the United States and a resident of ...., State of ...., whose post-office address is ...., administrator of the estate of C .... D ...., late a citizen of the United States and a resident of ...., State of ...., deceased (as by reference to the duly certified copy of letters of administration, hereto annexed, will more fully appear), prays that letters patent may be granted to him for the invention of the said C .... D .... for an improvement in .... set forth in the following specification; and he hereby appoints .... of .... (Rtgistration No. ....:...), his attorney (or agent), to prosecute this application and to transact all business in the Patent and Trademark Office connected therewith.

    (If no power of attorney is to be included in the application, omit the appointment of the attorney.)

    [The specification, which includes the description of the invention and the claims, is written here.]

    A .... B ...., the above-named petitioner, being sworn (or affirmed), deposes and says that he is a citizen of the United States of America and a resident of ...., that he is the administrator of the estate (or executor of the last will and testament) of C .... D ...., deceased, late a citizen of the United States and resident of ...., that he verily believes the said C .... D .... to be the original, first and sole inventor of the improvement in .... described and claimed in the foregoing specification; that he does not know and does not believe that the same was ever known or used before the invention thereof by the said C .... D ...., or patented or described in any printed publication in any country before the said invention thereof, or more than one year prior to this application, or in public use or on sale in the United States for more than one year prior to this application; that said invention has not been patented or make the subject of an inventor's certificate in any country foreign to the United States on an application filed by the said C .... D .... or his legal representatives or assigns more than 12 months prior to this application; that he acknowledges his duty to disclose information of which he is aware which is material to the examination of this application, and that no application for patent or inventor's certificate on said invention has been filed by the said C .... D .... or his representatives or assigns in any country foreign to the United States, except as follows: ....

              A.......................... B ....
                           (Signature)

ADMINISTRATOR, ETC.

STATE OF .... }
County of .... } ss:

    Sworn to and subscribed before me this .... day of ...., 19....
    [SEAL]

                  ....
                  (Signature of notary or officer)

                  ....
                  (Official character)

Figure 17.3. Patent application, administrator of estate of deceased inventor; power of attorney, oath.

.........................., being sworn (or affirmed), deposes and says that he is a citizen of the United States of America and resident of ...., that on ...., 19..., he filed application for patent Serial No. .... in the United States Patent and Trademark Office, that he verily believes himself to be the original, first and sole inventor of the improvement in .... described and claimed in the specification of said application for patent; that he does not know and does not believe that the same was ever known or used before his invention thereof, or patented or described in any printed publication in any country before his invention thereof, or more than one year prior to the date of said application, or in public use or on sale in the United States for more than one year prior to the date of said application; that said invention has not been patented or made the subject of an inventor's certificate before the date of said application in any country foreign to the United States on an application filed by him or his legal representatives or assigns more than twelve months prior to the date of said application; that he acknowledges his duty to disclose information of which he is aware which is material to the examination of this application, and that no application for patent or inventor's certificate on said invention has been filed by him or his representatives or assigns in any country foreign to the United States, except as follows: ....

....
(Inventor's full signature)

Sworn to and subscribed before me this .... day of ...., 19...,

....
(Signature of notary or officer)

[ꜱᴇᴀʟ]

....
(Official character)

Figure 17.4. Oath not accompanying application.

Tᴏ ᴛʜᴇ Cᴏᴍᴍɪssɪᴏɴᴇʀ ᴏғ Pᴀᴛᴇɴᴛs ᴀɴᴅ Tʀᴀᴅᴇᴍᴀʀᴋs:

Your petitioner, ..., a citizen of the United States and a resident of .... in the county of .... and State of ...., whose post-office address is ...., city of ...., State of ...., prays that letters patent may be granted to him for the new and original design for ...., set forth in the following specification; and he hereby appoints, ..., of ...., (Registration No. ....), his attorney (or agents), to prosecute this application and to transact all business in the Patent and Trademark Office connected therewith.

Be it known that I have invented a new, original, and ornamental design for .... of which the following is a specification, reference being had to the accompanying drawing, forming a part hereof.

The figure is a plan view of a ...., showing my new design.
I claim:

The ornamental design for a ...., as shown.

.................., the above-named petitioner being sworn (or affirmed), deposes and says that he is a citizen of the United States and resident of county of ...., State of ...., that he verily believes himself to be the original, first, and sole inventor of the design for .... described and claimed in the foregoing specification; that he does not know and does not believe that the same was ever known or used before his invention thereof, or patented or described in any printed publication in any country before his invention thereof, or more than one year prior to this application, or in public use or on sale in the United States for more than one year prior to this application; that said design has not been patented or made the subject of an inventor's certificate in any country foreign to the United States on an application filed by him or his legal representatives or assigns more than 6 months prior to this application; that he acknowledges his duty to disclose information of which he is aware which is material to the examination of this application, and that no application for patent or inventor's certificate on said design has been filed by him or his representatives or assigns in any country foreign to the United States, except as follows: ....

....
(Inventor's full signature)

Sworn to and subscribed before me this .... day of ...., 19....
[ꜱᴇᴀʟ]

....
(Signature of notary or officer)

....
(Official character)

Figure 17.5. Design specification oath.

To the Commissioner of Patents and Trademarks:

Your petitioner, ..., a citizen of the United States and a resident of ...., in the State of ...., whose post-office address is ...., prays that letters patent may be granted to him for the new and distinct variety of ...., set forth in the following specification; and he hereby appoints .... of .... (Registration No. ....), his attorney (or agent), to prosecute this application and to transact all business in the Patent and Trademark Office connected therewith.

(If no power of attorney is to be included in the application, omit the appointment of the attorney.)

[The specification, which includes the description of the invention and the claims, is written here.]

..................., the above-named petitioner, being sworn (or affirmed), deposes and says that he is a citizen of the United States of America and resident of ...., that he verily believes himself to be the original, first, and sole inventor of the new and distinct variety of .... described and claimed in the foregoing specification; that he has asexually reproduced the said new and distinct variety; that he does not know and does not believe that the same was ever known or used before his invention thereof, or patented or described in any printed publication in any country before his invention thereof, or more than one year prior to this application, or in public use or on sale in the United States for more than one year prior to this application; that said invention has not been patented or made the subject of an inventor's certificate in any country foreign to the United States on an application filed by him or his legal representatives or assigns more than 12 months prior to this application; that he acknowledges his duty to disclose information of which he is aware which is material to the examination of this application, and that no application for patent or inventor's certificate on said new and distinct variety of plant has been filed by him or his representatives or assigns in any country foreign to the United States, except as follow: ....

....
(Inventor's full signature)

State of .... } ss:
County of .... }
Sworn to and subscribed before me this .... day of ...., 19...,

....
(Signature of notary or officer)

[SEAL]

....
(Official character)

Figure 17.6. Plat patent application; power of attorney, oath.

To the Commissioner of Patents and Trademarks:

The undersigned having, on or about the .... day of ...., 19.....,
made application for letters patent for an improvement in ...., Serial Number ...., hereby appoints .... of ...., State of ...., Registration No. ...., his attorney (or agent), to prosecute said application, and to transact all business in the Patent and Trademark Office connected therewith.

....
(Signature)

Figure 17.7. Power of attorney or authorization of agent, not accompanying application.

To the Commissioner of Patents and Trademarks:

The undersigned having, on or about the .... day of ...., 19...., appointed ...., of ...., State of ...., his attorney (or agent) to prosecute an application for letters patent which application was filed on or about the .... day of .... 19...., for an improvement in ...., Serial Number ...., hereby revokes the power of attorney (or authorization of agent) then given.

....
(Signature)

Figure 17.8. Revocation of power of attorney or authorization of agent.

(No special form is prescribed for assignments, which may contain various provisions depending upon the agreement of the parties. The following two forms are specimens of assignments which have been used in some cases.)

WHEREAS, I, ..., of ...., did obtain Letters Patent of the United States for an improvement in .... No. ...., dated ....; and whereas, I am now the sole owner of said patent; and,

WHEREAS, ..., of ...., whose post-office address is ...., City of ...., and State of ...., is desirous of acquiring the entire interest in the same;

Now, THEREFORE, in consideration of the sum of .... dollars ($.........), the receipt of which is hereby acknowledged, and other good and valuable considerations, I, ..., by these presents do sell, assign, and transfer unto the said ...., the entire right, title, and interest in and to the said Letters Patent aforesaid; the same to be held and enjoyed by the said ...., for his own used and behoof, and for his legal representatives and assigns, to the full end of the term for which said Letters Patent are granted, as fully and entirely as the same would have been held by me had this assignment and sale not been made.

Executed, this .... day of ...., 19...., at ....

STATE .... ⎱ ss:
County of .... ⎰

Before me personally appeared said .... and acknowledged the foregoing instruments to be his free act and deed this .... day of ....,

....
(Notary Public)

[SEAL]

Figure 17.9. Assignment of patent.

WHEREAS, I, ..., of .... have invented certain new and useful Improvements in ...., for which an application for United States Letters Patent was filed on ...., Serial No. ...., [if the application has been prepared but not yet filed, state "for which an application for United States Letters Patent was executed on ....," instead] and

WHEREAS, ..., of ...., whose post-office address is ...., is desirous of acquiring the entire right, title and interest in the same;

Now, THEREFORE, in consideration of the sum of .... dollars ($.........), the receipt whereof is hereby acknowledged, and other good and valuable consideration, I, the said ...., by these presents do sell, assign and transfer unto said ...., the full and exclusive right to the said invention in the United States and the entire right, title, and interest in and to any and all Letters Patent which may be granted, therefore in the United States.

I hereby authorize and request the Commissioner of Patents and Trademarks to issue said Letters Patent to said ...., as the assignee of the entire right, title, and interest in and to the same, for his sole use and behoof; and for the use and behoof of his legal representatives, to the full end of the term for which said Letters Patent may be granted, as fully and entirely as the same would have been held by me had this assignment and sale not been made.

Executed this .... day of ...., 19...., at ....

....

STATE OF .... ⎱ ss:
County of .... ⎰

Before me personally appeared said .... and acknowledged the foregoing instrument to be his free act and deed this ...... day of ...., 19.....

....
(Notary Public)

[SEAL]

Figure 17.10. Assignment of application.

(Rules 65 and 68 of the Rules of Practice provide for a declaration in lieu of an oath in certain instances. The petition and specification preceded the declaration.)
................., the above-named petitioner .... declares that he is a citizen of the United States and resident of .... that he verily believes himself to be the original, first, and sole inventor of the improvement in ....
.... described and claimed in the annexed specification; that he does not know and does not believe that the same was ever known or used before .... invention thereof, or patented or described in any printed publication in any country before his invention thereof, or more than one year prior to this application, or in public use or on sale in the United States more than one year prior to this application; that said invention has not been patented in any country foreign to the United States on an application filed by him or his legal representatives or assigns more than twelve months prior to this application; that he acknowledge his duty to disclose information of which he is aware is material to the examination of this application, and that no application for patent on said invention has been filed by him or his representatives or assigns in any country foreign to the United States, except as follows: ....

The undersigned petitioner .... declare .... further that all statements made herein of .... own knowledge are true and that all statements made on information and belief are believed to be true; and further that these statements were made with the knowledge that willful false statements and the like so made are punishable by fine or imprisonment, or both, under section 1001 of Title 18 of the United States Code and that such willful false statements may jeopardize the validity of the application or any patent issuing thereon.
Inventor's full name or names ....

....
(Signature)

Date ....

Figure 17.11. Declaration that may be included in an application in lieu of an oath.

drawings must be readily understood by persons using the patent descriptions. The patent office publishes the following rules related to the standards for drawings.

1.84 *Standards for drawings.*

(a) *Paper and ink.* Drawings must be made upon paper which is flexible, strong, white, smooth, non-shiny and durable. Two-ply or three ply bristol board is preferred. The surface of the paper should be calendered and of a quality which will permit erasure and correction with India ink. India ink, or its equivalent in quality, is preferred for pen drawings to secure perfectly black solid lines. The use of white pigment to cover lines is not normally acceptable.

(b) *Size of sheet and margin.* The size of the sheets on which drawings are made may either be exactly 8½ by 14 inches (21.6 by 35.6 cm.) or exactly 21.0 by 29.7 cm. (DIN size A4). All drawing sheets in particular application must be the same size. One of the shorter sides of the sheet is regarded as its top. (1) On 8½ by 14 inch drawing sheets, the drawing must include a top margin of 2 inches (5.1 cm) and bottom and side margins of ¼ inch (6.4 mm.) from the edges, thereby leaving a "sight" precisely 8 by 11¾ inches (20.3 by 29.8 cm.) Margin border lines are not permitted. All work must be included within the "sight." The sheets may be provided with two ¼ inch (6.4 mm.) diameter holes having their centerlines spaced $^{11}/_{16}$ inch (17.5 mm.) below the top edge and 2¾ inches (7.0 cm.) apart, said holes being equally spaced from the respective side edges. (2) On 21.0 by 29.7 cm. drawing sheets, the drawing must include a top margin of at least 2.5 cm., a left side margin of 2.5 cm., a right side margin of 1.5 cm., and a bottom margin of 1.0 cm. Margin border lines are not permitted. All work must be contained within a sight size not to exceed 17 by 26.2 cm.

(c) *Character of lines.* All drawings must be made with drafting instruments or by a process which will give them satisfactory reproduction characteristics. Every line and letter must be durable, black, sufficiently dense and dark, uniformly thick and well defined; the weight of all lines and letters must be heavy enough to permit adequate reproduction. This direction applies to all lines however fine, to shading, and to lines representing cut surfaces in sectional views. All lines must be clean, sharp, and solid. Fine or crowded lines should be avoided. Solid black should not be used for sectional or surface shading. Freehand work should be avoided wherever it is possible to do so.

(d) Hatching and shading. (1) Hatching should be made by oblique parallel lines spaced sufficiently apart to enable the lines to be distinguished without difficulty. (2) Heavy lines on the shade side of objects should preferably be used except where they tend to thicken the work and obscure reference characters. The light should come from the upper left-hand corner at an angle of 45°. Surface delineations should preferably be shown by proper shading, which should be open.

(e) Scale. The scale to which a drawing is made ought to be large enough to show the mechanism without crowding when the drawing is reduced in size to two-thirds in reproduction, and views of portions of the mechanism on a larger scale should be used when necessary to show details clearly; two or more sheets should be used if one does not give sufficient room to accomplish this end, but the number of sheets should not be more than is necessary.

(f) Reference characters. The different views should be consecutively numbered figures. Reference numerals (and letters, but numerals are preferred) must be plain, legible and carefully formed, and not be encircled. They should, if possible, measure at least one-eighth of an inch (3.2 mm.) in height so that they may bear reduction to one twenty-fourth of an inch (1.1. mm.); and they may be slightly larger when there is sufficient room. They should not be so placed in the close and complex parts of the drawing as to interfere with a thorough comprehension of the same, and therefore should rarely cross or mingle with the lines. When necessarily grouped around a certain part, they should be placed at a little distance, at the closest point where there is available space, and connected by lines with the parts to which they refer. They should not be placed upon hatched or shaded surfaces but when necessary, a blank space may be left in the hatching or shading where the character occurs so that is shall appear perfectly distinct and separate from the work. The same part of an invention appearing in more than one view of the drawing must always be designated by the same character, and the same character must never be used to designate different parts. Reference signs not mentioned in the description shall appear in the drawing, and vice versa.

(g) Symbols, Legends. Graphical drawing symbols and other labeled representations may be used for conventional elements when appropriate, subject to approval by the Office. The elements for which such symbols and labeled representations are used must be adequately identified in the specification. While descriptive matter on drawings is not permitted, suitable legends may be used, or may be required in proper cases, as in diagrammatic views and flow sheets or to show materials or where labeled representations are employed to illustrate conventional elements. Arrows may be required in proper cases, to show direction of movement. The lettering should be as large as, or larger than, the reference characters.

(i) Views. The drawings must contain as many figures as may be necessary to show the invention; the figures should be consecutively numbered if possible in the order in which they appear. The figures may be plain, elevation, section, or perspective views, and detail views of portions of elements, on a larger scale if necessary, may also be used. Exploded views, with the separated parts of the same figure embraced by a bracket, to show the relationship or order of assembly of various parts are permissible. When necessary, a view of a large machine or device in its entirety may be broken and extended over several sheets if there is no loss in facility of understanding the view. Where figures on two or more sheets form in effect a single complete figure, the figures on the several sheets should be so

arranged that the complete figure can be understood by laying the drawing sheet adjacent to one another. The arrangement should be such that no part of any of the figures appearing on the various sheets are concealed and that the complete figure can be understood even though spaces will occur in the complete figure because of the margins on the drawing sheets. The plane upon which a sectional view is taken should be indicated on the general view by a broken line, the ends of which should be designated by numerals corresponding to the figure number of the sectional view and have arrows applied to indicate the direction in which the view is taken. A moved position may be shown by a broken line superimposed upon a suitable figure if this can be done without crowding, otherwise a separate figure must be used for this purpose. Modified forms of construction can only be shown in separate figures. Views should not be connected by projection lines nor should center lines be used.

(j) *Arrangements of views*. All views on the same sheet should stand in the same direction and, if possible, stand so that they can be read with the sheet held in an upright position. If views longer than the width of the sheet are necessry for the clearest illustration of the invention, the sheet may be turned on its side so that the top of the sheet with the appropriate top margin is on the right-hand side. One figure must not be placed upon another or within the outline of another.

(k) *Figure for Official Gazette*. The drawing should, as far as possible, be so planned that one of the views will be suitable for publication in the Official Gazette as the illustration of the invention.

(l) *Extraneous matter*. Identifying indicia (such as to the attorney's docket number, inventor's name, number of sheets, etc.) not to exceed 2¾ inches (7.0 cm.) in width may be placed in a centered location between the side edges within three-fourths inch (19.1 mm.) of the top edge. Authorized security markings may be placed on the drawings provided they are outside the illustrations and are removed when the material is declassified. Other extraneous matter will not be permitted upon the face of the drawing.

(m) *Transmission of drawings*. Drawings transmitted to the Office should be sent flat, protected by a sheet of heavy binder's board, or may be rolled for transmission in a suitable mailing tube: but must never be folded. If received creased or mutilated new drawings will be required. (See rule 1.152 for design drawings, 1.165 for plant drawings, and 1.174 for reissue drawings.)

The requirements relating to these drawings are strictly enforced. However, a drawing which doesn't comply with all of the rules or regulations may be accepted for the purpose of examination with a new drawing required later. The patent office also advises all applicants to employ competent draftsmen to make the drawings. The patent office may furnish drawings at your expense, although the time required varies, if you can't otherwise procure them.

Filing Fees

The basic filing fee is $340 (except for design or plant applications), to which is added certain additional charges for claims, depending on their number. An issue fee of $560 is required when a patent is to be granted. These amounts are reduced by 50% when the applicant is a small entity—that is, an independent inventor, a nonprofit organization, or a small business concern. An applicant must submit a verified statement to establish status as a small entity. In addition, maintenance fees are due 3½, 7½ and 11½ years after the patent is issued to keep it in force.

These filing fees are for the government only and do not include legal or attorney fees. You should understand up front that to obtain a patent in the limited state will cost several thousand dollars if you include attorney and other legal fees.

USE OF PATENT PENDING MARKING

If you make or sell patented articles, you are required to mark the articles with the word "patented" and the number of the patent. The penalty for failure to do this is that you may not recover damages from a patent infringer unless the infringer was notified of the infringement and continued to infringe after the notice. However, the marking of an article as patented when it is in fact not patented is against the law. Some inventors mark articles sold with the terms "patent applied for" or "patent pending." These phrases have no legal effect, but they warn that an application for a patent has been filed in the Patent and Trademark Office. Thus, a potential infringer knows that if he or she tools up to manufacture the item that has such a marking, when and if a patent is granted, he or she will be infringing on your patent and could be subject to a lawsuit. However, the protection afforded by a patent does not start until the actual grant of the patent. The law imposes a fine on those who use these terms falsely.

LIMITATIONS AND DISADVANTAGES OF PROTECTION WITH PATENTS

There are disadvantages and limitations to the use of patents. Here are some that you should consider before you apply for a patent through the patent office.

First, your patent can be designed around. That is, if your patent shows how to accomplish a certain task, you're only being given a patent for that particular method of accomplishing that task. Someone else can then see what you are doing, think of a different way to do the same task which does not infringe on your patent, and patent the new invention himself.

Infringement of a patent consists in the unauthorized making, using, or selling of your patented invention within the territory of the United States during the term of the patent. However, if the patent is infringed, the government itself will not sue. That's your job. You may sue for relief in the appropriate federal court and you may ask the court for an injunction to prevent the continuation of the infringement, and award of damages because of the infringement. However in such a suit, the defendant may raise the question of the validity of your patent. This is an important point. Your patent can be invalidated by the court even after it has already been granted to you. In fact, in one survey it was reported that 70% of patents that have been taken to court for infringement are actually invalidated. These inventors received nothing for their effort or for their expense in obtaining their patents, much less the court costs.

Another disadvantage of a patent is the cost. As stated, it will amount to several thousand dollars. And this only gets you a patent in the United States. Remember that a U.S. patent does not protect you in foreign countries, and each country has its own patent laws. While you can certainly obtain patents in foreign countries through your patent attorney, this will cost more money. Therefore, the cost of a patent must be weighed against its value prior to applying for it. Many inventors have the idea that it is possible to make a fortune simply by having a patent granted. This is not true.

Another disadvantage is the specifics on the invention required by the patent office. It is for this reason that many chemical processes, even though they can be patented, are not. It has been reported, for example, that the inventor of the paper which corrects typewriting mistakes made a gross error in patenting because the chemical would work over a large range of percentages of the impregnation of the paper, whereas the patent office required a specific percentage to the nearest tenth. From the information in the patent itself, many others were able to copy the idea simply by impregnating the paper with other amounts of the chemical. To prevent this sort of infringement, the formula for Coca Cola has never been patented and still remains a secret. However, if you decide to proceed, the end result is the U.S. patent shown in Figure 17.12. To illustrate the differences, a foreign patent for the same device is shown in Figure 17.13.

QUESTIONS AND ANSWERS ABOUT PATENTS

Following are 40 frequently asked questions about patents and their responses published by the Patent and Trademark Office of the Department of Commerce.[1]

Nature and Duration of Patents
1. Q. **What is a patent?**
   A. A patent is a grant issued by the United States Government giving an inventor the right to exclude all others from making, using, or selling his invention within the United States, its territories and possessions.
2. Q. **For how long a term of years is a patent granted?**
   A. Seventeen years from the date on which it is issued; except for patents on ornamental designs, which are granted for term 14 years.
3. Q. **May the term of a patent be extended?**
   A. Only by special act of Congress, and this occurs very rarely and only in most exceptional circumstances
4. Q. **Does the patentee continue to have any control over use of the invention after his patent expires?**
   A. No. Anyone has the free right to use an invention covered in an expired patent, so long as he does not use features covered in other unexpired patents in doing so.
5. Q. **On what subject matter may a patent be granted?**
   A. A patent may be granted to the inventor or discoverer of any new and useful process, machine, manufacture, or composition of matter, or any new and useful improvement thereof, or on any distinct and new variety of plant, other than a tuber-propagated plant, which is asexually reproduced, or on any new, original, and ornamental design for an article of manufacture.
6. A. **On what subject matter may a patent not be granted?**
   A. A patent may not be granted on a useless device, on printed matter, on a method of doing business, on an improvement in a device which would be obvious to a person skilled in the art, or on a machine which will not operate, particularly on an alleged perpetual motion machine.

Meaning of Words "Patent Pending"
7. Q. **What do the terms "patent pending" and "patent applied for" mean?**
   A. They are used by a manufacturer or seller of an article to inform the public that an application for patent on that article is on file in the Patent and Trademark Office. The law imposes a fine on those who use these terms falsely to deceive the public.

Patent Applications
8. Q. **I have made some changes and improvements in my invention after my patent application was filed in the Patent and Trademark Office. May I amend my patent application by adding description or illustration of these features?**

[1] From *Q and A About Patents*, U.S. Department of Commerce, Washington, D.C. (1979).

United States Patent [19]

Cohen

[11] 3,803,639

[45] Apr. 16, 1974

[54] **BODY ARMOUR JACKET**

[76] Inventor: **William A. Cohen,** 1556 N. Sierra Madre Villa, Pasadena, Calif. 91107

[22] Filed: **July 11, 1973**

[21] Appl. No.: **378,207**

[30] **Foreign Application Priority Data**

Oct. 4, 1972   Israel...................................... 40502

[52] **U.S. Cl.** 2/2.5
[51] **Int. Cl.** F41h 1/02
[58] **Field of Search** 2/2.5

[56] **References Cited**
UNITED STATES PATENTS

2,640,987	6/1903	Ehlers	2/2.5
2,743,446	5/1956	Persico et al.	2/2.5
2,748,391	6/1956	Lewis et al.	2/2.5
2,954,563	10/1960	DeGrazio	2/2.5
3,130,414	4/1964	Bailey et al.	2/2.5
3,392,406	7/1968	Pernini et al.	2/2.5

Primary Examiner—Alfred R. Guest
Attorney, Agent, or Firm—Benjamin J. Barish

[57]   **ABSTRACT**

A body armour jacket, which may be easily donned and doffed and may be conveniently opened for purposes of comfort or ventilation, includes a front body assembly and a back body assembly, the front body assembly comprising a right armour section, a left armour section, and a center armour flap. The ends of the right and left armour sections are in abutting relationship and are fastened together by a fastener. The center armour flap is hinged to one of the sections along a line spaced from its abutting end and is fastenable by another fastener to the other section along a line spaced from its abutting end, such that the center armour flap, when closed, bridges the abutting ends of both sections.

7 Claims, 4 Drawing Figures

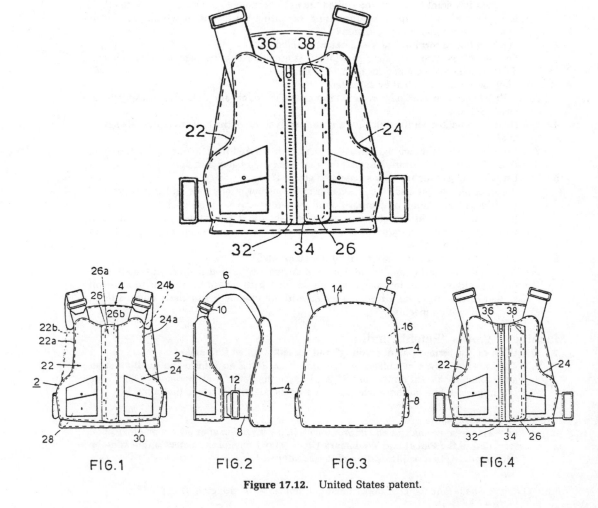

Figure 17.12.   United States patent.

FIG.1   FIG.2   FIG.3   FIG.4

1

BODY ARMOUR JACKET

BACKGROUND OF THE INVENTION

The present invention relates to body armour jackets such as are used by soldiers and policemen to provide 5 body protection against small arms fire, shrapnel, and the like.

A number of body armour jackets have been designed. In one type, the front assembly of the jacket includes a fabric carrier and a one-piece armour insert. 10 Such a jacket, however, is not openable from the front and therefore is inconvenient to don and doff, sometimes uncomfortable to wear, and difficult to ventilate. Another known form of body armour jacket is made of flexible armour, such as ballistic nylon, and includes a 15 front closure arrangement by overlapping the armour on the inside. Such an arrangement, however, would not be satisfactory with rigid armour, as distinguished from flexible armour, since rigid armour would produce undue discomfort in the chest and abdominal re- 20 gions because of the armour rigidity.

Insofar as I am aware, a rigid armour body jacket having a front closure has not yet been devised. An object of the present invention is to provide such a body 25 armour jacket.

SUMMARY OF THE INVENTION

According to the invention, there is provided a body armour jacket including a front body assembly and a back body assembly joined thereto, characterized in 30 that the front body assembly comprises a right armour section, a left armour section, and a center armour flap. The ends of the right and left armour sections are in abutting relationship and are fastened together by a 35 first openable and closable fastener. The center armour flap is hinged to one of said sections along a line spaced from its abutting end and is fastenable by a second openable and closable fastener to the other of said sections along a line spaced from its abutting end, such 40 that the center armour flap, when closed, bridges the abutting ends of both said armour sections.

According to another feature of the invention, the right and left armour sections and said center armour flap each comprises a fabric carrier and a rigid armour 45 plate insert.

In the preferred embodiment of the invention described below, the center armour flap is hinged to one of these sections by stitching. Also, the first mentioned fastener is a slide-fastener, and the second-mentioned 50 fastener comprises a series of snap-fasteners.

According to a further features, the front body assembly is joined to the back body assembly by adjustable shoulder and waist straps.

Such a body armour jacket, since it is provided with 55 a front closure, may be easily donned and doffed, and may be conveniently opened when desired for purposes of comfort or ventilation.

Further features and advantages of the invention will be apparent from the description below. 60

BRIEF DESCRIPTION OF THE DRAWINGS

The invention is herein described, by way of example only, with reference to the accompanying drawings, 65 wherein:

FIG. 1 is a front elevational view of a body armour jacket constructed in accordance with the invention;

2

FIG. 2 is a side elevational view of the body armour jacket of FIG. 1;

FIG. 3 is a rear elevational view of the body armour jacket of FIG. 1; and

FIG. 4 is a front elevational view corresponding to FIG. 1 but illustrating the center armour flap in its open position to permit opening and closing the front closure fastener.

DESCRIPTION OF THE PREFERRED EMBODIMENT

The body armour jacket illustrated in the drawings comprises a front assembly, generally designated 2, and a back assembly, generally designated 4, both joined together by adjustable shoulder straps 6 and adjustable waist straps 8. The straps are made adjustable by the provision of buckles 10 in the shoulder straps, and buckles 12 in the waist straps.

The back assembly, as shown in FIG. 3, comprises a single fabric carrier 14 and a single rigid armour plate insert 16 disposed within the fabric carrier. The shoulder straps 6 and waist straps 8 are fixed, as by stitching, to the fabric carrier 14.

Front assembly 2, is made of three parts, namely a right armour section 22, a left armour section 24, and a center armour flap 26. Each of the foregoing is also made of a fabric carrier (22a, 24a, 26a), and a rigid armour plate insert (22b, 24b, 26b) carried within its respective fabric carrier. If desired, the fabric carriers of the right and left sections may also be formed with pockets as shown at 28 and 30, respectively.

As shown particularly in FIG. 4 (wherein the center armour flap 26 is pivoted open), the ends of the right and left sections 2 and 4 are disposed in abutting relationship and are fastened together by an openable and closable slide-fastener 32, e.g., a zip-fastener. The center armour flap 26 is hingedly mounted, as by stitching, to the left armour section 24 along line 34, which line is spaced from the abutting end of that section. In addition, the center flap is fastenable to the right armour section by a line of snap fasteners, the female snaps 36 of which are located along a line on the fabric carrier 24a of the right section 24 spaced inwardly from its abutting end, and the male snaps 38 of which are located along a line on the fabric carrier 26a of the center armour flap 26 spaced slightly from the corresponding end of the flap.

The arrangement is such that when the center armour flap 26 is closed (FIG. 1), its rigid armour insert 26b completely bridges the abutting ends of the right and left armour inserts 22b, 24b of the sections. The armour insert 26b of the center flap thus provides armour portection for the region occupied by the front closure 32.

It will thus be seen that the body armour jacket illustrated may be opened from the front merely by detaching snaps 36, 38, thereby permitting the center armour flap to be pivoted open; and then opening the center slide-fastener 32 to open the jacket. To close the jacket, slide-fastener 32 is closed, and then fasteners 38 are snapped into fasteners 36 to close the center armour flap 26.

The armour inserts may be rigid reinforced fiberglass or ceramic. The invention could also be used with soft armour inserts, such as nylon.

It will thus be seen that the body armour jacket illustrated is provided with a front closure system which

Figure 17.12. (Continued)

3

permits the jacket to be conveniently donned, doffed and opened for purposes of comfort or ventilation.

Many modifications, variations, and other applications of the illustrated embodiment will be apparent.

What is claimed is:

1. A body armour jacket including a front body assembly and a back body assembly joined thereto, characterized in that the front body assembly comprises a right armour section, a left armour section, and a center armour flap, the end of the right and left armour sections being in abutting relationship and being fastened together by a first openable and closable fastener, the centre armour flap being hinged to one of said sections along a line spaced from its abutting end and being fastenable by a second openable and closable fastener to the other of said sections along a line spaced from its abutting end such that the center armour flap, when closed, bridges the abutting ends of both said armour sections.

4

2. A jacket according to claim 1, wherein said right and left armour sections and said center armour flap each comprises a fabric carrier and a rigid armour plate insert.

3. A jacket according to claim 1, wherein said center armour flap is hinged to said one section by stitching.

4. A jacket according to claim 1, wherein said first fastener is a slide-fastener.

5. A jacket according to claim 1, wherein said second fastener comprises a line of snap-fasteners.

6. A jacket according to claim 1, wherein said front body assembly is joined to the back body assembly by adjustable shoulder and waist straps.

7. A jacket according to claim 1, wherein said back body assembly comprises a fabric carrier and a rigid armour plate insert.

* * * * *

Figure 17.12. (Continued)

PATENT SPECIFICATION (11) 1 378 609

(21) Application No. 40631/73 (22) Filed 29 Aug. 1973 (19)

(31) Convention Application No. 40502 (32) Filed 4 Oct. 1972 in

(33) Israel (IL)

(44) Complete Specification published 27 Dec. 1974 ·

(51) International Classification F41H 1/02

(52) Index at acceptance
A3V 1A5A

(54) AN ARMOUR JACKET

(71) I, WILLIAM ALAN COHEN, of 1556 North Sierra Madre Villa, Pasadena, California, United States of America, do hereby declare the invention, for which I
5 pray that a patent may be granted to me, and the method by which it is to be performed, to be particularly described in and by the following statement:—

The present invention relates to body
10 armour jackets such as are used by soldiers and policemen to provide body protection against small arms fire, shrapnel, and the like.

A number of body armour jackets have
15 been proposed. In one type, the front assembly of the jacket includes a fabric carrier and a one-piece armour insert. Such a jacket, however, is not openable from the front and therefore is inconvenient to
20 put on and take off, sometimes uncomfortable to wear, and difficult to ventilate.

According to the present invention there is provided a body armour jacket including a front assembly and a back assembly
25 joined thereto, the front assembly comprising a right armour section, a left armour section, and a centre armour flap, the free side edges of the right and left armour sections being intended to be disposed in
30 mutually abutting relationship when the jacket is worn and being provided with a first openable and closable fastener to fasten together said abutting edges, and the centre armour flap being hinged to one of said
35 sections along a line spaced from said free side edge of said one section and being fastenable by a second openable and closable fastener to the other of said sections along a line spaced from said free side
40 edge of said other section such that the centre armour flap, when closed, bridges said free side edges of both said armour sections.

The right and left armour sections and
45 the centre armour flap each comprise a fabric carrier and a rigid armour plate insert.

In the preferred embodiment of the invention described below, the centre armour
50 flap is hinged to one of these sections by

[Price 25p]

stitching. Also, the first mentioned fastener is a sliding clasp fastener, and the second-mentioned fastener comprises a series of press-stud fasteners.

The front assembly may be joined to 55 the back assembly by adjustable shoulder and waist straps.

Such a body armour jacket, since it is provided with a front closure, may be easily put on and taken off, and may be 60 conveniently opened when desired for purposes of comfort or ventilation.

The invention will now be described in more detail, by way of example only, with reference to the accompanying drawings, 65 in which:—

Fig. 1 is a front elevational view of a body armour jacket;

Fig. 2 is a side elevational view of the body armour jacket of Fig. 1; 70

Fig. 3 is a rear elevational view of the body armour jacket of Fig. 1; and

Fig. 4 is a front elevational view corresponding to Fig. 1 but illustrating the centre armour flap in its open position to permit 75 opening and closing of the front closure fastener.

The body armour jacket illustrated in the drawings comprises a front assembly, generally designated 2, and a back 80 assembly, generally designated 4, both joined together by adjustable shoulder straps 6 and adjustable waist straps 8. The straps are made adjustable by the provision of buckles 10 in the shoulder straps, and 85 buckles 12 in the waist straps.

The back assembly, as shown in Fig. 3, comprises a single fabric carrier 14 and a single rigid armour plate insert 16 disposed within the fabric carrier. The shoulder 90 straps 6 and waist straps 8 are fixed, as by stitching, to the fabric carrier 14.

Front assembly, 2, is made of three parts, namely a right armour section 22, a left armour section 24, and a centre armour 95 flap 26. Each of the foregoing is also made of a fabric carrier 22a, 26a, and a rigid armour plate insert 22b, 24b, 26b, carried within its respective fabric carrier. If desired, the fabric carriers of the right 100

Figure 17.13. Foreign patent.

and left sections may also be formed with pockets as shown at 28 and 30, respectively.

As shown particularly in Fig. 4 (wherein the centre armour flap 26 is pivoted open), the adjacent edges of the right and left sections 22 and 24 are disposed in abutting relationship and are fastened together by an openable and closable sliding clasp fastener 32, i.e. zip-fastener. The centre armour flap 26 is hingedly mounted, as by stitching, to the left armour section 24 along line 34, which line is spaced from said abutting side edge of that section. In addition, the centre flap is fastenable to the right armour section by a line of press-stud fasteners, the female members 36 of which are located along a line on the fabric carrier 22a of the right section 22 spaced inwardly from its abutting side edge, and the male members 38 of which are located along a line on the fabric carrier 26a of the centre armour flap 26 spaced slightly from the corresponding free side edge of the flap.

The arrangement is such that when the centre armour flap 26 is closed (Fig. 1), its rigid armour insert 26b completely bridges the abutting side edges of the right and left armour inserts 22b, 24b of the sections. The armour insert 26b of the centre flap thus provides armour protection for the region occupied by the front fastener 32.

It will thus be seen that the body armour jacket illustrated may be opened from the front merely by detaching press-stud fastener members 36, 38, thereby permitting the centre armour flap to be pivoted open; and then opening the centre sliding-clasp fastener 32 to open the jacket. To close the jacket, sliding-clasp fastener 32 is closed, and then fastener members 38 are snapped into fastener members 36 to close the centre armour flap 26.

The armour inserts may be of rigid reinforced fibre-glass or ceramic. The invention could also be used with soft armour inserts, such as nylon.

It will thus be seen that the body armour jacket illustrated is provided with a front closure system which permits the jacket to be conveniently put on and taken off and opened for purposes of comfort or ventilation.

WHAT I CLAIM IS:—

1. A body armour jacket including a front assembly and a back assembly joined thereto, the front assembly comprising a right armour section, a left armour section, and a centre armour flap, the free side edges of the right and left armour sections being intended to be disposed in mutually abutting relationship when the jacket is worn and being provided with a first openable and closable fastener to fasten together said abutting edges, and the centre armour flap being hinged to one of said sections along a line spaced from said free side edge of said one section and being fastenable by a second openable and closable fastener to the other of said sections along a line spaced from said free side edge of said other section such that the centre armour flap, when closed, bridges said free side edges of both said armour sections.

2. A jacket as claimed in claim 1, wherein the right and left armour sections and the centre armour flap each comprise a fabric carrier and a rigid armour plate insert.

3. A jacket as claimed in claim 1 or claim 2, wherein the centre armour flap is hinged to said one section by stitching.

4. A jacket as claimed in any one of claims 1 to 3, wherein said second fastener comprises a line of press-stud fasteners.

5. A jacket as claimed in any one of Claims 1 to 4, wherein said front assembly is joined to the back assembly by adjustable shoulder and waist straps.

6. A jacket as claimed in any one of Claims 1 to 5, wherein said back assembly comprises a fabric carrier and a rigid armour plate insert.

7. A body armour jacket substantially as herein described with reference to and as illustrated in the accompanying drawings.

MARKS & CLERK,
Chartered Patent Agents,
57 & 58 Lincoln's Inn Fields,
London WC1A 3LS.
Agents for the Applicant.

Printed for Her Majesty's Stationery Office by Burgess & Son (Abingdon), Ltd.—1974.
Published at The Patent Office, 25 Southampton Buildings, London, WC2A 1AY
from which copies may be obtained.

Figure 17.13. (Continued)

1378609   COMPLETE SPECIFICATION

1 SHEET   *This drawing is a reproduction of the Original on a reduced scale*

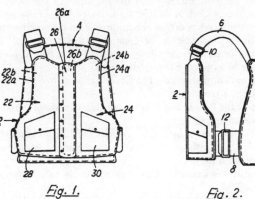
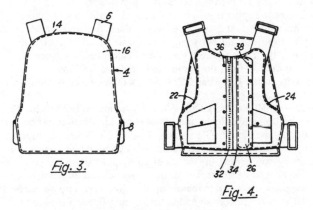

Figure 17.13. (Continued)

A. No. The law specifically provides that new matter shall not be introduced into the disclosure of a patent application. However, you should call the attention of your attorney or agent promptly to any such changes you may make or plan to make, so that he may take or recommend any steps that may be necessary for your protection.

9. Q. **How does one apply for a patent?**
   A. By making the proper application to the Commissioner of Patents and Trademarks, Washington, D.C. 20231.

10. **What is the best way to prepare an application?**
   A. As the preparation and prosecution of an application are highly complex proceedings they should preferably be conducted by an attorney trained in this specialized practice. The Patent and Trademark Office therefore advises inventors to employ a patent attorney or agent who is registered in the Patent and Trademark Office. No attorney or agent not registered in the Patent and Trademark Office may prosecute applications. The pamphlet entitled *Attorneys and Agents Registered to Practice Before the U.S. Patent and Trademark Office*, contains an alphabetical and geographical list of persons on the Patent and Trademark Office register.

   See Question 40 for source.

11. Q. **Of what does a patent application consist?**
   A. An application fee, a petition, a specification and claims describing and defining the invention, an oath or declaration, and a drawing if the invention can be illustrated.

12. Q. **What are the Patent and Trademark Office fees in connection with filing of an application for patent and issuance of the patent?**

A. A filing fee of $340 except for design or plant patents plus certain additional charges for claims depending on their number and the manner of their presentation are required when the application is filed. A final or issue fee of $560 if the patent is to be granted. These amounts are reduced by 50% when the applicant is a small entity—an independent inventor, a nonprofit organization, or a small business concern. This final fee is not required until your application is allowed by the Patent and Trademark Office.

13. Q. **Are models required as part of the application?**

A. Only in the most exceptional cases. The Office has the power to require that a model be furnished, but rarely exercises it.

14. Q. **Is it necessary to go the Patent and Trademark Office in Washington to transact business concerning patent matters?**

A. No; most business with the Patent and Trademark Office is conducted by correspondence. Interviews regarding pending applications can be arranged with examiners if necessary, however, and are often helpful.

15. Q. **Can the Patent and Trademark Office give advice as to whether an inventor should apply for a patent?**

A. No. It can only consider the patentability of an invention when this question comes regularly before it in the form of a patent application.

16. Q. **Is there any danger that the Patent and Trademark Office will give others information contained in my application while it is pending?**

A. No. All patent applications are maintained in the strictest secrecy until the patent is issued. After the patent is issued, however, the Patent and Trademark Office file containing the application and all correspondence leading up to issuance of the patent is made available in the Patent Search Room for inspection by anyone, and copies of these files may be purchased from the Patent and Trademark Office.

17. Q. **May I write to the Patent and Trademark Office directly about my application after it is filed?**

A. The Patent and Trademark Office will answer an applicant's inquiries as to the status of the application, and inform him whether his application has been rejected, allowed, or is awaiting action by the Patent and Trademark Office. However, if you have a patent attorney or agent the Patent and Trademark Office cannot correspond with both you and the attorney concerning the merits of your application. All comments concerning your invention should be forwarded through your patent attorney or agent.

18. Q. **What happens when two inventors apply separately for a patent for the same invention?**

A. An "interference" is declared and testimony may be submitted to the Patent and Trademark Office to determine which inventor is entitled to the patent. Your attorney or agent can give you further information about this if it becomes necessary.

19. Q. **Can the period allowed by the Patent and Trademark Office for response to an office action in a pending application be extended?**

A. No. This time period required by the examiner cannot be extended, but it may be reduced to not less than thirty days. The application will become abandoned unless proper response is received in the Patent and Trademark Office within the time allowed.

20. Q. **May applications be examined out of their regular order?**

A. No; all applications are examined in the order in which they are filed, except under certain very special conditions.

When to Apply for Patent

21. Q. **I have been making and selling my invention for the past 13 months and have not filed any patent application. Is it too late for me to apply for patent?**

A. Yes. A valid patent may not be obtained if the invention was in public use or on sale in this country for more than one year prior to the filing of your patent application. Your own use and sale of the invention for more than a year before your application is filed will bar your right to a patent just as effectively as though this use and sale had been done by someone else.

22. Q. **I published an article describing my invention in a magazine 13 months ago. Is it too late to apply for patent?**

A. Yes. The fact that you are the author of the article will not save your patent application. The law provides that the inventor is not entitled to a patent if the invention has been described in a printed publication anywhere in the world more than a year before his patent application is filed.

Who May Obtain a Patent

23. Q. Is there any restriction as to persons who may obtain a United States patent?

A. No. Any inventor may obtain a patent regardless of age or sex, by complying with the provisions of the law. A foreign citizen may obtain a patent under exactly the same conditions as a United States citizen.

24. Q. If two or more persons work together to make an invention, to whom will the patent be granted?

A. If each had a share in the ideas forming the invention, they are joint inventors and a patent will be issued to them jointly on the basis of a proper patent application filed by them jointly. If on the other hand one of these persons has provided all of the ideas of the invention, and the other has only followed instructions in making it, the person who contributed the ideas is the sole inventor and the patent application and patent should be in his name alone.

25. Q. If one person furnishes all of the ideas to make an invention and another employs him or furnishes the money for building and testing the invention, should the patent application be filed by them jointly?

A. No. The application must be signed, executed, sworn to, and filed in the Patent and Trademark Office, in the name of the true inventor. This is the person who furnishes the ideas, not the employer or the person who furnishes the money.

26. Q. May a patent be granted if an inventor dies before filing his application?

A. Yes; the application may be filed by the inventor's executor or administrator.

27. Q. While in England this summer, I found an article on sale which was very ingenious and has not been introduced into the United States or patented or described. May I obtain a United States patent on this invention?

A. No. A United States patent may be obtained only by the true inventor, not by someone who learns of an invention of another.

Ownership and Sale of Patent Rights

28. Q. May the inventor sell or otherwise transfer his right to his patent or patent application to someone else?

A. Yes. He may sell all or any part of his interest in the patent application or patent to anyone by a properly worded assignment. The application must be filed in the Patent and Trademark Office as the invention of the true inventor, however and not as the invention of the person who has purchased the invention from him.

29. Q. Is it advisable to conduct a search of patents and other records before applying for a patent?

A. Yes; if it is found that the device is shown in some prior patent it is useless to make application. By making a search beforehand the expense involved in filing a needless application is often saved.

Patent Searching

30. Q. Where can a search be conducted?

A. In the Search Room of the Patent and Trademark Office at Crystal Plaza, 2021 Jefferson Davis Highway, Arlington, Virginia. Classified and numerically arranged sets of United States and foreign patents are kept there for public use.

31. Q. Will the Patent and Trademark Office make searches for individuals to help them decide whether to file patent applications?

A. No. But it will assist inventors who come to the Patent and Trademark Office by helping them to find the proper patent classes in which to make searches. For a reasonable fee it will furnish lists of patents in any class and subclass.

Technical Knowledge Available from Patents

32. Q. I have not made an invention but have encountered a problem. Can I obtain knowledge through patents of what has been done by others to solve the problem?

A. The patents in the Patent Search Room contain a vast wealth of technical information and suggestions, organized in a manner which will enable you to review those most closely related to your field of interest. You may come to Arlington and review these patents, or engage a patent practitioner to do this for you and to send you copies of the patents most closely related to your problem.

33. Q. Can I make a search or obtain technical information from patents at locations other than the Patent Search Room?

A. Yes. The libraries listed previously have sets of patent copies numerically arranged in bound volumes, and these patents may be used for search or other information purposes as discussed in the answer to Question 34.

34. Q. **How can technical information be found in a library collection of patents arranged in bound volume in numerical order?**

A. You must first find out from the *Manual of Classification* in the library the Patent classes and subclasses which cover the field of your invention or interest. You can then, by referring to microfilm reels or volumes of the *Index of Patents* in the library identify the patents in these subclasses and, thence, look at them in the bound volumes. Further information on this subject may be found in the leaflet *Obtaining Information from Patents*, a copy of which may be requested from the Patent and Trademark Office.

Infringement of Others' Patents

35. Q. **If I obtain a patent on my invention, will that protect me against the claims of others who assert that I am infringing their patents when I make, use, or sell my own invention?**

A. No. There may be a patent of a more basic nature on which your invention is an improvement. If your invention is a detailed refinement or feature of such a basically protected invention, you may not use it without the consent of the patentee, just as no one will have the right to use your patented improvement without your consent. You should seek competent legal advice before starting to make or sell or use your invention commercially, even though it is protected by a patent granted to you.

Enforcement of Patent Rights

36. Q. **Will the Patent and Trademark Office help me to prosecute others if they infringe the rights granted to me by my patent?**

A. No. The Patent and Trademark Office has no jurisdiction over questions relating to the infringement of patent rights. If your patent is infringed you may sue the infringer in the appropriate United States court at your own expense.

Patent Protection in Foreign Countries

37. Q. **Does a United States patent give protection in foreign countries?**

A. No. The United States patent protects your invention only in this country. If you wish to protect your invention in foreign countries, you must file an application in the Patent Office of each such country within the time permitted by law. This may be quite expensive, both because of the cost of filing and prosecuting the individual patent applications, and because of the fact that most foreign countries require payment of taxes to maintain the patents in force. You should inquire of your practitioner about these costs before you decide to file in foreign countries.

How to Obtain Further Information

38. Q. **How does one obtain information as to patent applications, fees, and other details concerning patents?**

A. By ordering a pamphlet entitled *General Information Concerning Patents*. See Question 40 for sources.

39. Q. **How can I obtain information about the steps I should take in deciding whether to try to obtain a patent, in securing the best possible patent protection, and in developing and marketing my invention successfully?**

A. By ordering a pamphlet entitled *Patents and Inventions—An Information Aid to Inventors*. See Question 40 for source.

40. Q. **How can I obtain copies of the pamphlets mentioned in the answers to Questions 10, 38, and 39?**

A. These pamphlets may be purchased from the Superintendent of Documents, Washington, D.C. 20402, or through any district office of the U.S. Department of Commerce.

WHAT IS A COPYRIGHT?

A copyright is a form of protection given to the authors of original works of authorship, be they literary, dramatic, musical, artistic, or even certain other types of intellectual works. Section 106 of the U.S. Copyright Act generally gives the owner of the copyright the exclusive rights to do and to authorize the following:

1. To reproduce a copyrighted work in copies or phono records
2. To prepare derivative works based upon the copyrighted work
3. To distribute copies of phonorecords of the copyrighted work to the public by sale or other transfer of ownership, or by rent or lease or lending
4. In the case of literary, musical, dramatic, and choreographic works, pantomimes, motion pictures, and other audiovisual works, to perform the copyrighted work publicly
5. In case of literary, musical, dramatic, choreographic, and sculptural works, including the individual images of motion picture or audiovisual works, to display the copyrighted work publicly

It is illegal for anyone to violate any of the rights provided to the owner by the copyright. However, these rights are not unlimited in their scope, and Sections 107 through 118 of the Copyright Act provide for limitations.

Typical of items which can be copyrighted are the following: literary works, musical works including any accompanying words; dramatic works including any accompanying music; pantomimes and choreographic works; pictorial, graphic and sculptural works; motion pictures and other audiovisual works; and sound recordings. This list is, however, not all-inclusive. For example, a computer program, software, is registerable as a literary work. Maps are also registerable as pictorial, graphic, or sculptural works, and so forth. All of these can be copyrighted.

WHAT CAN'T BE COPYRIGHTED?

There are several categories of material that are not eligible for copyright protection. These include: (1) works that have not been fixed in a tangible form of expression, for example, works that have not been written down, recorded, or photographed; (2) titles, names, short phrases, and slogans, mere symbols or designs, mere variations of typographic ornamentation, lettering, or coloring, mere listings of ingredients or contents; (3) ideas, procedures, methods, systems, processes, concepts, principles, discoveries, or devices, as distinguished from a description, explanation, or illustration; (4) works consisting entirely of information that is common property and containing no original authorship. Examples here would include standard calendars, height and weight charts, tape measures and rules, schedules of sporting events, and lists of tables taken from public documents or other common sources.

WHO CAN COPYRIGHT?

As with a patent, only the author or someone deriving his or her rights through the author can rightfully claim copyright. It is important to realize that, unlike a patent, a copyright is done automatically and does not require an attorney even for registration. The procedures for copyright registration are very simple. Copyright protection exists from the time the work is created in any fixed form.

The copyright in the work of authorship immediately becomes the property of the author who created it. Now, there is an exception to this if you are working for someone else. In this case, it is the employer, not the employee, who is considered the author, as you come under a copyright statute defining "work for hire," which is work prepared by an employee within the scope of his or her employment, or a work specially ordered or commissioned for use as a contribution to a collective work.

If there are two or more authors of a joint work, all are co-owners of the copyright unless there are agreements to the contary.

HOW TO APPLY FOR A COPYRIGHT

As we've said, a copyright is secured automatically upon creation. The way in which copyright protection is secured under a new law in the United States is sometimes confused with the way it worked under the old law. Under the old copyright law, copyright was secured by publication with the copyright notice or registration in the copyright office. However, under the new law, no publication or registration or other action in the copyright office is required to secure copyright. You should also recognize that this differs from a patent which must actually be granted by the Patent and Trademark Office.

Prior to 1978 when the new copyright law came into effect, copyright was secured by act of publication with the notice of copyright, publication meaning the distribution of copies of a work to the public by sale or other transfer of ownership, or by rental, lease, or lending. Even though publication is no longer required for copyright, the concept of publication is important in the copyright law because when a work is published, several important consequences follow:

1. Works that are published with a notice of copyright in the United States are subject to mandatory deposit with the Library of Congress.
2. Publication of a work can affect the limitations on the exclusive rights of the copyright owner that are set forth in the new law.
3. The year of publication is used in determining the length of the copyright protection for anonymous and pseudonymous works, when the author's identity is not in the records of the Copyright Office, and for works made for hire.
4. Deposit requirements of published works differ from those of registration of unpublished works.

Now, if you are publishing your work, let's talk first about the notice of copyright. The copyright notice should have three elements:

1. The symbol, a little "c" in a circle, ©, or the word "copyright" or the abbreviation "copr." (I would recommend the © plus the word "copyright," since in some countries this will give you additional international protection.)
2. The year of first publication of whatever it is you are publishing
3. The name of the owner of the copyright

Thus, a typical copyright would read as follows: Copyright © by William A. Cohen, 1990

If you are copyrighting phonograph records or similar items, instead of ©, use this symbol: ℗ In the same fashion, put down the year of first publication and the name of the owner of the copyright.

HOW TO REGISTER YOUR COPYRIGHT

Remember, you receive your copyright automatically. However, there are several advantages to registering your copyright with the U.S. Copyright Office. Here are a few:

1. There will be public record of your claim.
2. Registration may be necessary before infringement suits may be filed in court.
3. If made before or within five years of publication, registration will establish *prima facie* evidence in court of the validity of the copyright and facts stated on the copyright certificate.
4. If registration is made prior to an infringement of the work or registration is made within three months after publication of the work, the copyright owner will qualify in the courts for an award of statutory damages and attorney's fees. Otherwise, only an award of actual damages and profits is available to the copyright owner.

Under the new law, registration may be made at any time within the life of the copyright. It is highly recommended.

Unlike patenting, copyrighting can be done by yourself without professional help. It is also very inexpensive to do, costing at the present time no more than $10 per copyrighted work. Basically you need to submit only three things: (1) a completed application form, (2) the fee of $10 per application, and (3) a deposit of the work being registered. The copy requirements may vary in different situations. In general, they are as follows:

1. If the work is unpublished, one complete copy or phonorecord
2. If the work was first published in the United States on or after January 1, 1978, two complete copies or phonorecords of the best edition
3. If the work was first published in the United States before January 1, 1978, two complete copies or phonorecords of the work as first published
4. If the work was first published outside the United States, whenever published, one complete copy or phonorecord of the work as first published
5. If the work is a contribution to a collective work and published after January 1, 1978, one complete copy or phonorecord of the best edition of the collective work

To obtain copies of the application forms, write to the Register of Copyrights, Library of Congress, Washington, D.C. 20559 or call the copyright office hotline (202) 287-9100. Sample forms are contained in Figures 17.14 through 17.21.

You should request Form TX if you are registering a published or unpublished nondramatic literary work. Form PA is for published and unpublished works of the performing arts, musical and dramatic works, pantomimes and choreographic works, motion pictures, and other audiovisual works. Form VA is for

Filling Out Application Form TX

Detach and read these instructions before completing this form. Make sure all applicable spaces have been filled in before you return this form.

BASIC INFORMATION

When to Use This Form: Use Form TX for registration of published or unpublished non-dramatic literary works, excluding periodicals or serial issues. This class includes a wide variety of works: fiction, non-fiction, poetry, textbooks, reference works, directories, catalogs, advertising copy, compilations of information, and computer programs. For periodicals and serials, use Form SE.

Deposit to Accompany Application: An application for copyright registration must be accompanied by a deposit consisting of copies or phonorecords representing the entire work for which registration is to be made. The following are the general deposit requirements as set forth in the statute:

Unpublished Work: Deposit one complete copy (or phonorecord).

Published Work: Deposit two complete copies (or phonorecords) of the best edition.

Work First Published Outside the United States: Deposit one complete copy (or phonorecord) of the first foreign edition.

Contribution to a Collective Work: Deposit one complete copy (or phonorecord) of the best edition of the collective work.

The Copyright Notice: For published works, the law provides that a copyright notice in a specified form "shall be placed on all publicly distributed copies from which the work can be visually perceived." Use of the copyright notice is the responsibility of the copyright owner and does not require advance permission from the Copyright Office. The required form of the notice for copies generally consists of three elements: (1) the symbol "©", or the word "Copyright," or the abbreviation "Copr."; (2) the year of first publication; and (3) the name of the owner of copyright. For example: "© 1981 Constance Porter." The notice is to be affixed to the copies "in such manner and location as to give reasonable notice of the claim of copyright."

For further information about copyright registration, notice, or special questions relating to copyright problems, write:

Information and Publications Section, LM-455
Copyright Office
Library of Congress
Washington, D.C. 20559

LINE-BY-LINE INSTRUCTIONS

1 SPACE 1: Title

Title of This Work: Every work submitted for copyright registration must be given a title to identify that particular work. If the copies or phonorecords of the work bear a title (or an identifying phrase that could serve as a title), transcribe that wording *completely* and *exactly* on the application. Indexing of the registration and future identification of the work will depend on the information you give here.

Previous or Alternative Titles: Complete this space if there are any additional titles for the work under which someone searching for the registration might be likely to look, or under which a document pertaining to the work might be recorded.

Publication as a Contribution: If the work being registered is a contribution to a periodical, serial, or collection, give the title of the contribution in the "Title of this Work" space. Then, in the line headed "Publication as a Contribution," give information about the collective work in which the contribution appeared.

2 SPACE 2: Author(s)

General Instructions: After reading these instructions, decide who are the "authors" of this work for copyright purposes. Then, unless the work is a "collective work," give the requested information about every "author" who contributed any appreciable amount of copyrightable matter to this version of the work. If you need further space, request additional Continuation sheets. In the case of a collective work, such as an anthology, collection of essays, or encyclopedia, give information about the author of the collective work as a whole.

Name of Author: The fullest form of the author's name should be given. Unless the work was "made for hire," the individual who actually created the work is its "author." In the case of a work made for hire, the statute provides that "the employer or other person for whom the work was prepared is considered the author."

What is a "Work Made for Hire"? A "work made for hire" is defined as: (1) "a work prepared by an employee within the scope of his or her employment"; or (2) "a work specially ordered or commissioned for use as a contribution to a collective work, as a part of a motion picture or other audiovisual work, as a translation, as a supplementary work, as a compilation, as an instructional text, as a test, as answer material for a test, or as an atlas, if the parties expressly agree in a written instrument signed by them that the work shall be considered a work made for hire." If you have checked "Yes" to indicate that the work was "made for hire," you must give the full legal name of the employer (or other person for whom the work was prepared). You may also include the name of the employee along with the name of the employer (for example: "Elster Publishing Co., employer for hire of John Ferguson").

"Anonymous" or "Pseudonymous" Work: An author's contribution to a work is "anonymous" if that author is not identified on the copies or phonorecords of the work. An author's contribution to a work is "pseudonymous" if that author is identified on the copies or phonorecords under a fictitious name. If the work is "anonymous" you may: (1) leave the line blank; or (2) state " anonymous" on the line; or (3) reveal the author's identity. If the work is "pseudonymous" you may : (1) leave the line blank; or (2) give the pseudonym and identify it as such (for example: "Huntley Haverstock, pseudonym"); or (3) reveal the author's name, making clear which is the real name and which is the pseudonym (for example: "Judith Barton, whose pseudonym is Madeline Elster"). However, the citizenship or domicile of the author **must** be given in all cases.

Dates of Birth and Death: If the author is dead, the statute requires that the year of death be included in the application unless the work is anonymous or pseudonymous. The author's birth date is optional, but is useful as a form of identification. Leave this space blank if the author's contribution was a "work made for hire."

Author's Nationality or Domicile: Give the country of which the author is a citizen, or the country in which the author is domiciled. Nationality or domicile **must** be given in all cases.

Nature of Authorship: After the words "Nature of Authorship" give a brief general statement of the nature of this particular author's contribution to the work. Examples: "Entire text"; "Coauthor of entire text"; "Chapters 11-14"; "Editorial revisions"; "Compilation and English translation"; "New text."

Figure 17.14. Filling out application form TX.

406

3 SPACE 3: Creation and Publication

General Instructions: Do not confuse "creation" with "publication." Every application for copyright registration must state "the year in which creation of the work was completed." Give the date and nation of first publication only if the work has been published.

Creation: Under the statute, a work is "created" when it is fixed in a copy or phonorecord for the first time. Where a work has been prepared over a period of time, the part of the work existing in fixed form on a particular date constitutes the created work on that date. The date you give here should be the year in which the author completed the particular version for which registration is now being sought, even if other versions exist or if further changes or additions are planned.

Publication: The statute defines "publication" as "the distribution of copies or phonorecords of a work to the public by sale or other transfer of ownership, or by rental, lease, or lending"; a work is also "published" if there has been an "offering to distribute copies or phonorecords to a group of persons for purposes of further distribution, public performance, or public display." Give the full date (month, day, year) when, and the country where, publication first occurred. If first publication took place simultaneously in the United States and other countries, it is sufficient to state "U.S.A."

4 SPACE 4: Claimant(s)

Name(s) and Address(es) of Copyright Claimant(s): Give the name(s) and address(es) of the copyright claimant(s) in this work even if the claimant is the same as the author. Copyright in a work belongs initially to the author of the work (including, in the case of a work made for hire, the employer or other person for whom the work was prepared). The copyright claimant is either the author of the work or a person or organization to whom the copyright initially belonging to the author has been transferred.

Transfer: The statute provides that, if the copyright claimant is not the author, the application for registration must contain "a brief statement of how the claimant obtained ownership of the copyright." If any copyright claimant named in space 4 is not an author named in space 2, give a brief, general statement summarizing the means by which that claimant obtained ownership of the copyright. Examples: "By written contract"; "Transfer of all rights by author"; "Assignment"; "By will." Do not attach transfer documents or other attachments or riders.

5 SPACE 5: Previous Registration

General Instructions: The questions in space 5 are intended to find out whether an earlier registration has been made for this work and, if so, whether there is any basis for a new registration. As a general rule, only one basic copyright registration can be made for the same version of a particular work.

Same Version: If this version is substantially the same as the work covered by a previous registration, a second registration is not generally possible unless: (1) the work has been registered in unpublished form and a second registration is now being sought to cover this first published edition; or (2) someone other than the author is identified as copyright claimant in the earlier registration, and the author is now seeking registration in his or her own name. If either of these two exceptions apply, check the appropriate box and give the earlier registration number and date. Otherwise, do not submit Form TX; instead, write the Copyright Office for information about supplementary registration or recordation of transfers of copyright ownership.

Changed Version: If the work has been changed, and you are now seeking registration to cover the additions or revisions, check the last box in space 5, give the earlier registration number and date, and complete both parts of space 6 in accordance with the instructions below.

Previous Registration Number and Date: If more than one previous registration has been made for the work, give the number and date of the latest registration.

6 SPACE 6: Derivative Work or Compilation

General Instructions: Complete space 6 if this work is a "changed version," "compilation," or "derivative work," and if it incorporates one or more earlier works that have already been published or registered for copyright, or that have fallen into the public domain. A "compilation" is defined as "a work formed by the collection and assembling of preexisting materials or of data that are selected, coordinated, or arranged in such a way that the resulting work as

a whole constitutes an original work of authorship." A "derivative work" is "a work based on one or more preexisting works." Examples of derivative works include translations, fictionalizations, abridgments, condensations, or "any other form in which a work may be recast, transformed, or adapted." Derivative works also include works "consisting of editorial revisions, annotations, or other modifications" if these changes, as a whole, represent an original work of authorship.

Preexisting Material (space 6a): For derivative works, complete this space and space 6b. In space 6a identify the preexisting work that has been recast, transformed, or adapted. An example of preexisting material might be: "Russian version of Goncharov's 'Oblomov'." Do not complete space 6a for compilations.

Material Added to This Work (space 6b): Give a brief, general statement of the new material covered by the copyright claim for which registration is sought. **Derivative work** examples include: "Foreword, editing, critical annotations"; "Translation"; "Chapters 11-17." If the work is a **compilation**, describe both the compilation itself and the material that has been compiled. Example: "Compilation of certain 1917 Speeches by Woodrow Wilson." A work may be both a derivative work and compilation, in which case a sample statement might be: "Compilation and additional new material."

7 SPACE 7: Manufacturing Provisions

General Instructions: The copyright statute currently provides, as a general rule, that the copies of a published work "consisting preponderantly of nondramatic literary material in the English language" be manufactured in the United States or Canada in order to be lawfully imported and publicly distributed in the United States. If the work being registered is unpublished or not in English, leave this space blank. Complete this space if registration is sought for a published work "consisting preponderantly of nondramatic literary material that is in the English language." Identify those who manufactured the copies and where those manufacturing processes were performed. As an exception to the manufacturing provisions, the statute prescribes that, where manufacture has taken place outside the United States or Canada, a maximum of 2000 copies of the foreign edition may be imported into the United States without affecting the copyright owners' rights. For this purpose, the Copyright Office will issue an Import Statement upon request and payment of a fee of $3 at the time of registration or at any later time. For further information about import statements, write for Form IS.

8 SPACE 8: Reproduction for Use of Blind or Physically Handicapped Individuals

General Instructions: One of the major programs of the Library of Congress is to provide Braille editions and special recordings of works for the exclusive use of the blind and physically handicapped. In an effort to simplify and speed up the copyright licensing procedures that are a necessary part of this program, section 710 of the copyright statute provides for the establishment of a voluntary licensing system to be tied in with copyright registration. Copyright Office regulations provide that you may grant a license for such reproduction and distribution solely for the use of persons who are certified by competent authority as unable to read normal printed material as a result of physical limitations. The license is entirely voluntary, nonexclusive, and may be terminated upon 90 days notice.

How to Grant the License: If you wish to grant it, check one of the three boxes in space 8. Your check in one of these boxes, together with your signature in space 10, will mean that the Library of Congress can proceed to reproduce and distribute under the license without further paperwork. For further information, write for Circular R63.

9,10,11 SPACE 9, 10, 11: Fee, Correspondence, Certification, Return Address

Deposit Account: If you maintain a Deposit Account in the Copyright Office, identify it in space 9. Otherwise leave the space blank and send the fee of $10 with your application and deposit.

Correspondence (space 9): This space should contain the name, address, area code, and telephone number of the person to be consulted if correspondence about this application becomes necessary.

Certification (space 10): The application can not be accepted unless it bears the date and the **handwritten signature** of the author or other copyright claimant, or of the owner of exclusive right(s), or of the duly authorized agent of author, claimant, or owner of exclusive right(s).

Address for Return of Certificate (space 11): The address box must be completed legibly since the certificate will be returned in a window envelope.

Figure 17.14. (Continued)

FORM TX

UNITED STATES COPYRIGHT OFFICE

REGISTRATION NUMBER

_____

| TX | TXU |

EFFECTIVE DATE OF REGISTRATION

_____ _____ _____
Month   Day   Year

DO NOT WRITE ABOVE THIS LINE. IF YOU NEED MORE SPACE, USE A SEPARATE CONTINUATION SHEET.

1

TITLE OF THIS WORK ▼

PREVIOUS OR ALTERNATIVE TITLES ▼

PUBLICATION AS A CONTRIBUTION If this work was published as a contribution to a periodical, serial, or collection, give information about the collective work in which the contribution appeared.   **Title of Collective Work ▼**

If published in a periodical or serial give: **Volume ▼**   **Number ▼**   **Issue Date ▼**   **On Pages ▼**

2

a

NAME OF AUTHOR ▼

DATES OF BIRTH AND DEATH
Year Born ▼   Year Died ▼

Was this contribution to the work a "work made for hire"?
☐ Yes
☐ No

AUTHOR'S NATIONALITY OR DOMICILE
Name of Country
OR { Citizen of ▶ _____
     Domiciled in ▶ _____

WAS THIS AUTHOR'S CONTRIBUTION TO THE WORK
Anonymous?   ☐ Yes ☐ No
Pseudonymous?   ☐ Yes ☐ No
If the answer to either of these questions is "Yes," see detailed instructions.

NATURE OF AUTHORSHIP Briefly describe nature of the material created by this author in which copyright is claimed. ▼

NOTE

Under the law, the "author" of a "work made for hire" is generally the employer, not the employee (see instructions). For any part of this work that was "made for hire" check "Yes" in the space provided, give the employer (or other person for whom the work was prepared) as "Author" of that part, and leave the space for dates of birth and death blank.

b

NAME OF AUTHOR ▼

DATES OF BIRTH AND DEATH
Year Born ▼   Year Died ▼

Was this contribution to the work a "work made for hire"?
☐ Yes
☐ No

AUTHOR'S NATIONALITY OR DOMICILE
Name of country
OR { Citizen of ▶ _____
     Domiciled in ▶ _____

WAS THIS AUTHOR'S CONTRIBUTION TO THE WORK
Anonymous?   ☐ Yes ☐ No
Pseudonymous?   ☐ Yes ☐ No
If the answer to either of these questions is "Yes," see detailed instructions.

NATURE OF AUTHORSHIP Briefly describe nature of the material created by this author in which copyright is claimed. ▼

c

NAME OF AUTHOR ▼

DATES OF BIRTH AND DEATH
Year Born ▼   Year Died ▼

Was this contribution to the work a "work made for hire"?
☐ Yes
☐ No

AUTHOR'S NATIONALITY OR DOMICILE
Name of Country
OR { Citizen of ▶ _____
     Domiciled in ▶ _____

WAS THIS AUTHOR'S CONTRIBUTION TO THE WORK
Anonymous?   ☐ Yes ☐ No
Pseudonymous?   ☐ Yes ☐ No
If the answer to either of these questions is "Yes," see detailed instructions.

NATURE OF AUTHORSHIP Briefly describe nature of the material created by this author in which copyright is claimed. ▼

3

YEAR IN WHICH CREATION OF THIS WORK WAS COMPLETED This information must be given in all cases.
◀ Year

DATE AND NATION OF FIRST PUBLICATION OF THIS PARTICULAR WORK
Complete this information ONLY if this work has been published.
Month ▶ _____ Day ▶ _____ Year ▶ _____
◀ Nation

4

See instructions before completing this space.

COPYRIGHT CLAIMANT(S) Name and address must be given even if the claimant is the same as the author given in space 2.▼

TRANSFER If the claimant(s) named here in space 4 are different from the author(s) named in space 2, give a brief statement of how the claimant(s) obtained ownership of the copyright.▼

DO NOT WRITE HERE / OFFICE USE ONLY

APPLICATION RECEIVED

ONE DEPOSIT RECEIVED

TWO DEPOSITS RECEIVED

REMITTANCE NUMBER AND DATE

MORE ON BACK ▶
• Complete all applicable spaces (numbers 5-11) on the reverse side of this page.
• See detailed instructions.
• Sign the form at line 10.

DO NOT WRITE HERE

Page 1 of _____ pages

Figure 17.14. *(Continued)*

FORM TX

☐ CORRESPONDENCE
Yes

☐ DEPOSIT ACCOUNT
FUNDS USED

FOR
COPYRIGHT
OFFICE
USE
ONLY

DO NOT WRITE ABOVE THIS LINE. IF YOU NEED MORE SPACE, USE A SEPARATE CONTINUATION SHEET.

PREVIOUS REGISTRATION Has registration for this work, or for an earlier version of this work, already been made in the Copyright Office?

☐ Yes ☐ No If your answer is "Yes," why is another registration being sought? (Check appropriate box) ▼

☐ This is the first published edition of a work previously registered in unpublished form.

☐ This is the first application submitted by this author as copyright claimant.

☐ This is a changed version of the work, as shown by space 6 on this application.

If your answer is "Yes," give: **Previous Registration Number** ▼ _____ **Year of Registration** ▼ _____

5

DERIVATIVE WORK OR COMPILATION Complete both space 6a & 6b for a derivative work; complete only 6b for a compilation.

a. Preexisting Material Identify any preexisting work or works that this work is based on or incorporates. ▼

b. Material Added to This Work Give a brief, general statement of the material that has been added to this work and in which copyright is claimed. ▼

6

See instructions
before completing
this space.

MANUFACTURERS AND LOCATIONS If this is a published work consisting preponderantly of nondramatic literary material in English, the law may require that the copies be manufactured in the United States or Canada for full protection. If so, the names of the manufacturers who performed certain processes, and the places where these processes were performed **must** be given. See instructions for details.

Names of Manufacturers ▼ _____ **Places of Manufacture** ▼

7

REPRODUCTION FOR USE OF BLIND OR PHYSICALLY HANDICAPPED INDIVIDUALS A signature on this form at space 10, and a check in one of the boxes here in space 8, constitutes a non-exclusive grant of permission to the Library of Congress to reproduce and distribute solely for the blind and physically handicapped and under the conditions and limitations prescribed by the regulations of the Copyright Office: (1) copies of the work identified in space 1 of this application in Braille (or similar tactile symbols); or (2) phonorecords embodying a fixation of a reading of that work; or (3) both.

a ☐ Copies and Phonorecords   b ☐ Copies Only   c ☐ Phonorecords Only

8

See instructions.

DEPOSIT ACCOUNT If the registration fee is to be charged to a Deposit Account established in the Copyright Office, give name and number of Account.

Name ▼ _____ **Account Number** ▼ _____

9

CORRESPONDENCE Give name and address to which correspondence about this application should be sent. Name/Address/Apt/City/State/Zip ▼

Area Code & Telephone Number ▶ _____

Be sure to
give your
daytime phone
◀ number.

CERTIFICATION* I, the undersigned, hereby certify that I am the

Check one ▶

☐ author
☐ other copyright claimant
☐ owner of exclusive right(s)
☐ authorized agent of _____

of the work identified in this application and that the statements made by me in this application are correct to the best of my knowledge.

Name of author or other copyright claimant, or owner of exclusive right(s) ▲

10

Typed or printed name and date ▼ If this is a published work, this date must be the same as or later than the date of publication given in space 3.

_____ date ▶ _____

✍ **Handwritten signature (X)** ▼

MAIL CERTIFI-CATE TO

Certificate will be mailed in window envelope

Name ▼

Number/Street/Apartment Number ▼

City/State/ZIP ▼

Have you:
• Completed all necessary spaces?
• Signed your application in space 10?
• Enclosed check or money order for $10 payable to *Register of Copyrights*?
• Enclosed your deposit material with the application and fee?

MAIL TO: Register of Copyrights, Library of Congress, Washington, D.C. 20559.

11

⬩U.S. GOVERNMENT PRINTING OFFICE: 1987:181—531/60,006

August 1987—100,000

Figure 17.14. (Continued)

Filling Out Application Form PA

Detach and read these instructions before completing this form. Make sure all applicable spaces have been filled in before you return this form.

BASIC INFORMATION

When to Use This Form: Use Form PA for registration of published or unpublished works of the performing arts. This class includes works prepared for the purpose of being "performed" directly before an audience or indirectly "by means of any device or process." Works of the performing arts include: (1) musical works, including any accompanying words; (2) dramatic works, including any accompanying music; (3) pantomimes and choreographic works; and (4) motion pictures and other audiovisual works.

Deposit to Accompany Application: An application for copyright registration must be accompanied by a deposit consisting of copies or phonorecords representing the entire work for which registration is to be made. The following are the general deposit requirements as set forth in the statute:

Unpublished Work: Deposit one complete copy (or phonorecord).

Published Work: Deposit two complete copies (or phonorecords) of the best edition.

Work First Published Outside the United States: Deposit one complete copy (or phonorecord) of the first foreign edition.

Contribution to a Collective Work: Deposit one complete copy (or phonorecord) of the best edition of the collective work.

Motion Pictures: Deposit *both* of the following: (1) a separate written description of the contents of the motion picture; and (2) for a published work, one complete copy of the best edition of the motion picture; or, for an unpublished work, one complete copy of the motion picture or identifying material. Identifying material may be either an audiorecording of the entire soundtrack or one frame enlargement or similar visual print from each 10-minute segment.

The Copyright Notice: For published works, the law provides that a copyright notice in a specified form "shall be placed on all publicly distributed copies from which the work can be visually perceived." Use of the copyright notice is the responsibility of the copyright owner and does not require advance permission from the Copyright Office. The required form of the notice for copies generally consists of three elements: (1) the symbol "©", or the word "Copyright," or the abbreviation "Copr."; (2) the year of first publication; and (3) the name of the owner of copyright. For example: "© 1981 Constance Porter." The notice is to be affixed to the copies "in such manner and location as to give reasonable notice of the claim of copyright."

For further information about copyright registration, notice, or special questions relating to copyright problems, write:

> Information and Publications Section, LM-455
> Copyright Office
> Library of Congress
> Washington, D.C. 20559

PRIVACY ACT ADVISORY STATEMENT Required by the Privacy Act of 1974 (P.L. 93-579)

The authority for requesting this information is title 17, U.S.C., secs. 409 and 410. Furnishing the requested information is voluntary. But if the information is not furnished, it may be necessary to delay or refuse registration and you may not be entitled to certain relief, remedies, and benefits provided in chapters 4 and 5 of title 17, U.S.C.

The principal uses of the requested information are the establishment and maintenance of a public record and the examination of the application for compliance with legal requirements.

Other routine uses include public inspection and copying, preparation of public indexes, preparation of public catalogs of copyright registrations, and preparation of search reports upon request.

NOTE: No other advisory statement will be given in connection with this application. Please keep this statement and refer to it if we communicate with you regarding this application.

LINE-BY-LINE INSTRUCTIONS

1 SPACE 1: Title

Title of This Work: Every work submitted for copyright registration must be given a title to identify that particular work. If the copies or phonorecords of the work bear a title (or an identifying phrase that could serve as a title), transcribe that wording *completely* and *exactly* on the application. Indexing of the registration and future identification of the work will depend on the information you give here. If the work you are registering is an entire "collective work" (such as a collection of plays or songs), give the overall title of the collection. If you are registering one or more individual contributions to a collective work, give the title of each contribution, followed by the title of the collection. Example: "'A Song for Elinda' in *Old and New Ballads for Old and New People.*"

Previous or Alternative Titles: Complete this space if there are any additional titles for the work under which someone searching for the registration might be likely to look, or under which a document pertaining to the work might be recorded.

Nature of This Work: Briefly describe the general nature or character of the work being registered for copyright. Examples: "Music"; "Song Lyrics"; "Words and Music"; "Drama"; "Musical Play"; "Choreography"; "Pantomime"; "Motion Picture"; "Audiovisual Work."

2 SPACE 2: Author(s)

General Instructions: After reading these instructions, decide who are the "authors" of this work for copyright purposes. Then, unless the work is a "collective work," give the requested information about every "author" who contributed any appreciable amount of copyrightable matter to this version of the work. If you need further space, request additional Continuation Sheets. In the case of a collective work, such as a songbook or a collection of plays, give information about the author of the collective work as a whole.

Name of Author: The fullest form of the author's name should be given. Unless the work was "made for hire," the individual who actually created the work is its "author." In the case of a work made for hire, the statute provides that "the employer or other person for whom the work was prepared is considered the author."

What is a "Work Made for Hire"? A "work made for hire" is defined as: (1) "a work prepared by an employee within the scope of his or her employment"; or (2) "a work specially ordered or commissioned for use as a contribution to a collective work, as a part of a motion picture or other audiovisual work, as a translation, as a supplementary work, as a compilation, as an instructional text, as a test, as answer material for a test, or as an atlas, if the parties expressly agree in a written instrument signed by them that the work shall be considered a work made for hire." If you have checked "Yes" to indicate that the work was "made for hire," you must give the full legal name of the employer (or other person for whom the work was prepared). You may also include the name of the employee along with the name of the employer (for example: "Elster Music Co., employer for hire of John Ferguson").

"Anonymous" or "Pseudonymous" Work: An author's contribution to a work is "anonymous" if that author is not identified on the copies or phonorecords of the work. An author's contribution to a work is "pseudonymous" if that author is identified on the copies or phonorecords under a fictitious name. If the work is "anonymous" you may: (1) leave the line blank; or (2) state "anonymous" on the line; or (3) reveal the author's identity. If the work is "pseudonymous" you may: (1) leave the line blank; or (2) give the pseudonym and identify it as such (for example: "Huntley Haverstock, pseudonym"); or (3) reveal the author's name, making clear which is the real name and which is the pseudonym (for example: "Judith Barton, whose pseudonym is Madeline Elster"). However, the citizenship or domicile of the author **must** be given in all cases.

Dates of Birth and Death: If the author is dead, the statute requires that the year of death be included in the application unless the work is anonymous or pseudonymous. The author's birth date is optional, but is useful as a form of identification. Leave this space blank if the author's contribution was a "work made for hire."

Author's Nationality or Domicile: Give the country of which the author is a citizen, or the country in which the author is domiciled. Nationality or domicile **must** be given in all cases.

Nature of Authorship: Give a brief general statement of the nature of this particular author's contribution to the work. Examples: "Words"; "Co-Author of Music"; "Words and Music"; "Arrangement"; "Co-Author of Book and Lyrics"; "Dramatization"; "Screen Play"; "Compilation and English Translation"; "Editorial Revisions."

Figure 17.15. Filling out application form PA.

3 SPACE 3: Creation and Publication

General Instructions: Do not confuse "creation" with "publication." Every application for copyright registration must state "the year in which creation of the work was completed." Give the date and nation of first publication only if the work has been published.

Creation: Under the statute, a work is "created" when it is fixed in a copy or phonorecord for the first time. Where a work has been prepared over a period of time, the part of the work existing in fixed form on a particular date constitutes the created work on that date. The date you give here should be the year in which the author completed the particular version for which registration is now being sought, even if other versions exist or if further changes or additions are planned.

Publication: The statute defines "publication" as "the distribution of copies or phonorecords of a work to the public by sale or other transfer of ownership, or by rental, lease, or lending"; a work is also "published" if there has been an "offering to distribute copies or phonorecords to a group of persons for purposes of further distribution, public performance, or public display." Give the full date (month, day, year) when, and the country where, publication first occurred. If first publication took place simultaneously in the United States and other countries, it is sufficient to state "U.S.A."

4 SPACE 4: Claimant(s)

Name(s) and Address(es) of Copyright Claimant(s): Give the name(s) and address(es) of the copyright claimant(s) in this work even if the claimant is the same as the author. Copyright in a work belongs initially to the author of the work (including, in the case of a work made for hire, the employer or other person for whom the work was prepared). The copyright claimant is either the author of the work or a person or organization to whom the copyright initially belonging to the author has been transferred.

Transfer: The statute provides that, if the copyright claimant is not the author, the application for registration must contain "a brief statement of how the claimant obtained ownership of the copyright." If any copyright claimant named in space 4 is not an author named in space 2, give a brief, general statement summarizing the means by which that claimant obtained ownership of the copyright. Examples: "By written contract"; "Transfer of all rights by author"; "Assignment"; "By will." Do not attach transfer documents or other attachments or riders.

5 SPACE 5: Previous Registration

General Instructions: The questions in space 5 are intended to find out whether an earlier registration has been made for this work and, if so, whether there is any basis for a new registration. As a general rule, only one basic copyright registration can be made for the same version of a particular work.

Same Version: If this version is substantially the same as the work covered by a previous registration, a second registration is not generally possible unless: (1) the work has been registered in unpublished form and a second registration is now being sought to cover this first published edition; or (2) someone other than the author is identified as copyright claimant in the earlier registration, and the author is now seeking registration in his or her own name. If either of these two exceptions apply, check the appropriate box and give the

earlier registration number and date. Otherwise, do not submit Form PA; instead, write the Copyright Office for information about supplementary registration or recordation of transfers of copyright ownership.

Changed Version: If the work has been changed, and you are now seeking registration to cover the additions or revisions, check the last box in space 5, give the earlier registration number and date, and complete both parts of space 6 in accordance with the instructions below.

Previous Registration Number and Date: If more than one previous registration has been made for the work, give the number and date of the latest registration.

6 SPACE 6: Derivative Work or Compilation

General Instructions: Complete space 6 if this work is a "changed version," "compilation," or "derivative work," and if it incorporates one or more earlier works that have already been published or registered for copyright, or that have fallen into the public domain. A "compilation" is defined as "a work formed by the collection and assembling of preexisting materials or of data that are selected, coordinated, or arranged in such a way that the resulting work as a whole constitutes an original work of authorship." A "derivative work" is "a work based on one or more preexisting works." Examples of derivative works include musical arrangements, dramatizations, translations, abridgments, condensations, motion picture versions, or "any other form in which a work may be recast, transformed, or adapted." Derivative works also include works "consisting of editorial revisions, annotations, or other modifications" if these changes, as a whole, represent an original work of authorship.

Preexisting Material (space 6a): Complete this space and space 6b for derivative works. In this space identify the preexisting work that has been recast, transformed, or adapted. For example, the preexisting material might be: "French version of Hugo's 'Le Roi s'amuse'." Do not complete this space for compilations.

Material Added to This Work (space 6b): Give a brief, general statement of the **additional** new material covered by the copyright claim for which registration is sought. In the case of a derivative work, identify this new material. Examples: "Arrangement for piano and orchestra"; "Dramatization for television"; "New film version"; "Revisions throughout; Act III completely new." If the work is a compilation, give a brief, general statement describing both the material that has been compiled **and** the compilation itself. Example: "Compilation of 19th Century Military Songs."

7,8,9 SPACE 7, 8, 9: Fee, Correspondence, Certification, Return Address

Deposit Account: If you maintain a Deposit Account in the Copyright Office, identify it in space 7. Otherwise leave the space blank and send the fee of $10 with your application and deposit.

Correspondence (space 7): This space should contain the name, address, area code, and telephone number of the person to be consulted if correspondence about this application becomes necessary.

Certification (space 8): The application cannot be accepted unless it bears the date and the **handwritten signature** of the author or other copyright claimant, or of the owner of exclusive right(s), or of the duly authorized agent of the author, claimant, or owner of exclusive right(s).

Address for Return of Certificate (space 9): The address box must be completed legibly since the certificate will be returned in a window envelope.

MORE INFORMATION

How To Register a Recorded Work: If the musical or dramatic work that you are registering has been recorded (as a tape, disk, or cassette), you may choose either copyright application Form PA or Form SR, Performing Arts or Sound Recordings, depending on the purpose of the registration.

Form PA should be used to register the underlying musical composition or dramatic work. Form SR has been developed specifically to register a "sound recording" as defined by the Copyright Act—a work resulting from the "fixation of a series of sounds," separate and distinct from the underlying musical or dramatic work. Form SR should be used when the copyright claim is limited to the sound recording itself. (In one instance, Form SR may also be used to file for a copyright registration for both kinds of works—see (4) below.) Therefore:

(1) File Form PA if you are seeking to register the musical or dramatic work, not the "sound recording," even though what you deposit for copyright purposes may be in the form of a phonorecord.

(2) File Form PA if you are seeking to register the audio portion of an audiovisual work, such as a motion picture soundtrack; these are considered integral parts of the audiovisual work.

(3) File Form SR if you are seeking to register the "sound recording" itself, that is, the work that results from the fixation of a series of musical, spoken, or other sounds, but not the underlying musical or dramatic work.

(4) File Form SR if you are the copyright claimant for both the underlying musical or dramatic work and the sound recording, and you prefer to register both on the same form.

(5) File both forms PA and SR if the copyright claimant for the underlying work and sound recording differ, or you prefer to have separate registration for them.

"Copies" and "Phonorecords": To register for copyright, you are required to deposit "copies" or "phonorecords." These are defined as follows:

Musical compositions may be embodied (fixed) in "copies," objects from which a work can be read or visually perceived, directly or with the aid of a machine or device, such as manuscripts, books, sheet music, film, and videotape. They may also be fixed in "phonorecords," objects embodying fixations of sounds, such as tapes and phonograph disks, commonly known as phonograph records. For example, a song (the work to be registered) can be reproduced in sheet music ("copies") or phonograph records ("phonorecords"), or both.

Figure 17.15. (Continued)

PA   PAU

EFFECTIVE DATE OF REGISTRATION

Month   Day   Year

DO NOT WRITE ABOVE THIS LINE. IF YOU NEED MORE SPACE, USE A SEPARATE CONTINUATION SHEET.

1

TITLE OF THIS WORK ▼

PREVIOUS OR ALTERNATIVE TITLES ▼

NATURE OF THIS WORK ▼ See instructions

2

a

NAME OF AUTHOR▼

DATES OF BIRTH AND DEATH
Year Born ▼   Year Died ▼

Was this contribution to the work a "work made for hire"?
☐ Yes
☐ No

AUTHOR'S NATIONALITY OR DOMICILE
Name of Country
OR { Citizen of ▶
Domiciled in ▶

WAS THIS AUTHOR'S CONTRIBUTION TO THE WORK
Anonymous?   ☐ Yes ☐ No
Pseudonymous?   ☐ Yes ☐ No

If the answer to either of these questions is "Yes," see detailed instructions.

NATURE OF AUTHORSHIP Briefly describe nature of the material created by this author in which copyright is claimed. ▼

NOTE

Under the law, the "author" of a "work made for hire" is generally the employer, not the employee (see instructions). For any part of this work that was "made for hire" check "Yes" in the space provided, give the employer (or other person for whom the work was prepared) as "Author" of that part, and leave the space for dates of birth and death blank.

b

NAME OF AUTHOR ▼

DATES OF BIRTH AND DEATH
Year Born ▼   Year Died ▼

Was this contribution to the work a "work made for hire"?
☐ Yes
☐ No

AUTHOR'S NATIONALITY OR DOMICILE
Name of country
OR { Citizen of ▶
Domiciled in ▶

WAS THIS AUTHOR'S CONTRIBUTION TO THE WORK
Anonymous?   ☐ Yes ☐ No
Pseudonymous?   ☐ Yes ☐ No

If the answer to either of these questions is "Yes," see detailed instructions.

NATURE OF AUTHORSHIP Briefly describe nature of the material created by this author in which copyright is claimed. ▼

c

NAME OF AUTHOR ▼

DATES OF BIRTH AND DEATH
Year Born ▼   Year Died ▼

Was this contribution to the work a "work made for hire"?
☐ Yes
☐ No

AUTHOR'S NATIONALITY OR DOMICILE
Name of Country
OR { Citizen of ▶
Domiciled in ▶

WAS THIS AUTHOR'S CONTRIBUTION TO THE WORK
Anonymous?   ☐ Yes ☐ No
Pseudonymous?   ☐ Yes ☐ No

If the answer to either of these questions is "Yes," see detailed instructions.

NATURE OF AUTHORSHIP Briefly describe nature of the material created by this author in which copyright is claimed. ▼

3

YEAR IN WHICH CREATION OF THIS WORK WAS COMPLETED This information must be given in all cases.
◀ Year

DATE AND NATION OF FIRST PUBLICATION OF THIS PARTICULAR WORK
Complete this information ONLY if this work has been published.
Month ▶   Day ▶   Year ▶
◀ Nation

4

See instructions before completing this space.

COPYRIGHT CLAIMANT(S) Name and address must be given even if the claimant is the same as the author given in space 2.▼

TRANSFER If the claimant(s) named here in space 4 are different from the author(s) named in space 2, give a brief statement of how the claimant(s) obtained ownership of the copyright.▼

APPLICATION RECEIVED

ONE DEPOSIT RECEIVED

TWO DEPOSITS RECEIVED

REMITTANCE NUMBER AND DATE

DO NOT WRITE HERE
OFFICE USE ONLY

MORE ON BACK ▶
• Complete all applicable spaces (numbers 5-9) on the reverse side of this page.
• See detailed instructions.   • Sign the form at line 8.

DO NOT WRITE HERE
Page 1 of_____pages

Figure 17.15. (Continued)

DO NOT WRITE ABOVE THIS LINE. IF YOU NEED MORE SPACE, USE A SEPARATE CONTINUATION SHEET.

PREVIOUS REGISTRATION Has registration for this work, or for an earlier version of this work, already been made in the Copyright Office?

☐ Yes ☐ No If your answer is "Yes," why is another registration being sought? (Check appropriate box) ▼

☐ This is the first published edition of a work previously registered in unpublished form.

☐ This is the first application submitted by this author as copyright claimant.

☐ This is a changed version of the work, as shown by space 6 on this application.

If your answer is "Yes," give: **Previous Registration Number** ▼   **Year of Registration** ▼

5

DERIVATIVE WORK OR COMPILATION   Complete both space 6a & 6b for a derivative work; complete only 6b for a compilation.

a. Preexisting Material   Identify any preexisting work or works that this work is based on or incorporates. ▼

b. Material Added to This Work   Give a brief, general statement of the material that has been added to this work and in which copyright is claimed.▼

6

See instructions
before completing
this space.

DEPOSIT ACCOUNT   If the registration fee is to be charged to a Deposit Account established in the Copyright Office, give name and number of Account.

Name ▼   **Account Number** ▼

7

CORRESPONDENCE   Give name and address to which correspondence about this application should be sent.   Name/Address/Apt/City/State/Zip ▼

Area Code & Telephone Number ▶

Be sure to
give your
daytime phone
◀ number

CERTIFICATION*   I, the undersigned, hereby certify that I am the

Check only one ▼

☐ author

☐ other copyright claimant

☐ owner of exclusive right(s)

☐ authorized agent of_____
                Name of author or other copyright claimant, or owner of exclusive right(s) ▲

8

of the work identified in this application and that the statements made
by me in this application are correct to the best of my knowledge.

Typed or printed name and date ▼ If this is a published work, this date must be the same as or later than the date of publication given in space 3.

_____ date ▶ _____

✍ Handwritten signature (X) ▼

**MAIL
CERTIFI-
CATE TO**

**Certificate
will be
mailed in
window
envelope**

Name ▼

Number/Street/Apartment Number ▼

City/State/ZIP ▼

Have you:
● Completed all necessary
  spaces?
● Signed your application in space
  8?
● Enclosed check or money order
  for $10 payable to *Register of
  Copyrights?*
● Enclosed your deposit material
  with the application and fee?

MAIL TO: Register of Copyrights.
Library of Congress. Washington.
D.C. 20559.

9

* 17 U.S.C. § 506(e): Any person who knowingly makes a false representation of a material fact in the application for copyright registration provided for by section 409, or in any written statement filed in connection with the application, shall be fined not more than $2,500.

☆U.S. GOVERNMENT PRINTING OFFICE: 1987:181—531 60,001

August 1987—60,000

Figure 17.15.   (*Continued*)

Filling Out Application Form VA

Detach and read these instructions before completing this form. Make sure all applicable spaces have been filled in before you return this form.

BASIC INFORMATION

When to Use This Form: Use Form VA for copyright registration of published or unpublished works of the visual arts. This category consists of "pictorial, graphic, or sculptural works," including two-dimensional and three-dimensional works of fine, graphic, and applied art, photographs, prints and art reproductions, maps, globes, charts, technical drawings, diagrams, and models.

What Does Copyright Protect? Copyright in a work of the visual arts protects those pictorial, graphic, or sculptural elements that, either alone or in combination, represent an "original work of authorship." The statute declares: "In no case does copyright protection for an original work of authorship extend to any idea, procedure, process, system, method of operation, concept, principle, or discovery, regardless of the form in which it is described, explained, illustrated, or embodied in such work."

Works of Artistic Craftsmanship and Designs: "Works of artistic craftsmanship" are registrable on Form VA, but the statute makes clear that protection extends to "their form" and not to "their mechanical or utilitarian aspects." The "design of a useful article" is considered copyrightable "only if, and only to the extent that, such design incorporates pictorial, graphic, or sculptural features that can be identified separately from, and are capable of existing independently of, the utilitarian aspects of the article."

Labels and Advertisements: Works prepared for use in connection with the sale or advertisement of goods and services are registrable if they contain "original work of authorship." Use Form VA if the copyrightable material in the work you are registering is mainly pictorial or graphic; use Form TX if it consists mainly of text. **NOTE:** Words and short phrases such as names, titles, and slogans cannot be protected by copyright, and the same is true of standard symbols, emblems, and other commonly used graphic designs that are in the public domain. When used commercially, material of that sort can sometimes be protected under state laws of unfair competition or under the Federal trademark laws. For information about trademark registration, write to the Commissioner of Patents and Trademarks, Washington, D.C. 20231.

Deposit to Accompany Application: An application for copyright registration must be accompanied by a deposit consisting of copies representing the entire work for which registration is to be made.

Unpublished Work: Deposit one complete copy.

Published Work: Deposit two complete copies of the best edition.

Work First Published Outside the United States: Deposit one complete copy of the first foreign edition.

Contribution to a Collective Work: Deposit one complete copy of the best edition of the collective work.

The Copyright Notice: For published works, the law provides that a copyright notice in a specified form "shall be placed on all publicly distributed copies from which the work can be visually perceived." Use of the copyright notice is the responsibility of the copyright owner and does not require advance permission from the Copyright Office. The required form of the notice for copies generally consists of three elements: (1) the symbol "©", or the word "Copyright," or the abbreviation "Copr."; (2) the year of first publication; and (3) the name of the owner of copyright. For example: "© 1981 Constance Porter." The notice is to be affixed to the copies "in such manner and location as to give reasonable notice of the claim of copyright."

For further information about copyright registration, notice, or special questions relating to copyright problems, write:

Information and Publications Section, LM-455
Copyright Office, Library of Congress, Washington, D.C. 20559

LINE-BY-LINE INSTRUCTIONS

1 SPACE 1: Title

Title of This Work: Every work submitted for copyright registration must be given a title to identify that particular work. If the copies of the work bear a title (or an identifying phrase that could serve as a title), transcribe that wording *completely* and *exactly* on the application. Indexing of the registration and future identification of the work will depend on the information you give here.

Previous or Alternative Titles: Complete this space if there are any additional titles for the work under which someone searching for the registration might be likely to look, or under which a document pertaining to the work might be recorded.

Publication as a Contribution: If the work being registered is a contribution to a periodical, serial, or collection, give the title of the contribution in the "Title of This Work" space. Then, in the line headed "Publication as a Contribution," give information about the collective work in which the contribution appeared.

Nature of This Work: Briefly describe the general nature or character of the pictorial, graphic, or sculptural work being registered for copyright. Examples: "Oil Painting"; "Charcoal Drawing"; "Etching"; "Sculpture"; "Map"; "Photograph"; "Scale Model"; "Lithographic Print"; "Jewelry Design"; "Fabric Design."

2 SPACE 2: Author(s)

General Instructions: After reading these instructions, decide who are the "authors" of this work for copyright purposes. Then, unless the work is a "collective work," give the requested information about every "author" who contributed any appreciable amount of copyrightable matter to this version of the work. If you need further space, request additional Continuation Sheets. In the case of a collective work, such as a catalog of paintings or collection of cartoons by various authors, give information about the author of the collective work as a whole.

Name of Author: The fullest form of the author's name should be given. Unless the work was "made for hire," the individual who actually created the work is its "author." In the case of a work made for hire, the statute provides that "the employer or other person for whom the work was prepared is considered the author."

What is a "Work Made for Hire"? A "work made for hire" is defined as: (1) "a work prepared by an employee within the scope of his or her employment"; or (2) "a work specially ordered or commissioned for use as a contribution to a collective work, as a part of a motion picture or other audiovisual work, as a translation, as a supplementary work, as a compilation, as an instructional text, as a test, as answer material for a test, or as an atlas, if the parties expressly agree in a written instrument signed by them that the work shall be considered a work made for hire." If you have checked "Yes" to indicate that the work was "made for hire," you must give the full legal name of the employer (or other person for whom the work was prepared). You may also include the name of the employee along with the name of the employer (for example: "Elster Publishing Co., employer for hire of John Ferguson").

"Anonymous" or "Pseudonymous" Work: An author's contribution to a work is "anonymous" if that author is not identified on the copies or phonorecords of the work. An author's contribution to a work is "pseudonymous" if that author is identified on the copies or phonorecords under a fictitious name. If the work is "anonymous" you may: (1) leave the line blank; or (2) state "anonymous" on the line; or (3) reveal the author's identity. If the work is "pseudonymous" you may: (1) leave the line blank; or (2) give the pseudonym and identify it as such (for example: "Huntley Haverstock, pseudonym"); or (3) reveal the author's name, making clear which is the real name and which is the pseudonym (for example: "Henry Leek, whose pseudonym is Priam Farrel"). However, the citizenship or domicile of the author **must** be given in all cases.

Dates of Birth and Death: If the author is dead, the statute requires that the year of death be included in the application unless the work is anonymous or pseudonymous. The author's birth date is optional, but is useful as a form of identification. Leave this space blank if the author's contribution was a "work made for hire."

Figure 17.16. Filling out application form VA.

Author's Nationality or Domicile: Give the country of which the author is a citizen, or the country in which the author is domiciled. Nationality or domicile **must** be given in all cases.

Nature of Authorship: Give a brief general statement of the nature of this particular author's contribution to the work. Examples: "Painting"; "Photograph"; "Silk Screen Reproduction"; "Co-author of Cartographic Material"; "Technical Drawing"; "Text and Artwork."

3 SPACE 3: Creation and Publication

General Instructions: Do not confuse "creation" with "publication." Every application for copyright registration must state "the year in which creation of the work was completed." Give the date and nation of first publication only if the work has been published.

Creation: Under the statute, a work is "created" when it is fixed in a copy or phonorecord for the first time. Where a work has been prepared over a period of time, the part of the work existing in fixed form on a particular date constitutes the created work on that date. The date you give here should be the year in which the author completed the particular version for which registration is now being sought, even if other versions exist or if further changes or additions are planned.

Publication: The statute defines "publication" as "the distribution of copies or phonorecords of a work to the public by sale or other transfer of ownership, or by rental, lease, or lending"; a work is also "published" if there has been an "offering to distribute copies or phonorecords to a group of persons for purposes of further distribution, public performance, or public display." Give the full date (month, day, year) when, and the country where, publication first occurred. If first publication took place simultaneously in the United States and other countries, it is sufficient to state "U.S.A."

4 SPACE 4: Claimant(s)

Name(s) and Address(es) of Copyright Claimant(s): Give the name(s) and address(es) of the copyright claimant(s) in this work even if the claimant is the same as the author. Copyright in a work belongs initially to the author of the work (including, in the case of a work made for hire, the employer or other person for whom the work was prepared). The copyright claimant is either the author of the work or a person or organization to whom the copyright initially belonging to the author has been transferred.

Transfer: The statute provides that, if the copyright claimant is not the author, the application for registration must contain "a brief statement of how the claimant obtained ownership of the copyright." If any copyright claimant named in space 4 is not an author named in space 2, give a brief, general statement summarizing the means by which that claimant obtained ownership of the copyright. Examples: "By written contract"; "Transfer of all rights by author"; "Assignment"; "By will." Do not attach transfer documents or other attachments or riders.

5 SPACE 5: Previous Registration

General Instructions: The questions in space 5 are intended to find out whether an earlier registration has been made for this work and, if so, whether there is any basis for a new registration. As a rule, only one basic copyright registration can be made for the same version of a particular work.

Same Version: If this version is substantially the same as the work covered by a previous registration, a second registration is not generally possible unless: (1) the work has been registered in unpublished form and a second registration is now being sought to cover this first published edition; or (2) someone other than the author is identified as copyright claimant in the earlier registration, and the author is now seeking registration in his or her own name. If either of these two exceptions apply, check the appropriate box and give the earlier registration number and date. Otherwise, do not submit Form VA; instead, write the Copyright Office for information about supplementary registration or recordation of transfers of copyright ownership.

Changed Version: If the work has been changed, and you are now seeking registration to cover the additions or revisions, check the last box in space 5, give the earlier registration number and date, and complete both parts of space 6 in accordance with the instructions below.

Previous Registration Number and Date: If more than one previous registration has been made for the work, give the number and date of the latest registration.

6 SPACE 6: Derivative Work or Compilation

General Instructions: Complete space 6 if this work is a "changed version," "compilation," or "derivative work," and if it incorporates one or more earlier works that have already been published or registered for copyright, or that have fallen into the public domain. A "compilation" is defined as "a work formed by the collection and assembling of preexisting materials or of data that are selected, coordinated, or arranged in such a way that the resulting work as a whole constitutes an original work of authorship." A "derivative work" is "a work based on one or more preexisting works." Examples of derivative works include reproductions of works of art, sculptures based on drawings, lithographs based on paintings, maps based on previously published sources, or "any other form in which a work may be recast, transformed, or adapted." Derivative works also include works "consisting of editorial revisions, annotations, or other modifications" if these changes, as a whole, represent an original work of authorship.

Preexisting Material (space 6a): Complete this space **and** space 6b for derivative works. In this space identify the preexisting work that has been recast, transformed, or adapted. Examples of preexisting material might be "Grunewald Altarpiece"; or "19th century quilt design." Do not complete this space for compilations.

Material Added to This Work (space 6b): Give a brief, general statement of the **additional** new material covered by the copyright claim for which registration is sought. In the case of a derivative work, identify this new material. Examples: "Adaptation of design and additional artistic work"; "Reproduction of painting by photolithography"; "Additional cartographic material"; "Compilation of photographs." If the work is a compilation, give a brief, general statement describing both the material that has been compiled **and** the compilation itself. Example: "Compilation of 19th Century Political Cartoons."

7,8,9 SPACE 7, 8, 9: Fee, Correspondence, Certification, Return Address

Deposit Account: If you maintain a Deposit Account in the Copyright Office, identify it in space 7. Otherwise leave the space blank and send the fee of $10 with your application and deposit.

Correspondence (space 7): This space should contain the name, address, area code, and telephone number of the person to be consulted if correspondence about this application becomes necessary.

Certification (space 8): The application cannot be accepted unless it bears the date and the **handwritten signature** of the author or other copyright claimant, or of the owner of exclusive right(s), or of the duly authorized agent of the author, claimant, or owner of exclusive right(s).

Address for Return of Certificate (space 9): The address box must be completed legibly since the certificate will be returned in a window envelope.

MORE INFORMATION

Form of Deposit for Works of the Visual Arts

Exceptions to General Deposit Requirements: As explained on the reverse side of this page, the statutory deposit requirements (generally one copy for unpublished works and two copies for published works) will vary for particular kinds of works of the visual arts. The copyright law authorizes the Register of Copyrights to issue regulations specifying "the administrative classes into which works are to be placed for purposes of deposit and registration, and the nature of the copies or phonorecords to be deposited in the various classes specified." For particular classes, the regulations may require or permit "the deposit of identifying material instead of copies or phonorecords," or "the deposit of only one copy or phonorecord where two would normally be required."

What Should You Deposit? The detailed requirements with respect to the kind of deposit to accompany an application on Form VA are contained in the Copyright Office Regulations. The following does not cover all of the deposit requirements, but is intended to give you some general guidance.

For an Unpublished Work, the material deposited should represent the entire copyrightable content of the work for which registration is being sought.

For a Published Work, the material deposited should generally consist of two complete copies of the best edition. Exceptions: (1) For certain types of works, one complete copy may be deposited instead of two. These include greeting cards, postcards, stationery, labels, advertisements, scientific drawings, and globes; (2) For most three-dimensional sculptural works, and for certain two-dimensional works, the Copyright Office Regulations require deposit of identifying material (photographs or drawings in a specified form) rather than copies; and (3) Under certain circumstances, for works published in five copies or less or in limited, numbered editions, the deposit may consist of one copy or of identifying reproductions.

Figure 17.16. (Continued)

FORM VA

UNITED STATES COPYRIGHT OFFICE

REGISTRATION NUMBER

VA   VAU

EFFECTIVE DATE OF REGISTRATION

Month   Day   Year

DO NOT WRITE ABOVE THIS LINE. IF YOU NEED MORE SPACE, USE A SEPARATE CONTINUATION SHEET.

1

TITLE OF THIS WORK ▼

NATURE OF THIS WORK ▼ See instructions

PREVIOUS OR ALTERNATIVE TITLES ▼

PUBLICATION AS A CONTRIBUTION If this work was published as a contribution to a periodical, serial, or collection, give information about the collective work in which the contribution appeared.   **Title of Collective Work ▼**

If published in a periodical or serial give: **Volume ▼**   **Number ▼**   **Issue Date ▼**   **On Pages ▼**

2

a

NAME OF AUTHOR ▼

DATES OF BIRTH AND DEATH
Year Born ▼   Year Died ▼

Was this contribution to the work a "work made for hire"?
☐ Yes
☐ No

AUTHOR'S NATIONALITY OR DOMICILE
Name of Country
OR { Citizen of ▶
Domiciled in ▶

WAS THIS AUTHOR'S CONTRIBUTION TO THE WORK
Anonymous?   ☐ Yes ☐ No
Pseudonymous?   ☐ Yes ☐ No

If the answer to either of these questions is "Yes," see detailed instructions.

NATURE OF AUTHORSHIP Briefly describe nature of the material created by this author in which copyright is claimed. ▼

NOTE

Under the law, the "author" of a "work made for hire" is generally the employer, not the employee (see instructions). For any part of this work that was "made for hire" check "Yes" in the space provided, give the employer (or other person for whom the work was prepared) as "Author" of that part, and leave the space for dates of birth and death blank.

b

NAME OF AUTHOR ▼

DATES OF BIRTH AND DEATH
Year Born ▼   Year Died ▼

Was this contribution to the work a "work made for hire"?
☐ Yes
☐ No

AUTHOR'S NATIONALITY OR DOMICILE
Name of country
OR { Citizen of ▶
Domiciled in ▶

WAS THIS AUTHOR'S CONTRIBUTION TO THE WORK
Anonymous?   ☐ Yes ☐ No
Pseudonymous?   ☐ Yes ☐ No

If the answer to either of these questions is "Yes," see detailed instructions.

NATURE OF AUTHORSHIP Briefly describe nature of the material created by this author in which copyright is claimed. ▼

c

NAME OF AUTHOR ▼

DATES OF BIRTH AND DEATH
Year Born ▼   Year Died ▼

Was this contribution to the work a "work made for hire"?
☐ Yes
☐ No

AUTHOR'S NATIONALITY OR DOMICILE
Name of Country
OR { Citizen of ▶
Domiciled in ▶

WAS THIS AUTHOR'S CONTRIBUTION TO THE WORK
Anonymous?   ☐ Yes ☐ No
Pseudonymous?   ☐ Yes ☐ No

If the answer to either of these questions is "Yes," see detailed instructions.

NATURE OF AUTHORSHIP Briefly describe nature of the material created by this author in which copyright is claimed. ▼

3

YEAR IN WHICH CREATION OF THIS WORK WAS COMPLETED This information must be given in all cases.
◀ Year

DATE AND NATION OF FIRST PUBLICATION OF THIS PARTICULAR WORK
Complete this information Month ▶ _____ Day ▶ _____ Year ▶ _____
ONLY if this work has been published.
◀ Nation

4

See instructions before completing this space.

COPYRIGHT CLAIMANT(S) Name and address must be given even if the claimant is the same as the author given in space 2.▼

TRANSFER If the claimant(s) named here in space 4 are different from the author(s) named in space 2, give a brief statement of how the claimant(s) obtained ownership of the copyright.▼

APPLICATION RECEIVED

ONE DEPOSIT RECEIVED

TWO DEPOSITS RECEIVED

REMITTANCE NUMBER AND DATE

DO NOT WRITE HERE
OFFICE USE ONLY

MORE ON BACK ▶
• Complete all applicable spaces (numbers 5-9) on the reverse side of this page.
• See detailed instructions.
• Sign the form at line 8.

DO NOT WRITE HERE

Page 1 of _____ pages

Figure 17.16. (Continued)

416

EXAMINED BY ....

CHECKED BY ....

☐ CORRESPONDENCE
  Yes

☐ DEPOSIT ACCOUNT
  FUNDS USED

FORM VA

FOR
COPYRIGHT
OFFICE
USE
ONLY

DO NOT WRITE ABOVE THIS LINE. IF YOU NEED MORE SPACE, USE A SEPARATE CONTINUATION SHEET.

PREVIOUS REGISTRATION Has registration for this work, or for an earlier version of this work, already been made in the Copyright Office?

☐ Yes ☐ No If your answer is "Yes," why is another registration being sought? (Check appropriate box) ▼

☐ This is the first published edition of a work previously registered in unpublished form.

☐ This is the first application submitted by this author as copyright claimant.

☐ This is a changed version of the work, as shown by space 6 on this application.

If your answer is "Yes," give: **Previous Registration Number ▼**   **Year of Registration ▼**

5

DERIVATIVE WORK OR COMPILATION Complete both space 6a & 6b for a derivative work; complete only 6b for a compilation.

a. **Preexisting Material** Identify any preexisting work or works that this work is based on or incorporates. ▼

_____

_____

b. **Material Added to This Work** Give a brief, general statement of the material that has been added to this work and in which copyright is claimed. ▼

_____

_____

6

See instructions
before completing
this space.

DEPOSIT ACCOUNT If the registration fee is to be charged to a Deposit Account established in the Copyright Office, give name and number of Account.
Name ▼   **Account Number ▼**

_____

7

CORRESPONDENCE Give name and address to which correspondence about this application should be sent.   Name/Address/Apt/City/State/Zip ▼

_____

_____

_____
                    Area Code & Telephone Number ▶

Be sure to
give your
daytime phone
◀ number.

CERTIFICATION* I, the undersigned, hereby certify that I am the

Check only one ▼

☐ author

☐ other copyright claimant

☐ owner of exclusive right(s)

☐ authorized agent of_____
          Name of author or other copyright claimant, or owner of exclusive right(s) ▲

of the work identified in this application and that the statements made
by me in this application are correct to the best of my knowledge.

Typed or printed name and date ▼ If this is a published work, this date must be the same as or later than the date of publication given in space 3.

_____ **date ▶** _____

☞   **Handwritten signature (X) ▼**

8

**MAIL
CERTIFI-
CATE TO**

Certificate
will be
mailed in
window
envelope

Name ▼

Number/Street/Apartment Number ▼

City/State/ZIP ▼

Have you:
● Completed all necessary
  spaces?
● Signed your application in space
  8?
● Enclosed check or money order
  for $10 payable to *Register of
  Copyrights?*
● Enclosed your deposit material
  with the application and fee?

MAIL TO: Register of Copyrights,
Library of Congress, Washington,
D.C. 20559.

9

* 17 U.S.C. § 506(e): Any person who knowingly makes a false representation of a material fact in the application for copyright registration provided for by section 409, or in any written statement filed in
connection with the application, shall be fined not more than $2,500.

☆ U.S. GOVERNMENT PRINTING OFFICE: 1987—181—531/60,009   August 1987—60,000

Figure 17.16. (Continued)

Filling Out Application Form SR

Detach and read these instructions before completing this form. Make sure all applicable spaces have been filled in before you return this form.

BASIC INFORMATION

When to Use This Form: Use Form SR for copyright registration of published or unpublished sound recordings. It should be used where the copyright claim is limited to the sound recording itself, and it may also be used where the same copyright claimant is seeking simultaneous registration of the underlying musical, dramatic, or literary work embodied in the phonorecord.

With one exception, "sound recordings" are works that result from the fixation of a series of musical, spoken, or other sounds. The exception is for the audio portions of audiovisual works, such as a motion picture soundtrack or an audio cassette accompanying a filmstrip; these are considered a part of the audiovisual work as a whole.

Deposit to Accompany Application: An application for copyright registration of a sound recording must be accompanied by a deposit consisting of phonorecords representing the entire work for which registration is to be made.

Unpublished Work: Deposit one complete phonorecord.

Published Work: Deposit two complete phonorecords of the best edition, together with "any printed or other visually perceptible material" published with the phonorecords.

Work First Published Outside the United States: Deposit one complete phonorecord of the first foreign edition.

Contribution to a Collective Work: Deposit one complete phonorecord of the best edition of the collective work.

The Copyright Notice: For published sound recordings, the law provides that a copyright notice in a specified form "shall be placed on all publicly distributed phonorecords of the sound recording." Use of the copyright notice is the responsibility of the copyright owner and does not require advance permission from the Copyright Office. The required form of the notice for phonorecords of sound recordings consists of three elements: (1) the symbol "℗" (the letter "P" in a circle); (2) the year of first publication of the sound recording; and (3) the name of the owner of copyright. For example: "℗ 1981 Rittenhouse Record Co." The notice is to be "placed on the surface of the phonorecord, or on the label or container, in such manner and location as to give reasonable notice of the claim of copyright." For further information about copyright, write:
Information and Publications Section, LM-455
Copyright Office, Library of Congress, Washington, D.C. 20559

LINE-BY-LINE INSTRUCTIONS

1 SPACE 1: Title

Title of This Work: Every work submitted for copyright registration must be given a title to identify that particular work. If the phonorecords or any accompanying printed material bear a title (or an identifying phrase that could serve as a title), transcribe that wording completely and exactly on the application. Indexing of the registration and future identification of the work may depend on the information you give here.

Nature of Material Recorded: Indicate the general type or character of the works or other material embodied in the recording. The box marked "Literary" should be checked for nondramatic spoken material of all sorts, including narration, interviews, panel discussions, and training material. If the material recorded is not musical, dramatic, or literary in nature, check "Other" and briefly describe the type of sounds fixed in the recording. For example: "Sound Effects"; "Bird Calls"; "Crowd Noises."

Previous or Alternative Titles: Complete this space if there are any additional titles for the work under which someone searching for the registration might be likely to look, or under which a document pertaining to the work might be recorded.

2 SPACE 2: Author(s)

General Instructions: After reading these instructions, decide who are the "authors" of this work for copyright purposes. Then, unless the work is a "collective work," give the requested information about every "author" who contributed any appreciable amount of copyrightable matter to this version of the work. If you need further space, request additional Continuation Sheets. In the case of a collective work, such as a collection of previously published or registered sound recordings, give information about the author of the collective work as a whole. If you are submitting this Form SR to cover the recorded musical, dramatic, or literary work as well as the sound recording itself, it is important for space 2 to include full information about the various authors of all of the material covered by the copyright claim, making clear the nature of each author's contribution.

Name of Author: The fullest form of the author's name should be given. Unless the work was "made for hire," the individual who actually created the work is its "author." In the case of a work made for hire, the statute provides hat "the employer or other person for whom the work was prepared is considered the author."

What is a "Work Made for Hire"? A "work made for hire" is defined as: (1) "a work prepared by an employee within the scope of his or her employment"; or (2) "a work specially ordered or commissioned for use as a contribution to a collective work, as a part of a motion picture or other audiovisual work, as a translation, as a supplementary work, as a compilation, as an instructional text, as a test, as answer material for a test, or as an atlas, if the parties expressly agree in a written instrument signed by them that the work shall be considered a work made for hire." If you have checked "Yes" to indicate that the work was "made for hire," you must give the full legal name of the employer (or other person for whom the work was prepared). You may also include the name of the employee along with the name of the employer (for example: "Elster Record Co., employer for hire of John Ferguson").

"Anonymous" or "Pseudonymous" Work: An author's contribution to a work is "anonymous" if that author is not identified on the copies or phonorecords of the work. An author's contribution to a work is "pseudonymous" if that author is identified on the copies or phonorecords under a fictitious name. If the work is "anonymous" you may: (1) leave the line blank; or (2) state "anonymous" on the line; or (3) reveal the author's identity. If the work is "pseudonymous" you may: (1) leave the line blank; or (2) give the pseudonym and identify it as such (for example: "Huntley Haverstock, pseudonym"); or (3) reveal the author's name, making clear which is the real name and which is the pseudonym (for example: "Judith Barton, whose pseudonym is Madeline Elster"). However, the citizenship or domicile of the author **must** be given in all cases.

Dates of Birth and Death: If the author is dead, the statute requires that the year of death be included in the application unless the work is anonymous or pseudonymous. The author's birth date is optional, but is useful as a form of identification. Leave this space blank if the author's contribution was a "work made for hire."

Author's Nationality or Domicile: Give the country of which the author is a citizen, or the country in which the author is domiciled. Nationality or domicile **must** be given in all cases.

Nature of Authorship: Give a brief general statement of the nature of this particular author's contribution to the work. If you are submitting this Form SR to cover both the sound recording and the underlying musical, dramatic, or literary work, make sure that the precise nature of each author's contribution is reflected here. Examples where the authorship pertains to the recording: "Sound Recording"; "Performance and Recording"; "Compilation and Remixing of Sounds." Examples where the authorship pertains to both the recording and the underlying work: "Words, Music, Performance, Recording"; "Arrangement of Music and Recording"; "Compilation of Poems and Reading."

Figure 17.17. Filling out application form SR.

3 SPACE 3: Creation and Publication

General Instructions: Do not confuse "creation" with "publication." Every application for copyright registration must state "the year in which creation of the work was completed." Give the date and nation of first publication only if the work has been published.

Creation: Under the statute, a work is "created" when it is fixed in a copy or phonorecord for the first time. Where a work has been prepared over a period of time, the part of the work existing in fixed form on a particular date constitutes the created work on that date. The date you give here should be the year in which the author completed the particular version for which registration is now being sought, even if other versions exist or if further changes or additions are planned.

Publication: The statute defines "publication" as "the distribution of copies or phonorecords of a work to the public by sale or other transfer of ownership, or by rental, lease, or lending"; a work is also "published" if there has been an "offering to distribute copies or phonorecords to a group of persons for purposes of further distribution, public performance, or public display." Give the full date (month, day, year) when, and the country where, publication first occurred. If first publication took place simultaneously in the United States and other countries, it is sufficient to state "U.S.A."

4 SPACE 4: Claimant(s)

Name(s) and Address(es) of Copyright Claimant(s): Give the name(s) and address(es) of the copyright claimant(s) in this work even if the claimant is the same as the author. Copyright in a work belongs initially to the author of the work (including, in the case of a work made for hire, the employer or other person for whom the work was prepared). The copyright claimant is either the author of the work or a person or organization to whom the copyright initially belonging to the author has been transferred.

Transfer: The statute provides that, if the copyright claimant is not the author, the application for registration must contain "a brief statement of how the claimant obtained ownership of the copyright." If any copyright claimant named in space 4 is not an author named in space 2, give a brief, general statement summarizing the means by which that claimant obtained ownership of the copyright. Examples: "By written contract"; "Transfer of all rights by author"; "Assignment"; "By will." Do not attach transfer documents or other attachments or riders.

5 SPACE 5: Previous Registration

General Instructions: The questions in space 5 are intended to find out whether an earlier registration has been made for this work and, if so, whether there is any basis for a new registration. As a rule, only one basic copyright registration can be made for the same version of a particular work.

Same Version: If this version is substantially the same as the work covered by a previous registration, a second registration is not generally possible unless: (1) the work has been registered in unpublished form and a second registration is now being sought to cover this first published edition; or (2) someone other than the author is identified as copyright claimant in the earlier registration, and the author is now seeking registration in his or her own name. If either of these two exceptions apply, check the appropriate box and give the earlier registration number and date. Otherwise, do not submit Form SR; instead, write the Copyright Office for information about supplementary registration or recordation of transfers of copyright ownership.

Changed Version: If the work has been changed, and you are now seeking registration to cover the additions or revisions, check the last box in space 5, give the earlier registration number and date, and complete both parts of space 6 in accordance with the instructions below.

Previous Registration Number and Date: If more than one previous registration has been made for the work, give the number and date of the latest registration.

6 SPACE 6: Derivative Work or Compilation

General Instructions: Complete space 6 if this work is a "changed version," "compilation," or "derivative work," and if it incorporates one or more earlier works that have already been published or registered for copyright, or that have fallen into the public domain, or sound recordings that were fixed before February 15, 1972. A "compilation" is defined as "a work formed by the collection and assembling of preexisting materials or of data that are selected, coordinated, or arranged in such a way that the resulting work as a whole constitutes an original work of authorship." A "derivative work" is "a work based on one or more preexisting works." Examples of derivative works include recordings reissued with substantial editorial revisions or abridgments of the recorded sounds, and recordings republished with new recorded material, or "any other form in which a work may be recast, transformed, or adapted." Derivative works also include works "consisting of editorial revisions, annotations, or other modifications" if these changes, as a whole, represent an original work of authorship.

Preexisting Material (space 6a): Complete this space **and** space 6b for derivative works. In this space identify the preexisting work that has been recast, transformed, or adapted. For example, the preexisting material might be: "1970 recording by Sperryville Symphony of Bach Double Concerto." Do not complete this space for compilations.

Material Added to This Work (space 6b): Give a brief, general statement of the **additional** new material covered by the copyright claim for which registration is sought. In the case of a derivative work, identify this new material. Examples: "Recorded performances on bands 1 and 3"; "Remixed sounds from original multitrack sound sources"; "New words, arrangement, and additional sounds." If the work is a compilation, give a brief, general statement describing both the material that has been compiled **and** the compilation itself. Example: "Compilation of 1938 Recordings by various swing bands."

7,8,9 SPACE 7, 8, 9: Fee, Correspondence, Certification, Return Address

Deposit Account: If you maintain a Deposit Account in the Copyright Office, identify it in space 7. Otherwise leave the space blank and send the fee of $10 with your application and deposit.

Correspondence (space 7): This space should contain the name, address, area code, and telephone number of the person to be consulted if correspondence about this application becomes necessary.

Certification (space 8): The application cannot be accepted unless it bears the date and the **handwritten signature** of the author or other copyright claimant, or of the owner of exclusive right(s), or of the duly authorized agent of the author, claimant, or owner of exclusive right(s).

Address for Return of Certificate (space 9): The address box must be completed legibly since the certificate will be returned in a window envelope.

MORE INFORMATION

"Works": "Works" are the basic subject matter of copyright; they are what authors create and copyright protects. The statute draws a sharp distinction between the "work" and "any material object in which the work is embodied."

"Copies" and "Phonorecords": These are the two types of material objects in which "works" are embodied. In general, **"copies"** are objects from which a work can be read or visually perceived, directly or with the aid of a machine or device, such as manuscripts, books, sheet music, film, and videotape. **"Phonorecords"** are objects embodying fixations of sounds, such as audio tapes and phonograph disks. For example, a song (the "work") can be reproduced in sheet music ("copies") or phonograph disks ("phonorecords"), or both.

"Sound Recordings": These are "works," not "copies" or "phonorecords." "Sound recordings" are "works that result from the fixation of a series of musical, spoken, or other sounds, but not including the sounds accompanying a motion picture or other audiovisual work." Example: When a record company issues a new release, the release will typically involve two distinct "works": the "musical work" that has been recorded, and the "sound recording" as a separate work in itself. The material objects that the record company sends out are "phonorecords": physical reproductions of both the "musical work" and the "sound recording."

Should You File More Than One Application? If your work consists of a recorded musical, dramatic, or literary work, and both that "work," and the sound recording as a separate "work," are eligible for registration, the application form you should file depends on the following:

File Only Form SR if: The copyright claimant is the same for both the musical, dramatic, or literary work and for the sound recording, and you are seeking a single registration to cover both of these "works."

File Only Form PA (or Form TX) if: You are seeking to register only the musical, dramatic, or literary work, not the sound recording. Form PA is appropriate for works of the performing arts; Form TX is for nondramatic literary works.

Separate Applications Should Be Filed on Form PA (or Form TX) and on Form SR if: (1) The copyright claimant for the musical, dramatic, or literary work is different from the copyright claimant for the sound recording; or (2) You prefer to have separate registrations for the musical, dramatic, or literary work and for the sound recording.

Figure 17.17. (*Continued*)

FORM SR
UNITED STATES COPYRIGHT OFFICE

REGISTRATION NUMBER

SR   SRU

EFFECTIVE DATE OF REGISTRATION

Month   Day   Year

DO NOT WRITE ABOVE THIS LINE. IF YOU NEED MORE SPACE, USE A SEPARATE CONTINUATION SHEET.

1   **TITLE OF THIS WORK ▼**

PREVIOUS OR ALTERNATIVE TITLES ▼

NATURE OF MATERIAL RECORDED ▼ See instructions.
- ☐ Musical   ☐ Musical-Dramatic
- ☐ Dramatic   ☐ Literary
- ☐ Other _____

2   a

NAME OF AUTHOR ▼   **DATES OF BIRTH AND DEATH**
Year Born ▼   Year Died ▼

Was this contribution to the work a "work made for hire"?
- ☐ Yes
- ☐ No

AUTHOR'S NATIONALITY OR DOMICILE Name of Country
OR { Citizen of ▶_____
{ Domiciled in ▶_____

WAS THIS AUTHOR'S CONTRIBUTION TO THE WORK
Anonymous? ☐ Yes ☐ No
Pseudonymous? ☐ Yes ☐ No
If the answer to either of these questions is "Yes," see detailed instructions.

NATURE OF AUTHORSHIP Briefly describe nature of the material created by this author in which copyright is claimed. ▼

NOTE

Under the law, the "author" of a "work made for hire" is generally the employer, not the employee (see instructions). For any part of this work that was "made for hire" check "Yes" in the space provided, give the employer (or other person for whom the work was prepared) as "Author" of that part, and leave the space for dates of birth and death blank.

b

NAME OF AUTHOR ▼   **DATES OF BIRTH AND DEATH**
Year Born ▼   Year Died ▼

Was this contribution to the work a "work made for hire"?
- ☐ Yes
- ☐ No

AUTHOR'S NATIONALITY OR DOMICILE Name of country
OR { Citizen of ▶_____
{ Domiciled in ▶_____

WAS THIS AUTHOR'S CONTRIBUTION TO THE WORK
Anonymous? ☐ Yes ☐ No
Pseudonymous? ☐ Yes ☐ No
If the answer to either of these questions is "Yes," see detailed instructions.

NATURE OF AUTHORSHIP Briefly describe nature of the material created by this author in which copyright is claimed. ▼

c

NAME OF AUTHOR ▼   **DATES OF BIRTH AND DEATH**
Year Born ▼   Year Died ▼

Was this contribution to the work a "work made for hire"?
- ☐ Yes
- ☐ No

AUTHOR'S NATIONALITY OR DOMICILE Name of Country
OR { Citizen of ▶_____
{ Domiciled in ▶_____

WAS THIS AUTHOR'S CONTRIBUTION TO THE WORK
Anonymous? ☐ Yes ☐ No
Pseudonymous? ☐ Yes ☐ No
If the answer to either of these questions is "Yes," see detailed instructions.

NATURE OF AUTHORSHIP Briefly describe nature of the material created by this author in which copyright is claimed. ▼

3   **YEAR IN WHICH CREATION OF THIS WORK WAS COMPLETED** This information must be given in all cases.
_____ ◀ Year

DATE AND NATION OF FIRST PUBLICATION OF THIS PARTICULAR WORK
Complete this information ONLY if this work has been published.
Month ▶_____ Day ▶_____ Year ▶_____ ◀ Nation

4   **COPYRIGHT CLAIMANT(S)** Name and address must be given even if the claimant is the same as the author given in space 2.▼

See instructions before completing this space.

TRANSFER If the claimant(s) named here in space 4 are different from the author(s) named in space 2, give a brief statement of how the claimant(s) obtained ownership of the copyright.▼

DO NOT WRITE HERE OFFICE USE ONLY

APPLICATION RECEIVED

ONE DEPOSIT RECEIVED

TWO DEPOSITS RECEIVED

REMITTANCE NUMBER AND DATE

MORE ON BACK ▶
- Complete all applicable spaces (numbers 5-9) on the reverse side of this page.
- See detailed instructions.
- Sign the form at line 8.

DO NOT WRITE HERE
Page 1 of _____ pages

Figure 17.17. (Continued)

DO NOT WRITE ABOVE THIS LINE. IF YOU NEED MORE SPACE, USE A SEPARATE CONTINUATION SHEET.

PREVIOUS REGISTRATION   Has registration for this work, or for an earlier version of this work, already been made in the Copyright Office?

☐ Yes ☐ No   If your answer is "Yes," why is another registration being sought? (Check appropriate box) ▼

☐ This is the first published edition of a work previously registered in unpublished form.

☐ This is the first application submitted by this author as copyright claimant.

☐ This is a changed version of the work, as shown by space 6 on this application.

If your answer is "Yes," give: **Previous Registration Number** ▼   **Year of Registration** ▼

5

DERIVATIVE WORK OR COMPILATION   Complete both space 6a & 6b for a derivative work; complete only 6b for a compilation.

a. Preexisting Material   Identify any preexisting work or works that this work is based on or incorporates. ▼

b. Material Added to This Work   Give a brief, general statement of the material that has been added to this work and in which copyright is claimed. ▼

6

See instructions
before completing
this space.

DEPOSIT ACCOUNT   If the registration fee is to be charged to a Deposit Account established in the Copyright Office, give name and number of Account.

Name ▼   **Account Number** ▼

7

CORRESPONDENCE   Give name and address to which correspondence about this application should be sent.   Name/Address/Apt/City/State/Zip ▼

Area Code & Telephone Number ▶

Be sure to
give your
daytime phone
◀ number.

CERTIFICATION*   I, the undersigned, hereby certify that I am the

Check one ▼

☐ author

☐ other copyright claimant

☐ owner of exclusive right(s)

☐ authorized agent of_____
                        Name of author or other copyright claimant, or owner of exclusive right(s) ▲

of the work identified in this application and that the statements made
by me in this application are correct to the best of my knowledge.

Typed or printed name and date ▼ If this is a published work, this date must be the same as or later than the date of publication given in space 3.

                                                                      date ▶ _____

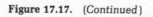   Handwritten signature (X) ▼

8

**MAIL
CERTIFI-
CATE TO**

**Certificate
will be
mailed in
window
envelope**

Name ▼

Number/Street/Apartment Number ▼

City/State/ZIP ▼

Have you:
• Completed all necessary
  spaces?
• Signed your application in space
  8?
• Enclosed check or money order
  for $10 payable to *Register of
  Copyrights?*
• Enclosed your deposit material
  with the application and fee?

MAIL TO: Register of Copyrights,
Library of Congress, Washington,
D.C. 20559.

9

Figure 17.17.   (*Continued*)

Filling Out Application Form SE

Detach and read these instructions before completing this form. Make sure all applicable spaces have been filled in before you return this form.

BASIC INFORMATION

When To Use This Form: Use a separate Form SE for registration of each individual issue of a serial, Class SE. A serial is defined as a work issued or intended to be issued in successive parts bearing numerical or chronological designations and intended to be continued indefinitely. This class includes a variety of works: periodicals; newspapers; annuals; the journals, proceedings, transactions, etc., of societies. Do not use Form SE to register an individual contribution to a serial. Request Form TX for such contributions.

Deposit to Accompany Application: An application for copyright registration must be accompanied by a deposit consisting of copies or phonorecords representing the entire work for which registration is to be made. The following are the general deposit requirements as set forth in the statute:

Unpublished Work: Deposit one complete copy (or phonorecord).

Published Work: Deposit two complete copies (or phonorecords) of the best edition.

Work First Published Outside the United States: Deposit one complete copy (or phonorecord) of the first foreign edition.

Mailing Requirements: It is important that you send the application, the deposit copy or copies, and the $10 fee together in the same envelope or package. The Copyright Office cannot process them unless they are received together. Send to: *Register of Copyrights, Library of Congress, Washington, D.C. 20559.*

The Copyright Notice: For published works, the law provides that a copyright notice in a specified form "shall be placed on all publicly distributed copies from which the work can be visually perceived." Use of the copyright notice is the responsibility of the copyright owner and does not require advance permission from the Copyright Office. The required form of the notice for copies generally consists of three elements: (1) the symbol "©"; or the word "Copyright," or the abbreviation "Copr."; (2) the year of first publication; and (3) the name of the owner of copyright. For example: "© 1981 National News Publishers, Inc." The notice is to be affixed to the copies "in such manner and location as to give reasonable notice of the claim of copyright." For further information about copyright registration, notice, or special questions relating to copyright problems, write:

Information and Publications Section, LM-455
Copyright Office, Library of Congress, Washington, D.C. 20559

LINE-BY-LINE INSTRUCTIONS

1 SPACE 1: Title

Title of This Serial: Every work submitted for copyright registration must be given a title to identify that particular work. If the copies or phonorecords of the work bear a title (or an identifying phrase that could serve as a title), copy that wording *completely* and *exactly* on the application. Give the volume and number of the periodical issue for which you are seeking registration. The "Date on copies" in space 1 should be the date appearing on the actual copies (for example: "June 1981," "Winter 1981"). Indexing of the registration and future identification of the work will depend on the information you give here.

Previous or Alternative Titles: Complete this space only if there are any additional titles for the serial under which someone searching for the registration might be likely to look, or under which a document pertaining to the work might be recorded.

2 SPACE 2: Author(s)

General Instructions: After reading these instructions, decide who are the "authors" of this work for copyright purposes. In the case of a serial issue, the organization which directs the creation of the serial issue as a whole is generally considered the author of the "collective work" (see "Nature of Authorship") whether it employs a staff or uses the efforts of volunteers. Where, however, an individual is independently responsible for the serial issue, name that person as author of the "collective work."

Name of Author: The fullest form of the author's name should be given. In the case of a "work made for hire," the statute provides that "the employer or other person for whom the work was prepared is considered the author." If this issue is a "work made for hire," the author's name will be the full legal name of the hiring organization, corporation, or individual. The title of the periodical should not ordinarily be listed as "author" because the title itself does not usually correspond to a legal entity capable of authorship. When an individual creates an issue of a serial independently and not as an "employee" of an organization or corporation, that individual should be listed as the "author."

Author's Nationality or Domicile: Give the country of which the author is a citizen, or the country in which the author is domiciled. Nationality or domicile **must** be given in all cases. The citizenship of an organization formed under United States Federal or state law should be stated as "U.S.A."

What is a "Work Made for Hire"? A "work made for hire" is defined as: (1) "a work prepared by an employee within the scope of his or her employment"; or (2) "a work specially ordered or commissioned for use as a contribution to a collective work, as a part of a motion picture or other audiovisual work, as a translation, as a supplementary work, as a compilation, as an instructional text, as a test, as answer material for a test, or as an atlas, if the parties expressly agree in a written instrument signed by them that the work shall be considered a work made for hire." An organization that uses the efforts of volunteers in the creation of a "collective work" (see "Nature of Authorship") may also be considered the author of a "work made for hire" even though those volunteers were not specifically paid by the organization. In the case of a "work made for hire," give the full legal name of the employer and check "Yes" to indicate that the work was made for hire. You may also include the name of the employee along with the name of the employer (for example: "Elster Publishing Co., employer for hire of John Ferguson").

"Anonymous" or "Pseudonymous" Work: Leave this space **blank** if the serial is a "work made for hire." An author's contribution to a work is "anonymous" if that author is not identified on the copies or phonorecords of the work. An author's contribution to a work is "pseudonymous" if that author is identified on the copies or phonorecords under a fictitious name. If the work is "anonymous" you may: (1) leave the line blank; or (2) state "anonymous" on the line; or (3) reveal the author's identity. If the work is "pseudonymous" you may: (1) leave the line blank; or (2) give the pseudonym and identify it as such (for example: "Huntley Haverstock, pseudonym"); or (3) reveal the author's name, making clear which is the real name and which is the pseudonym (for example: "Judith Barton, whose pseudonym is Madeline Elster"). However, the citizenship or domicile of the author **must** be given in all cases.

Dates of Birth and Death: Leave this space blank if the author's contribution was a "work made for hire." If the author is dead, the statute requires that the year of death be included in the application unless the work is anonymous or pseudonymous. The author's birth date is optional, but is useful as a form of identification.

Nature of Authorship: Give a brief statement of the nature of the particular author's contribution to the work. If an organization directed, controlled and supervised the creation of the serial issue as a whole, check the box "collective work." The term "collective work" means that the author is responsible for compilation and editorial revision, and may also be responsible for certain individual contributions to the serial issue. Further examples of "Authorship" which may apply both to organizational and to individual authors are "Entire text"; "Entire text and/or illustrations"; "Editorial revision, compilation, plus additional new material."

Figure 17.18. Filling out application form SE.

3 SPACE 3: Creation and Publication

General Instructions: Do not confuse "creation" with "publication." Every application for copyright registration must state "the year in which creation of the work was completed." Give the date and nation of first publication only if the work has been published.

Creation: Under the statute, a work is "created" when it is fixed in a copy or phonorecord for the first time. Where a work has been prepared over a period of time, the part of the work existing in fixed form on a particular date constitutes the created work on that date. The date you give here should be the year in which this particular issue was completed.

Publication: The statute defines "publication" as "the distribution of copies or phonorecords of a work to the public by sale or other transfer of ownership, or by rental, lease, or lending"; a work is also "published" if there has been an "offering to distribute copies or phonorecords to a group of persons for purposes of further distribution, public performance, or public display." Give the full date (month, day, year) when, and the country where, publication of this particular issue first occurred. If first publication took place simultaneously in the United States and other countries, it is sufficient to state "U.S.A."

4 SPACE 4: Claimant(s)

Name(s) and Address(es) of Copyright Claimant(s): This space must be completed. Give the name(s) and address(es) of the copyright claimant(s) of this work even if the claimant is the same as the author named in space 2. Copyright in a work belongs initially to the author of the work (including, in the case of a work made for hire, the employer or other person for whom the work was prepared). The copyright claimant is either the author of the work or a person or organization to whom the copyright initially belonging to the author has been transferred.

Transfer: The statute provides that, if the copyright claimant is not the author, the application for registration must contain "a brief statement of how the claimant obtained ownership of the copyright." A transfer of copyright ownership (other than one brought about by operation of law) must be in writing. If any copyright claimant named in space 4 is not an author named in space 2, give a brief, general statement describing the means by which that claimant obtained ownership of the copyright from the original author. Examples: "By written contract"; "Written transfer of all rights by author"; "Assignment"; "Inherited by will." Do not attach the actual document of transfer or other attachments or riders.

5 SPACE 5: Previous Registration

General Instructions: This space applies only rarely to serials. Complete space 5 if this particular issue has been registered earlier or if it contains a substantial amount of material that has been previously registered. Do not complete this space if the previous registrations are simply those made for earlier issues.

Previous Registration:
a. Check this box if this issue has been registered in unpublished form and a second registration is now sought to cover the first published edition.
b. Check this box if someone other than the author is identified as copyright claimant in the earlier registration and the author is now seeking registration in his or her own name. If the work in question is a contribution to a collective work, as opposed to the issue as a whole, file Form TX, not Form SE.
c. Check this box (and complete space 6) if this particular issue, or a substantial portion of the material in it, has been previously registered and you are now seeking registration for the additions and revisions which appear in this issue for the first time.

Previous Registration Number and Date: Complete this line if you checked one of the boxes above. If more than one previous registration has been made for the issue or for material in it, give only the number and year date for the latest registration.

6 SPACE 6: Derivative Work or Compilation

General Instructions: Complete space 6 if this issue is a "changed version," "compilation," or "derivative work," which incorporates one or more earlier works that have already been published or registered for copyright, or that have fallen into the public domain. Do not complete space 6 for an issue consisting of entirely new material appearing for the first time, such as a new issue of a continuing serial. A "compilation" is defined as "a work formed by the collection and assembling of preexisting materials or of data that are se-lected, coordinated, or arranged in such a way that the resulting work as a whole constitutes an original work of authorship." A "derivative work" is "a work based on one or more preexisting works." Examples of derivative works include translations, fictionalizations, abridgments, condensations, or "any other form in which a work may be recast, transformed, or adapted." Derivative works also include works "consisting of editorial revisions, annotations, or other modifications" if these changes, as a whole, represent an original work of authorship.

Preexisting Material (space 6a): For derivative works, complete this space and space 6b. In space 6a identify the preexisting work that has been recast, transformed, adapted, or updated. Example: "1978 Morgan Co. Sales Catalog." Do not complete space 6a for compilations.

Material Added to This Work (space 6b): Give a brief, general statement of the new material covered by the copyright claim for which registration is sought. **Derivative work** examples include: "Editorial revisions and additions to the Catalog"; "Translation"; "Additional material." If a periodical issue is a **compilation**, describe both the compilation itself and the material that has been compiled. Examples: "Compilation of previously published journal articles"; "Compilation of previously published data." An issue may be both a derivative work and a compilation, in which case a sample statement might be: "Compilation of [describe] and additional new material."

7 SPACE 7: Manufacturing Provisions

General Instructions: The copyright statute currently provides, as a general rule, that the copies of a published work "consisting preponderantly of nondramatic literary material in the English language" be manufactured in the United States or Canada in order to be lawfully imported and publicly distributed in the United States. If the work being registered is unpublished or not in English, leave this space blank. Complete this space if registration is sought for a published work "consisting preponderantly of nondramatic literary material that is in the English language." Identify those who manufactured the copies and where those manufacturing processes were performed. As an exception to the manufacturing provisions, the statute prescribes that, where manufacture has taken place outside the United States or Canada, a maximum of 2000 copies of the foreign edition may be imported into the United States without affecting the copyright owners' rights. For this purpose, the Copyright Office will issue an Import Statement upon request and payment of a fee of $3 at the time of registration or at any later time. For further information about import statements, write for Form IS.

8 SPACE 8: Reproduction for Use of Blind or Physically Handicapped Individuals

General Instructions: One of the major programs of the Library of Congress is to provide Braille editions and special recordings of works for the exclusive use of the blind and physically handicapped. In an effort to simplify and speed up the copyright licensing procedures that are a necessary part of this program, section 710 of the copyright statute provides for the establishment of a voluntary licensing system to be tied in with copyright registration. Copyright Office regulations provide that you may grant a license for such reproduction and distribution solely for the use of persons who are certified by competent authority as unable to read normal printed material as a result of physical limitations. The license is entirely voluntary, nonexclusive, and may be terminated upon 90 days notice.

How to Grant the License: If you wish to grant it, check one of the three boxes in space 8. Your check in one of these boxes, together with your signature in space 10, will mean that the Library of Congress can proceed to reproduce and distribute under the license without further paperwork. For further information, write for Circular R63.

9,10,11 SPACE 9, 10, 11: Fee, Correspondence, Certification, Return Address

Deposit Account: If you maintain a Deposit Account in the Copyright Office, identify it in space 9. Otherwise leave the space blank and send the fee of $10 with your application and deposit.

Correspondence (space 9): This space should contain the name, address, area code, and telephone number of the person to be consulted if correspondence about this application becomes necessary.

Certification (space 10): The application cannot be accepted unless it bears the date and the **handwritten signature** of the author or other copyright claimant, or of the owner of exclusive right(s), or of the duly authorized agent of the author, claimant, or owner of exclusive right(s).

Address for Return of Certificate (space 11): The address box must be completed legibly since the certificate will be returned in a window envelope.

Figure 17.17. (Continued)

423

FORM SE
UNITED STATES COPYRIGHT OFFICE

REGISTRATION NUMBER

_____

U

EFFECTIVE DATE OF REGISTRATION

_____

Month   Day   Year

DO NOT WRITE ABOVE THIS LINE. IF YOU NEED MORE SPACE, USE A SEPARATE CONTINUATION SHEET.

1 TITLE OF THIS SERIAL ▼

Volume ▼   Number ▼   Date on Copies ▼   Frequency of Publication ▼

PREVIOUS OR ALTERNATIVE TITLES ▼

---

2 **a** NAME OF AUTHOR ▼

DATES OF BIRTH AND DEATH
Year Born ▼   Year Died ▼

Was this contribution to the work a "work made for hire"?
☐ Yes
☐ No

AUTHOR'S NATIONALITY OR DOMICILE
Name of Country
OR { Citizen of ▶ _____
    { Domiciled in ▶ _____

WAS THIS AUTHOR'S CONTRIBUTION TO THE WORK
Anonymous?   ☐ Yes ☐ No
Pseudonymous?   ☐ Yes ☐ No
If the answer to either of these questions is "Yes," see detailed instructions.

NATURE OF AUTHORSHIP   Briefly describe nature of the material created by this author in which copyright is claimed. ▼
☐ Collective Work   Other:

NOTE

Under the law, the "author" of a "work made for hire" is generally the employer, not the employee (see instructions). For any part of this work that was "made for hire" check "Yes" in the space provided, give the employer (or other person for whom the work was prepared) as "Author" of that part, and leave the space for dates of birth and death blank.

b NAME OF AUTHOR ▼

DATES OF BIRTH AND DEATH
Year Born ▼   Year Died ▼

Was this contribution to the work a "work made for hire"?
☐ Yes
☐ No

AUTHOR'S NATIONALITY OR DOMICILE
Name of country
OR { Citizen of ▶ _____
    { Domiciled in ▶ _____

WAS THIS AUTHOR'S CONTRIBUTION TO THE WORK
Anonymous?   ☐ Yes ☐ No
Pseudonymous?   ☐ Yes ☐ No
If the answer to either of these questions is "Yes," see detailed instructions.

NATURE OF AUTHORSHIP   Briefly describe nature of the material created by this author in which copyright is claimed. ▼
☐ Collective Work   Other:

c NAME OF AUTHOR ▼

DATES OF BIRTH AND DEATH
Year Born ▼   Year Died ▼

Was this contribution to the work a "work made for hire"?
☐ Yes
☐ No

AUTHOR'S NATIONALITY OR DOMICILE
Name of Country
OR { Citizen of ▶ _____
    { Domiciled in ▶ _____

WAS THIS AUTHOR'S CONTRIBUTION TO THE WORK
Anonymous?   ☐ Yes ☐ No
Pseudonymous?   ☐ Yes ☐ No
If the answer to either of these questions is "Yes," see detailed instructions.

NATURE OF AUTHORSHIP   Briefly describe nature of the material created by this author in which copyright is claimed. ▼
☐ Collective Work   Other:

---

3 YEAR IN WHICH CREATION OF THIS ISSUE WAS COMPLETED   This information must be given in all cases.
◀ Year

DATE AND NATION OF FIRST PUBLICATION OF THIS PARTICULAR ISSUE
Complete this information ONLY if this work has been published.
Month ▶ _____ Day ▶ _____ Year ▶ _____
◀ Nation

---

4 COPYRIGHT CLAIMANT(S) Name and address must be given even if the claimant is the same as the author given in space 2.▼

See instructions before completing this space.

TRANSFER If the claimant(s) named here in space 4 are different from the author(s) named in space 2, give a brief statement of how the claimant(s) obtained ownership of the copyright.▼

DO NOT WRITE HERE OFFICE USE ONLY

APPLICATION RECEIVED

ONE DEPOSIT RECEIVED

TWO DEPOSITS RECEIVED

REMITTANCE NUMBER AND DATE

MORE ON BACK ▶
• Complete all applicable spaces (numbers 5-11) on the reverse side of this page
• See detailed instructions.   • Sign the form at line 10.

DO NOT WRITE HERE

Page 1 of _____ pages

Figure 17.18.   (Continued)

424

DO NOT WRITE ABOVE THIS LINE. IF YOU NEED MORE SPACE, USE A SEPARATE CONTINUATION SHEET.

PREVIOUS REGISTRATION   Has registration for this issue, or for an earlier version of this particular issue, already been made in the Copyright Office?

☐ **Yes** ☐ **No**   If your answer is "Yes," why is another registration being sought? (Check appropriate box) ▼

a. ☐ This is the first published version of an issue previously registered in unpublished form.

b. ☐ This is the first application submitted by this author as copyright claimant.

c. ☐ This is a changed version of this issue, as shown by space 6 on this application.

If your answer is "Yes," give: **Previous Registration Number** ▼   **Year of Registration** ▼

5

DERIVATIVE WORK OR COMPILATION   Complete both space 6a & 6b for a derivative work; complete only 6b for a compilation.

a. Preexisting Material   Identify any preexisting work or works that this work is based on or incorporates. ▼

b. Material Added to This Work   Give a brief, general statement of the material that has been added to this work and in which copyright is claimed. ▼

6

See instructions before completing this space.

MANUFACTURERS AND LOCATIONS   If this is a published work consisting preponderantly of nondramatic literary material in English, the law may require that the copies be manufactured in the United States or Canada for full protection. If so, the names of the manufacturers who performed certain processes, and the places where these processes were performed **must** be given. See instructions for details.

Names of Manufacturers ▼   **Places of Manufacture** ▼

7

REPRODUCTION FOR USE OF BLIND OR PHYSICALLY HANDICAPPED INDIVIDUALS   A signature on this form at space 10, and a check in one of the boxes here in space 8, constitutes a non-exclusive grant of permission to the Library of Congress to reproduce and distribute solely for the blind and physically handicapped and under the conditions and limitations prescribed by the regulations of the Copyright Office: (1) copies of the work identified in space 1 of this application in Braille (or similar tactile symbols); or (2) phonorecords embodying a fixation of a reading of that work; or (3) both.

    a ☐ Copies and Phonorecords   **b** ☐ Copies Only   **c** ☐ Phonorecords Only

8

See instructions.

DEPOSIT ACCOUNT   If the registration fee is to be charged to a Deposit Account established in the Copyright Office, give name and number of Account.

Name ▼   **Account Number** ▼

9

CORRESPONDENCE   Give name and address to which correspondence about this application should be sent. Name/Address/Apt/City/State/Zip ▼

Area Code & Telephone Number ▶

Be sure to give your daytime phone number.

CERTIFICATION*   I, the undersigned, hereby certify that I am the

Check one ▶

☐ author
☐ other copyright claimant
☐ owner of exclusive right(s)
☐ authorized agent of _____

Name of author or other copyright claimant, or owner of exclusive right(s) ▲

of the work identified in this application and that the statements made by me in this application are correct to the best of my knowledge.

10

Typed or printed name and date ▼ If this is a published work, this date must be the same as or later than the date of publication given in space 3.

_____ date ▶ _____

👉 **Handwritten signature (X)** ▼

MAIL CERTIFI-CATE TO

Certificate will be mailed in window envelope

Name ▼

Number/Street/Apartment Number ▼

City/State/ZIP ▼

Have you:
- Completed all necessary spaces?
- Signed your application in space 10?
- Enclosed check or money order for $10 payable to *Register of Copyrights*?
- Enclosed your deposit material with the application and fee?

MAIL TO: Register of Copyrights. Library of Congress. Washington. D.C. 20559.

11

* 17 U.S.C. § 506(e): Any person who knowingly makes a false representation of a material fact in the application for copyright registration provided for by section 409, or in any written statement filed in connection with the application, shall be fined not more than $2,500.

☆U.S. GOVERNMENT PRINTING OFFICE: 1982-361-278/59

Sept. 1982—210,000

Figure 17.18.   (*Continued*)

THIS FORM:
- Can be used solely as an adjunct to a basic application for copyright registration.
- Is not acceptable unless submitted together with Form TX, Form PA, or Form VA.
- Is acceptable only if the group of works listed on it all qualify for a single copyright registration under 17 U.S.C. § 408 (c)(2).

ADJUNCT APPLICATION
for Copyright Registration for a Group of Contributions to Periodicals

WHEN TO USE FORM GR/CP: Form GR/CP is the appropriate adjunct application form to use when you are submitting a basic application on Form TX, Form PA, or Form VA, for a group of works that qualify for a single registration under section 408(c)(2) of the copyright statute.

WHEN DOES A GROUP OF WORKS QUALIFY FOR A SINGLE REGISTRATION UNDER 17 U.S.C. §408 (c)(2)? The statute provides that a single copyright registration for a group of works can be made if **all** of the following conditions are met:

(1) All of the works are by the same author, who is an individual (not an employer for hire); and

(2) All of the works were first published as contributions to periodicals (including newspapers) within a twelve-month period; and

(3) Each of the contributions as first published bore a separate copyright notice, and the name of the owner of copyright in the work (or an abbreviation or alternative designation of the owner) was the same in each notice; and

(4) One copy of the entire periodical issue or newspaper section in which each contribution was first published must be deposited with the application; and

(5) The application must identify each contribution separately, including the periodical containing it and the date of its first publication.

How to Apply for Group Registration:

First: Study the information on this page to make sure that all of the works you want to register together as a group qualify for a single registration.

Second: Turn this page over and read through the detailed instructions for group registration. Decide which form you should use for the basic registration (Form TX for nondramatic literary works; or Form PA for musical, dramatic, and other works of the performing arts; or Form VA for pictorial and graphic works). Be sure that you have all of the information you need before you start filling out both the basic and the adjunct application forms.

Third: Complete the basic application form, following the detailed instructions accompanying it **and the special instructions on the reverse of this page**.

Fourth: Complete the adjunct application on Form GR/CP and mail it, together with the basic application form and the required copy of each contribution, to: Register of Copyrights, Library of Congress, Washington, D.C. 20559. Unless you have a Deposit Account in the Copyright Office, your application and copies must be accompanied by a check or money order for $10, payable to: *Register of Copyrights*.

Figure 17.19. Adjunct application for copyright registration for a group of contributions to periodicals.

ADJUNCT APPLICATION
for
Copyright Registration for a
Group of Contributions to Periodicals

- Use this adjunct form only if your are making a single registration for a group of contributions to periodicals, and you are also filing a basic application on Form TX, Form PA, or Form VA. Follow the instructions, attached.

- Number each line in Part B consecutively. Use additional Forms GR/CP if you need more space.

- Submit this adjunct form with the basic application form. Clip (do not tape or staple) and fold all sheets together before submitting them.

FORM GR/CP
UNITED STATES COPYRIGHT OFFICE

REGISTRATION NUMBER
TX   PA   VA

EFFECTIVE DATE OF REGISTRATION

. . . .
(Month)   (Day)   (Year)

FORM GR/CP RECEIVED

Page _____ of _____ pages

DO NOT WRITE ABOVE THIS LINE. FOR COPYRIGHT OFFICE USE ONLY

(A) **Identification of Application**

IDENTIFICATION OF BASIC APPLICATION:
- This application for copyright registration for a group of contributions to periodicals is submitted as an adjunct to an application filed on: (Check which)

☐ Form TX   ☐ Form PA   ☐ Form VA

IDENTIFICATION OF AUTHOR AND CLAIMANT: (Give the name of the author and the name of the copyright claimant in all of the contributions listed in Part B of this form. The names should be the same as the names given in spaces 2 and 4 of the basic application.)

Name of Author: . . . .

Name of Copyright Claimant: . . . .

(B) **Registration For Group of Contributions**

COPYRIGHT REGISTRATION FOR A GROUP OF CONTRIBUTIONS TO PERIODICALS: (To make a single registration for a group of works by the same individual author, all first published as contributions to periodicals within a 12-month period (see instructions), give full information about each contribution. If more space is needed, use additional Forms GR/CP.)

☐
Title of Contribution: . . . .
Title of Periodical: . . . . Vol. . . . . No. . . . . Issue Date . . . . Pages. . . . . .
Date of First Publication:. . . . . Nation of First Publication . . . .
        (Month) (Day) (Year)   (Country)

☐
Title of Contribution: . . . .
Title of Periodical: . . . . Vol. . . . . No. . . . . Issue Date . . . . Pages. . . . . .
Date of First Publication:. . . . . Nation of First Publication . . . .
        (Month) (Day) (Year)   (Country)

☐
Title of Contribution: . . . .
Title of Periodical: . . . . Vol. . . . . No. . . . . Issue Date . . . . Pages. . . . . .
Date of First Publication:. . . . . Nation of First Publication . . . .
        (Month) (Day) (Year)   (Country)

☐
Title of Contribution: . . . .
Title of Periodical: . . . . Vol. . . . . No. . . . . Issue Date . . . . Pages. . . . . .
Date of First Publication:. . . . . Nation of First Publication . . . .
        (Month) (Day) (Year)   (Country)

☐
Title of Contribution: . . . .
Title of Periodical: . . . . Vol. . . . . No. . . . . Issue Date . . . . Pages. . . . . .
Date of First Publication:. . . . . Nation of First Publication . . . .
        (Month) (Day) (Year)   (Country)

☐
Title of Contribution: . . . .
Title of Periodical: . . . . Vol. . . . . No. . . . . Issue Date . . . . Pages. . . . . .
Date of First Publication:. . . . . Nation of First Publication . . . .
        (Month) (Day) (Year)   (Country)

☐
Title of Contribution: . . . .
Title of Periodical: . . . . Vol. . . . . No. . . . . Issue Date . . . . Pages. . . . . .
Date of First Publication:. . . . . Nation of First Publication . . . .
        (Month) (Day) (Year)   (Country)

Figure 17.18. *(Continued)*

DO NOT WRITE ABOVE THIS LINE. FOR COPYRIGHT OFFICE USE ONLY

☐ Title of Contribution: ....
Title of Periodical: .... Vol...... No...... Issue Date........ .... Pages........
Date of First Publication:.. Nation of First Publication....................................
(Month)   (Day)   (Year)   (Country)

Ⓑ
Continued

☐ Title of Contribution: ....
Title of Periodical: .... Vol...... No...... Issue Date......... Pages........
Date of First Publication:.. Nation of First Publication....................................
(Month)   (Day)   (Year)   (Country)

☐ Title of Contribution: ....
Title of Periodical: .... Vol...... No...... Issue Date......... Pages........
Date of First Publication:.. Nation of First Publication....................................
(Month)   (Day)   (Year)   (Country)

☐ Title of Contribution: ....
Title of Periodical: .... Vol...... No...... Issue Date......... Pages........
Date of First Publication:.. Nation of First Publication....................................
(Month)   (Day)   (Year)   (Country)

☐ Title of Contribution: ....
Title of Periodical: .... Vol...... No...... Issue Date......... Pages........
Date of First Publication:.. Nation of First Publication....................................
(Month)   (Day)   (Year)   (Country)

☐ Title of Contribution: ....
Title of Periodical: .... Vol...... No...... Issue Date......... Pages........
Date of First Publication:.. Nation of First Publication....................................
(Month)   (Day)   (Year)   (Country)

☐ Title of Contribution: ....
Title of Periodical: .... Vol...... No...... Issue Date......... Pages........
Date of First Publication:.. Nation of First Publication....................................
(Month)   (Day)   (Year)   (Country)

☐ Title of Contribution: ....
Title of Periodical: .... Vol...... No...... Issue Date......... Pages........
Date of First Publication:.. Nation of First Publication....................................
(Month)   (Day)   (Year)   (Country)

☐ Title of Contribution: ....
Title of Periodical: .... Vol...... No...... Issue Date......... Pages........
Date of First Publication:.. Nation of First Publication....................................
(Month)   (Day)   (Year)   (Country)

☐ Title of Contribution: ....
Title of Periodical: .... Vol...... No...... Issue Date......... Pages........
Date of First Publication:.. Nation of First Publication....................................
(Month)   (Day)   (Year)   (Country)

☐ Title of Contribution: ....
Title of Periodical: .... Vol...... No...... Issue Date......... Pages........
Date of First Publication:.. Nation of First Publication....................................
(Month)   (Day)   (Year)   (Country)

☆ U.S. GOVERNMENT PRINTING OFFICE: 1978—261-022/12   Apr. 1978—300,000

Figure 17.19.   (Continued)

PROCEDURE FOR GROUP REGISTRATION

TWO APPLICATION FORMS MUST BE FILED

When you apply for a single registration to cover a group of contributions to periodicals, you must submit two application forms:

(1) A basic application on either Form TX, or Form PA, or Form VA. It must contain all of the information required for copyright registration except the titles and information concerning publication of the contributions.

(2) An adjunct application on Form GR/CP. The purpose of this form is to provide separate identification for each of the contributions and to give information about their first publication, as required by the statute.

WHICH BASIC APPLICATION FORM TO USE

The basic application form you choose to submit should be determined by the nature of the contributions you are registering. As long as they meet the statutory qualifications for group registration (outlined on the reverse of this page), the contributions can be registered together even if they are entirely different in nature, type, or content. However, you must choose which of three forms is generally the most appropriate on which to submit your basic application:

Form TX: for nondramatic literary works consisting primarily of text. Examples are fiction, verse, articles, news stories, features, essays, reviews, editorials, columns, quizzes, puzzles, and advertising copy.

Form PA: for works of the performing arts. Examples are music, drama, choreography, and pantomimes.

Form VA: for works of the visual arts. Examples are photographs, drawings, paintings, prints, art reproductions, cartoons, comic strips, charts, diagrams, maps, pictorial ornamentation, and pictorial or graphic material published as advertising.

If your contributions differ in nature, choose the form most suitable for the majority of them. However, if any of the contributions consists preponderantly of nondramatic text matter in English, you should file Form TX for the entire group. This is because Form TX is the only form containing spaces for information about the manufacture of copies, which the statute requires to be given for certain works.

REGISTRATION FEE FOR GROUP REGISTRATION

The fee for registration of a group of contributions to periodicals is $10, no matter how many contributions are listed on Form GR/CP. Unless you maintain a Deposit Account in the Copyright Office, the registration fee must accompany your application forms and copies. Make your remittance payable to: *Register of Copyrights.*

WHAT COPIES SHOULD BE DEPOSITED FOR GROUP REGISTRATION?

The application forms you file for group registration must be accompanied by one complete copy of each contribution listed in Form GR/CP, exactly as the contribution was first published in a periodical. The deposit must consist of the entire issue of the periodical containing the contribution; or, if the contribution was first published in a newspaper, the deposit should consist of the entire section in which the contribution appeared. Tear sheets or proof copies are not acceptable for deposit.

COPYRIGHT NOTICE REQUIREMENTS

For published works, the law provides that a copyright notice in a specified form "shall be placed on all publicly distributed copies from which the work can be visually perceived." The required form of the notice generally consists of three elements: (1) the symbol "©", or the word "Copyright", or the abbreviation "Copr."; (2) the year of first publication of the work; and (3) the name of the owner of copyright in the work, or an abbreviation or alternative form of the name. For example: "© 1978 Samuel Craig".

Among the conditions for group registration of contributions to periodicals, the statute establishes two requirements involving the copyright notice:

(1) Each of the contributions as first published must have borne a separate copyright notice; and

(2) "The name of the owner of copyright in the work, or an abbreviation by which the name can be recognized, or a generally known alternative designation of the owner" must have been the same in each notice.

HOW TO FILL OUT THE BASIC APPLICATION FORM WHEN APPLYING FOR GROUP REGISTRATION

In general, the instructions for filling out the basic application (Form TX, Form PA, or Form VA) apply to group registrations. In addition, please observe the following specific instructions:

Space 1 (Title): Do not give information concerning any of the contributions in space 1 of the basic application. Instead, in the block headed "Title of this Work", state: "See Form GR/CP, attached". Leave the other blocks in space 1 blank.

Space 2 (Author): Give the name and other information concerning the author of all of the contributions listed in Form GR/CP. To qualify for group registration, all of the contributions must have been written by the same individual author.

Space 3 (Creation and Publication): In the block calling for the year of creation, give the year of creation of the last of the contributions to be completed. Leave the block calling for the date and nation of first publication blank.

Space 4 (Claimant): Give all of the requested information, which must be the same for all of the contributions listed on Form GR/CP.

Other spaces: Complete all of the applicable spaces, and be sure that the form is signed in the certification space.

HOW TO FILL OUT FORM GR/CP

PART A: IDENTIFICATION OF APPLICATION

• **Identification of Basic Application:** Indicate, by checking one of the boxes, which of the basic application forms (Form TX, or Form PA, or Form VA) you are filing for registration.

• **Identification of Author and Claimant:** Give the name of the individual author exactly as it appears in line 2 of the basic application, and give the name of the copyright claimant exactly as it appears in line 4. These must be the same for all of the contributions listed in Part B of Form GR/CP.

PART B: REGISTRATION FOR GROUP OF CONTRIBUTIONS

• **General Instructions:** Under the statute, a group of contributions to periodicals will qualify for a single registration only if the application "identifies each work separately, including the periodical containing it and its date of first publication." Part B of the Form GR/CP provides lines enough to list 19 separate contributions; if you need more space, use additional Forms GR/CP. If possible, list the contributions in the order of their publication, giving the earliest first. Number each line consecutively.

• **Important:** All of the contributions listed on Form GR/CP must have been published within a single twelve-month period. This does not mean that all of the contributions must have been published during the same calendar year, but it does mean that, to be grouped in a single application, the earliest and latest contributions must not have been published more than twelve months apart. Example: Contributions published on April 1, 1978, July 1, 1978, and March 1, 1979, could be grouped together, but a contribution published on April 15, 1979, could not be registered with them as part of the group.

• **Title of Contribution:** Each contribution must be given a title that is capable of identifying that particular work and of distinguishing it from others. If the contribution as published bears a title (or an identifying phrase that could serve as a title), transcribe its wording completely and exactly.

• **Identification of Periodical:** Give the over-all title of the periodical in which the contribution was first published, together with the volume and issue number (if any) and the issue date.

• **Pages:** Give the number of the page of the periodical issue on which the contribution appeared. If the contribution covered more than one page, give the inclusive pages, if possible.

• **First Publication:** The statute defines "publication" as "the distribution of copies or phonorecords of a work to the public by sale or other transfer of ownership, or by rental, lease, or lending"; a work is also "published" if there has been an "offering to distribute copies or phonorecords to a group of persons for purposes of further distribution, public performance, or public display." Give the full date (month, day, and year) when, and the country where, publication of the periodical issue containing the contribution first occurred. If first publication took place simultaneously in the United States and other countries, it is sufficient to state "U.S.A."

NOTE: The advantage of group registration is that it allows any number of works published within a twelve-month period to be registered "on the basis of a single deposit, application, and registration fee." On the other hand, group registration may also have disadvantages under certain circumstances. If infringement of a published work begins before the work has been registered, the copyright owner can still obtain the ordinary remedies for copyright infringement (including injunctions, actual damages and profits, and impounding and disposition of infringing articles). However, in that situation—where the copyright in a published work is infringed before registration is made—the owner cannot obtain special remedies (statutory damages and attorney's fees) unless registration was made within three months after first publication of the work.

Figure 17.19. (*Continued*)

APPLICATION FOR
Renewal Registration

HOW TO REGISTER A RENEWAL CLAIM:

- **First:** Study the information on this page and make sure you know the answers to two questions:

   (1) What are the renewal time limits in your case?

   (2) Who can claim the renewal?

- **Second:** Turn this page over and read through the specific instructions for filling out Form RE. Make sure, before starting to complete the form, that the copyright is now eligible for renewal, that you are authorized to file a renewal claim, and that you have all of the information about the copyright you will need.

- **Third:** Complete all applicable spaces on Form RE, following the line-by-line instructions on the back of this page. Use typewriter, or print the information in dark ink.

- **Fourth:** Detach this sheet and send your completed Form RE to: Register of Copyrights, Library of Congress, Washington, D.C. 20559. Unless you have a Deposit Account in the Copyright Office, your application must be accompanied by a check or money order for $6, payable to: *Register of Copyrights*. Do not send copies, phonorecords, or supporting documents with your renewal application.

WHAT IS RENEWAL OF COPYRIGHT? For works originally copyrighted between January 1, 1950 and December 31, 1977, the statute now in effect provides for a first term of copyright protection lasting for 28 years, with the possibility of renewal for a second term of 47 years. If a valid renewal registration is made for a work, its total copyright term is 75 years (a first term of 28 years, plus a renewal term of 47 years). Example: For a work copyrighted in 1960, the first term will expire in 1988, but if renewed at the proper time the copyright will last through the end of 2035.

SOME BASIC POINTS ABOUT RENEWAL:

(1) There are strict time limits and deadlines for renewing a copyright.

(2) Only certain persons who fall into specific categories named in the law can claim renewal.

(3) The new copyright law does away with renewal requirements for works first copyrighted after 1977. However, copyrights that were already in their first copyright term on January 1, 1978 (that is, works originally copyrighted between January 1, 1950 and December 31, 1977) **still have to be renewed** in order to be protected for a second term.

TIME LIMITS FOR RENEWAL REGISTRATION: The new copyright statute provides that, in order to renew a copyright, the renewal application and fee must be received in the Copyright Office "within one year prior to the expiration of the copyright." It also provides that all terms of copyright will run through the end of the year in which they would otherwise expire. Since all copyright terms will expire on December 31st of their last year, all periods for renewal registration will run from December 31st of the 27th year of the copyright, and will end on December 31st of the following year.

To determine the time limits for renewal in your case:

(1) First, find out the date of original copyright for the work. (In the case of works originally registered in unpublished form, the date of copyright is the date of registration; for published works, copyright begins on the date of first publication.)

(2) Then add 28 years to the year the work was originally copyrighted.

Your answer will be the calendar year during which the copyright will be eligible for renewal, and December 31st of that year will be the renewal deadline. Example: a work originally copyrighted on April 19, 1957, will be eligible for renewal between December 31, 1984, and December 31, 1985.

WHO MAY CLAIM RENEWAL: Renewal copyright may be claimed only by those persons specified in the law. Except in the case of four specific types of works, the law gives the right to claim renewal to the individual author of the work, regardless of who owned the copyright during the original term. If the author is dead, the statute gives the right to claim renewal to certain of the author's beneficiaries (widow and children, executors, or next of kin, depending on the circumstances). The present owner (proprietor) of the copyright is entitled to claim renewal only in four specified cases, as explained in more detail on the reverse of this page.

CAUTION: Renewal registration is possible only if an acceptable application and fee are **received** in the Copyright Office during the renewal period and before the renewal deadline. If an acceptable application and fee are not received before the renewal deadline, the work falls into the public domain and the copyright cannot be renewed. The Copyright Office has no discretion to extend the renewal time limits.

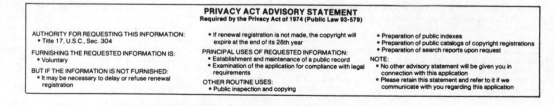

PRIVACY ACT ADVISORY STATEMENT
Required by the Privacy Act of 1974 (Public Law 93-579)

AUTHORITY FOR REQUESTING THIS INFORMATION:
- Title 17, U.S.C., Sec. 304

FURNISHING THE REQUESTED INFORMATION IS:
- Voluntary

BUT IF THE INFORMATION IS NOT FURNISHED:
- It may be necessary to delay or refuse renewal registration

- If renewal registration is not made, the copyright will expire at the end of its 28th year

PRINCIPAL USES OF REQUESTED INFORMATION:
- Establishment and maintenance of a public record
- Examination of the application for compliance with legal requirements

OTHER ROUTINE USES:
- Public inspection and copying

- Preparation of public indexes
- Preparation of public catalogs of copyright registrations
- Preparation of search reports upon request

NOTE:
- No other advisory statement will be given you in connection with this application
- Please retain this statement and refer to it if we communicate with you regarding this application

---

Figure 17.20. Application for renewal registration.

INSTRUCTIONS FOR COMPLETING FORM RE

SPACE 1: RENEWAL CLAIM(S)

• *General Instructions:* In order for this application to result in a valid renewal, space 1 must identify one or more of the persons who are entitled to renew the copyright under the statute. Give the full name and address of each claimant, with a statement of the basis of each claim, using the wording given in these instructions.

• *Persons Entitled to Renew:*

A. The following persons may claim renewal in all types of works except those enumerated in Paragraph B, below:
1. The author, if living. State the claim as: *the author.*
2. The widow, widower, and/or children of the author, if the author is not living. State the claim as: *the widow (widower) of the author* . . . .
(Name of author)

and/or *the child (children) of the deceased author* . . . .
(Name of author)

3. The author's executor(s), if the author left a will and if there is no surviving widow, widower, or child. State the claim as: *the executor(s) of the author*

. . . .
(Name of author)

4. The next of kin of the author, if the author left no will and if there is no surviving widow, widower, or child. State the claim as: *the next of kin of the deceased author* . . . . *there being no will.*
(Name of author)

B. In the case of the following four types of works, the proprietor (owner of the copyright at the time of renewal registration) may claim renewal:
1. Posthumous work (a work as to which no copyright assignment or other contract for exploitation has occurred during the author's lifetime). State the claim as: *proprietor of copyright in a posthumous work.*
2. Periodical, cyclopedic, or other composite work. State the claim as: *proprietor of copyright in a composite work.*
3. "Work copyrighted by a corporate body otherwise than as assignee or licensee of the individual author." State the claim as: *proprietor of copyright in a work copyrighted by a corporate body otherwise than as assignee or licensee of the individual author.* (This type of claim is considered appropriate in relatively few cases.)
4. Work copyrighted by an employer for whom such work was made for hire. State the claim as: *proprietor of copyright in a work made for hire.*

SPACE 2: WORK RENEWED

• *General Instructions:* This space is to identify the particular work being renewed. The information given here should agree with that appearing in the certificate of original registration.

• *Title:* Give the full title of the work, together with any subtitles or descriptive wording included with the title in the original registration. In the case of a musical composition, give the specific instrumentation of the work.

• *Renewable Matter:* Copyright in a new version of a previous work (such as an arrangement, translation, dramatization, compilation, or work republished with new matter) covers only the additions, changes, or other new material appearing for the first time in that version. If this work was a new version, state in general the new matter upon which copyright was claimed.

• *Contribution to Periodical, Serial, or other Composite Work:* Separate renewal registration is possible for a work published as a contribution to a periodical, serial, or other composite work, whether the contribution was copyrighted independently or as part of the larger work in which it appeared. Each contribution published in a separate issue ordinarily requires a separate renewal registration. However, the new law provides an alternative, permitting groups of periodical contributions by the same individual author to be combined under a single renewal application and fee in certain cases.

If this renewal application covers a single contribution, give all of the requested information in space 2. If you are seeking to renew a group of contributions, include a reference such as "See space 5" in space 2 and give the requested information about all of the contributions in space 5.

SPACE 3: AUTHOR(S)

• *General Instructions:* The copyright secured in a new version of a work is independent of any copyright protection in material published earlier. The only "authors" of a new version are those who contributed copyrightable matter to it. Thus, for renewal purposes, the person who wrote the original version on

which the new work is based cannot be regarded as an "author" of the new version, unless that person also contributed to the new matter.

• *Authors of Renewable Matter:* Give the full names of all authors who contributed copyrightable matter to this particular version of the work.

SPACE 4: FACTS OF ORIGINAL REGISTRATION

• *General Instructions:* Each item in space 4 should agree with the information appearing in the original registration for the work. If the work being renewed is a single contribution to a periodical or composite work that was not separately registered, give information about the particular issue in which the contribution appeared. You may leave this space blank if you are completing space 5.

• *Original Registration Number:* Give the full registration number, which is a series of numerical digits, preceded by one or more letters. The registration

number appears in the upper right hand corner of the certificate of registration.

• *Original Copyright Claimant:* Give the name in which ownership of the copyright was claimed in the original registration.

• *Date of Publication or Registration:* Give only one date. If the original registration gave a publication date, it should be transcribed here; otherwise the registration was for an unpublished work, and the date of registration should be given.

SPACE 5: GROUP RENEWALS

• *General Instructions:* A single renewal registration can be made for a group of works if **all** of the following statutory conditions are met: (1) all of the works were written by the same author, who is named in space 3 and who is or was an individual (not an employer for hire); (2) all of the works were first published as contributions to periodicals (including newspapers) and were copyrighted on their first publication; (3) the renewal claimant or claimants, and the basis of claims, as stated in space 1, is the same for all of the works; (4) the renewal application and fee are "received not more than 28 or less than 27 years after the 31st day of December of the calendar year in which all of the works were first published"; and (5) the renewal application identifies each work separately, including the periodical containing it and the date of first publication.

Time Limits for Group Renewals: To be renewed as a group, all of the contributions must have been first published during the same calendar year. For example, suppose six contributions by the same author were published on April 1, 1960, July 1, 1960, November 1, 1960, February 1, 1961, July 1, 1961, and March 1, 1962. The three 1960 copyrights can be combined and renewed at any time during 1988, and the two 1961 copyrights can be renewed as a group during 1989, but the 1962 copyright must be renewed by itself, in 1990.

Identification of Each Work: Give all of the requested information for each contribution. The registration number should be that for the contribution itself if it was separately registered, and the registration number for the periodical issue if it was not.

SPACES 6, 7 AND 8: FEE, MAILING INSTRUCTIONS, AND CERTIFICATION

• *Deposit Account and Mailing Instructions (Space 6):* If you maintain a Deposit Account in the Copyright Office, identify it in space 6. Otherwise, you will need to send the renewal registration fee of $6 with your form. The space headed "Correspondence" should contain the name and address of the person to be consulted if correspondence about the form becomes necessary

• *Certification (Space 7):* The renewal application is not acceptable unless it bears the handwritten signature of the renewal claimant or the duly authorized agent of the renewal claimant.

• *Address for Return of Certificate (Space 8):* The address box must be completed legibly, since the certificate will be returned in a window envelope.

Figure 17.20. (Continued)

REGISTRATION NUMBER

EFFECTIVE DATE OF RENEWAL REGISTRATION

....
(Month)   (Day)   (Year)

DO NOT WRITE ABOVE THIS LINE.   FOR COPYRIGHT OFFICE USE ONLY

①
Renewal Claimant(s)

RENEWAL CLAIMANT(S), ADDRESS(ES), AND STATEMENT OF CLAIM: (See Instructions)

1
Name..
Address...
Claiming as ....
(Use appropriate statement from instructions)

2
Name..
Address...
Claiming as ....
(Use appropriate statement from instructions)

3
Name..
Address...
Claiming as ....
(Use appropriate statement from instructions)

②
Work Renewed

TITLE OF WORK IN WHICH RENEWAL IS CLAIMED:

RENEWABLE MATTER:

CONTRIBUTION TO PERIODICAL OR COMPOSITE WORK:

Title of periodical or composite work: ....

If a periodical or other serial, give: Vol. .... No. .... Issue Date ....

③
Author(s)

AUTHOR(S) OF RENEWABLE MATTER:

④
Facts of Original Registration

ORIGINAL REGISTRATION NUMBER:

....

ORIGINAL COPYRIGHT CLAIMANT:

ORIGINAL DATE OF COPYRIGHT:

• If the original registration for this work was made in published form, give:

DATE OF PUBLICATION: .... (Month) (Day) (Year)

} OR {

• If the original registration for this work was made in unpublished form, give:

DATE OF REGISTRATION: .... (Month) (Day) (Year)

Figure 17.20.   (*Continued*)

EXAMINED BY: . . . .

CHECKED BY: . . . .

RENEWAL APPLICATION RECEIVED:

DEPOSIT ACCOUNT FUNDS USED: ☐

REMITTANCE NUMBER AND DATE:

FOR COPYRIGHT OFFICE USE ONLY

DO NOT WRITE ABOVE THIS LINE. FOR COPYRIGHT OFFICE USE ONLY

RENEWAL FOR GROUP OF WORKS BY SAME AUTHOR: To make a single registration for a group of works by the same individual author published as contributions to periodicals (see instructions), give full information about each contribution. If more space is needed, request continuation sheet (Form RE/CON).

⑤ Renewal for Group of Works

1
Title of Contribution: . . . .
Title of Periodical: . . . . Vol. . . . . . . No. . . . . Issue Date . . . .
Date of Publication: . . . . Registration Number: . . . .
(Month)   (Day)   (Year)

2
Title of Contribution: . . . .
Title of Periodical: . . . . Vol. . . . . . . No. . . . . Issue Date . . . .
Date of Publication: . . . . Registration Number: . . . .
(Month)   (Day)   (Year)

3
Title of Contribution: . . . .
Title of Periodical: . . . . Vol. . . . . . . No. . . . . Issue Date . . . .
Date of Publication: . . . . Registration Number: . . . .
(Month)   (Day)   (Year)

4
Title of Contribution: . . . .
Title of Periodical: . . . . Vol. . . . . . . No. . . . . Issue Date . . . .
Date of Publication: . . . . Registration Number: . . . .
(Month)   (Day)   (Year)

5
Title of Contribution: . . . .
Title of Periodical: . . . . Vol. . . . . . . No. . . . . Issue Date . . . .
Date of Publication: . . . . Registration Number: . . . .
(Month)   (Day)   (Year)

6
Title of Contribution: . . . .
Title of Periodical: . . . . Vol. . . . . . . No. . . . . Issue Date . . . .
Date of Publication: . . . . Registration Number: . . . .
(Month)   (Day)   (Year)

7
Title of Contribution: . . . .
Title of Periodical: . . . . Vol. . . . . . . No. . . . . Issue Date . . . .
Date of Publication: . . . . Registration Number: . . . .
(Month)   (Day)   (Year)

DEPOSIT ACCOUNT: (If the registration fee is to be charged to a Deposit Account established in the Copyright Office, give name and number of Account.)

Name: . . . .
Account Number: . . . .

CORRESPONDENCE: (Give name and address to which correspondence about this application should be sent.)

Name: . . . .
Address: . . . .
                                                                     (Apt.)
. . . .
(City)   (State)   (ZIP)

⑥ Fee and Correspondence

CERTIFICATION: I, the undersigned, hereby certify that I am the: (Check one)
☐ renewal claimant   ☐ duly authorized agent of: . . . .
                                                                (Name of renewal claimant)
of the work identified in this application, and that the statements made by me in this application are correct to the best of my knowledge.

☞   Handwritten signature: (X) . . . .

Typed or printed name: . . . .

Date: . . . .

⑦ Certification (Application must be signed)

. . . .
(Name)
. . . .
(Number, Street and Apartment Number)
. . . .
(City)   (State)   (ZIP code)

MAIL CERTIFICATE TO

(Certificate will be mailed in window envelope)

⑧ Address for Return of Certificate

U.S. GOVERNMENT PRINTING OFFICE: 1978—261-022/10

Apr. 1978—500,000

Figure 17.20. (Continued)

FORM CA

UNITED STATES COPYRIGHT OFFICE
LIBRARY OF CONGRESS
WASHINGTON, D.C. 20559

Application for
Supplementary Copyright Registration

To Correct or Amplify Information Given in the
Copyright Office Record of an Earlier Registration

What is "Supplementary Copyright Registration"? Supplementary registration is a special type of copyright registration provided for in section 408(d) of the copyright law.

Purpose of Supplementary Registration. As a rule, only one basic copyright registration can be made for the same work. To take care of cases where information in the basic registration turns out to be incorrect or incomplete, the law provides for "the filing of an application for supplementary registration, to correct an error in a copyright registration or to amplify the information given in a registration."

Earlier Registration Necessary. Supplementary registration can be made only if a basic copyright registration for the same work has already been completed.

Who May File. Once basic registration has been made for a work, any author or other copyright claimant, or owner of any exclusive right in the work, who wishes to correct or amplify the information given in the basic registration, may submit Form CA.

Please Note:

- Do not use Form CA to correct errors in statements on the copies or phonorecords of the work in question, or to reflect changes in the content of the work. If the work has been changed substantially, you should consider making an entirely new registration for the revised version to cover the additions or revisions.

- Do not use Form CA as a substitute for renewal registration. For works originally copyrighted between January 1, 1950 and December 31, 1977, registration of a renewal claim within strict time limits is necessary to extend the first 28-year copyright term to the full term of 75 years. This cannot be done by filing Form CA.

- Do not use Form CA as a substitute for recording a transfer of copyright or other document pertaining to rights under a copyright. Recording a document under section 205 of the statute gives all persons constructive notice of the facts stated in the document and may have other important consequences in cases of infringement or conflicting transfers. Supplementary registration does not have that legal effect.

How to Apply for Supplementary Registration:

First: Study the information on this page to make sure that filing an application on Form CA is the best procedure to follow in your case.

Second: Turn this page over and read through the specific instructions for filling out Form CA. Make sure, before starting to complete the form, that you have all of the detailed information about the basic registration you will need.

Third: Complete all applicable spaces on this form, following the line-by-line instructions on the back of this page. Use typewriter, or print the information in dark ink.

Fourth: Detach this sheet and send your completed Form CA to: Register of Copyrights, Library of Congress, Washington, D.C. 20559. Unless you have a Deposit Account in the Copyright Office, your application must be accompanied by a non-refundable filing fee in the form of a check or money order for $10 payable to: *Register of Copyrights.* Do not send copies, phonorecords, or supporting documents with your application, since they cannot be made part of the record of a supplementary registration.

What Happens When a Supplementary Registration is Made? When a supplementary registration is completed, the Copyright Office will assign it a new registration number in the appropriate registration category, and issue a certificate of supplementary registration under that number. The basic registration will not be expunged or cancelled, and the two registrations will both stand in the Copyright Office records. The supplementary registration will have the effect of calling the public's attention to a possible error or omission in the basic registration, and of placing the correct facts or the additional information on official record. Moreover, if the person on whose behalf Form CA is submitted is the same as the person identified as copyright claimant in the basic registration, the Copyright Office will place a note referring to the supplementary registration in its records of the basic registration.

PLEASE READ DETAILED INSTRUCTIONS ON REVERSE

Figure 17.21. Application for supplementary copyright registration.

REGISTRATION NUMBER

| TX | TXU | PA | PAU | VA | VAU | SR | SRU | RE |

Effective Date of Supplementary Registration

. . . .

MONTH   DAY   YEAR

DO NOT WRITE ABOVE THIS LINE. FOR COPYRIGHT OFFICE USE ONLY

Ⓐ
Basic Instructions

TITLE OF WORK:

REGISTRATION NUMBER OF BASIC REGISTRATION: | **YEAR OF BASIC REGISTRATION:**

NAME(S) OF AUTHOR(S): | **NAME(S) OF COPYRIGHT CLAIMANT(S):**

Ⓑ
Correction

LOCATION AND NATURE OF INCORRECT INFORMATION IN BASIC REGISTRATION:
Line Number . . . . Line Heading or Description . . . .

INCORRECT INFORMATION AS IT APPEARS IN BASIC REGISTRATION:

CORRECTED INFORMATION:

EXPLANATION OF CORRECTION: (Optional)

Ⓒ
Amplification

LOCATION AND NATURE OF INFORMATION IN BASIC REGISTRATION TO BE AMPLIFIED:
Line Number . . . . Line Heading or Description . . . .

AMPLIFIED INFORMATION:

EXPLANATION OF AMPLIFIED INFORMATION: (Optional)

Figure 17.21. (Continued)

EXAMINED BY:	FORM CA RECEIVED:	FOR COPYRIGHT OFFICE USE ONLY
CHECKED BY:		
CORRESPONDENCE: ☐ YES	REMITTANCE NUMBER AND DATE:	
REFERENCE TO THIS REGISTRATION ADDED TO BASIC REGISTRATION: ☐ YES · ☐ NO	DEPOSIT ACCOUNT FUNDS USED: ☐	

CONTINUATION OF: (Check which)   ☐ PART B OR   ☐ PART C

(D) Continuation

DEPOSIT ACCOUNT: If the registration fee is to be charged to a Deposit Account established in the Copyright Office. give name and number of Account:

Name . . . . Account Number . . . .

CORRESPONDENCE: Give name and address to which correspondence should be sent:

Name . . . . Apt. No. . . . .

Address . . . .
                    (Number and Street)   (City)   (State)   (ZIP Code)

(E) Deposit Account and Mailing Instructions

CERTIFICATION ✱ I, the undersigned, hereby certify that I am the: (Check one)

☐ author ☐ other copyright claimant ☐ owner of exclusive right(s) ☐ authorized agent of: . . . .
                                                                            (Name of author or other copyright claimant, or owner of exclusive right(s))

of the work identified in this application and that the statements made by me in this application are correct to the best of my knowledge.

☞   Handwritten signature: (X) . . . .

     Typed or printed name. . . . .

     Date: . . . .

✱ 17 USC §506(e): FALSE REPRESENTATION—Any person who knowingly makes a false representation of a material fact in the application for copyright registration provided for by section 409, or in any written statement filed in connection with the application. shall be fined not more than $2.500.

(F) Certification (Application must be signed)

. . . .
                                    (Name)

. . . .
                        (Number, Street and Apartment Number)

. . . .
             (City)   (State)   (ZIP code)

MAIL CERTIFICATE TO

(Certificate will be mailed in window envelope)

(G) Address for Return of Certificate

January 1984—60,000
☆ U.S. GOVERNMENT PRINTING OFFICE: 1984—421-278/510

Figure 17.21.   (Continued)

INSTRUCTIONS

For Completing FORM CA (Supplementary Registration)

PART A: BASIC INSTRUCTIONS

• *General Instructions:* The information in this part identifies the basic registration to be corrected or amplified. Each item must agree exactly with the information as it already appears in the basic registration (even if the purpose of filing Form CA is to change one of these items).

• *Title of Work:* Give the title as it appears in the basic registration, including previous or alternative titles if they appear.

• *Registration Number:* This is a series of numerical digits, pre-ceded by one or more letters. The registration number appears in the upper right hand corner of the certificate of registration.

• *Registration Date:* Give the year when the basic registration was completed.

• *Name(s) of Author(s) and Name(s) of Copyright Claim-ant(s):* Give all of the names as they appear in the basic registra-tion.

PART B: CORRECTION

• *General Instructions:* Complete this part **only** if information in the basic registration was incorrect at the time that basic registration was made. Leave this part blank and complete Part C, instead, if your purpose is to add, update, or clarify information rather than to rectify an actual error.

• *Location and Nature of Incorrect Information:* Give the line number and the heading or description of the space in the basic registration where the error occurs (for example: "Line number 3 . . . Citizenship of author").

• *Incorrect Information as it Appears in Basic Registration:* Transcribe the erroneous statement exactly as it appears in the basic registration.

• *Corrected Information:* Give the statement as it should have ap-peared.

• *Explanation of Correction (Optional):* If you wish, you may add an explanation of the error or its correction.

PART C: AMPLIFICATION

• *General Instructions:* Complete this part if you want to provide any of the following: (1) additional information that could have been given but was omitted at the time of basic registration; (2) changes in facts, such as changes of title or address of claimant, that have oc-curred since the basic registration; or (3) explanations clarifying infor-mation in the basic registration.

• *Location and Nature of Information to be Amplified:* Give the line number and the heading or description of the space in the basic registration where the information to be amplified appears.

• *Amplified Information:* Give a statement of the added, updated, or explanatory information as clearly and succinctly as possible.

• *Explanation of Amplification (Optional):* If you wish, you may add an explanation of the amplification.

PARTS D, E, F, G: CONTINUATION, FEE, MAILING INSTRUCTIONS AND CERTIFICATION

• *Continuation (Part D):* Use this space if you do not have enough room in Parts B or C.

• *Deposit Account and Mailing Instructions (Part E):* If you main-tain a Deposit Account in the Copyright Office, identify it in Part E. Otherwise, you will need to send the non-refundable filing fee of $10 with your form. The space headed "Correspondence" should contain the name and address of the person to be consulted if correspondence about the form becomes necessary.

• *Certification (Part F):* The application is not acceptable unless it bears the handwritten signature of the author, or other copyright clai-mant, or of the owner of exclusive right(s), or of the duly authorized agent of such author, claimant, or owner.

• *Address for Return of Certificate (Part G):* The address box must be completed legibly, since the certificate will be returned in a window envelope.

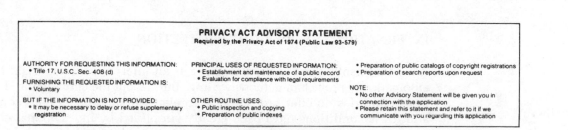

Figure 17.21. (Continued)

published and unpublished works of the visual arts, pictorial, graphic, and sculptural works. Form SR is for published and unpublished sound recordings. Form SE is for serials, works issued or intended to be issued in successive parts, bearing numerical or chronological designations and intended to be continued indefinitely (periodicals, newspapers, magazines, newsletters, annuals, journals, etc.). Form GR/CP is an adjunct application to be used for registration of a group of contributions to periodicals. Form RE is for renewals for works copyright under the law in effect through December 31, 1977. Finally, we have Form CA. It is for supplementary registration to correct or amplify information given in the copyright record of an earlier registration.

HOW LONG IS A COPYRIGHT VALID?

Under the new law, a work that is created, that is, fixed and in tangible form for the first time on or after January 1, 1978, is automatically protected from the moment of its creation and is ordinarily given a term enduring for the author's life, plus an additional 50 years after the author's death. If the work is a joint work prepared by two or more authors who did not work for hire, the terms lasts for 50 years after the last surviving author's death. For works made for hire and for anonymous and pseudonymous works, the duration of copyright will be 75 years from publication or 100 from creation, whichever is shorter.

Works that were created before the new law came into effect but have neither been published nor registered for copyright before January 1, 1978 have been automatically brought under the statute and are now given federal copyright protection. The duration of copyright for these works will generally be computed in the same way as for new works. However, all works in this category are guaranteed at least 25 years under statutory protection.

For works copyrighted before January 1, 1978, copyright was secured either on the date the work was published or on the date of registration if the work was registered in nonpublished form. In either case, a copyright lasted for a first term of 28 years from the first date that it was secured, and it was eligible for renewal once for an additional 28 years. Under the new copyright law, the renewal term has been extended from 28 to 47 years for copyrights that were subsisting on January 1, 1978. However, the copyright must be timely renewed to receive the 47-year period of added protection.

If you want a form for renewing a copyright which has already been registered, ask for Form RE. This is for claims to renew a copyright and for works copyrighted under the old law.

INTERNATIONAL COPYRIGHT PROTECTION

As with patents, there is no such thing as an international copyright that will automatically protect an author's writings throughout the entire world. However, most countries do offer protection to foreign works under certain conditions, and these conditions have been greatly simplified by international copyright treaties and conventions. The United States is a member of the Universal Copyright Convention (UCC) which came into force in 1955. Under this convention, a work by a national or domiciliary of a country that is a member of the Universal Copyright Convention or a work first published in a Universal Copyright Convention country may claim protection under the Universal Copyright Convention, as long as the work bears the notice of the copyright in the foreign position specified by the Universal Copyright Convention. It is for this reason that I advise that you use the word "copyright" as well as the symbol ©. However, any author who wants protection for his or her work in a particular country should find out about that specific country; if possible, he or she should do this before the work is published anywhere.

WHAT IS A TRADEMARK?

A trademark includes any word, name, symbol, device, or any combination thereof adopted and used by a manufacturer or merchant to identify his goods and distinguish them from those manufactured or sold by others. The primary function of the trademark is to indicate origin. However, it has other functions. Trademarks also guarantee the quality of the goods bearing the mark and through advertising help to create and maintain a demand for your product.

Rights in a trademark are acquired only by use, and the use must ordinarily continue if the rights so acquired are to be preserved. This means that although you may register a trademark in the Patent and Trademark Office, this by itself does not create or establish any exclusive right. Such registration is only recognition by the U.S. government of the right of the owner to use the mark in commerce to distinguish the mark from those of others.

TRADEMARKS YOU CANNOT REGISTER

Certain trademarks cannot be registered. This is so if the mark:

1. Does not function as a trademark to identify the goods or services as coming from a particular source; for example, the matter applied for is merely ornamentation
2. Is immoral, deceptive or scandalous
3. May disparage or falsely suggest a connection with persons, institutions, beliefs or national symbols, or bring them into contempt or disrepute
4. Consists of or simulates the flag or coat of arms or other insignia of the United States, or a State or municipality, or any foreign nation
5. Is the name, portrait or signature of a particular living individual, unless he has given written consent; or is the name, signature or portrait of a deceased President of the United States during the life of his widow, unless she has given her consent
6. So resembles a mark already registered in the PTO as to be likely, when applied to the goods of the applicant, to cause confusion, or to cause mistake, or to deceive
7. Is merely descriptive or deceptively misdescriptive of the goods or services
8. Is primarily geographically descriptive or deceptively misdescriptive of the goods or services of the applicant
9. Is primarily merely a surname

A mark will not be refused registration on the grounds listed in numbers 7, 8 and 9 if the applicant can show that, through use of the mark in commerce which can be controlled by the U.S. Congress, it has become distinctive so that it now identifies to the public the applicant's goods or services. Marks which are refused registration on the grounds listed in numbers 1, 7, 8 and 9 may be registered on the *Supplemental Register*, which contains terms or designs considered capable of distinguishing the party's goods or services, but that do not yet do so. If a mark is registered on the *Supplemental Register*, the registrant may bring suit for trademark infringement in the Federal courts, or may use the registration as a basis for filing in some foreign countries. None of the other benefits of Federal registration listed on pages 1 and 2 apply. In order to file an application on the *Supplemental Register*, the applicant must have made lawful use of the mark must have been in use in commerce for one year. (An application may be filed on the *Principal Register* as soon as the mark has been used in commerce.) An applicant may file an application on the *Principal Register* and, if appropriate, amend the application to the *Supplemental Register* for no additional fee.

BENEFITS OF REGISTRATION

While Federal registration is not necessary for trademark protection, registration on the Principal Register does provide certain advantages:

- The right to sue in Federal court for trademark infringement
- Recovery of profits, damages and costs in a Federal court infringement action and the possibility of treble damages and attorneys' fees
- Constructive notice of a claim of ownership (which eliminates a good faith defense for a party adopting the trademark subsequent to the registrant's date of registration)
- The right to deposit the registration with Customs in order to stop the importation of goods bearing an infringing mark
- Prima facie evidence of the validity of the registration, registrant's ownership of the mark and of registrant's exclusive right to use the mark in commerce in connection with the goods or services specified in the certificate
- The possibility of incontestability, in which case the registration constitutes conclusive evidence of the registrant's exclusive right, with certain limited exceptions, to use the registered mark in commerce
- Limited grounds for attacking a registration once it is five years old
- Availability of criminal penalties in an action for counterfeiting a registered trademark
- A basis for filing trademark applications in foreign countries

HOW TO REGISTER FOR A TRADEMARK

The application for registration for a trademark must be filed in the name of the owner of the mark. The owner may file and prosecute his own application for registration, or he or she may be represented by an attorney or other person authorized to practice in trademark cases.

There are four parts to the application for a trademark. They are as follows:

1. A written application
2. A drawing of the mark
3. Five specimens or facsimiles
4. The required filing fee

Let's look at each in turn.

Written Application Form[2]

The application must be written in English. Figures 17.22, 17.23, and 17.24 may be used for either a trademark or service mark application. Additional forms may be photocopied. The appropriate form for the type of applicant which is applying should be used. Unincorporated associations would generally use the "corporation" form. The following explanation covers each blank, beginning at the top.

Heading. Identify (a) the mark (e.g. "ERGO" or "ERGO and design") and (b) the class number(s) of the goods or services for which registration is sought. Classification is part of the PTO's administrative processing. The International Classification of Goods and Services is used (see reverse side of application form). The class may be left blank if the appropriate class number is not known.

Applicant. The application must be filed in the name of the owner of the mark. Specify, if an individual, applicant's name and citizenship; if a partnership, the names and citizenship of the general partners and the domicile of the partnership; if a corporation or association, the name under which it is incorporated and the State or foreign nation under the laws of which it is organized. Also indicate the applicant's post office address and, if an individual, place of residence.

Identification of Goods or Services. State briefly the *specific* goods or services for which the mark is used and for which registration is sought as shown in Figure 17.25.

Dates of Use. State the date of first use anywhere of the trademark on the goods or in connection with the services specified.

Applicant must also state its date of first use of the mark on the (goods or in connection with the services in commerce which may lawfully be regulated by Congress. The type of commerce must be identified [e.g. "interstate commerce" (shipment of goods from one state to another); or "commerce between the U.S. and (specify foreign country)"]. The date of first use in commerce may be the same as the date of first use of the mark anywhere, but it cannot be earlier.

Method of Use. State how the mark is used in connection with the goods or services specified, e.g. labels, packaging, or, for services only, advertising.

---

[2] From *Basic Facts About Trademarks*, U.S. Department of Commerce, Patent and Trademark Office, Washington, D.C. (1988).

<table>
<tr><td rowspan="3">**TRADEMARK APPLICATION, PRINCIPAL REGISTER, WITH DECLARATION**
(Individual)</td><td>MARK *(identify the mark)*</td></tr>
<tr><td>CLASS NO. *(if known)*</td></tr>
</table>

TO THE COMMISSIONER OF PATENTS AND TRADEMARKS:

NAME OF APPLICANT, AND BUSINESS TRADE NAME, IF ANY

BUSINESS ADDRESS

RESIDENCE ADDRESS

CITIZENSHIP OF APPLICANT

The above identified applicant has adopted and is using the trademark shown in the accompanying drawing for the following

goods: _____

_____

and requests that said mark be registered in the United States Patent and Trademark Office on the Principal Register established by the Act of July 5, 1946.

The trademark was first used on the goods on _____ ; was first used on the goods in
                                             (date)

_____ commerce on _____ ; and is now in use in such
   (type of commerce)   *(date)*

commerce.

The mark is used by applying it to _____

_____

and five specimens showing the mark as actually used are presented herewith.

_____
                              (name of applicant)

being hereby warned that willful false statements and the like so made are punishable by fine or imprisonment, or both, under Section 1001 of Title 18 of the United States Code and that such willful false statements may jeopardize the validity of the application or any registration resulting therefrom, declares that he/she believes himself/herself to be the owner of the trademark sought to be registered; to the best of his/her knowledge and belief no other person, firm, corporation, or association has the right to use said mark in commerce, either in the identical form or in such near resemblance thereto as may be likely, when applied to the goods of such other person, to cause confusion, or to cause mistake, or to deceive; the facts set forth in this application are true; and all statements made of his/her own knowledge are true and all statements made on information and belief are believed to be true.

_____
                              (signature of applicant)

_____
                              (date)

FORM PTO-1476FB (REV. 4-87)   U.S. DEPARTMENT OF COMMERCE/Patent and Trademark Office

Figure 17.22. Trademark application, principal register, with declaration (individual).

TRADEMARK APPLICATION, PRINCIPAL REGISTER, WITH DECLARATION (Partnership)	MARK *(identify the mark)*
	CLASS NO. *(if known)*

TO THE COMMISSIONER OF PATENTS AND TRADEMARKS:

NAME OF PARTNERSHIP

NAMES OF PARTNERS

BUSINESS ADDRESS OF PARTNERSHIP

CITIZENSHIP OF PARTNERS

The above identified applicant has adopted and is using the trademark shown in the accompanying drawing for the following

goods: _____

_____

and requests that said mark be registered in the United States Patent and Trademark Office on the Principal Register established by the Act of July 5, 1946.

The trademark was first used on the goods on _____ ; was first used on the goods in
                                                                  (date)

_____ commerce on _____ ; and is now in use in such
     (type of commerce)   *(date)*

commerce.

The mark is used by applying it to _____

_____

and five specimens showing the mark as actually used are presented herewith.

_____
(name of partner)

being hereby warned that willful false statements and the like so made are punishable by fine or imprisonment, or both, under Section 1001 of Title 18 of the United States Code and that such willful false statements may jeopardize the validity of the application or any registration resulting therefrom, declares that he/she believes himself/herself to be the owner of the trademark sought to be registered; to the best of his/her knowledge and belief no other person, firm, corporation, or association has the right to use said mark in commerce, either in the identical form or in such near resemblance thereto as may be likely, when applied to the goods of such other person, to cause confusion, or to cause mistake, or to deceive; the facts set forth in this application are true; and all statements made of his/her own knowledge are true and all statements made on information and belief are believed to be true.

_____
(signature of applicant)

_____
(date)

FORM PTO-1477FB (REV. 4-87)   U.S. DEPARTMENT OF COMMERCE/Patent and Trademark Office

Figure 17.23. Trademark application, principal register, with declaration (partnership).

<table>
<tr><td rowspan="2">TRADEMARK APPLICATION, PRINCIPAL
REGISTER, WITH DECLARATION
(Corporation)</td><td>MARK (identify the mark)</td></tr>
<tr><td>CLASS NO. (if known)</td></tr>
</table>

TO THE COMMISSIONER OF PATENTS AND TRADEMARKS:

NAME OF CORPORATION

STATE OR COUNTRY OF INCORPORATION

BUSINESS ADDRESS OF CORPORATION

The above identified applicant has adopted and is using the trademark shown in the accompanying drawing for the following

goods: _____

_____
and requests that said mark be registered in the United States Patent and Trademark Office on the Principal Register established by the Act of July 5, 1946.

The trademark was first used on the goods on _____ ; was first used on the goods in
(date)

_____ commerce on _____ ; and is now in use in such
(type of commerce)   *(date)*

commerce.

The mark is used by applying it to _____

_____
and five specimens showing the mark as actually used are presented herewith.

_____
(name of officer of corporation)
being hereby warned that willful false statements and the like so made are punishable by fine or imprisonment, or both, under Section 1001 of Title 18 of the United States Code and that such willful false statements may jeopardize the validity of the application or any registration resulting therefrom, declares that he/she is

_____
(official title)
of applicant corporation and is authorized to execute this instrument on behalf of said corporation; he/she believes said corporation to be the owner of the trademark sought to be registered; to the best of his/her knowledge and belief no other person, firm, corporation, or association has the right to use said mark in commerce, either in the identical form or in such near resemblance thereto as may be likely, when applied to the goods of such other person, to cause confusion, or to cause mistake, or to deceive; the facts set forth in this application are true; and all statements made of his/her own knowledge are true and all statements made on information and belief are believed to be true.

_____
(name of corporation)

By _____
(signature of officer of corporation, and official title of officer)

_____
(date)

Figure 17.24. Trademark application, principal register, with declaration (corporation).

Goods

1	Chemicals used in industry, science, photography, as well as in agriculture, horticulture, and forestry; unprocessed artificial resins; unprocessed plastics; manures; fire extinguishing compositions; tempering and soldering preparations; chemical substances for preserving foodstuffs; tanning substances; adhesives used in industry.
2	Paints, varnishes, lacquers; preservatives against rust and against deterioration of wood; colourants; mordants; raw natural resins; metals in foil and powder form for painters, decorators, printers and artists.
3	Bleaching preparations and other substances for laundry use; cleaning, polishing, scouring and abrasive preparations; soaps; perfumery, essential oils, cosmetics, hair lotions; dentifrices.
4	Industrial oils and greases; lubricants; dust absorbing, wetting and binding compositions; fuels (including motor spirit) and illuminants; candles, wicks.
5	Pharmaceutical, veterinary, and sanitary preparations; dietetic substances adapted for medical use, food for babies; plasters, materials for dressings material for stopping teeth, dental wax, disinfectants; preparations for destroying vermin; fungicides, herbicides.
6	Common metals and their alloys; metal building materials; transportable buildings of metal; materials of metal for railway tracks; non-electric cables and wires of common metal; ironmongery, small items of metal hardware; pipes and tubes of metal; safes; goods of common metal not included in other classes; ores
7	Machines and machine tools; motors (except for land vehicles); machine coupling and belting (except for land vehicles); agricultural implements; incubators for eggs.
8	Hand tools and implements (hand operated); cutlery; side arms; razors.
9	Scientific, nautical, surveying, electric, photographic, cinematographic, optical, weighing, measuring, signalling, checking (supervision), life-saving and teaching apparatus and instruments; apparatus for recording transmission or reproduction of sound or images; magnetic data carriers, recording discs; automatic vending machines and mechanisms for coin-operated apparatus; cash registers, calculating machines, data processing equipment and computers; fire-extinguishing apparatus.
10	Surgical, medical, dental, and veterinary apparatus and instruments, artificial limbs, eyes and teeth; orthopedic articles; suture materials.
11	Apparatus for lighting, heating, steam generating, cooking, refrigerating, drying, ventilating, water supply, and sanitary purposes.
12	Vehicles; apparatus for locomotion by land, air or water.
13	Firearms; ammunition and projectiles; explosives; fireworks.
14	Precious metals and their alloys and goods in precious metals or coated therewith, not included in other classes; jewelry, precious stones; horological and other chronometric instruments.
15	Musical instruments.
16	Paper and cardboard and goods made from these materials, not included in other classes; printed matter; bookbinding material; photographs; stationery; adhesives for stationery or household purposes; artists' materials; paint brushes; typewriters and office requisites (except furniture); instructional and teaching material (except apparatus); plastic materials for packaging (not included on other classes); playing cards; printers' type; printing blocks.
17	Rubber, gutta-percha, gum, asbestos, mica and goods made from these materials and not included in other classes; plastics in extruded form for use in manufacture; packing, stopping and insulating materials; flexible pipes, not of metal.
18	Leather and imitations of leather, and goods made from these materials and not included in other classes; animal skins, hides; trunks and travelling bags; umbrellas, parasols and walking sticks; whips, harness and saddlery.
19	Building materials (non-metallic); non-metallic rigid pipes for building; asphalt, pitch and bitumen; non-metallic transportable buildings; monuments, not of metal.
20	Furniture, mirrors, picture frames; goods (not included in other classes) of wood, cork, reed, cane, wicker, horn, bone, ivory, whalebone, shell, amber, mother-of-pearl, meerschaum and substitutes for all these materials, or of plastics.
21	Household or kitchen utensils and containers (not of precious metal or coated therewith); combs and sponges; brushes (except paint brushes); brush-making materials; articles for cleaning purposes; steel wool; unworked or semi-worked glass (except glass used in building); glassware, porcelain and earthenware, not included in other classes.
22	Ropes, string, nets, tents, awnings, tarpaulins, sails, sacks; and bags (not included other classes); padding and stuffing materials (except of rubber or plastics); raw fibrous textile materials.
23	Yarns and threads, for textile use.
24	Textile and textile goods, not included in other classes; bed and table covers.
25	Clothing, footwear, headgear.
26	Lace and embroidery, ribbons and braid; buttons, hooks and eyes, pins and needles; artificial flowers.
27	Carpets, rugs, mats and matting; linoleum and other materials for covering existing floors; wall hangings (non-textile).
28	Games and playthings; gymnastic and sporting articles not included in other classes; decorations for Christmas trees.
29	Meats, fish, poultry and game; meat extracts; preserved, dried and cooked fruits and vegetables; jellies, jams; eggs, milk and milk products; edible oils and fats; salad dressings; preserves.
30	Coffee, tea, cocoa, sugar, rice, tapioca, sago, artificial coffee; flour, and preparations made from cereals, bread, pastry and confectionery, ices; honey, treacle; yeast, baking-powder; salt, mustard, vinegar, sauces, (except salad dressings) spices; ice.
31	Agricultural, horticultural and forestry products and grains not included in other classes; living animals; fresh fruits and vegetables; seeds, natural plants and flowers; foodstuffs for animals; malt.
32	Beers; mineral and aerated waters and other non-alcoholic drinks; fruit drinks and fruit juices; syrups and other preparations for making beverages.
33	Alcoholic beverages (except beers).
34	Tobacco; smokers' articles; matches.

Services

35	Advertising and business.
36	Insurance and financial.
37	Construction and repair.
38	Communication.
39	Transportation and storage.
40	Material treatment.
41	Education and entertainment
42	Miscellaneous.

Figure 17.25. International schedule of classes of goods and services.

Execution. The application form must be dated and signed. By signing the form, the applicant is swearing that all the information in the application is believed to be true. If the applicant is an individual, the individual must execute it; if joint applicants, all must execute; if a partnership, one general partner must execute the application; and if a corporation or association, one officer of the organization must execute the application.

Drawing

The drawing is a representation of the mark as actually used on the goods or services. There are two types: (a) typed drawings and (b) special form drawings. All drawings must be made upon pure white durable nonshiny paper 8½" wide by 11" long. One of the shorter sides of the sheet should be regarded as its top. There must be a margin of at least one inch on the sides and bottom of the paper and at least one inch between the drawing of the mark and the heading. An application may contain only one drawing.

Heading. Across the top of the drawing, beginning one inch from the top edge and not exceeding one quarter of the sheet, list on separate lines applicant's name; post office address; date of first use; date of first use in commerce; and the goods or services recited in the application (or typical items of the goods or services if there are a large number). A typewritten heading is preferred.

Typed Drawing. If the mark is only words, or words and numerals, and the applicant does not wish the registration to be issued for a particular depiction of the words and/or numerals, the mark may be typed in capital letters in the center of the page.

Special Form Drawing. This form must be used if the applicant wishes the registration for the mark to be issued in a particular style, or if the mark contains a design element. The drawing of the mark must be done in black ink, either with an india ink pen or by a process which will give satisfactory reproduction characteristics. Every line and letter, including words, must be black. This applies to all lines, including lines used for shading. Half-tones and gray are not acceptable. All lines must be clean, sharp, and solid, and not be fine or crowded. A printer's proof or camera ready copy may be used if otherwise suitable. Photographs are not acceptable. Photocopies are acceptable only if they produce an unusually clear and sharp black and white rendering. The use of white pigment to cover lines is not acceptable.

The preferred size of the drawing of the mark is 2½" × 2½", and in no case may it be larger than 4" × 4". If the amount of detail in the mark precludes clear reduction to the required 4" × 4" size, such detail should not be shown in the drawing but should be verbally described in the body of the application.

Where color is a feature of a mark, the color or colors may be designated in the drawing by the linings shown in the following chart:

Specimens (Examples of Use)

Trademarks may be placed on the goods, or their containers, or on displays associated with the goods, or on tags or labels attached to the goods. The applicant must furnish five specimens showing examples of such use. The specimens may be identical or they may show five different types of uses.

The five specimens should be actual labels, tags, containers, displays, etc. as long as they are capable of being arranged flat and of a size not larger than 8½" × 13". Three-dimensional or bulky material submitted as examples cannot be accepted. When, due to the mode of applying or affixing the mark to the goods, or to the nature of the mark, specimens as indicated above cannot be furnished, five copies of a photograph or other reproduction, not larger than 8½" × 13" and clearly and legibly showing the mark on the goods, should be furnished.

Service Marks.   Examples of the mark as used in the sale or advertising of the services (e.g., brochures or advertisements) must be furnished unless it is impossible to do so because of the nature of the mark or the manner in which it is used, in which case some other representation must be submitted. In the case of service marks not used in printed or written form, three audio cassette recordings should be furnished.

Fees

The fee is $200 for each class of goods or services for which application is made. (See International Classification of Goods and Services, reverse side of application form.) At least $200 must be submitted for the application to be given a filing date. All payments should be made in United States specie, treasury notes, national bank notes, post office money order, or certified checks. Personal or business checks may be submitted, but the Patent and Trademark Office will cancel credit if payment cannot be collected. Money orders and checks should be made payable to the Commissioner of Patents and Trademarks. Money sent by mail to the Patent and Trademark Office will be at the risk of the sender; letters containing money (cash) should be registered. Remittances made from foreign countries must be payable and immediately negotiable in the United States for the full amount of the fee required.

BASES FOR RECEIVING A FILING DATE

1.   *Use in commerce.*   A foreign applicant using a mark in commerce which may lawfully be regulated by Congress may apply for registration in the same manner as residents of the United States.

2.   *Foreign registration.*   The application may be based upon a registration which the applicant has previously secured in its country of origin (if the U.S. and this country are parties to the same international trademark agreement or provide reciprocal registration rights). The application must be accompanied by a copy of the foreign registration, certified by the foreign office which issued the registration.

3.   *Foreign application.*   The U.S. application may be based on an application for registration filed in the applicant's country of origin (if the U.S. and this country are parties to the same international trademark agreement or provide reciprocal registration rights) as long as the U.S. application is filed within six months of the foreign filing. This entitles the applicant to a right of priority, giving it an effective filing date in the U.S. that is the same date as the foreign filing. Before the U.S. application will be approved, a certified copy of the foreign registration resulting from the foreign application must be submitted.

Use-related requirements. If the applicant relies on a foreign application or registration, and use in commerce is not asserted, the applicant must conform to the same requirements as applicants basing their applications on use in commerce, except that the following need not be submitted:

(a) Specimens;
(b) Date of first use of the mark or date of first use of the mark in commerce;
(c) The manner in which the mark is used on or in connection with the particular goods or services.

FOREIGN APPLICANTS

Domestic representative. Applicants not living in the United States must designate by a written document the name and address of some person resident in the United States on whom notices of process in proceedings affecting the mark may be served. This person will also receive all official communications unless the applicant is represented by an attorney in the United States.

COMMUNICATIONS WITH THE PATENT AND TRADEMARK OFFICE

The application and all other communications should be addressed to "The Commissioner of Patents and Trademarks, Washington, D.C., 20231." It is preferred that the applicant indicate its telephone number on the application form. Once a serial number is assigned, the applicant should refer to this number in all telephone and written communications.

TRADEMARK NOTICE

Once a Federal registration is issued, the registrant may give notice of registration by using the ® symbol, or the phrase "Registered in U.S. Patent and Trademark Office" or "Reg. U.S. Pat. & Tm. Off." Although it is not required, prior to registration many trademark owners use a TM or SM (if the mark identifies a service) symbol to indicate a claim of ownership, even if no Federal trademark application is pending.

RENEWAL OF TRADEMARKS

Trademarks are good for a 20-year period and may be renewed for periods of 20 years from the expiring period unless previously canceled or surrendered. However, between the fifth and sixth year after the date of the registration, the registrant must file an affidavit stating the mark is currently in use in commerce. If no affidavit is filed, the registration is cancelled.

TRADEMARK SEARCH LIBRARY

A record of all active registrations and pending applications is maintained by the PTO to help determine whether a previously registered mark exists which could prevent the registration of an applicant's mark. (See ground for refusal No. 6, above.) The search library is located near Washington, D.C. at Crystal Plaza 2, 2nd Floor, 2011 Jefferson Davis Highway, Arlington, VA 22022, and is open to the public free of charge Monday through Friday, 8:00 am to 5:30 pm. The PTO cannot advise prospective applicants of the availability of a particular mark prior to the filing of an application. The applicant may hire a private search company or law firm to perform a search if a search is desired before filing an application and the applicant is unable to visit the search library. The PTO cannot recommend any such companies, but the applicant may wish to consult listings for "Trademark Search Services" in the telephone directories or contact local bar associations for a list of attorneys specializing in trademark law.

FOR ADDITIONAL INFORMATION ON TRADEMARKS

The Federal registration of trademarks is governed by the Trademark Act of 1946, 15 U.S.C. Sec. 1051 et seq.; the Rules, 37 C.F.R. Part 2; and the Trademark Manual of Examining Procedure.

General Trademark or Patent Information: (703) 557-INFO

Status Information for Particular Trademark Applications: (703) 557-5249

SOURCES OF ADDITIONAL INFORMATION

The Concise Guide to Patents, Trademarks, and Copyrights, edited by Solomon J. Schepps, published by Bell Publishing Co., a division of Crown Publishers, Inc., 1 Park Avenue, New York, NY 10016.

Copyright Law of the United States of America, published by the United States Copyright Office, Library of Congress, Washington, DC 20559.

General Information Concerning Patents, published by the Superintendent of Documents, U.S. Government Printing Office, Washington DC 20402.

General Information Concerning Trademarks, published by the Superintendent of Documents, U.S. Government Printing Office, Washington, DC 20402.

The Inventors Patent Handbook, by Stacy V. Jones, published by Dial Press, 1 Dag Hammarskjold Plaza, New York, NY 10017.

Patent Attorneys and Agents Registered to Practice Before the U.S. Patent and Trademark Office, U.S. Government Printing Office, Washington, DC 20402.

Patent It by Hrand M. Munchergan, published by Tab Books, Inc., Blue Ridge Summit, PA 17214.

Patent It Yourself, by David Pressman, published by Nolo Press, 950 Parker St., Berkeley, CA 94710.

Patent and Trademark Forms Booklet, U.S. Government Printing Office, Washington, DC 20402.

18

Personnel Management

Personnel management is the management of people, and people, you will find, are the most important resource in your business. Chapter 16 covered how to find and hire new personnel. This chapter discusses developing job descriptions, wage scales, and compensation plans, doing performance appraisal and counseling your employees, dealing with disciplinary problems, motivating employees, terminating employees, and using temporary help services. Finally, it covers the major labor laws which affect your business.

PERFORMING A JOB ANALYSIS AND DEVELOPING JOB DESCRIPTIONS

Good job descriptions will assist you in hiring, in establishing wage scales and compensation, in constructing your performance appraisal, and in hiring temporary help services. In fact, good job descriptions are the basis of most actions that you must take in personnel management. The job description itself is based on a good prior job analysis. Job analysis is really a methodology for discovering the most important factors concerning a job in your company. The analysis answers the four major questions for the job description and job specification:

1. What physical and/or mental tasks does the worker perform? These may include cleaning, fabricating, planning, judging, managing, and numerous other functions.

2. How does the worker do the job—what methods are used and what equipment or machinery, if any, is involved? For example, does the job require use of a lathe, a cash register, a computer, and if a lathe is used, for what purpose is it used?

3. Why is the job done? In this part of the analysis, you should develop a short explanation of the objective of the job and how it relates to other jobs that are done in your company. Here you may indicate that your copywriter writes copy which is used in space and direct mail advertisements.

4. What qualifications are needed to perform this job? List knowledge, skills, training, personal characteristics, and so forth that are required of the worker. For example, a sales engineer may need a bachelor's degree in engineering, ability to get along with people, a pleasing personality, persuasiveness, and energy.

In summary, the job analysis provides a complete picture of the job that you want performed, including what the worker does, how he does it, his job's relationship to other jobs that must be performed, and knowledge, skills, training, and education that the worker must have in order to do the job.

Conducting a job analysis is not difficult. The easiest way is simply to sit down and think through the various aspects of the job as mentioned previously. If you already have an employee in the job and you wish to redefine it, you may speak with him or her and his or her supervisor. If not, you could talk with people in other companies who have similar jobs. You could also ask the employee or supervisor to list the duties and responsibilities and qualifications he or she feels are important in performing the job. You can then modify this information as appropriate. To assist you in doing this, use the job analysis outline shown in Figure 18.1. A complete example of this form is shown in Figure 18.2.

Now that you have completed the job analysis, you have the material necessary to develop a job description and job specification. There is a small distinction between job descriptions and job specifications. A job description is part of the job analysis which describes the responsibilities of the job, how the job is done, and how it ties in with other jobs in your business. The job specification part, which is used directly in your recruiting efforts, is that part of the analysis which describes those qualifications required of someone in order to do the job properly. Therefore, to prepare a job description, simply summarize the important facts about the job which you have analyzed. Write down in a clear, concise way the important information, including a job title that is descriptive of the position, a brief summary of the work to be performed, major responsibilities of the job including knowledge of equipment that may be necessary, decision making, and scheduling, major job duties that are performed only occasionally, and the relationship of the job to other positions in your firm, including whom the employee would supervise and to whom the employee would report. To assist you with this, use the outline for writing a job description contained in Figure 18.3. An example of this use is shown in Figure 18.4. Figure 16.2 in Chapter 16 shows an outline for writing a job specification. This is especially necessary for your hiring and recruiting effort. Figure 16.3 shows a simple job specification form completed.

WAGE SCALES AND COMPENSATION

How much to pay your employee for a particular job is very important. Unfortunately, the question has no simple answer. If you pay too little, your better employees will leave to do the same work elsewhere or to work on their own, and only the poorer, less motivated, and less able employees will remain to work for you for lower pay. On the other hand, overpaying has a drawback. You can be less competitive in the price you charge for the product or the service which you are offering.

Also, an important consideration is the fact that compensation is measured in more than mere dollars, and many compensation programs fail because the business does not recognize this as a fact. Back in the 1880s, Congress, in a serious cost reduction effort, failed to appropriate money for the salaries of army officers. Thus, army officers received no compensation whatsoever for such services as they rendered, and they were able to support their families at

Job title_____ Reporting to_____

What tasks will the employee perform?_____

_____

_____

_____

How will the employee accomplish the work?_____

_____

_____

_____

_____

Why will this job be done?_____

_____

_____

_____

_____

What qualifications are needed to perform this work?___ _____

_____

_____

_____

With whom inside and outside the organization will this employee interface?_____

_____

Figure 18.1. Job analysis form.

Special problems_____

_____

_____

_____

Figure 18.1.   (*Continued*)

Job title Buyer, Office Supplies   Reporting to Chief Buyer

What tasks will the employee perform? 1. Maintain a complete file of vendors

for office supplies. 2. Place purchase orders for office supplies. 3. Meet

with office supplies salespersons. Disseminate information about new types of supplies

that are available. 4. Negotiate lowest prices possible for office supplies bought.

How will the employee accomplish the work? Employee will have private office

and share secretary with two other buyers. Appointments and proposals will be

solicited by mail and/or telephone. Small budget will be available for purchase

of basic directories of office supply vendors and manufacturers.

Why will this job be done? Office supplies are needed to support

$20-million-a-year engineering consultant company.

_____

_____

What qualifications are needed to perform this work? Prior experience

as a buyer of office supplies. Knowledge of accounting procedures. Persuasiveness

Figure 18.2.   Completed job analysis form.

and good negotiating abilities.

_____

With whom inside and outside the organization will this employee interface?_____

Inside the organization, this employee will interface with all functional and _____

staff division chiefs. Outside the organization, with sales representatives of _____

the various office supply companies. _____

Special problems None _____

_____

_____

_____

Figure 18.2. (Continued)

_____

Title _____

Supervisor _____

Duties _____

_____

_____

Background requirements _____

_____

_____

Personal requirements _____

_____

_____

Figure 18.3. Outline for writing a job description.

Title <u>Office Supplies Buyer</u>

Supervisor <u>Chief Buyer</u>

Duties <u>Purchase office supplies for $20-million engineering consultant company.</u>

<u>Involves maintaining file of sources, contacting and meeting with salespeople</u>

<u>representing office supply companies, negotiating prices, and placing orders</u>

<u>for office supplies.</u>

Background requirements <u>Prior experience as a buyer of office supplies</u>

<u>and knowledge of accounting procedures.</u>

Personal requirements <u>Should be a persuasive person and a good</u>

<u>negotiator.</u>

Figure 18.4. Completed outline for writing a job description.

the subsistence level only because they were granted government quarters and were able to eat at government mess facilities. Yet, despite this drastic effort, there were no mass resignations. Clearly, the compensation that was received was other than in dollars, for these officers continued to work without pay for almost two years.

Compensation obviously does consist of elements other than salary. These include working environment, terms of employment, status, and fringe benefits. We'll come back to salary, but, because of their importance, let's look at these other elements first.

Working Environment

Working environment is an extremely important element of compensation. It encompasses a wide range of factors. These include working conditions, the facilities in which your workers work, and the *esprit de corps* that you as the president of a company are able to develop in the group of employees that work for you.

Terms of Employment

Terms of employment also include many different aspects, both tangible and intangible. These can include the security that your company offers, the hours of work, the number of holidays and vacation days and their length, sick days, and many similar items.

Status

Status may come from your company and its relative position in the industry as well as from the title which you give the job that the employee holds. If yours is a small company, it may at first appear unlikely that you have anything to offer in the way of status. However, imaginative titles for the various jobs that people do for you as employees can create status. In fact, it can be a major portion of the compensation which you pay to your employees.

Fringe Benefits

There are basically two types of fringe benefits. There are those that everyone who works for you will receive and those that are reserved for key personnel. Certain fringe benefits have become very common with many companies, even small ones. These include life insurance policies, retirement plans, medical and hospital insurance, and the like. In many cases such supplements to salary will be expected. If you are trying to recruit someone who already has one or more of these benefits at his or her current place of employment, you will find that it will be difficult to hire this person if you cannot duplicate the benefits offered. Fringe benefits for key personnel include stock options, use of a car, club memberships, and so on. These fringe benefits for key personnel can be even larger than the salary element of compensation.

Bonuses

Bonuses are an addition to the normal salary. For maximum benefit to you, they should be tied in some way to the performance of the individual as well as to the performance of your company. You must be very careful with bonuses. Used correctly, a bonus element of compensation can help motivate maximum performance. Used incorrectly, it can cause frustration and hurt your personnel policies and the performance of your company.

The Salary Component of Compensation

In determining the salary component, consider the following principles:

1. Higher pay should be given for work requiring more knowledge, skill, or physical exertion.
2. Pay should be competitive with that given for similar work in other companies.

3. Total earnings should reflect the employee's contribution to the performance of your company.

4. So far as possible, pay scales should be known to all employees.

5. Overqualified employees should not be paid more or at least not very much more than fully qualified employees for the same position and same work.

6. You should strive to be as fair as possible in the application of these basic principles of salary compensation, as well as in compensation in general for your employees.

DEVELOPING A COMPENSATION PACKAGE

The first step in developing a total compensation package for a position is to document all the nonsalary elements including insurance, unique things about your company, the title you have given the job, and others. You should also endeavor to find out what compensation other firms are paying for similar work. You can obtain such data from professional organizations and associations, industrial organizations, your local chamber of commerce, the U.S. Bureau of Labor Statistics, independent management consultants, and executive recruiters. Once you have gotten these data, you can list them on a form such as that shown in Figure 18.5. You should endeavor to quantify in dollars those factors that are quantifiable. Naturally, some intangibles cannot be quantified, such as stability of employment, the reputation of your company in the industry, or a job title. But you should document these factors as shown in Figure 18.6. The

Job title

Company	Salary	Bonus	Life Insurance	Health insurance	Retirement plan	Other Quantitative	Total Quantitative	Non-quantifiable

Figure 18.5. Form for compensation comparisons.

Job title

Company	Salary	Bonus	Life Insurance	Health Insurance	Retirement Plan	Other Quantitative	Total Quantitative	Non-quantifiable
A	$28-40 K	—	$1,000	$1,000	$1,500	2 weeks vacation (.7-1.1 K)	$32.2-46.6 K	Very stable employment situation
B	$27-32 K	—	$1,000	$1,000	$1,500	Auto = $2 K 2 weeks vacation (.7-1.2 K)	$31.2-48.7 K	Frequent layoffs and turnover
C	$26-36 K	—	$1,000	$1,000	$1,500	2 weeks vacation (.6-1 K)	$30.1-40.5 K	Best reputation in industry
D	$27-40 K	5-10% of base salary	$1,000	$1,000	$2,000	Savings plan: 5% of salary 2 weeks vacation (.7-1.1 K)	$33.4-49.6 K	Company will fund additional schooling
E	$28-35 K	.5-1.0 K	$1,000	$1,000	$2,000	2 weeks vacation (.7-1 K)	$33.2-41 K	Traditionally rapid promotion
F	$28-40 K	—	$1,000	$1,000	$1,000	2 weeks vacation (.7-1 K)	$31.7-44 K	Outstanding location
Survey of 200 firms in industry	$25-46 K	80 unknown	Unknown	Unknown	Unknown	Unknown	$25-46 K	—

Figure 18.6. Completed form for compensation comparisons.

final result of this work should be a range of quantitative compensation figures along with a list of important intangible variables that you are offering.

You should develop the compensation package for every position in your organization. Do not finalize any until all have been analyzed. In this way, you will insure that the system that you're putting together for your firm will be cohesive, make sense, and be fair to all. One way of making sure that the various positions in your company do hang together is to categorize them: professional, skilled worker, and unskilled worker. Then, within these general groupings, a point system can be used to establish these relationships using the following four steps:

1. *Select the relevant factors.* In this case, you select factors which are applicable to your particular situation, including your objectives, type of work being performed, and other factors. Each factor should represent a characteristic of the work which you feel is significant. In rating professional individuals for your company, you may consider education, experience, leadership ability required, level of responsibility, and number of individuals supervised.

2. *Define the factors by points.* Whatever factors you have established must now be defined by points. One way of doing this is to use 100 points as maximum and break down various levels of achievement for whatever factors you are analyzing. If you are analyzing the education factor, a doctorate may be worth 100 points; a master's degree required, 75 points; bachelor's degree required, 50 points; or no degree required for the position, 25 points. Other factors might be point-defined as shown in Figure 18.7.

3. *Weight the factors.* After you have defined the number of points for each factor, you must weight them to help you decide on the relative importance of each of these factors for performing the work. No matter how many factors are considered or their relative weighting by percentage, the total number must equal 100%. Therefore, with the factors described previously, you might decide on a weighting for a specific professional job as follows:

Education required	5%
Experience required	25%
Leadership ability required	30%
Level of responsibility for the job	30%
Number of people supervised	10%
Total	100%

4. *Perform the necessary calculations.* The final step necessary is to make calculations for each position. You do this by reviewing the job specifications that you developed earlier, applying points for each factor, and multiplying the number of points by the factor weighting. Let's look at an example here using the weighting we have established for the factors in item 3 above. If we have specified a bachelor's degree, it is worth 50 points (Figure 18.7). In the weighting given in item 3 above, education is 5%. Therefore, 50 points times 5% is 2.5 points. If the experience required is less than five years, Figure 18.7 gives us 20 points. Again, referring above to our weighting, we see that experience is worth 25%, so 20 points times 25% is 5 points. We will say that little leadership ability is required for this job. This, according to Figure 18.7, is worth 50 points. Fifty points times the 30% weighting

Note: These point definitions are for examples only. You must break
down whatever factors you are analyzing to assign points for various levels
of achievement in the same way, but the point assignment break down you
use depends on your particular situation.

EDUCATION	Points	LEADERSHIP ABILITY	Points
No degree required	25	No leadership ability required	25
Bachelor's Degree requrired	50	Little leadership ability re'd	50
Master's Degree required	75	Some leadership ability req'd	75
Doctor's Degree required	100	Much leadership ability req'd	100

EXPERIENCE		LEVEL OF JOB RESPONSIBILITY	
Less than 5 years req'd	25	Responsible for less than $250,000	25
Less than 10 years req'd	50	Responsible for less than $500,000	50
Less than 20 years req'd	75	Responsible for less than $ 1 mil	75
20 or more years req'd	100	Responsible for $1 mil or more	100

TECHNICAL ABILITY		NUMBER OF INDIVIDUAL SUPERVISED	
No technical ability req'd	25	No personnel supervised	25
Little technical ability req'd	50	1-50 personnel supervised	50
Some technical ability req'd	75	51-100 personnel supervised	75
Much technical ability req'd	100	More than 100 personnel supervised	100

Figure 18.7.   Point method for salary/compensation evaluation: point definitions.

found above equals 15 points. The level of job responsibility is less than $1
million per year. Figure 18.7 says this is 25 points. The weighting for this
is 30%, which times the 25 points equals 6 points. Finally, we will assume
that this position is nonsupervisory. According to Figure 18.7, no individuals
supervised equals 20 points and in our weighting this is 10%. So, the result
is 2 points. The grand total of the above is:

$$
\begin{array}{r}
2.5 \\
5.0 \\
15.0 \\
6.0 \\
\underline{2.0} \\
30.5 \text{ points}
\end{array}
$$

This would therefore be considered a 30.5-point professional position. This
total is recorded and will be compared with totals for other positions that
you calculate. You can make final adjustments among the compensation
packages based on these point differences.

HOW TO ADMINISTER YOUR COMPENSATION SYSTEM

If you administer your compensation system in a fair and effective way, you will obtain and keep good employees. To do this, consider the following as reasons to increase salary:

1. Merit increases to recognize performance and contribution
2. Tenure increases for time spent working at your company
3. Increases for market and economic conditions depending upon supply and demand for certain types of employees
4. Promotion increases for employees assigned to higher level jobs

To allow for these increases, a planned and scheduled review should be accomplished for all your employees, generally on a yearly basis, either all at one time or on anniversary of hire. This annual review should consider all of these factors regarding a pay and salary increase. However, salary increases should not be automatic or tied to a cost of living benefit. Further, merit increases should not be made unless performance actually warrants it. To do otherwise will demotivate your employees for high performance and eventually make the prices that you must charge for your goods or services noncompetitive.

PERFORMANCE APPRAISAL AND COUNSELING

Performance appraisal and counseling are essential for your company, and a well-designed performance appraisal system will enable you to do the following:

1. Select individuals for promotion fairly and wisely
2. Determine merit increases fairly
3. Identify individual needs for special training
4. Provide an opportunity for a complete discussion of performance, career goals, progress, organizational policies, and other areas of interest to you and your employees
5. Obtain feedback from your employees

Performance appraisal systems can be rather informal, especially for the small company. However, they should always be documented, both for reference in the future and to enable you to compare different employees and their performance.

There are seven basic methods for performance appraisal. These are:

1. Graphic rating scale
2. Forced distribution
3. Forced choice
4. Critical incidents
5. Ranking
6. Essay appraisals
7. Management by objectives

III. PERFORMANCE FACTORS *Specific example of performance required*	NOT OBSERVED OR NOT RELEVANT	FAR/ BELOW STANDARD	BELOW/ STANDARD	MEETS STANDARD	ABOVE/ STANDARD	WELL/ ABOVE STANDARD
1. JOB KNOWLEDGE *(Depth, currency, breadth)*	O	☐	☐	☐	☐	☐
2. JUDGMENT AND DECISIONS *(Consistent, accurate, effective)*	O	☐	☐	☐	☐	☐
3. PLAN AND ORGANIZE WORK *(Timely, creative)*	O	☐	☐	☐	☐	☐
4. MANAGEMENT OF RESOURCES *(Manpower and material)*	O	☐	☐	☐	☐	☐
5. LEADERSHIP *(Initiative, accept responsibility)*	O	☐	☐	☐	☐	☐
6. ADAPTABILITY TO STRESS *(Stable, flexible, dependable)*	O	☐	☐	☐	☐	☐
7. ORAL COMMUNICATION *(Clear, concise, confident)*	O	☐	☐	☐	☐	☐
8. WRITTEN COMMUNICATION *(Clear, concise, organized)*	O	☐	☐	☐	☐	☐
9. PROFESSIONAL QUALITIES *(Attitude, dress, cooperation, bearing)*	O	☐	☐	☐	☐	☐
10. HUMAN RELATIONS *(Equal opportunity participation, sensitivity)*		☐	☐	☐	☐	☐

Figure 18.8.   Example of the graphic rating scale.

The Graphic Rating Scale

The graphic rating scale is a scale which can be either numerical or descriptive in which an individual is rated on a variety of attributes which you feel are important for the particular job. Because it can be numerical, the method allows for a total score and therefore easy comparison if you have large numbers of personnel. Since each factor has a score, it is easy to identify those areas in which an individual may be doing well or may need to improve. An example of a graphic rating scale is shown in Figure 18.8.

Forced Distribution

In the forced distribution method, whoever is doing the performance appraisal must rate a certain number of individuals and place each number into a different percentage category—for example, upper 25%, middle 50%, lower 25%—

according to some criteria. The forced distribution scale is also used when there are large numbers of people to be rated. One advantage of the forced distribution system over the graphic rating scale by itself is that it eliminates the danger that the rater will be either too severe or too lenient, since he or she must place everyone in one category or another. However, forced distribution also has a major disadvantage in that it assumes that all groups have identical percentages of poor, fair, or outstanding performance, which is, of course, highly unlikely.

Forced Choice

The forced choice method of rating forces the appraiser to choose a most and least descriptive statement about the individual being rated out of several statements that are listed together in the same group. A number of these groups make up a rating form. A typical forced choice group is shown in Figure 18.9.

In using this method, some of the raters' choices are disregarded by whoever is analyzing the results. These include those descriptions that are not highly relevant to the job which the individual is performing. The main advantage in forced choice rating is that it also minimizes the rate of bias. Research has also shown some evidence that forced choice rating correlates better with productivity than many other types of ratings. However, forced choice does have serious drawbacks. It is expensive, and the forms must be specially prepared and specially administered.

Critical Incidents

With the critical incidents method, the appraiser begins by making up a list of requirements that are considered critical to the performance of the job. This can be done with the assistance of the job description and job specification which you prepared earlier. Once the list of critical requirements is prepared, the rater notes incidents during the rating period, both positive and negative, which pertain to each of the critical requirements listed. The main advantage of this system is that it provides specific examples of performance rather than generalities to discuss during the counseling period of performance appraisal. The difficulty is trying to compare the ratings of one individual and another based solely on such nonquantitative data. However, the critical incident method does adapt very well to the purposes of a small company.

	Most	Least
1. Exhibits a high degree of technical knowledge	( )	( )
2. Carries out assignment reliably	( )	( )
3. Demonstrates good judgment	( )	( )
4. Knows how to deal with people	( )	( )

Figure 18.9. Forced choice group.

Ranking

The ranking method is very easy, especially if you have a small number of employees. You simply rank the individuals reporting to you, starting with your best individual and proceeding down the list to your worst. Clearly, ranking is very valuable in determining such things as promotions, raises, layoffs and the like. However, it is of very little use during an interview or during the annual salary review, and the question of fairness may be raised regarding comparing individuals performing totally different jobs and having totally different functions within your company.

Essay Appraisals

With the essay appraisal, the rater simply writes a descriptive essay on the individual performance during the period of rating. Essays may make use of critical incidents, and they are very useful because of this for the evaluation interview and for documenting recommendations for promotion and other personnel actions. Again, the problem is one of making comparisons among different performances; also, these essays may be time consuming to accomplish.

Management by Objectives

Management by objectives (MBO) is both a performance rating method and a style of management. It provides for specific quantifiable performance goals that are decided upon by you and the individual rated at the beginning of the performance rating period. At the end of the performance rating period, which is usually a year, you sit down with the employee and review these agreed-upon goals. In doing this, you are also critiquing actual performance.

There are clearly advantages to using MBO. These include a closer relationship between you and your employees, the fact that your subordinates have the opportunity to discuss problems with you that otherwise they might not bring up for discussion, and the focus on future performance rather than the past. However, there are also serious problems in using MBO. These include the facts that the goal may be set too low, that MBO stresses those things that are quantifiable when many goals that you wish the employee to reach during the oncoming year may not be quantifiable, and that MBO does not encourage flexibility. Therefore, if company goals are changed during the period of rating, MBO goals must be changed as well. If you don't do this, then the MBO goals may bear no relationship to the direction that you want to see your company take.

Any of the above methods of performance appraisal can work for your company. However, you should be sure that the method of performance appraisal adopted is spelled out clearly to all your employees and also that you use a standard appraisal form for use on all your employees and by managers who may be doing appraisals. A typical form, regardless of which performance appraisal method is used, should include such job performance factors as dependability, initiative, job knowledge, volume of work accomplished, the quality of performance, results achieved, ability to work with others in your firm, and effectiveness in dealing with others outside of your company, including customers, suppliers and so forth.

While the annual, semiannual, or biannual performance appraisal is an excellent time to sit down with your employee and discuss past performance, counseling should never be reserved for such occasions. Of course, you should see your employees if you are dissatisfied with the job they are doing, and counsel them one-on-one as to what you expect and why they are not performing up to your expectations. In fact, to keep communications open and your organization running smoothly, you may want to have periodic talks with key employees whether or not you have something specific to say. That is, a one-on-one meeting is useful just to review their problems, how they feel about their job and the way they are doing it, and what can be done and what you can do in order for them to be able to do it better. We might conclude that although the performance appraisal is an excellent tool and your employees should be counseled whenever you use it, do not make this the only counseling you ever have with your employees.

DEALING WITH DISCIPLINARY PROBLEMS

You may not like confrontations with employees over disciplinary problems. Few do. But, in a way, it is a cost of doing business. You can minimize disciplinary problems by creating an atmosphere of mutual trust and understanding and common purpose in which all of your employees know your company rules, as well as the reasons for them, and therefore do everything possible to support them.

Now, some rules may be common to all firms, including those pertaining to absenteeism, tardiness, drunkenness, theft, and so forth. However, above and beyond this, here are a few guidelines for establishing company rules which will help foster the positive climate of discipline which you are seeking.

1. The rules and standards which you establish must be reasonable and perceived to be reasonable by your employees.
2. Whatever rules you establish, they should be communicated so they are known and they are understood by all employees. This means not only that the words are understood, but that the reasoning behind them and why they are essential are understood as well.
3. There should be no favoritism. What is expected of one employee should be expected of all employees.
4. Even though you have established rules which all employees are expected to adhere to, if some extenuating circumstances exist which make a rule either extraordinarily harsh or unreasonable, it should be modified for that specific instance.
5. Your employees should be aware of the fact that they can and should tell you if they are dissatisfied with rules they consider unfair or unreasonable, and that you will consider modification of these rules or elimination if the rule is in fact as they perceive it to be.
6. The punishment for breaking certain important rules should be spelled out and should be understood by your employees.
7. When you are developing these rules, you should consult your employees before adopting them.
8. There should always be an appeals procedure available so that an employee who feels that you have made an unfair decision in applying the rule can be heard.

HOW TO MOTIVATE YOUR EMPLOYEES

The Importance of Motivation

Motivation is extremely important. Nonmotivated employees can have several negative effects on your business. These include friction on the job, substandard output in quality, a high turnover of employees, absenteeism, tardiness, and many of the disciplinary problems which you wish to avoid. It is a fact that motivated employees are the most productive and will produce to their maximum abilities for your company.

Over the years, researchers have developed different theories regarding motivation. Among these are Frederick Taylor, who felt that motivation should be primarily through economic means, and Frederick Hertzberg, who discovered a number of job satisfiers and dissatisfiers and developed the theory that motivation could be achieved primarily through something called "job enrichment." Other theories would have employees participate more in the management of the company and in general decision making, or would have motivation depend primarily upon management style. A summary of the various means of motivation discussed above indicate that there are 15 things you can do to promote motivation among employees in your company. You should practice them as much as possible in your day-to-day management.

Fifteen Ways to Promote Motivation in Your Company

1. Care about the people who work for you. The people who work for you don't have to become friends, but they are people and you should recognize them as such. You should be concerned with their problems and their opportunities both on the job and off.

2. Take responsibility for your actions. This means that when you make a mistake, you should acknowledge it freely and don't try to blame it on an employee.

3. Be tactful with your employees. They are not pieces of machinery. They have feelings, thoughts, and ambitions. Therefore, they deserve respect and to be treated with tact.

4. Give praise when a job is well done. If your employee does something good, show that you appreciate it by your public recognition.

5. So far as possible, foster independence in your employees. Let them have as much authority and responsibility as they can handle.

6. Be willing to learn from your employees. You are not an expert on everything. Acknowledge expertise of those who work for you.

7. Always exhibit enthusiasm and confidence. Enthusiasm and confidence are catching, and if you are enthusiastic and confident, your employees will be also.

8. Keep open lines of communication to your employees so they can express their opinions, even if they disagree with you.

9. If your employee has a problem doing his or her job, don't just give orders. Give as much help as you can in order to allow your employee to do the job as best as he or she can.

10. Set standards for yourself and your company. Communicate these standards to your employees.

11. Always let your employees know where they stand—when you are happy with them and when you are unhappy. Never let them be in doubt.

12. Keep your employees informed about what's going on in the way of future plans in your company. If your employees can understand "the big picture," they can help you better by orienting their jobs to your overall objectives.

13. Encourage initiative, innovation, and ingenuity in your employees. Don't turn off ideas submitted by someone who works for you simply because he or she is not supposed to come up with ideas. Good ideas are hard to come by, and you want all you can get.

14. Be aware of your own prejudices and biases toward certain people. Do not allow these prejudices or biases to interfere with the way you treat them or your evaluation of their performance.

15. Always be flexible. The fact that you have done something one way since you started your business does not mean that it has been done right. Always be ready to change for something better.

If you will follow these 15 pieces of advice, you will have better motivation and higher performance from your employees.

TERMINATION

Sometimes it will be necessary to terminate employees for cause. This should never be taken lightly. Remember that in hiring an individual you have invested considerable time and effort. You have invested further effort in training your employee to do the job. If possible, prior to dismissal, a warning and a second chance should be given. However, sometimes dismissal is absolutely required. To keep some employees, either because of violation of rules or their low level of performance, will pull down the performance of other employees and cause problems with morale and motivation.

In terminating an employee, you should have an exit interview in which you inform them forthrightly but tactfully why they are being released. Don't be angry or unpleasant. Remember that this employee, even though he or she may not work for you again, will probably work for someone else in the future. Further, regardless of his or her performance for you, this person may work for someone else quite satisfactorily.

Here is some further guidance on termination:

1. Warn and counsel an employee whose dismissal is contemplated prior to the dismissal decision.

2. Once it is definitely decided to dismiss an employee, do not delay.

3. Hold a termination interview with the employee, explaining tactfully but straightforwardly the reasons for termination.

4. Be sure that you have the employee's correct forwarding address and telephone number.

5. Pay all wages that are due to the employee.

6. If severance pay is part of the contract, be sure that it is paid.

7. Maintain a file on terminated employees which includes the reasons for termination.

8. Respond to any requests for information from the Workers' Compensation Disability Insurance or Unemployment Insurance Board if your terminated employee applies for any of these benefits.

USING TEMPORARY HELP SERVICES

Sometimes it is better for your company to use temporary labor rather than permanent labor. Such services may be necessary when a rush order comes in or the work load suddenly increases but you know that it will drop back to a normal level after the rush order is completed. Temporary help may be necessary during time of sickness of many of your employees or when a key employee is ill, or a special project or seasonal demand must be fulfilled. Under these circumstances, bring in temporary help is far better than hiring and then having to fire, lay off, or pay for services which are not being fully utilized.

TEMPORARY HELP SERVICES VERSUS HIRING YOUR OWN TEMPORARY HELP

Before considering temporary help of any kind, you should consider paying overtime for additional work from your present employees. However, sometimes this isn't possible, either because they are already working overtime, or for some other reason. Once you decide on temporary help, you have two choices. One choice is to hire your own temporary help. The problems are having to find this help and the expense for hiring. If you go to a temporary help service, you avoid these difficulties. A temporary help service has already hired these individuals as its own employees. Therefore, they are fully covered by insurance and generally understand the specific types of jobs that you may have for them. In essence, you are relieved of any problems with recruiting, interviewing, screening, testing, and training. Of course, there are some disadvantages. These include the fact that although the individual may be competent for the type of work being done, he or she does not know your particular company and some orientation may be necessary before the job will be done exactly as you want.

There are about a thousand firms in the temporary help industry in the United States. They are usually located near large population centers. You can generally find these firms in the yellow pages of your telephone book. Look under employment—temporary, or employment—contractors, temporary help. The cost will vary depending upon the firm, the location, and other relevant factors. It will be higher than the basic salary or wage you would pay for a similar permanent employee. This is because for this one price you are paying not only for the hours worked but for other things such as payroll taxes, Social Security, workers' compensation, and, of course, the expenses and profits of the temporary help firm. William Olsten, president of the Olsten Corp. of New York, recommends planning early for successful use of temporary help. He gives the following three general planning procedures if you decide that temporary help is necessary.[1]

---

[1] *Pointers on Using Temporary-Help Services*, Small Business Administration (1979).

1. What to do when the time comes
2. Preparing for the temporary employee
3. The work begins

What to Do When the Time Comes

When the time comes that you need extra help and you want to place an order with a temporary-help service, take these steps:

ONE—Estimate your needs. Decide what the specific requirements of the job are. Exactly what talents do you need? How long will you need the employee?

Don't ask for someone with higher qualifications than the work calls for—the cost will be unnecessarily high. On the other hand, don't try to economize by getting underqualified help and then expecting the worker to carry out tasks that he or she isn't prepared to handle.

TWO—Give the temporary-help service full information. If the temporary-personnel firm is to help you get the best results at the lowest possible cost, you must give its people detailed information about the work to be done. Tell them the nature of your business, the working hours, when and how long you'll need help, the skills required, the types of equipment to be operated. You may want to send samples of the work to be done, if it is feasible, for example, with various clerical tasks. Be sure to give the exact location of your business, transportation available, parking information, and the name and title of the person to whom the temporary employee is to report

Preparing for the Temporary Employee

A few steps taken before the temporary employee reports for work will do much to make the association a success, both for the employee and for you.

ONE—Arrange for supervision. Appoint one of your permanent employees to supervise the temporary employee and check on the progress of the work from time to time. Be sure this supervisor understands the job to be done and just what his own responsibility is.

TWO—Tell your permanent employees. It's a good idea to let your staff know that you are taking on extra help and that it will be temporary. Explain why the extra help is needed and ask them to cooperate with the new employee in any way possible.

THREE—Prepare the physical facilities. Have everything ready before the temporary worker arrives. The work to be done should be organized and laid out so that the employee can begin producing with a minimum of time spent in adjusting to the job and the surroundings. See that the materials needed are available and the equipment is in place and in good working order.

FOUR—Plan the workload. Don't set up schedules that are impossible to complete within the time you allot. Try to stay within the time limits you gave the temporary-help service, but plan to extend the time period, if necessary, rather than crowd the employee. Rushing and overwork can result in costly mistakes.

FIVE—Prepare detailed instructions. Describe your type of business, the products you manufacture or the services you offer. Be specific in outlining the procedures your company follows. Most employees of temporary-help services adjust quickly to the methods of an individual firm because of their varied experience.

The Work Begins

You've made all the preparations. The employee has arrived and is ready to start work. What now? How do you get a temporary worker started? What should you expect? What if you're not satisfied.

This is the crucial stage of the relation between your company and the temporary employee. Get off to a good start and the rest will go smoothly.

ONE—Help the employee settle in. Receive the temporary employee as you would receive one hired on a permanent basis. Make him feel like a member of your team. Explain where to hang coats, the location of the washroom, the lunch hour, coffee breaks, and so on.

Introduce the temporary employee to the permanent employee who will supervise the work.

Introduce the temporary employee also to permanent employees in the same department. Explain that "Miss Jones will be here for a few days to help out." Or, "John will be here this week to help get out the rush job."

TWO—Explain the job. Go over the work assignment and the instructions. Explain company routines. Make your directions as simple as possible and provide samples of the work to be done. If the work is complex, explain it clearly and make certain that your explanation is understood. Assure the temporary employee of your staff's cooperation and willingness to help, and show your own interest and concern.

THREE—Don't expect the impossible. How much can you expect from a temporary employee? Fully as much as you contracted for with the service firm. Most employees of temporary-personnel services perform well. They are experienced and versatile. Because they have worked for a variety of businesses, they have learned to adapt quickly to a new situation, and they know that future assignments depend on their doing satisfactory work.

But don't expect the impossible. Don't overload temporary employees—make a slight allowance for the fact that they are not familiar with your business and its operations. Check the work occasionally, ask for any questions, never leave the employee feeling stranded or left out. At the same time, don't make him nervous by hovering over him. And don't push or prod too much.

MAJOR LABOR LAWS THAT AFFECT YOUR BUSINESS

It is important that you know and obey the major labor laws that can affect your business. Following is a list and description developed by the U.S. Department of Labor.[2]

Black Lung Benefits Act (Title IV Federal Mine and Safety Health Act of 1977 as Amended)

Benefits to Disabled Coal Miners. This act is designed to offer medical treatment and monthly payments to coal miners totally disabled from pneumoconiosis (black lung) arising from employment in the Nation's coal mines. This act also

---

[2] *Major Laws Administered by the U.S. Department of Labor Which Affect Small Business*, U.S. Department of Labor, Office of the Assistant Secretary for Administration and Management, San Francisco, CA (1987).

provides benefits to the miner's dependents and to certain survivors of miners who died due to or while totally disabled from pneumoconiosis.

Regulations.   20 CFR Chapters 718, 722, 725, 726, 727

Administration of the Law.   Employment Standards Administration, Office of Workers' Compensation Programs, Division of Coal Mine Workers' Compensation.

Information.   Contact specialist in the National Office:

James DeMarce, Associate Director
Division of Coal Mine Workers' Compensation
Washington, DC 20210
(202) 523-6692

Consumer Credit Production Act—Title III

Limitations on Withholding Wages to Satisfy Creditors.   This Title of the act, the Federal wage garnishment law, limits the amount of an employee's disposable earnings which may be withheld in any one week by an employer to satisfy creditors. "Disposable earnings" means that part of an employee's earnings remaining after deduction of any amount required by law to be withheld. Restrictions on the amount that may be garnished in a week do not apply to bankruptcy court orders and debts for State or Federal taxes. The law also prohibits an employer from discharging an employee whose earnings have been subjected to garnishment for any one indebtedness.

Regulations.   29 CFR Chapter 870.

Administration of the Law.   Employment Standards Administration, Wage-Hour Division.

Information.   Contact Wage-Hour offices in your region:

Employment Standards Administration
Wage-Hour Division
71 Stevenson Street, Suite 905
San Francisco, CA 94105
(415) 995-5414

Contract Work Hours and Safety Standards Act

Overtime Pay; Safety and Health Requirements.   This law and its implementing regulations require that all laborers and mechanics employed by contractors or subcontractors in the performance of most Federal service contracts exceeding $2,500, Federally funded construction contracts exceeding $2,000, and supply contracts between $2,500 and $10,000* be paid overtime compensation at a rate of not less than one and one-half times their basic rates of pay for all hours

---

* Supply contracts in excess of $10,000 are subject to the Walsh-Healey Public Contracts Act.

worked in excess of 40 in a workweek. The Act also includes safety and health provisions.

Regulations.   48 CFR 22.3; 29 CFR 5.

Administration of the Law.   Employment Standards Administration, Wage-Hour Division. [Safety and health requirements are administered by the Occupational Safety and Health Administration (OSHA)]

Information.   Contact local specialist in your region:

> Employment Standards Administration
> Wage-Hour Division
> 71 Stevenson Street, Suite 905
> San Francisco, CA 94105
> (415) 995-5414

> Occupational Safety and Health Administration
> 71 Stevenson Street, Suite 415
> San Francisco, CA 94105
> (415) 995-5672

or local OSHA Area Office.

Davis-Bacon and Related Acts

Wage Rates and Fringe Benefits for Laborers and Mechanics under Construction Contracts.   This law is applicable to most Federal and federally assisted contracts in excess of $2,000 for the construction, alteration, or repair, including painting and decorating, of public buildings or public works. It provides that all laborers and mechanics employed under such contracts be paid the wage rates and fringe benefits found by the Department of Labor to be prevailing on similar projects for corresponding classifications of laborers and mechanics in the locality and included in a wage decision in the contract. A contract which is subject to the Davis-Bacon Act or most of the related Acts is also subject to the Copeland (Anti-Kickback) Act which prohibits illegal deductions or kickbacks of wages. Such contracts also require the submission of certified payroll records on a weekly basis to the contracting agency.

Regulations.   48 CFR 22.4; 29 CFR 1, 3, and 5.

Administration of the Law.   Employment Standards Administration, Wage-Hour Division.

Information.   Contact local specialist in your region:

> Employment Standards Administration
> Wage-Hour Division
> 71 Stevenson Street, Suite 905
> San Francisco, CA 94105
> (415) 995-5414

Employee Retirement Income Security Act of 1974 (ERISA)

Protection of Employees in Private Pension and Welfare Plans.   The purpose of this law is to protect the interests of participants and beneficiaries in employee pension and welfare benefit plans. The Act requires reporting and disclosure of plan and financial information to the U.S. Department of Labor as well as to plan participants and beneficiaries; it also establishes fiduciary standards to safeguard plan assets. In addition, the law requires that pension plans meet minimum participation, vesting and funding standards. Finally, it establishes a program insuring the pension benefits of individuals in certain types of pension plans that terminate. With limited exceptions, the law applies to all private employee pension and welfare benefit plans, regardless of size. Public plans are not covered.

Regulations.   29 CFR Chapter XXV.

Administration of the Law.   Pension and Welfare Benefits Administration.

Information.   Contact the office serving your area:

Area Office	*Jurisdiction*
71 Stevenson street P.O. Box 3455, Suite 915 San Francisco, CA 94119-3455 (415) 995-5400	The San Francisco Area Office serves the 48 northern California counties which include Monterey, Kings, Tulare, Inyo, and all counties north thereof. In addition the San Francisco Area Office also covers the state of Nevada.
909 First Avenue, Room 3135 Seattle, WA 98174 (206) 442-4244	The Seattle District Office, who is under the San Francisco Area Office, has jurisdiction over Washington, Utah, Idaho, Oregon and Alaska. The joint efforts of both offices overlap in the above mentioned areas.
3660 Wilshire Blvd., Suite 718 Los Angeles, CA 90010 (213) 252-7556	The Los Angeles Area Office has jurisdiction over the ten southern California counties not previously mentioned in the above part. Los Angeles also governs the states of Arizona and Hawaii .

Executive Order 11246, as Amended (Parts II, III, and IV)

Equal Employment Opportunity.   The order requires that equal employment opportunity provided to all persons without regard to race, color, religion, sex, or national origin, employed or seeking employment with Government econtractos or subcontractors. It also applies to construction contractors who are performing on construction projects being built with Federal financial assistance.

Applicability.   Government contracts, subcontracts and Federally assisted construction contracts in excess of $10,000 and government contracts and subcontracts which accumulate (or may be expected to accumulate) to $10,000 in any 12-month period.

Regulations.   41 CFR Chapter 60.

Administration of the Law.   Employment Standards Administration, Office of Federal Contract Compliance Programs.

Information.   Contact local specialist in your region:

Employment Standards Administration
Office of Federal Contract Compliance Program
71 Stevenson Street, Suite 910
San Francisco, CA 94105
(415) 995-5422

Fair Labor Standards Act of 1938, as Amended

Minimum Wages, Overtime and Equal Pay,* Child Labor.   This law establishes minimum wages, overtime pay, equal pay,* recordkeeping and child labor standards for employees individually engaged in or producing goods for interstate commerce, and for all employees employed in certain enterprises described in the Act, unless a specific exemption applies. Employers must comply with the Act's requirements with respect to their covered employees who are not specifically exempt.

Regulations.   29 CFR 511-800.

Administration of the Law.   Employment Standards Administration, Wage-Hour Division.

Information.   Contact Wage-Hour offices in your region:

Employment Standards Administration
Wage-Hour Division
71 Stevenson Street, Suite 905
San Francisco, CA 94105
(415) 995-5414

Federal Employee's Compensation Act, as Amended

Federal Employee Benefits.   This law provides for payment of worker's compensation benefits to civil officers and employees of all branches of the Federal Government and to specific categories of other workers and of enrollees under certain programs including some programs under the Job Training Partnership Act of 1982.

Regulations.   20 CFR Chapters 10 and 25.

---

* Under the President's Reorganization Plan #1 of 1978, the enforcement responsibility for the equal pay provisions of the Fair Labor Standards Act was transferred to the Equal Employment Opportunity Commission effective July 1, 1979.

Administration of the Law. Employment Standards Administration, Office of Worker's Compensation Programs, Division of Federal Employee's Compensation.

Information. Contact local specialist in your region:

Employment Standards Administration
Worker's Compensation Programs
Division of Federal Employees' Compensation
71 Stevenson Street, Suite 225
San Francisco, CA 94105
(415) 995-5699

Federal Mine Safety and Health Act of 1977

Safety and Health Protection of U.S. Miners. This statute places more than 20,000 underground and surface coal and noncoal mining operations under a single federal law that protects the safety and health of our nation's nearly one-million miners. The Act repeals the Federal Metal and Nonmetallic Mine Safety Act, and amends the Federal Coal Mine Health and Safety Act of 1969, to contain some new stronger provisions, and to cover both coal and noncoal mines.

On March 9, 1978, the effective date of the Act, responsibility for administering and enforcing federal mine safety and health law was transferred from the U.S. Department of the Interior to the U.S. Department of Labor. The Act created the Mine Safety and Health Administration (MSHA) headed by the Assistant Secretary of Labor.

MSHA carries out the Act's provisions through mandatory safety and health inspections of each mine, engineering studies, education and training programs and development of standards aimed at elimination of hazardous practices and conditions in the mines.

In addition, section 504 of the Act is an amendment to the Small Business Act, administered by the Small Business Administration, and provides that small businesses operating coal mines may receive assistance in altering equipment, facilities, or operations in order to meet federal mine safety and health requirements.

Regulations. 30 CFR 1-199.

Administration of the Law. Mine Safety and Health Administration.

Information. Contact Public Information Officer:

Wayne E. Zeneman
Director
Office of Information and Public Affairs
Mine Safety and Health Administration
U.S. Department of Labor
4015 Wilson Blvd.
Arlington, VA 22203
Phone: (703) 235-1452

Job Corps

Training Program.   Job Corps is a vocational and educational training program for youth between the ages of 16 through 21. The training is provided at residential centers throughout the United States. These centers are operated by both private contractors and federal agencies. Participation in the Job Corps program is free for eligible youth.

Regulation.   20 CFR Parts 675 and 684.

Administration of the Law.   Employment and Training Administration Job Corps

Information.   Contact local Job Corps office:

> Regional Director
> Office of Job Corps
> U.S. Department of Labor
> Employment & Training Administration
> 71 Stevenson Street, Suite 1015
> San Francisco, CA 94105
> (415) 995-5451

Job Training Partnership Act of 1982

Training Programs.   Employers can participate in Job Training Partnership Act programs through the Private Industry Council (PIC) established for each Service Delivery Area under the Job Training Act (JTPA) and a variety of apprenticeship and on-the-job training programs. The Governor of each State has the responsibility for designating Service Delivery Areas within the State.

The PICs, composed primarily of representatives of business and industry in the Service Delivery Area, carry major responsibility for preparation of the job training plan and for designation of entities to provide training and services to those who are in need of them.

Employers participating in on-the-job training programs can receive payments covering training costs during the training period. The payment is based on a percentage of the participant's wages. JTPA program operators, or other certifying agencies, will screen and refer eligible workers and can arrange for participant classroom training, counseling orientation, and other supportive services. These services are provided without cost to the employer. Employers retain the right to make the final selection from among those referred.

Regulations.   20 CFR 626-638.

Administration of the Law.   Employment and Training Administration.

Information.   Contact local specialist in your region:

> Employment and Training Administration
> Associate Regional Administrator

Job Training Partnership Act
71 Stevenson Street, Suite 820, P.O. Box 3767
San Francisco, CA 94119-3767
(415) 995-5905

Longshore and Harbor Worker's Compensation Act

Worker's Compensation Benefit. This act provides benefits to certain employees disabled from injuries incurred upon the navigable waters of the United States or adjoining areas customarily used by employers in maritime employment.

The Longshore Act has been extended by the Defense Base Act, which covers employees of contractors with the United States outside the continental U.S. the Outer Continental Shelf Lands Act, which provides coverage to certain offshore oil workers; and the Nonappropriated Fund Instrumentalities Act, which provides for benefits for civilian employees in nonappropriated funds instrumentalities, e.g. post exchanges and commissaries.

Regulations. 20 CFR 701-704.

Administration of the Law. Employment Standards Administration, Office of Worker's Compensation Programs, Division of Longshore and Harbor Worker's Compensation.

Information. Contact local specialist in your region:

Employment Standards Administration
Office of Worker's Compensation Program
Division of Longshore and Harbor Workers' Compensation
Assistant Deputy Commissioner
71 Stevenson Street, Suite 210
San Francisco, CA 94105
(415) 995-5705

Migrant and Seasonal Agricultural Worker Protection Act

Employment Protection for Migrant and Seasonal Agricultural Workers. This law requires agricultural employers, agricultural associations, and farm labor contractors to observe certain labor standards when employing migrant and seasonal agricultural workers, unless exemptions apply. The Act establishes, among other things, specific requirements with respect to recordkeeping, wage payment, disclosure, housing and transportation and requires that farm labor contractors register with U.S. Department of Labor.

Regulations. 29 CFR 500.

Administration of the Law. Employment Standards Administration, Wage-Hour Division.

Information. Contact Wage-Hour offices in your region:

Employment Standards Administration
Wage-Hour Division
71 Stevenson Street, Suite 905
San Francisco, CA 94105
(415) 995-5414

Occupational Safety and Health Act of 1970

Safe and Healthful Conditions in the Workplace.   This statute covers all employers engaged in business affecting interstate commerce and who have one or more employees. However, to avoid duplication of effort among agencies, the Act does not apply to working conditions of employees where other Federal agencies exercise statutory authority to prescribe or enforce standards or regulations affecting occupational safety or health.

Under this law, covered employers must furnish their employees a safe and healthful workplace. Employers also must comply with standards and with applicable recordkeeping and reporting requirements specified in regulations issued by the Occupational Safety and Health Administration (OSHA). Some States, operating under OSHA-approved State plans, conduct their own occupational safety and health programs.

In addition to standards promulgation and enforcement, OSHA sponsors consultation, and training/education programs to encourage voluntary compliance. In all States, employers may request the services of consultants who advise about compliance with OSHA, but who are not inspectors and do not issue citations for non-compliance. Priority for consultation is given to small business employers. OSHA training and education materials and services may be obtained from local agency area offices.

Regulations.   29 CFR 1900-1999.

Administration of the Law.   Occupational Safety and Health Administration (OSHA).

Information.   Contact local specialist in your region:

Occupational Safety and Health Administration
Office of the Regional Administrator
71 Stevenson Street, Suite 415
San Francisco, CA 94105
(415) 995-5672

Rehabilitation Act of 1973, as Amended (29 USC 793: P.L. 93-112, Sec. 503)

Equal Employment of Qualified Handicapped Persons.   Under Section 503 of the Act, Government contractors and subcontractors are required to take affirmative action to employ and to advance in employment qualified handicapped individuals.

Applicability.   All Government contracts and subcontracts for personal property and nonpersonal services in excess of $2,500.

Regulations. 41 CFR Part 60-741.

Administration of the Law. Employment Standards Administration, Office of Federal Contract Compliance Programs.

Information. Contact local specialist in your region:

Employment Standards Administration
Office of Federal Contract Compliance Programs
71 Stevenson Street, Suite 910
San Francisco, CA 94105
(415) 995-5422

Service Contract Act of 1965, as Amended

Wage Rates and Fringe Benefits for Service Employees under Service Contracts. This law is applicable to employees performing work under Federal contracts and subcontracts which are principally for services, as follows:

(1) Contracts of $2,500 or less—Payment of not less than the minimum wage provided in Section 6(a)(1) of the Fair Labor Standards Act.

(2) Contracts over $2,500—Payment of not less than the wage rates and fringe benefits found by the Department of Labor to be prevailing in the locality or in certain cases, wage rates and fringe benefits contained in a predecessor contractor's collective bargaining agreement, as provided in a wage determination, included in the contract.

The law also contains recordkeeping and safety and health requirements.

Regulations. 48 CFR 22.10; 29 CFR 4.

Administration of the Law. Employment Standards Administration, Wage-Hour Division. [Safety and health provisions are administered by the Occupational Safety and Health Administration (OSHA).]

Information. Contact Wage-Hour offices in your region:

Employment Standards Administration
Wage-Hour Division
71 Stevenson Street, Suite 905
San Francisco, CA 94105
(415) 995-5414

Occupational Safety and Health Administration
Office of the Regional Administrator
71 Stevenson Street, Suite 415
San Francisco, CA 94105
(415) 995-5672

Social Security Act of 1935, as Amended

Unemployment Insurance Laws.   Unemployment insurance is a joint Federal-State program incorporating certain basic standards set forth in the Social Security Act and the Federal Unemployment Tax Act. Each State requires employers who come under its unemployment insurance law to pay taxes based on their payroll. The State legislature fixes the rate of tax on employers and has enacted experience rating provisions which allow an employer's tax to vary according to the amount of benefits paid to former workers or other methods provided by State law for measuring the risk of unemployment. Each State law specifies the conditions under which workers may receive benefits, the amounts they may receive, and the number of weeks they may draw benefits. The Federal Government pays the costs of administering these laws and permits employers to credit State contributions paid, or from which they are excused under the State experience-rating provisions, against the Federal tax imposed by the Federal Unemployment Tax Act.

Regulations.   20 CFR 601, 604, 609, 614, 625, 638, 640, 650 and 29 CFR 21.

Administration of the Law.   Employment and Training Administration, Unemployment Insurance Service and Individual State Employment Service Offices.

Information.   Contact local Employment Security or Job Service office:

Employment and Training Administration
Associate Regional Administrator for Unemployment Insurance
71 Stevenson Street, Suite 825, P.O. Box 3767
San Francisco, CA 94119-3767
(415) 995-5486

Trade Act of 1974—Title II, Chapter 2, as Amended

Adjustment Assistance to Workers Adversely Impacted by Increased Import Competition.   This law provides assistance to workers who become totally or partially separated from employment because of increased import competition. Such assistance may consist of training, job search and relocation allowances, special help in finding a new job, and weekly cash benefits equal to the level of regular unemployment compensation payable in the separated worker's state (A worker must exhaust all unemployment insurance benefits available in his state before collecting weekly cash benefits under the Trade Act.).

Petitioning worker groups may be certified eligible to apply for worker adjustment assistance if the Department determines that increased imports of articles like or directly competitive with those produced by the petitioning worker's firm contributed importantly to decreased sales and/or production and to worker separations.

Regulations.   20 CFR Part 617 (proposed).

Administration of the Law.   Employment and Training Administration, Office of Trade Adjustment Assistance. Program benefits administered through the Unemployment Insurance Service and individual State Employment Security Agencies.

Information.   Contact specialist in your region:

Employment and Training Administration
Associate Regional Administrator for Unemployment Insurance
71 Stevenson Street, Suite 825, P.O. Box 3767
San Francisco, CA 94119-3767
(415) 995-5486

Veterans' Employment Emphasis under Federal Contracts (Title 38, U.S. Code, Section 2012)

Emphasis on Employment and Advancement of Veterans by Federal Government Contractors and Subcontractors.   The law requires that Federal government contractors and subcontractors take affirmative action to employ and to advance in employment qualified special disabled and Vietnam-era veterans. Such Government contractors and subcontractors are required to list suitable employment openings with the nearest local State Employment Service office.

A Local Veteran's Employment Representative is located in each local State Employment Service office to provide employment advice and assistance to veterans. A veteran, to whom the provisions apply, may contact the regional office of the Office of Federal Contract Compliance Programs, if it appears that a contractor or subcontractor has failed to comply.

Applicability.   All Government contracts and subcontracts of $10,000 or more.

Regulations.   41 CFR Subpart 60-250.

Administration of the Law.   The law is administered by two Department of Labor Agencies: (1) Employment Standards Administration, Office of Federal Contract Compliance Programs; responsible for enforcement; (2) Assistant Secretary for Veteran's Employment and Training; responsible for employment assistance.

Information.   Contact local specialists in your region:

Employment Standards Administration
Office of Federal Contract Compliance Programs
71 Stevenson Street, Suite 910
San Francisco, CA 94105
(415) 995-5422

Veterans Employment & Training Service
Regional Office
71 Stevenson Street, Suite 705
San Francisco, CA 94105
(415) 995-5544

Disabled Veterans' Outreach Program and Local Veterans' Employment Representatives (Title 38, United States Code, Sections 2003A

and 2004, respectively)
Section 2003A Disabled Veteran Outreach Program (DVOP)
Section 2004 Local Veterans' Employment Representative (LVER)

Veterans' Job Placement Assistance.   The Veterans' Employment and Training Service provides grants to State Employment Security Agencies for specialized veteran services positions under the Disabled Veteran Outreach Program and the Local Veterans' Employment Representative program. Each DVOP specialist provides services only to eligible veterans in accordance with the priorities established in the law. These services include the provision of job referral and placement services which are free to employers and veterans, the promotion and development of subsidized and unsubsidized training opportunities with employers and special emphasis on outreach to disabled and Vietnam veterans. In addition, Local Veterans' Employment Representatives make certain that veterans are given preferential assistance through the Job Service. They promote and facilitate veteran job placement and training through regular contacts with employers, labor unions, veterans' organizations and community organizations and assist both employers and veterans meet their employment needs. All other staff in local Employment Service offices are also required to provide priority services to veterans.

Regulation.   20 CFR Part 652, Subpart B.

Administration of the Law.   Veterans' Employment and Training Service.

Information.   Contact local Employment Services/Job Service office:

Veterans Employment and Training Service
Regional Office
71 Stevenson Street, Suite 705
San Francisco, CA 94105
(415) 995-5544

Veterans' Job Training Act (P.L. 98-77, as Amended)

Employer Incentive to Hire Veterans.   Although not a permanent program, this is considered one of the best incentive packages ever for hiring and training a qualified veteran. The Veterans Administration will pay an employer half the veteran's entry wages up to $10,000 for up to nine months or 15 months for veterans with a disability rating of 30 percent or more.

A veteran must have served during the Korean Conflict (6/27/50 to 1/31/55) or the Vietnam Era (8/5/64 to 5/7/75), and have been unemployed for 10 of the 15 immediately preceding weeks. The veteran must also have been discharged from active military service under conditions other than dishonorable, or have been discharged because of service-connected disability.

Employers must certify they intend to hire the veteran upon completion of training. Adequate training facilities must be available; wages and benefits must be no less than those normally paid; and training cannot be for a position for which the veteran already qualifies.

Veterans and potential employers alike must apply for certification with any local Job Service Office or VA Regional Office. Since this is not a permanent program, interested parties should contact those offices concerning dates by which application must be made.

Regulations. None.

Administration of the Law Jointly. Veterans Administration and Department of Labor, Assistant Secretary for Veterans' Employment and Training.

Information. Contact local Job Service office or VA Regional office:

Veterans Employment and Training Service
Regional Office
71 Stevenson Street, Suite 705
San Francisco, CA 94105
(415) 995-5544

Veterans' Reemployment Rights (Title 38, U.S. Code, Sections 2021-2026)

Reemployment Rights of Veterans. This law provides that any employee enlisting in or inducted into the Armed Services of the United States, shall be restored to the position that he otherwise would have achieved but for his military service with attendant seniority, status and rate of pay, if still qualified to perform.

If, by reason of disability sustained or aggravated during military service, the individual is unable to perform in the job, the person shall be offered another appropriate position. If there are complaints, the Department of Labor investigates and attempts to resolve the problem.

Under somewhat similar provisions, it also provides statutory protection to employees who leave their positions to perform training duty with the National Guard or Reserves.

Applicability. All private employers regardless of size or number of employees and all State and local governmental entities.

Regulations. None.

Administration of the Law. Office of Assistant Secretary of Labor for Veterans' Employment and Training, Veterans' Employment and Training Service.

Information. Contact Veterans' Employment and Training Service:

Regional Office
71 Stevenson Street, Suite 705
San Francisco, CA 94105
(415) 995-5544

Wagner-Peyser Act of 1933, as Amended

Employment Service/Job Service. Under this law, employers are assisted in obtaining qualified workers for their labor force needs, in filling jobs requiring special skills or other needs, in developing personnel management tools, and in identifying and resolving internal work force problems such as turnover, absenteeism, and special recruitment difficulties. Local Job Service offices screen and counsel job applicants and provide employers with a variety of labor market information. In virtually every major urban area and 43 states, the Job Service operates a computerized job bank, updated daily to list job openings.

Regulations.   20 CFR 652.

Administration of the Law.   Employment and Training Administration, U.S. Employment Service and affiliated State Job Service Offices.

Information.   Local office, Job Service or Employment Service:

Employment and Training Administration
Director, United States Employment Services, Region IX
71 Stevenson Street, Suite 805, P.O. Box 3767
San Francisco, CA 94119-3767
(415) 995-5494

Walsh-Healey Public Contracts Act

Minimum Wages, Overtime, Child Labor, Safety and Health, Convict Labor, and Manufacturer and Regular Dealer Requirements in Supply Contracts.   This law is applicable to most Federal contracts in excess of $10,000 for the manufacture or furnishing of materials, supplies, articles, and equipment. The law and the regulations require that contractors be either manufacturers or regular dealers, and that they pay their employees performing on covered contracts at least the minimum wage, determined by the Secretary of Labor to prevail for similar work (the rate provided in Section 6(a)(1) of the Fair Labor Standards Act) and overtime compensation at rates not less than one and one-half times the employees' basic rates of pay for all hours worked in excess of 40 in a work week. The Act also prohibits the employment of minors under 16 years of age and of convict labor (except under certain conditions) on contract work, and contains safety and health provisions.

Regulations.   48 CFR 22.6; 41 CFR 50-201; 41 CFR 50-202; 41 CFR 50-206.

Administration of the Law.   Employment Standards Administration, Wage-Hour Division.
[Safety and health provisions are administered by the Occupational Safety and Health Administration (OSHA), except for those dealing with coal mines, which are enforced by the Mine Safety and Health Administration (MSHA).]

Information.   Contact local specialists in your region:

Employment Standards Administration
Wage-Hour Division
71 Stevenson Street, Suite, 905
San Francisco, CA 94105
(415) 995-5414

Occupational Safety and Health Administration
71 Stevenson Street, Suite 415
San Francisco, CA 94105
(415) 995-5672

Work Incentive (WIN) Program

Employment and Training. The Work Incentive (WIN) Program is an employment assistance program that provides employment, training and social supportive services such as child care, housing assistance, medical services, etc., to public welfare applicants and recipients in order to enable them to become self supporting and independent of welfare assistance.

All welfare applicants and recipients, unless otherwise exempt because of age, disability, or other factors, must register with the WIN program. After registration and appraisal, an employability plan may call for job search, institutional training, work experience, on-the-job training, referral, or other services as needed to obtain employment. Job ready WIN registrants may be placed or obtain employment with both public or private sector employers.

Authorization. Social Security Act, Parts IV A and IV C as amended.

Administration of the Law. Employment and Training Administration, U.S. Department of Labor and Family Support Administration, U.S. Department of Health and Human Services.

Information. Contact local specialists in your region:

Employment and Training Administration
Director of Work Incentive Program
71 Stevenson Street, Suite 805, P.O. Box 3767
San Francisco, CA 94119-3767
(415) 995-5491

SOURCES OF ADDITIONAL INFORMATION

Affirmative Action and Equal Employment: A Guide Book, published by the U.S. Government Printing Office, Washington, DC 20402.

Compensation, by Robert E. Sibson, published by the American Management Association, 135 West 50th Street, New York, NY 10020.

Effective Psychology for Managers, by Mortimer R. Feinberg, published by Prentice-Hall, Inc., Englewood Cliffs, NJ 07632.

Grievance Handling: 101 Guides for Supervisors, by Walter E. Baer, published by the American Management Association, 135 West 50th Street, New York, NY 10020.

Handbook of Modern Personnel Administration, edited by Joseph J. Famularo, published by McGraw-Hill Book Co., 1221 Avenue of the Americas, New York, NY 10020.

Handbook of Wage and Salary Administration, by Milton L. Rock, published by McGraw-Hill Book Co., 1221 Avenue of the Americas, New York, NY 10020.

The OSHA Compliance Manual, by Donald C. Petersen, published by McGraw-Hill Book Co., 1221 Avenue of the Americas, New York, NY 10020.

Personnel Management, by Michael J. Jucius, published by Richard Irwin, Inc., 1818 Ridge Road, Homewood, IL 60430.

Personnel, The Human Problems of Management, 3rd edition, by George Strauss and Leonard R. Sayles, published by Prentice-Hall, Inc., Englewood Cliffs, NJ 07632.

19

How to Avoid Getting Ripped Off

Unfortunately, crime is rising in the United States. In fact, in just five years losses due to crime in small business have risen more than 100%, and this percentage is based on official figures, which involve only reported crimes. Probably, in actuality, the number of crimes is even higher. The subject of crime is very important to a small business. In fact, the Small Business Administration says that crime contributes to 30 to 40% of business failures. Furthermore, a small business is 35 times as likely to be a victim of crime as a large business.

In this chapter, we are going to cover the methods of preventing major crimes for small business owners. These crimes include:

1. Burglary
2. Robbery
3. Shoplifting
4. Internal theft
5. Bad checks

BURGLARY

Burglary is any unlawful entry to commit a felony or a theft, whether or not force was used to gain entrance. Statistics show that burglaries have doubled in the past several years, and so it is a major crime with which small business must contend.

Prevention of Burglary

There are methods that can prevent burglary in your small business. These include: locks, alarm systems, key control, lighting, burglar-resistant windows, window screens, safes, guards or patrols, watchdogs, and frequent cash deposits. Let's look at each in turn.

Locks. Locks are important because even if they fail to keep a burglar out, the burglar must force his or her way onto your premises. This is important because in many standard burglary insurance policies, you must have evidence of a forced entry in order to collect.

According to the Small Business Administration, most experts on locks consider the pin-tumbler cylinder lock to provide the best security. Such a lock has a variable number of pins. You should consider a lock with at least five pins, as burglars can easily pick one with fewer pins. It is also wise to utilize dead-bolt locks. A dead-bolt lock is one having a lock bolt that must be moved positively by turning the knob or key without action of a spring. It cannot be opened by sliding a piece of flexible material or tool between the door edge or door jamb. If you use a double cylinder dead-bolt lock, the door cannot be opened without a key on either side. This is important, especially in the case of glass doors, because if the burglar breaks the glass and attempts to open the door merely by reaching through, he or she will not be able to do so. A double cylinder dead-bolt lock also provides protection in the case where a thief remains concealed during the day and then attempts to break out with his loot (your goods) after closing time. It is advisable to be particularly careful about the rear door in a store since burglars tend to favor rear doors. You may consider barring it in addition to locking it. All locks should be installed by a competent locksmith; even the best lock available will not be effective in preventing burglaries if it is not installed properly.

Alarm Systems. A silent central station burglar alarm generally is better protection than a local alarm such as a siren or a bell. This is because a silent alarm will alert only the specialist who knows how to handle the burglary and will not notify the burglar of his detection as will a loud local alarm system. On the other hand, if your intention is to frighten the burglar off prior to his entrance, it is the better type of protection.

Regardless of whether you want a silent alarm or a local alarm, there is a wide choice of sensory devices available for the system that you adopt. These include: ultrasonic detectors, photo beams, radar motion detectors, vibration detectors, and auxiliary equipment such as an automatic phone dialer which notifies the police when the alarm system has been triggered.

Each type of alarm has advantages and disadvantages, depending on your situation. Therefore, it is recommended that you have professional guidance in determining which alarm is best for you. For example, local alarms may be useless in areas that are not frequently patrolled or in secluded neighborhoods.

Key Control. Key control is as important as the lock the key opens. You should avoid key duplication by having the key stamped, "Do not duplicate." You should caution employees who have access to keys not to leave store keys with parking lot attendants or anywhere else where someone may gain access to them. You should keep a record of each of your keys and who has custody of it at any given time. When employees leave your employ or if a key is lost, you should install new locks and issue new keys. Don't use the same key for outside doors as for the door to your office. Remember that if you use a master key, it will weaken your security system since one key will open all locks. Do not have your keys plainly marked as to specific store or specific lock. Use a code with key numbers. Do everything possible to make it tougher for a potential burglar.

Lighting. Burglars prefer the darkness because of the protection that it offers. Therefore, illuminating exterior and interior parts of your premises at night will discourage burglars. In addition, indoor lighting allows police or patrol cars to see silhouettes in your store. Silhouettes help them to spot something amiss.

It is possible to control lighting with a photoelectric eye system which will turn on your lights automatically at dusk and turn them off at dawn. This saves you a trip on weekends, and means one less thing for you to remember to do.

Burglar-Resistant Windows. Windows, especially storefront windows that offer a burglar access to the store's interior, are very vulnerable to hit-and-run attacks by burglars who will break the glass, enter the store or perhaps open the window only, steal something, and leave immediately. The likelihood of such an attack's occurring can be reduced by using tempered glass, laminated glass, or impact-resistant plastic windows.

Window Screens. Steel mesh screens or bars are available to give added protection to windows, transom skylights, ventilator shafts, air vents, and manholes. Such protection is particularly important in screening areas that are not in view, as they are an excellent route of entry and exit for burglars. Heavy window screens or gratings are also available to protect show windows. After closing time, these screens are shut and locked into place and allow no room for entry of an object that could break your window.

Safes. Many safes are available which can provide excellent protection for your money and other valuables. Along these lines, you should recognize that a fire-resistant safe is not necessarily burglar resistant. In fact, being made of fire-retardant materials may make it easy to break open if it is not also burglar resistant. Note that the word is "resistant." Any safe can be broken open if the burglar has enough time. Because of this, many burglars will attempt to carry a small safe off rather than try to open it on your premises.

While many types of burglar-resistant safes are available, the "E" safe is considered adequate under most situations. "E" safes are more expensive; however, many insurance companies will give a reduction in premiums for use of this type of safe.

Four precautions regarding your safe will help to reduce burglaries.

1. Bolt the safe to the building structure. As noted earlier, burglars may attempt to carry your safe off. Surprisingly, even some very heavy safes have been carted off by enterprising thieves. Beware!
2. In the case of a store, put the safe where it can be seen from the street, if possible. Also, make sure that the safe is well lighted by night.
3. Never leave the combination to your safe on store premises.
4. When an employee who knows your safe combination leaves your employ, always change the combination to your safe.

Guards on Patrols. Special and private guards and private police patrols can be hired to stay on your premises during certain hours or check your store at regular intervals. Such private help may also assist you in training your employees and auditing your store for areas which may give easy access to potential burglaries.

Although the cost of private guards and police patrols is not low and may be prohibitive for a particularly small operation, you may be able to get around this by banding together with several stores, all of you contributing to a common fund for this purpose. Private guards and police patrols can be located in the yellow pages of your telephone book.

Watchdogs. Watchdogs are very valuable in preventing burglaries since they confront the potential burglar with an immediate physical threat. Also, word of your watchdog soon gets around and may even deter the attempt. You need not own your own watchdog; you may be able to rent them for a monthly rate of several hundred dollars. Again, check the yellow pages of your telephone book.

Frequent Cash Deposits. One sure way to minimize losses is to make frequent bank deposits. In fact, having little cash on hand provides little motivation for a burglar to take the risk of attempting to burglarize your business.

ROBBERY

Technically, robbery is stealing or taking anything of value by force, violence, or the use of fear. Robbery is the fastest growing crime in the United States. Also, the greatest increase has been found in retail stores where holdups alone have increased 75% in recent times. Note that robbery is a violent crime and in the majority of cases the robber uses a weapon. As a result, robbery victims are frequently hurt. So it is naturally in your interest to do everything possible to prevent robbery.

Prevention of Robbery

Some of the means to prevent burglaries will also prevent robberies. For example, frequent cash deposits will remove some of the motivation, but you must be very careful here. The sight of the money may trigger a robbery. Therefore, it is wise to vary your hours and routes to the bank if possible, and not carry your deposits in obvious money containers. An armored car service may be of value here. Such services offer a safe alternative with pickup items scheduled to meet your needs with guaranteed delivery. Special safes may also be available in conjunction with an armored car service. These special safes, known as dual control safes, can only be unlocked jointly by the armored car guard and the store owner.

Another unique safe which is helpful in preventing robberies is a safe with an inner compartment, with a special drop slot for cash deposits. Such a safe works on the same principle as a dual control safe—the advantage being that only the manager or owner of the store as opposed to the cashier has access to the second compartment once the cash has been deposited.

The Importance of Opening and Closing Routines. Special routines for opening and closing your store may be of great assistance in preventing robberies. This should be a two-man job. When you open the store, the second man observes your actions as you open, enter, and check the burglar alarm. If you do not reappear at a prearranged time, this should be the signal for your "second man" to call the police. If everything is all right, the owner would reappear and signal to the assistant. The closing routine at night should be similar, with the assistant again waiting outside and observing.

A trained guard dog can be of value in preventing robbery. A guard dog would be in your presence at all times and would be trained to attack anyone who threatens you. These guard dogs can't be rented because of the personal nature of the defense—they usually must be owned by the store owner.

Physical Deterrents.   Certain devices will assist you in minimizing the effect of robberies once they take place. One is a surveillance camera which, if robbers know it exists, may also act as a deterrent. Other types of silent alarms, including footrail switches, cash door contacts, and holdup buttons, can also be of great assistance in catching robbers once the act has taken place. A handgun may also be of use during a robbery, if it is legal and *if you are trained in its use.* On the other hand, you must be aware of the risk that if you use your handgun the robber will probably use his as well.

Cautions on Night Calls.   You should be particularly cautious if you are called at night to return to your business for some purpose. If the reason given is a malfunction of your burglar alarm system, you should phone the police department and ask that someone meet you at your place of business. If the problem is some sort of repair that must be done, make sure to phone the repair company and ask that the service truck meet you. Call before you leave your home, not from the store. If you arrive at your store and do not see the police car or the repair truck, don't park near your store or enter it. Verify all phone calls you receive after store hours.

SHOPLIFTING

Shoplifting is the most commonplace of all small business crimes, and currently shoplifters are stealing more than $2 billion worth of merchandise annually. Everything that you can do to spot, deter, apprehend, prosecute, and prevent shoplifting is much to the advantage of your business and other businesses across the country.

Types of Shoplifters

If you can learn to spot a shoplifter, it will help a great deal in shoplifting prevention. Addison H. Verrill, chairman of Dale System, Inc., Garden City, New York, describes shoplifters as falling into five categories.

Juvenile Offenders.   Juvenile offenders account for approximately 50% of all shoplifters. They usually steal on a dare or simply for a thrill, and often they expect store owners and the courts not to prosecute fully because of their age. Sometimes they enter stores in groups or gangs in an attempt to intimidate the owner. The best prevention here is to prosecute, remembering that this usually is the first type of theft committed by youngsters who later commit much more serious crimes.

Impulse Shoplifters.   Impulse shoplifters may appear to be perfectly respectable people. The theft is not premeditated, but occurs upon the sudden presentation of an opportunity, at which time the shoplifter falls to the temptation provided. The best prevention here is to insure that you have structured deterrents into your store to remove opportunities and temptations for shoplifting.

Alcoholics, Vagrants, and Drug Addicts. In this category fall people whose physiological dependency requires them to commit theft. Because of their other problems, very frequently these criminals are clumsy or erratic in their behavior, and for this reason they may be easier to detect than other types of shoplifters. However, at the same time, you must remember that such people may be under the influence of drugs and may be armed as well as violent. It is best to leave the apprehension of such people to the police.

Kleptomaniacs. Persons suffering from kleptomania have a driving psychological need to steal. Frequently they have little or no use for the items they steal and could easily afford to pay for the items. However, unless you are a psychologist or a psychiatrist, you can probably do nothing special to prevent theft by this group.

Professionals. Professionals make up the final category of shoplifters. These individuals are usually highly skilled and may be difficult to spot. They tend to steal items which can be quickly resold, such as high-demand consumer goods including televisions, stereos, and other smaller appliances. Shoplifting professionals may case a store well in advance of the actual theft. Again, your most effective defense is proper deterrence with the layout of your store and alert, well-trained personnel.

Tactics of Shoplifters

Another way to help prevent shoplifting and be able to spot shoplifters is to know what tactics they use in accomplishing their theft. Basic shoplifter tactics include putting on clothes and simply walking out wearing them. Another common tactic is for two or more shoplifters to work as a team; while one or more use some tactic to distract the store owner or salesperson, the other or others commit the theft. Another tactic is simply to switch price tags and in this way to pay lower prices for more expensive items. Many shoplifters will use a palming tactic whereby the merchandise to be taken is placed under a handkerchief, between the folds of a newspaper, or with some similar item used to cover the item which is shoplifted. Common items such as pocketbooks, umbrellas, baby strollers, briefcases, are also used as depositories for items that are shoplifted, or the shoplifter may slip the item into a pocket of a jacket or within a dress. Professionals are a little more sophisticated, using items known as booster boxes, which are empty cartons disguised in gift wrappings. These booster boxes have hidden openings which allow shoplifters to pick up the item quickly without being observed. Professionals may also use hooker belts, which are worn around the waist. These hooker belts support hooks on which stolen items can be attached. You should be aware of all of these tactics and similar tactics used by shoplifters.

Deterring Shoplifters

To deter shoplifters, you must take four basic actions. These are: educating your employees as to what to expect or what to do, planning your store keeping shoplifters in mind, using protective equipment, and using protective personnel.

Educating Your Employees. You should brief your employees regarding shoplifter tactics as well as the various types of shoplifters. You should also instruct them to watch for suspicious-looking shoppers and shoppers carrying possible concealing devices such as those described. If you operate a clothing store, your salespeople should keep careful count of the number of items carried into and out of dressing rooms. Employees should be especially aware of groups of shoppers who enter the store together and who may be trying diversionary tactics. The salespeople should also be watchful of individuals who handle a great deal of merchandise, but take an especially long time to make the decision. Watch for loitering of customers in any one area and customers who only shop during certain hours when sales personnel on duty are few. Individual employees accepting payment for goods such as cashiers should be careful of switched price labels and purchased items which can be containers for stolen goods, such as garbage cans or tool boxes.

Frequently, local police conduct training seminars for store personnel. Such courses can be very helpful in showing you and your personnel how to spot shoplifters, and teaching you the latest methods of prevention. To find out if such training is available, contact your local police.

Planning Store Layout. It is unfortunate that you must consider shoplifters when you are planning the layout of your store. But this is a fact, and not to do so would be a terrible mistake which would cost you dearly in lost merchandise. Therefore, do plan your store with deterrents in mind. Some of these are: maintaining adequate lighting in all areas of the store, maintaining merchandise displayed in standard groups of three or four items per display so that your salespeople will notice when something is missing, keeping small items of high value behind a counter or in a locked case with sales personnel on duty, keeping your displays neat (it is easier to spot an item missing from an orderly display than from one in disarray), positioning your cash register so that it provides complete and unobstructed views of aisles of goods, and having your display cases which contain all of your expensive items locked. Finally, if fire regulations permit, you should lock all exits which are not to be used by your customers. Those exits which are not locked should have alarm systems attached to them which make a noise when someone enters or leaves. Close and block off unused checkout aisles.

Using Protective Equipment. These devices can greatly decrease the amount of shoplifting to which your store is subjected. It includes two-way mirrors, one-way viewing mirrors, peepholes, closed circuit television, and convex wall mirrors. The use of special electronic tags will prevent much shoplifting. If someone attempts to leave when electronic tags are not removed or rendered inoperative, an alarm goes off. Other tags are almost tamper-proof because they are either attached to hard-to-break plastic string or constructed in such a fashion that they cannot easily be removed or switched. Price labels marked by rubber stamps or pricing machines are also very useful in preventing removal and switching, and are better than either felt-marked or pencil-marked price tags since they cannot be switched, or the amount altered. You can also institute a system to alert your employees as to whether a package has been paid for or not. For example, you can instruct your cashiers or salespeople to staple receipts to the outside of all packages that have been paid for. A simple system but it works.

Protective Personnel. Another method of preventing or deterring shoplifting is using protective personnel. These include detectives disguised as customers who can better observe what is going on in your store than your salespeople can, and uniformed guards who stand as visual deterrents to shoplifting.

Apprehending Shoplifters

Apprehension of shoplifters is very critical. It must be done with some finesse, because you certainly don't want to disturb your regular customers or collar an innocent person. Not only will you lose future sales, but you could be sued. Therefore, apprehension should be carefully thought out and policies established beforehand. In general, in order to make shoplifting charges stick, you must do the following:

1. See the shoplifter take or conceal store merchandise
2. Positively identify the merchandise as belonging to you
3. Testify that it was taken by the shoplifter with the intent to steal
4. Prove that the merchandise was not paid for

Failure to meet these basic criteria leaves you open to counter-charges of false arrest. You must remember that false arrest does not necessarily mean arrest by police, but may simply mean that you have prevented a customer from conducting normal activities. Therefore, you should be extremely careful about this point and check regarding laws pertaining to shoplifting in your state with your lawyer or your local police or both. Be especially careful that the shoplifter is not able to dump the merchandise after you have decided to arrest him. In fact, a good rule is: if you lose sight of the shoplifter for even an instant, forget it. If the shoplifter succeeded in getting rid of the merchandise, you could be in for a lot of trouble.

INTERNAL THEFT

According to the SBA, loss due to theft amounts to between 1 and 7% of sales, of which dishonest employees account for two-thirds. The Department of Commerce further estimates that dishonest employees are responsible for 75 to 80% of all retail shortages. The most common type of internal theft is embezzlement in which cash is received and your employee merely pockets it without making a record of the sale. A slightly more complicated type of internal theft or embezzlement is called "lapping." With this type of theft, the embezzler withholds receipts such as payments on accounts receivable temporarily, perhaps with the intent to repay. The amount withheld is eventually paid by "borrowing" from yet another account which is intended to be a payment on accounts receivable. In this way, borrowing may increase and the amounts grow larger and larger; in fact, sometimes this type of fraud may run on for years and years, and when it is finally detected the amount is in the tens or even hundreds of thousands of dollars.

Internal theft is frequently concealed, and therefore you must look for clues to the fact that it is going on. Here are six different occurrences which should lead to an investigation to see if an embezzler is ripping you off.

1. *Decline or unusually small increase in cash or credit sales.* This could mean that some sales are not being recorded.

2. *Increase in overall sales returns.* This might mean a concealment of accounts receivable payments.

3. *Inventory shortages.* This could be caused by fictitious purchases, unrecorded sales, or some other means of theft.

4. *Profit declines and expense increases.* This could be a sign that cash is being taken from your accounts in some way.

5. *Slow collection.* This could be a device concealing lapping mentioned previously.

6. *Unusual bad debt writeoffs.* This could cover some sort of internal theft scheme.

In general, there are two major ways to cut down on internal theft. These are:

1. Screening your employees
2. Controlling your business operations and removing theft hazards

Screening employees we have talked about before, especially as it pertains to your hiring practices as discussed in an earlier chapter. Five areas for potential theft and ways to prevent this theft are recommended by Saul D. Astor, president of Management Safeguards, Inc., of New York City.[1]

Pricing

Loosely controlled pricing procedures constitute a major cause of inventory "shrinkage."

Case in Point. Items in a thrift store were ticketed in pencil. Moreover, some tickets were unmarked. Since the store was inadequately staffed, many customers marked down prices, switched tickets, or wrote in their own prices.

Antitheft Pointers

Price items by machine or rubber stamp, not by handwriting.

Permit only authorized employees to set prices and mark merchandise.

Make *unannounced* spot checks to be sure that actual prices agree with authorized prices and price charge records.

Refunds

Refunds provide dishonest employees an easy means to ply their trade. There are more ways to lose money on returns or refunds than the average retailer dreams possible.

Case in Point. In one store, many returned items were marked down to a fraction of cost because of damage. It was easy for clerks to get authorization to buy "as is" merchandise. When they were armed with an okay, they substituted first-grade items for "as is" stock.

---

[1] Saul D. Astor, *Preventing Retail Theft*, Small Business Administration (1978).

Antitheft Pointers

Insist on a merchandise inspection by someone other than the person who
made the sale.

Match items to the return vouchers and then return the merchandise back
into stock as quickly as possible.

Keep a tight control on all credit documents. Spot check customers by mail
or telephone to make sure they got their refunds.

Popular Salespeople

The popular salesperson is a great asset—providing he or she is popular for
the right reasons. However, many salespeople win "fans" because of the deals
they swing and the favors they grant.

Case in Point. Customers stood in line to wait for one veteran saleswoman.
They refused to be served by anyone else. And no wonder! She switched tickets
for many "special" customers, giving them substantial markdowns. Store losses
amounted to about $300 a week—not including $25 a week in increased commissions for the crook.

Antitheft Pointers

The popular salesperson may be your biggest asset. But don't take it for
granted. Find out for yourself *why* he or she is so well liked.

Pay special attention to the salesperson who is visited by too many personal
friends. To discourage such socializing, some retailers hire people who
live outside the immediate store vicinity.

Cash Handling

The cashier's post is particularly vulnerable to theft. The experienced cash
handler with larceny on his or her mind can rob a store blind in a hundred
and one ways.

Case in Point. A store owner's sales were high, but his profits were dragging.
The cause was traced to a cashier who rang up only some of the items bought
by his "customers." In most cases, he didn't ring "put-downs" at all. (A "put-
down" is the right amount of cash which a customer leaves on the counter
when he rushes out without waiting for his tape.)

Antitheft Pointers

Keep a sharp eye open for signals—nods, winks, and so on—between cashiers
and customers.

Pay special attention to cashiers when they are surrounded by clusters of
people.

Be alert to the use of over-ring slips to cover up shortages.

Watch for items bypassed when ringing up sales.

Check personal checks to make sure they are not being used to cover up
shortages.

Use a professional shopper to check for violations of cash register and related procedures.

Backdoor Thefts

Large-scale theft is carried on more often through the back than the front door. Hundreds, even thousands, of dollars worth of merchandise can be stolen within a few seconds.

Case in Point.   A stock clerk parked his car at the receiving dock. He kept his trunk closed but unlocked. At 12:30 P.M., when the shipping-receiving manager was at lunch, the stock clerk threw full cartons of shoes into his trunk and then slammed it locked. Elapsed time: 18 seconds.

Antitheft Pointers

Have a secondary check by a worker or a salesperson on all incoming shipments.

Insist on flattening all trash cartons and make spot checks of trash after hours.

Prohibit employees from parking near receiving door or dock.

Keep receiving door *locked* when not in use. Make sure locked door cannot be raised a few inches. A receiving door should be opened only by a supervisor who remains in area until it's relocked.

Alarm on door should ring until turned off with key held by store manager.

Distribute door keys carefully and change lock cylinders periodically.

The Bank of America, in its excellent booklet "Crime Prevention for Small Business," recommends instituting several control measures to reduce the danger of internal theft. First, key job cross-checks in which one person orders the merchandise while another records hours worked and a third makes out payroll checks. This may be difficult or impractical for all small businesses, but you could divide duties so that employees do not have excessive control over your operations. Cash register controls are important since it is here that employees have direct access to incoming cash. Therefore, each checker should be responsible for his or her own cash drawer, counting all cash receipts at the beginning of the shift and signing the register tape. The customer should receive a sales receipt for every transaction. In this way, individuals at the cashier's station are prevented from pocketing cash or underringing a sale and pocketing the difference, since the customer would notice this and call attention to the incorrect ring-up. You must be sure that whoever is operating the cash register immediately replaces tape, since it is possible to ring up with no tape in the machine and in that way not record any sales. Checking all incoming merchandise against purchase invoices insures that quantities, prices, shipping charges, and other conditions are correct. Keeping storage rooms locked and allowing access only under supervision will eliminate the opportunities for theft through this quarter. Paying by serially numbered checks will control disbursements. Keeping checks under lock and key, along with check-writing equipment, will help control this source of possible theft. Voiding all paid bills or invoices will insure that they can't be used a second time, and if you establish firm price and discount policies, unauthorized discounts will be unlikely.

Christopher J. Moran, CPA, a partner in A. M. Pullen and Company of Greensboro, North Carolina, recommends the following 16 precautions.[2]

Ounces of Prevention

There are many steps an owner-manager can take to cut down on the possibility of losses through embezzlement. Do you take the following precautions?

1. Check the background of prospective employees. Sometimes you can satisfy yourself by making a few telephone calls or writing a few letters. In other cases, you may want to turn the matter over to a credit bureau or similar agency to run a background check. (Keep in mind that the rights of individuals must be preserved in furnishing, receiving, and using background information.)

2. Know your employees to the extent that you may be able to detect signs of financial or other personal problems. Build up rapport so that they feel free to discuss such things with you in confidence.

3. See that no one is placed on the payroll without authorization from you or a responsible official of the company. If you have a personnel department, require that it approve additions to the payroll as a double check.

4. Have the company mail addressed to a post office box rather than your place of business. In smaller cities, the owner-manager may want to go to the post office himself to collect the mail. In any event, you or your designated keyman should personally open the mail and make a record at that time of cash and checks received. Don't delude yourself that checks or money orders payable to your company can't be converted into cash by an enterprising embezzler.

5. Either personally prepare the daily cash deposits or compare the deposits made by employees with the record of cash and checks received. Make sure you get a copy of the duplicate deposit slip or other documentation from the bank. make it a habit to go to the bank and make the daily deposit yourself as often as you can. If you delegate these jobs, make an occasional spot check to see that nothing is amiss.

6. Arrange for bank statements and other correspondence from banks to be sent to the same post office box, and personally reconcile all bank statements with your company's books and records. The owner-manager who has not reconciled the statements for some time may want to get oriented by the firm's outside accountant.

7. Personally examine all canceled checks and endorsements to see if there is anything unusual. This also applies to payroll checks.

8. Make sure that an employee in a position to mishandle funds is adequately bonded. Let him know that fidelity coverage is a matter of company policy rather than any feeling of mistrust on your part. If a would-be embezzler knows that a bonding company also has an interest in what he does, he may think twice before helping himself to your funds.

[2] Christopher J. Moran, *Preventing Embezzlement*, Small Business Administration (1977).

9. Spot check your accounting records and assets to satisfy yourself that all is well and that your plan of internal control is being carried out.

10. Personally approve unusual discounts and bad-debt writeoffs. Approve or spot check credit memos and other documentation for sales returns and allowances.

11. Don't delegate the signing of checks and approval of cash disbursements unless absolutely necessary and never approve any payment without sufficient documentation or prior knowledge of the transaction.

12. Examine all invoices and supporting data before signing checks. Make sure that all merchandise was actually received and the price seems reasonable. In many false purchase schemes, the embezzler neglects to make up receiving forms or other records purporting to show receipt of merchandise.

13. Personally cancel all invoices at the time you sign the checks to prevent double payment through error or otherwise.

14. Don't sign blank checks. Don't leave a supply of signed blank checks when you go on vacation.

15. Inspect all prenumbered checkbooks and other prenumbered forms from time to time to insure that checks or forms form the backs of the books have not been removed and possibly used in a fraudulent scheme.

16. Have the preparation of the payroll and the actual paying of employees handled by different persons, especially when cash is involved.

BAD CHECKS

The Department of Commerce estimates that more than $2 billion worth of losses a year can be attributed solely to bad checks. It's worth your effort to prevent a portion of this huge amount from coming out of your pocket. You will be a lot less likely to accept bad checks if you (1) require identification, and (2) consider certain key points before you hand over the cash.

Require Identification

You should always require identification to make sure that the person presenting you with a check is the same person whose name is printed on the check. It is better to require at least two pieces of identification. Usually, these should be a driver's license and a major credit card. Recording information such as the serial number from the driver's license and the number from the credit card will help to deter the person from passing the bad check, and it will also help locate the individual if the check turns out to be bad.

Of course, identification is not foolproof. Any identification can be forged. However, some pieces of identification are more difficult to forge than others. The following types of identification are more difficult and are therefore better for check cashing purposes: automobile operator's license, automobile registration card, credit cards, government passes, and identification cards issued by companies that carry a photograph, description, and signature.

The following cards are not good identification because they are easily forged: Social Security cards, business cards, club organization cards, bank books, work permits, insurance cards, learner's permits, letters, birth certificates, library cards, and voter registration cards.

Check Key Points

The following key points should be considered when the check and pieces of identification are presented.

1. Compare signature from the check with signature on the identification.
2. If the check is written for a nonlocal bank, make sure the customer's out-of-town as well as his local address and telephone are written on the back of the check.
3. Check the date, including day, month, and year. Do not accept checks that are not dated or postdated, or checks on which the date is more than 30 days past.
4. Be sure that the numerical amount agrees with the amount written in in numerals.
5. Be sure that the check is legibly written, signed in ink, and does not have any erasures or written-over amounts.
6. Be sure that you are the payee, or your firm is. If a check is a two-party check, that is, a check which is written to the individual presenting you with the check and is to be endorsed over to you, be sure that you get full information and take special care.
7. It is safer to take personal checks only for the exact amount of purchase. Of course, whether you do this or not is your decision.
8. Set a limit on the amount that you will cash a check for. Post the amount for your customers to see and accept none beyond that amount except for amount of purchase.
9. Statistically, checks with low serial numbers are returned more often than checks with higher numbers. Therefore, be especially cautious about low numbers.
10. Statistically, bad checks tend to be in the $25 to $35 range, according to the Small Business Administration. Be particularly careful of checks around this amount or under $50.
11. Look for lack of concern about the price of the merchandise purchased. Lack of concern may indicate that the check is no good.

Bad Check Protection Services and Equipment

Certain devices and services will assist you in minimizing bad checks. You can photograph the individual who cashes the check with a Polaroid camera. This procedure is definitely a deterrent since bad check passers do not want to be photographed. There is a check verification service available in many states for a small monthly fee. A central computer contains only negative information about check passers. You can get this information as a participating businessperson by calling a central number and giving the customer's driver's license number. Another mechanical deterrent available is a fingerprint register. This fingerprint register works without the traditional black, messy ink. It involves only one thumbprint on the back of the check which is registered by the machine. Obviously, bad check passers do not wish to be fingerprinted either.

You can find out more about check protection equipment by checking in the yellow pages of your telephone directory and also by talking with other merchants who are using similar devices.

You Are Under No Obligation to Take a Check

Never forget that you are not obligated to take anyone's check, even if the individual presents identification and all of the key points described above are positive. Naturally, you may wish to do so in order to make a sale and for good will. However, Leonard Kolodny, who is the manager of the Retail Bureau of the Metropolitan Washington Board of Trade, Washington, D.C., recommends that you not accept a check if:

1. The person presenting it appears to be intoxicated
2. The customer acts at all suspiciously
3. The check has an old date
4. The check is dated in advance

Kolodny also recommends that you not tell a customer that you cannot accept his check because he is a college student or lives in a bad neighborhood, or give a similar response. If you respond in such a way as to appear to discriminate when refusing to cash a check, you may be in violation of a state or federal law on discrimination.

SOURCES OF ADDITIONAL INFORMATION

Mind Your Own Business, by Norman Jaspen, published by Prentice-Hall, Inc., Englewood Cliffs, NJ 07632.

Protect Your Business Against Crime—A Guide for the Small Businessman, published by Drake Publishers, Inc., New York, NY 10017.

Shop Lifting and Shrinkage Protection for Stores, by Loren E. Edwards, published by Charles C. Thomas, 301 East Lawrence Avenue, Springfield, IL 62717.

Sticky Fingers, by William W. McCullough, published by AMACOM, a division of the American Management Association, 135 West 50th Street, New York, NY 10020.

20

How the Computer Can Revolutionize Your Business

In previous chapters I've talked about use of computers for financial management, tax preparation and planning, record keeping, and to a certain extent, marketing. I now want to tell you that this is only scratching the surface. A computer will do more to raise your productivity than any other single tool I can think of. If you have never used a computer before, or have done so only to play "Pac-Man" or "Space Invaders," you are in for a real treat.

But first, if you harbor any doubts about using a computer, let me tell you are not alone. I also was once numbered in this category. I could think of nothing that a computer could do that (I thought) I couldn't accomplish with pencil, paper, or maybe a typewriter. I told friends that if I adopted a computer as an aid to my writing, this would cause my productivity to decline. My method of book writing in those days was to develop a detailed chapter outline, and then to dictate my book on audiotape. My typist would type out a draft from the tape. I would correct this and return it to my typist for a corrected copy. I couldn't see how I could beat that until computers came on the market at a reasonable price that would type out my dictation. I was wrong.

HOW THE COMPUTER TURNED MY BUSINESS PRACTICE UPSIDE DOWN

My wife, Nurit, got into computing first. She was working on her doctoral dissertation in clinical psychology and insisted that a computer could save her lots of time. As I completed my own doctoral dissertation some years earlier without a computer, I wasn't really convinced. Whenever I needed computing done for research, I could have it done at the big mainframe at the university, and as for my writing . . . well, I already explained that. But as you might have guessed, she got one anyway.

I was amazed how easily she mastered the computer, and even more shocked at how quickly she could revise entire chapters of her dissertation as it developed without having to retype it. When I reviewed her work, I was also surprised at the complete lack of typographical errors, and the neatness of the printout. Unlike many typewriters, the right side of the page was as even as the left. This process was as easy as the stroke of a key and is called "justification." Further, the entire document could be stored on a floppy disk. Any time she wanted to work on it, she simply put the disk in the computer. What a space saver!

I didn't waste any time in getting her to teach me how to use this simple word-processing program for my correspondence. Boy, did I save time! If I misspelled a word, no longer did I need to white out or otherwise fix my mistake. If I completed some correspondence, and found I had left out an important paragraph, I didn't need to do the whole letter over. I just inserted the paragraph in the right place and printed it out. Further, no more typos. There was a spelling program on another disk. You just loaded that up and your spelling mistakes disappeared.

Then came the day that I went on contract for a college textbook. A textbook is different from a regular book in that not only must you write the basic text, but your publisher usually wants additional ancillary materials. In my case I had to furnish a 500-page instructor's manual and another manual with 2,100 multiple-choice and true/false questions. Further, the publisher wants these additional materials as "camera ready copy." This means that instead of type-setting, the publisher simply takes a picture of each page that you furnish and reproduces that . . . so your manuscript has to be letter perfect and error free. Naturally, I turned to the computer. But to speed things up, I combined my old method with the computer. I did a detailed outline and made an audiotape which I sent to my typist. But instead of sending me a corrected manuscript, I had my typist work with her computer with the same word-processing program that I used. She sent me a disk which I put in my computer. I made the corrections I wanted, and printed the final camera ready copy myself.

HOW THE COMPUTER CAN DOUBLE AND TRIPLE YOUR PRODUCTIVITY

The word processing by itself allowed me to double the work I turned out in a given amount of time . . . and the quality of work was better too. But I soon discovered other things that I could do with my computer that saved me time, money, and made all of my business operations more efficient. Here are a few that I haven't discussed in previous chapters.

DESKTOP PUBLISHING

In the bad old days, I used to pay a graphic artist to do my layout and typesetting for brochures, flyers, or booklets. This usually cost a minimum of a $100 or more per job and took at least a week before I could even proofread. Now, using a software program costing a couple of hundred dollars, I can do everything myself in short order. I have a full choice of dozens of different typefaces and sizes. As a bonus, I don't have to wait, and except for my own time constraints, or the time constraints of people I hire to help me out from time to time, I get the work done immediately and never need to wait. I don't mean that I never use a graphic artist now. But much of the routine work I can do myself.

The same is true of overhead transparencies that I use for my seminars. It used to take at least a week, and there were always typos, some of which I caught too late to have corrected. With a desktop publishing program, all that is past. I do all my own stuff, with the advantages I mentioned above.

Of course, I am able to save all of my material, so that if I ever want it again, or want it with minor changes, it's a piece of cake to make the changes and print the new material out.

MAILING ADVERTISEMENTS USING MERGE

There are all sorts of programs around that let you merge your customer list with a particular salesletter. This means that every letter is personalized to that individual customer. What once had to be done by someone else can now be done by you at home. Your program will address both letters and envelopes. This is especially valuable for relatively small mailings for which it isn't cost effective to have done by a lettershop.

LET THE COMPUTER FIX YOUR WRITING

I mentioned earlier that programs exist to correct your spelling. But there are also programs available to correct your grammar, programs to give you choices of the words you may want to use (a thesaurus program), programs that will help you to write so that your writing is more readable, and so on. A computer software program probably can't turn you into an instant professional writer, but it certainly can turn you into a more competent one. If you want help with copywriting for your ads, there are programs for this also. One called "Headliner" creates headlines, theme lines, slogans, and jingles. Another program from the same company will help you in picking the perfect name for your product or service. When you consider that there are companies around that charge several thousand dollars for this chore, you can appreciate just what an advantage it is to be able to do this for yourself.

MAKING FORECASTS AND PLANS

One of the most common computer uses for business is that of the spreadsheet. A spreadsheet program can be used to do sophisticated calculations, provide data for graphs, do forecasts, view results by changing various "what if" variables, estimate costs, and the like. Basically, a spreadsheet is simply a chart with rows and columns filled with numbers. But the beauty of this type of program is that you can do the formula calculations to fill in these rows and columns with hundreds of accurate numerical results almost instantly. In Chapter 15 I showed you how to develop a business/marketing plan without a computer. But sure enough, there are software programs around to assist you with developing plans of all types incorporating the spreadsheet concept.

ANALYZING POTENTIAL EMPLOYEES

Big companies pay big fees to consultants to obtain complete psychological evaluations on potential key employees. Even this has been computerized and you can obtain programs in which you input data by merely answering questions posed by the program based on a short interview you have with the candidate.

The output tells you how the individual is likely to behave under different situations, as well as how best to influence him or her. If you want to use handwriting analysis as an assist in evaluation, these kinds of programs are available as well.

MARKETING RESEARCH

There are probably hundreds of marketing research programs available. They will help you not only to design your research tool, but to analyze your data and interpret the results as well.

BUSINESS SIMULATION

If you want to fine tune your business decision-making tools, there are programs around that will place you in a number of business situations requiring you to make tactical and strategic business decisions. The programs analyze your decisions and teach you to consider factors that you may not have considered. Thus you can learn some things by experience without experiencing the hard knocks and loss of time and money that usually goes with learning in the real world.

Of course there are many other things that a computer can do for including maintaining your list of customers, finding new customers for you, and doing media research. Buy a device called a modem which attaches to your computer and your telephone and you'll be able to access data banks of information all over the country and do research on things, people, and companies right from your home. I hope I've said enough to show you what a computer might be able to do for you. If you are interested in any of the programs I've described, go to your local business software store. They can show you most of these programs, and a lot more. If you live in a town that doesn't have a store that sells software, go to your newsstand and get a copy of one of the many computer magazines that are now being published. You will not only see many programs advertised and described right in the magazine, but you can obtain catalogues from companies that publish hundreds of other programs that can help you run and build your business.

WHAT YOU NEED TO KNOW ABOUT COMPUTERS

First let me say that you really don't need to know much. But if you are unfamiliar with computers, it all seems confusing. I'm going to clear up that confusion right now. When you buy a computer, you need a keyboard, the computer proper, one or more disk drives, a visual indictor (called a monitor), and a printer.

The keyboard attaches to the computer and is very similar to the one on a typewriter. It has a few more keys, but that's no problem. The instructions that come with any program you buy tells you what keys to press to get the computer to do what you want. As may be obvious, the keyboard is used to tell the computer what to do. If you're writing (the term used in dealing with computers is "word processing"), each time you push a key, you're telling the computer to make that mark on the screen of your monitor, which may be either color or monochrome. For most purposes, the single color is fine.

The disk drives work like a record player. You play your computer programs on them. The programs themselves are on the disks. The programs are known as "software." If you have an IBM type of personal computer, the disks are floppy disks 5¼" in diameter. If you use an Apple Macintosh, the disk is 3½" in diameter. These smaller disks may be physically hard rather than floppy, but for reasons that will be made clear in a minute they are not known as "hard disks." Other computers use one or the other of these types.

One important software program that comes on a disk is the DOS, or Disk Operating System. The Microsoft DOS which I use is currently in version 3.10. As with all software programs, when a new version comes out, the number increases. Thus the previous version of Microsoft DOS was 2.11. The DOS runs your computer system. It manages the communications among all these devices: computer, keyboard, monitor, printer, and so on, and helps other programs to run. The newest version as I write this is 4.01.

Now back to the hard disk I noted earlier in passing. In addition to containing software programs that you may want to run, disks are also used for storing data: your advertising brochure, customer lists, sales letters, and so forth. Each disk allows you to store 1,440,000 bits or 1.44 megabytes of information. Now I know that this sounds like a lot. You will soon discover that it's not. The beauty of a hard disk is that depending on what hard disk you buy, it will store 10, 20, 40, 60, or even greater megabytes of data. What this means is that programs and data you want stored can all go on a hard disk. The speed and convenience of accessing this data compared with using soft disks will truly amaze you. Now one way or another, you're going to need two disk drives. My recommendation is to start right off with a one hard disk and one regular disk drive. You need the one regular disk drive to input new programs that you buy. How many megabytes for your hard disk? Once again, my general advice is more than you think. Once you start using a computer—and you see more potential for it in your business—your needs grow exponentially and fast.

WHAT KIND OF COMPUTER SHOULD YOU BUY?

Whatever computer you buy, make certain that it has at least 640Kb RAM. "RAM" stands for Random Access Memory, and "Kb" means "kilobyte" that is, 1,000 bytes. This is a description of your computer's power. Less than 640Kb of RAM will deny you access to many business software programs that you may want to use. The two biggest personal computer types on the market today are the IBM/IBM compatibles and Apple's Macintosh. The biggest advantage of the IBM types are the amount of software available. Everybody and his brother develops software for the IBMs. For the Macintosh, it's probably ease of use. With the MacIntosh use of a "mouse" is standard. A mouse is a pointing device. You point to a symbol on the screen, click a button on your mouse, and the computer reacts to a command. For many operations, this is faster and easier than using the conventional keyboard. However, you can also buy a mouse for your IBM or IBM compatible. I have a so-called IBM clone, and use the mouse in conjunction with desktop publishing. I do not recommending buying a computer by mail until you get more experience. There are always a few things that just don't seem to go right. Sure, most companies have telephone numbers that you can call, even toll-free numbers. Still, getting a busy signal when you are in a hurry or running up a large telephone bill while someone walks you through the problem is not my idea of fun. Buy it locally, and your initial problems with setup are much diminished . . . even though you can probably buy more cheaply through the mail.

WHAT KIND OF PRINTER TO BUY

There are three basic kinds of printers: dot matrix, letter quality, and laser. The dot matrix is fast, but every letter is formed of little dots, and it's not much good for letters or advertisements or communicating with someone outside of your company. Letter-quality printers use the typewriter style of daisy wheels. The printing looks great. The problems are speed (you may think this isn't important, but wait until you spend several hours to print out a lengthy document) and lack of graphic capability. The laser printers solve all of the above. The problem is that they'll set you back a minimum of $1,100 currently. I've used all three, and it really depends a lot on the kind of work you want your computer for and how much you can afford. There are also near letter quality printers available now. They are dot matrix also, but the number of dots per inch is a lot higher than the older models. These represent a compromise between standard dot matrix and laser. They're a lot cheaper, but are still not laser quality.

SOURCES OF ADDITIONAL INFORMATION

The Art of Desktop Publishing, 2nd edition, by Tony Bove, Cherly Rhodes, and Wes Thomas, published by Bantam Books, 666 Fifth Avenue, New York, NY 10103.

The Macintosh Advisor, by Cynthia Harriman and Bencion Calica, published by Hayden Books, 4300 West 62nd Street, Indianapolis, IN 46268.

Managing Your Hard Disk, by Don Berliner, published by Que Corporation, P.O. Box 90, Carmel, IN 46032.

123 Made Easy, by Mary Campbell, published by Osbourne/McGraw-Hill, 2600 Tenth Street, Berkeley, CA 94710.

The Personal Computer in Business Book, by Peter A. McWilliams, published by Prelude Press, Box 69773, Los Angeles, CA 90069.

Webster's New World Dictionary of Computer Terms, compiled by Laura Darcy and Louise Boston, published by Simon and Schuster, Inc., One Gulf + Western Plaza, New York, NY 10023.

Appendix I

SBA Field Offices

City, State, Zip	Address	Phone	Type*
Northeast			
Albany, NY 12207	445 Broadway, Rm. 222	(518)472-6300	POD
Augusta, ME 04330	40 Western Ave., Rm. 512	(207)622-8378	DO
Boston, MA 02110	60 Batterymarch St., 10th Fl.	(617)223-3204	RO
Boston, MA 02222	10 Causeway St., Rm. 265	(617)565-5590	DO
Buffalo, NY 14202	111 W. Huron St., Rm. 1311	(716)846-4301	BO
Camden, NJ 08104	2600 Mt. Ephrain Ave.	(609)757-5183	POD
Concord, NH 03301	55 Pleasant St., Rm. 210	(603)225-1400	DO
Elmira, NY 14901	333 E. Water St., 4th Fl.	(607)734-8130	BO
Fairlawn, NJ 07410	15-01 Broadway, 1st Fl.	(201)794-8195	DAO
Hartford, CT 06106	330 Main St., 2nd Fl.	(203)240-4700	DO
Melville, NY 11747	35 Pinelawn Rd., Rm. 102E	(516)454-0750	BO
Montpelier, VT 05602	87 State St., Rm. 205	(802)828-4474	DO
Newark, NJ 07102	60 Park Pl., 4th Fl.	(201)645-2434	DO
New York, NY 10278	26 Federal Plaza, Rm. 29-118	(212)264-7772	RO
New York, NY 10278	26 Federal Plaza, Rm. 3100	(212)264-4355	DO
Providence, RI 02903	380 Westminister Mall, 5th Fl.	(401)528-4586	DO
Rochester, NY 14614	100 State St., Rm. 601	(716)263-6700	POD
Springfield, MA 01103	1550 Main St., Rm. 212	(413)785-0268	BO
Syracuse, NY 13260	100 S. Clinton St., Rm. 1071	(315)423-5383	DO
Mid-Atlantic			
Baltimore, MD 21202	10 N. Calvert St., 3rd Fl.,	(301)962-4392	DO
Charleston, WV 25301	550 Eagan St., Ste. 309	(304)348-5220	BO
Clarksburg, WV 26301	168 W. Main St., 5th Fl.	(304)623-5631	DO
Harrisburg, PA 17101	100 Chestnut St., Ste. 309	(717)782-3840	BO
Philadelphia, PA 19004	231 St. Asaphs Rd., Ste. 640-W	(215)596-5889	RO
Philadelphia, PA 19004	231 St. Asaphs Rd., Ste. 400-E	(215)596-5889	DO
Pittsburgh, PA 15222	960 Penn Ave., 5th Fl.	(412)644-2780	DO
Richmond, VA 23240	400 N. 8th St., Rm. 3015	(804)771-2617	DO
Washington, DC 20036	1111 18th St. NW, 6th Fl.	(202)634-4950	DO
Wilkes-Barre, PA 18701	20 N. Pennsylvania Ave., Rm. 2327	(717)826-6497	BO
Wilmington, DE 19801	844 King St., Rm. 5207	(302)573-6294	BO
Southeast			
Atlanta, GA 30367	1375 Peachtree St. NE, 5th Fl.	(404)347-2797	RO
Atlanta, GA 30309	1720 Peachtree Rd. NW, 6th Fl.	(404)347-4749	DO
Atlanta, GA 30308	120 Ralph McGill St., 14th Fl.	(404)347-3771	DAO
Charlotte, NC 28202	222 S. Church St., Rm. 300	(704)371-6563	DO
Columbia, SC 29201	1835 Assembly St., Rm. 358	(803)765-5376	DO
Coral Gables, FL 33146	1320 S. Dixie Hwy., Ste. 501	(305)536-5521	DO
Jacksonville, FL 32202	400 W. Bay St., Rm. 261	(904)791-3782	DO
Statesboro, GA 30458	52 N. Main St., Rm. 225	(912)489-8719	POD
Tampa, FL 33602	700 Twiggs St., Rm. 607	(813)228-2594	POD
W. Palm Beach, FL 33407	3500 45th St., Ste. 6	(305)689-2223	POD
Midwest			
Cedar Rapids, IA 52402	373 Collins Rd. NE, Rm. 100	(319)399-2571	DO
Chicago, IL 60604	230 S. Dearborn St., Rm. 510	(312)353-0359	RO
Chicago, IL 60604	219 S. Dearborn St., Rm. 437	(312)353-4528	DO
Cincinnati, OH 45202	550 Main St., Rm. 5028	(513)684-2814	BO
Cleveland, OH 44199	1240 E. 9th St., Rm. 317	(216)522-4180	DO

City, State, Zip	Address	Phone	Type*
Midwest (continued)			
Columbus, OH 43215	85 Marconi Blvd., Rm. 512	(614)469-6860	DO
Des Moines, IA 50309	210 Walnut St., Rm. 749	(515)284-4422	DO
Detroit, MI 48226	477 Michigan Ave., Rm. 515	(313)226-6075	DO
Eau Claire, WI 54701	500 S. Barstow Commons, Rm. 17	(715)834-9012	POD
Indianapolis, IN 46204	575 N. Pennsylvania St., Rm. 578	(317)269-7272	DO
Kansas City, MO 64106	911 Walnut St., 13th Fl.	(816)374-5288	RO
Kansas City, MO 64106	1103 Grand Ave., 6th Fl.	(816)374-3419	DO
Madison, WI 53703	212 E. Washington Ave., Rm. 213	(608)264-5261	DO
Marquette, MI 49885	300 S. Front St.	(906)225-1108	BO
Milwaukee, WI 53203	310 W. Wisconsin Ave., Rm. 400	(414)291-3941	BO
Minneapolis, MN 55403	100 N. 6th St., Ste. 610	(612)349-3550	DO
Omaha, NE 68154	11145 Mill Valley Rd.	(402)221-4691	DO
St. Louis, MO 63101	815 Olive St., Rm. 242	(314)425-6600	DO
Springfield, IL 62701	4 N. Old State Capitol Plaza, 1st Fl.	(217)492-4416	BO
Springfield, MO 65805	309 N. Jefferson St., Rm. 150	(417)864-7670	BO
Wichita, KS 67202	110 E. Waterman St., 1st Fl.	(316)269-6571	DO
South			
Birmingham, AL 35203	2121 8th Ave. N, Ste. 200	(205)731-1344	DO
Gulfpot, MS 39501	One Hancock Plaza, Ste. 1001	(601)863-4449	BO
Jackson, MS 39269	100 W. Capitol St., Ste. 322	(601)965-0121	DO
Little Rock, AR 72201	320 W. Capitol Ave., Rm. 601	(501)378-5871	DO
Louisville, KY 40202	600 Federal Pl., Rm. 188	(502)582-5976	DO
Nashville, TN 37219	404 James Robertson Pkwy., Ste. 1012	(615)736-5881	DO
New Orleans, LA 70112	1661 Canal St., Ste. 2000	(504)589-6685	DO
Shreveport, LA 71101	500 Fannin St., Rm. 8A08	(318)226-5196	POD
Northwest			
Anchorage, AK 99513	8th & C Sts.	(907)271-4022	DO
Billings, MT 59101	2601 First Ave. N., Rm. 216	(406)657-6047	POD
Boise, ID 83702	1020 Main St., Ste. 290	(208)334-1696	DO
Casper, NY 82602	100 E. B St., Rm. 4001	(307)261-5761	DO
Fargo, ND 58102	657 2nd Ave. N., Rm. 218	(701)237-5771	DO
Helena, MT 59626	301 S. Park, Rm. 528	(406)449-5381	DO
Portland, OR 97204	1220 S.W. Third Ave., Rm. 676	(503)423-5221	DO
Seattle, WA 98121	2615 4th Ave., Rm. 440	(206)442-5676	RO
Seattle, WA 98174	915 Second Ave., Rm. 1792	(206)442-5534	DO
Sioux Falls, SD 57102	101 S. Main Ave., Ste. 101	(801)524-5800	DO
Spokane, WA 99201	W. 920 Riverside Ave., Rm. 651	(509)456-3783	DO
West			
Agana, GM 96910	Pacific Daily News Bldg., Rm. 508	(671)472-7277	BO
Denver, CO 80202	999 18th St., N. Tower	(303)294-7001	RO
Denver, CO 80202	721 19th St., Rm. 407	(303)844-2607	DO
Fresno, CA 93721	2202 Monterey St., Ste. 108	(209)487-5189	DO
Honolulu, HI 96850	300 Ala Moana, Rm. 2213	(808)541-2990	DO
Las Vegas, NV 89125	301 E. Stewart St., Rm. 301	(702)388-6611	DO
Los Angeles, CA 90071	350 S. Figueroa St., 6th Fl.	(213)894-2956	DO
Reno, NV 89505	50 S. Virginia St., Rm. 238	(702)784-5268	POD
Sacramento, CA 95814	660 J St., Rm. 215	(916)551-1445	BO
Sacramento, CA 95853	77 Cadillac Dr., Ste. 158	(916)978-4578	DAO
Salt Lake City, UT 84138	125 S. State St., Rm. 2237	(801)524-5800	DO
San Diego, CA 92188	880 Front St., Rm. 4829	(619)293-5440	DO
San Francisco, CA 94102	450 Golden Gate Ave.	(415)556-7487	RO
San Francisco, CA 94105	211 Main St., 4th Fl.	(415)974-0642	DO
Santa Ana, CA 92701	2700 N. Main St., Rm. 400	(714)836-2494	BO
Southwest			
Albuquerque, NM 87100	5000 Marble Ave. NE, Rm. 320	(505)262-6171	DO
Austin, TX 78701	300 E. 8th St., Rm. 520	(512)482-5288	POD
Corpus Christi, TX 78401	400 Main St., Ste. 403	(512)888-3331	BO
Dallas, TX 75235	8625 King George Dr., Bldg. C	(214)767-7643	RO
Dallas, TX 75242	1100 Commerce St., Rm. 3C36	(214)767-0605	DO
El Paso, TX 79935	10737 Gateway W., Ste. 320	(915)541-7586	DO
Fort Worth, TX 76102	819 Taylor St., Rm. 10A27	(817)334-3613	BO
Grand Prairie, TX 75051	2306 Oak Lane, Ste. 110	(214)767-7571	DAO
Harlingen, TX 78550	222 E. Van Buren St., Rm. 500	(512)427-8533	DO
Houston, TX 77054	2525 Murworth, Ste. 112	(713)660-4401	DO
Lubbock, TX 79401	1611 Tenth St., Ste. 200	(806)743-7462	DO
Marshall, TX 75670	505 E. Travis, Rm. 103	(214)935-5257	POD
Oklahoma City, OK 73102	200 N.W. 5th St., Ste. 670	(405)231-4301	DO

City, State, Zip	Address	Phone	Type*
Southwest (continued)			
Phoenix, AZ 85004	2005 N. Central Ave., 5th Fl.	(602)261-3732	DO
San Antonio, TX 78206	727 E. Durango St., Rm. A513	(512)229-6250	DO
Tucson, AZ 85701	300 W. Congress St., Box FB-33	(602)629-6715	POD
Caribbean			
Hato Rey, PR 00918	Carlos Chardon Ave., Rm. 691	(809)753-4002	DO
St. Croix, VI 00820	4C & 4D Este Sion Frm, Rm. 7	(809)773-3480	POD
St. Thomas, VI 00801	Veterans Dr., Rm. 210	(809)774-8530	POD

* Type: RO = regional office, DO = district office, BO = branch office, POD = post of duty, DAO = disaster area office.

Appendix II

Minority Business Development Agency Directory

Northeast

Office of Field Operations
New York Regional Office
26 Federal Plaza, Rm. 37-20
New York, NY 10278
(212)264-3262
FTS 264-3262

Boston District Office
10 Causeway St., Rm. 418
Boston, MA 02222
(617)835-6850
FTS 835-6850

Mid-Atlantic

Office of Field Operations
Washington Regional Office
14th and Constitution Aves. NW, Rm. 6711
Washington, D.C. 20230
(202)377-8275
FTS 377-8275

Philadelphia District Office
9436 Federal Office Bldg.
600 Arch St.
Philadelphia, PA 19106
FTS 597-9236

Pittsburgh District Office
614–16 Federal Office Bldg.
1000 Liberty Ave.
Pittsburgh, PA 15222
FTS 722-6659

South

Office of Field Operations
Atlanta Regional Office
1371 Peachtree St. NE, Ste. 505
Atlanta, GA 30309
(404)881-4091
FTS 257-4091

Miami District Office
928 Federal Office Bldg.
51 S.W. First Ave.
Miami, FL 33130
(305)350-5054
FTS 350-5054

Midwest

Office of Field Operations
Chicago Regional Office
55 E. Monroe St., Ste. 1440
Chicago, IL 60603
(312)353-0182
FTS 353-0182

West

Office of Field Operations
San Francisco Regional Office
221 Main Street, Room 1280
San Francisco, CA 94102
(415)974-9597
FTS 454-9597

Los Angeles District Office
2500 Wilshire Blvd., Ste. 908
Los Angeles, CA 90057
(213)894-7157
FTS 798-7157

Southwest

Office of Field Operations
Dallas Regional Office
1100 Commerce St., Rm. 7B23
Dallas, TX 75242
(214)767-8001
FTS 729-8001

Appendix III

Small Business Organizations and Contacts

There are many organizations throughout the nation that represent small business interests. The following list of general small business organizations is by no means exhaustive but does represent several of the major organizations that deal with the federal government on a regular and ongoing basis.

Center for Small Business
Chamber of Commerce of the United States
1615 H St. NW
Washington DC 20062
(202)659-6180

Coalition of Small and Independent Business Assoc.
Council of Smaller Enterprises
690 The Huntingdon Bldg.
Cleveland, OH 44115
(216)621-3300

Independent Business Assoc. of Wisconsin
7635 Bluemound Rd.
Milwaukee, WI 53214
(414)258-7055

National Assoc. of Small Business Investment Cos.
618 Washington Bldg.
Washington, DC 20005
(202)638-3411

National Business League
4324 Georgia Ave. NW
Washington, DC 20011
(202)829-5900

National Economic Development Assoc.
1636 R St. NW
Washington, DC 20009
(202)232-1666

National Federation of Independent Business
490 L'Enfant Plaza East SW, Ste. 3206
Washington, DC 20024
(202)554-9000

National Small Business Assoc.
1604 K St. NW
Washington, DC 20006
(202)296-7400

New York Assoc. of Small Business Councils
1500 One MONY Plaza
Syracuse, NY 13202
(315)422-1343

Smaller Business Assoc. of New England
69 Hickory Dr.
Waltham, MA 02994
(617)890-9070

Smaller Manufacturers Council
339 Boulevard of the Allies
Pittsburgh, PA 15222
(412)391-1622

Appendix IV

Business Services Directory

Office of Business Liaison

The Office of Business Liaison informs the business community of department and administration resources, policies, and programs; informs department and administration officials of the critical issues facing the business community; promotes private-sector involvement in departmental policymaking and program development; and guides individuals and firms through the channels of the federal government through the Business Assistance Program.

Office of the Director	(202)377-3942
Outreach Program	(202)377-1360
Business Assistance Program	(202)377-3176

Bureau of the Census

The Census Bureau produces detailed statistical information for the nation. Information is available on population, housing, agriculture, manufacturing, retail trade, service industries, wholesale trade, foreign trade, mining, transportation, construction, and the revenues and expenditures of state and local governments. The Bureau also produces statistical studies of many foreign countries.

User Services

General Information	(301)763-4100
Data User Training	(301)763-1510
Geographic Information	(301)763-5270
Product Information (print, map)	(301)763-4100
Map Orders	(812)288-3212

Government, Commerce, and Industry Subjects

Agriculture Data	(301)763-1113
Business Data (retail, wholesale, services)	(301)763-7564
Construction Statistics	(301)763-7163
Government Data	(301)763-7366
Industry Data	(301)763-7800
Manufacturers' Data	(301)763-7666

Population, Housing, and Income Subjects

Housing Data	(301)763-2881
International Statistics	(301)763-2870
Neighborhood Statistics (1980 Census)	(301)763-2358
Population Data (age, race, income, education, etc.)	(301)763-5020
Special Demographic Studies	(301)763-7720

Government, Commerce, and Civic Relations

	(301)763-2436

Regional Assistance

Atlanta, GA	(404)347-2274
Boston, MA	(617)223-0226
Charlotte, NC	(704)371-6144
Chicago, IL	(312)353-0980
Dallas, TX	(214)767-0625
Denver, CO	(303)234-3924
Detroit, MI	(313)226-7742
Kansas City, KS	(913)236-3731
Los Angeles, CA	(213)209-6612
New York, NY	(212)264-3860
Philadelphia, PA	(215)597-8313
Seattle, WA	(206)442-7080
For a detailed telephone contact list	(301)763-2436

Bureau of Economic Analysis

The Bureau of Economic Analysis measures and analyzes U.S. economic activity. Its economic accounts provide basic information on economic growth, inflation, regional development, and the nation's role in the world economy.

Public Information Office	(202)523-0777
National Income and Wealth Division (gross national product, price measures, personal income, corporate profits)	(202)523-0669
Statistical Indicators Division (composite indexes of leading, coincident, and lagging indicators)	(202)523-0535
Business Outlook Division (survey of plant and equipment expenditures)	(202)523-0874
Interindustry Economics Division (input–output accounts)	(202)523-0683
Regional Economic Measurement Division (projections of state, county, and SMSA personal income and employment)	(202)523-0966
Balance of Payments Division (estimates of international transactions)	(202)523-0620
International Investment Division (survey of U.S. direct investment abroad and foreign direct investment in the United States)	(202)523-0547

National Technical Information Service

National Technical Information Service (NTIS) disseminates technical information to the public. Through NTIS, businesses, educators, state and local governments and private individuals can buy the products of government-sponsored research. Technical documents, software, data files, and varying levels of intellectual properties are sold to national and international interests.

General Information	(703)487-4600
Document Orders	(703)487-4650
Rush Handling	(703)487-4700
Toll Free	(800)336-4700
Subscriptions	(703)487-4630
Customer Service	(703)487-4660
Database Services	(703)487-4805

Government Inventions and Patents	(703)487-4732
International Affairs	(703)487-4820
Washington, D.C. Bookstore	(202)377-0365
Accounting	(703)487-4770
Telecopier of 3M Facsimile Service	(703)321-8547

Office of Productivity, Technology, and Innovation

Office of Productivity and Innovation seeks to improve public policies that advance private-sector productivity, technological innovation, and competition.

Public Affairs	(202)377-0944
General Policy Issues	(202)377-1091
Productivity Issues and Human Resources. (Compares models for interfirm productivity.)	(202)377-2058
Commerce Productivity Center. (Improves productivity.)	(202)377-0940
Commercialization of Federal Technology. (Business access to federally funded technology.)	(202)377-0659
Industrial Technology Partnerships. (Counsels on R&D limited partnerships and cooperative R&D.)	(202)377-5913
International Joint Ventures. (Promotes bilateral and multilateral formation.)	(202)377-0944
Sensitivity Analysis. (Recommends new technologies.)	(202)377-0661
Metric Information	(202)377-0944
Small Technology-Based Businesses/State and Local Governments. (Recommends technological innovation models for economic development.)	(202)377-8111

Economic Development Administration

The Economic Development Administration provides financial and technical assistance to economically distressed areas of the nation in order to stimulate economic growth and create jobs.

Public Affairs	(202)377-5113

Regional Office Assistance

Philadelphia, PA	(215)597-4603

Connecticut, Delaware, District of Columbia, Maine, Maryland, Massachusetts, New Hampshire, New Jersey, New York, Pennsylvania, Puerto Rico, Rhode Island, Vermont, Virginia, Virgin Islands, and West Virginia

Atlanta, Georgia	(404)881-7401

Alabama, Florida, Georgia, Kentucky, Mississippi, North Carolina, South Carolina, and Tennessee

Denver, Colorado	(303)844-4714

Colorado, Iowa, Kansas, Missouri, Montana, Nebraska, North Dakota, South Dakota, Utah, and Wyoming

Chicago, Illinois	(312)353-7707

Illinois, Indiana, Michigan, Minnesota, Ohio, and Wisconsin

Seattle, Washington	(206)442-0596

Alaska, American Samoa, Arizona, California, Guam, Hawaii, Idaho, Nevada, Oregon, and Washington

Austin, Texas	(512)482-5461

Arkansas, Louisiana, New Mexico, Oklahoma, and Texas

International Trade Administration

The International Trade Administration (ITA) provides a broad array of programs and services developed to help American companies get started in exporting or expand export operations of manufactured goods, nonagricultural commodities, and services. The agency also participates in formulating and implementing U.S. foreign trade and economic policies. It assures that exports of U.S. high technology equipment and data are controlled in accordance with national security, short supply, and foreign-policy objectives and guards against illegal diversion of exports. In addition, ITA administers legislation that helps U.S. industry and labor counter unfair foreign trade practices.

Public Affairs	(202)377-3808

ITA services and activities fall within four operating units:

THE U.S. AND FOREIGN COMMERCIAL SERVICE—the framework within which ITA gathers accurate and timely commercial information, distributes it through a worldwide network of trade specialists, and provides in-depth counseling, assistance, and support to the business community:

Headquarters	(202)377-5777
Caribbean Basin Business Information Center	(202)377-2527
Domestic Operations	(202)377-4767
Export Counseling	(202)377-3181
Export Promotion Services:	
Foreign Market Analysis and Contact Programs	(202)377-1468
Trade Event Programs	(202)377-4231
Foreign Operations	(202)377-1599
Alabama—Birmingham	(205)264-1331
Alaska—Anchorage	(907)271-5041
Arizona—Phoenix	(602)261-3285
Arkansas—Little Rock	(501)378-5794
California—Los Angeles	(213)209-6707
*California—Santa Ana	(714)836-2461
California—San Diego	(619)293-5395
California—San Francisco	(415)556-5860
Colorado—Denver	(303)844-3246
Connecticut—Hartford	(203)722-3530
Florida—Miami	(305)536-5267
*Florida—Clearwater	(813)461-0011
*Florida—Jacksonville	(904)791-2796
*Florida—Orlando	(305)425-1234
*Florida—Tallahassee	(904)488-6469
Georgia—Atlanta	(404)881-7000
Georgia—Savannah	(912)944-4204
Hawaii—Honolulu	(808)546-8694
*Idaho—Boise	(208)334-2470
Illinois—Chicago	(312)353-4450
*Illinois—Palatine	(312)397-3000 ext.532
Illinois—Rockford	(815)987-8100
Indiana—Indianapolis	(317)269-6214
Iowa—Des Moines	(515)284-4222
*Kansas—Wichita	(316)269-6160
Kentucky—Louisville	(502)582-5066
Louisiana—New Orleans	(504)589-6546
*Maine—Augusta	(207)622-8249
Maryland—Baltimore	(301)962-3560
*Maryland—Rockville	(301)251-2345
Massachusetts—Boston	(617)223-2312
Michigan—Detroit	(313)226-3650
*Michigan—Grand Rapids	(616)456-2411
Minnesota—Minneapolis	(612)349-3338
Mississippi—Jackson	(601)965-4388
Missouri—Kansas City	(816)374-3142
Missouri—St. Louis	(314)425-3302
Nebraska—Omaha	(402)221-3664
Nevada—Reno	(702)784-5203
*New Jersey—Trenton	(609)896-4222
New Mexico—Albuquerque	(505)766-2386
New York—Buffalo	(716)846-4191
New York—New York	(212)264-0634
*New York—Rochester	(716)263-6480
North Carolina—Greensboro	(919)378-5345
Ohio—Cincinnati	(513)684-2944
Ohio—Cleveland	(216)522-4750
Oklahoma—Oklahoma City	(405)231-5302
*Oklahoma—Tulsa	(918)581-7650
Oregon—Portland	(503)221-3001
Pennsylvania—Philadelphia	(215)597-2866
Pennsylvania—Pittsburgh	(412)644-2850
Puerto Rico—San Juan	(809)753-4555
*Rhode Island—Providence	(401)528-5104 ext. 22
South Carolina—Columbia	(803)765-5345

District Offices (continued)

South Carolina—Charleston	(803)724-4361
*Tennessee—Memphis	(901)521-4137
Tennessee—Nashville	(615)736-5161
*Texas—Austin	(512)472-5059
Texas—Dallas	(214)767-0542
Texas—Houston	(713)229-2578
Utah—Salt Lake City	(801)524-5116
Virginia—Richmond	(804)771-2246
Washington—Seattle	(206)442-5616
*Washington—Spokane	(509)456-4557
West Virginia—Charleston	(304)347-5123
Wisconsin—Milwaukee	(414)291-3473

*Denotes Branch Office

TRADE DEVELOPMENT—the industry unit responsible for formulating trade policy and promotion activities:

Headquarters	(202)377-1461
Aerospace	(202)377-8228
Automotive	(202)377-0554
Chemicals and Allied Products	(202)377-0128
Consumer Goods	(202)377-0337
Computer and Business Equipment	(202)377-0572
Energy	(202)377-1466
Export Trading Companies	(202)377-5131
Forest Products and Domestic Construction	(202)377-0384
General Industrial Machinery	(202)377-5455
Instrumentation	(202)377-5466
Medical Services	(202)377-0550
Major Projects and International Construction	(202)377-5225
Metals, Minerals, and Commodities	(202)377-0575
Micro Electronics & Instrumentation	(202)377-2587
Service Industries	(202)377-3575
Special Industrial Machinery	(202)377-0302
Telecommunications	(202)377-4466
Textiles	(202)377-5078
Trade Information Analysis	(202)377-1316
Export Statistics and Trade Data (Foreign)	(202)377-4211
Export Statistics and Trade Data (Domestic)	(202)377-4211

INTERNATIONAL ECONOMIC POLICY—the office organized on a country and regional basis which gives market-specific counsel to American business:

Headquarters	(202)377-3022
GATT Divison	(202)377-3681
International Organizations	(202)377-3227

U.S. Trade by Region

Africa	(202)377-2175
Canada	(202)377-3643
	or 0849
Caribbean Basin & Mexico	(202)377-2527
Eastern Europe	(202)377-2645
European Community	(202)377-5276
Israel Information Center	(202)377-4652
Japan	(202)377-4527
Near East	(202)377-4441
Pacific Basin	(202)377-3875
Peoples Republic of China and Hong Kong	(202)377-3583
South America	(202)377-2436
South Asia	(202)377-2954
U.S.S.R	(202)377-4655
Western Europe	(202)377-5341

TRADE ADMINISTRATION—the office responsible for safeguarding the national interest through effective administration of U.S. trade laws:

Headquarters	(202)377-1455
Export Administration	(202)377-5491
Emergency Licensing Requests	(202)377-2752
	or 4811

License Status	(202)377-2752
Publications	(202)377-8731
Seminars	(202)377-8731
Trade Fair Licenses	(202)377-4811
Regulations and Policy Information	(202)377-4811
Export Enforcement	(202)377-8252
Anti-Boycott Compliance	(202)377-2381
Field Offices:	
California—Los Angeles	(818)904-6019
California—San Jose	(408)466-4204
New York—New York	(212)264-3950
Virginia—Springfield	(703)487-4950
Import Administration	(202)377-1780

Quick Reference List

Aeronautical Chart Sales	(301)436-6990
Business Assistance	(202)377-3176
Commerce Speakers	(202)377-1360
Copyright Information*	(202)287-8700
Consumer Information	(202)377-5001
District Export Councils	(202)377-4767
Energy-Related Inventions, Evaluation	(301)975-4000
Export	
Counseling	(202)377-3181
Export Trading Companies	(202)377-5131
License/Application	(202)377-4811
Fish Exports/Imports	(202)673-5478
Fishery Management Plans	(202)673-5263
Foreign Trade Zones	(202)377-2862
Freight Rates**	(202)426-5812
Industry/Products Information	(202)377-1461
Metric Information	(202)377-0944
Micro Computer Information Exchange	(301)948-5717
Minority-Owned Business	(202)377-8015
Nautical Chart Sales	(301)436-6990
NTIS Sales Desk	(703)487-4650
Overseas Customer Lists	(202)377-3022
Overseas Marketing	(202)377-3022
Overseas Trade Fairs	(202)377-8220
Patent & Trademark Information	(703)557-3080
Productivity Enhancement Information	(202)377-0940
Procurement	
Bidder's List	(202)377-3387
Commerce Buy List	(202)377-3387
MBDA Profile System	(202)377-2414
NOAA Opportunities	(202)377-1537
Small Business	(202)377-1472
Women-Owned Business	(202)377-1472
Federal Procurement Conferences	(202)377-2975
Publications	
"Business America" Magazine	(202)377-3251
Commerce Business Daily	(202)377-4868
Domestic Economic Development	(202)377-5113
NBS Reference Materials	(301)975-2012
NTIA Publication Information	(202)377-1551
Sea Grant Research	(301)443-8923
Small Business	
Assistance	(202)377-3176
Procurement/Set Asides	(202)377-1472
Standards & Codes for Products	(301)975-4036
Statistics	
Business Cycles	(202)523-0535
Capital Investment	(202)523-0874
Gross National Product	(202)523-0669
Foreign Travelers to U.S.	(202)377-0140
Housing Starts	(301)763-5731
Income Data	(301)763-5020
International Trade Balance	(202)523-0620
Personal Income by County	(202)523-0951
Population	(301)763-5020
Price Indexes	(202)523-0828
Retail Trade Data	(301)763-4100
Trade Statistics	(202)377-2185
Technology	
International Joint Ventures	(202)377-0944
National Joint Ventures	(202)377-5914

Small Business	(202)377-8111
Time of Day	(303)499-7111
Travel	
"America, Catch the Spirit."	(202)377-4752
Tourism Information (Inbound)	(202)377-4752
Weather	
Climate for Farming	(301)763-4690
Forecast	
U.S. Eastern Cities	(301)899-3244
U.S. Western Cities	(301)899-3249
Past Conditions	(202)673-5381
Tide & Water Levels	(301)443-8441
Women-Owned Business	(202)377-1472

  * Handled by the Library of Congress
 ** Handled by the Maritime Commission

Minority Business Development Agency

Minority Business Development Agency (MBDA) provides an array of management, marketing, financial, and technical assistance to the nation's minority businesses through business development centers, minority business trade organizations, and MBDA research and field offices.

Public Affairs	(202)377-1936
Enterprise Development (Minority Business Development Centers, Indian Business, and Rural Business Assistance)	(202)377-3816
Resource Development (Minority Business Trade Associations, state and local governments)	(202)377-5770
Advocacy, Research, and Information	(202)377-3163
Field Operations	(202)377-8015
Atlanta, GA	(404)257-4091
Chicago, IL	(312)353-0182
Dallas, TX	(214)767-8001
New York, NY	(212)264-3262
San Francisco, CA	(415)974-9597
Washington, DC	(202)377-8275

National Bureau of Standards

The National Bureau of Standards is the nation's measurement laboratory for industry, science, and technology.

General Information	(301)975-2000
Research and Technology Applications	(301)975-3088
Industrial Research Associate Program	(301)975-3087
Information Resource and Services Division	(301)975-2786
Publication and Program Inquiries	(301)975-3058
Product Standards Policy	(301)975-4000
Standards and Codes Information. (Custom searches identify pertinent codes and standards from a database of 240,000 documents.)	(301)975-4029
Laboratory Accreditation	(301)975-4016
Weights and Measures	(301)975-4004
General Agreement on Tariffs and Trade (GATT)	(301)975-4023
Contracting Office	(301)975-6336
Purchasing Office	(301)975-6351
Small Business Specialist	(301)975-6343
Standard Reference Materials. (Materials characteristics for physical or chemical properties or composition.)	(301)975-2027
Standards Reference Data. (Physical and chemical data for industrial design, energy, environment, and health applications.)	(301)975-2208
Physical Measurement Services. (Calibration of standards and test instruments for measuring quantities such as density, electrical quantities, optical, mechanical, radiation, and thermal quantities.)	(301)975-2007
Center for Radiation Research. (Methods, calibrations, and products essential to the measurement of radiation for health care, nuclear energy, radiation processing, and radiation safety.)	(301)975-6093
Center for Chemical Physics. (Measurement methods and services for industry in surface science, molecular spectroscopy, chemical kinetics, and thermodynamics.)	(301)975-2500

Center for Analytical Chemistry. (Measurement methods and services for analysis of chemicals in medicine, energy, and pollution control.)	(301)975-3145
Institute for Materials Science and Engineering. (Measurement methods and services to evaluate materials such as gases, ceramics, metals, and polymers; failures and substitution questions.)	(301)975-5659
Institute for Computer Sciences and Technology	(301)975-2822
Center for Programming Science and Technology. (Standards and guidelines related for programming languages, software engineering, data management, computer security, and systems selection and evaluation.)	(301)975-3240
Center for Computer Systems Engineering. (Standards and guidelines related to computer system components, computer network protocols, local and area networks, and computer-based office systems.)	(301)975-2904
Office of Energy-Related Inventions. (Inventions evaluated for technical validity and commercial feasibility.)	(301)975-4000
Law Enforcement Standards Laboratory. (Technical data for standards used by law enforcement officials to evaluate commercial products.)	(301)975-2757
Center for Applied Mathematics. (Statistical models, computational methods, math tables, handbooks, and manuals.)	(301)975-2732
Center for Electronics and Electrical Engineering. (Engineering data, measurement methods, standards, and technical services.)	(301)975-2220
Center for Manufacturing Engineering. (Basic metrology, automation, and control support for discrete part manufacturers and others.)	(301)975-3400
Center for Building Technology. (Performance criteria and measurement technology for building owners, occupants, designers, builders, manufacturers, and regulatory authorities.)	(301)975-5903
Center for Fire Research. (Engineering data, methods, and practices, measurement and test methods for fire safety.)	(301)975-4600
Center for Chemical Engineering. (Measurement data, standards, and services for fluids, solids, and gases.)	(303)497-5108

National Oceanic and Atmospheric Administration

The National Oceanic and Atmospheric Administration conducts research and gathers data about the oceans, atmosphere, space, and sun.

Under Secretary for National Oceanic and Atmospheric Administration	(202)377-3436
Legislative Affairs	(202)377-4981
Constituent Affairs	(202)377-5118
Business Contact	(202)377-1537
Congressional Affairs	(202)377-4981

Major line organizations within NOAA include:

National Marine Fisheries Service

Public Affairs	(202)673-5445
Constituent Affairs, Enforcement, Fishery Industry Services, International Fishery Programs, Protected Marine Species, Habitat Conservation Programs, Fishery Management Plans	(202)763-5429

National Weather Service

Public Affairs	(301)427-7622
Industrial Meteorology, Meteorological Services, Marine Services, Natural Hazard Awareness, Agricultural Services, Climate Analysis Center	(301)427-7258

National Ocean Service

Public Affairs	(202)377-8090
Constituent Affairs	(301)443-8031

Nautical & Aeronautical Chart Sales, Nautical Chart Information, Aeronautical Chart Information, Aerial Photographs, Geodetic Information Center, Tides & Water Level Services, Ocean Services, National Marine Pollution Program, Diving Program, Coastal Zone Programs, Marine & Estuarine Programs, Ocean Minerals &
Energy   (301)436-6990

National Environmental Satellite, Data, and Information Service

Public Affairs	(202)377-8090
	or (301)763-4690

Constituent Affairs, Data Collection & Direct Broadcast, Landsat Customer Services, Retrospective Satellite Data Services, Oceanographic Data Services, Geological and Solar-Terrestrial Data Services, Climate Data Services, Climate Impact Assessment, Research & Technology Applications

(301)763-7820

Oceanic & Atmospheric Research

Public Affairs	(202)377-8090

Constituent Affairs, Sea Grant Program, University Affairs
(301)443-8344

Environmental Research Laboratory (ERL) Boulder, Colorado: Public Affairs, Solar Flare & Proton Event Forecasting
(303)497-6286

National Telecommunications and Information Administration

National Telecommunications and Information Administration is the President's principal adviser on domestic and international telecommunications policy.

Assistant Secretary	(202)377-1840
Public Affairs	(202)377-1551
International Affairs	(202)377-1866
Policy Analysis & Development	(202)377-1880
Policy Coordination & Management	(202)377-1800
Spectrum Management	(202)377-1850
Telecommunications Applications	(202)377-5802
Telecommunication Research	(303)497-3484

Office of Consumer Affairs

The Office of Consumer Affairs works to improve companies' customer relations and the quality of goods and services.

Office of the Director	(202)377-5001

Office of Small and Disadvantaged Business Utilization

The Office of Small and Disadvantaged Business Utilization advocates the use of small and/or disadvantaged businesses as well as women-owned businesses for fulfilling the procurement needs of the Department of Commerce.

Office of the Director	(202)377-3387

Patent & Trademark Office

General Information	(703)557-3080
Public Affairs	(703)557-3341
International Patents & Trademarks	(703)557-3065
Patent Public Search Room	(703)557-2276
Trademark Public Search Room	(703)557-3281

Regional Assistance

Patent Depository Libraries

General Information	(800)368-2532

The libraries listed receive current issues of the U.S. patents and maintain backfile collections of earlier-issued patents. These collections vary from library to library. All libraries offer CASSIS (Classification and Search Support Information System), which provides direct, on-line access to Patent & Trademark Office data.

Alabama

Auburn University Libraries	(205)826-4500
	Ext. 21
Birmingham Public Library	(205)226-3680

Alaska

Anchorage Municipal Libraries	(907)264-4481

Arizona

Tempe: Science Library, Arizona State University	(602)965-7607

Arkansas

Little Rock: Arkansas State Library	(501)371-2090

California

Los Angeles Public Library	(213)612-3273
Sacramento: California State Library	(916)322-4572
San Diego Public Library	(619)236-5813
Sunnyvale: Patent Information Clearinghouse	(408)738-5580

Colorado

Denver Public Library	(303)571-2122

Delaware

Newark: University of Delaware Library	(302)738-2238

Florida

Fort Lauderdale: Broward County Main Library	(305)357-7444
Miami-Dade Public Library	(305)579-5001

Georgia

Atlanta: Price Gilbert Memorial Library, Georgia Institute of Technology	(404)894-4508

Idaho

Moscow: University of Idaho Library	(208)885-6235

Illinois

Chicago Public Library	(312)269-2865
Springfield: Illinois State Library	(217)782-5430

Indiana

Indianapolis-Marion County Public Library	(317)269-1706

Louisiana

Baton Rouge: Troy H. Middleton Library, Louisiana State University	(504)388-2570

Maryland

College Park: Engineering and Physical Sciences Library, University of Maryland	(301)454-3037

Massachusetts

Amherst: Physical Sciences Library, University of Massachusetts	(413)545-1370
Boston Public Library	(617)536-5400
	Ext. 265

Michigan

Ann Arbor: Engineering Transportation Library, University of
   Michigan   (313)764-7494
Detroit Public Library   (313)833-1450

Minnesota

Minneapolis Public Library & Information
   Center   (612)372-6570

Missouri

Kansas City: Linda Hall Library   (816)363-4600
St. Louis Public Library   (314)241-2288
                                Ext. 390

Montana

Butte: Montana College of Mineral Science and Technology
   Library   (406)496-4283

Nebraska

Lincoln: University of Nebraska-Lincoln, Engineering Library
                             (402)472-3411

Nevada

Reno: University of Nevada Library   (702)784-6579

New Hampshire

Durham: University of New Hampshire Library (603)862-1777

New Jersey

Newark Public Library   (201)733-7815

New Mexico

Albuquerque: University of New Mexico
   Library   (505)277-5441

New York

Albany: New York State Library   (518)474-5125
Buffalo and Erie County Public Library (716)856-7525
                                Ext. 267
New York Public Library   (212)714-8529

North Carolina

Raleigh: D.H. Hill Library, N.C. State
   University   (919)737-3280

Ohio

Cincinnati & Hamilton County, Public Library (513)369-6936
Cleveland Public Library   (216)623-2870
Columbus: Ohio State University   (614)422-6286
Toledo/Lucas County Public Library (419)255-7055
                                Ext. 212

Oklahoma

Stillwater: Oklahoma State University Library (405)624-6546

Oregon

Salem: Oregon State Library   (503)378-4277

Pennsylvania

Cambridge Springs: Alliance College Library (814)398-2098
Philadelphia: Franklin Institute Library (215)448-1227

Pittsburgh: Carnegie Library of Pittsburgh (412)622-3138
University Park: Pattee Library, Pennsylvania State University
                             (814)865-4861

Rhode Island

Providence Public Library   (401)521-8726

South Carolina

Charleston: Medical University of South Carolina Library
                             (803)792-2372

Tennessee

Memphis & Shelby County Public Library and Information
   Center   (901)725-8876

Texas

Austin: McKinney Engineering Library, University of Texas
                             (512)471-1610
College Station: Sterling C. Evans Library, Texas A&M
   University   (409)845-2551
Dallas Public Library   (214)749-4176
Houston: The Fondren Library, Rice University (713)527-8101
                              Ext.2587

Utah

Salt Lake City: Marriott Library, University
   of Utah   (801)581-8394

Washington

Seattle: Engineering Library, University of Washington
                             (206)543-0740

Wisconsin

Madison: Kurt F. Wendt Engineering Library, University of
   Wisconsin   (608)262-6845
Milwaukee Public Library   (414)278-3247

United States Travel and Tourism Administration

This office is designed to develop and carry out a comprehensive
program to stimulate travel to the United States by residents
of foreign countries. In order to increase U.S. exports of goods
and services through tourism, USTTA works to increase foreign
demand, remove barriers, encourage small- and medium-size
exporters. Additionally, USTTA provides accurate and timely
statistics and data, forms partnerships with state and local
governments, and develops international marketing strategies
for the private and public sector.

Under Secretary for Travel and Tourism   (202)377-0136
Tourism Marketing. (Develops cooperative advertising and
   promotion activities; conducts travel trade shows, seminars,
   familiarization tours and missions; operates consumer
   information centers.)   (202)377-4752
Field Operations. (International congress and regional offices
   in Australia, Japan, Canada, Mexico, France, West
   Germany, and the United Kingdom.)   (202)377-4554
Policy and Planning   (202)377-5211
Research. (Compiles foreign visitor arrival and expenditure
   statistics.)   (202)377-4028

Appendix V

Small Business Administration Business Plan and Qualifications Résumé

(Each item should be completed, if none or not applicable so state).

I. Firm Identification:

Name _____

Trade Name _____

Address _____

         Street   P.O. Box

_____

       City   County   State   Zip

Business Phone _____ _____ Home Phone _____ _____

      Area code   Number   Area Code   Number

Type of Business _____ SIC Code _____

Employees Identification Number _____ Tax Exemption No. _____

Number of Employees: _____ as of _____

Indicate if supply, service, construction or concession _____

Month and Year Business Established _____

Fiscal Year Ends _____

Is concern organized for profit?   Yes ☐   No ☐

Is concern associated in any way with a non-profit organization?

                    Yes ☐   No ☐

If yes, specify name of non-profit organization and the nature of the association ____

_____

_____

Does concern and affiliates meet small business size standard as defined in Part 121 SBA Rules and Regulations?   Yes ☐   No ☐

If answer is *no*, Divestitute Agreement must be submitted.

II. List other types and locations of business in which firm is or has recently been engaged.

Types of Business: _____

Address of Facility: _____

_____

Presently Operating: Yes ☐   No ☐   If operating, how long? _____

III. Ownership:

A. Type of Ownership

      Sole Proprietorship ☐

      Partnership ☐   (Attach copy of partnership agreement.)

Corporation ☐ (Attach copy of certificate from Secretary of State, Articles of State, Articles of Incorporation, and By-Laws.)

If corporation: Total no. of shares authorized: _____

Total no. of shares issued: _____

B. Is concern owned and controlled by one or more persons who have been deprived of the opportunity to develop and maintain a competitive position in the economy because of social or economic disadvantages? Yes ☐ No ☐

C. Name and address of all stockholders and/or partners and their ethnic identification; i.e., Aleuts, Black American, Eskimo, Indian, Oriental, Spanish-American, White American, etc.

Name	Address	*Number and Class of Shares	Office Held	Ethnic Ident.
_____	_____	_____	_____	_____
_____	_____	_____	_____	_____
_____	_____	_____	_____	_____
_____	_____	_____	_____	_____
_____	_____	_____	_____	_____
_____	_____	_____	_____	_____

[1] Attach copy of Stock Certificate(s) issued.

D. Attach copy of all Divestiture and/or Ownership Agreements.

E. Attach personal financial statement on above principals (SBA Form 413 may be used to submit this statement).

F. SBA Form 912, "Statement of Personal History" must be completed according to the instructions contained therein and submitted with this Business Plan and Qualifications Resume.

G. Show names of social and/or economic disadvantaged persons listed in III C above. Give a narrative summary of cultural, social, chronic economic circumstances and background on each to support disadvantaged status. (Continue on separate sheet as necessary.)

Name: _____
Narrative Summary:

Name: _____
Narrative Summary:

Name: _____
Narrative Summary:

Name: _____
Narrative Summary:

H. List all entities that owners, directors, officers, partners and managers of applicant have a financial interest in or hold a management or board position. If none, so state.

Name of Entity	Name of Person	Position Held	% or Ownership
_____	_____	_____	_____
_____	_____	_____	_____
_____	_____	_____	_____
_____	_____	_____	_____

I.   Have any of the above firms received or applied for 8(a) approval:

Yes ☐   No ☐   If yes, identify _____

VI.   Company History: (Narrative of purpose chronological development, problems and successes).

V.   Product or Service: (Narrative of characteristics, uses and applicability to commercial market. Nature of work performed with own forces, area of operations).

VI.   A.   Management: (A copy of this form must be completed by all directors, officers and senior management personnel.)

1.   Name: _____   2.   Age ____   3.   Sex ____

4.   Marital Status _____   5.   Social Security Number _____

6.   Military Serial Number _____

7.   Present Position: (Include description of duties)

8.   Other jobs and positions held and salaries.

9.   Formal schooling

10.   Technical training and qualifications

11.   Management training

12.   Military Experience

(a)   Branch of   Place of   Period of   MOS   Rank
      Service   Service   Service

      _____   _____   _____   ____   _____

      _____   _____   _____   ____   _____

    (b) Service Schools attended and date of attendance

            _____

            _____

            _____

  B. List professional, management and technical resource support to be received by your company. (Attach copies of all Management and Technical Support Agreements.)

Name	Address	Phone	Service Performed	Compensation to Be Paid
____	____	____	____	____
____	____	____	____	____
____	____	____	____	____
____	____	____	____	____

  C. Diagram Organizational Chart of Firm.

VII. **Marketing:**
    A. **Market Area:**

    B. **Market Potential:**

    C. **Commercial Customers:**

    D. **Government Customers:** (Include name and phone number of contracting officers and small business specialist contacted).

    E. **Competitors**

    F. **Advantage over Competitors**

    G. **Pricing and Bidding Procedures** (attach sample of pricing and bidding documents)

    H. **Sales Forecast by Product or Service Category**

    I. **Sales and Distribution Plan** (Including advertising pricing, credit terms, etc.):

    J. **Business Plan Graph** (Reflect commercial and non 8(a) government sales, 8(a) projected support, and break-even point).

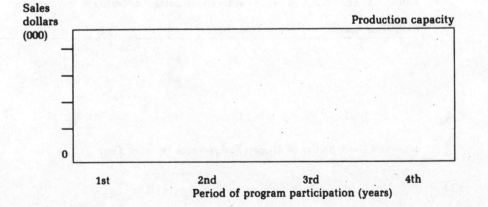

K. Break-Even chart (Reflect income from sales, fixed cost, variable cost and break-even point).

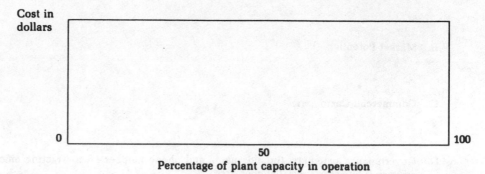

Cost in
dollars

0   50   100

Percentage of plant capacity in operation

VIII. Production:
A. Plant: (Include location, total square footage, and layout and sketch of office and storage areas. Also include copy of lease deed or proposed lease).

B. Equipment:

Quantity	Description	Age	Buying or Leasing	Cost

C. Equipment Layout and Production Flow Plan:

D. Supervisory Personnel (names and responsibilities):

E. Labor Skill and Source (detailed list by classification, number and pay rate):

Skill Classification	Number	Pay Rate	Source

F. Materials Used, Source of Supply, and Average Delivery Time:

L. Licenses and Certificates in Effect:

Type	Amount	Place of Issue
_____	_____	_____
_____	_____	_____
_____	_____	_____

M. List trade association and other organizations of which company is a member.

N. Labor Agreements in effect.

O. Contracts with suppliers

P. List law suits in force or pending

Q. Patents, royalties, etc.

R. Product research and development

S. Annual sales volume in dollars required for company to breakeven. $____

VII. Statement of Cooperation:
I understand that if approved for participation in the 8(a) Program I will assume certain obligations as listed below. I understand and agree that if I do not meet these obligations, Small Business Administration may, in its sole discretion, remove me from further participation. I further understand that SBA cannot assure the availability of 8(a) contracts to my company, either now or in the future.

I pledge to use my best efforts to develop my business by actively soliciting business (either commercial or competitive Federal) in accordance with the projections made in my business plan.

I pledge to provide SBA with timely and accurate financial information which will consist of at least quarterly profit or loss statements and quarterly balance sheet. The income from 8(a) contracts is to be shown separately from other income. If requested, I will provide such other information as may be required.

H.   List of Loans or Loan Guarantees Provided by the Small Business Administration:

Names and Address of Lender	Loan Number	Original Amount of Loan	Amount Outstanding
_____	_____	_____	_____
_____	_____	_____	_____
_____	_____	_____	_____

I.   Outline of Business Goals: (Necessary to become competitive)

Annual Sales $_____   Current Ratio_____ to_____

Annual Profits $_____   Debt to Net_____ to_____
                                         Worth Ratio

Bondability $_____   Estimated number of_____ to_____
                                         years to become competitive

J.   Additional Equipment Necessary to Conduct Competitive Business:

Description	Purchase Cost	Lease Cost
_____	$_____	$_____
_____	$_____	$_____
_____	$_____	$_____
_____	$_____	$_____
_____	$_____	$_____
_____	$_____	$_____
_____	$_____	$_____
_____	$_____	$_____
Total	$_____	$_____Per Month

K. Other Resources Needed to Become Competitive:

Type	Amount	Anticipated Source
_____	_____	_____
_____	_____	_____
_____	_____	_____

I further agree that any duly authorized representative of the Small Business Administration shall have access to and the right to examine any pertinent books, documents, papers, and records involving transactions related to any contract awarded under the 8(a) Program.

To the best of my ability, I will put into practice the business methods and advice provided to me by Small Business Administration. I will discuss with appropriate SBA personnel any major changes or long-term commitments prior to entering into such commitments.

I will conduct my business affairs in an ethical manner.

I hereby certify that I have not paid fees to third parties, whether directly or indirectly, in the process of obtaining 8(a) subcontracts. If such fees have been paid, or contracted to be paid, I attach full details of such agreement.

I further certify that the statements contained in this application and attachments are true and correct to the best of my knowledge and belief.

Signature of Authorized Officer of Firm	Title of Officer	Date

Technical and Management Assistance Agreement:

The undersigned requests the SBA to provide technical and management assistance in connection with this Business Plan and Qualifications Resume. It is understood that said assistance shall be performed free of charge. I hereby authorize SBA to furnish information and data contained in the Business Plan and Qualifications Resume to those persons providing this company with technical and management assistance. All information will be treated in strict confidence.

In consideration of this assistance, I hereby waive all claims arising therefrom against SBA and aforeferenced persons.

Signature of Authorized Officer of Firm	Title of Officer	Date

XI. Other Pertinent Information:

A. Contracts or Jobs In-House:

Customer & Representative	Description	Amount ($)	%Completed	Scheduled Completion
_____	_____	_____	_____	_____
_____	_____	_____	_____	_____
_____	_____	_____	_____	_____
_____	_____	_____	_____	_____
_____	_____	_____	_____	_____
_____	_____	_____	_____	_____

B. Average Monthly Billings—$:

C. Record of Surety and Fidelity Bonds:

Date	Job or Person	Type of Bond	Amount	Surety Company	Agent or Agency
____	____	____	____	____	____
____	____	____	____	____	____
____	____	____	____	____	____
____	____	____	____	____	____
____	____	____	____	____	____
____					

D. Contracts or Jobs Completed within the Last Two Years

Customer	Description	Amount ($)
_____	_____	_____
_____	_____	_____
_____	_____	_____
_____	_____	_____
_____	_____	_____
_____	_____	_____

_____   _____   _____

_____   _____   _____

_____   _____   _____

_____   _____   _____

_____   _____   _____

_____   _____   _____

E.   Schedule of Insurance:

Company	Coverage	Amount	Expiration Date	Agents or Agency
_____	_____	_____	_____	_____
_____	_____	_____	_____	_____
_____	_____	_____	_____	_____
_____	_____	_____	_____	_____

F.   Bank and Trade Reference:

Name and Address	Contact Person and Position
_____	_____
_____	_____
_____	_____
_____	_____

G.   Availability of credit and Financial Assistance:

Source	Amount	Terms	Degree of Commitment (Attach any documentation of commitment
_____	_____	_____	_____
_____	_____	_____	_____
_____	_____	_____	_____

G. Shipping Facilities and Accessibility to Transportation:

H. Quality Control System:

I. Workforce Classified as Disadvantaged and Training Programs:

J. Expansion Capability:

IX. Operational Plan:

X. Financial:
Attach year-end and current business balance sheet on applicant and affiliates, year-end and current profit and loss statements on applicant and affiliates, aging of accounts receivable and payables on applicant, monthly cash flow for twelve months on applicant and annual detail projection for two years on applicant.

A. Sales History: (Applicant)

	FY_____	FY_____	FY_____	Year-end to date as of _____
Commercial	_____	_____	_____	_____
Government 8(a)	_____	_____	_____	_____
Government Other	_____	_____	_____	_____
Total _____		_____	_____	_____

B. Profits of Losses (Applicant)

			Year-end to
FY_____	FY_____	FY_____	date as of_____
_____	_____	_____	_____

C. Projection (Applicant)

	1st Year	2nd Year	3rd Year	4th Year
8(a) Projected support	_____	_____	_____	_____
Commercial sales	_____	_____	_____	_____
Other government	_____	_____	_____	_____
Total	_____	_____	_____	_____

Note: Projected 8(a) support should decline with each progressive year. Commercial and other Government sales should increase.

D. Condensed Balance Sheets History (Applicant):

Current as of____		FY ending 19___	
C/A_____	C/L_____	C/A_____	C/L_____
F/A_____	LT/L_____	F/A_____	LT/L_____
O/A_____	N/W_____	O/A_____	N/W_____
Total_____	_____	_____	_____

FY Ending 19___		FY Ending 19___	
C/A_____	C/L_____	C/A_____	C/L_____
F/A_____	LT/L_____	F/A_____	LT/L_____
O/A_____	N/W_____	O/A_____	N/W_____
Total_____	_____	_____	_____

Key: C/A—current assets   O/A—other assets   LT/L—Long term liabilities
     F/A—Fixed assets   C/L—current liabilities   N/W—Networth

E. Sales History (Affiliates—Sponsors)

Name of Affiliate_____

	FY_____	FY_____	FY_____	Year end to date as of_____
Commercial	_____	_____	_____	_____
Government	_____	_____	_____	_____
Total	_____	_____	_____	_____

F. Condensed Balance Sheets (Affiliates—Sponsors)

Name of Affiliate_____

Current as of____		FY Ending 19___	
C/A_____	C/L_____	C/A_____	C/L_____
F/A_____	LT/L_____	F/A_____	LT/L_____
O/A_____	N/W_____	O/A_____	N/W_____
Total_____	_____	_____	_____

FY Ending 19___		FY Ending 19___	
C/A_____	C/L_____	C/A_____	C/L_____
F/A_____	LT/L_____	F/A_____	LT/L_____
O/A_____	N/W_____	O/A_____	N/W_____
Total_____	_____	_____	_____

Appendix VI

Guide to Free Tax Services Provided by the IRS

The Internal Revenue Service makes available free help and guidance concerning federal tax rules and policies. The following excerpts from the IRS's *Guide to Free Tax Services* (Publication No. 910) contain sources of information that may be useful to you in dealing with business tax issues and problems.

Answers to Federal Tax Questions

Note: If the telephone number is not preceded by 1-800, it is a local number and should be used only if you are not calling long distance.

Alabama

1-800-424-1040

Alaska

Anchorage, 561-7484
Elsewhere, 1-800-424-1040

Arizona

Phoenix, 257-1233
Elsewhere, 1-800-424-1040

Arkansas

1-800-424-1040

California

Please call the telephone number
shown in the white pages of your
local telephone directory under
U.S. Government, Internal
Revenue Service, Federal Tax
Assistance.

Colorado

Denver, 825-7041
Elsewhere, 1-800-424-1040

Connecticut

1-800-424-1040

Delaware

1-800-424-1040

District of Columbia

488-3100

Florida

Jacksonville, 354-1760
Elsewhere, 1-800-424-1040

Georgia

Atlanta, 522-0050
Elsewhere, 1-800-424-1040

Hawaii

Oahu, 541-1040
Elsewhere, 1-800-424-1040

Idaho

1-800-424-1040

Illinois

Chicago, 435-1040
Elsewhere, 1-800-424-1040

Indiana

Indianapolis, 269-5477
Elsewhere, 1-800-424-1040

Iowa

Des Moines, 283-0523
Elsewhere, 1-800-424-1040

Kansas

1-800-424-1040

Kentucky

1-800-424-1040

Louisiana

1-800-424-1040

Maine

1-800-424-1040

Maryland

Baltimore, 962-2590
Montgomery County, 488-3100
Prince George's County, 488-3100
Elsewhere, 1-800-424-1040

Massachusetts

Boston, 523-1040
Elsewhere, 1-800-424-1040

Michigan

Detroit, 237-0800
Elsewhere, 1-800-424-1040

Minnesota

Minneapolis, 291-1422
St. Paul, 291-1422
Elsewhere, 1-800-424-1040

Mississippi

1-800-424-1040

Missouri

St. Louis, 342-1040
Elsewhere, 1-800-424-1040

Montana

1-800-424-1040

Nebraska

Omaha, 422-1500
Elsewhere, 1-800-424-1040

Nevada

1-800-424-1040

New Hampshire

1-800-424-1040

New Jersey

Newark, 622-0600
Elsewhere, 1-800-424-1040

New Mexico

1-800-424-1040

New York

Bronx, 732-0100
Brooklyn, 596-3770
Buffalo, 855-3955
Manhattan, 732-0100
Nassau, 222-1131
Queens, 596-3770
Rockland County, 997-1510
Staten Island, 596-3770
Suffolk, 724-5000
Westchester County, 997-1510
Elsewhere, 1-800-424-1040

North Carolina

1-800-424-1040

North Dakota

1-800-424-1040

Ohio

Cincinnati, 621-6281
Cleveland, 522-3000
Elsewhere, 1-800-424-1040

Oklahoma

1-800-424-1040

Oregon

Eugene, 485-8286
Portland, 221-3960
Salem, 581-8721
Elsewhere, 1-800-424-1040

Pennsylvania

Philadelphia, 574-9900
Pittsburgh, 281-0112
Elsewhere, 1-800-424-1040

Puerto Rico

San Juan Metro Area, 753-4040
Isla DDD, 753-4549

Rhode Island

1-800-424-1040

South Carolina

1-800-424-1040

South Dakota

1-800-424-1040

Tennessee

Nashville, 259-4601
Elsewhere, 1-800-424-1040

Texas

Dallas, 742-2440
El Paso, 532-6116
Ft. Worth, 263-9229
Houston, 965-0440
Elsewhere, 1-800-424-1040

Utah

1-800-424-1040

Vermont

1-800-424-1040

Virginia

Bailey's Crossroads, 557-9230
Richmond, 649-2361
Elsewhere, 1-800-424-1040

Washington

Seattle, 442-1040
Elsewhere, 1-800-424-1040

West Virginia

1-800-424-1040

Wisconsin

Milwaukee, 271-3780
Elsewhere, 1-800-424-1040

Wyoming

1-800-424-1040

Telephone Assistance Services for deaf taxpayers who have access to TV/telephone — TTY equipment.

Indiana residents, 1-800-382-4059

Elsewhere in U.S., including Alaska, Hawaii, Virgin Islands, and Puerto Rico, 1-800-428-4732

Hours of Operation

8:00 A.M. to 6:45 P.M. EST (Jan. 1 – April 15)
8:00 A.M. to 4:30 P.M. EST (April 16 – Dec. 31)

Tele-Tax

The IRS has a telephone service, Tele-Tax, that provides automated refund information and recorded tax information on about 150 topics covering such areas as filing requirements, dependents, itemized deductions, and tax credits. Tele-Tax is available 24 hours a day, 7 days a week, to taxpayers using push-button (tone-signaling) telephones, and Monday through Friday, during office hours, to taxpayers using pushbutton (pulse dial) or rotary (dial) phones.

To use Tele-Tax, select, by number, the topic you wish to hear. Call the appropriate phone number listed below. If you have a push-button (tone signaling) phone, follow the recorded instructions. If you have a rotary (dial) or push-button (pulse-tone), ask the IRS operator for the topic number you want to hear.

Alabama

1-800-554-4477

Alaska

1-800-554-4477

Arizona

Phoenix, 252-4909
Elsewhere, 1-800-554-4477

Arkansas

1-800-554-4477

California

Counties of Amador, Calaveras,

Contra Costa, Marin, and San Joaquin,
1-800-428-4032
Los Angeles, 617-3177
Oakland, 839-4245
Elsewhere, 1-800-554-4477

Colorado

Denver, 592-1118
Elsewhere, 1-800-554-4477

Connecticut

1-800-554-4477

Delaware

1-800-554-4477

District of Columbia

628-2929

Florida

Jacksonville, 353-9579
Elsewhere, 1-800-554-4477

Georgia

Atlanta, 331-6572
Elsewhere, 1-800-554-4477

Hawaii

1-800-554-4477

Idaho

1-800-554-4477

Illinois

Chicago, 829-6397
Springfield, 789-0489
Elsewhere, 1-800-554-4477

Indiana

Indianapolis, 634-1550
Elsewhere, 1-800-554-4477

Iowa

1-800-554-4477

Kansas

1-800-554-4477

Kentucky

1-800-554-4477

Louisiana

1-800-554-4477

Maine

1-800-554-4477

Maryland

Baltimore, 244-7306
Elsewhere, 1-800-554-4477

Massachusetts

Boston, 523-8602
Elsewhere, 1-800-554-4477

Michigan

Detroit, 961-4282
Elsewhere, 1-800-554-4477

Minnesota

St. Paul, 224-4288
Elsewhere, 1-800-554-4477

Mississippi

1-800-554-4477

Missouri

St. Louis, 241-4700
Elsewhere, 1-800-554-4477

Montana

1-800-554-4477

Nebraska

Omaha, 221-3324
Elsewhere, 1-800-554-4477

Nevada

1-800-554-4477

New Hampshire

1-800-554-4477

New Jersey

Newark, 624-1223
Elsewhere, 1-800-554-4477

New Mexico

1-800-554-4477

New York

Brooklyn, 858-4461
Buffalo, 856-9320
Manhattan, 406-4080
Queens, 858-4461
Staten Island, 858-4461
Elsewhere, 1-800-554-4477

North Carolina

1-800-554-4477

North Dakota

1-800-554-4477

Ohio

Cincinnati, 421-0329
Cleveland, 522-3037
Elsewhere, 1-800-554-4477

Oklahoma

1-800-554-4477

Oregon

Portland, 294-5363
Elsewhere, 1-800-554-4477

Pennsylvania

Philadelphia, 592-8946
Pittsburgh, 281-3120
Elsewhere, 1-800-554-4477

Rhode Island

1-800-554-4477

South Carolina

1-800-554-4477

South Dakota

1-800-554-4477

Tennessee

Nashville, 242-1541
Elsewhere, 1-800-554-4477

Texas

Dallas, 767-1792
Houston, 850-8801
Elsewhere, 1-800-554-4477

Utah

1-800-554-4477

Vermont

1-800-554-4477

Virginia

Richmond, 771-2369
Elsewhere, 1-800-554-4477

Washington

Seattle, 343-7221
Elsewhere, 1-800-554-4477

West Virginia

1-800-554-4477

Wisconsin

Milwaukee, 291-1783
Elsewhere, 1-800-554-4477

Wyoming

1-800-554-4477

Tele-Tax Topic Numbers and Subjects

Topic No.	Subject
	IRS Procedures and Services
101	IRS help available—Volunteer tax assistance programs, toll-free telephone, walk-in assistance, and outreach program
102	Tax assistance for handicapped individuals and the deaf
103	Small business tax workshops—Tax help for new businesses
104	Problem resolution program—Special help for problem situations
105	Public libraries—Tax information tapes and reproducible tax forms
106	Examination procedures and how to prepare for an audit
107	The collection process
108	Tax fraud—How to report
109	Special enrollment examination to practice before IRS

Topic No.	Subject
110	Organizations—How to apply for exempt status
111	Audit appeal rights
112	Electronic filing
999	Local information
	Filing Requirements, Filing Status, Exemptions
151	Who must file?
152	Which form—1040, 1040A, or 1040EZ?
153	When, where, and how to file
154	Filing requirements for a dependent child
155	Filing as single
156	Filing joint or separate
157	Filing as head of household
158	Filing as qualifying widow/widower
159	Filing status for separated individuals
160	Dependent—Who can be claimed?
161	Dependent child—Divorced or separated parents

Free Tax Publications

The Internal Revenue Service publishes many free publications to help you with your taxes. Some are listed here. You may order these free publications and forms by using the addresses in this appendix or you can call IRS toll-free at 1-800-424-3676.

GENERAL PUBLICATIONS

17 Your Federal Income Tax. This publication can help you prepare your own return. It takes you through the return and explains the tax laws that cover salaries and wages, interest and dividends, itemized deductions, rental income, gains and losses and adjustments to income (such as alimony, reimbursed employee business expenses, and IRA contributions). Examples illustrate typical situations. Filled-in forms and schedules show how to report income and deductions. The Tax Table, Tax Rate Schedules, and earned income credit tables are included in this publication.

Forms 1040, 1040A, 1040EZ, Schedules A, B, D, E, R, SE, Forms W-2, 2106, 2119, 2441, 3903.

586A The Collection Process (Income Tax Accounts). This booklet explains your rights and duties as a taxpayer who owes tax. It also explains the legal obligation of the Internal Revenue Service to collect overdue taxes, and the way this obligation is fulfilled.

556 Examination of Returns, Appeal Rights, and Claims for Refund. This publication may be helpful if your return is examined by the IRS. It explains that returns are normally examined to verify the correctness of reported income, exemptions, or deductions, and it describes what appeal rights you have if you disagree with the results of the examination. The publication also explains the procedures for the examination of items of partnership income, deduction, gain, loss, and credit. Information is given on how to file a claim for refund, the time for filing a claim for refund, and the limit on the amount of refund.

Forms 1040X and 1120X.

GENERAL SMALL BUSINESS PUBLICATIONS

334 Tax Guide for Small Business. This book explains some federal tax laws that apply to businesses. It describes the four major forms of business organizations—sole proprietorship, partnership, corporation, and S corporation—and explains the tax responsibilities of each.

This publication is divided into eight parts. The first part contains general information on business organization and accounting practices. Part II discusses the tax aspects of accounting for the assets used in a business.

Parts III and IV explain how to figure your business income for tax purposes. They describe the kinds of income you must report and the different types of business deductions you can take.

Part V discusses the rules that apply when you sell or exchange business assets or investment property. It includes chapters of capital gains and losses, and on involuntary conversions, such as theft and casualty losses. The chapters in Part VI bring together some specific tax considerations for each of the four major forms of business organizations.

Part VII looks at some of the credits that can reduce your income tax, and some of the other taxes you may have to pay in addition to income tax. It also discusses the information returns that may have to be filed. The last part shows how to fill out the main income tax forms businesses use.

Schedule C (Form 1040), Forms 1065, 1120, 1120-A, 1120S, Schedule K-1 (Form 1065), Forms 4562 and 4797.

583 Information for Business Taxpayers. This publication shows sample records that a small business can use if it operates as a sole proprietorship. Records like these will help you prepare complete and accurate tax returns and make sure you pay only the tax you owe. This publication also discusses the taxpayer identification number businesses must use, information returns businesses may have to file, and the kinds of business taxes businesses may have to pay.

Schedule C (Form 1040), and Form 4562.

557 Tax-Exempt Status for Your Organization. This publication discusses how organizations become recognized as exempt from federal income tax under section 501(a) of the Internal Revenue Code. (These include organizations described in section 501(c).) The publication explains how to get an appropriate ruling or determination letter recognizing the exemption, and it gives other information that applies generally to all exempt organizations.

Forms 990, 1023, and 1024.

LEGAL STRUCTURES

541 Tax Information on Partnerships. Forms 1065, 4797, and Schedules D, K, and K-1 (Form 1065).

542 Tax Information on Corporations. Forms 1120 and 1120-A.

589 Tax Information on S Corporations. Form 1120S and Schedule K-1 (Form 1120S).

BUSINESS PROCEDURES AND PRACTICES

538 Accounting Periods and Methods. This publication explains which accounting periods and methods can be used for figuring federal taxes, and how to apply for approval to change from one period or method to another. Almost all individual taxpayers have the calendar year as their tax period and use the cash method.

Forms 1128 and 3115.

908 Bankruptcy. This publication explains the income tax aspects of bankruptcy and discharge of debt for individuals and small businesses.

Forms 1040, 1041, 1120.

551 Basis of Assets. This publication explains how to determine the basis of property. The basis of property you buy is usually its cost. If you received property in some other way, such as by gift or inheritance, you normally must use a basis other than cost.

535 Business Expenses. This publication discusses such business expenses as pay for your employees; fringe benefits; rental expenses; interest; taxes; insurance; employee benefit plans; and certain education expenses of yourself and your employees. It also outlines the choice to capitalize certain business expenses; discusses amortization and depletion; covers some business expenses that may be deductible in some circumstances and not deductible in others; and points out some expenses that are not deductible.

917 Business Use of a Car. This publication explains the expenses that you may deduct for the business use of your car. The publication also discusses the taxability of the use of a car provided by an employer, and it explains new rules for deducting car expenses.

587 Business Use of Your Home. This publication can help you decide if you qualify to deduct certain expenses for using part of your home in your business. Deductions for the business use of a home computer are also discussed.

Schedule C (Form 1040), and Form 4562.

549 Condemnations and Business Casualties and Thefts. This publication can help you figure your gain or loss if you have property that is condemned or if you sell or exchange it under threat or imminence of condemnation.

The publication also explains the deduction for casualties and thefts to business property. Casualties are events such as hurricanes, earthquakes, tornadoes, fires, floods, vandalism, and car accidents.

Forms 4797 and 4864.

548 Deduction for Bad Debts. This publication explains that if someone owes you money and you cannot collect on the debt, you may be able to claim a deduction for a bad debt. For a bad debt to qualify for the deduction, there must be a true creditor-debtor relationship between you and the person or organization that owes you the money. There must be a legal obligation to pay you a fixed sum of money. You must realize a loss because of your inability to collect the money owed to you.

534 Depreciation. This publication discusses the various methods of depreciation, including the new modified accelerated cost recovery system (MACRS). This publication covers:

—What can be depreciated
—Section 179 deduction
—MACRS-assets placed in service after 1986
—ACRS-assets placed in service after 1980 and before 1987
—The limitations for passenger automobiles and other "listed property" placed in service after June 18, 1984
—Methods used for assets placed in service before 1981 and for assets not qualifying for ACRS and MACRS
—Example with a filled-in Form 4562. Form 4562.

561 Determining the Value of Donated Property. This publication can help donors and appraisers determine the value of property (other than cash) that is given to qualified organizations. It explains what kind of information you need to support a charitable deduction you claim on your return.

Form 8283.

596 Earned Income Credit. This publication discusses who may receive the earned income credit, and how to figure and claim the credit. It also discusses how to receive advance payments of the earned income credit.

Forms W-5, 1040, and 1040A.

1244 Employee's Daily Record of Tips (Form 4070-A) and

Employee's Report of Tips to Employer (Form 4070). This publication explains how you must report tips if you are an employee who receives tips. Copies of the monthly tip report you must give your employer are included, as well as a daily list you can use for your own records.

Forms 4070 and 4070-A.

794 Favorable Determination Letter. This publication explains the effect of the new law upon your determination letter, points out some operational features that may affect the qualified status of your employee benefit plan, and provides information on the reporting requirements for your plan.

349 Federal Highway Use Tax on Heavy Vehicles. This publication explains which trucks, truck-tractors, and buses are subject to the federal use tax on heavy highway motor vehicles, which is one source of funds for the national highway construction program. The tax is due from the person in whose name the vehicle is either registered or required to be registered. The publication tells how to figure and pay the tax due.

Beginning July 1, 1987, heavy highway vehicles from Canada and Mexico that are used on U.S. highways are subject to the tax.

1048 Filing Requirements for Employee Benefit Plans. Forms 5500, 5500-C, 5500-R, and 5500EZ.

378 Fuel Tax Credits. This publication explains the credit or refund allowed for the federal excise taxes paid on certain fuels, and the income tax credit available when alcohol is used as a fuel.

Forms 4136 and 6478.

572 General Business Credit. This publication explains the general business credit, including the investment credit, the low-income housing credit, the jobs credit, and the research credit. It also describes transition property qualifying for the investment credit, which was repealed for most property placed in service after 1985.

Forms 3800, 4255, 8586, and 5884.

590 Individual Retirement Arrangements (IRAs). This publication explains the benefits of having an individual retirement arrangement (IRA) and provides information on current deductions, tax responsibilities, and the "rollover" from one IRA to another. An IRA is a savings plan that lets you set aside money for your retirement. Your contributions to an IRA are tax deductible and the

BUSINESS PROCEDURES AND PRACTICES (cont.)

earnings in your IRA are not taxed until they are distributed to you.

Topics covered include:
—Who may set up an IRA
—Setting up an IRA
—Deductible and non-deductible contributions
—Excess contributions
—Distributions
—Rollovers.

Forms 5329 and 8606.

916 Information Returns. This publication provides general information about the rules for reporting payments to nonemployees and transactions with other persons. This publication also provides information on taxpayer identification numbers, information on backup withholding, and an explanation of the penalties relating to information returns.

Forms 1099 Series; W-2G; 1098, 4789; 5498; 8300; 8308; 8362.

545 Interest Expense. This publication explains what items may and may not be deducted as interest, which is an amount paid for the use of borrowed money. Where on the return you deduct interest depends on whether you borrowed the money for personal use, for rental or royalty property, or for your business.

Schedule A (Form 1040).

537 Installment Sales. This publication discusses sales arrangements that provide for part or all of the selling price to be paid in a later year. These arrangements are "installment sales." If you finance the buyer's purchase of your property, instead of having the buyer get a loan or mortgage from a bank, you probably have an installment sale.

Form 6252.

550 Investment Income and Expenses. This publication explains which types of investment income are and are not taxable, when the income is taxed, and how to report it on your tax return. The publication discusses the treatment of tax shelters and investment-related expenses. The publication also explains how to figure your gain or loss when you sell or trade your investment property.

Schedules B and D (Form 1040).

1212 List of Original Issue Discount Instruments. This publication explains the tax treatment of original issue discount (OID). It describes how brokers and other middlemen, who may hold the debt instruments as nominees for the owners, should report OID to IRS and to the owners on Forms 1099-OID or 1099-INT; and how owners of OID debt instruments should report OID on their income tax returns.

The publication gives rules for figuring the discount amount to report each year, if required. It also gives tables that IRS has compiled regarding certain publicly traded OID debt instruments, including short-term U.S. Treasury securities.

Schedule B (Form 1040) and Forms 1099-OID and 1099-INT.

529 Miscellaneous Deductions. This publication discusses expenses you generally may take as miscellaneous deductions on Schedule A (Form 1040), such as employee expenses and expenses of producing income. It does not discuss other itemized deductions, such as the ones for charitable contributions, moving expenses, interest, taxes, or medical and dental expenses.

Schedule A (Form 1040).

521 Moving Expenses. This publication explains how, if you changed job locations last year, or started a new job, you may be able to deduct your moving expenses. You may qualify for a deduction whether you are self-employed or an employee. The expenses must be connected with starting work at your new job location. You must meet a distance test and a time test. You also may be able to deduct expenses of moving to the United States if you retire while living and working overseas or if you are a survivor or dependent of a person who died while living and working overseas. The publication also discusses changes to moving expense deductions and how they may affect your tax return.

To deduct your allowable moving expenses, you must itemize your deductions. You should use Form 3903, Moving Expenses, if your move is within or to the United States or its possessions. You should use Form 3903F, Foreign Moving Expenses, if your move is outside the United States or its possessions.

Forms 3903, 3903F, and 4782.

564 Mutual Fund Distributions. This publication discusses the federal income tax treatment of distributions paid or allocated to you as an individual shareholder of a mutual fund. A comprehensive example shows distributions made by a mutual fund with illustrations of Form 1099-DIV and Form 1040.

Form 1040, Schedule B (Form 1040), and Form 1099-DIV.

536 Net Operating Losses

925 Passive Activity and At-Risk Rules. This publication covers the rules that limit passive activity losses and credits and the at-risk limits.

Form 8582.

552 Recordkeeping for Individuals and a List of Tax Publications. This publication can help you decide what records to keep and how long to keep them for tax purposes. These records will help you prepare your income tax returns so that you will pay only your correct tax. If you keep a record of your expenses during the year, you may find that you can reduce your taxes by itemizing your deductions. Deductible expenses include medical and dental bills, interest, contributions, and taxes.

531 Reporting Income from Tips. This publication gives advice about keeping track of cash and charge tips and explains that all tips received are subject to federal income tax. Social security or railroad retirement tax may also be due if tips total $20 or more a month. The publication also explains the rules about the information that employers must report to the Internal Revenue Service about their employees' tip income.

Forms 4070 and 4070A.

544 Sales and Other Dispositions of Assets. This publication explains how to figure gain and loss on various transactions, such as trading or selling an asset, and it explains the tax results of different types of gains and losses. Not all transactions result in taxable gains or deductible losses, and not all gains are taxed the same way.

Schedule D (Form 1040), and Form 4797.

533 Self-Employment Tax. This publication explains the self-employment tax, which is a social security tax for people who work for themselves. It is similar to the social security tax withheld from the pay of wage earners.

Social security benefits are available to people who are self-employed just as they are to wage earners. Your payments of self-employment tax contribute to your coverage under the social security system.

Schedule SE (Form 1040).

560 Self-Employed Retirement Plans. This publication discusses retirement plans for self-employed persons and certain partners in partnerships. These retirement plans are sometimes called Keogh plans or HR-10 plans.

If you set up a retirement plan that meets certain legal requirements, you may be able to deduct your payments to the plan. In addition, income earned by the plan will be tax-free until it is distributed.

598 Tax on Unrelated Business Income of Exempt Organizations. This publication explains the unrelated business income tax provisions that apply to most tax-exempt organizations. An organization that regularly operates a trade or business that is not substantially related to its exempt purpose may be taxed on the income from this business. Generally, a tax-exempt organization with gross income of $1,000 or more from an unrelated trade or business must file a return.
Form 990-T.

571 Tax-Sheltered Annuity Programs for Employees of Public Schools and Certain Tax-Exempt Organizations. This publication explains the rules concerning employers qualified to buy tax-sheltered annuities, eligible employees who may participate in the program, the amounts that may be excluded from income, and the taxation of benefits when they are received.
Form 5330.

463 Travel, Entertainment, and Gift Expenses. This publication explains what expenses you may deduct for business-related travel, entertainment, and gifts. It also discusses the reporting and recordkeeping requirements for these expenses. It includes the new limits on meals and entertainment.
The publication summarizes the deduction and substantiation rules for employees, self-employed persons (including independent contractors), and employers (including corporations and partnerships).
Form 2106.

DOING BUSINESS OUTSIDE THE U.S.

686 Certification for Reduced Tax Rates in Tax Treaty Countries. This publication explains how U.S. citizens, residents, and domestic corporations may certify to a treaty country that they are entitled to treaty benefits.

514 Foreign Tax Credit for U.S. Citizens and Resident Aliens. This publication may help you if you paid foreign income tax. You may be able to take a foreign tax credit or deduction to avoid the burden of double taxation. The pamphlet explains which foreign taxes qualify and how to figure your credit or deduction.
Form 1116.

593 Income Tax Benefits for U.S. Citizens and Residents Who Go

Overseas. This publication briefly reviews various U.S. tax provisions that apply to U.S. citizens or resident aliens who live or work abroad and expect to receive income from foreign sources.

597 Information on the United States-Canada Income Tax Treaty. This publication reproduces the entire text of the U.S.-Canada income tax treaty, and also gives an explanation of certain treaty provisions that often apply to U.S. citizens or residents who have Canadian sourced income. There is also a discussion that deals with certain tax problems that may be encountered by Canadian residents who temporarily work in the United States.

54 Tax Guide for U.S. Citizens and Resident Aliens Abroad. This publication discusses the tax situations of U.S. citizens and resident aliens who live and work abroad, or who have income from foreign countries. In particular, it explains the rules for excluding income and excluding or deducting certain housing costs. Answers are provided to questions that taxpayers ask most often about taxes for people living overseas.
Forms 2555, 1116, and 1040, Schedule SE (Form 1040).

570 Tax Guide for U.S. Citizens Employed in U.S. Possessions. Forms 4563 and 5074.

901 U.S. Tax Treaties

ALIENS AND VISITORS

513 Tax Information for Visitors to the United States. This publication can familiarize you with the general requirements of U.S. income tax laws for foreign visitors, who may have to file a U.S. income tax return during their visit.
Forms 1040C, 1040NR, 2063, and 1040-ES(-NR).

927 Tax Obligations of Legalized Aliens. This bilingual publication discusses, in English and Spanish, the tax obligations of previously undocumented aliens who are applying for resident status under the immigration amnesty program.

519 U.S. Tax Guide for Aliens. This comprehensive publication gives guidelines on how to determine U.S. tax status and figure U.S. tax.
Resident aliens, like U.S. citizens, generally are taxed on income from all sources, both in and outside the United States. Nonresident aliens generally are taxed only on income from sources in the United States. This income

may be from investments or from business activities such as performing personal services in the United States. An income tax treaty may reduce the standard 30% tax rate on nonresident aliens' investment income. Their business income is taxed at the same graduated rates that apply to U.S. citizens or residents.
Aliens admitted to the United States with permanent immigration visas are resident aliens, while temporary visitors generally are nonresident aliens. Aliens with other types of visas may be resident aliens or nonresident aliens, depending on the length and nature of their stay.
Forms 1040, 1040C, 1040NR, 2063, and Schedule A (Form 1040).

REAL ESTATE

527 Rental Property. This publication defines rental income, discusses rental expenses, and explains how to report them both on your return. It also covers casualty losses on rental property, passive activity limits, at-risk rules pertaining to rental property, and the sale of rental property.
Schedule E (Form 1040), Forms 4562 and 4797.

530 Tax Information for Owners of Homes, Condominiums, and Cooperative Apartments. This publication gives information about home ownership and federal taxes. It explains how to determine basis, how to treat settlement and closing costs, and how to treat repairs and improvements you make. The publication discusses itemized deductions for mortgage interest, real estate taxes, and casualty and theft losses. It also explains the mortgage interest credit and the residential energy credit carryforward.

SPECIAL BUSINESSES

225 Farmer's Tax Guide. This publication explains how federal tax laws apply to farming. It gives examples of typical farming situations and discusses the kinds of farm income you must report and the different deductions you can take.
Form 1040, Schedule F (Form 1040), Schedules A, D, SE (Form 1040), Forms 4136, 4255, 4562, 4684, 4797, and 6251.

1045 Information for Tax Practitioners

595 Tax Guide for Commercial Fishermen. This publication describes the federal tax laws as they apply to the fishing business. It is intended for sole proprietors

SPECIAL BUSINESSES (cont.)

who use Schedule C (Form 1040) to report profit or loss from fishing. This guide does not cover corporations or partnerships.

The publication's 17 chapters each give tax information about a different aspect of the fishing business. The last chapter gives an example of a fisherman's record-keeping system and sample tax forms.

Schedule C (Form 1040), Forms 1099— MISC, 4562, and 4797.

911 Tax Information for Direct Sellers. This publication may help you if you are a "direct seller," a person who sells consumer products to others on a person-to-person basis. Many direct sellers sell door-to-door, at sales parties, or by appointment in someone's home. Information on figuring your income from direct sales as well as the kinds of expenses you may be entitled to deduct is also provided.

Schedules C and SE (Form 1040) and Form 4562.

578 Tax Information for Private Foundations and Foundation Managers. This publication covers tax matters of interest to private foundations and their managers, including the tax classification of the foundation, filing requirements, the tax on net investment income, and various excise taxes on transactions that violate the foundation rules.

Form 990PF.

IF YOU EMPLOY OTHERS

51 Circular A, Agricultural Employer's Tax Guide. Form 943.

15 Circular E, Employer's Tax Guide. Every employer automatically receives this publication on its revision and every person who applies for an employer identification number receives a copy.

Forms 940, 941, and 941E.

179 Circular PR, Guia Contributiva Federal Para Patronos Puertorriqueños (Federal Tax Guide for Employers in Puerto Rico). Forms W-3PR, 940PR, 941PR, 942PR, and 943PR.

80 Circular SS, Federal Tax Guide for Employers in the Virgin Islands, Guam, and American Samoa. Forms 940, 941SS and 943.

539 Employment Taxes. This publication explains the responsibility you may have, if you have employees, to withhold federal income tax from their wages. You may also have to pay social security taxes (FICA) and federal unemployment tax (FUTA). The publication also discusses the rules for advance payment of the earned income credit and the rules for reporting and allocating tips.

Forms 940 and 941.

594 The Collection Process (Employment Tax Accounts). This booklet explains your rights and duties as a taxpayer who owes employer's quarterly federal taxes. It also explains how we fulfill the legal obligation of the Internal Revenue Service to collect these taxes. It is not intended as a precise and technical analysis of the law.

515 Withholding of Tax on Nonresident Aliens and Foreign Corporations. This publication provides information for withholding agents who are required to withhold and report tax on payments to nonresident aliens and foreign corporations. Also included are three tables listing U.S. tax treaties and some of the treaty provisions that provide for reduction or exemption from withholding for certain types of income.

Forms 1042 and 1042S, 1001, 4224, 8233, 1078, 8288, 8288-A and W-8.

Where to Send Your Order for Free Forms and Publications

Send your order to the "Forms Distribution Center" for your state.

Alabama—P.O. Box 9903, Bloomington, IL 61799
Alaska—P.O. Box 12626, Fresno, CA 93778
Arizona—P.O. Box 12626, Fresno, CA 93778
Arkansas—P.O. Box 9903, Bloomington, IL 61799
California—P.O. Box 12626, Fresno, CA 93778
Colorado—P.O. Box 12626, Fresno, CA 93778
Connecticut—P.O. Box 25866, Richmond, VA 23260
Delaware—P.O. Box 25866, Richmond, VA 23260
District of Columbia—P.O. Box 25866, Richmond, VA 23260
Florida—P.O. Box 25866, Richmond, VA 23260
Georgia—P.O. Box 25866, Richmond, VA 23260
Hawaii—P.O. Box 12626, Fresno, CA 93778
Idaho—P.O. Box 12626, Fresno, CA 93778
Illinois—P.O. Box 9903, Bloomington, IL 61799
Indiana—P.O. Box 9903, Bloomington, IL 61799
Iowa—P.O. Box 9903, Bloomington, IL 61799
Kansas—P.O. Box 9903, Bloomington, IL 61799
Kentucky—P.O. Box 9903, Bloomington, IL 61799
Louisiana—P.O. Box 9903, Bloomington, IL 61799
Maine—P.O. Box 25866, Richmond, VA 23260
Maryland—P.O. Box 25866, Richmond, VA 23260
Massachusetts—P.O. Box 25866, Richmond, VA 23260
Michigan—P.O. Box 9903, Bloomington, IL 61799
Minnesota—P.O. Box 9903, Bloomington, IL 61799
Mississippi—P.O. Box 9903, Bloomington, IL 61799
Missouri—P.O. Box 9903, Bloomington, IL 61799
Montana—P.O. Box 12626, Fresno, CA 93778
Nebraska—P.O. Box 9903, Bloomington, IL 61799
Nevada—P.O. Box 12626, Fresno, CA 93778
New Hampshire—P.O. Box 25866, Richmond, VA 23260
New Jersey—P.O. Box 25866, Richmond, VA 23260

New Mexico—P.O. Box 12626, Fresno, CA 93778
New York—P.O. Box 25866, Richmond, VA 23260
North Carolina—P.O. Box 25866, Richmond, VA 23260
North Dakota—P.O. Box 9903, Bloomington, IL 61799
Ohio—P.O. Box 9903, Bloomington, IL 61799
Oklahoma—P.O. Box 9903, Bloomington, IL 61799
Oregon—P.O. Box 12626, Fresno, CA 93778
Pennsylvania—P.O. Box 25866, Richmond, VA 23260
Puerto Rico—P.O. Box 25866, Richmond, VA 23260
Rhode Island—P.O. Box 25866, Richmond, VA 23260
South Carolina—P.O. Box 25866, Richmond, VA 23260
South Dakota—P.O. Box 9903, Bloomington, IL 61799
Tennessee—P.O. Box 9903, Bloomington, IL 61799
Texas—P.O. Box 9903, Bloomington, IL 61799
Utah—P.O. Box 12626, Fresno, CA 93778
Vermont—P.O. Box 25866, Richmond, VA 23260
Virginia—P.O. Box 25866, Richmond, VA 23260
Virgin Islands—V. I. Bureau of Internal Revenue, P.O. Box 3186, St. Thomas, VI 00801
Washington—P.O. Box 12626, Fresno, CA 93778
West Virginia—P.O. Box 25866, Richmond, VA 23260
Wisconsin—P.O. Box 9903, Bloomington, IL 61799
Wyoming—P.O. Box 12626, Fresno, CA 93778
Foreign Addresses—Taxpayers with mailing addresses in foreign countries should send their order to either: Forms Distribution Center, P.O. Box 25866, Richmond, VA 23260; or Forms Distribution Center, P.O. Box 12626, Fresno, CA 93778, whichever is closer. Send letter requests for other forms and publications to: Forms Distribution Center, P.O. Box 25866, Richmond, VA 23260.

Appendix VII

Directory of Small Business Investment Companies

This appendix is adapted from the government's *Directory of Operating Small Business Investment Companies*. It is the most recent publication available. However, addresses, phone numbers, and names of officers change frequently. Before mailing material to any of the SBICs listed here, try contacting the company by phone to verify the address and name of officer.

This directory is an alphabetical listing by state of Small Business Investment Companies (including branch offices). These companies have received licenses from SBA and their licenses remain outstanding. This list does not include currently licensed SBICs that are in the process of surrendering their licenses or that are subject to legal proceedings that may terminate their licenses.

This directory does not purport to characterize the relative merits, as investment companies or otherwise, of the listed licensees. Inclusion on this list should not be interpreted as approval of a company's operations or as a recommendation by the SBA.

This directory is composed of two parts:

Part I—Small Business Investment Companies.
Part II—301 (d) Small Business Investment Companies. (These licensees are limited to assisting small businesses owned by socially or economically disadvantaged persons.)

Key: Following each address, where relevant, the following abbreviations are used:

DL = date of license.
PC = private capital, $.
SBAL = SBA leverage, $.
IP = investment policy (C = communications, CA = Chinese Americans, CM = communications media, D = diversified, EF = export finance, EI = energy industries, FOR = food retailers, FR = franchised retailers, GS = grocery stores, LPA = lodging places and amusements, M = medical, MG = major group, RE = real estate, RES = real estate specialist, T = transportation, VM = vending machines).
OC = owner code (1 = bank dominated, 50% or more owned by bank or bank holding company; 2 = bank associated, 10–49% owned by bank or bank holding company; 3 = financial organization other than bank or bank holding company, public or nonpublic; 4 = non-financial company, public or nonpublic; 5 = 40' Act company). Ownership code followed by "P" signifies partnership.

Part I—SBIC Licensees

Alabama

First SBIC of Alabama
David Delaney, Pres.
16 Midtown Park E.
Mobile, AL 36606
(205)476-0700   DL: 7/20/78
PC: 2,166,700   SBAL: 6,500,000
IP: D   OC: 5

Hickory Venture Capital Corp.
J. Thomas Noojin, Pres.

699 Gallatin St., Ste. A-2
Huntsville, AL 35801
(205)539-1931   DL: 3/28/85
PC: 8,000,000   SBAL: 0
IP: D   OC: 1

Remington Fund, Inc. (The)
Lana Sellers, Pres.
1927 First Ave. N.
Birmingham, AL 35202
(205)324-7709   DL: 5/16/86

PC: 3,000,100   SBAL: 0
IP: D   OC: 5

Alaska

Alaska Business Investment Corp.
James Cloud, V.P.
301 W. Northern Lights Blvd.
Mail: P.O. Box 100600; Anchorage
99510
Anchorage, AK 99510

541

Alaska (continued)

(907)278-2071   DL: 12/10/82
PC: 2,500,000   SBAL: 0
IP: D   OC: 1

Arizona

Northwest Venture Partners
(Main Office: Minneapolis, MN)
88777 E. Via de Ventura, Ste. 335
Scottsdale, AZ 85258
(602)483-8940

Norwest Growth Fund, Inc.
(Main Office: Minneapolis, MN)
88777 E. Via de Ventura, Ste. 335
Scottsdale, AZ 85258
(602)483-8940

Rocky Mountain Equity Corp.
Anthony J. Nicoli, Pres.
4530 Central Ave.
Phoenix, AZ 85012
(602)274-7534   DL: 9/22/81
PC: 600,000   SBAL: 500,000
IP: D   OC: 5

Valley National Investors, Inc.
John M. Holliman III, V.P. & Mngr.
201 N. Central Ave., Ste. 900
Phoenix, AZ 85004
(602)261-1577   DL: 4/4/84
PC: 15,000,000   SBAL: 0
IP: D   OC: 1

Wilbur Venture Capital Corp.
Jerry F. Wilbur, Pres.
4575 S. Palo Verde, Ste. 305
Tucson, AZ 85714
(602)747-5999   DL: 5/11/87
PC: 1,000,000   SBAL: 0
IP: D   OC: 5

Arkansas

Small Business Inv. Capital, Inc.
Charles E. Toland, Pres.
10003 New Benton Hwy.
Mail: P.O. Box 3627
Little Rock, AR 72203
(501)455-6599   DL: 3/6/75
PC: 1,150,000   SBAL: 2,750,000
IP: GS   OC: 4

Southern Ventures, Inc.
Jeffrey A. Doose, Pres. & Dir.
605 Main St., Ste. 202
Arkadelphia, AR 71923
(501)246-9627   DL: 11/30/88
PC: 1,250,000   SBAL: 0
IP: D   OC: 5

California

AMF Financial, Inc.
William Temple, V.P.
4330 La Jolla Village Dr., Ste. 110
San Diego, CA 92122
(619)546-0167   DL: 10/26/82
PC: 626,000   SBAL: 0
IP: D   OC: 5

Atalanta Investment Co., Inc.
(Main Office: New York, NY)
141 El Camino Dr.
Beverly Hills, CA 90212
(213)273-1730

BNP Venture Capital Corp.
Edgerton Scott II, Pres.
3000 Sand Hill Rd.

Bldg. 1, Ste. 125
Menlo Park, CA 94025
(415)854-1084   DL: 10/12/84
PC: 1,550,000   SBAL: 0
IP: D   OC: 1

Bancorp Venture Capital, Inc.
Arthur H. Bernstein, Pres.
11812 San Vicente Blvd.
Los Angeles, CA 90049
(213)820-7222   DL: 5/4/84
PC: 2,250,000   SBAL: 2,250,000
IP: D   OC: 1

BankAmerica Ventures, Inc.
Patrick Topolski, Pres.
555 California St.
San Francisco, CA 94104
(415)953-3001   DL: 11/12/59
PC: 22,500,000   SBAL: 0
IP: 45% MG 26 & 38   OC: 1

CFB Venture Capital Corp.
Richard J. Roncaglia, V.P.
530 B. St., Third Fl.
San Diego, CA 92101
(619)230-3304   DL: 8/30/83
PC: 1,000,000   SBAL: 0
IP: D   OC: 1

CFB Venture Capital Corp.
(Main Office: San Diego, CA)
350 California St., Mezz.
San Francisco, CA 94104
(415)445-0594

Citicorp Venture Capital, Ltd.
(Main Office: New York, NY)
2 Embarcadero Pl.
2200 Geny Rd., Ste. 203
Palo Alto, CA 94303
(415)424-8000

City Ventures, Inc.
Warner Heineman, V. Chmn.
400 N. Roxbury Dr.
Beverly Hills, CA 90210
(213)550-5709   DL: 6/4/82
PC: 2,000,000   SBAL: 0
IP: D   OC: 1

Crosspoint Investment Corp.
Max Simpson, Pres. & Chief F.O.
1951 Landings Dr.
Mountain View, CA 94043
(415)968-0930   DL: 9/26/79
PC: 667,500   SBAL: 600,000
IP: D   OC: 3

Developers Equity Capital Corp.
Larry Sade, Chmn. of the Board
1880 Century Park East, Ste. 311
Los Angeles, CA 90067
(213)277-0330   DL: 6/12/74
PC: 677,000   SBAL: 1,010,000
IP: RE   OC: 5

Draper Associates, a California LP
Bill Edwards, Pres.
c/o Timothy C. Draper
3000 Sand Hill Rd., Bldg. 4, #235
Menlo Park, CA 94025
(415)854-1712   DL: 9/12/79
PC: 2,015,000   SBAL: 6,000,000
IP: D   OC: 5-P

First Interstate Capital, Inc.
Ronald J. Hall, Mng. Dir.
5000 Birch St., Ste. 10100
Newport Beach, CA 92660
(714)253-4360   DL: 7/5/78

PC: 15,000,000   SBAL: 0
IP: D   OC: 1

First SBIC of Calif.
Tim Hay, Pres.
650 Town Center Dr., 17th Fl.
Costa Mesa, CA 92626
(714)556-1964   DL: 1/29/60
PC: 25,000,000   SBAL: 0
IP: D   OC: 1

First SBIC of Calif.
(Main Office: Costa Mesa, CA)
5 Palo Alto Sq., Ste. 938
Palo Alto, CA 94306
(415)424-8011

First SBIC of Calif.
(Main Office: Costa Mesa, CA)
155 N. Lake Ave., Ste. 1010
Pasadena, CA 91109
(818)304-3451

G C & H Partners
James C. Gaither, G. P.
One Maritime Plaza, 20th Fl.
San Francisco, CA 94110
(415)981-5252   DL: 4/30/84
PC: 1,287,176   SBAL: 900,000
IP: D   OC: 5-P

Hamco Capital Corp.
William R. Hambrecht, Pres.
235 Montgomery St.
San Francisco, CA 94104
(415)576-3635   DL: 3/1/82
PC: 3,990,238   SBAL: 11,000,000
IP: D   OC: 5

Imperial Ventures, Inc.
H. Wayne Snavely, Pres.
9920 S. Lacienega Blvd.
Mail: P.O. Box 92991; L.A. 90009
Inglewood, CA 90301
(213)417-5888   DL: 8/31/78
PC: 3,001,781   SBAL: 0
IP: D   OC: 1

Jupiter Partners
John M. Bryan, Pres.
600 Montgomery St., 35th Fl.
San Francisco, CA 94111
(415)421-9990   DL: 10/26/62
PC: 3,253,720   SBAL: 4,500,000
IP: 50% MG 36   OC: 5-P

Latigo Capital Partners, II
Robert A. Peterson, G.P.
1800 Century Park E., Ste. 430
Los Angeles, CA 90067
(213)556-2666   DL: 9/20/85
PC: 1,015,000   SBAL: 1,000,000
IP: D   OC: 5

Marwit Capital Corp.
Martin W. Witte, Pres.
180 Newport Ctr. Dr., Ste. 200
Newport Beach, CA 92660
(714)640-6234   DL: 5/3/62
PC: 1,031,178   SBAL: 2,000,000
IP: D   OC: 5

Merrill Pickard Anderson & Eyre I
Steven L. Merrill, Pres.
Two Palo Alto Sq., Ste. 425
Palo Alto, CA 94306
(415)856-8880   DL: 11/26/80
PC: 28,083,735   SBAL: 0
IP: D   OC: 1-P

Metropolitan Venture Co., Inc.
Rudolph J. Lowy, Chmn. of the Board

5757 Wilshire Blvd., Ste. 670
Los Angeles, CA 90036
(213)938-3488   DL: 9/30/81
PC: 1,000,000   SBAL: 1,000,000
IP: D   OC: 5

New West Partners II
Timothy P. Haidinger, Mngr.
4350 Executive Dr., Ste. 206
San Diego, CA 92121
(619)457-0723   DL: 2/17/87
PC: 1,003,123   SBAL: 1,000,000
IP: D   OC: 5

New West Partners II
(Main Office: San Diego, CA)
4600 Campus Dr., Ste. 103
Newport Beach, CA 92660
(714)756-8940

PBC Venture Capital Inc.
Henry L. Wheeler, Mngr.
1408 18th St.
Mail: P.O. Box 6008; Bakersfield 93386
Bakersfield, CA 93301
(805)395-3555   DL: 9/28/80
PC: 550,000   SBAL: 0
IP: D   OC: 1

Peerless Capital Co., Inc.
Robert W. Lautz, Jr., Pres.
675 S. Arroyo Pkwy., Ste. 320
Pasadena, CA 91105
(818)577-9199   DL: 7/11/86
PC: 1,000,000   SBAL: 0
IP: D   OC: 5

Ritter Partners
William C. Edwards, Pres.
150 Isabella Ave.
Atherton, CA 94025
(415)854-1555   DL: 10/18/62
PC: 3,228,802   SBAL: 4,500,000
IP: 50% MG 36   OC: 5-P

Round Table Capital Corp.
Richard Dumke, Pres.
655 Montgomery St., Ste. 700
San Francisco, CA 94111
(415)392-7500   DL: 4/28/80
PC: 900,000   SBAL: 2,700,000
IP: D   OC: 5

San Joaquin Capital Corp.
Chester Troudy, Pres.
1415 18th St., Ste. 306
Mail: P.O. Box 2538
Bakersfield, CA 93301
(805)323-7581   DL: 5/11/62
PC: 1,086,971   SBAL: 3,235,000
IP: D   OC: 5

Seaport Ventures, Inc.
Michael Stopler, Pres.
525 B. St., Ste. 630
San Diego, CA 92101
(619)232-4069   DL: 11/22/82
PC: 1,355,452   SBAL: 2,000,000
IP: D   OC: 5

Union Venture Corp.
Jeffrey Watts, Pres.
445 S. Figueroa St.
Los Angeles, CA 90071
(213)236-4092   DL: 9/30/67
PC: 23,550,000   SBAL: 0
IP: D   OC: 1

VK Capital Co.
Franklin Van Kasper, G.P.
50 California St., Ste. 2350
San Francisco, CA 94111

(415)391-5600   DL: 2/7/86
PC: 1,050,505   SBAL: 500,000
IP: D   OC: 5-P

Vista Capital Corp.
Frederick J. Howden, Jr., Chmn.
5080 Shoreham Pl., Ste. 202
San Diego, CA 92122
(619)453-0780   DL: 2/2/83
PC: 568,501   SBAL: 0
IP: D   OC: 5

Walden Capital Partners
Arthur S. Berliner, Pres.
750 Battery St., 7th Fl.
San Francisco, CA 94111
(415)391-7225   DL: 12/17/74
PC: 1,294,227   SBAL: 3,350,000
IP: D   OC: 2-P

Wells Fargo Capital Corp.
Ms. Sandra J. Menichelli, V.P. & G.M.
420 Montgomery St., 9th Fl.
San Francisco, CA 94163
(415)396-2059   DL: 11/15/88
PC: 2,000,000   SBAL: 0
IP: D   OC: 1

Westamco Investment Co.
Leonard G. Muskin, Pres.
8929 Wilshire Blvd., Ste. 400
Beverly Hills, CA 90211
(213)652-8288   DL: 7/24/61
PC: 800,000   SBAL: 0
IP: 66⅔% RE   OC: 4

Colorado

Associated Capital Corp.
Rodney J. Love, Pres.
4891 Independence St., Ste. 201
Wheat Ridge, CO 80033
(303)420-8155   DL: 11/16/76
PC: 2,125,000   SBAL: 6,750,000
IP: GS   OC: 4

UBD Capital, Inc.
Allan R. Haworth, Pres.
1700 Broadway
Denver, CO 80274
(303)863-6329   DL: 10/23/85
PC: 2,000,000   SBAL: 0
IP: D   OC: 1

Connecticut

AB SBIC, Inc.
Adam J. Bozzuto, Pres.
275 School House Rd.
Cheshire, CT 06410
(203)272-0203   DL: 11/17/76
PC: 500,000   SBAL: 1,000,000
IP: GS   OC: 4

All State Venture Capital Corp.
Ceasar N. Anquillare, Pres.
The Bishop House
32 Elm St., P.O. Box 1629
New Haven, CT 06506
(203)787-5029   DL: 11/2/62
PC: 1,000,000   SBAL: 0
IP: D   OC: 3

Capital Impact Corp.
William D. Starbuck, Pres.
961 Main St.
Bridgeport, CT 06601
(203)384-5670   DL: 3/1/85
PC: 7,216,171   SBAL: 9,000,000
IP: D   OC: 1

Capital Resource Co. of Connecticut
I. Martin Fierberg, Mng. Part.
699 Bloomfield Ave.
Bloomfield, CT 06002
(203)243-1114   DL: 3/23/77
PC: 976,365   SBAL: 2,855,000
IP: D   OC: 5-P

Dewey Investment Corp.
George E. Mrosek, Pres.
101 Middle Tpke. W.
Manchester, CT 06040
(203)649-0654   DL: 4/9/62
PC: 510,650   SBAL: 910,000
IP: D   OC: 5

First Connecticut SBIC
David Engelson, Pres.
177 State St.
Bridgeport, CT 06604
(203)366-4726   DL: 5/6/60
PC: 9,402,322   SBAL: 27,950,000
IP: 50% RE   OC: 6

First New England Capital, LP
Richard C. Klaffky, Pres.
255 Main St.
Hartford, CT 06106
(203)728-5200   DL: 3/25/88
PC: 5,000,000   SBAL: 0
IP: D   OC: 2-P

Marcon Capital Corp.
Martin A. Cohen, Pres.
49 Riverside Ave.
Westport, CT 06880
(203)226-6893   DL: 10/23/75
PC: 776,550   SBAL: 2,250,000
IP: D   OC: 4

Northeastern Capital Corp.
Joseph V. Ciaburri, Chmn. & CEO
209 Church St.
New Haven, CT 06510
(203)865-4500   DL: 3/8/61
PC: 1,000,951   SBAL: 2,120,000
IP: D   OC: 6

Regional Financial Enterprises, L.P.
Robert M. Williams, Mng. Part.
36 Grove St.
New Canaan, CT 06840
(203)966-2800   DL: 7/1/80
PC: 10,107,679   SBAL: 13,000,000
IP: D   OC: 1-P

SBIC of Connecticut Inc. (The)
Kenneth F. Zarrilli, Pres.
1115 Main St.
Bridgeport, CT 06603
(203)367-3282   DL: 1/31/61
PC: 617,160   SBAL: 1,250,000
IP: D   OC: 6

Delaware

Morgan Investment Corp.
William E. Pike, Chmn.
902 Market St.
Wilmington, DE 19801
(302)651-2500   DL: 12/10/87
PC: 30,000,000   SBAL: 0
IP: D   OC: 2

D.C.

Allied Investment Corp.
David J. Gladstone, Pres.
1666 K. St., N.W., Ste. 901
Washington, DC 20006
(202)331-1112   DL: 12/23/59

D.C. (continued)

PC: 4,784,708   SBAL: 14,350,000
IP: D   OC: 6

American Security Capital Corp., Inc.
William G. Tull, Pres.
730 Fifteenth St. N.W.
Washington, DC 20013
(202)624-4843   DL: 8/13/84
PC: 2,500,000   SBAL: 1,500,000
IP: D   OC: 1

DC Bancorp Venture Capital Co.
Allan A. Weissburg, Pres.
1801 K. St., N.W.
Washington, DC 20006
(202)955-6970   DL: 7/18/85
PC: 1,500,000   SBAL: 2,000,000
IP: D   OC: 2

Washington Ventures, Inc.
Kenneth A. Swain, Pres.
1320 18th St., N.W., Ste. 300
Washington, DC 20036
(202)895-2560   DL: 12/3/86
PC: 2,000,000   SBAL: 3,250,000
IP: D   OC: 1

Florida

Allied Investment Corp.
(Main Office: Washington, DC)
Exec. Office Ctr., Ste. 305
2770 N. Indian River Blvd.
Vero Beach, FL 32960
(407)778-5556

First North Florida SBIC
J.B. Higdon, Pres.
1400 Gadsden St.
P.O. Box 1021
Quincy, FL 32351
(904)875-2600   DL: 12/17/60
PC: 1,500,108   SBAL: 2,500,000
IP: GS   OC: 5

Gold Coast Capital Corp.
William I. Gold, Pres.
3550 Biscayne Blvd., Rm. 601
Miami, FL 33137
(305)576-2012   DL: 12/22/59
PC: 680,000   SBAL: 1,930,092
IP: D   OC: 5

J & D Capital Corp.
Jack Carmel, Pres.
12747 Biscayne Blvd.
North Miami, FL 33181
(305)893-0303   DL: 7/9/80
PC: 694,106   SBAL: 2,050,000
IP: D   OC: 5

Market Capital Corp.
E. E. Eads, Pres.
1102 N. 28th St.
P.O. Box 22667
Tampa, FL 33630
(813)247-1357   DL: 3/24/64
PC: 786,000   SBAL: 1,800,000
IP: GS   OC: 4

Quantum Capital Partners, Ltd.
Michael E. Chaney, Pres.
2400 E. Commercial Blvd., Ste. 814
Fort Lauderdale, FL 33308
(305)776-1133   DL: 7/7/82
PC: 1,500,000   SBAL: 4,000,000
IP: D   OC: 5-P

Southeast Venture Capital Ltd. I
James R. Fitzsimons, Jr., Pres.

3250 Miami Ctr.
100 Chopin Plaza
Miami, FL 33131
(305)379-2005   DL: 1/8/68
PC: 5,970,420   SBAL: 5,500,000
IP: D   OC: 1-P

Western Financial Capital Corp.
(Main Office: Dallas, TX)
1380 N.E. Miami Gardens Dr., Ste. 225
N. Miami Beach, FL 33179
(305)949-5900

Georgia

Investor's Equity, Inc.
I. Walter Fisher, Pres.
2629 First National Bank Tower
Atlanta, GA 30383
(404)523-3999   DL: 8/10/61
PC: 3,083,700   SBAL: 0
IP: D   OC: 5

North Riverside Capital Corp.
Tom Barry, Pres.
50 Technology Park/Atlanta
Norcross, GA 30092
(404)446-5556   DL: 8/24/84
PC: 3,010,500   SBAL: 7,500,000
IP: D   OC: 5

Hawaii

Bancorp Hawaii SBIC
James D. Evans, Jr., Pres.
111 S. King St., Ste. 1060
Honolulu, HI 96813
(808)521-6411   DL: 2/17/84
PC: 2,000,000   SBAL: 500,000
IP: D   OC: 1

Illinois

ANB Venture Corp.
Kurt L. Liljedahl, Exec. V.P.
33 N. LaSalle St.
Chicago, IL 60690
(312)855-1554   DL: 9/11/87
PC: 10,000,000   SBAL: 0
IP: D   OC: 1

Alpha Capital Venture Partners, L.P.
Andrew H. Kalnow, G.P.
3 First National Plaza, 14th Fl.
Chicago, IL 60602
(312)372-1556   DL: 4/23/84
PC: 4,867,307   SBAL: 0
IP: D   OC: 2-P

Business Ventures Inc.
Milton Lefton, Pres.
20 N. Wacker Dr., Ste. 550
Chicago, IL 60606
(312)346-1580   DL: 10/31/83
PC: 564,750   SBAL: 600,000
IP: D   OC: 5

Continental Illinois Venture Corp.
John L. Hines, Pres.
209 S. LaSalle St.
Mail: 231 S. LaSalle St.
Chicago, IL 60693
(312)828-8023   DL: 4/2/70
PC: 25,200,450   SBAL: 0
IP: D: OC: 1

First Capital Corp. of Chicago
John A. Canning, Jr., Pres.
3 First National Plaza, Ste. 1330
Chicago, IL 60670
(312)732-5400   DL: 6/8/61

PC: 91,771,742   SBAL: 3,600,000
IP: D   OC: 1

Frontenac Capital Corp.
David A. R. Dullum, Pres.
208 S. LaSalle St., Rm. 1900
Chicago, IL 60604
(312)368-0047   DL: 12/29/76
PC: 6,245,622   SBAL: 3,600,000
IP: D   OC: 2

Heller Equity Capital Corp.
Robert E. Koe, Pres.
200 N. LaSalle St., 10th Fl.
Chicago, IL 60601
(312)621-7200   DL: 9/19/80
PC: 2,015,000   SBAL: 0
IP: D   OC: 5

Mesirow Capital Partners SBIC, Ltd.
James C. Tyree, Pres. of C.G.P.
1355 LaSalle St., Ste. 3910
Chicago, IL 60603
(312)443-5773   DL: 7/7/82
PC: 1,250,000   SBAL: 5,000,000
IP: D   OC: 5-P

Walnut Capital Corp.
Burton W. Kanter, Chmn. of the Board
208 S. LaSalle St.
Chicago, IL 60604
(312)346-2033   DL: 11/7/83
PC: 5,123,800   SBAL: 10,000,000
IP: D   OC: 5

Indiana

1st Source Capital Corp.
Eugene L. Cavanaugh, Jr., V.P.
100 N. Michigan St.
Mail: P.O. Box 1602; South Bend
46634
South Bend, IN 46601
(219)236-2180   DL: 12/23/83
PC: 2,500,000   SBAL: 0
IP: D   OC: 1

Circle Ventures, Inc.
Robert Salyers, Pres.
2502 Roosevelt Ave.
Indianapolis, IN 46218
(317)636-7242   DL: 8/19/83
PC: 1,000,000   SBAL: 500,000
IP: D   OC: 5

Equity Resource Co., Inc.
Michael J. Hammes, V.P.
One Plaza Pl.
202 S. Michigan St.
South Bend, IN 46601
(219)237-5255   DL: 12/27/83
PC: 2,000,000   SBAL: 0
IP: D   OC: 1

Raffensperger Hughes Venture Corp.
Samuel B. Sutphin, Pres.
20 N. Meridian St.
Indianapolis, IN 46204
(317)635-4551   DL: 5/5/88
PC: 1,050,000   SBAL: 0
IP: D   OC: 5

White River Capital Corp.
Thomas D. Washburn, Pres.
500 Washington St.
Mail: P.O. Box 929
Columbus, IN 47201
(812)372-0111   DL: 3/31/82
PC: 1,048,000   SBAL: 0
IP: D   OC: 1

Iowa

MorAmerica Capital Corp.
David R. Schroder, V.P.
800 American Bldg.
Cedar Rapids, IA 52401
(319)363-8249   DL: 9/30/59
PC: 5,000,000   SBAL: 10,650,440
IP: D   OC: 3

Kansas

Kansas Venture Capital, Inc.
Larry J. High, Pres.
First National Bank Tower, Ste. 825
One Townsite Plaza
Topeka, KS 66603
(913)233-1368   DL: 6/17/77
PC: 3,740,690   SBAL: 0
IP: D   OC: 3

Kentucky

Financial Opportunities, Inc.
Gary Duerr, Mngr.
6060 Dutchman's Ln.
Mail: PO Box 35710; Louisville, KY
40232
Louisville, KY 40205
(502)451-3800   DL: 10/17/74
PC: 900,000   SBAL: 2,700,000
IP: D   OC: 4

Mountain Ventures, Inc.
Jerry A. Rickett, Exec. V.P.
London Bank & Trust Bldg.
400 S. Main St., 4th Fl.
London, KY 40741
(606)864-5175   DL: 12/19/78
PC: 1,640,000   SBAL: 0
IP: D   OC: 5

Wilbur Venture Capital Corp.
(Main Office: Tucson, AZ)
400 Fincastle Bldg.
3rd & Broadway
Louisville, KY 40202
(502)585-1214

Louisiana

Capital for Terrebonne, Inc.
Hartwell A. Lewis, Pres.
27 Austin Dr.
Houma, LA 70360
(504)868-3930   DL: 1/24/78
PC: 750,000   SBAL: 480,000
IP: D   OC: 5

Louisiana Equity Capital Corp.
G. Lee Griffin, Pres.
451 Florida St.
Baton Rouge, LA 70821
(504)389-4421   DL: 2/21/74
PC: 4,260,639   SBAL: 0
IP: D   OC: 1

Maine

Maine Capital Corp.
David M. Coit, Pres.
Seventy Center St.
Portland, ME 04101
(207)772-1001   DL: 8/7/80
PC: 1,000,000   SBAL: 1,000,000
IP: D   OC: 1

Maryland

First Maryland Capital, Inc.
Joseph A. Kenary, Pres.

107 W. Jefferson St.
Rockville, MD 20850
(301)251-6630   DL: 7/12/84
PC: 616,600   SBAL: 0
IP: D   OC: 5

Greater Washington Investments, Inc.
Don A. Christensen, Pres.
5454 Wisconsin Ave.
Chevy Chase, MD 20815
(301)656-0626   DL: 2/9/60
PC: 8,485,655   SBAL: 4,000,000
IP: D   OC: 6

Jiffy Lube Capital Corp.
Eleanor C. Harding, Pres.
6000 Metro Dr.
Mail: PO Box 17223; Baltimore 21203-
7223
Baltimore, MD 21215
(301)764-3234   DL: 12/9/87
PC: 2,000,000   SBAL: 1,200,000
IP: D   OC: 5

Massachusetts

Advent Atlantic Capital Co., LP
David D. Croll, Mng. Part.
45 Milk St.
Boston, MA 02109
(617)338-0800   DL: 11/28/83
PC: 4,956,680   SBAL: 6,000,000
IP: D   OC: 5-P

Advent IV Capital Co.
David D. Croll, Mng. Part.
45 Milk St.
Boston, MA 02109
(617)338-0800   DL: 7/27/82
PC: 12,050,000   SBAL: 3,000,000
IP: D   OC: 5-P

Advent Industrial Capital Co., LP
David Croll, Mng. Part.
45 Milk St.
Boston, MA 02109
(617)338-0800   DL: 11/9/84
PC: 3,326,400   SBAL: 7,000,000
IP: D   OC: 3-P

Advent V Capital Co., LP
David D. Croll, Mng. Part.
45 Milk St.
Boston, MA 02109
(617)338-0800   DL: 9/5/84
PC: 29,075,000   SBAL: 29,000,000
IP: D   OC: 5-P

Atlas II Capital Corp.
Joost E. Tjaden, Pres.
101 Federal St., 4th Fl.
Boston, MA 02110
(617)951-9420   DL: 7/27/82
PC: 1,000,000   SBAL: 500,000
IP: D   OC: 5

BancBoston Ventures, Inc.
Paul F. Hogan, Pres.
100 Federal St.
Mail: P.O. Box 2016 Stop 01-31-08
Boston, MA 02110
(617)434-2441   DL: 5/8/59
PC: 25,000,000   SBAL: 0
IP: D   OC: 1

Bever Capital Corp.
Joost E. Tjaden, Pres.
101 Federal St., 4th Fl.
Boston, MA 02110
(617)951-9420   DL: 10/31/83

PC: 1,000,000   SBAL: 1,500,000
IP: D   OC: 5

Boston Hambro Capital Co.
Edwin Goodman, Pres. of Corp., G.P.
160 State St., 9th Fl.
Boston, MA 02109
(617)523-7767   DL: 1/4/80
PC: 5,942,914   SBAL: 2,000,000
IP: D   OC: 5-P

Business Achievement Corp.
Michael L. Katzeff, Pres.
1172 Beacon St., Ste. 202
Newton, MA 02161
(617)965-0550   DL: 8/8/63
PC: 550,000   SBAL: 1,570,000
IP: D   OC: 5

Chestnut Capital International II LP
David D. Croll, Mng. Part.
45 Milk St.
Boston, MA 02109
(617)338-0800   DL: 7/10/85
PC: 6,729,124   SBAL: 12,500,000
IP: D   OC: 5-P

Chestnut Street Partners, Inc.
David D. Croll, Pres.
45 Milk St.
Boston, MA 02109
(617)574-6763   DL: 12/3/86
PC: 3,750,000   SBAL: 5,000,000
IP: D   OC: 5

First Capital Corp. of Chicago
(Main Office: Chicago, IL)
133 Federal St., 6th Fl.
Boston, MA 02110
(617)542-9185

First United SBIC, Inc.
Alfred W. Ferrara, V.P.
135 Will Dr.
Canton, MA 02021
(617)828-6150   DL: 10/29/76
PC: 600,000   SBAL: 0
IP: D   OC: 4

Fleet Venture Resources, Inc.
(Main Office: Providence, RI)
Carlton V. Klein, V.P.
60 State St.
Boston, MA 02109
(617)367-6700

Mezzanine Capital Corp.
David D. Croll, Pres.
45 Milk St.
Boston, MA 02109
(617)574-6752   DL: 5/28/87
PC: 30,000,000   SBAL: 25,000,000
IP: D   OC: 4

Milk Street Partners, Inc.
Richard H. Churchill, Jr., Pres.
45 Milk St.
Boston, MA 02109
(617)574-6723   DL: 9/17/87
PC: 1,000,000   SBAL: 0
IP: D   OC: 5

Monarch-Narragansett Ventures, Inc.
George W. Siguler, Pres.
One Financial Plaza
Springfield, MA 01102
(413)781-3000   DL: 12/8/86
PC: 10,000,000   SBAL: 18,970,000
IP: D   OC: 3

New England Capital Corp.
Z. David Patterson, V.P.

Massachusetts (continued)

One Washington Mall, 7th Fl.
Boston, MA 02108
(617)573-6400   DL: 8/21/61
PC: 15,000,000   SBAL: 0
IP: D   OC: 1

Northeast SBI Corp.
Joseph Mindick, Treas.
16 Cumberland St.
Boston, MA 02115
(617)267-3983   DL: 5/7/74
PC: 378,802   SBAL: 1,130,000
IP: D   OC: 5

Orange Nassau Capital Corp.
Joost E. Tjaden, Pres.
101 Federal St., 4th Fl.
Boston, MA 02110
(617)951-9420   DL: 7/8/81
PC: 2,000,000   SBAL: 1,000,000
IP: D   OC: 5

Pioneer Ventures Ltd. Partnership
Christopher W. Lynch, Mng. Part.
60 State St.
Boston, MA 02109
(617)742-7825   DL: 11/20/86
PC: 5,157,122   SBAL: 0
IP: D   OC: 3-P

Shawmut National Capital Corp.
Steven James Lee, Pres.
One Federal St., 30th Fl.
Boston, MA 02211
(617)556-4700   DL: 12/27/67
PC: 6,000,000   SBAL: 0
IP: D   OC: 1

Stevens Capital Corp.
Edward Capuano, Pres.
168 Stevens St.
Fall River, MA 02721
(617)679-0044   DL: 6/21/84
PC: 506,000   SBAL: 0
IP: D   OC: 5

UST Capital Corp.
Walter Dick, Pres.
40 Court St.
Boston, MA 02108
(617)726-7137   DL: 10/6/61
PC: 1,752,800   SBAL: 2,000,000
IP: D   OC: 1

Vadus Capital Corp.
Joost E. Tjaden, Pres.
101 Federal St., 4th Fl.
Boston, MA 02110
(617)951-9420   DL: 11/3/81
PC: 2,000,000   SBAL: 1,000,000
IP: D   OC: 5

Michigan

Michigan Tech Capital Corp.
Clark L. Pellegrini, Pres.
Technology Park
601 W. Sharon Ave.; P.O. Box 364
Houghton, MI 49931
(906)487-2970   DL: 8/20/82
PC: 642,500   SBAL: 0
IP: D   OC: 5

Minnesota

FBS SBIC, Ltd. Partnership
John M. Murphy, Jr., Mng. Agent
1100 First Bank Pl. E.
Minneapolis, MN 55480
(612)370-4764   DL: 9/27/84

PC: 11,183,320   SBAL: 0
IP: D   OC: 1-P

North Star Ventures II, Inc.
Terrence W. Glarner, Pres.
150 S. Fifth St., Ste. 3400
Minneapolis, MN 55402
(612)333-1133   DL: 5/17/84
PC: 6,663,585   SBAL: 13,020,000
IP: D   OC: 5

Northland Capital Venture Partnership
George G. Barnum, Jr., Pres.
613 Missabe Bldg.
Duluth, MN 55802
(218)722-0545   DL: 6/30/67
PC: 773,822   SBAL: 800,000
IP: D   OC: 5-P

Northwest Venture Partners
Robert F. Zicarelli, Mng. G.P.
2800 Piper Jaffray Tower
222 S. Ninth St.
Minneapolis, MN 55402
(612)372-8770   DL: 10/13/83
PC: 50,446,962   SBAL: 0
IP: D   OC: 2-P

Norwest Growth Fund, Inc.
Daniel J. Haggerty, Pres.
2800 Piper Jaffray Tower
222 S. Ninth St.
Minneapolis, MN 55402
(612)372-8770   DL: 2/25/60
PC: 16,350,000   SBAL: 18,504,000
IP: D   OC: 1

Shared Ventures, Inc.
Howard W. Weiner, Pres.
6550 York Ave., South, Ste. 419
Edina, MN 55435
(612)925-3411   DL: 9/18/81
PC: 752,000   SBAL: 1,200,000
IP: D   OC: 5

Missouri

Bankers Capital Corp.
Raymond E. Glasnapp, Pres.
3100 Gillham Rd.
Kansas City, MO 64109
(816)531-1600   DL: 2/12/76
PC: 632,000   SBAL: 1,010,000
IP: D   OC: 5

Capital for Business, Inc.
James B. Hebenstreit, Pres.
1000 Walnut, 18th Fl.
Kansas City, MO 64106
(816)234-2357   DL: 10/15/59
PC: 6,000,000   SBAL: 0
IP: D   OC: 1

Capital for Business, Inc.
(Main Office: Kansas City, MO)
11 S. Meramec, Ste. 804
St. Louis, MO 63105
(314)854-7427

MBI Venture Capital Investors, Inc.
Anthony Sommers, Pres.
850 Main St.
Kansas City, MO 64105
(816)471-1700   DL: 12/11/84
PC: 5,500,000   SBAL: 0
IP: D   OC: 1

MorAmerica Capital Corp.
(Main Office: Cedar Rapids, IA)
911 Main St., Ste. 2724A
Commerce Tower Bldg.

Kansas City, MO 64105
(816)842-0114

United Missouri Capital Corp.
Joe Kessinger, Mngr.
1010 Grand Ave.
Mail: P.O. Box 419226; K.C., MO 64141
Kansas City, MO 64106
(816)556-7333   DL: 9/21/84
PC: 2,500,000   SBAL: 0
IP: D   OC: 1

Nebraska

First of Nebraska Investment Corp.
Dennis O'Neal, Mng. Off.
One First National Ctr., Ste. 701
Omaha, NE 68102
(402)633-3585   DL: 11/25/88
PC: 1,000,000   SBAL: 0
IP: D   OC: 1

United Financial Resources Corp.
Dennis L. Schulte, Mngr.
6211 L. St.
Mail: P.O. Box 1131
Omaha, NE 68101
(402)734-1250   DL: 7/7/83
PC: 500,000   SBAL: 500,000
IP: GS   OC: 5

Nevada

Enterprise Finance Cap. Development Corp.
Robert S. Russell, Sr., Pres.
First Interstate Bank of Nevada Bldg.
One E. First Street, Ste. 1100
Reno, NV 89501
(702)329-7797   DL: 12/29/83
PC: 1,000,000   SBAL: 800,000
IP: D   OC: 5

New Hampshire

VenCap, Inc.
Richard J. Ash, Pres.
1155 Elm St.
Manchester, NH 03101
(603)644-6100   DL: 1/10/85
PC: 1,403,911   SBAL: 1,200,000
IP: D   OC: 5

New Jersey

Bishop Capital, L.P.
Charles J. Irish
58 Park Pl.
Newark, NJ 07102
(201)623-0171   DL: 8/27/87
PC: 3,000,000   SBAL: 1,000,000
IP: D   OC: 2-P

ESLO Capital Corp.
Leo Katz, Pres.
212 Wright St.
Newark, NJ 07114
(201)242-4488   DL: 5/31/79
PC: 639,323   SBAL: 1,500,000
IP: D   OC: 5

First Princeton Capital Corp.
Michael D. Feinstein, Pres.
Five Garret Mountain Plaza
West Paterson, NJ 07424
(201)278-8111   DL: 3/8/83
PC: 1,202,048   SBAL: 2,250,000
IP: D   OC: 5

Monmouth Capital Corp.
Eugene W. Landy, Pres.

125 Wycoff Rd.
Midland Nat. Bank Bldg., P.O. Box
335
Eatontown, NJ 07724
(201)542-4927   DL: 5/28/61
PC: 2,083,247   SBAL: 3,670,000
IP: D   OC: 6

Tappan Zee Capital Corp.
Karl Kirschner, Pres.
201 Lower Notch Rd.
Little Falls, NJ 07424
(201)256-8280   DL: 11/16/63
PC: 750,000   SBAL: 2,250,000
IP: 66% RE   OC: 5

Unicorn Ventures II, L.P.
Frank P. Diassi, G.P.
6 Commerce Dr.
Cranford, NJ 07016
(201)276-7880   DL: 10/9/84
PC: 4,553,000   SBAL: 4,000,000
IP: D   OC: 5-P

Unicorn Ventures, Ltd.
Frank P. Diassi, Pres.
6 Commerce Dr.
Cranford, NJ 07016
(201)276-7880   DL: 11/10/81
PC: 2,508,513   SBAL: 6,000,000
IP: D   OC: 5-P

United Jersey Venture Capital, Inc.
Stephen H. Paneyko, Pres.
301 Carnegie Ctr., P.O. Box 2066
Princeton, NJ 08540
(609)987-3490   DL: 1/20/87
PC: 1,000,000   SBAL: 0
IP: D   OC: 1

New Mexico

Albuquerque SBIC
Albert T. Ussery, Pres.
501 Tijeras Ave., N.W.
P.O. Box 487
Albuquerque, NM 87103
(505)247-0145   DL: 11/16/77
PC: 552,000   SBAL: 1,500,000
IP: D   OC: 5

Equity Capital Corp.
Jerry A. Henson, Pres.
119 E. Marcy St., Ste. 101
Santa Fe, NM 87501
(505)988-4273   DL: 1/24/84
PC: 962,720   SBAL: 1,250,000
IP: D   OC: 5

Southwest Capital Investments, Inc.
Martin J. Roe, Pres.
The Southwest Bldg.
3500-E Comanche Rd., N.E.
Albuquerque, NM 87107
(505)884-7161   DL: 4/30/76
PC: 830,552   SBAL: 2,480,000
IP: D   OC: 3

United Mercantile Capital Corp.
Joe Justice, Gen. Mgr.
2400 Louisiana Blvd., Bldg. 4, Ste.
101
Mail: P.O. Box 37487; Albuquerque
87176
Albuquerque, NM 87110
(505)883-8201   DL: 11/16/76
PC: 629,888   SBAL: 1,200,000
IP: D   OC: 5

New York

767 Ltd. Partnership
H. Wertheim and H. Mallement, G.P.
767 Third Ave.
New York, NY 10017
(212)838-7776   DL: 6/18/84
PC: 1,515,152   SBAL: 1,500,000
IP: D   OC: 5-P

ASEA-Harvest Partners II
Harvey Wertheim, G.P.
767 Third Ave.
New York, NY 10017
(212)838-7776   DL: 10/9/84
PC: 1,016,559   SBAL: 1,000,000
IP: D   OC: 5-P

American Commercial Capital Corp.
Gerald J. Grossman, Pres.
310 Madison Ave., Ste. 1304
New York, NY 10017
(212)986-3305   DL: 12/30/82
PC: 1,000,000   SBAL: 3,000,000
IP: D   OC: 5

American Energy Investment Corp.
John J. Hoey, Chmn. of the Board
645 Fifth Ave., Ste. 1900
New York, NY 10022
(212)688-7307   DL: 2/20/81
PC: 2,500,000   SBAL: 0
IP: EI   OC: 5

Amev Capital Corp.
Martin Orland, Pres.
One World Trade Ctr., 50th Fl.
New York, NY 10048
(212)775-9100   DL: 8/14/79
PC: 5,500,000   SBAL: 8,000,000
IP: D   OC: 5

Atalanta Investment Co., Inc.
L. Mark Newman, Chmn. of the Board
450 Park Ave.
New York, NY 10022
(212)832-1104   DL: 6/22/79
PC: 5,422,321   SBAL: 11,800,000
IP: D   OC: 4

BT Capital Corp.
James G. Hellmuth, Dpty. Chmn.
280 Park Ave.—10 West
New York, NY 10017
(212)850-1916   DL: 11/10/72
PC: 78,310,944   SBAL: 25,500,000
IP: D   OC: 1

Boston Hambro Capital Co.
(Main Office: Boston, MA)
17 E. 71st St.
New York, NY 10021
(212)288-9106

Bridger Capital Corp.
Seymour L. Wane, Pres.
645 Madison Ave., Ste. 810
New York, NY 10022
(212)888-4004   DL: 4/5/88
PC: 2,005,000   SBAL: 4,000,000
IP: D   OC: 5

CMNY Capital L.P.
Robert Davidoff, G.P.
77 Water St.
New York, NY 10005
(212)437-7078   DL: 3/14/62
PC: 3,400,000   SBAL: 13,100,000
IP: D   OC: 3-P

Central New York SBIC
Albert Wertheimer, Pres.

351 S. Warren St.
Syracuse, NY 13202
(315)478-5026   DL: 4/28/61
PC: 150,000   SBAL: 0
IP: VM   OC: 4

Chase Manhattan Capital Corp.
Gustav H. Koven, Pres.
1 Chase Manhattan Plaza, 23rd Fl.
New York, NY 10081
(212)552-6275   DL: 8/2/62
PC: 24,785,000   SBAL: 0
IP: D   OC: 1

Chemical Venture Capital Assoc.
Jeffrey C. Walker, Mng. Gen. Part.
277 Park Ave., 10th Fl.
New York, NY 10172
(212)310-7578   DL: 10/22/84
PC: 69,384,413   SBAL: 0
IP: D   OC: 1-P

Citicorp Venture Capital, Ltd.
William Comfort, Chmn. of the Bd.
399 Park Ave., 6th Fl.
New York, NY 10043
(212)559-1127   DL: 12/18/67
PC: 127,197,602   SBAL: 10,000,000
IP: D   OC: 1

Clinton Capital Corp.
Mark Scharfman, Pres.
79 Madison Ave., Ste. 800
New York, NY 10016
(212)696-4334   DL: 10/22/80
PC: 12,000,000   SBAL: 35,000,000
IP: D   OC: 5

Croyden Capital Corp.
Lawrence D. Gorfinkle, Pres.
45 Rockefeller Plaza, Ste. 2165
New York, NY 10111
(212)974-0184   DL: 5/23/84
PC: 1,457,963   SBAL: 1,000,000
IP: D   OC: 5

Diamond Capital Corp.
Steven B. Kravitz, Pres.
805 Third Ave., Ste. 1100
New York, NY 10017
(212)838-1255   DL: 1/21/88
PC: 2,000,000   SBAL: 0
IP: D   OC: 5

Edwards Capital Co.
Edward H. Teitlebaum, Pres.
215 Lexington Ave., Ste. 805
New York, NY 10016
(212)686-2568   DL: 6/22/79
PC: 7,200,000   SBAL: 18,450,000
IP: T   OC: 5-P

F/N Capital Ltd. Partnership
Raymond A. Lancaster, Pres.
One Norstar Plaza
Albany, NY 12207
(518)447-4050   DL: 11/29/88
PC: 3,600,000   SBAL: 0
IP: D   OC: 1-P

Fairfield Equity Corp.
Matthew A. Berdon, Pres.
200 E. 42nd Street
New York, NY 10017
(212)867-0150   DL: 11/16/61
PC: 997,109   SBAL: 2,400,000
IP: D   OC: 5

Ferranti High Technology, Inc.
Sandford R. Simon, Pres. & Dir.
515 Madison Ave.
New York, NY 10022

New York (continued)

(212)688-9828   DL: 5/31/83
PC: 3,000,000   SBAL: 1,000,000
IP: D   OC: 5

Fifty-Third St. Ventures, L.P.
Patricia Cloherty & Dan Tessler, G.P.
155 Main St.
Cold Spring, NY 10516
(914)265-5167   DL: 7/29/76
PC: 5,790,251   SBAL: 7,960,000
IP: D   OC: 5-P

Franklin Corp. SBIC (The)
Norman S. Strobel, Pres.
767 Fifth Ave.
G.M. Bldg., 23rd Fl.
New York, NY 10153
(212)486-2323   DL: 9/17/59
PC: 10,003,114   SBAL: 8,640,000
IP: D   OC: 6

Fundex Capital Corp.
Howard Sommer, Pres.
525 Northern Blvd.
Great Neck, NY 11021
(516)466-8551   DL: 5/18/78
PC: 1,801,000   SBAL: 4,650,000
IP: D   OC: 5

GHW Capital Corp.
Philip Worlitzer, V.P.
25 W. 45th St., Ste. 707
New York, NY 10036
(212)869-4584   DL: 11/13/85
PC: 1,000,000   SBAL: 0
IP: D   OC: 1

Genesee Funding, Inc.
A. Keene Bolton, Pres.
100 Corporate Woods
Rochester, NY 14623
(716)272-2332   DL: 11/26/86
PC: 1,000,000   SBAL: 0
IP: D   OC: 5

Hanover Capital Corp. (The)
Geoffrey T. Selzer, Pres.
150 E. 58th St., Ste. 2710
New York, NY 10155
(212)980-9670   DL: 6/22/61
PC: 1,000,001   SBAL: 1,875,000
IP: D   OC: 5

Intergroup Venture Capital Corp.
Ben Hauben, Pres.
230 Park Ave.
New York, NY 10017
(212)661-5428   DL: 8/7/78
PC: 502,500   SBAL: 0
IP: D   OC: 5

Interstate Capital Co., Inc.
David Scharf, Pres.
380 Lexington Ave.
New York, NY 10017
(212)986-7333   DL: 10/22/80
PC: 1,250,000   SBAL: 3,500,000
IP: D   OC: 5

Irving Capital Corp.
Andrew McWethy, Pres.
1290 Ave. of the Americas
New York, NY 10104
(212)408-4800   DL: 12/6/76
PC: 16,400,000   SBAL: 0
IP: D   OC: 1

Kwiat Capital Corp.
Sheldon F. Kwiat, Pres.
576 Fifth Ave.

New York, NY 10036
(212)391-2461   DL: 9/25/81
PC: 510,000   SBAL: 500,000
IP: D   OC: 5

M & T Capital Corp.
William Randon, Pres.
One M & T Plaza
Buffalo, NY 14240
(716)842-5881   DL: 12/29/67
PC: 5,007,486   SBAL: 0
IP: D   OC: 1

MH Capital Investors, Inc.
Edward L. Kock III, Pres.
270 Park Ave.
New York, NY 10017
(212)286-3222   DL: 11/6/86
PC: 20,000,000   SBAL: 0
IP: D   OC: 1

Multi-Purpose Capital Corp.
Eli B. Fine, Pres.
5 W. Main St., Rm. 207
Elmsford, NY 10523
(914)347-2733   DL: 3/18/63
PC: 210,300   SBAL: 165,000
IP: D   OC: 5

NYBDC Capital Corp.
Robert W. Lazar, Pres.
41 State St.
Albany, NY 12207
(518)463-2268   DL: 11/2/73
PC: 500,000   SBAL: 770,000
IP: D   OC: 4

NYSTRS/NV Capital, Ltd. Partnership
Raymond A. Lancaster, Pres.
One Norstar Plaza
Albany, NY 12207
(518)447-4050   DL: 2/7/86
PC: 6,750,730   SBAL: 0
IP: D   OC: 2-P

NatWest USA Capital Corp.
Orville G. Aarons, G. Mngr.
175 Water St.
New York, NY 10038
(212)602-1200   DL: 2/6/86
PC: 20,000,000   SBAL: 0
IP: D   OC: 1

Norstar Capital Inc.
Raymond A. Lancaster, Pres.
One Norstar Plaza
Albany, NY 12207
(518)447-4043   DL: 4/12/85
PC: 5,396,925   SBAL: 0
IP: D   OC: 1

Norwood Venture Corp.
Mark R. Littell, Pres.
145 W. 45th St., Ste. 1211
New York, NY 10036
(212)869-5075   DL: 8/18/80
PC: 5,000,000   SBAL: 9,000,000
IP: D   OC: 5

Onondaga Venture Capital Fund, Inc.
Irving W. Schwartz, Exec. V.P.
327 State Tower Bldg.
Syracuse, NY 13202
(315)478-0157   DL: 9/30/87
PC: 2,502,500   SBAL: 0
IP: D   OC: 5

Preferential Capital Corp.
Bruce Bayroff, Sec.-Treas.
16 Court St.
Brooklyn, NY 11241
(718)855-2728   DL: 9/14/79

PC: 509,380   SBAL: 1,000,000
IP: D   OC: 5

Pyramid Ventures, Inc.
John Popovitch, Treas.
280 Park Ave.—10 West
New York, NY 10015
(212)850-1934   DL: 6/26/87
PC: 16,002,501   SBAL: 0
IP: D   OC: 1

Questech Capital Corp.
John E. Koonce, Pres.
320 Park Ave., 3rd Fl.
New York, NY 10022
(212)891-7500   DL: 6/26/81
PC: 5,000,000   SBAL: 12,000,000
IP: D   OC: 5

R & R Financial Corp.
Imre Rosenthal, Pres.
1451 Broadway
New York, NY 10036
(212)790-1441   DL: 4/27/62
PC: 505,000   SBAL: 300,000
IP: D   OC: 3

Rand SBIC, Inc.
Donald Ross, Pres.
1300 Rand Bldg.
Buffalo, NY 14203
(716)853-0802   DL: 5/5/76
PC: 1,605,000   SBAL: 1,800,000
IP: D   OC: 6

Realty Growth Capital Corp.
Alan Leavit, Pres.
271 Madison Ave.
New York, NY 10016
(212)983-6880   DL: 3/29/63
PC: 1,000,000   SBAL: 280,000
IP: D   OC: 5

Republic SBI Corp.
Robert V. Treanor, Sr. V.P.
452 Fifth Ave.
New York, NY 10018
(212)930-8639   DL: 4/4/88
PC: 2,000,000   SBAL: 0
IP: D   OC: 1

SLK Capital Corp.
Edward A. Kerbs, Pres.
115 Broadway, 20th Fl.
New York, NY 10006
(212)587-8800   DL: 1/27/88
PC: 1,000,000   SBAL: 0
IP: D   OC: 5

Small Bus. Electronics Investment
Corp.
Stanley Meisels, Pres.
1220 Peninsula Blvd.
Hewlett, NY 11557
(516)374-0743   DL: 9/1/60
PC: 600,000   SBAL: 0
IP: D   OC: 5

Southern Tier Capital Corp.
Harold Gold, Sec.–Treas.
55 S. Main St.
Liberty, NY 12754
(914)292-3030   DL: 6/28/61
PC: 350,111   SBAL: 800,000
IP: MG 70 (hotels and rooming
houses)   OC: 5

Sterling Commercial Capital, Inc.
Harvey L. Granat, Pres.
175 Great Neck Rd., Ste. 404
Great Neck, NY 11021
(516)482-7374   DL: 10/3/88

PC: 2,500,000   SBAL: 0
IP: D   OC: 5

TLC Funding Corp.
Philip G. Kass, Pres.
141 S. Central Ave.
Hartsdale, NY 10530
(914)683-1144   DL: 2/29/80
PC: 1,250,000   SBAL: 2,940,000
IP: D   OC: 5

Tappan Zee Capital Corp.
(Main Office: Little Falls, NJ)
120 N. Main St.
New City, NY 10956
(914)634-8890

Telesciences Capital Corp.
Mike A. Petrozzo, Contact
26 Broadway, Ste. 841
New York, NY 10004
(212)425-0320   DL: 9/14/78
PC: 1,250,000   SBAL: 0
IP: D   OC: 4

Vega Capital Corp.
Victor Harz, Pres.
720 White Plains Rd.
Scarsdale, NY 10583
(914)472-8550   DL: 8/5/68
PC: 2,402,861   SBAL: 5,990,000
IP: D   OC: 6

Venture SBIC, Inc.
Arnold Feldman, Pres.
249-12 Jericho Tpke.
Floral Park, NY 11001
(516)352-0068   DL: 11/23/77
PC: 612,000   SBAL: 1,800,000
IP: D   OC: 5

WFG-Harvest Partners, Ltd.
Harvey J. Wertheim, G.P.
767 Third Ave.
New York, NY 10017
(212)838-7776   DL: 9/30/85
PC: 3,026,412   SBAL: 0
IP: D   OC: 1-P

Winfield Capital Corp.
Stanley M. Pechman, Pres.
237 Mamaroneck Ave.
White Plains, NY 10605
(914)949-2600   DL: 4/19/72
PC: 1,100,000   SBAL: 3,300,000
IP: D   OC: 5

Wood River Capital Corp.
Thomas A. Barron, Pres.
667 Madison Ave.
New York, NY 10022
(212)750-9420   DL: 5/9/79
PC: 15,512,000   SBAL: 31,000,000
IP: D   OC: 5

North Carolina

Delta Capital, Inc.
Alex B. Wilkins, Jr., Pres.
227 N. Tryon St., Ste. 201
Charlotte, NC 28202
(704)372-1410   DL: 11/29/61
PC: 1,250,000   SBAL: 5,000,000
IP: 50% RE   OC: 3

Falcon Capital Corp.
P.S. Prasad, Pres.
400 W. Fifth St.
Greenville, NC 27834
(919)752-5918   DL: 4/14/64
PC: 604,237   SBAL: 1,000,000
IP: D   OC: 5

Heritage Capital Corp.
William R. Starnes, Pres.
2095 Two First Union Ctr.
Charlotte, NC 28282
(704)334-2867   DL: 10/21/61
PC: 2,050,265   SBAL: 3,500,114
IP: 50% RE   OC: 3

Kitty Hawk Capital, Ltd. Partnership
Walter H. Wilkinson, Pres.
Independence Ctr., Ste. 1640
Charlotte, NC 28246
(704)333-3777   DL: 7/23/80
PC: 1,905,000   SBAL: 3,000,000
IP: D   OC: 5-P

NCNB SBIC Corp.
Troy S. McCrory, Jr., Pres.
One NCNB Plaza—T05—2
Charlotte, NC 28255
(704)374-5583   DL: 7/19/84
PC: 2,500,000   SBAL: 0
IP: D   OC: 1

NCNB Venture Co., L.P.
S. Epes Robinson, G.P.
One NCNB Plaza, T-39
Charlotte, NC 28255
(704)374-5723   DL: 7/19/84
PC: 20,176,039   SBAL: 0
IP: D   OC: 1-P

Ohio

A.T. Capital Corp.
Robert C. Salipante, Pres.
900 Euclid Ave., T-18
Mail: P.O. Box 5937
Cleveland, OH 44101
(216)687-4970   DL: 6/4/84
PC: 9,760,000   SBAL: 0
IP: D   OC: 1

Capital Funds Corp.
Carl G. Nelson, Chief Inv. Off.
800 Superior Ave.
Cleveland, OH 44114
(216)344-5774   DL: 12/9/60
PC: 5,700,000   SBAL: 0
IP: C   OC: 1

Clarion Capital Corp.
Morton A. Cohen, Pres.
35555 Curtis Blvd.
Eastlake, OH 44094
(216)953-0555   DL: 9/25/68
PC: 8,891,858   SBAL: 10,040,000
IP: D   OC: 6

First Ohio Capital Corp.
David J. McMacken, G. Mngr.
606 Madison Ave.
Mail: P.O. Box 2061; Toledo, OH 43603
Toledo, OH 43604
(419)259-7146   DL: 4/14/82
PC: 2,450,000   SBAL: 1,300,000
IP: D   OC: 1

Gries Investment Co.
Robert D. Gries, Pres.
1500 Statler Office Tower
Cleveland, OH 44115
(216)861-1146   DL: 3/24/64
PC: 682,961   SBAL: 1,432,400
IP: D   OC: 5

JRM Capital Corp.
H.F. Meyer, Pres.
110 W. Streetsboro St.
Hudson, OH 44236

(216)656-4010   DL: 9/18/75
PC: 550,000   SBAL: 310,000
IP: GS   OC: 4

National City Capital Corp.
Michael Sherwin, Pres.
629 Euclid Ave.
Cleveland, OH 44114
(216)575-2491   DL: 2/8/79
PC: 2,501,791   SBAL: 4,530,000
IP: D   OC: 1

SeaGate Venture Mngmnt., Inc.
Charles A. Brown, V.P.
245 Summit St., Ste. 1403
Toledo, OH 43603
(419)259-8605   DL: 7/19/85
PC: 1,010,000   SBAL: 1,000,000
IP: D   OC: 1

Tamco Investors (SBIC) Inc.
Nathan H. Monus, Pres.
375 Victoria Rd.
Youngstown, OH 44515
(216)792-3811   DL: 6/21/77
PC: 350,000   SBAL: 1,050,000
IP: GS   OC: 4

Oklahoma

Alliance Business Investment Co.
Barry Davis, Pres.
17 E. Second St.
One Williams Ctr., Ste. 2000
Tulsa, OK 74172
(918)584-3581   DL: 8/12/59
PC: 3,480,502   SBAL: 3,860,000
IP: D   OC: 5

Western Venture Capital Corp.
William B. Baker, Chief Op. Off.
4880 S. Lewis
Tulsa, OK 74105
(918)749-7981   DL: 8/3/81
PC: 2,007,500   SBAL: 5,000,000
IP: D   OC: 2

Oregon

First Interstate Capital, Inc.
(Main Office: Newport Beach, CA)
227 S.W. Pine St., Ste. 200
Portland, OR 97204
(503)223-4334

Northern Pacific Capital Corp.
John J. Tennant, Jr., Pres.
1201 S.W. 12th Ave., Ste. 608
Mail: P.O. Box 1658; Portland, OR 97207
Portland, OR 97205
(503)241-1255   DL: 1/18/62
PC: 911,464   SBAL: 500,000
IP: D   OC: 5

Norwest Growth Fund, Inc.
(Main Office: Minneapolis, MN)
1300 S.W. 5th St., Ste. 3108
Portland, OR 97201
(503)223-6622

U.S. Bancorp Capital Corp.
Stephen D. Fekety, Pres.
111 S.W. Fifth Ave., Ste. 1570
Portland, OR 97204
(503)275-5860   DL: 3/5/81
PC: 1,730,000   SBAL: 0
IP: D   OC: 1

Pennsylvania

Capital Corp. of America
Martin M. Newman, Pres.
225 S. 15th St., Ste. 920
Philadelphia, PA 19102
(215)732-1666   DL: 8/9/84
PC: 1,302,135   SBAL: 1,240,000
IP: D   OC: 6

Enterprise Venture Cap. Corp. of Pa.
Don Cowie, C.E.O.
227 Franklin St., Ste. 215
Johnstown, PA 15901
(814)535-7597   DL: 9/11/85
PC: 1,147,649   SBAL: 0
IP: D   OC: 1

Erie SBIC
George R. Heaton, Pres.
32 W. 8th St., Ste. 615
Erie, PA 16501
(814)453-7964   DL: 7/19/85
PC: 1,080,000   SBAL: 1,000,000
IP: D   OC: 5

Fidelcor Capital Corp.
Bruce H. Luehrs, Pres.
123 S. Broad St.
Philadelphia, PA 19109
(215)985-7287   DL: 1/14/88
PC: 5,100,000   SBAL: 0
IP: D   OC: 1

First SBIC of California
(Main Office: Costa Mesa, CA)
Daniel A. Dye, Contact
P.O. Box 512
Washington, PA 15301
(412)223-0707

First Valley Capital Corp.
Matthew W. Thomas, Pres.
640 Hamilton Mall, 8th Fl.
Allentown, PA 18101
(215)776-6760   DL: 8/19/83
PC: 510,000   SBAL: 0
IP: D   OC: 1

Franklin Corp. SBIC (The)
(Main Office: New York, NY)
Plymouth Meeting Exec. Congress
Suite 461-610 W. Germantown Pike
Plymouth Meeting, PA 19462

Meridian Capital Corp.
Joseph E. Laky, Pres.
Ste. 222, Blue Bell West
650 Skippack Pike
Blue Bell, PA 19422
(215)278-8907   DL: 7/22/77
PC: 2,571,715   SBAL: 0
IP: D   OC: 1

Meridian Venture Partners
Raymond R. Rafferty, G.P.
The Fidelity Court Bldg.
259 Radnor-Chester Rd.
Radnor, PA 19087
(215)293-0210   DL: 2/24/87
PC: 5,000,000   SBAL: 0
IP: D   OC: 5-P

PNC Capital Corp.
Gary J. Zentner, Pres.
Pittsburgh National Bldg.
Fifth Ave. and Wood St.
Pittsburgh, PA 15222
(412)355-2245   DL: 8/12/82
PC: 5,044,971   SBAL: 0
IP: D   OC: 1

Rhode Island

Domestic Capital Corp.
Nathaniel B. Baker, Pres.
815 Reservoir Ave.
Cranston, RI 02910
(401)946-3310   DL: 12/11/84
PC: 500,000   SBAL: 1,000,000
IP: D   OC: 1

Fleet Venture Resources, Inc.
Robert M. Van Degna, Pres.
111 Westminster St.
Providence, RI 02903
(401)278-6770   DL: 12/18/67
PC: 10,207,604   SBAL: 1,500,000
IP: D   OC: 1

Moneta Capital Corp.
Arnold Kilberg, Pres.
285 Governor St.
Providence, RI 02906
(401)861-4600   DL: 5/4/84
PC: 1,002,500   SBAL: 1,500,000
IP: D   OC: 5

Old Stone Capital Corp.
Arthur C. Barton, Pres.
One Old Stone Sq., 11th Fl.
Providence, RI 02903
(401)278-2559   DL: 7/20/61
PC: 6,991,500   SBAL: 7,270,000
IP: D   OC: 3

Wallace Capital Corp.
Lloyd W. Granoff, Pres.
170 Westminister St., Ste. 300
Providence, RI 02903
(401)273-9191   DL: 12/22/86
PC: 1,015,000   SBAL: 0
IP: D   OC: 4

South Carolina

Carolina Venture Cap. Corp.
Thomas H. Harvey III, Pres.
14 Archer Rd.
Hilton Head Isl., SC 29928
(803)842-3101   DL: 1/19/81
PC: 792,100   SBAL: 700,000
IP: D   OC: 5

Charleston Capital Corp.
Henry Yaschik, Pres.
111 Church St., P.O. Box 328
Charleston, SC 29402
(803)723-6464   DL: 6/21/61
PC: 1,012,409   SBAL: 1,000,000
IP: D   OC: 5

Floco Investment Co., Inc. (The)
William H. Johnson, Sr., Pres.
Highway 52 North
Mail: P.O. Box 919; Lake City, SC
29560
Scranton, SC 29561
(803)389-2731   DL: 7/5/61
PC: 491,900   SBAL: 0
IP: FOR   OC: 5

Lowcountry Investment Corp.
Joseph T. Newton, Jr., Pres.
4444 Daley St.
P.O. Box 10447
Charleston, SC 29411
(803)554-9880   DL: 7/28/60
PC: 1,908,950   SBAL: 1,620,000
IP: GS   OC: 4

Reedy River Ventures
John M. Sterling, Pres.
233 E. Main St., Ste. 202

Mail: P.O. Box 17526
Greenville, SC 29606
(803)232-6198   DL: 7/16/81
PC: 2,607,300   SBAL: 3,200,000
IP: D   OC: 5-P

Tennessee

Financial Resources, Inc.
Milton Picard, Chmn. of the Board
2800 Sterick Bldg.
Memphis, TN 38103
(901)527-9411   DL: 3/21/62
PC: 1,000,320   SBAL: 0
IP: D   OC: 5

Leader Capital Corp.
James E. Pruitt Jr., Pres.
158 Madison Ave.
P.O. Box 708; Memphis 38101-0708
Memphis, TN 38101
(901)578-2405   DL: 6/23/86
PC: 1,485,000   SBAL: 0
IP: D   OC: 3

Texas

Alliance Business Investment Co.
(Main Office: Tulsa, OK)
911 Louisiana
One Shell Plaza, Ste. 3990
Houston, TX 77002
(713)224-8224

Brittany Capital Co.
Steve Peden, Part.
1525 Elm St.
2424 LTV Tower
Dallas, TX 75201
(214)954-1515   DL: 8/4/69
PC: 1,000,000   SBAL: 3,200,000
IP: D   OC: 5-P

Business Capital Corp.
James E. Sowell, Chmn. of the Board
4809 Cole Ave., Ste. 250
Dallas, TX 75205
(214)522-3739   DL: 9/30/82
PC: 510,000   SBAL: 800,000
IP: D   OC: 5

Capital Marketing Corp.
Ray Ballard, Mngr.
100 Nat Gibbs Dr.
P.O. Box 1000
Keller, TX 76248
(817)656-7309   DL: 6/24/68
PC: 11,155,106   SBAL: 32,460,000
IP: GS   OC: 4

Capital Southwest Venture Corp.
William R. Thomas, Pres.
12900 Preston Rd., Ste. 700
Dallas, TX 75230
(214)233-8242   DL: 7/13/61
PC: 5,794,784   SBAL: 16,000,000
IP: D   OC: 6

Central Texas SBI Corp.
David G. Horner, Pres.
P.O. Box 2600
Waco, TX 76702
(817)753-6461   DL: 3/29/62
PC: 600,000   SBAL: 0
IP: D   OC: 1

Charter Venture Group, Inc.
Winston C. Davis, Pres.
2600 Citadel Plaza Dr., Ste. 600
Houston, TX 77008
(713)863-0704   DL: 10/10/80

PC: 1,000,000   SBAL: 1,000,000
IP: D   OC: 1

Citicorp Venture Capital, Ltd.
(Main Office: New York, NY)
717 N. Harwood, Ste. 2920-LB87
Dallas, TX 75201
(214)880-9670

Energy Assets, Inc.
Laurence E. Simmons, Exec. V.P.
4900 Republic Bank Ctr.
700 Lousiana
Houston, TX 77002
(713)236-9999   DL: 4/12/79
PC: 1,233,109   SBAL: 500,000
IP: EI   OC: 4

Enterprise Capital Corp.
Fred Zeidman, Pres.
4543 Post Oak Pl., #130
Houston, TX 77027
(713)621-9444   DL: 5/8/70
PC: 5,000,000   SBAL: 12,000,000
IP: D   OC: 3

FCA Investment Co.
Robert S. Baker, Chmn.
3000 Post Oak, Ste. 1790
Houston, TX 77056
(713)965-0061   DL: 8/19/85
PC: 1,017,000   SBAL: 240,000
IP: D   OC: 5

First Interstate Cap. Corp. of Texas
Richard S. Smith, Pres.
1000 Louisiana, 7th Fl.
Mail: P.O. Box 3326; Houston, TX
77253
Houston, TX 77002
(713)224-6611   DL: 11/1/79
PC: 19,057,008   SBAL: 19,000,000
IP: D   OC: 1

Ford Capital, Ltd.
C. Jeff Pan, Pres.
1525 Elm St.
Mail: P.O. Box 2140; Dallas, TX 75221
Dallas, TX 75201
(214)954-0688   DL: 10/6/86
PC: 8,045,500   SBAL: 0
IP: D   OC: 1-P

Houston Partners, SBIP
Harvard Hill, Pres., CGP
Capital Center Penthouse
401 Louisiana
Houston, TX 77002
(713)222-8600   DL: 11/19/85
PC: 1,656,477   SBAL: 2,200,000
IP: D   OC: 5-P

MCap Corp.
J. Wayne Gaylord, Mngr.
1717 Main St., 6th Fl.
Momentum Pl.
Dallas, TX 75201
(214)939-3131   DL: 3/31/88
PC: 3,500,000   SBAL: 0
IP: D   OC: 1

MVenture Corp.
Wayne Gaylord, Pres.
1717 Main St., 6th Fl. — Momentum
Pl.
Mail: P.O. Box 662090; Dallas, TX
75266
Dallas, TX 75201
(214)939-3131   DL: 12/8/76
PC: 16,250,000   SBAL: 35,000,000
IP: D   OC: 1

Mapleleaf Capital Ltd.
Edward Fink, Pres.
55 Waugh, Ste. 710
Houston, TX 77007
(713)880-4494   DL: 10/6/80
PC: 3,000,002   SBAL: 5,000,000
IP: D   OC: 2-P

Mid-State Capital Corp.
Smith E. Thomasson, Pres.
510 N. Valley Mills Dr.
Waco, TX 76710
(817)772-9220   DL: 3/4/85
PC: 1,400,000   SBAL: 0
IP: D   OC: 2

Neptune Capital Corp.
Richard C. Strauss, Pres.
5956 Sherry Ln., Ste. 800
Dallas, TX 75225
(214)739-1414   DL: 12/23/86
PC: 1,062,707   SBAL: 0
IP: D   OC: 5

Omega Capital Corp.
Theodric E. Moor, Jr., Pres.
755 S. 11th St., Ste. 250
Mail: P.O. Box 2173
Beaumont, TX 77704
(409)832-0221   DL: 8/12/82
PC: 530,000   SBAL: 500,000
IP: D   OC: 5

Republic Venture Group, Inc.
Robert H. Wellborn, CEO
325 N. St. Paul 2829 Tower II
Mail: P.O. Box 655961; Dallas, TX
75265
Dallas, TX 775201
(214)922-3500   DL: 6/26/61
PC: 36,000,044   SBAL: 9,000,000
IP: D   OC: 1

Revelation Resources, Ltd.
Mr. Chris J. Mathews, Mngr.
2929 Allen Pkwy., Ste. 1705
Houston, TX 77019
(713)526-5623   DL: 1/12/88
PC: 1,123,605   SBAL: 0
IP: D   OC: 5-P

Rust Capital Ltd.
Jack A. Morgan, Part.
114 W. 7th St., Ste. 500
Austin, TX 78701
(512)482-0806   DL: 5/4/79
PC: 7,000,000   SBAL: 12,000,000
IP: D   OC: 3-P

SBI Capital Corp.
William E. Wright, Pres.
6305 Beverly Hill Ln.
Mail: P.O. Box 570368; Houston, TX
77257
Houston, TX 77057
(713)975-1188   DL: 10/22/81
PC: 2,250,000   SBAL: 2,700,000
IP: D   OC: 5

San Antonio Venture Group, Inc.
Domingo Bueno, Pres.
2300 W. Commerce St.
San Antonio, TX 78207
(512)223-3633   DL: 3/23/78
PC: 1,051,000   SBAL: 500,000
IP: D   OC: 4

South Texas SBIC
Kenneth L. Vickers, Pres.
120 S. Main St.
P.O. Box 1698

Victoria, TX 77902
(512)573-5151   DL: 5/8/61
PC: 1,500,000   SBAL: 1,000,000
IP: D   OC: 1

Southwestern Venture Cap. of Texas,
Inc.
James A. Bettersworth, Pres.
1336 E. Court St.
P.O. Box 1719
Seguin, TX 78155
(512)379-0380   DL: 11/24/80
PC: 1,326,000   SBAL: 1,000,000
IP: D   OC: 2

Southwestern Venture Cap. of Texas,
Inc.
(Main Office: Seguin, TX)
1250 N.E. Loop 410, Ste. 300
San Antonio, TX 78209
(512)822-9949

Sunwestern Capital Corp.
Thomas W. Wright, Pres.
3 Forest Plaza
12221 Merit Dr., Ste. 1300
Dallas, TX 75251
(214)239-5650   DL: 3/7/83
PC: 2,324,372   SBAL: 5,500,000
IP: D   OC: 5

Sunwestern Ventures, Ltd.
Thomas W. Wright, Pres.
3 Forest Plaza
12221 Merit Dr., Ste. 1300
Dallas, TX 75251
(214)239-5650   DL: 10/22/84
PC: 10,076,928   SBAL: 25,500,000
IP: D   OC: 5-P

Texas Commerce Investment Co.
Fred Lummis, V.P.
Texas Commerce Bank Bldg., 30th Fl.
712 Main St.
Houston, TX 77002
(713)236-4719   DL: 6/9/82
PC: 8,700,000   SBAL: 0
IP: D   OC: 1

UNCO Ventures, Inc.
John Gatti, Pres.
909 Fannin St., 7th Fl.
Houston, TX 77010
(713)853-2422   DL: 9/30/88
PC: 3,000,000   SBAL: 0
IP: D   OC: 2

Wesbanc Ventures, Ltd.
Stuart Schube, Gen. Part.
520 Post Oak Blvd., Ste. 130
Houston, TX 77027
(713)622-9595   DL: 5/28/85
PC: 2,530,000   SBAL: 1,500,000
IP: D   OC: 1-P

Western Financial Capital Corp.
Mrs. Marion Rosemore, Pres.
17772 Preston Rd., Ste. 101
Dallas, TX 75252
(214)380-0044   DL: 2/22/80
PC: 4,046,744   SBAL: 10,640,000
IP: M   OC: 6

Vermont

Queneska Capital Corp.
Albert W. Coffrin, III, Pres.
123 Church St.
Burlington, VT 05401
(802)865-1806   DL: 4/25/88
PC: 1,500,000   SBAL: 0
IP: D   OC: 1

Virginia

Crestar Capital
A. Hugh Ewing, III, Mng. G.P.
9 S. 12th St., 3rd Fl.
Richmond, VA 23219
(804)643-7358   DL: 10/29/84
PC: 9,100,000   SBAL: 7,500,000
IP: D   OC: 1

James River Capital Assoc.
A. Hugh Ewing, Mng. Part.
9 S. 12th St.
Mail: P.O. Box 1776; Richmond, VA
23219
Richmond, VA 23214
(804)643-7323   DL: 5/15/81
PC: 1,144,875   SBAL: 2,500,000
IP: D   OC: 5-P

Metropolitan Capital Corp.
John B. Toomey, Pres.
2550 Huntington Ave.
Alexandria, VA 22303
(703)960-4698   DL: 12/2/70
PC: 2,238,418   SBAL: 3,090,000
IP: D   OC: 4   .

Sovran Funding Corp.
David A. King, Jr., Pres.
Sovran Ctr., 6th Fl.
One Commercial Plaza
Mail: P.O. Box 600
Norfolk, VA 23510
(804)441-4041   DL: 2/11/85
PC: 10,000,000   SBAL: 3,000,000
IP: D   OC: 1

Tidewater SBI Corp.
Gregory H. Wingfield, Pres.
1214 First Virginia Bank Tower
101 St. Paul's Blvd.
Norfolk, VA 23510
(804)627-2315   DL: 2/5/65
PC: 1,000,000   SBAL: 500,000
IP: D   OC: 4

Washington

Capital Resource Corp.
T. Evans Wyckoff, Pres.

1001 Logan Bldg.
Seattle, WA 98101
(206)623-6550   DL: 5/19/80
PC: 1,087,373   SBAL: 1,000,000
IP: D   OC: 5

Northwest Business Investment Corp.
C. Paul Sandifur, Pres.
929 W. Sprague Ave.
Spokane, WA 99204
(509)838-3111   DL: 3/16/61
PC: 238,680   SBAL: 0
IP: D   OC: 5

Seafirst Capital Corp.
David R. West, Exec. V.P.
Columbia Seafirst Ctr.
701 Fifth Ave., P.O. Box 34103
Seattle, WA 98124
(206)358-7441   DL: 6/18/80
PC: 3,000,000   SBAL: 5,500,000
IP: D   OC: 1

U.S. Bancorp Capital Corp.
(Main Office: Portland, OR)
1415 Fifth Ave.
Seattle, WA 98171
(206)344-8105

Washington Trust Equity Corp.
John M. Snead, Pres.
Washington Trust Financial Ctr.
P.O. Box 2127
Spokane, WA 99210
(509)455-3821   DL: 2/21/80
PC: 705,000   SBAL: 0
IP: D   OC: 1

Wisconsin

Banc One Venture Corp.
H. Wayne Foreman, Pres.
111 E. Wisconsin Ave.
Milwaukee, WI 53202
(414)765-2274   DL: 5/2/84
PC: 6,000,000   SBAL: 2,000,000
IP: D   OC: 1

Bando-McGlocklin Capital Corp.
George Schonath, Investment Adv.
13555 Bishops Ct., Ste. 225
Brookfield, WI 53005
(414)784-9010   DL: 9/2/80
PC: 7,175,113   SBAL: 21,520,000
IP: D   OC: 5

Capital Investments, Inc.
Robert L. Banner, V.P.
Commerce Bldg., Ste. 400
744 N. Fourth St.
Milwaukee, WI 53203
(414)273-6560   DL: 5/25/59
PC: 4,806,833   SBAL: 7,580,000
IP: D   OC: 6

M & I Ventures Corp.
Jon T. Byrnes, Pres.
770 N. Water St.
Milwaukee, WI 53202
(414)765-7910   DL: 8/19/85
PC: 5,448,370   SBAL: 0
IP: D   OC: 1

MorAmerica Capital Corp.
(Main Office: Cedar Rapids, IA)
600 E. Mason St.
Milwaukee, WI 53202
(414)276-3839

Super Market Investors, Inc.
David H. Maass, Pres.
23000 Roundy Dr.
Mail: P.O. Box 473; Milwaukee 53202
Pewaukee, WI 53072
(414)547-7999   DL: 1/25/79
PC: 500,000   SBAL: 750,000
IP: GS   OC: 4

Wisconsin Community Capital, Inc.
Paul J. Eble, Pres.
1 S. Pinckney St., Ste. 500
Madison, WI 53703
(608)256-3441   DL: 12/17/85
PC: 1,005,000   SBAL: 0
IP: D   OC: 5

Part II—301(d) Licensees

Alabama

Alabama Capital Corp.
David C. Delaney, Pres.
16 Midtown Park East
Mobile, AL 36606
(205)476-0700   DL: 7/28/81
PC: 1,550,000   SBAL: 4,650,000
IP: D   OC: 5

Alabama Small Business Investment
Co.
Harold Gilchrist, Mngr.
206 N. 24th St.
Birmingham, AL 35203
(205)324-5234   DL: 4/5/88
PC: 1,005,000   SBAL: 0
IP: D   OC: 1

Tuskegee Capital Corp.
A. G. Bartholomew, Pres.
4453 Richardson Rd.
Hampton Hall Bldg.
Montgomery, AL 36108
(205)281-8059   DL: 2/9/83

PC: 850,000   SBAL: 0
IP: D   OC: 5

Alaska

Calista Business Investment Corp.
Alex Raider, Pres.
503 E. Sixth Ave.
Anchorage, AK 99501
(907)277-0425   DL: 3/31/83
PC: 750,000   SBAL: 750,000
IP: D   OC: 5

Arkansas

Capital Management Services, Inc.
David L. Hale, Pres.
1910 N. Grant St., Ste. 200
Little Rock, AR 72207
(501)664-8613   DL: 3/14/79
PC: 1,406,310   SBAL: 2,500,000
IP: D   OC: 5

Power Ventures, Inc.
Dorsey D. Glover, Pres.

829 Highway 270 N.
Malvern, AR 72104
(501)332-3695   DL: 2/26/81
PC: 500,000   SBAL: 1,000,000
IP: D   OC: 5

California

ABC Capital Corp.
Anne B. Cheng, Pres.
610 E. Live Oak Ave.
Arcadia, CA 91006
(818)570-0653   DL: 1/9/85
PC: 1,000,000   SBAL: 3,000,000
IP: D   OC: 5

Allied Business Investors, Inc.
Jack Hong, Pres.
428 S. Atlantic Blvd., Ste. 201
Monterey Park, CA 91754
(818)289-0186   DL: 12/29/82
PC: 600,000   SBAL: 1,200,000
IP: D   OC: 5

Ally Finance Corp.
Percy P. Lin, Pres.
9100 Wilshire Blvd., Ste. 408
Beverly Hills, CA 90212
(213)550-8100   DL: 6/4/82
PC: 600,000   SBAL: 950,000
IP: D   OC: 5

Asian American Capital Corp.
David Der, Pres.
1251 W. Tennyson Rd., Ste. 4
Hayward, CA 94544
(415)887-6888   DL: 2/23/81
PC: 638,200   SBAL: 1,000,000
IP: D   OC: 5

Astar Capital Corp.
George Hsu, Pres.
7282 Orangethorpe Ave., Ste. 8
Buena Park, CA 90621
(714)739-2218   DL: 11/6/86
PC: 1,020,000   SBAL: 3,060,000
IP: D   OC: 5

Bentley Capital
John Hung, Pres.
592 Vallejo St., Ste. 2
San Francisco, CA 94133
(415)362-2868   DL: 8/27/87
PC: 1,500,000   SBAL: 1,490,000
IP: D   OC: 5

Best Finance Corp.
Vincent Lee, Gen. Mgr.
1814 W. Washington Blvd.
Los Angeles, CA 90007
(213)731-2268   DL: 6/24/87
PC: 1,001,200   SBAL: 2,000,000
IP: D   OC: 5

Business Equity and Development
Corp.
Leon M.N. Garcia, Pres./CEO
767 N. Hill St., Ste. 401
Los Angeles, CA 90012
(213)613-0916   DL: 3/19/70
PC: 1,877,532   SBAL: 1,000,000
IP: D   OC: 5

Calsafe Capital Corp.
Bob T.C. Chang, Chmn. of the Board
240 S. Atlantic Blvd.
Alhambra, CA 91801
(818)289-4080   DL: 12/28/88
PC: 1,000,000   SBAL: 0
IP: D   OC: 5

Charterway Investment Corp.
Harold H. M. Chuang, Pres.
222 S. Hill St., Ste. 800
Los Angeles, CA 90012
(213)687-8539   DL: 4/4/84
PC: 1,597,336   SBAL: 3,000,000
IP: D   OC: 5

Continental Investors, Inc.
Lac Thantrong, Pres.
8781 Seaspray Dr.
Huntington Beach, CA 92646
(714)964-5207   DL: 6/18/80
PC: 2,000,000   SBAL: 5,000,000
IP: D   OC: 5

Equitable Capital Corp.
John C. Lee, Pres.
855 Sansome St.
San Francisco, CA 94111
(415)434-4114   DL: 3/8/79
PC: 642,995   SBAL: 1,505,000
IP: D   OC: 5

First American Capital Funding, Inc.
Luu TranKiem, Chmn.
38 Corporate Park, Ste. B
Irvine, CA 92714
(714)660-9288   DL: 5/2/84
PC: 823,250   SBAL: 2,202,000
IP: D   OC: 5

Helio Capital, Inc.
Chester Koo, Pres.
5900 S. Eastern Ave., Ste. 136
Commerce, CA 90040
(213)721-8053   DL: 9/20/85
PC: 1,000,000   SBAL: 2,000,000
IP: D   OC: 5

LaiLai Capital Corp.
Hsing-Jong Duan, Pres. & Gen. Mngr.
223 E. Garvey Ave., Ste. 228
Monterey, CA 91754
(818)288-0704   DL: 11/24/82
PC: 1,000,000   SBAL: 2,000,000
IP: D   OC: 5

Magna Pacific Investments
David Wong, Pres.
700 N. Central Ave., Ste. 245
Glendale, CA 91203
(818)547-0809   DL: 12/3/85
PC: 1,000,000   SBAL: 1,080,000
IP: D   OC: 5

Myriad Capital, Inc.
Felix Chen, Pres.
328 S. Atlantic Blvd., Ste. 200A
Monterey Park, CA 91754
(818)570-4548   DL: 9/16/80
PC: 1,334,530   SBAL: 5,338,120
IP: D   OC: 5

New Kukje Investment Co.
George Su Chey, Pres.
3670 Wilshire Blvd., Ste. 418
Los Angeles, CA 90010
(213)389-8679   DL: 1/10/85
PC: 1,020,000   SBAL: 1,000,000
IP: D   OC: 5

Opportunity Capital Corp.
J. Peter Thompson, Pres.
One Fremont Pl.
39650 Liberty St., Ste. 425
Fremont, CA 94538
(415)651-4412   DL: 9/23/71
PC: 2,526,043   SBAL: 2,180,500
IP: D   OC: 2

Positive Enterprises, Inc.
Kwok Szeto, Pres.
399 Arguello St.
San Francisco, CA 94118
(415)386-6606   DL: 6/6/80
PC: 505,000   SBAL: 505,000
IP: D   OC: 5

RSC Financial Corp.
Frederick K. Bae, Pres.
323 E. Matilija Road, #208
Ojai, CA 93023
(805)646-2925   DL: 9/28/72

San Joaquin Business Investment
Group, Inc.
Joe Williams, Pres.
2310 Tulare St., Ste. 140
Fresno, CA 93721
(209)233-3580   DL: 4/23/88
PC: 1,000,000   SBAL: 0
IP: D   OC: 5

Colorado

Colorado Invesco, Inc.
1999 Broadway, Ste. 2100
Denver, CO 80202
(303)293-2431   DL: 6/18/84
PC: 1,020,600   SBAL: 560,000
IP: D   OC: 5

D.C.

Allied Financial Corp.
David J. Gladstone, Pres.
1666 K. St., N.W., Ste. 901
Washington, DC 20006
(202)331-1112   DL: 8/9/83
PC: 6,000,000   SBAL: 12,000,000
IP: D   OC: 6

Broadcast Capital, Inc.
John E. Oxendine, Pres.
1771 N. St., N.W., Ste. 421
Washington, DC 20036
(202)429-5393   DL: 11/26/80
PC: 3,050,000   SBAL: 5,800,000
IP: C   OC: 5

Consumers United Capital Corp.
Ester M. Carr-Davis, Pres.
2100 M. St., N.W.
Washington, DC 20037
(202)872-5274   DL: 4/22/85
PC: 1,008,000   SBAL: 0
IP: D   OC: 4

Fulcrum Venture Capital Corp.
C. Robert Kemp, Chmn.
1030 15th St., N.W., Ste. 203
Washington, DC 20005
(202)785-4253   DL: 7/5/78
PC: 2,000,000   SBAL: 2,000,000
IP: D   OC: 3

Minority Broadcast Investment Corp.
Walter L. Threadgill, Pres.
1200 18th St., N.W., Ste. 705
Washington, DC 20036
(202)293-1166   DL: 8/7/79
PC: 1,000,100   SBAL: 1,500,100
IP: C   OC: 5

Syncom Capital Corp.
Herbert P. Wilkins, Pres.
1030 15th St., N.W., Ste. 203
Washington, DC 20005
(202)293-9428   DL: 7/10/78
PC: 2,250,000   SBAL: 6,125,000
IP: C   OC: 4

Florida

Allied Financial Corp.
(Main Office: Washington, D.C.)
Exec. Office Ctr., Ste. 305
2770 N. Indian River Blvd.
Vero Beach, FL 32960
(407)778-5556

First American Lending Corp. (The)
Roy W. Talmo, Chmn.
1926 10th Ave. N.
Mail: P.O. Box 24660; W. Palm Beach
33416
Lake Worth, FL 33461
(305)533-1511   DL: 9/27/79
PC: 500,000   SBAL: 800,000
IP: D   OC: 1

Ideal Financial Corp.
Ectore T. Reynaldo, Gen. Mngr.
780 N.W. 42nd Ave., Ste. 303

Florida (continued)

Miami, FL 33126
(305)442-4665   DL: 3/7/83
PC: 500,000   SBAL: 1,000,000
IP: D   OC: 5

Pro-Med Investment Corp.
(Main Office: Dallas, TX)
1380 N.E. Miami Gardens Dr., Ste. 225
N. Miami Beach, FL 33179
(305)949-5900

Venture Group, Inc.
Ellis W. Hitzing, Pres.
5433 Buffalo Ave.
Jacksonville, FL 32208
(904)353-7313   DL: 4/25/83
PC: 500,000   SBAL: 500,000
IP: D   OC: 5

Georgia

Renaissance Capital Corp.
Samuel B. Florence, Pres.
161 Spring St., NW, Ste. 610
Atlanta, GA 30303
(404)658-9061   DL: 12/5/86
PC: 1,000,000   SBAL: 0
IP: D   OC: 5

Hawaii

Pacific Venture Capital, Ltd.
Dexter J. Taniguchi, Pres.
222 S. Vineyard St.
PH.1
Honolulu, HI 96813
(808)521-6502   DL: 6/25/80
PC: 1,000,000   SBAL: 700,000
IP: D   OC: 4

Illinois

Amoco Venture Capital Co.
Gordon E. Stone, Pres.
200 E. Randolph Dr.
Chicago, IL 60601
(312)856-6523   DL: 12/22/70
PC: 3,676,750   SBAL: 6,603,000
IP: D   OC: 4

Chicago Community Ventures, Inc.
Phyllis George, Pres.
104 S. Michigan Ave., Ste. 215–218
Chicago, IL 60603
(312)726-6084   DL: 6/14/72
PC: 1,005,000   SBAL: 2,005,000
IP: D   OC: 4

Combined Fund, Inc. (The)
E. Patric Jones, Pres.
1525 E. 53rd St.
Chicago, IL 60615
(312)753-9650   DL: 5/4/71
PC: 1,100,250   SBAL: 1,629,000
IP: D   OC: 1

Neighborhood Fund, Inc. (The)
James Fletcher, Pres.
1950 E. 71st St.
Chicago, IL 60649
(312)684-8074   DL: 4/3/78
PC: 730,000   SBAL: 950,000
IP: D   OC: 1

Peterson Finance and Investment Co.
James S. Rhee, Pres.
3300 W. Peterson Ave., Ste. A
Chicago, IL 60659
(312)583-6300   DL: 2/7/84
PC: 1,035,000   SBAL: 1,520,000
IP: D   OC: 2

Tower Ventures, Inc.
Robert T. Smith, Pres.
Sears Tower, BSC 43-50
Chicago, IL 60684
(312)875-0571   DL: 6/30/75
PC: 2,000,000   SBAL: 3,000,000
IP: D   OC: 4

Kentucky

Equal Opportunity Finance, Inc.
Franklin Justice, Jr., V.P. & Mngr.
420 Hurstbourne Ln., Ste. 201
Louisville, KY 40222
(502)423-1943   DL: 9/24/70
PC: 1,456,591   SBAL: 1,600,000
IP: D   OC: 4

Louisiana

SCDF Investment Corp.
Martial Mirabeau, Mngr.
1006 Surrey St., P.O. Box 3885
Lafayette, LA 70502
(318)232-3769   DL: 4/26/73
PC: 2,700,010   SBAL: 3,119,549
IP: D   OC: 4

Maryland

Albright Venture Capital, Inc.
William A. Albright, Pres.
1355 Piccard Dr., Ste. 380
Rockville, MD 20850
(301)921-9090   DL: 8/10/79
PC: 505,000   SBAL: 750,000
IP: D   OC: 5

Security Financial and Investment
Corp.
Han Y. Cho, Pres.
7720 Wisconsin Ave., Ste. 207
Bethesda, MD 20814
(301)951-4288   DL: 12/29/83
PC: 510,000   SBAL: 500,000
IP: D   OC: 5

Massachusetts

Argonauts MESBIC Corp. (The)
Mr. Chi Fu Yeh, Pres.
2 Vernon St., P.O. Box 2411
Framingham, MA 01701
(508)820-3430   DL: 6/17/88
PC: 1,000,000   SBAL: 0
IP: D   OC: 5

New England MESBIC, Inc.
Etang Chen, Pres.
530 Turnpike St.
North Andover, MA 01845
(617)688-4326   DL: 10/26/82
PC: 500,000   SBAL: 1,500,000
IP: D   OC: 5

Transportation Capital Corp.
(Main Office: New York, NY)
45 Newbury St, Ste. 207
Boston, MA 02116
(617)536-0344

Michigan

Dearborn Capital Corp.
Michael LaManes, Pres.
P.O. Box 1729
Dearborn, MI 48121
(313)337-8577   DL: 12/14/78
PC: 2,156,957   SBAL: 1,000,000
IP: D   OC: 4

Metro-Detroit Investment Co.
William J. Fowler, Pres.

30777 Northwestern Hwy., Ste. 300
Farmington Hill, MI 48018
(313)851-6300   DL: 6/1/78
PC: 2,000,000   SBAL: 6,000,000
IP: GS   OC: 4

Motor Enterprises, Inc.
James Kobus, Mngr.
3044 W. Grand Blvd.
Detroit, MI 48202
(313)556-4273   DL: 4/13/70
PC: 1,500,000   SBAL: 2,000,000
IP: D   OC: 4

Mutual Investment Co., Inc.
Jack Najor, Pres.
21415 Civic Center Dr.
Mark Plaza Bldg., Ste. 217
Southfield, MI 48076
(313)557-2020   DL: 4/21/80
PC: 1,964,094   SBAL: 5,808,000
IP: D   OC: 5

Minnesota

Capital Dimensions Ventures Fund,
Inc.
Dean R. Pickerell, Pres.
Two Appletree Sq., Ste. 244
Minneapolis, MN 55425
(612)854-3007   DL: 1/29/79
PC: 7,342,662   SBAL: 10,000,000
IP: D   OC: 4

Mississippi

Sun-Delta Capital Access Ctr., Inc.
Howard Boutte, Jr., V.P.
819 Main St.
Greenville, MS 38701
(601)335-5291   DL: 9/25/79
PC: 1,258,100   SBAL: 0
IP: D   OC: 5

New Jersey

Capital Circulation Corp.
Judy Kao, Mngr.
208 Main St.
Fort Lee, NJ 07024
(201)947-8637   DL: 3/28/85
PC: 1,000,000   SBAL: 2,000,000
IP: D   OC: 5

Formosa Capital Corp.
Philp Chen, Pres.
1037 Rte. 46 East, Unit C-208
Clifton, NJ 07013
(201)916-0016   DL: 8/22/85
PC: 1,000,000   SBAL: 2,000,000
IP: D   OC: 5

Rutgers Minority Investment Co.
Oscar Figueroa, Pres.
92 New St.
Newark, NJ 07102
(201)648-5287   DL: 7/28/70
PC: 1,499,000   SBAL: 905,000
IP: D   OC: 4

Transpac Capital Corp.
Tsuey Tang Wang, Pres.
1037 Rte. 46 East
Clifton, NJ 07013
(201)470-0706   DL: 5/28/87
PC: 1,000,000   SBAL: 2,000,000
IP: D   OC: 5

Zaitech Capital Corp.
Mr. Fu-Tong Hsu, Pres.
1037 Rte. 46 East, Unit C-201
Clifton, NJ 07013

(201)365-0047   DL: 6/5/86
PC: 1,000,000   SBAL: 1,000,000
IP: D   OC: 5

New Mexico

Assoc. Southwest Investors, Inc.
John R. Rice, Gen. Mngr.
2400 Louisiana N.E.
Bldg. #4, Ste. 225
Albuquerque, NM 87110
(505)881-0066   DL: 12/9/71
PC: 717,000   SBAL: 1,700,000
IP: D   OC: 4

New York

American Asian Capital Corp.
Howard H. Lin, Pres.
130 Water St., Ste. 6-L
New York, NY 10005
(212)422-6880   DL: 11/12/76
PC: 503,000   SBAL: 500,000
IP: D   OC: 5

Avdon Capital Corp.
A. M. Donner, Pres.
1413 Ave. J
Brooklyn, NY 11230
(718)692-0950   DL: 4/21/83
PC: 1,000,000   SBAL: 2,500,000
IP: D   OC: 5

CVC Capital Corp.
Jeorg G. Klebe, Pres.
131 E. 62th St.
New York, NY 10021
(212)319-7210   DL: 3/22/78
PC: 3,255,000   SBAL: 6,000,000
IP: C, RE, EF   OC: 5

Capital Investors & Management Corp.
Rose Chao, Mngr.
210 Canal St., Ste. 607
New York, NY 10013
(212)964-2480   DL: 2/6/80
PC: 900,000   SBAL: 1,500,000
IP: D   OC: 5

Cohen Capital Corp.
Edward H. Cohen, Pres.
8 Freer St., Ste. 185
Lynbrook, NY 11563
(516)887-3434   DL: 3/1/78
PC: 710,000   SBAL: 1,300,000
IP: D   OC: 5

Columbia Capital Corp.
Mark Scharfman, Pres.
79 Madison Ave., Ste. 800
New York, NY 10016
(212)696-4334   DL: 9/9/83
PC: 3,831,343   SBAL: 3,660,000
IP: D   OC: 5

East Coast Venture Capital, Inc.
Zindel Zelmanovitch, Pres.
313 W. 53rd St., 3rd Fl.
New York, NY 10019
(212)245-6460   DL: 7/14/86
PC: 1,000,000   SBAL: 2,000,000
IP: D   OC: 5

Elk Associates Funding Corp.
Gary C. Granoff, Pres.
600 Third Ave., 38th Fl.
New York, NY 10016
(212)972-8550   DL: 7/24/80
PC: 5,487,808   SBAL: 8,785,000
IP: T   OC: 5

Equico Capital Corp.
Duane Hill, Pres.

135 W. 50th St., 11th Fl.
New York, NY 10020
(212)641-7650   DL: 5/7/71
PC: 10,550,000   SBAL: 10,295,000
IP: D   OC: 4

Everlast Capital Corp.
Frank J. Segreto, Gen. Mgr. & V.P.
350 Fifth Ave., Ste. 2805
New York, NY 10118
(212)695-3910   DL: 7/30/84
PC: 2,840,000   SBAL: 5,400,000
IP: D   OC: 5

Exim Capital Corp.
Victor K. Chun, Pres.
290 Madison Ave.
New York, NY 10017
(212)683-3375   DL: 1/5/79
PC: 660,000   SBAL: 1,800,000
IP: D   OC: 5

Fair Capital Corp.
Robert Yet Sen Chen, Pres.
c/o Summit Assoc.
3 Pell St., 2nd Fl.
New York, NY 10013
(212)608-5866   DL: 9/27/82
PC: 508,000   SBAL: 500,000
IP: D   OC: 5

Freshstart Venture Capital Corp.
Zindel Zelmanovich, Pres.
313 W. 53rd St., 3rd Fl.
New York, NY 10019
(212)265-2249   DL: 2/24/83
PC: 708,525   SBAL: 2,310,000
IP: D   OC: 5

Hanam Capital Corp.
Dr. Yul Chang, Pres.
One Penn Plaza, Ground Floor
New York, NY 10119
(212)714-9830   DL: 5/6/87
PC: 1,021,000   SBAL: 0
IP: D   OC: 5

Hop Chung Capital Investors, Inc.
Yon Hon Lee, Pres.
185 Canal St., Rm. 303
New York, NY 10013
(212)219-1777   DL: 7/18/80
PC: 510,000   SBAL: 1,000,000
IP: D   OC: 5

Horn & Hardart Capital Corp.
Gerald Zarin, V.P.
30 Fifth Ave.
New York, NY 10019
(212)484-9600   DL: 9/11/85
PC: 1,000,000   SBAL: 0
IP: D   OC: 5

Ibero American Investors Corp.
Emilio Serrano, Pres.
38 Scio St.
Rochester, NY 14604
(716)262-3440   DL: 9/28/79
PC: 1,246,471   SBAL: 1,897,000
IP: D   OC: 5

Intercontinental Capital Funding
Corp.
James S. Yu, Pres.
60 E. 42nd St., Ste. 740
New York, NY 10165
(212)286-9642   DL: 9/30/81
PC: 500,000   SBAL: 1,750,000
IP: D   OC: 5

International Paper Cap. Formation,
Inc.
(Main Office: Memphis, TN)

Frank Polney, Mngr.
Two Manhattanville Rd.
Purchase, NY 10577
(914)397-1578

Japanese American Capital Corp.
Stephen C. Huang, Pres.
19 Rector St.
New York, NY 10006
(212)964-4077   DL: 8/7/79
PC: 525,000   SBAL: 1,490,000
IP: D   OC: 5

Jardine Capital Corp.
Evelyn Sy Dy, Pres.
109 Lafayette St., Unit 204
New York, NY 10038
(212)941-0966   DL: 12/22/86
PC: 1,000,000   SBAL: 2,000,000
IP: D   OC: 5

Manhattan Central Capital Corp.
David Choi, Pres.
1255 Broadway, Rm. 405
New York, NY 10001
(212)684-6411   DL: 6/11/87
PC: 1,000,000   SBAL: 1,000,000
IP: D   OC: 5

Medallion Funding Corp.
Alvin Murstein, Pres.
205 E. 42nd St., Ste. 2020
New York, NY 10017
(212)682-3300   DL: 6/23/80
PC: 9,234,000   SBAL: 21,734,000
IP: T   OC: 5

Minority Equity Cap. Co., Inc.
Donald F. Greene, Pres.
275 Madison Ave.
New York, NY 10016
(212)686-9710   DL: 5/17/71
PC: 2,615,747   SBAL: 3,104,046
IP: D   OC: 4

Monsey Capital Corp.
Shamuel Myski, Pres.
125 Route 59
Monsey, NY 10952
(914)425-2229   DL: 1/17/85
PC: 1,257,040   SBAL: 3,000,000
IP: D   OC: 5

New Oasis Capital Corp.
James Huang, Pres.
114 Liberty St., Ste. 304
New York, NY 10006
(212)349-2804   DL: 2/6/80
PC: 500,000   SBAL: 1,500,000
IP: D   OC: 5

North American Funding Corp.
Franklin F. Y. Wong, V.P. & Gen. Mgr.
177 Canal St.
New York, NY 10013
(212)226-0080   DL: 3/5/81
PC: 500,000   SBAL: 1,500,000
IP: D   OC: 5

Pan Pac Capital Corp.
Dr. In Ping Jack Lee, Pres.
121 E. Industry Ct.
Deer Park, NY 11729
(516)586-7653   DL: 6/11/80
PC: 503,000   SBAL: 1,505,000
IP: D   OC: 5

Pierre Funding Corp.
Elias Debbas, Pres.
605 Third Ave.
New York, NY 10016
(212)490-9540   DL: 1/22/81
PC: 2,762,074   SBAL: 7,111,800
IP: T   OC: 5

New York (continued)

Situation Venture Corp.
Sam Hollander, Pres.
502 Flushing Ave.
Brooklyn, NY 11205
(718)855-1835   DL: 2/16/77
PC: 1,000,200   SBAL: 3,000,000
IP: D   OC: 5

Square Deal Venture Capital Corp.
Mordechai Z. Feldman, Pres.
805 Avenue L.
Brooklyn, NY 11230
(718)692-2924   DL: 9/28/79
PC: 546,000   SBAL: 1,200,000
IP: D   OC: 5

Taroco Capital Corp.
David R. C. Chang, Pres.
19 Rector St., 35th Fl.
New York, NY 10006
(212)344-6690   DL: 9/10/76
PC: 1,010,000   SBAL: 3,030,000
IP: CA   OC: 5

Transportation Capital Corp.
Melvin L. Hirsch, Pres.
60 E. 42nd St., Ste. 3115
New York, NY 10165
(212)697-4885   DL: 6/23/80
PC: 6,561,380   SBAL: 10,148,333
IP: D   OC: 5

Triad Capital Corp. of New York
Lorenzo J. Barrera, Pres.
960 Southern Blvd.
Bronx, NY 10459
(212)589-6541   DL: 11/25/83
PC: 545,253   SBAL: 500,000
IP: D   OC: 2

Trico Venture, Inc.
Avruhum Donner, Pres.
1413 Avenue J
Brooklyn, NY 11230
(718)692-0950   DL: 6/27/86
PC: 1,000,000   SBAL: 1,700,000
IP: D   OC: 5

United Capital Investment Corp.
Paul Lee, Pres.
60 E. 42nd St., Ste. 1515
New York, NY 10165
(212)682-7210   DL: 2/5/85
PC: 1,030,000   SBAL: 3,000,000
IP: D   OC: 5

Venture Opportunities Corp.
A. Fred March, Pres.
110 E. 59th St., 29th Fl.
New York, NY 10022
(212)832-3737   DL: 12/1/78
PC: 875,000   SBAL: 2,300,000
IP: D   OC: 5

Watchung Capital Corp.
S. T. Jeng, Pres.
431 Fifth Ave., 5th Fl.
New York, NY 10016
(212)889-3466   DL: 2/19/80
PC: 500,000   SBAL: 1,000,000
IP: D   OC: 5

Yang Capital Corp.
Maysing Yang, Pres.
41-40 Kissena Blvd.
Flushing, NY 11355
(516)482-1578   DL: 4/12/83
PC: 500,000   SBAL: 1,500,000
IP: D   OC: 5

Yusa Capital Corp.
Christopher Yeung, Chmn. of the
Board
622 Broadway
New York, NY 10012
(212)420-1350   DL: 7/31/84
PC: 1,035,000   SBAL: 2,000,000
IP: D   OC: 5

North Carolina

Business Capital Inv. Co., Inc.
Christopher S. Liu, Mngr.
327 South Road
High Point, NC 27260
(919)889-8334   DL: 12/29/88
PC: 1,000,000   SBAL: 0
IP: D   OC: 5

Ohio

Center City MESBIC, Inc.
Michael A. Robinson, Pres.
Centre City Office Bldg., Ste. 762
40 S. Main St.
Dayton, OH 45402
(513)461-6164   DL: 7/29/81
PC: 500,000   SBAL: 500,000
IP: D   OC: 5

Rubber City Capital Corp.
Jesse T. Williams, Pres.
1144 E. Market St.
Akron, OH 44316
(216)796-9167   DL: 8/14/85
PC: 1,000,000   SBAL: 0
IP: D   OC: 5

Pennsylvania

Alliance Enterprise Corp.
W. B. Priestley, Pres.
1801 Market St., 3rd Fl.
Philadelphia, PA 19103
(215)977-3925   DL: 10/20/71
PC: 3,030,200   SBAL: 2,700,000
IP: D   OC: 4

Greater Phila. Venture Capital Corp.,
Inc.
Martin Newman, Mngr.
920 Lewis Tower Bldg.
225 S. Fifteenth St.
Philadelphia, PA 19102
(215)732-3415   DL: 3/31/72
PC: 760,981   SBAL: 1,505,000
IP: D   OC: 2

Salween Financial Services, Inc.
Dr. Ramarao Naidu, Pres.
228 N. Pottstown Pike
Exton, PA 19341
(215)524-1880   DL: 7/1/83
PC: 800,000   SBAL: 725,000
IP: D   OC: 5

Puerto Rico

North America Inv. Corp.
Santigo Ruz Betacourt, Pres.
Banco CTR #1710, M. Rivera Av Stop
34
Mail: PO BX 1831 Hato Rey Sta., PR
00919
Hato Rey, PR 00936
(809)751-6178   DL: 11/7/74
PC: 1,075,000   SBAL: 2,250,000
IP: D   OC: 5

Tennessee

Chickasaw Capital Corp.
Tom Moore, Pres.
67 Madison Ave.
Memphis, TN 38147
(901)523-6404   DL: 8/30/77
PC: 500,000   SBAL: 500,000
IP: D   OC: 1

International Paper Cap. Formation,
Inc.
John G. Herman, V.P. and Controller
International Place I
6400 Poplar Ave., 10-74
Memphis, TN 38197
(901)763-6282   DL: 11/5/81
PC: 1,000,000   SBAL: 1,000,000
IP: D   OC: 5

Tennessee Equity Capital Corp.
Walter S. Cohen, Pres.
1102 Stonewall Jackson Ct.
Nashville, TN 37220
(615)373-4502   DL: 1/19/79
PC: 837,000   SBAL: 1,670,000
IP: D   OC: 5

Tennessee Venture Capital Corp.
Wendell P. Knox, Pres.
162 Fourth Ave. North, Ste. 125
Mail: P.O. Box 2567
Nashville, TN 37219
(615)244-6935   DL: 9/28/79
PC: 500,000   SBAL: 500,000
IP: D   OC: 5

Valley Capital Corp.
Lamar J. Partridge, Pres.
8th Floor Krystal Bldg.
100 W. Martin Luther King Blvd.
Chattanooga, TN 37402
(615)265-1557   DL: 10/8/82
PC: 1,145,000   SBAL: 600,000
IP: D   OC: 5

Tennessee Venture Capital Corp.
Osbie L. Howard, Pres.
152 Beale St., Ste. 401
Mail: P.O. Box 300; Memphis, TN
38101
Memphis, TN 38101
(901)527-6091   DL: 12/16/82
PC: 1,250,000   SBAL: 0
IP: D   OC: 5

Texas

Chen's Financial Group, Inc.
Samuel S. C. Chen, Pres.
1616 W. Loop South, Ste. 200
Houston, TX 77027
(713)850-0879   DL: 3/5/84
PC: 1,000,000   SBAL: 3,000,000
IP: D   OC: 5

Evergreen Capital Co., Inc.
Shen-Lim Lin, Chmn. & Pres.
8502 Tybor Dr., Ste. 201
Houston, TX 77074
(713)778-9770   DL: 7/7/83
PC: 1,851,000   SBAL: 4,000,000
IP: D   OC: 5

MESBIC Financial Corp. of Dallas
Donald R. Lawhorne, Pres.
12655 N. Central Expressway, Ste. 814
Dallas, TX 75243
(214)991-1597   DL: 2/26/70
PC: 4,050,000   SBAL: 3,050,000
IP: D   OC: 2

MESBIC Financial Corp. of Houston
Lynn H. Miller, Pres.
811 Rusk, Ste. 201
Houston, TX 77002
(713)228-8321   DL: 11/12/76
PC: 1,546,450   SBAL: 854,000
IP: D   OC: 2

Minority Enterprise Funding, Inc.
Frederick C. Chang, Pres.
17300 El Camino Real, Ste. 107-B
Houston, TX 77058
(713)488-4919   DL: 3/9/79
PC: 1,000,000   SBAL: 2,650,000
IP: D   OC: 5

Pro-Med Investment Corp.
Mrs. Marion Rosemore, Pres.
17772 Preston Rd., Ste. 101
Dallas, TX 75252
(214)380-0044   DL: 11/28/86
PC: 2,000,000   SBAL: 3,000,000
IP: D   OC: 6

Southern Orient Capital Corp.
Min H. Liang, Pres.
2419 Fannin, Ste. 200
Houston, TX 77002
(713)225-3369   DL: 12/29/80
PC: 550,000   SBAL: 1,650,000
IP: D   OC: 5

United Oriental Capital Corp.
Don J. Wang, Pres.
908 Town & Country Blvd., Ste. 310
Houston, TX 77024
(713)461-3909   DL: 7/7/82
PC: 1,000,000   SBAL: 3,700,000
IP: D   OC: 5

Virginia

East West United Investment Co.
Bui Dung, Pres.
815 W. Broad St.
Falls Church, VA 22046
(703)237-7200   DL: 1/22/76

PC: 500,000   SBAL: 1,500,000
IP: D   OC: 5

Washington Finance and Investment
Corp.
Chang H. Lie, Pres.
100 E. Broad, St.
Falls Church, VA 22046
(703)534-7200   DL: 6/3/82
PC: 1,005,000   SBAL: 3,000,000
IP: D   OC: 5

Wisconsin

Future Value Ventures, Inc.
William P. Beckett, Pres.
622 N. Water St., Ste. 500
Milwaukee, WI 53202
(414)278-0377   DL: 11/9/84
PC: 1,020,000   SBAL: 1,000,000
IP: D   OC: 5

Index